BEYOND KLIMT

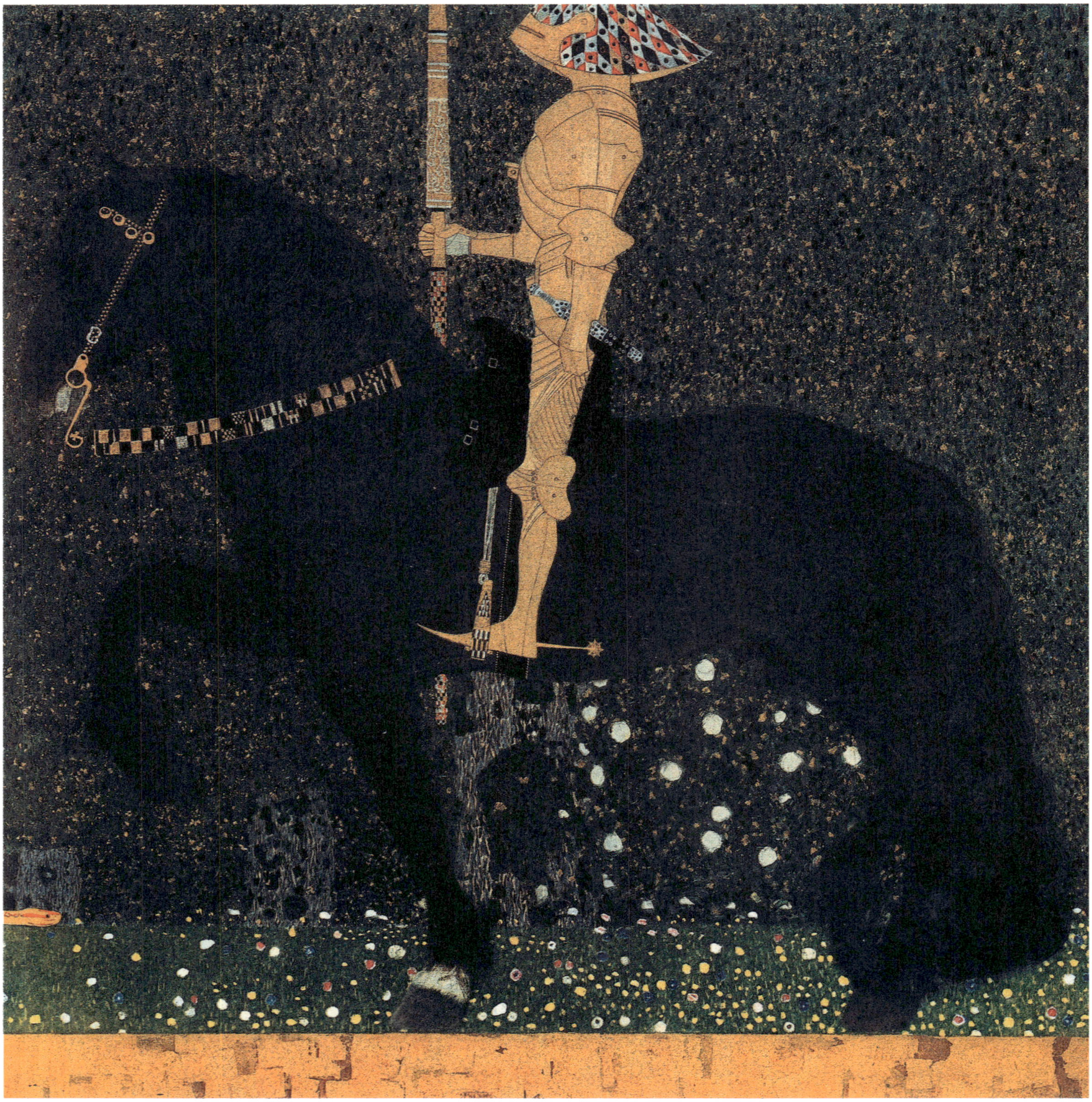

Gustav Klimt
The Golden Knight, 1903
Aichi Prefectural Museum of Art, Nagoya

BEYOND KLIMT

New Horizons in Central Europe

HIRMER

Content

Foreword

The outbreak of World War I in 1914 marked an incisive break in the history of Europe. It caused political, economic, and social turmoil, in particular the dissolution of the Austria-Hungarian Dual Monarchy. The end of the war thus also represented the end of an era. And with the death of Gustav Klimt, Egon Schiele, Koloman Moser, and Otto Wagner, the golden era of fin-de-siècle Vienna also appeared to have come to an end. Did the upheavals caused by the war lead to a hiatus or even a decline in the art of the successor states of the Habsburg Monarchy?

This exhibition examines the degree to which the ideational form and content of art were influenced by the events of the time. The developments in the art of this region until around 1938 are investigated from an artistic point of view rather than on the basis of political borders.

World War I fragmented the international artist networks and destroyed artists' careers, be it as a result of the fighting or on account of the physical and psychological aftermath of the war. Many artists witnessed the horrors of war and commented on the events as reporters, propagandists, critics, or compassionate observers.

The exhibition looks at the consequences of this rupture for artists, the limitations it entailed, the new prospects it opened up, and the continuities that remained.

Many artists took the opportunity to participate in the new political beginning, used their work to process the trauma they had experienced, or called for a new, universal humanism. The breakup of the former multinational state and the political orientation of the young nation-states left its mark. The defeat of the Republic of Councils in Hungary in 1919 led to an exodus of the avant-garde to neighboring states, in many cases to the newly formed Republic of Austria. Artists used magazines to communicate beyond political borders, formed groups with shared interests, or congregated in artistic centers.

This was particularly true of artists from the lands of the former Habsburg Monarchy. Their participation in movements such as Abstraction-Création, Surrealism, the Bauhaus, or in the *International Exhibition of New Theater Technology* in Vienna in 1924 bears witness to the priority placed on artistic identity rather than an ethnic or political one. The same applies to the trend toward a new realism, which cannot be explained in terms of the political orientation or geographical or linguistic identity of the artists involved. It demonstrates that art does not stop at political or national boundaries but should be seen in a larger context of cultural identification.

While artists had persistently found new and creative ways of communicating with their colleagues during the interwar years, innovative artistic developments were brought to a standstill by the start of World War II. The mutual recognition of cultural points of contact was pushed into the background by the political situation. The exhibition offers an opportunity to rediscover and reestablish this interrupted continuity and to foster a new understanding and perception.

After Vienna, the exhibition travels to the Centre for Fine Arts in Brussels (BOZAR), during the third Austrian Presidency of the European Council. The dialog between the Belvedere and BOZAR has proved fruitful in finding a thought-provoking narrative for visitors in both cities. The partnership between Austria and the Centre for Fine Arts in Brussels goes back a long way, starting with the *Masterpieces from Vienna* exhibition in 1947. As a house of the arts in the capital of Europe, BOZAR looks at Austria from a European angle. In 1998, it hosted *Austria im Rosennetz*, conceived by its curator Harald Szeemann as a series of "curiosity cabinets" portraying the state of mind of the country. In 2006, *Yearning for Beauty* highlighted the intellectual and physical bridge between Vienna and Brussels by presenting the Wiener Werkstätte and the Stoclet House together. Now, *Beyond Klimt* focuses on the generation that restored the artistic fabric after the war. The exhibition bears witness to the mobility of artists, their artworks, and their evolving ideas during a defining period for Europe.

We should like to express our gratitude first of all to the exhibition curator Alexander Klee for his inspired concept, which sheds new light on the interwar years, and for its bold implementation. We are also extremely grateful to the Hungarian National Gallery and its Director General László Baán for the loan of a number of key works, as well as to all other lenders for their generous support. Our thanks go as well to the Austrian Federal Ministry of Foreign Affairs and Federal Chancellery for promoting synergies between our cultural institutions.

The accomplished design for the Belvedere exhibition was created by the architect Gerhard Veigel. Within the Belvedere, we would like to thank our assistant curators Stephanie Auer and Miroslav Haľák for their tireless efforts, and Kristof Viola and Tanja Angermann-Cekinmez from Exhibition Management for their professional supervision of the project. Thanks are also due to Eva Lahnsteiner from Publication Management for the production of the catalogue. Finally, a big thank-you to the entire Belvedere team, who have been instrumental in the success of the exhibition.

At BOZAR, we should like to express our special gratitude to H. E. Willem van de Voorde, ambassador of Belgium to Austria, Slovakia, Slovenia, and Bosnia & Herzegovina, for his help and support. We should also like specially to thank the Austrian Foreign Ministry and the Austrian Federal Chancellery for the synergies they have fostered between our cultural institutions.

Last but not least we would like to thank the entire BOZAR team for their unceasing dedication to the realization of this project—in particular exhibition coordinator Ann Geeraerts, responsible for the exhibition management in Brussels, technical coordinator Nicolas Bernus, publication manager Gunther De Wit, who helped with the catalogue production, and Kurt De Boodt for his contribution to the overall exhibition narrative, which is also reflected in this publication.

Stella Rollig
CEO and Artistic Director, Belvedere, Vienna

Paul Dujardin
Director-General and Artistic Director, BOZAR, Centre for Fine Arts, Brussels

Sophie Lauwers
Head of Exhibitions, BOZAR, Centre for Fine Arts, Brussels

The Dissolution of the Habsburg Monarchy and its Aftermath in the Interwar Period

Arnold Suppan

When, on June 28, 1914, Archduke Franz Ferdinand and his consort Sophie were assassinated in Sarajevo by the young Bosnian Serb terrorist Gavrilo Princip—who was supported by Colonel Dragutin Dimitrijević, chief of the intelligence service of the Serbian General Staff—the diplomatic system left the governments in Vienna, Belgrade, Berlin, Saint Petersburg, Paris, and London considerable room for political maneuver. But in all capitals "war parties" were preparing to manage a chain reaction. The Emperor-King Franz Joseph and his ministers and generals in Vienna and Budapest failed to realize that their response to the Serbian irredentism would provoke a European war, mobilizing all enemies of the Dual Monarchy. But responsibility also lies with the other state chancelleries in Saint Petersburg, Berlin, Paris, and London: "All of them fought because they decided that fighting was better than the alternative, and all were convinced that not going to war would risk their great-power status."[1] So, World War I became a struggle among empires, a top-down war.

World War I, with its heavy mobilization of peoples, weapons, and ideologies, increased nationalist tensions to a level beyond anything previously experienced. In August 1914, there was "an unfamiliar sensation that perhaps the Monarchy was not going to die after all, but was instead experiencing a strange rebirth." All its nations, throughout all classes, professions, and creeds, including many intellectuals (among them Sigmund Freud, Hugo von Hofmannsthal, Arthur Schnitzler, Georg Trakl, Oskar Kokoschka, and Ludwig Wittgenstein), initially shared this feeling. Massive pro-war demonstrations took place not only in Vienna, Graz, and Innsbruck, but also in Budapest, Kraków, Zagreb, Ljubljana, Sarajevo, and Prague. "Many young men viewed the war as a great adventure, a test of their manhood, a chance for glory and renown."[2]

The Austro-Hungarian armies, not prepared for a great war, fought many battles involving heavy losses against the Russian armies in Galicia, Bukovina, Carpathian Ruthenia, and Volhynia, against the Serbian armies in Serbia and Montenegro, from May 1915 against the Italian armies at the Isonzo and in Trentino, and from August 1916 against the Romanian armies in Transylvania. Because of the defeats in Galicia (e. g., at the fortress of Przemyśl) and in Serbia, the Imperial-Royal Army needed German help against the Russian and Serbian armies, which it also required in 1916 against Romania and in 1917 against Italy (Karfeit/Caporetto). In September 1916, the German Emperor took supreme command of all forces of the Central Powers, invoking the concept of *Nibelungentreue* to encourage its weaker ally. More than any previous war, World War I became a war of industrialized mass slaughter, with armies using the highly destructive capacity of machine guns, rapid-fire rifles and cannons, heavy artillery, trench mortars, high explosives, grenades, flamethrowers, and poison gas. Ultimately, all the military engagements by Austria-Hungary in this "total war" resulted in enormous casualties: 1.2 million soldiers killed in action, 3.5 million wounded, 2.5 million prisoners of war, 600,000 refugees, 400,000 civilian fatalities.[3]

The war also increased pressure within the Monarchy: economic life, administration, and the judiciary system itself were subject to an absolutist wartime regime. Even more problematic in the escalating ethnic fighting was the increasing condemnation of Pan-Slavism, Pan-Serbism, and Pan-Russianism among the German-Austrian and Magyar middle classes. "The language of segregation, caricature, and demonization turned into a quintessential culture of discrimination and organized hatred." (Oto Luthar) From August 1914, Ruthenes, Poles, and Jews were fleeing en masse from Galicia and Bukovina to Silesia, Moravia, Lower Austria, Vienna, and Prague, followed by evacuations and deportations from Bosnia-Herzegovina, the Littoral, and Trentino. Around the same time, persecutions commenced of Serbian, Croatian, Slovene, Ruthenian/Ukrainian, and Czech politicians, lawyers, journalists, academics, teachers, priests, and others who had been nationally and politically active leading up to 1914. There was an interminable series of prosecutions for high treason, e.g., against the Czech politicians Karel Kramář and Alois Rašín. On the front, the consistent German and Magyar doubts about the "reliability" of the Slavic regiments were unwarranted, as these suffered demonstrably heavy casualties on the Balkan, Galician, and, later, the Italian fronts. Unfortunately, the Emperor and the Army High Command saw the main reasons for desertion not in poor leadership but in the personal failure of soldiers and in nationalist agitation.[4]

For Austria-Hungary and Germany, World War I became a kind of "national economic suicide." (Gerald D. Feldman) The introduction of the economic model of a state-planned national economy with a form of state capitalism worked better for the Western Powers than for the Central Powers, not least thanks to Wall Street support. The common economic area of the German Empire and the Habsburg Monarchy was not large enough to balance the British, French, and American blockade—not even in coalition with the Ottoman Empire and Bulgaria, or after the occupation of Russian Poland, Lithuania, Ukraine, Walachia, Serbia, Montenegro, and Macedonia. In the larger cities of the Bohemian and Austrian lands, people, especially women, were queueing outside the shops: in autumn 1914 for flour and bread, in early 1915 for milk and potatoes, in autumn 1915 for oil, in March 1916 for coffee, the next month for sugar, in July 1916 for soap. The coal supply still functioned in Budapest, Prague, Kraków, and Ljubljana, but not in Vienna and Zagreb. There were rumors of profiteering by "coffee-house types." People were shouting: "Hoarder, usurer, Galician, Jew!" The Jews became convenient scapegoats for social and economic ills. Ninety percent of the letters handled at the *Zensurstellen* (censorship offices) reported food shortages. The militarization of the war industry workforce helped contain large-scale strikes; in January 1918, the field army even sent troops from the Eastern Front, where the Russian Bolsheviks had ended the war against the Central Powers in December 1917.[5]

"When […] Emperor Charles showed that a separate peace was in vain and when he became a vassal of Germany, a revision of policy became necessary. […] Austria-Hungary must be practically blotted out as an empire. It should be partitioned among the nationalities of which it is composed. As a great power it should no longer exist." (Robert Lansing)

Nonetheless, the "imperial mission" of Austria-Hungary was losing its momentum. During the war, political, economic, and social power shifted more and more from the imperial center Vienna and the royal center Budapest to the new power centers Prague, Kraków, Lwów (Lviv), Zagreb, and Ljubljana, which were supported by the Entente Powers via national councils in exile. And the Habsburg Empire's "nationalities"—encouraged by Lenin's and Wilson's concept of national self-determination (above all a propaganda slogan against the Habsburgs and Ottomans)— now demanded not only national autonomy but their own nation-states. Perhaps the transformation of the imperial structure into a federal union of autonomous societies would have spelled the end of the imperial concept and the Habsburg Empire, even if it had not been destroyed by war and revolution. However, the fate of the Dual Monarchy was tied to the military fortunes of Germany, not least because of secret initiatives by Emperor Charles to conclude a separate peace treaty. In Spa, on May 12, 1918, the emperors William II and Charles I agreed on a long-term treaty between the two empires, calling for military union and a maximum of economic cooperation. Now the French, British, and Italians—and later also the Americans—intensified nationalist propaganda against the Habsburg Monarchy, although all of them had already declared war on Austria-Hungary long before this. On May 30, 1918, the US Secretary of State, Robert Lansing, stated that, because "the Prussians will have to all intents won the war, […] Austria-Hungary must be practically blotted out as an empire. It should be partitioned among all nationalities of which it is composed. As a great power it should no longer exist."[6]

In the end, the Habsburg Monarchy fell because it lost a world war against the Entente of France, Britain, Italy, the United States, and Japan. With the gradual collapse of its political, economic, social, and administrative structures, the Austro-Hungarian Empire lost its ability to continue total warfare. When the Germans offered President Wilson an armistice, the Joint Council of Ministers in Vienna did the same, asking for peace negotiations based on the Fourteen Points. However, on October 18, 1918, Wilson stated he was "no longer at liberty to accept the mere 'autonomy' of these peoples as the basis for peace," but was "obliged to insist that they, and not he, shall be the judges of what action of the Austro-Hungarian government will satisfy their aspirations and their conception of their rights and destiny as members of the family of nations." A year later, the Czech historian Josef Pekař identified this statement as the "death sentence" for the Habsburg Monarchy. "The material as well as the ideological armoury of independent Habsburg imperial rule was exhausted. […] The Habsburgs had evidently lost the battle for publicity as well as the military contest."[7] Emperor-King Charles and more than six hundred years of Habsburg rule became irrelevant overnight.

"Complete incapacity of the rulers, absolute demoralization and disorganization, general insecurity," was the verdict of the Viennese doctor and poet, Arthur Schnitzler. The moral indignation against the war found passionate expression in the Viennese writer and critic Karl Kraus's monumental masterpiece *Die letzten Tage der Menschheit (The Last Days of Mankind)*, written in the fateful years between 1915 and 1917, though—obviously—not published until 1922. Kraus proposed that men were fighting because of the jingoistic propaganda of a censored and cynical press. He depicted

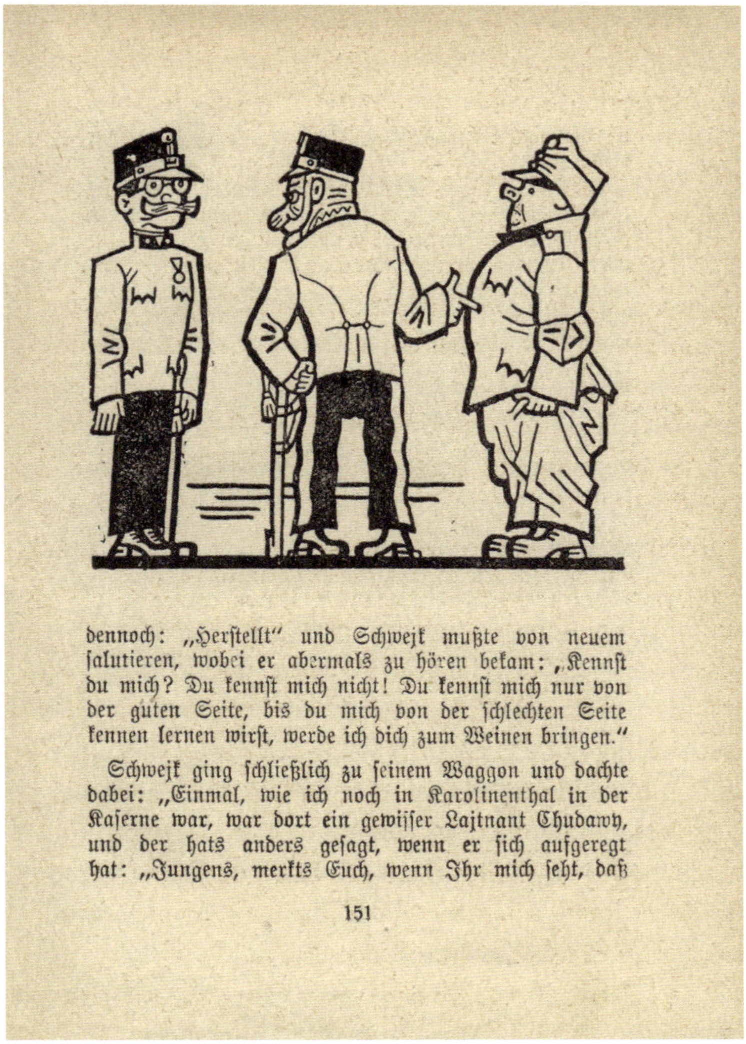

dennoch: „Herstellt“ und Schwejk mußte von neuem salutieren, wobei er abermals zu hören bekam: „Kennst du mich? Du kennst mich nicht! Du kennst mich nur von der guten Seite, bis du mich von der schlechten Seite kennen lernen wirst, werde ich dich zum Weinen bringen.“

Schwejk ging schließlich zu seinem Waggon und dachte dabei: „Einmal, wie ich noch in Karolinenthal in der Kaserne war, war dort ein gewisser Lajtnant Chudawy, und der hats anders gesagt, wenn er sich aufgeregt hat: „Jungens, merkts Euch, wenn Ihr mich seht, daß

151

Jaroslav Hašek, *Die Abenteuer des braven Soldaten Schwejk während des Weltkrieges*, (German translation of the Czech novel *The Good Soldier Švejk*), with illustrations by Josef Lada, vol. 3, Prague 1926

the war mainly as "a criminal plot of military adventurers and of greedy businessmen, a conscious conspiracy plot of scoundrels and idiots against the people." The Hungarian poet Endre Ady claimed from the outset that this was "a war of the Prussian Junkers, the Habsburgs, and the Magyar upper-class bandits." The Czech author Jaroslav Hašek acerbically lampooned an inept bureaucracy and corrupt administration in his famous novel *Osudy dobrého vojáka Švejka za světové války (The Good Soldier Švejk and His Fortunes in the World War)*, originally written in 1921–22 and containing one hilarious adventure after another (fig. 1). And in his short story *Hrvatski bog Mars (The Croatian God Mars)*, the Croatian author Miroslav Krleža expressed his dismay about the inhumanity of the Imperial and Royal military apparatus.[8] However, the Central Europe of the Habsburgs with its Baroque culture, its enlightened civilization, its rule of law, and its protection of minorities against increasing nationalism was coming to an end. It was left to Robert Musil's *Kakania*, Joseph Roth's *Radetzky Marsch*, and Stefan Zweig's *Die Welt von Gestern (The World of Yesterday)* to immortalize it in literature.[9]

The outcome of World War I transformed the entire area of East-Central and Southeastern Europe. Instead of being ruled by four large empires—Russia, Germany, Austria-Hungary, and the Ottoman Empire—it became a region consisting of a dozen small and medium-sized nation-states: Finland, Estonia, Latvia, Lithuania, Poland, Czechoslovakia, Austria, Hungary, Romania, Bulgaria, Yugoslavia, Greece, and Albania. In his Four Principles of February 11, 1918, Wilson had demanded that "every territorial settlement involved in this war must be made in the interest and for the benefit of the populations concerned." However, the majority of the new nation-states became so more *de jure*, rather than *de facto*, because most of them contained any number of national and religious minorities: Germans, Jews, Belarusians, Ukrainians/Ruthenes, Russians, Poles, Czechs, Slovaks, Magyars, Croats, Slovenes, Albanians, Bulgarians, and Turks—altogether some thirty million people. The burning question since the peace treaties of Versailles, Saint-Germain, Trianon, and Neuilly in 1919–20, has therefore been whether the new post-Versailles system was better than the previous one. Obviously, the principle of self-determination was violated several times: in Eastern Poland and Gdańsk, in the Bohemian and Slovakian borderlands, in Maramureş, Crişana, Banat, Bačka, Baranya, in the Littoral, Istria, and South Tyrol, in Bukovina, southern Bessarabia, Dobruja, Caribrod, Bosilegrad, and in Thrace.[10]

"The war had destroyed political systems, ruined economies, divided societies, and opened vistas onto radically utopian visions of a better world" (Ian Kershaw). Most of the East-Central European lands suffered from disrupted industrial production and lack of food and/or coal. The old railway system, on which the Habsburg economy had depended, came to a halt as each newly formed state claimed ownership of the rolling stock. In many regions of the former Habsburg Monarchy unemployment was high and undernourished men, women, and children in rags were everywhere. The two million inhabitants of Vienna were particularly affected, because the new Budapest administration stopped food supplies and the new regime in Prague placed an embargo on coal. Immediately after the war, latent nationalist tensions expressed themselves in bitter disputes over contested borders and trade barriers. Class conflict overlaid ethnic, territorial, and economic clashes "to produce a boiling cauldron of violent animosity." New forms of violence (plundering, looting, and poaching by war returnees, Red Guards in Vienna, Legionnaires in Prague, Red and White Terror in Hungary) threatened public order. Over and above that, the threat of a Bolshevik takeover felt very real—not only in Berlin but also in Vienna and Budapest. Moreover, the underlying anti-Semitism, already in existence before 1914, now manifested itself in accusations that the Bolshevist movement was led by Jews.[11]

While the October Revolution in Russia, the postwar upheavals in Germany, and the disintegration of the Habsburg Monarchy created a power vacuum, Poland recovered its independence. The new frontiers to Germany, however, remained in question, partly because of the division of Upper Silesia (following a plebiscite) and partly because of the creation of the Free City of Danzig (now Gdańsk). Since the Peace Conference had been unable to establish Poland's eastern frontiers, the new Polish army was now forced to fight against the Red Army and won the largely Ukrainian and Belarusian borderlands between Poland and Bolshevik Russia. With the aid of French credits, the Poles built a new harbor in Gdynia. However, at that very moment, the two traditional "giants," now resurrected as great powers—the German Reich and the Soviet Union (since 1922)—began to exploit the minority issue against Poland.[12]

President Thomas G. Masaryk and Foreign Minister Edvard Beneš had won international support for the creation of Czechoslovakia as a large state in East-Central Europe from the German-Bohemian Egerland in the west to Carpathian Ruthenia in the east. At the Peace Conference, Beneš combined arguments of national self-determination of the Czechs and Slovaks, historic political rights, economic necessity, and strategic considerations with fake statistics. Although the German-Bohemian spokesmen sent notes to President Wilson protesting against the "imperialistic encroachments of the Czech State," the French Foreign Minister Pichon rejected the German-Austrian government's suggestion of a plebiscite and arbitration. While Beneš warned the Prague government to "avoid all struggles and bloody riots in the German parts of Bohemia," he initiated a policy of *faits accomplis* in order to secure the territories claimed by the new state. In November and December 1918, Czech troops occupied the German-populated towns and villages in Bohemia, Moravia, and Silesia without major incidents. On March 4, 1919, the German Social Democratic Party organized demonstrations against a ruling by the Czechoslovak government banning Germans in the Bohemian lands from taking part in elections for the Viennese parliament. This time the Czechoslovak government did not hesitate to use armed force: fifty-four demonstrators were killed. Meanwhile, in Paris, Beneš pushed the Allied Council of Ten to approve a strategically defensible and economically strong Czechoslovakia to help replace German and Austrian influence in the area. Since the French government wanted to weaken Germany, the Allies tacitly tolerated the absorption of the German borderlands into Czechoslovakia.[13]

The armistice agreement between the Allies and Hungary, signed in Belgrade on November 13, 1918, stated explicitly that all Hungarian territory, with the exception of Croatia-Slavonia, was to remain under Hungarian administration. The Prague government, however, denied Hungarian sovereignty over the Slovak counties, appealed to the right of self-determination for the Slovaks, and threatened military action. With the help of the French and Italian military missions, the Czechoslovak army tried to establish its authority in Slovakia. But the situation escalated when Béla Kun's Communist government in Budapest conducted a successful campaign against eastern Slovakia. Nonetheless, in June 1919, the Council of Four established the new borders of Hungary and the Hungarian Red Army was forced to retreat. As a result of the early occupation of southern Hungary by Serbian troops, there was not much discussion at the Peace Conference about the new border between Hungary and Yugoslavia; only Pécs and the Banat remained contested. While the Serbian troops had to retreat from the coal mines at Pécs, the Banat was divided between Romania and Yugoslavia.[14]

At the turn of 1918/19, following regional battles between South Slavic and Carinthian and Styrian troops in south-eastern Carinthia and Lower Styria, a US field mission touring the Slovene-German Maribor region and south-eastern Carinthia reported: "There are many Slovenes who do not wish to join Yugoslavia [...]—we strongly recommend that the final frontier between Austria and Yugoslavia in the province of Carinthia be drawn along the watershed of the Karawanken mountains." But the Yugoslav delegation in Paris protested at the Council of Ten and, on February 18, demanded a demarcation line including the German-Austrian cities of Klagenfurt and Villach. Marshal Foch told the Yugoslavs: "Whatever you have occupied shall remain in your possession." Nevertheless, the Commission des Affaires Roumaines et Yugoslaves recommended a plebiscite in Lower Carinthia and, on May 12, Clemenceau, Lloyd George, and Wilson took its advice. Wilson in particular defended this decision in the face of several Yugoslav interventions. In the plebiscite on October 10, 1920, monitored by British, French, and Italian officers, 59 percent of the population decided to remain in Austria. The Austrian side had thus successfully won over almost half of the Slovene-speaking population.[15]

Soon after the Carinthian plebiscite, the Belgrade government had to negotiate an agreement with the new Italian government. In the Treaty of Rapallo, signed on November 12, 1920, Italy kept the whole Littoral, Trieste, and Istria, the islands of Cres and Lošinj, though in Dalmatia only the city of Zadar and the islands of Lastovo and Palagruža. Rijeka was to become a buffer state between the two countries, but, in 1924, was divided between Italy and Yugoslavia. However, half a million Croats and Slovenes in Italy became new minorities without minority rights. The same applied to the 220,000 Germans in South Tyrol, who became victims of the British and French promise made to Italy at the secret Treaty of London, in April 1915.[16]

On the subject of the peace treaties of Saint-Germain, Trianon, and Neuilly, the British historian Zara Steiner judged astutely: "The treaties with Austria, Hungary, and Bulgaria were far harsher and more vindictive that the one with Germany. The Austrian and Hungarian settlements were punitive in the extreme; the former was left in a perilous economic state, and the latter, if economically viable, was so stripped of territories and people as to guarantee its revisionist status."[17]

With the help of the Great Powers—France, Great Britain, and the United States—Poland, Czechoslovakia, Romania, and Yugoslavia were created as "associated" victorious powers. The Polish, Czech, Romanian, and Serbian elites tried to consolidate their power through nationalist ideologies and centralist measures in constitution, administration, education, and power politics (particularly the group around Marshal Piłsudski in Warsaw, the *hrad* ("castle") around President Masaryk in Prague, and the "courts" of King Ferdinand I in Bucharest and King Alexander I in Belgrade). These measures in particular curtailed the rights of the German, Magyar, Ukrainian, Russian, Jewish, and other minorities, especially in Eastern Poland, Bessarabia, Slovakia, and Slovenia, to a lesser extent also in West Prussia, Bukovina, the Bohemian lands, and Vojvodina.

After 1918, Poland, Czechoslovakia, Romania, and Yugoslavia with their German, Magyar, and Ukrainian minorities—and with Germany, the Soviet Union, Austria, and Hungary as their neighbors—suffered repeated setbacks resulting from a variety of factors. These included conflicts over border demarcations; government-enforced "de-Germanization," "de-Russification," "de-Austrianization," and "de-Magyarization;" the "nostrification" of foreign companies; the land reform and confiscation of estates; the lack of political participation by national minorities until 1925; and discriminatory trade restrictions between the "winning" and "losing" countries. Above all, the psychological factor of humiliation must not be underestimated. It is for this reason that the large majority of the almost four million Ukrainians, more than one million Germans and Belarusians respectively, and 150,000 Lithuanians refused to recognize Poland as their nation-state, and that 3.2 million Sudeten Germans and 760,000 Magyars did not regard Czechoslovakia as their country—by definition the nation-state of the "Czechoslovak nation," with "Czechoslovak" as its official language. The same was true for the 1.6 million Magyars and 720,000 Germans in Transylvania, Maramureş, Crişana, and the eastern Banat, as well as the 440,000 Danube Swabians and 40,000 Germans in Slovenia, and the 470,000 Magyars in Vojvodina, who did not develop an allegiance to the nation-state of the Serbs, Croats, and Slovenes, with "Serbo-Croatian" as its official language. Incidentally, none of the German and Magyar minority groups were allowed to play a role in shaping the new constitutions. Interwar Polish, Czech, Slovak, Magyar, Romanian, Serbian, Croatian, Slovene, and German nationalists promoted a particular ideal of "national democracy," in which principles such as minority rights and self-determination centered around collective rights rather than on principles of liberal individualism. However, shrill nationalism gained momentum as a result of class conflicts between the capitalist class and major landowners on one side and the "proletariat" and the masses of small peasants on the other.[18]

Many German, Hungarian, Czech, Polish, Romanian, Serbian, Croatian, Slovene, and Italian members of the Austrian and

Hungarian parliaments and of the Bohemian, Moravian, Silesian, Galician, Bukovinian, Croatian-Slavonian, Dalmatian, Istrian, Trieste, Gorizian, Styrian and Tyrolean Diets after 1918 became deputies in the Austrian, Hungarian, Czechoslovak, Polish, Romanian, Yugoslav, and Italian parliaments. Several deputies became ministers, some of them even prime ministers: the Austrians Karl Renner and Michael Mayr, the Czechs Karel Kramář, Jan Šrámek, Antonín Švehla, and Vlastimil Tusar, the Slovak Milan Hodža, the Polish Wincenty Witos, the Romanian Alexandru Vaida-Voievod, the Slovene Anton Korošec, and the Italian Alcide De Gasperi. Between 1918 and 1935, the Czech member of the Austrian *Reichsrat*, Tomáš Garrigue Masaryk, even became President of Czechoslovakia. After 1945, Renner became Austrian State Chancellor for a second time and then Federal President, while De Gasperi became Prime Minister of Italy. It is an open question whether they had learned their ethnicizing politics and policy of "muddling through" from Austria-Hungary.[19]

Despite propaganda slogans of "Away from Rome, away from Vienna!" in Prague and Belgrade, the development of Austrian and Hungarian secondary and higher education in the final decades before World War I had left the Monarchy's successor states with a manifold legacy. The governments in Warsaw, Prague, Budapest, Bucharest, and Belgrade used educational institutions and the army as instruments of national integration. Both old and new national universities were elitist and had relatively few students. Czechoslovakia found itself well supplied with educated Czech public officials, academics, teachers, physicians, and lawyers. However, since the Slovaks had no secondary or higher education in their own language during the final decades of rule from Budapest, nearly 22,000 Czech bureaucrats, educators, and professionals came to take up positions in Slovakia in the 1920s. The northern parts of Yugoslavia (Slovenia, Croatia-Slavonia, and Vojvodina) showed some parallels with Czechoslovakia regarding regional differences in the supply of educated professionals and public officials after 1918. Although, under Austrian rule, the Slovenes had no university, they still enjoyed higher levels of education than did the Serbs, Bosnians, Montenegrins, Albanians, and Macedonians. During the interwar period, Slovenes were thus able to find positions in Yugoslavia's central bureaucracy far in excess of their small share of population.[20]

With the rich heritage of Austria-Hungary, Czechoslovakia had been able to mobilize huge productive forces, gain an important body of knowledge, create enormous material wealth, and enrich its natural surroundings. The Czechoslovak foreign minister Beneš therefore feared a customs union with Austria and Hungary, as he explained to *Delnické Listy* in 1920: "The Czechs had fought not for political freedom—for this they had enjoyed to a certain extent before the war [sic!, A. S.]—but for their economic independence, and therefore the scheme for a confederation of the Danubian States, or even of a 'Customs Union', is out of the question for the Czechoslovak Republic. A political union with Austria and Hungary would mean that these countries would gain influence in our internal affairs: Austria by the way of the Germans living in our State, Hungary through the Magyars in Slovakia. The unfavorable economic conditions of Austria and Hungary form an obstacle to an economic union [...]."[21]

Beneš fought against both, the danger of an annexation of Austria to the German Reich as well as the danger of a restoration of the Habsburgs in Vienna or Budapest. On March 21, 1931, when the Austrian and the German foreign ministers announced their plan of a customs union, France and Czechoslovakia protested sharply, and were joined in this by Romania and Yugoslavia. Great Britain demanded that it be examined by the Council of the League of Nations and the Permanent International Court in The Hague. Charles Fenwick, editor of the *American Journal of International Law*, later criticized this decision-making: "[...] the governments of Great Britain and France were singularly lacking in statesmanship when they set their hands not only against the political union of Austria and Germany, but even against a restricted customs union which might have brought economic relief to Austria without necessity of closer political ties. [...] the withdrawal of prohibitions against it would have eased the political situation and would have greatly strengthened the democratic forces both in Austria and in Germany."[22]

Since, following the Locarno Pact of October 1925, the German Reich became not only a member of the League of Nations but also of the League Council, its importance to Poland, Czechoslovakia, Romania, and Yugoslavia was reinforced, as it now had a voice in the evaluation of minority treaties. On the other hand, the Great Depression created an even greater schism between the Sudeten Germans and Czechoslovakia—regardless of their political "activism" after 1926. The drop in exports in Sudeten German light industry and the decrease in spa tourism resulted in large-scale unemployment: as many as 525,000 men and women, i.e., 35 percent of the employable population. In their view, the Prague government did not do enough to counteract this problem. When, in February/March 1938, Milan Hodža's government finally accepted the demands of the younger generation of German "activists" (for public works contracts for local contractors and labor in the border regions and for proportional minority representation in government administration), it was too little, too late. By then, many Sudeten Germans were already looking toward Nazi Germany and pinning their hopes on Hitler and his promises to end mass unemployment. When the Sudeten German Party started to demand political, economic, and cultural autonomy within Czechoslovakia, the Nazi propaganda skillfully unmasked the fiction of Czechoslovakia as a nation-state. In summary, the leading Czech politicians "did not master [the Sudeten German] challenge in the 1920s, and they could not master it in the 1930s."[23]

The different parties in the Yugoslav parliament fought over the constitution, land reform, unification of administration, and public education. When, on June 20, 1928, a Montenegrin deputy of the Belgrade parliament shot two Croat deputies and wounded three others, among them the Croat peasant leader Stjepan Radić, who died some weeks later, political relations between Belgrade and Zagreb broke down completely. Even King Alexander I was shocked: "We cannot stay together with the Croats. Since we cannot, it would be better to separate. The best way to do this would be to effect a peaceful separation, like Sweden and Norway did." However, in 1929, King Alexander abolished the 1921 constitution, introduced a royal dictatorship, changed the country's name to "Kingdom of Yugoslavia," and strengthened the centralist administration by dividing the land into nine provinces (*banovine*) and the district of Belgrade; six of these regions and the capital had a Serbian majority.[24]

> "The war had destroyed political systems, ruined economies, divided societies, and opened vistas onto radically utopian visions of a better world." (Ian Kershaw)

The severe agricultural crisis beginning in the late 1920s forced Yugoslavia to look for new export markets and led to a rapprochement with the German Reich. Another reason for the Yugoslav approach to Nazi Germany was the Balkan policy of Benito Mussolini, who, in March 1933, proposed a Four Power Pact, a cooperation of Britain, France, Italy, and Germany, to address all European issues, including the revision of some German and Hungarian borders. In the meantime, the Zagreb lawyer Ante Pavelić, from September 1927 to January 1929 a member of the Yugoslav parliament, had organized the Ustaša movement as a terrorist organization and found support from émigrés in Italy, Austria, Germany, Hungary, and Bulgaria. On October 9, 1934, a Macedonian revolutionary, supported by three members of the Ustaše movement, killed King Alexander and the French foreign minister Louis Barthou in Marseille. In debates within the League of Nations, Yugoslavia accused Hungary of partial responsibility for the assassination because the criminals had been trained in Hungary. The Italian government ordered for all five to six hundred members of the Ustaše movement in Italy to be disarmed and sent most of them to camps on the Lipari Islands.[25]

Until the German-Austrian agreement in July 1936, Belgrade, Bucharest, and Prague feared a restoration of the Habsburgs in Vienna more than the *Anschluss* (annexation). On March 25, 1937, as a result of the new foreign policy of Prince Regent Paul and Prime Minister Milan Stojadinović, Italy and Yugoslavia signed a treaty of friendship and non-aggression. Italy's foreign minister Galeazzo Ciano believed that an alliance between Italians and South Slavs could smooth a possible annexation of Austria to Germany. Indeed, when Stojadinović visited Hitler in Berlin in January 1938, all the Reich Chancellor was interested in was Yugoslavia's attitude toward the annexation. Hitler managed to convince Stojadinović that Germany had no territorial but only economic interests in the Adriatic Sea and the Balkans, would not accept a restoration of the Habsburgs in Austria, and would respect the Yugoslav borders. Stojadinović duly declared: "Yugoslavia considers the Austrian question a clear interior question of the German people."[26] Hitler was very pleased.

The population of the Republic of (German-) Austria struggled with the transformation of Austrian identity from an imperial to a republican one, not least on account of the legacy of the Monarchy, the complexities of Habsburg imperialism, and the issue of German nationalism. Most of the new "Austrians" preferred to call themselves German-Austrian, particularly the Pan-Germans and Social Democrats, demanding a union with the Weimar Republic. Many mass organizations as well as student corporations cultivated the German-Austrian relationship in many forms, such as the huge Pan-German celebration of singers in Vienna in commemoration of the hundredth anniversary of the death of Franz Schubert in July 1928. During the 1920s, not only political relations between Berlin and Vienna increased, but also many personal links in law and business, between scientists, writers, and artists, and also in tourism. However, in 1927, following a miscarriage of justice, the Justizpalast was set on fire by Social Democrat demonstrators and eighty-nine people were killed (including four police officers) when the police used firearms to get the riot under control. After that incident, both sides were more inclined to call for the imprisonment of opponents or to resort to violence, especially in Vienna. Although the Treaty of Saint-Germain had forbidden all paramilitary groups, both the Christian Social *Heimwehr* (Home Guard) and the Social Democrat *Republikanischer Schutzbund* (Republican Defence League) assembled arsenals and threatened with mass demonstrations. As the country's two large parties lacked a shared commitment to patriotism, the Social Democrats under the leadership of Otto Bauer refused an offer by the Christian Social leader Ignaz Seipel, in 1931, to form a "grand coalition," and the governing Christian Social Party became partly dependent on the anti-democratic, fascist-leaning *Heimatblock*. Both parties had clearly overlooked the fact that this helped the National Socialists who—after their election successes in Germany in 1932—were clamoring for new elections. So, the Viennese Christian Socials found themselves on a "march between two abysses"—between the National Socialists and the Austro-Marxists.[27]

With the appointment of Hitler as Reich Chancellor, the government of Federal Chancellor Engelbert Dollfuss in Austria—with the help of Mussolini—fought with dictatorial measures against the increasing influence of Austria's (and Germany's) National Socialists, who responded with terrorist acts, including the murder of Dollfuss in July 1934. The new Chancellor Kurt Schuschnigg continued the policy of delimitation, but—after Mussolini's arrangement with Hitler (in January 1936)—was forced, for both political and economic reasons, into a compromise with Berlin (in July 1936). In *Mein Kampf,* Hitler had already revealed his plans for Austria and the motives behind them: German-Austria must "return" to the great German motherland. Only the conquest of Austria, with its strategically important location right in the center of the continent, could pave the way for the conquest of other European territories. Furthermore, Hitler had his eye on the industrial potential of Austria and Vienna's gold and foreign exchange reserves. As a matter of fact, when the German army marched into Austria on March 12, 1938, Hitler was cheered by hundreds of thousands of Austrians on his way from Braunau via Linz to Vienna. The Nazi regime quickly organized a plebiscite. The *Anschluss* was supported not only the National Socialists and the former *Grossdeutsche*, but also by the Catholic bishops, the four Superintendents of the Lutheran Church, and some of the Social Democrat leaders. Meanwhile, Jews, Christian Social, Legitimist, Social Democrat, and Communist functionaries were arrested or otherwise excluded from the vote. On April 10, 1938, 99 percent of the electorate voted in favor of the "reunification" of Germany and Austria, in other words, for annexation.[28]

Hitler's policy for the occupation of Czechoslovakia was not based on a coherent strategy, but developed gradually as part of his military, political, and economic objectives. No doubt, Hitler exploited the bitterness and anxieties after Versailles, the mass unemployment of the Great Depression, and the paranoid hatred of Jews and Bolsheviks. When, on November 5, 1937, he formulated a policy that called for the conquest and dismembering of Czechoslovakia and control of Bohemia, Moravia, and Silesia, rather than "freeing" the Sudeten Germans, as he claimed, Hitler's main objective was to incorporate the rich industrial potential of the Bohemian lands, the armaments of the Czechoslovak army, and Prague's gold and foreign exchange reserves into the German war economy.

Following the *Anschluss* of Austria in March 1938, the Sudeten German Party began to support National Socialism publicly and called for the recognition of the Sudeten German ethnic group as a legal entity and for compensation "for the injustices inflicted upon Sudeten Germans since 1918." Now Hitler used the call for self-determination of the Sudeten Germans as an instrument to destroy Czechoslovakia's parliamentary democracy. Britain and France, caught in their own World War I propaganda and the fiction of appeasement policy, backed down in the face of Hitler's threat. After the Sudeten German Party won 85 percent of the German vote in the local elections held in May and June 1938, its leader Konrad Henlein systematically refused the proposals for autonomy put forward by President Beneš and the Prague government, as part of a carefully planned delaying tactic.

When, at the party congress of the NSDAP in Nuremberg on September 12, Hitler pledged his support for the Sudeten Germans, many of them interpreted this as encouragement to stage an uprising. The Prague government was forced to declare a state of emergency and Prime Minister Chamberlain got on a plane to visit Hitler at the Berghof. There, Chamberlain accepted Hitler's demand of the secession of the *Sudetenland*, meaning all regions of Czechoslovakia with a German majority. The British and French governments presented this secession to Beneš and the Czechoslovak government in the form of an ultimatum and Prague accepted on September 21. However, Hitler then added further demands, also on behalf of Poland and Hungary. Chamberlain left Germany without result and the new Prague government ordered a general mobilization. On the one hand, Hitler was threatening with war, on the other he promised that "once this problem is solved there exist no further territorial problems for Germany in Europe." To keep the peace, the British Foreign Office and the German *Auswärtiges Amt* (Ministry of Foreign Affairs) asked Mussolini to act as mediator and Hitler agreed. In the afternoon of September 29, 1938, Hitler, Mussolini, Chamberlain, and Daladier met in Munich. They negotiated the modalities for the secession of all territories of Bohemia, Moravia, and Silesia with a 51 percent German-Czech ratio, based on the last Austrian prewar census of 1910. After suffering the humiliation of having his country's destiny decided without being consulted, Beneš resigned. Czechoslovakia's military alliances with France and the Soviet Union turned out to be worthless. "What Hitler had in mind at Munich was the ultimate creation [...] of a new order in Eastern Europe generally."[29]

On October 21, 1938, despite an overwhelming majority of the British and French parliaments voting for the Munich Agreement, Hitler signed a military directive for the *Wehrmacht* that included provisions for the liquidation of the remainder of the Czecho-Slovak state. While Poland took the Teschen (Cieszyn) region, the German-Italian arbitration on November 2, 1938, gave Hungary the southern strip of Slovakia and Carpathian Ruthenia, including Komárno/Komárom and Kassa/Košice. On October 6, 1938, Hlinka's Slovak People's Party had already declared Slovakian autonomy, and the Roman Catholic priest Jozef Tiso became head of the Slovak government. When the central government fought with the autonomous government over positions in the administration, the police, and the army, the new Czecho-Slovak president Emil Hácha dismissed the Slovak prime minister. Hitler invited Tiso to Berlin and gave him a clear choice: an immediate declaration of independence or the prospect of the division of Slovakia between Hungary, Poland, and Germany. No doubt the Slovaks served Hitler "only as willing pawns in a much larger game." On the next day, March 14, 1939, Tiso presented a report of his Berlin talks to the Slovak parliament, which duly proceeded to declare an independent "Slovak state." Now Hitler immediately called Hácha back to Berlin and, in the early hours of March 15, 1939, forced him to accept the rule of the German Reich. The next morning, German troops entered Prague and Brno. A day later, Hitler proclaimed the creation of the Protectorate Bohemia and Moravia. To his secretaries he said: "I will go down as the greatest German in history." The policy of appeasement, meanwhile, lay shattered in the ruins of the Czechoslovakian state.[30]

The postwar settlement had started to become undone from 1935 onward. Italy, Germany, and the Soviet Union opposed the demands of the Disarmament Conference in Geneva and started a new arms race. The 1930s became a decade of dictators, particularly of the totalitarian dictators Hitler, Stalin, and Mussolini. But when Hitler attempted to provoke a war in September 1938, there was no enthusiasm, not even in Germany. Nonetheless, when, on August 23, 1939, foreign ministers Molotov and Ribbentrop signed a non-aggression pact between the Soviet Union and Germany, together with a secret protocol delineating spheres of interest in Poland, Romania, and the Baltic, the world order had been turned upside down once and for all. Stefan Zweig, exiled in Britain, wrote on September 3, 1939, that the new war would be "a thousand times worse than 1914. [...] I am expecting everything from those criminals. What a breakdown of civilization."[31]

1 James J. Sheehan, *Where Have All the Soldiers Gone? The Transformation of Modern Europe* (Boston/New York, 2008), pp. 58–59; Christopher Clark, *The Sleepwalkers. How Europe Went to War in 1914* (London, 2012), pp. xxi–xxix.
2 Sheehan 2008 (see note 1), p. 60.
3 Manfried Rauchensteiner, *The First World War and the End of the Habsburg Monarchy, 1914–1918* (Vienna/Cologne/Weimar, 2014), pp. 936–54. By comparison, Germany lost more than 2 million soldiers killed in action, Russia 1.8 million, France 1.3 million, Great Britain 930,000, the Ottoman Empire 800,000, Italy 650,000, Serbia and Montenegro 300,000, Romania 250,000, Belgium 100,000, Bulgaria 100,000, and the USA 50,000. (Spencer C. Tucker and Priscilla Mary Roberts, *Encyclopedia of World War I* [Santa Barbara, 2005]).
4 Helmut Rumpler, ed., *Die Habsburgermonarchie 1848–1918*, vol. 11: *Die Habsburgermonarchie und der Erste Weltkrieg*, part 1 (Vienna, 2016), pp. 1–37.
5 Adam Tooze, *The Deluge: The Great War, America and the Remaking of the Global Order, 1916–1931* (New York, 2014), pp. 199–200; Richard G. Plaschka, Horst Haselsteiner, and Arnold Suppan, *Innere Front: Militärassistenz, Widerstand und Umsturz in der Donaumonarchie 1918* (Vienna, 1974), vol. 1, pp. 59–90.
6 Josef Kalvoda, *The Genesis of Czechoslovakia* (Boulder, Col./New York, 1986), pp. 294–95; Ivo Banac, *The National Question in Yugoslavia: Origins, History, Politics* (Ithaca/London, 1984), pp. 115–40.
7 R. J. W. Evans, "Communicating Empire: The Habsburgs and their Critics, 1700–1919," *Transactions of the Royal Society*, vol. 19 (2000), pp. 117–38.
8 Arthur Schnitzler, *Tagebuch 1917–1919*, ed. Werner Welzig (Vienna, 1985), pp. 189–201; Karl Kraus, *Die letzten Tage der Menschheit* (Vienna, 1922); Jaroslav Hašek, *The Good Soldier Švejk and his Fortunes in the World* (London, 1973); Miroslav Krleža, *Hrvatski bog Mars* (Graz/Vienna/Cologne, 1964); Péter Hanák, *The Garden and the Workshop: Essays on the Cultural History of Vienna and Budapest* (Princeton, 1998) p. 96; Ian Kershaw, *To Hell and Back: Europe 1914–1949* (London, 2015), p. 88.
9 Robert Musil, *Der Mann ohne Eigenschaften*, 2 vols. (Berlin, 1930/31); Joseph Roth, *Radetzkymarsch* (Berlin, 1932); Stefan Zweig, *Die Welt von Gestern* (Stockholm, 1944); cf. William M. Johnston, *The Austrian Mind: An Intellectual and Social History, 1848–1938* (Berkeley/Los Angeles/London, 1972).
10 Arnold Suppan, *Hitler–Beneš–Tito: Konflikt, Krieg und Völkermord in Ostmittel- und Südosteuropa*, 3 vols. (Vienna, [3]2017), vol. 3, map 1.
11 Ian Kershaw, *To Hell and Back: Europe, 1914–1949* (London, 2015), pp. 93–99; Ota Konrád, "Two post-war paths: popular violence in the Bohemian lands and in Austria in the aftermath of World War I," *Nationalities Papers* (2017), pp. 1–17.
12 Piotr S. Wandycz, *The Price of Freedom: A History of East Central Europe from the Middle Ages to the Present* (London/New York, 1992), pp. 201–35.
13 Klaus Koch, Walter Rauscher, and Arnold Suppan, eds., *Außenpolitische Dokumente der Republik Österreich 1918–1938* (ADÖ), vol. 2: *Im Schatten von Saint-Germain* (Vienna/Munich, 1994), doc. 190, 191, 213, 226, 226A-F, 267, 267A, 273, 274, 302, 312, 348.
14 Magda Ádám, György Litván, and Mária Ormos, eds., *Documents Diplomatiques Français sur l'histoire du basin des Carpates 1918–1932*, vol. I (Budapest, 1993), doc. 33, 61, 204, 249, 323, 427.
15 Arnold Suppan, *Jugoslawien und Österreich 1918–1938: Bilaterale Außenpolitik im europäischen Umfeld* (Vienna/Munich, 1996), pp. 468–656.
16 Marina Cattaruzza, *L'Italia e il confine orientale 1866–2006* (Bologna, 2007), pp. 113–64.
17 Zara Steiner, *The Lights That Failed: European International History 1919–1933* (Oxford, 2005), p. 99. On December 31, 1999, *The Economist* asserted that the war's final crime was a peace treaty "whose harsh terms would ensure a second war."
18 Joseph Rothschild, *East Central Europe between the Two World Wars*, 6th ed. (Seattle/London, 1990), pp. 3–25; Wandycz (see note 12), pp. 213–14. While the Jews constituted over forty percent of great industrialists and almost twenty percent of big landowners in Hungary, ninety percent of the Jews in Poland were unassimilated, used the Yiddish language, and lived in a world apart.
19 Cf. the biographies in *Österreichisches Biographisches Lexikon 1815–1950*, Austrian Academy of Sciences, 15 vols. (Graz/Cologne/Vienna, 1957–2018).
20 Suppan 2017 (see note 10), vol. 1, pp. 366–86, 561–84; Jaroslav Kučera, *Minderheit im Nationalstaat: Die Sprachenfrage in den tschechisch-deutschen Beziehungen 1918–1938* (Munich, 1999); Peter Štih, Vasko Simoniti, and Peter Vodopivec, *Slowenische Geschichte: Gesellschaft–Politik–Kultur* (Graz, 2008), pp. 311–55.
21 Frederick Hertz, *The Economic Problem of the Danubian States: A Study in Nationalism* (London, 1947), pp. 64–66.
22 Charles Fenwick, "Editorial Comment: Fuit Austria," *American Journal of International Law*, no. 32 (1938), p. 312.
23 Elizabeth Wiskemann, *Czechs and Germans: A Study of the Struggle in the Historic Provinces of Bohemia and Moravia* (London/New York/Toronto, 1938); Gerhard Weinberg, *Hitler's Foreign Policy 1933–1939: The Road to World War II* (New York, 2010), p. 86.
24 Banac 1984 (see note 6), pp. 379–405; *R. W. Seton-Watson i Jugoslaveni. Korespondencija 1906–1941. R. W. Seton-Watson and the Yugoslavs: Correspondence 1906–1941*, vol. 2: 1918–1941 (Zagreb/London, 1976), pp. 193–200.
25 Bogdan Krizman, *Ante Pavelić i Ustaše* (Zagreb, 1983), pp. 158–86.
26 "Protocols of Neurath and Stojadinović, Berlin, January 17, 1938," Arhiv Jugoslavije, zbirka Stojadinovića, F-24; Suppan 1996 (see note 15), p. 1214.
27 Walter Goldinger and Dieter A. Binder, *Geschichte der Republik Österreich 1918–1938* (Vienna/Munich 1992), pp. 73–83, 137–59; Ernst Hanisch, *Der lange Schatten des Staates: Österreichische Gesellschaftsgeschichte im 20. Jahrhundert* (Vienna, 1994), pp. 154–64, 285–94.
28 Gottfried-Karl Kindermann, *Österreich als Angriffsziel und Gegner des Nationalsozialismus 1933–1938* (Vienna, 2002); Hanisch 1994 (see note 27), pp. 337–47.
29 Fritz Taubert, ed., *Mythos München/Le Mythe de Munich/The Myth of Munich* (Munich, 2002); Martin Zückert, *Zwischen Nationsidee und staatlicher Realität* (Munich, 2006), pp. 282–98; Suppan (see note 10), pp. 490–522.
30 Ľubomir Lipták, "Slovakia in the 20th Century," in Elena Mannová, ed., *A Concise History of Slovakia* (Bratislava, 2000), pp. 256–59; Ian Kershaw, *Hitler 1936–1945: Nemesis* (New York/London, 2000), p. 171–73.
31 Kershaw 2015 (see note 11), pp. 341–45.

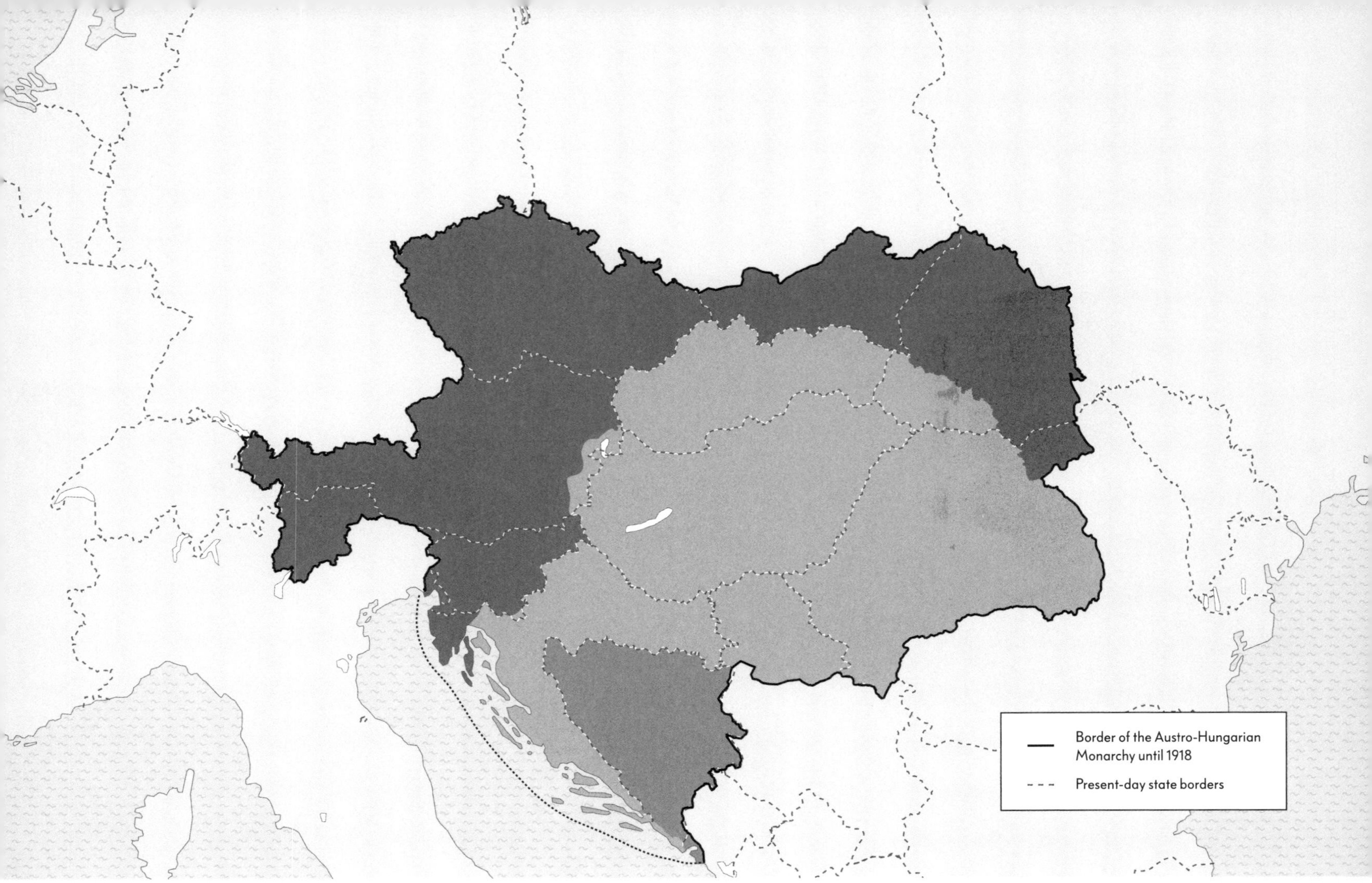

The Austro-Hungarian Monarchy until 1918
and today's political borders

border—Grenze:

Grenze, früher auch Gränze geschrieben, ist spätmhd. aus dem Polnischen entlehnt und von dem östlichen Kolonisationsgebiet aus allmählich durchgedrungen statt des einheimischen Mark. Häufig auf das Gebiet des Unräumlichen übertragen, z. B. ohne Grenzen ist dein Glück, sich in den angewiesenen Grenzen halten, keine Grenzen kennen.

Hermann Paul, *Deutsches Wörterbuch* (Halle, 1908), p. 225

Grenze F. ist eines der wenigen Lehnwörter slavischen Ursprungs: poln.=russ. granica, tschech. hranice ‚Grenzstein, Grenze', zu poln. gran, russ. grani, tschech. hrana ‚Ecke'. Im 13. Jh. ist das Wort für das Ordensland Preußen nachgewiesen als grenicze oder granizze. Von dort aus verbreitete es sich nach Westen und in die nordischen Sprachen: schwed. gräns, dän. grænse. Die Schreibung gränitze, gräinitze erscheint noch im 17. Jh., und Granitz, Gränitz wird noch 1909 als bair.=österr. gebucht.

Alfred Götze, ed., *Trübners Deutsches Wörterbuch,* vol. 3, G–H (Berlin, 1939), p. 236

German

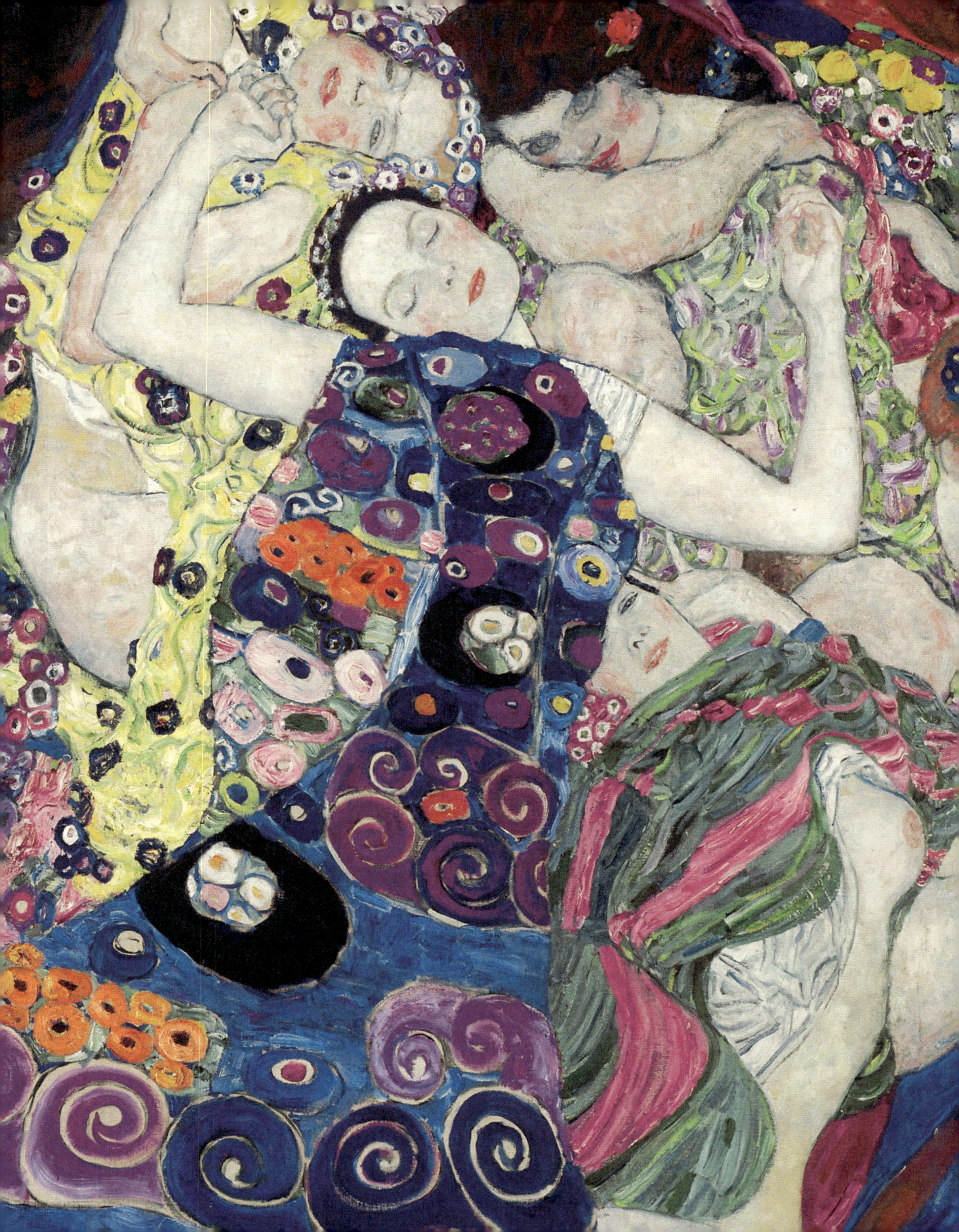

Gustav Klimt, *The Virgin*, 1913 (detail), National Gallery in Prague

A Artistic Diversity at the End of the Habsburg Monarchy

Gustav Klimt's Late Work and his Relationship with the New Viennese Avant-Garde

Franz Smola

KLIMT—A EUROPEAN JUGENDSTIL PAINTER

By around 1900, Gustav Klimt had risen to become Austria's greatest and most famous artist. In the preceding years of the 1880s and 1890s, he had worked with his brother Ernst and Franz Matsch on numerous wall and ceiling paintings, their pronounced realism and subjugation to their architectural setting largely in keeping with the style of late Historicism. In his Faculty Paintings for the ceiling of the Great Hall at the University of Vienna, a project that began in the late 1890s, Klimt first emerged as an artist who, rather than courting public approval, adhered solely to his own ideas. The Faculty Paintings' first presentations at the Vienna Secession between 1900 and 1903 unleashed fierce public debates about the degree of eroticism and ugliness permissible in art. These monumental works undoubtedly represented a crucial step in Klimt's artistic emancipation and his development into one of the preeminent Jugendstil painters in Vienna and in Europe as a whole (fig. 1).

One of Klimt's essential contributions to Jugendstil painting was the astonishing realism of his figural depictions, in which both taboo-defying eroticism and unconcealed ugliness are introduced in an allegorical context.

In 1897, the Vereinigung bildender Künstler Österreichs—Secession (Association of Austrian Artists—Secession) was founded, with Klimt as its first president, followed in 1898 by the opening of its exhibition hall designed by Joseph Maria Olbrich. This provided Klimt with a suitable forum in which to present his artworks for maximum public impact. The high point in this respect was a major Klimt exhibition staged by the artist at the Secession in 1903. One year before, the fourteenth exhibition featured probably Klimt's most important contribution to the Secession: the Beethoven Frieze. Its new linear and planar style coupled with extremely thin, elongated bodies influenced young artists like Egon Schiele and Oskar Kokoschka who would soon turn to Expressionism.

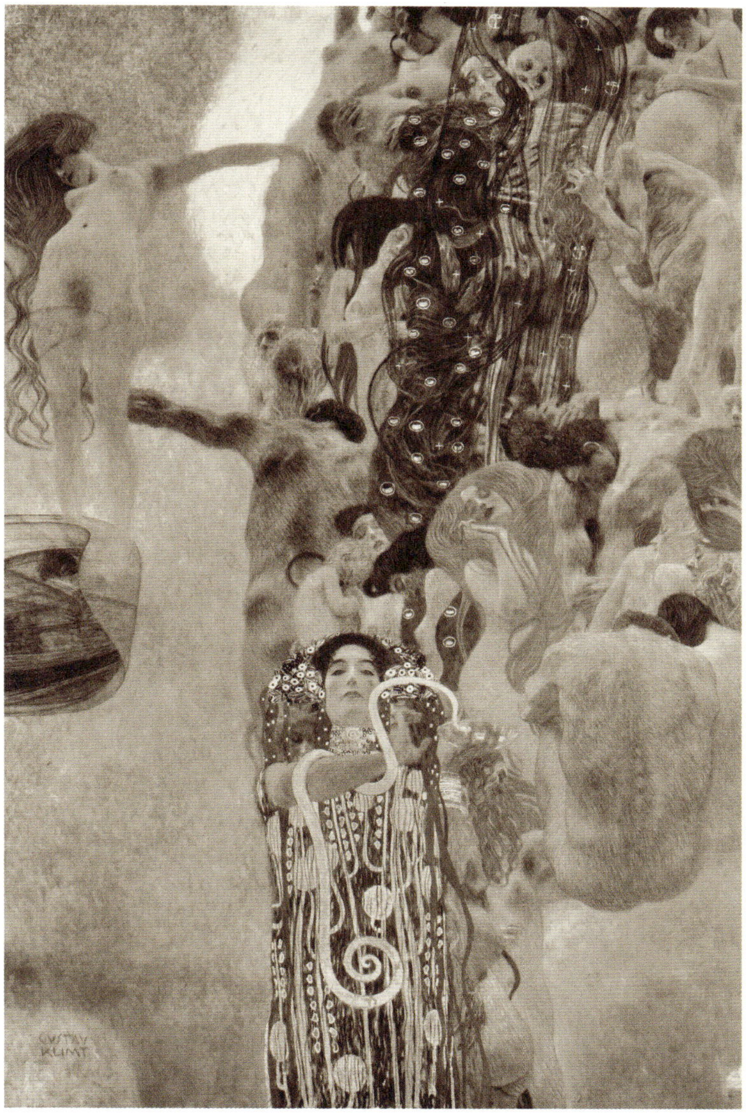

Fig. 1
Gustav Klimt
Medicine, 1900–07
Destroyed in a fire at Schloss Immendorf, Lower Austria, 1945

One of Klimt's essential contributions to Jugendstil painting was the astonishing realism of his figural depictions, in which both taboo-defying eroticism and unconcealed ugliness are introduced in an allegorical context, such as in the Faculty Paintings. On the other hand, hardly any other artists in this period ascribed as much importance to autonomous ornament, verging on the abstract, as Klimt. He incorporated ornament into his allegorical pictures and brilliantly executed portraits in an extremely original way. Unlike the highly controversial Faculty Paintings, Klimt's allegories and portraits suffused with ornament were generally praised and admired. His painting *The Kiss* (*Lovers*, fig. 2), begun in 1907, was bought by the Austrian state immediately after its first exhibition at the 1908 Kunstschau—the first work by the artist to be purchased for the recently founded Moderne Galerie.

THE SPLIT WITH THE SECESSION

Quarrels arising from personnel matters and diverging views about art eventually led to Klimt's spectacular split with the Secession in 1905, in which he was joined by a number of his allies.

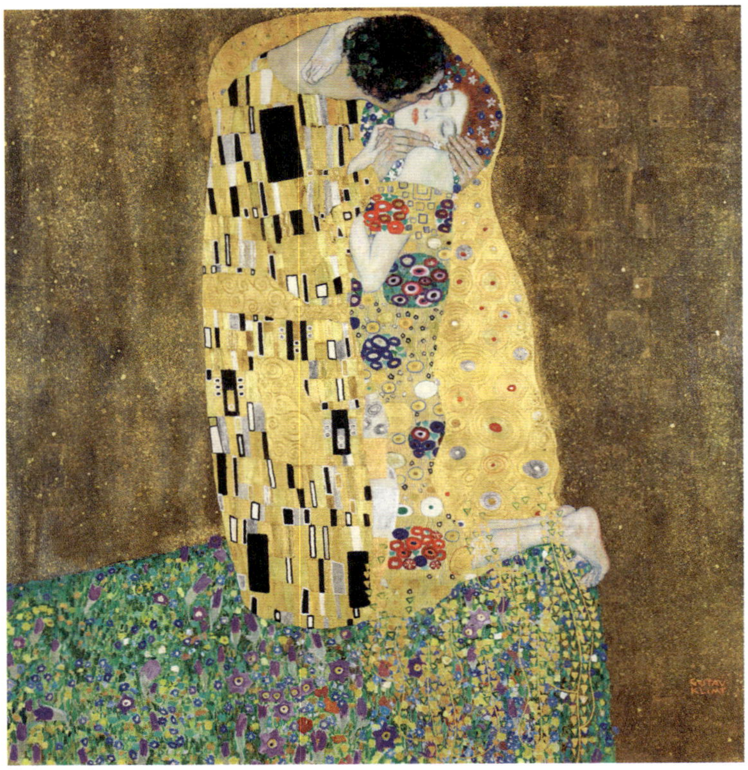

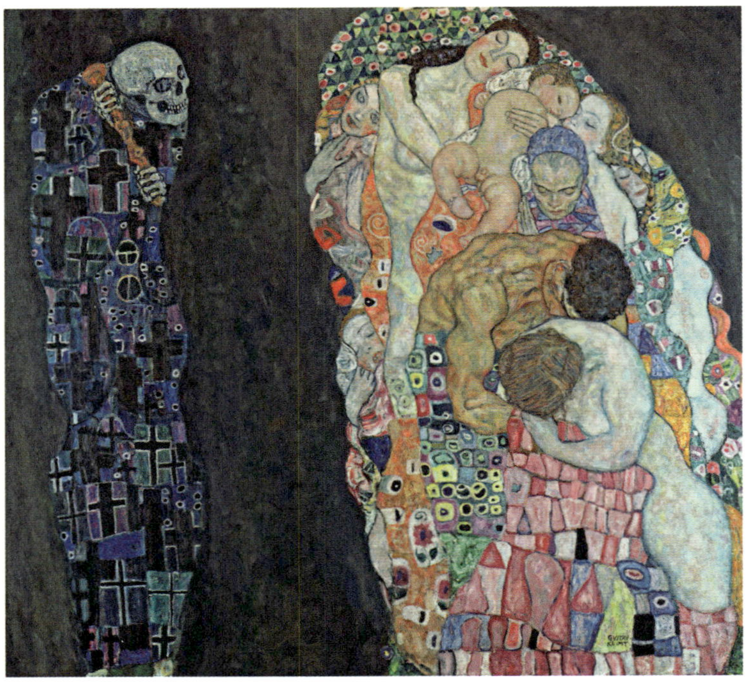

Fig. 2
Gustav Klimt
The Kiss (Lovers), 1907/08, with reworkings through to 1909
Belvedere, Vienna

Fig. 3
Gustav Klimt
Death and Life, 1910/11, reworked 1915/16
Leopold Museum, Vienna

However, this also entailed the loss of a platform for his art and the media attention this brought. The gap was filled by the Kunstschau exhibitions organized by Klimt and his artist group in 1908 and 1909. At the 1908 Kunstschau, with its rich and varied insights into the latest developments in the fine and applied arts, design, and architecture, the sixteen paintings by the master exhibited in the "Klimt chapel"—as it was dubbed by art writers—were the show's main attraction.[1]

However, on the international stage, the art of Jugendstil had long since been replaced by the avant-garde movement, which was rapidly evolving during this period and was followed with interest in Vienna. Here the groundwork was laid by exhibitions such as those at Galerie Miethke, then run by Klimt's close friend and colleague Carl Moll, where solo shows were devoted to artists like Vincent van Gogh (1906) and Paul Gauguin (1907).[2] From around 1910, an avant-garde art movement also began to develop in Vienna, now combined under the descriptor of "early Viennese Expressionism."[3] Oskar Kokoschka, Egon Schiele, Max Oppenheimer, Anton Kolig, Anton Faistauer, Albert Paris Gütersloh, and Felix Albrecht Harta are among the artists grouped under this label.

In December 1909, the inaugural exhibition of the Neukunstgruppe, the artists' association formed by Schiele, caused a sensation, while also being the first show in which Schiele's work received significant attention.[4] A veritable scandal, on the other hand, was sparked by Kokoschka's series of psychologically penetrating portraits at the *Sonderausstellung Malerei und Plastik* in February 1911, an exhibition organized by the Neukunstgruppe at the Hagenbund's premises.[5] In January 1912, an impressive display of the new forces on Vienna's art scene could be appreciated at Budapest's Müvésház (Artists' House) in a show featuring the preeminent members of the Neukunstgruppe as well as Kokoschka and Arnold Schönberg.[6] A further opportunity for a joint presentation of the new Viennese avant-garde was provided by the Sonderbund exhibition in Cologne in the summer of 1912. Alongside spectacular displays devoted to individual artists (van Gogh, Cézanne, and Munch, for example), it featured the most modern artists from selected European countries. Austria's contribution included artworks by Kokoschka, Schiele, Kolig, Faistauer, Gütersloh, and Harta.[7] In these impressive manifestations of the latest movements in art, the exponents of Jugendstil and the various Secessions were nowhere to be seen. These artists did, however, continue to organize their own exhibitions. Revealingly, a large exhibition showcasing mainly German art, in which Jugendstil continued to play an important role, was organized in Dresden almost in parallel with the Cologne Sonderbund show. Eight paintings by Klimt were included in this exhibition, and Viennese applied

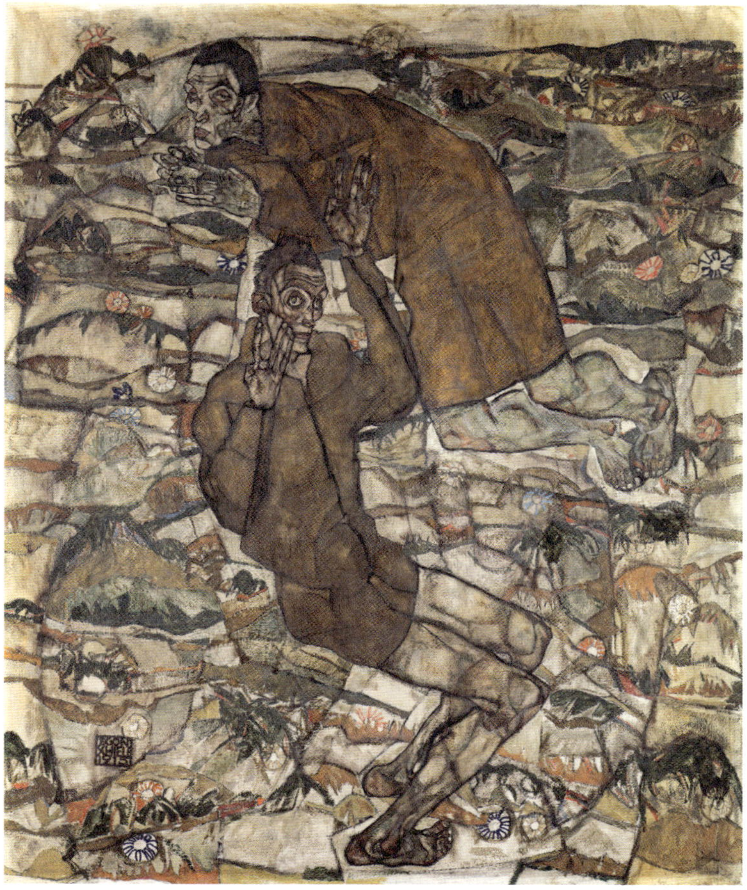

art featured prominently, especially works from the Wiener Werkstätte. By contrast, there were only two works by Kokoschka on display and not a single painting by Schiele.[8]

The situation for the Viennese avant-garde changed suddenly at the turn of the year 1912/13, when the Klimt Group decided to include all members of the Neukunstgruppe in its Bund Österreichischer Künstler (Union of Austrian Artists). Consequently, Klimt's work was now shown together with works by the "young artists," as he called them, at exhibitions organized by the Union. This new approach was first put to the test at the Bund Österreichischer Künstler exhibition in Budapest in March 1913. It featured ten paintings by Klimt, a lavish display of the Wiener Werkstätte's achievements, as well as exponents of Expressionism, such as Kokoschka and Schiele, who contributed three paintings each.[9]

KLIMT AND WORLD WAR I

The outbreak of World War I in the fall of 1914 caused a sudden hiatus in the activities of the international avant-garde art scene. For the vast majority of artists in the vanguard of artistic innovation, most of whom were born in the 1880s, the war tore a deep hole in their artistic career. Their generation was the one hardest hit by conscription, and many of these young artists were forced to do military service of one form or another, either directly, by fighting on the front, as in the case of Oskar Kokoschka and Herbert Boeckl, or as war painters working for the War Press Office, such as, for example, Anton Kolig, Wilhelm Thöny, and Felix Albrecht Harta. Schiele got off comparatively lightly and was involved mainly in guard duties and office work. But for all of them the opportunities to continue their work as artists were hugely curtailed.

"Exhibiting with me: Klimt, four pictures, including 'Death and Life,' which has been completely repainted; my 'Transfiguration' will hang opposite to this, his largest painting."

(Egon Schiele)

Gustav Klimt was fifty-two when the war started and did not have to worry about being called up to fight. For the most part, he was able to continue working undisturbed.[10] At this time, Klimt's late phase emerged, in which portraits and landscapes were to play an ever-greater role, while allegorical themes receded noticeably into the background. In terms of style, his late work saw the brushwork become more accentuated. A comparison of the paintings predating 1910 with those after 1914 strikingly reveals the more dynamic brushstrokes and broader application of paint. Klimt's former meticulous style of painting, for which he had been so admired by contemporaries, was now very much a thing of the past.

In view of the highly personal cosmos of ideas throughout Klimt's earlier works, with hardly a hint about current events in any of his pictures, it comes as little surprise that there is also no reference to the war in any of his post-1914 paintings. At such a tumultuous time, the idylls and beauty

Fig. 4
Egon Schiele
Transfiguration (*The Blind II*), 1915
Leopold Museum, Vienna

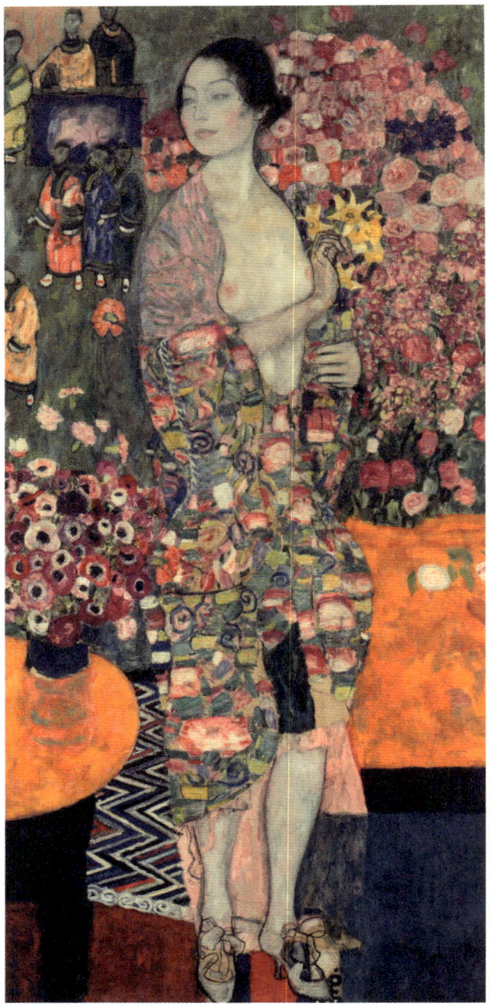

◂ Fig. 5
Gustav Klimt
The Dancer, 1916/17
Private collection, New York, courtesy of the Neue Galerie

Fig. 6 ▸
Wiener Werkstätte salesroom in New York, 1922
Gustav Klimt's *The Dancer* (1916/17) can be seen in the background

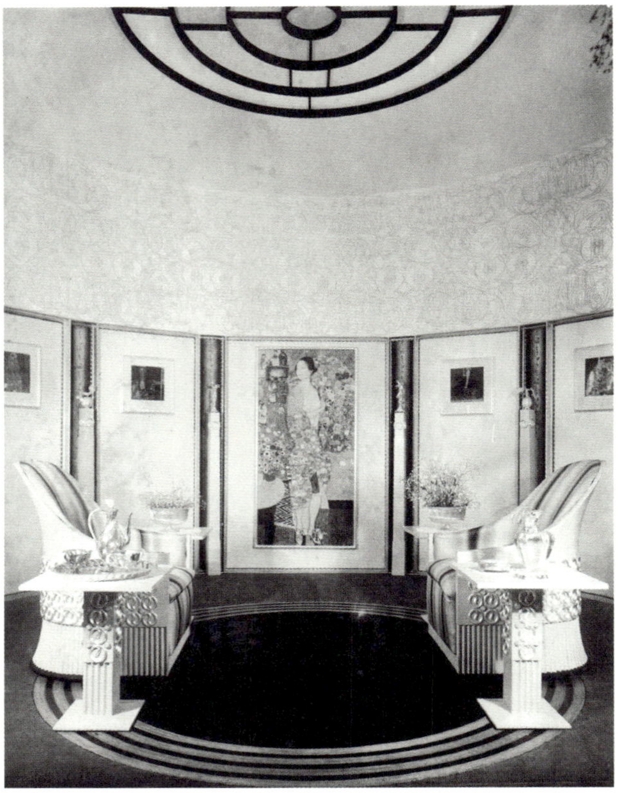

magically conjured by Klimt in his paintings seem strangely detached from reality. This approach, which could be characterized as a type of artistic escapism, can also be found in the work of other artists from Klimt's generation, such as Carl Moll and Koloman Moser, likewise exponents of the Secession style, whose motifs similarly reveal no inkling of the war.

EXHIBITIONS DURING THE WAR

In spite of the growing impact of the war, cultural life in the city remained astonishingly active. Exhibitions in Vienna, and also in the cities of other nations involved in the war, carried on with surprising continuity. Members of the Vienna Kunstschau, for instance, organized a guest exhibition at the Berlin Secession in January and February 1916.[11] Here, perhaps for the first time, the selection of works showed that the young Expressionists were gradually gaining equal status to Klimt, whose dominant position was beginning to wane. Three of Klimt's paintings were shown in Berlin together with three pictures by Schiele and a total of seven works by Kokoschka. Furthermore, Klimt's *Death and Life* (fig. 3), which the master had just finished reworking and was now presenting this new version to the public for the first time, was exhibited in the same room as Schiele's recently completed large-scale painting *Transfiguration (The Blind II*, fig. 4). The young Schiele gave a rapturous report about this to his brother-in-law Anton Peschka: "Exhibiting with me: Klimt, four pictures, including 'Death and Life,' which has been completely repainted; my 'Transfiguration' will hang opposite to this, his largest painting."[12] This direct comparison between Klimt's and Schiele's paintings is illuminating inasmuch as both works explore the same subject, namely the question of how to depict death. Klimt chose the traditional skeleton for his interpretation, while Schiele took a far more modern approach by expressing death in the faces and the waning gazes of two dying men.

The growing predominance of the "young artists" and Klimt's diminishing importance was even more pronounced at the presentation of the Austrian avant-garde in Stockholm, in neutral Sweden, in September 1917.[13] It featured extensive bodies of work by Klimt, Schiele, Kokoschka, Faistauer, Albin Egger-Lienz, and Anton Hanak, in which, even just in terms of numbers, Klimt was less prominent than some of his colleagues. Thirteen of Klimt's paintings were included, in contrast to fifteen by Schiele and fifteen by Kokoschka. Klimt had long ceased to be the brightest star outshining all others and was now merely one artist among many.

KLIMT'S LATE PAINTING STYLE

At home, on the other hand, Klimt had long been enjoying a kind of special status. Already during his lifetime, he was seen to stand apart from the established art scene. This arose in part from his increasingly withdrawn lifestyle, as the artist deliberately isolated himself at his Hietzing garden studio and, as a result, became more and more solitary, detached from the art scene, the public, and also his younger colleagues. But, above all, his works, which right until the end continued to adhere to the aesthetic ideals of Jugendstil, were increasingly at odds with the expressive painting culture that was strongly emerging in Austria. Klimt's style seemed more and more like an exoticism outside of the norm.

In particular Klimt's luxurious portraits of women, basking in a dreamy vibrancy, must have seemed like an anachronism to contemporaries facing the bitter realities of the war years. Nevertheless, they were still very much in demand, as the artist's many portrait commissions during the war demonstrate. Evidently, he was satisfying the need of *haute-bourgeois* society for fashionable extravagance, luxury, and glamor. One of the special characteristics of Klimt's late female portraits is his penchant for sumptuous floral landscapes, for instance in the form of floral patterned dresses or abundant flower arrangements on fabric wall hangings in the backgrounds of his pictures. A striking example is *The Dancer* of 1916/17 (fig. 5), originally perhaps a portrait of Ria Munk, which was later reworked by Klimt.

In those years, flowers also emerged as the main motif in the designs of the Wiener Werkstätte, with which Klimt had enjoyed close ties since its foundation in 1903.[14] Under Dagobert Peche, the foremost designer at the time, floral decor evolved into the dominant motif in metalwork, jewelry, wallpaper designs, and textiles. Remarkably, the Wiener Werkstätte managed to safeguard the production of its elite, artistically sophisticated artefacts throughout the difficult war years, even opening new branches (for example in Geneva and New York) amidst the austerity of the postwar period. In the 1920s, this predilection for floral designs developed seamlessly into an elegant, fashionable Art Deco style. Klimt's aesthetic portraits were the perfect addition to the luxurious, stylish environments in which the Wiener Werkstätte products were showcased, as contemporary photos of the New York salesroom exemplify (fig. 6). Presumably, Klimt would have continued to paint portraits defined by luxurious beauty, had the master been granted a longer life.

The allegorical compositions, to which Klimt still occasionally turned in his final years, similarly stand out like lone monoliths in the art landscape of the time. The large-scale painting *The Bride* (fig. 7), which the master worked on from 1917 but was never able to complete, is one such example. The subject of a visionary dream scene with a throng of partially nude, partially clothed female figures had appeared in similar earlier compositions by the artist, such as the painting *The Virgin* of 1913 (fig. 8) or the group representing Life in *Death and Life* (fig. 3). Here, Klimt had already explored the interplay between concealing and revealing, camouflage, and introducing fragments of the naked body, and

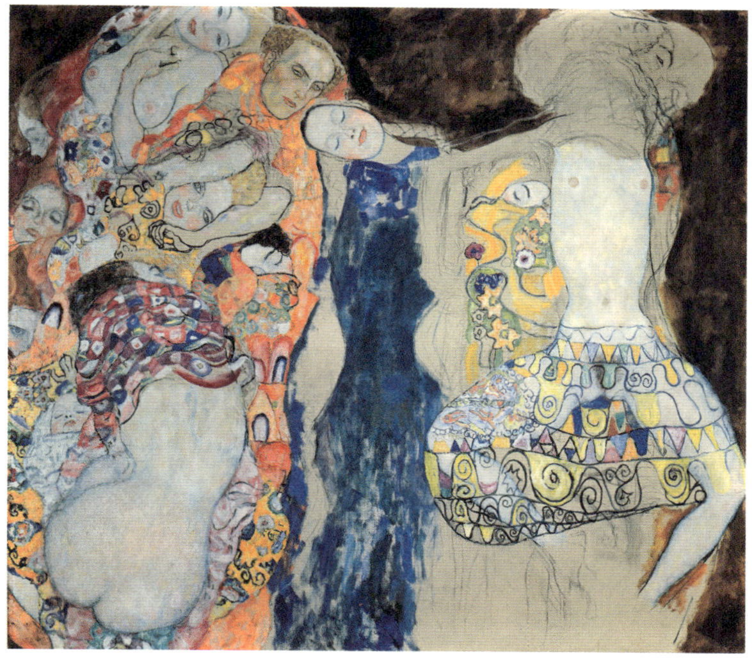

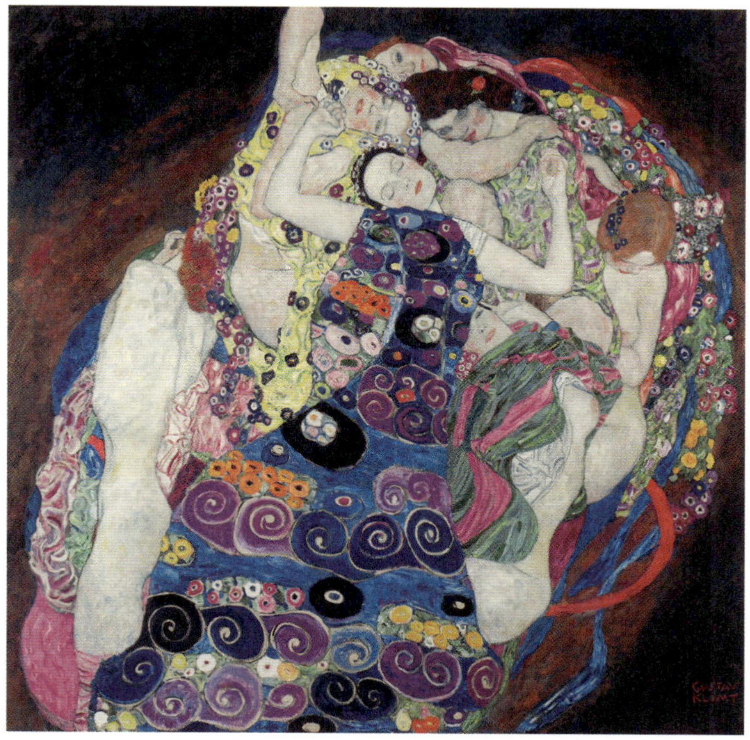

Fig. 7
Gustav Klimt
The Bride, 1917/18
Belvedere, Vienna, on loan from the Gustav Klimt | Wien 1900 Private Foundation, 2014

Fig. 8
Gustav Klimt
The Virgin, 1913
National Gallery in Prague

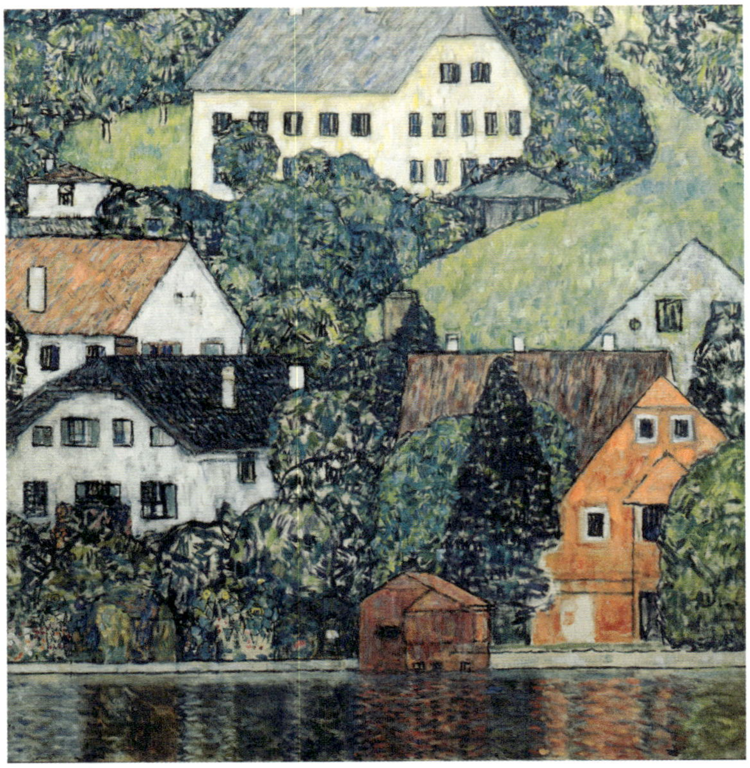

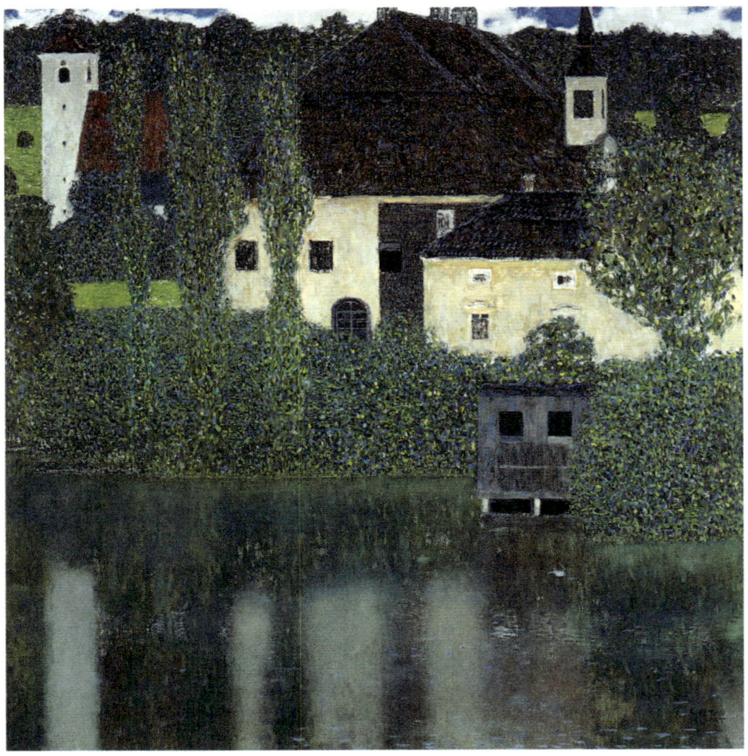

Fig. 9
Gustav Klimt
Houses at Unterach on the Attersee, 1915/16
Private collection

Fig. 10
Gustav Klimt
Schloss Kammer on the Attersee I (Wasserschloss), 1908
National Gallery in Prague

he continued this approach in *The Bride* (fig. 7). If the female nude in the right half of the painting was indeed to be accompanied by Death, as Marian Bisanz-Prakken argues, based on the skull that is merely suggested on the canvas, Klimt would have been continuing the theme of "Death and Maiden" already found in many other variations in his earlier paintings.[15]

Klimt also demonstrated astonishing perseverance in his landscapes, right up until the end of his life. Even during the war years, he never abandoned his annual ritual of summer sojourns in the countryside, the source of his repertoire of landscape motifs, nor did he ever stray from the dimensions and formats consistently adopted in his landscapes in previous years. Nevertheless, in Klimt's late landscapes in particular, a certain stylistic change can be detected. *Houses at Unterach on the Attersee* (fig. 9), for instance, painted in the years 1915 and 1916, is characterized by an emphasis on clearly distinguished, boldly outlined planes of color. A certain abruptness in the composition is also undeniable. These characteristics are completely absent from the Attersee paintings only a few years earlier, such as *Schloss Kammer on the Attersee I (Wasserschloss)* of 1908 (fig. 10), in which the master aspired to a dreamy, romanticized narrative with soft transitions between the motifs. In his late landscapes, Klimt had undoubtedly moved away from the sinuous elegance of Secessionist art.

Klimt's late drawings also reveal an astonishingly modern quality. He increasingly abandoned the self-contained line and developed a distinctive, dynamic rhythm, using agitated, swiftly applied strokes. A pinnacle in Klimt's late graphic art is represented by the many preliminary studies for the above-mentioned large canvas *The Bride* (fig. 7). These reveal new, almost expressive strokes in which Klimt has left the aesthetic, flowing lines of his earlier works far behind (fig. 11).[16]

KLIMT'S SIGNIFICANCE AFTER HIS DEATH

In the years after 1914, Klimt's colleagues increasingly saw his work as belonging to the past. Immediately after his sudden death in February 1918, the master of Jugendstil was elevated, once and for all, to a mythical cult figure. It is therefore no surprise that Carl Moll's survey of the previous one hundred years of Viennese painting, which opened at Kunsthaus Zürich three months after Klimt's death, became the first posthumous tribute to the master's art. It included no less than fourteen of his paintings.[17] A further tribute was the purchase, in 1919, of *Medicine*, one of the three monumental Faculty Paintings, for the Österreichische Galerie, an acquisition August Lederer helped organize and Ferdinand Bloch-Bauer, Sonja Knips, and Hugo Koller co-funded.[18]

However, there was no solo exhibition immediately following Klimt's death,

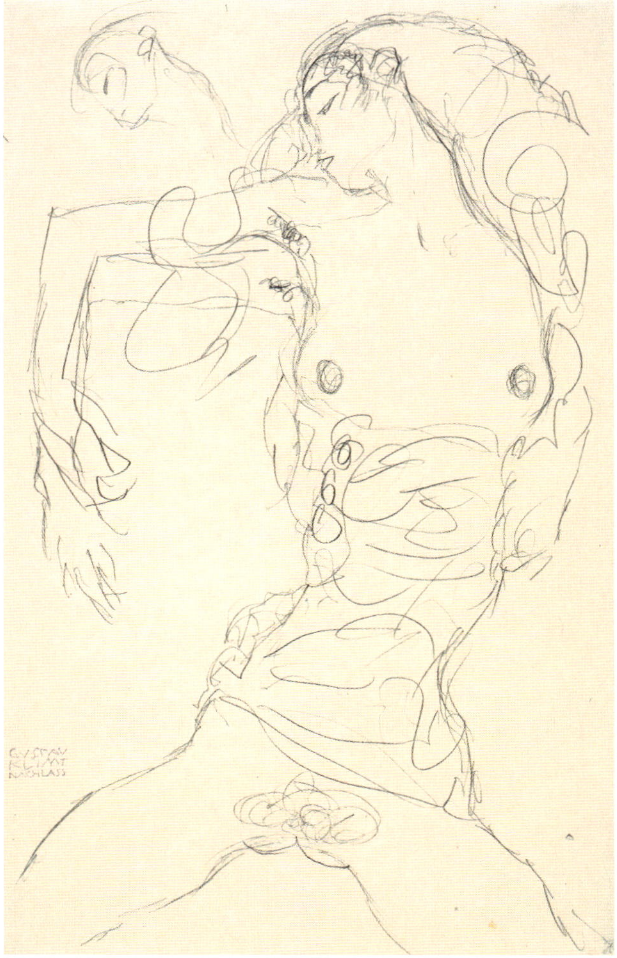

nor in the ensuing years. Only a few smaller shows of Klimt's work were presented at some of Vienna's commercial galleries. Exhibitions of his drawings and sketches, for example, were staged at Galerie Nebehay in June 1919 and at Galerie Würthle in May 1920. In May 1926, the Neue Galerie under Otto Kallir held a small Klimt exhibition including loans from the August and Serena Lederer collection.[19] Occasionally, paintings by Klimt were included in exhibitions organized by the Bund Österreichischer Künstler; examples include *Adam and Eve* (p. 63) at the 1920 Kunstschau[20] and the unfinished painting *The Bride* (fig. 7) at the 1925 Kunstschau.[21]

It was not until the tenth anniversary of Klimt's death that the master was remembered in two commemorative exhibitions. In March and April 1928, the Neue Galerie held an exhibition with around fifteen Klimt paintings, the majority from the collection of Paul Stiassny.[22] A few weeks later, the Secession staged a major Klimt retrospective with seventy-six paintings and numerous drawings and sketches. This was organized by an exhibition committee composed of prominent names, such as Berta Zuckerkandl, Bruno Grimschitz, and the two Vienna city councilors Julius Lindner and Julius Tandler, while Klimt's colleagues Josef Hoffmann, Carl Moll, and Alfred Roller revived the flair of earlier Secession exhibitions.[23] Contemporary reviews of the exhibition largely saw Klimt's art as historical, with his landscapes most highly praised, an opinion shared by Arthur Roessler.[24] One year later, Klimt's work became musealized once and for all with the reopening of the Moderne Galerie at the Orangery of the Lower Belvedere, where Klimt's art has been the main attraction ever since.[25]

Fig. 11
Gustav Klimt
Reclining Female Semi-Nude, study for *The Bride*, c. 1917
Leopold Museum, Vienna

1 Dietrun Otten, "Die Klimtgruppe: Malerei auf der Kunstschau 1908," in *Gustav Klimt und die Kunstschau 1908*, eds. Agnes Husslein-Arco and Alfred Weidinger, exh. cat. Belvedere, Vienna (Munich/Berlin/London/New York, 2008), pp. 156–75, here pp. 168–72.
2 Tobias G. Natter, *Die Galerie Miethke: Eine Kunsthandlung im Zentrum der Moderne*, exh. cat. Jüdisches Museum der Stadt Wien (Vienna, 2003), pp. 201, 205.
3 Patrick Werkner, *Physis und Psyche: Der österreichische Frühexpressionismus* (Vienna/Munich, 1986).
4 Tobias G. Natter and Thomas Trummer, eds., *Die Tafelrunde: Egon Schiele und sein Kreis*, exh. cat. Österreichische Galerie Belvedere, Vienna (Cologne, 2006), pp. 47–54.
5 Werner J. Schweiger, *Der junge Kokoschka: Leben und Werk. 1904–1914* (Vienna/Munich, 1983), pp. 165–96; Natter/Trummer 2006 (see note 4), pp. 55–57; Sabine Fellner, "Störenfriede: Der Schrecken der Avantgarde von Makart bis Nitsch," in *Störenfriede: Der Schrecken der Avantgarde von Makart bis Nitsch*, ed. Sabine Fellner, exh. cat. Lentos Kunstmuseum, Linz (Vienna, 2008), pp. 11–31, here p. 21.
6 *A Neukunst Wien 1912*, Müvésház, Budapest, January 1912; Franz Smola, "Neukunst und Klimtgruppe: Wiens Avantgarde in Budapest 1912/13," in *Zeit des Aufbruchs: Budapest und Wien zwischen Historismus und Avantgarde*, ed. Wilfried Seipel, exh. cat. Kunsthistorisches Museum, Vienna (Vienna/Milan, 2003), pp. 525–32, here pp. 525–27.
7 Franz Smola, "Der österreichische Beitrag zur Kölner Sonderbundausstellung 1912," in *1912—Mission Moderne: Die Jahrhundertschau des Sonderbundes*, ed. Barbara Schaefer, exh. cat. Wallraf-Richartz-Museum & Fondation Corboud, Cologne (Cologne, 2012), pp. 177–91.
8 *Grosse Kunstausstellung*, Städtischer Ausstellungspalast, Dresden, May 1 to October 15, 1912.
9 *Kollektiv-Ausstellung des Bundes Österreichischer Künstler und Gustav Klimt*, Müvésház (Artists' House), Budapest, March 1913; András Zwickl, "Das siegreiche Vordringen der modernen Bestrebungen: Kunst aus Österreich im Müvésház (Künstlerhaus)," in Seipel 2003 (see note 6), pp. 513–23, here pp. 516–17.
10 See Christian M. Nebehay, *Gustav Klimt: Dokumentation* (Vienna, 1969), p. 503.
11 *Katalog der Wiener Kunstschau in der Berliner Secession*, exh. cat. Berlin Secession (Berlin, 1916).
12 Letter from Egon Schiele to Anton Peschka, December 16, 1915 (autograph), whereabouts unknown; Leopold Museum, Vienna / Egon Schiele Autograph Database, ID: 951 (autograph is also accessible online at http://www.egonschiele.at [accessed on October 12, 2017]).
13 *Österrikiska konstutställningen*, Liljevalchs Konsthall, Stockholm, September 1917; Elizabeth Clegg, "War and Peace at the 1917 Stockholm 'Austrian Art Exhibition'," *The Burlington Magazine*, no. 1315, vol. 154, October 2012, pp. 676–88.
14 Janis Staggs, "Bejeweled Portraits and Painted Jewels," in *Klimt and the Women of Vienna's Golden Age: 1900-1918*, ed. Tobias G. Natter, exh. cat. Neue Galerie—Museum for German and Austrian Art, New York (Munich/London/New York, 2016), pp. 210–39.
15 Marian Bisanz-Prakken, "Gustav Klimt: The Late Work: New Light on *The Virgin* and *The Bride*," in *Gustav Klimt: The Ronald S. Lauder and Serge Sabarsky Collections*, ed. Renée Price, exh. cat. Neue Galerie—Museum for German and Austrian Art, New York (Munich/Berlin/London/New York, 2007), pp. 105–27, here pp. 124–27.
16 Marian Bisanz-Prakken, *Gustav Klimt: Die Zeichnungen*, exh. cat. Albertina, Vienna (Munich, 2012), pp. 254–56.
17 *Ein Jahrhundert Wiener Malerei*, Kunsthaus Zürich, May 12 to June 16, 1918.
18 Sophie Lillie, "Der Zeit ihren Klimt: Gustav Klimt im Spannungsfeld zwischen Politik und Gesellschaft," in *Klimt: Die Sammlung des Wien Museums*, ed. Ursula Storch, exh. cat. Wien Museum (Ostfildern, 2012), pp. 38–45, here p. 41.
19 Marie-Catherine Tessmar-Pfohl, "Die Neue Galerie von 1923 bis 1938: Kunsthandel und Kunstpolitik im Wien der Zwischenkriegzeit" (master's thesis, University of Vienna, 2003), p. 60.
20 Elizabeth Clegg, *Art, Design and Architecture in Central Europe 1890–1920* (New Haven/London, 2006), pp. 230–31; Matthias Boeckl, "Die Kunstschau 1909," in *Gustav Klimt—Josef Hoffmann: Pioniere der Moderne*, eds. Agnes Husslein-Arco and Alfred Weidinger, exh. cat. Belvedere, Vienna (Munich/London/New York, 2011), pp. 288–97, here p. 297.
21 Franz Smola, "Robin Christian Andersen: Leben und Werk. Mit einem Werkverzeichnis aller künstlerischen Arbeiten" (PhD dissertation, University of Vienna, 2017), pp. 157–58.
22 Tessmar-Pfohl 2003 (see note 19), p. 62.
23 *Klimt-Gedächtnis-Ausstellung*, Secession, Vienna, June 27 to July 31, 1928; Tessmar-Pfohl 2003 (see note 19), p. 62; Lillie 2012 (see note 18), pp. 38–45, here pp. 40–41.
24 A.R., "Gedächtnisausstellung Gustav Klimt," *Wiener Neueste Nachrichten*, April 7, 1928, quoted from Tessmar-Pfohl 2003 (see note 19), p. 62.
25 Lillie 2012 (see note 18), pp. 38–45, here p. 41.

In Search of a Tradition of the Future: Notes on Several Czech Artists From Preisler to Filla

Markéta Theinhardt

In the last year of the First World War, the Czech art scene was mourning the loss of two great artists. On April 27, 1918, Jan Preisler died of pneumonia at the age of 46, and on November 27, Bohumil Kubišta, twelve years Preisler's junior, succumbed to the Spanish flu. Preisler's obituary, which was published in the first postwar edition of *Volné směry* (Free Directions), the mouthpiece of the Mánes Association of Fine Artists, gave its author Vincenc Beneš (1883–1979) an opportunity to appraise the artistic aspirations of both generations of artists. Beneš himself belonged to the second generation: He was a member of Osma (The Eight), like Kubišta, joined the Skupina výtvarných umělců (Group of Visual Artists), and then rejoined the Mánes group in 1917. In the "battle of the Cubists" in 1913/14, Beneš, the creator of *Tram No. 4* (1912/13, The National Gallery in Prague), an emblematic work produced in the spirit of Analytical Cubism, defended the positions of "orthodox" Cubism, also underpinning his arguments with theory. However, with his 1915 *Military Funeral* (The National Gallery in Prague), he drew a line under Cubism's analytical, fragmented vision in favor of an emotional, holistic composition. This marked the beginning of his *retour à l'ordre.*

Transformations of this kind were not unusual at the time. The experience of war had no doubt sent convulsions through Europe's cultural and ethical foundations, but there also seems to have been a growing awareness that the exploration of form had been pushed to its very limits. This was also the observation made by Beneš in his obituary for Jan Preisler: "Our motto was entirely different from that of the preceding generation. Theirs was freedom, flexibility, independence, nature, emotion, life—for us it was the battle for artistic form. Thus, we fell for the opposite extreme: formalism. Both approaches to art run counter to one another, but must come together in a common focus if they are to reach the domain of art at all. The former proceeded from nature, life, and emotion, and their aim was to elevate their experience to the heights of art. The latter were equipped with diverse—sometimes useless—insights, and their aim was, generally speaking, to fill forms derived from logic with feeling and life. [...] Yet the strokes remained but strokes, the contrasts but contrasts, and the totality of the image simply refused to coalesce into a single vibrating space. We fared thus because we did not want to be 'painters by the grace of God,' but conscious creators ready to act at any moment."[1]

The example of French art was particularly apparent in the circle surrounding the Mánes group and its associated avant-garde. The group's exhibitions and publications, consistently dedicated to French art, caused the French model to become firmly embedded in art theory, a development that was also partly due to the efforts of Julius Meier-Graefe, an art historian whom Prague held in particularly high esteem. In his introduction to the catalogue accompanying *Les indépendants*, an exhibition of new French painting organized by Mánes in 1910, the young art historian Antonín Matějček not only formulated the first definition of Expressionism, but also offered an analysis of the significance of the "padres" of modern art, in particular Cézanne. A year prior to the foundation of the Skupina výtvarných umělců, a splinter group of artists that broke away from Mánes, prompted by recent trends in Paris, Matějček reiterated the "law," the logic of composition.

In his obituary for Preisler, Vincenc Beneš appears to regret and question all of this: "We envied the French for their creative aplomb, as well as their artistic successes. We knew that, to some extent, it could all be ascribed to France's national tradition. But we assumed that this tradition was based on an exacting knowledge of the laws of form, passed down from generation to generation, from master to student. We attempted to penetrate this closed circle in order to discover the secret of this remarkable creative endeavor. That was a mistake. Tradition is something that transcends the personal; something intangible, only accessible to the members of a chosen people. The so-called painterly laws are for the most part individual and only revealed to some after many years of persistent, systematic labor." Beneš concludes: "Yes, in the picture everything must be justified and in its rightful place, but not according to the logic of the mind, but according to the logic of artistic truth and feeling."[2]

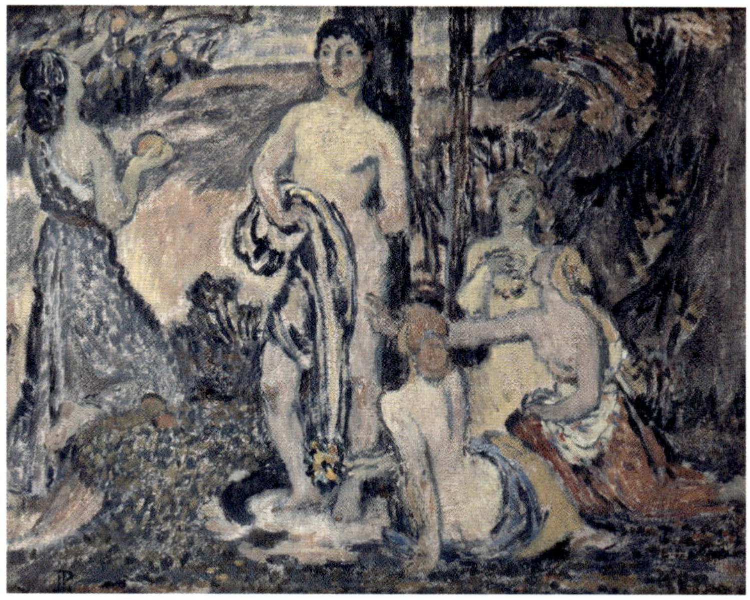

Fig. 1
Jan Preisler
Temptation (Bathing), 1916/17
Karlovy Vary Art Gallery

Against this background, it becomes clearer why Preisler was seen as such a key figure among the first generation of Mánes members (and not just by Beneš). Preisler's work seemed to combine the feeling (Beneš even refers to Slavic lyricism) and the knowledge of form, enriched by

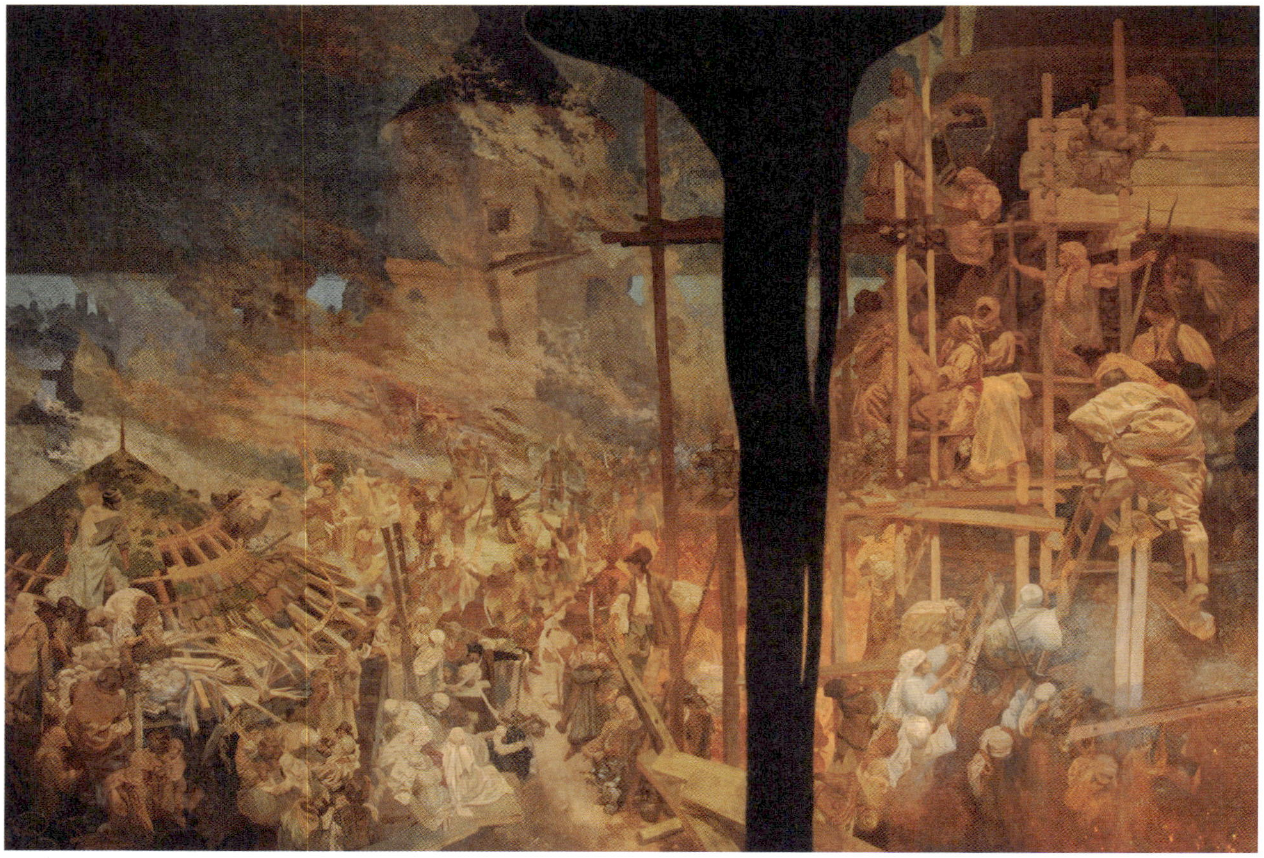

Fig. 2
Alfons Mucha
The Defense of Szigetvár against the Turks by the Ban of Croatia Nikola Šubić Zrinski in 1566, 1914
Prague City Gallery

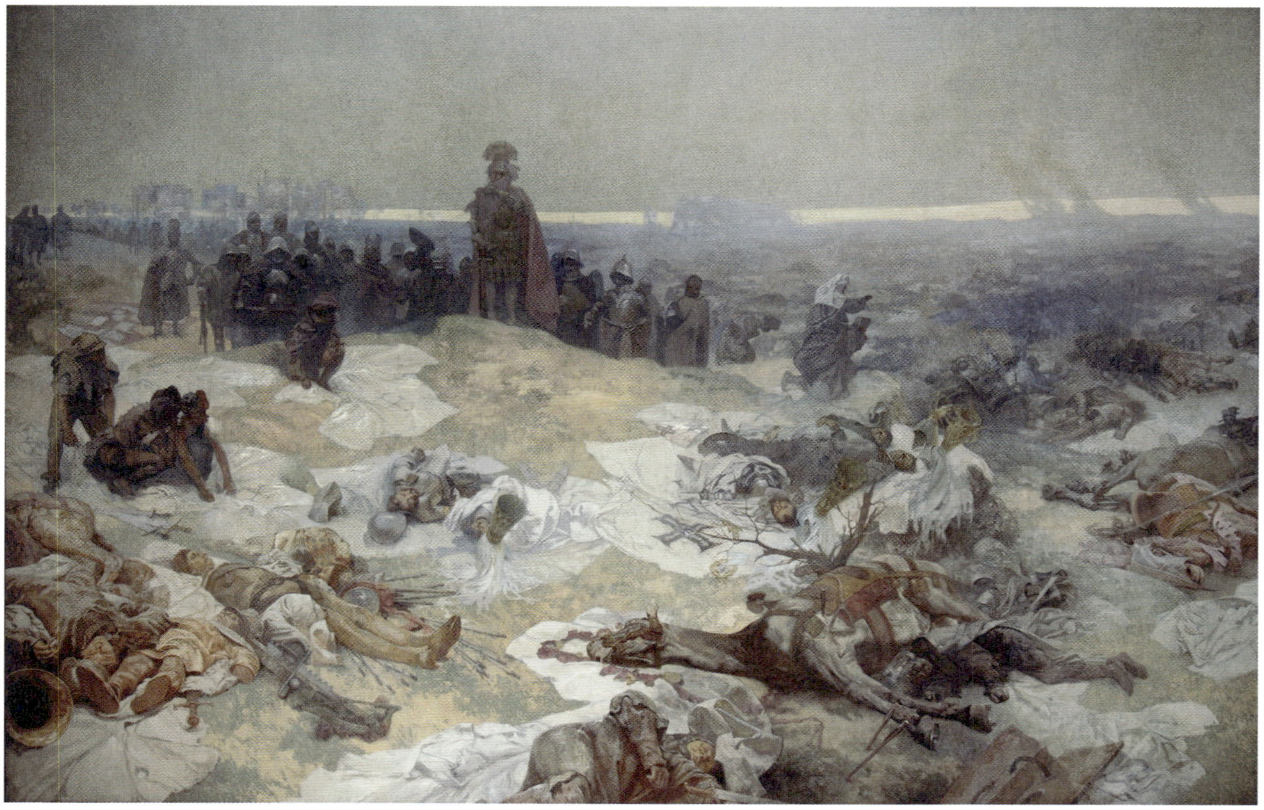

Fig. 3
Alfons Mucha
After the Battle of Grunwald in 1410, 1924
Prague City Gallery

his contact with the younger generation, composition, proportions, and, above all, by coloration, contrast, and the modeling of space through color. Preisler, who—according to the aforementioned criteria—really aspired toward the picture as a unified organism, had painstakingly worked through countless studies in pursuit of "perfection." In his works he had increasingly reduced the "content" until really only two motifs remained: bathing and seduction, through which he strove toward an increasingly classical style. Preisler was a decorator in the mold of Pierre Puvis de Chavannes, whose works the artist would have encountered in Vienna. However, during his relatively late visit to Paris in 1906, he was particularly fascinated by the work of Paul Gaugin. In his final pictures, so Beneš, Preisler's true, intrinsic artistic genius was revealed in the fact that these, despite their small size, seem like monumental decorations (fig. 1).[3]

"Our motto was entirely different from that of the preceding generation. Theirs was freedom, flexibility, independence, nature, emotion, life—for us it was the battle for artistic form." (Vincenc Beneš)

Rather than nationalistic scenes, the themes of Preisler's monumental decorations were tranquil, intimate portrayals of ideals, as in his 1910–12 works for Prague's Municipal House. This prestige building, erected primarily for the Czech community in the nationally divided city of Prague, was also to present a stage for artistic endeavors. Alfons Mucha, the grand master of the Art Nouveau, who had risen to fame in Paris, was particularly interested in carrying out the decorations for the Municipal House, even at the price of not being paid for his work, which was perceived as disloyal by many of his colleagues. In keeping with the tradition of monumental decoration, Mucha, who was roughly one artistic generation older than Preisler, gave his paintings for the Municipal House an ideological slant (*The Slavic Concord*, 1910/11). This work was intimately linked with the colossal *Slav Epic*, a project which Mucha started in 1910 in order to bequeath the entire piece, which was exhibited in 1928 at the functionalist Trade Fair Palace in Prague, to the "Czech people." Following the logic of the avant-garde, Mucha's enterprise should have been viewed as an extreme outlier in the hopelessly outdated genre of history painting. Only that, in this work, Mucha developed a number of remarkable artistic strategies that gave the project, both as a whole and in its individual components (including studies, photographs, and other materials), the power to pose crucial questions about civilization and existence (fig. 2, 3; pp. 66–68).

Bohumil Kubišta, who died of the Spanish flu in November 1918, belonged to the younger generation of artists, whose aspirations Vincenc Beneš describes from his own experience in his obituary for Jan Preisler. Together with Emil Filla, Kubišta was the driving force behind the theory and practice of a group of young artists known as Osma, and, like Filla, he soon adopted a Cubist formal language, although he never became a member of the Skupina výtvarných umělců. Kubišta's catastrophic financial situation, which had almost driven him to suicide at the end of his second visit to Paris in 1910, finally improved in 1913 when he joined the military as an officer and was stationed in Pula. At the end of 1914, he was involved in the sinking of the French submarine Curie and decorated for his services, a fact that was received with unease by the Francophile cultural circles in Prague. Nevertheless, Kubišta was one of the first officers to pledge allegiance to the new republic of Czechoslovakia in Prague in October 1918.

These events accompanied the painter's final years of creativity. Kubišta, whose works were presented across the international avant-garde exhibition network, was among those artists who gradually began to question the French "artistic model." Cubism, which had been elevated to an ideology among Czech avant-garde circles, became less important to the painter, who was obsessed by mathematics and the divine proportion (golden ratio)—despite the fact that he had developed his own particular variant of the style, which focused on the human psyche. He outlined his thoughts in a letter to his friend, the painter Jan Zrzavý, a founding member of the Symbolist Sursum Society (1912), and in an essay written around the same time entitled "On the Spiritual Essence of the Modern Age."[4] In their enthusiasm for the atavistic destructive power of the mechanisms of war, Kubišta's "war paintings" are similar to comparable Futurist works; however, the artist no longer looked to Futurism for inspiration (pp. 122–23). Of increasing interest to Kubišta were simple stereometric forms, as primal and mysterious as Sumerian busts and idols (pp. 92–93). Zrzavý's stereometric, spiritualistic-mysterious mannequins and expressive head portraits were produced in a lasting symbiosis with the ideas of his mentor Kubišta (pp. 102, 104–05).

Cubism or, rather, its definition, was the touchstone of the prewar Czech avant-garde. Not long after the foundation, in 1911, of the

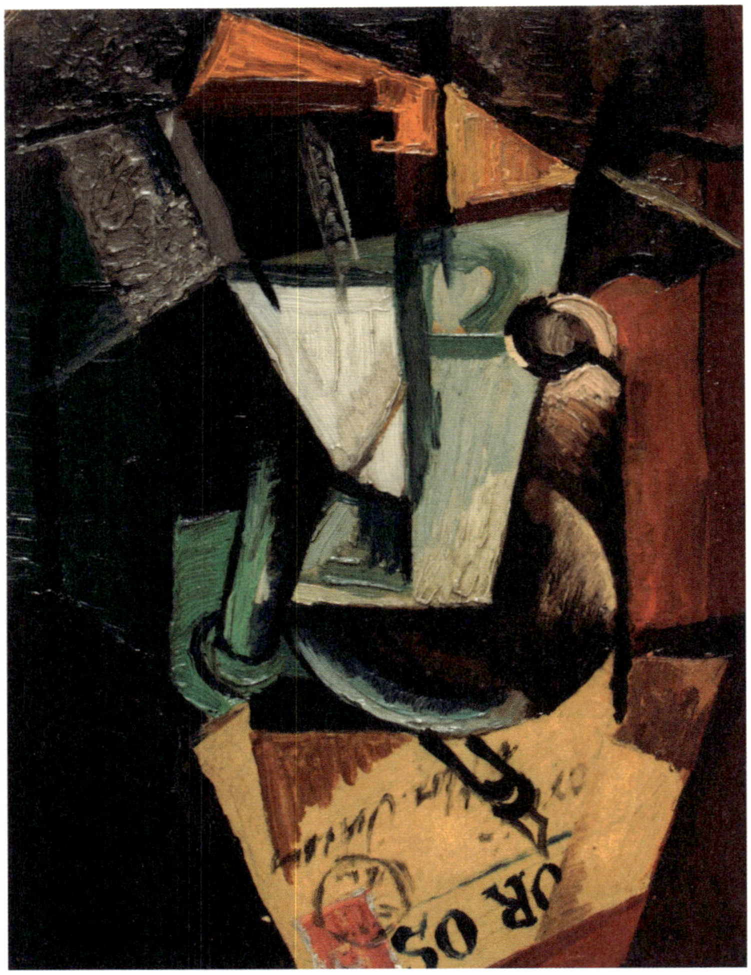

Fig. 4
Antonín Procházka
Still Life with Pitcher, c. 1914
Archive of the Aleš South Bohemian Gallery

Skupina výtvarných umělců—a group that, along with painters and sculptors (such as Otto Gutfreund), also included architects, which gave the phenomenon of Czech Cubism its special ideological status—creative differences were arising among its members by the end of 1912. As a result, Josef Čapek and Václav Špála, who saw Cubism more as a useful instrument for the achievement of formal freedom, rather than a logically cohesive construction, left the group. In 1914, shortly before the outbreak of war, two competing exhibitions were held: In February, the Mánes group opened *Modern Art*, an exhibition organized by the French writer and critic Alexandre Mercereau, displaying mainly works by the Salon Cubists and members of the Puteaux Group (Delaunay, Duchamp-Villon, Gleizes, La Fresnaye, Lhote, Metzinger, Villon, and others), alongside works by Czech artists such as Josef Čapek, Bohumil Kubišta, and Václav Špála. Running in parallel at the Prague Municipal House was the sixth exhibition of the Skupina výtvarných umělců, featuring works by Beneš, Filla, Gutfreund, Procházka, and others; paintings and graphic works by Munch, Derain, Picasso, Braque, and Pechstein; and statuettes from the Belgian Congo and Cameroon. This deeply polemic, even "fratricidal" (as it was described by the poet and critic S.K. Neumann) juxtaposition was a further prefiguration of the Czech avant-gardist's eventual *retour à l'ordre*.[5]

With Neumann's aid, Josef Čapek, Václav Špála, and Jan Zrzavý, who was to cultivate Bohumil Kubišta's memory, formed the Tvrdošíjní (The Stubborn Ones), the only continuation of the prewar avant-garde groups. Many of these artists, especially Josef Čapek, developed a complex, symbolistic Primitivist style. Upon returning from the Netherlands after the war, Emil Filla, the most prominent representative of the Czech prewar avant-garde and a "convinced Cubist," started exploring, one could say on a revised level, genres painted in the Classical style, particularly still life, as pure, cohesive, aesthetically effective constructions. Other avant-gardists, too, conducted explorations into the genres of painting: Špála experimented with landscape and still life; Procházka with still life, and Otto Gutfreund, who had worked toward a purely Constructivist form during his internment in France, produced sculptures in the spirit of New Objectivity (p. 310). Emil Filla, who, much like his great role model Picasso, was always receptive to new artistic movements (such as Surrealism), in the late 1930s—like Picasso—also gave his work a political dimension, as in the series of paintings and drawings produced at the time of growing threat, in which he referenced folk tradition and its elevation to artistic mythos by the nineteenth-century Neoclassicist Josef Mánes (p. 367).[6]

1 Vincenc Beneš, "Jan Preisler," in *Volné směry*, yr. 20, 1919/20, p. 10.
2 Beneš (see note 1), p. 11.
3 For more on Preisler, cf. *Jan Preisler 1872–1918*, ed. Petr Wittlich, exh. cat., Municipal House, Prague (Prague, 2003).
4 Mahulena Nešlehová, *Bohumil Kubišta* (Prague, 1984), pp. 171–72; Bohumil Kubišta, "O duchovní podstatě moderní doby," in *Česká kultura*, no. 14/15, October 9, 1914, pp. 217–21; see also Karel Srp, *Bohumil Kubišta. Zářivý krystal*, exh. cat., Galerie výtvraného umění v Ostravě (Řevnice, 2014).
5 On Cubism, see, for example, Miroslav Lamač, *Osma a Skupina výtvarných umělců 1907–1917* (Prague, 1988); Vojtěch Lahoda, *Český kubismus* (Prague, 1996).
6 Vojtěch Lahoda, *Emil Filla* (Prague, 2007).

Beyond Rippl-Rónai: Expressionist Trends in Hungarian Art

Gergely Barki

LOOKING TO FRANCE AND THE LEADING ROLE OF THE PAINTER JÓZSEF RIPPL-RÓNAI

The “isms” defining the new movements in early twentieth-century art were manifested in various ways in the countries of the Austro-Hungarian Empire. One striking difference between the Austrian and Hungarian capitals was that modern artists in Budapest and the Hungarian provinces looked to Paris, while the artists who shaped Austrian Modernism avoided the French capital, even to some extent ignoring it, and created an independent artistic center in Vienna. Nowadays, the international reputation of the former pioneers in Hungarian art is eclipsed by their Austrian counterparts. Hungarian artists did not climb to the same lofty heights in the international art-historical canon as the Austrians Klimt, Schiele, and Kokoschka, most associated with the artistic heyday of Vienna after 1900. The fact that a small group of Hungarian artists, including the painter József Rippl-Rónai, one of the most influential personalities on the Hungarian art scene, were more famous in Paris a century ago than their Austrian colleagues does nothing to alter this assessment. Interviewing Henri Matisse at his country studio in 1911, a Hungarian journalist asked whether the Fauve master knew Klimt—he did not. But Matisse did know several Hungarian painters, as his Académie included students from Hungary. The French artist also vividly remembered Rippl-Rónai and enquired about his latest works.[1] The Musée d’Orsay in Paris now holds five times as many works by Rippl-Rónai as by Klimt. This, of course, does not mean that the world knows the Austrian “painter prince” less well than his Hungarian colleague, for nothing could be further from the truth. Klimt went on to become a world star, so immensely famous that even the most prominent museums cannot honor him enough in their presentations of his work. In view of Rippl-Rónai’s reputation and the importance of his oeuvre, however, it is not too much of an exaggeration to claim that he represents approximately the same for Hungary as Klimt does for Austria, while also differing from him in many respects.

Rippl-Rónai represents the archetype of the Hungarian artist who was practically unknown in his home country at the beginning of his career, yet was at the vanguard of artistic innovation in France. He joined the Nabis and was already highly successful in Paris in the years prior to 1900, whereas his works only became well known in his native Hungary in the early twentieth century. His first solo exhibition in 1906 finally brought him greater recognition in Hungary, too. Around this time, he became a role model for the younger generation, many of whom followed his example and left for Paris. This first generation of Hungarian artists in Paris predominantly absorbed the spirit of Post-Impressionism, spreading this influence to their colleagues when they traveled home in summer. However, in the years between 1906 and 1908, several Hungarian artists were already gathering around the Fauves and their leader Matisse. For example, between 1906 and 1908, Róbert Berény and Béla Czóbel exhibited at the Salon d’Automne and the Salon des Indépendants in the same room as the Fauves, while Vilmos Perlrott-Csaba and Géza Bornemisza, among others, were students at the Acádemie Matisse.[2] They attended the famous Saturday evening soirées at Gertrude and Leo Stein’s apartment, soon encountering Picasso and his new style. However, this first generation, now known as the “Hungarian Fauves,” did not engage fully with Cubism. It was a group of younger Hungarian art students who, between 1912 and 1914, formed a genuine Hungarian Cubist colony in

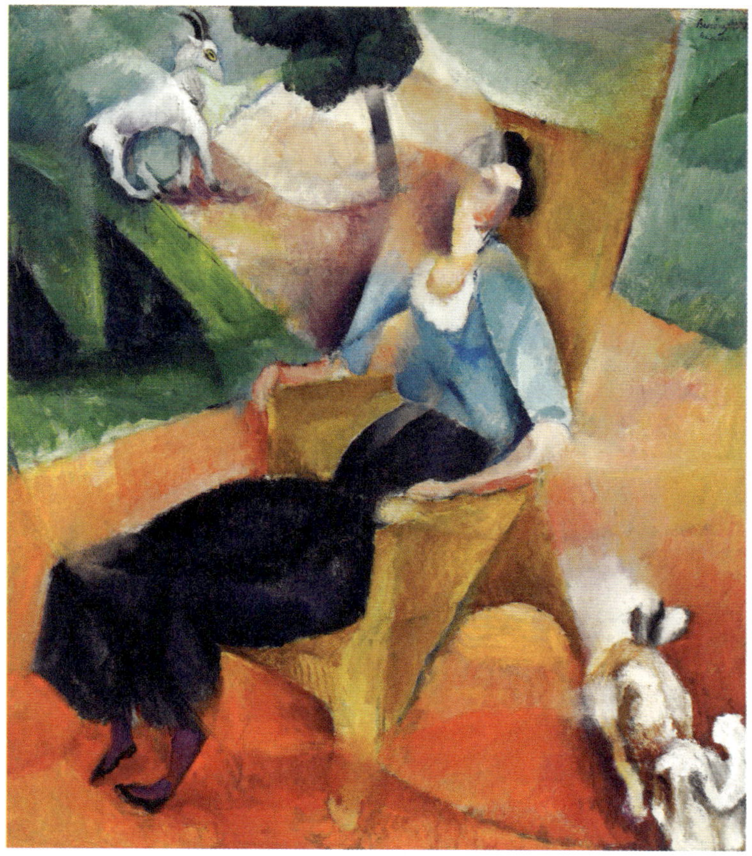

Fig. 1
Róbert Berény
Lady in an Armchair, 1912, Collection László & Hajni Iván, Monaco

Paris, with the Académie de La Palette under Henri Le Fauconnier and Jean Metzinger as its center. The sculptor József Csáky and the painters Alfréd Réth and Imre Szobotka stand out from this group. Together with other Hungarian artists, they exhibited at the Salon d’Automne in one room with the French Cubists, and were also affiliated with them in other ways, while remaining completely unknown in Hungary.

Meanwhile, József Rippl-Rónai developed a novel technique in Hungary, dubbed the “corn kernels” style, which had little in common with other developments in art at the time. He remained dedicated to Impressionism and Post-Impressionism, never straying from its path nor adhering to Fauvism, although some of his paintings from this period reveal echoes of this style. His painting *French Soldiers Marching* (p. 61), recently acquired by the Musée d'Orsay, seems to reveal an affinity to the Futurists in its approach, despite the fact that Rippl-Rónai was entirely unsympathetic toward this movement.

THE FIRST HUNGARIAN EXPRESSIONISTS

Rippl-Rónai nevertheless had friendly ties with a group of much younger artists who had also visited Paris but were opposed to the Impressionism he championed, their work later evolving into the Expressionist style. At their first exhibition, at the turn of the year 1909/10, the group of artists, which later became known as A Nyolcak (The Eight), were united in their aim to reject Impressionism, although their own styles were widely disparate.[3] This stylistic diversity was even more evident at their second exhibition in 1911, while only four of the founder members participated in the third and final exhibition at the end of 1912. At this show, the work of Róbert Berény and Lajos Tihanyi most perturbed Budapest's audience, both artists close to Expressionism in their endeavors. In an interview ten years later, Berény stated: "We were the ones who started painting in an Expressionist style and this resulted in a dramatic revolution in Hungarian painting. This movement was, of course, not abstract, not in the slightest, yet it only depicted of the outside world what the painter's innermost self felt when looking at his object. The revolution in composition went hand in hand with this new approach."[4] Contemporary press reviews and the painters' own accounts hardly convey that these artists were, in fact, raising the banner of Expressionism. However, a novel published at the time of The Eight's last exhibition, written by Gyula Török, who was in contact with the group, documents that at least some of the artists explicitly defined themselves as Expressionists.[5] It is also no coincidence that The Eight represented Hungary at the 1912 Sonderbund exhibition in Cologne, the first international show of Expressionism.[6] Here Berény's highly expressive paintings, in which the artist captured the essence of Freudian psychoanalysis he knew so well (fig. 1), and the Cubo-Expressionist works by Lajos Tihanyi were most prominent, as they were again at the group's exhibition at Vienna's Kunstsalon Brüko two years later. Several years after this, Tihanyi also participated in Lajos Kassák's *Aktivizmus* (Activism) movement and, reflecting the group's orientation, presented Expressionist pictures at a solo show at the exhibition space of the magazine *MA* on October 15, 1918.

> **"We were the ones who started painting in an Expressionist style and this resulted in a dramatic revolution in Hungarian painting."**
>
> (Róbert Berény)

PSEUDO-EXPRESSIONISTS DURING WORLD WAR I AND THE REVOLUTIONS

The outbreak of World War I halted all further development of The Eight group in its tracks. In Berény's work, it even caused a hiatus and a stylistic regression. Apart from his revolutionary poster calling people *To Arms! To Arms!* for the Hungarian Republic of Councils in 1919 (p. 168), none of his works from this time can be related to Expressionism and even the abovementioned poster can only be labeled Expressionist on account of its verve and vehemence. This is unusual inasmuch as the events of the war, simply by virtue of their tragic character, generally inspired artists to depict their experiences in an expressive way even if they had little connection with Expressionism as a style. Examples of this include the harrowing images by Baron László Mednyánszky, an exponent of *Atmospheric Impressionism* ("Stimmungsimpressionismus"), that were painted in situ on the battlefield (pp. 132–33). Mednyánszky's much earlier series of paintings depicting vagrants—also highly expressive—can only be loosely associated with Expressionism. Similarly, János Vaszary, although his painting style does reveal affinities, cannot be clearly categorized as an Expressionist, despite the fact that his pictures from this time—and not only the battle scenes—are charged with Expressionist force (p. 131).

KASSÁK!

During the war years, a new counter-culture emerged as if out of the blue, the earliest manifestations of which can be explicitly linked with Expressionism, its movements abroad and exponents at home. The driving force behind this avant-garde movement was the young writer Lajos Kassák, an extremely talented organizer who was active in almost every field of visual culture, a creator of the new and revolutionary. The pronounced antiwar sentiment of *A Tett*, a magazine Kassák founded in 1915, is regarded as one of the boldest examples of Expressionism in Hungary. Similarly, the magazine *MA*, which he brought out in 1916 after its predecessor *A Tett* was banned, was closely aligned with Expressionism, as were the artists it

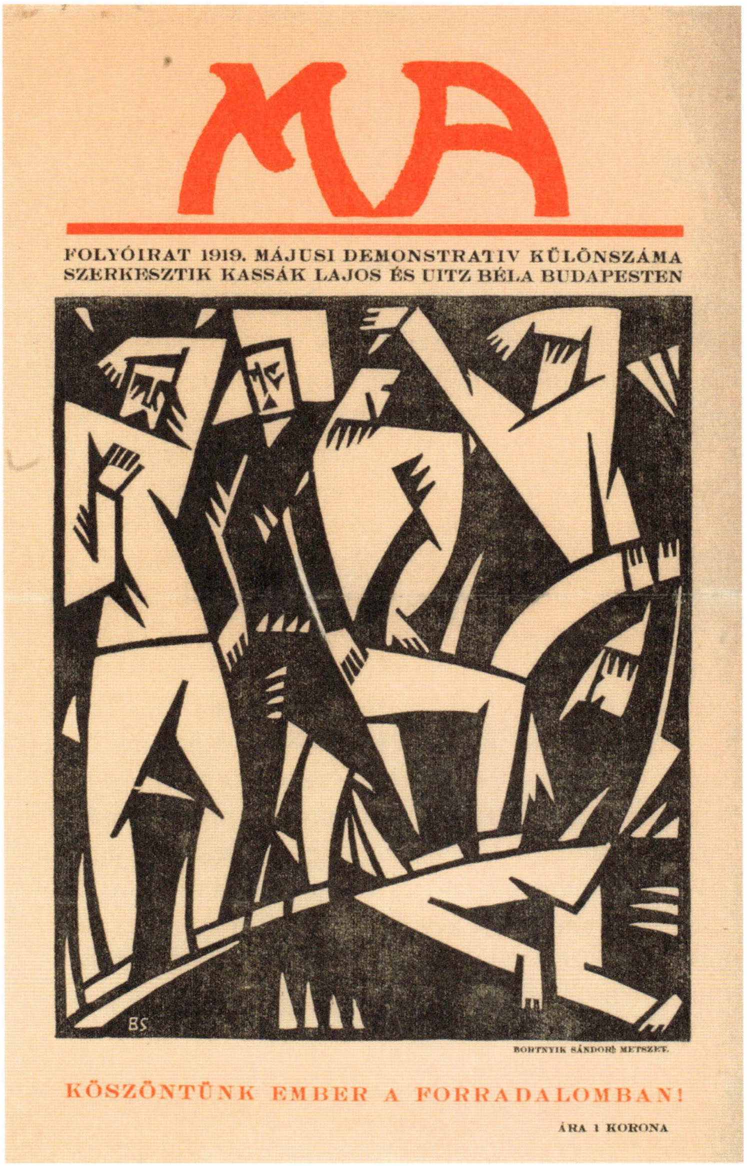

Fig. 2
Sándor Bortnyik
Front cover of *MA*, yr. 4, no. 5,
Vienna 1919

featured. Kassák offered these artists, some of whom he had discovered himself, various opportunities at *MA*'s editorial offices and the private gallery in his apartment. He promoted the art of his brother-in-law Béla Uitz as well as the Expressionist works of artists such as Lajos Tihanyi, József Nemes-Lampérth, Sándor Bortnyik, János Schadl, János Mattis-Teutsch, Béla Kádár, and others. This was achieved not only by means of exhibitions but also through accompanying lecture evenings and reproductions of their paintings, graphic works, and, mainly, linocuts published in his magazine and as postcards.

Kassák also introduced other Modernist movements in his publications. Alongside Cubism, he gave an enthusiastic welcome to Futurism, which had met with a hostile reception in Hungary. Nevertheless, in these early years (1916–18) it was Expressionism he championed. The Expressionism of the Activist painters gathered around Kassák differed in many ways from its forms in Germany or even in Austria. This divergence is perhaps best appreciated in the contemporary works of Sándor Bortnyik, which represent the heated, Activist character of Expressionism, often fired up with pathos and political passion, rather than a subjective stylization (fig. 2). It is no coincidence that during the period of the Hungarian Republic of Councils in 1919, even posters by artists who had not joined the *MA* circle and the Activists reveal stylistic similarities (pp. 167–68).

Kassák's extremely wide network of international connections had strong ties with Herwarth Walden, the prophetic leader of Expressionism, and the magazine *Der Sturm*. This was not a one-sided relationship, as Walden's interest in Mattis-Teutsch, and also in Hungarian avant-garde artists such as Moholy-Nagy, Péri, Bortnyik, Kádár, Ebnéth, and Kassák clearly demonstrates. Mattis-Teutsch's linocuts, which Kassák had already published in *MA* in 1917, were met with great interest from Herwarth Walden and he included these in the August 1918 issue of *Der Sturm* in addition to exhibiting the artist's work in Berlin in 1921.

EMIGRATION AND EXPRESSIONISM

After the collapse of the 1919 Republic of Councils, the leaders of the Hungarian avant-garde were forced to emigrate. Kassák and his circle continued their work in Vienna, where he published the magazine *MA* until he returned to Hungary in 1926. Echoing the trend at *Der Sturm*, Kassák also turned toward Constructivism; he changed his artistic orientation and he, too, developed his own artistic theory and created works he called "Pictorial Architecture."

Many of Hungary's émigré artists left Vienna; many broke with Kassák or went on to Berlin, where Hungarian and other émigrés from

East-Central Europe played an important role in Expressionism's continuing florescence. Included among them were four artists from the former group The Eight. Berény preferred composing at this time. He participated in the activities of the left-wing November Group, designed film sets, drew caricatures for the satirical paper *Ulk,* and explored psychoanalysis. His paintings from this period have been lost and we know his stylized, expressive works mainly from reproductions (fig. 3). Tihanyi, previously a member of the Activists, painted his most mature Expressionist pictures at this time, including portraits with an extraordinary evocative power, although his style became more geometric and Constructivist while in Berlin (pp. 72, 212–13). Even Károly Kernstok could not escape the influence of his colleagues and the German Expressionists, despite the fact that he had rejected this movement in the past. Béla Czóbel, who was in fact only a member of The Eight on paper, did not arrive in Berlin from Budapest but from the Netherlands. He had started developing his Expressionist pictorial compositions in Amsterdam, before moving to Bergen aan Zee to the north of the Dutch city, and finally continuing this process in Berlin (fig. 4). Although, like his colleagues, he never appeared on the radar of *Der Sturm,* he did develop close connections with the German Expressionists, especially the Brücke artists and the galleries that exhibited their works.

In the first half of the 1920s, artists from East-Central Europe had a decisive influence on *Der Sturm*'s gallery program, with the Hungarians playing a key role. János Mattis-Teutsch's début was an exhibition together with Paul Klee in the summer of 1921, and thereafter he had ample opportunity to present his *Soul Flowers,* as he later called them—images that reveal a close semblance to abstract Expressionism. Walden also regularly reproduced his linocuts on the title pages of *Der Sturm* (fig. 5). Mattis-Teutsch joined Die Abstrakten (The Abstract Artists), a group formed out of *Der Sturm*'s abstract Expressionists, and continued exhibiting for years, his works also featuring in the annual Grosse Berliner Kunstausstellung. Soon, however, he returned to his figural compositions and dedicated himself increasingly to monumental works, such as murals. (pp. 86–88, 208–09)

The next Hungarian artist from *Der Sturm* was Aurél Bernáth, most of whose expressive pictorial experiments, with their structured approach to space, have unfortunately been lost or destroyed. Although Ernő Kállai placed him on a pedestal in his key work *Neue Malerei in Ungarn* (New Painting in Hungary),[7] presenting him as one of the most promising figures in Hungarian Expressionism and the era, all we have now is a portfolio of graphic art, which he had finished in Vienna but was exhibited at Der Sturm gallery, and several black-and-

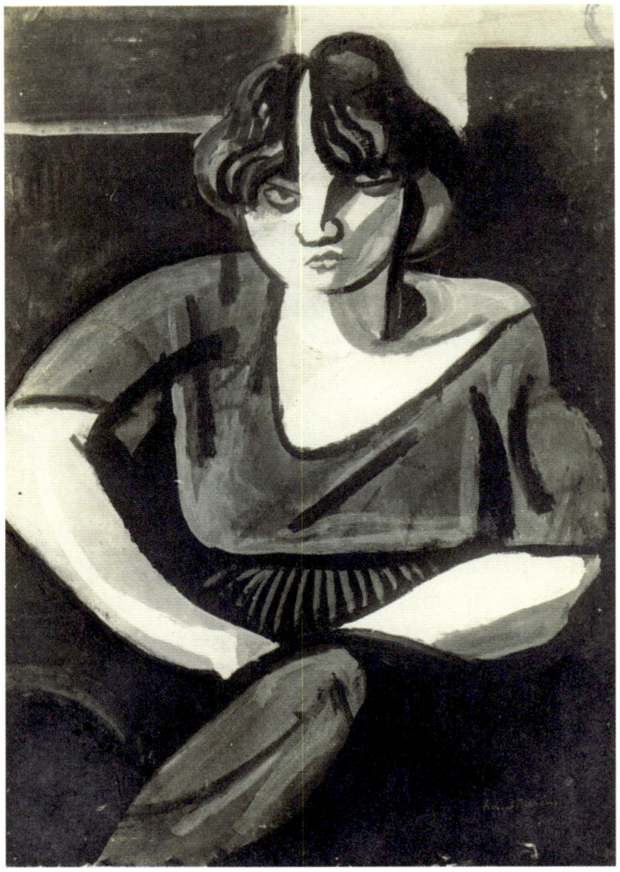

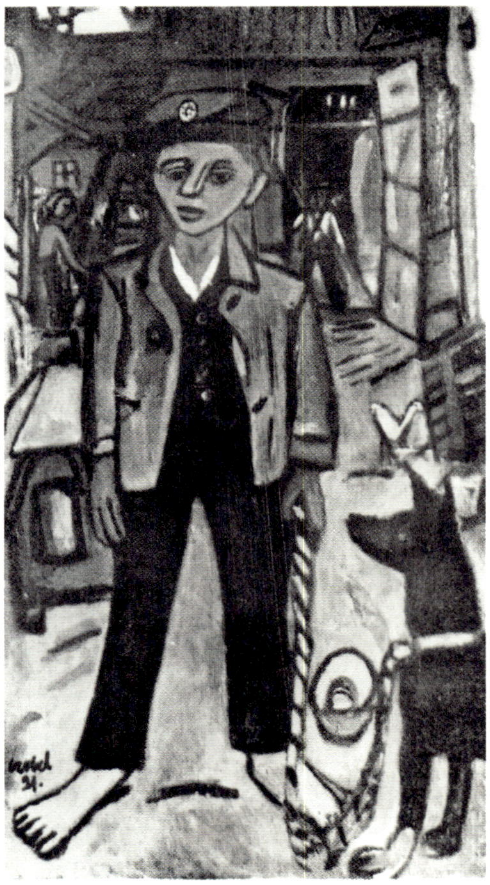

Fig. 3
Róbert Berény
Portrait of a Lady, 1921
Whereabouts unknown

Fig. 4
Béla Czóbel
Boy with Dog, 1921
Whereabouts unknown

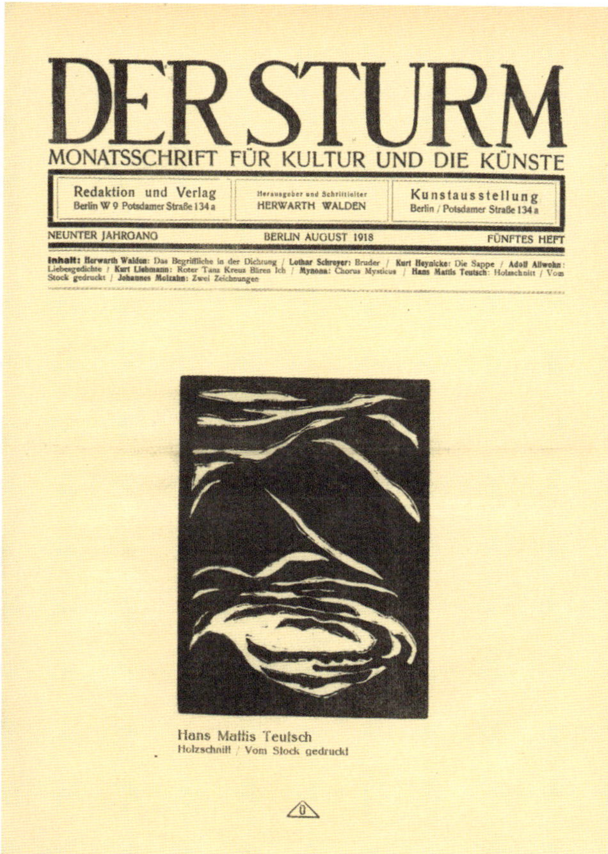
DER STURM
MONATSSCHRIFT FÜR KULTUR UND DIE KÜNSTE

Redaktion und Verlag Berlin W 9 Potsdamer Straße 134 a	Herausgeber und Schriftleiter HERWARTH WALDEN	Kunstausstellung Berlin / Potsdamer Straße 134 a

NEUNTER JAHRGANG BERLIN AUGUST 1918 FÜNFTES HEFT

Inhalt: **Herwarth Walden:** Das Begriffliche in der Dichtung / **Lothar Schreyer:** Bruder / **Kurt Heynicke:** Die Sappe / **Adolf Allwohn:** Liebesgedichte / **Kurt Liebmann:** Roter Tanz Kreuz Bären Ich / **Mynona:** Chorus Mysticus / **Hans Mattis Teutsch:** Holzschnitt / Vom Stock gedruckt / **Johannes Molzahn:** Zwei Zeichnungen

Hans Mattis Teutsch
Holzschnitt / Vom Stock gedruckt

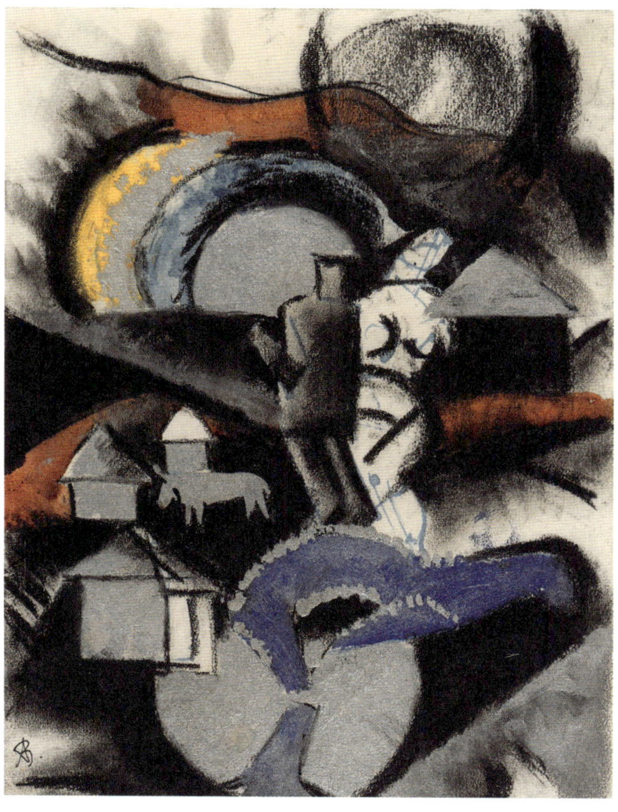

Fig. 5
János Mattis-Teutsch
Front cover of
Der Sturm, yr. 9,
no. 5, Berlin 1918

Fig. 6
Aurél Bernáth
Primitive Apotheosis, study for
The Red Animal, 1924, Museum
of Fine Arts — Hungarian
National Gallery, Budapest

white reproductions (fig. 6) to help us build a picture of the works with which he aimed to attract Walden's attention.

Der Sturm gallery presented the latest experiments by those Hungarian artists who no longer worked under the umbrella of Expressionism but had moved on to Constructivism. One of these was László Péri, a frequently exhibited artist who was even allocated a space in the gallery at Walden's apartment, as well as László Moholy-Nagy, who later continued his work as an acclaimed teacher at the Bauhaus.

This special emphasis on Hungary at Der Sturm gallery can be explained, aside from the gallery's openness toward the East, by Walden's sojourn in Budapest in November 1923, where he gave lectures about Expressionism and took the opportunity to seek out artists and works for his gallery. Thanks to this visit, Béla Kádár and Hugó Scheiber, two Expressionists from Budapest, were to become regular fixtures in exhibitions at Der Sturm gallery, with abundant reproductions of their work appearing in the magazine. Kádár was the only Hungarian to attract the attention of Nell, Walden's wife, with works reminiscent of Chagall and Campendonk, that combined the stylizing forms of the avant-garde with folkloric and Biblical motifs. Nell Walden purchased ten of his paintings at his first exhibition (fig. 8). Scheiber's world, on the other hand, with his exciting, entertaining depictions typifying the modern, bustling life in metropolitan Berlin, was more to the taste of her husband, because these pictures were then, as they are now, extremely easy to sell. By the same token, Walden also saw market opportunities in the portraits painted by Scheiber (fig. 7).

EXPRESSIONIST TRENDS IN HUNGARY BETWEEN THE TWO WORLD WARS

The political atmosphere after the lost war and the failed revolutions was not favorable to the continued existence of avant-garde movements, and the vacuum that followed the mass exodus of artists with modern views could be keenly felt. On the other hand, these tragic historical circumstances also served to strengthen Expressionist trends for a number of reasons. In his monograph about modern Hungarian painting, Lajos Németh, whose chapter on "Hungarian Expressionism" strangely only starts in this period, wrote: "From the variety of Expressionism's psychological subject matter it emerged that its formal language expressed the tragic zeitgeist of the trauma after the social cataclysm, the ideological crisis, and the mystical, religiously inspired yearning for the new, as well as the deliberate adoption of socially-engaged activity."[8] All these variations are represented by Hungarian artists of the time, who tackled the styles of Expressionism in different ways. Expressionism's sociocritical side was addressed most fiercely by Gyula Derkovits.

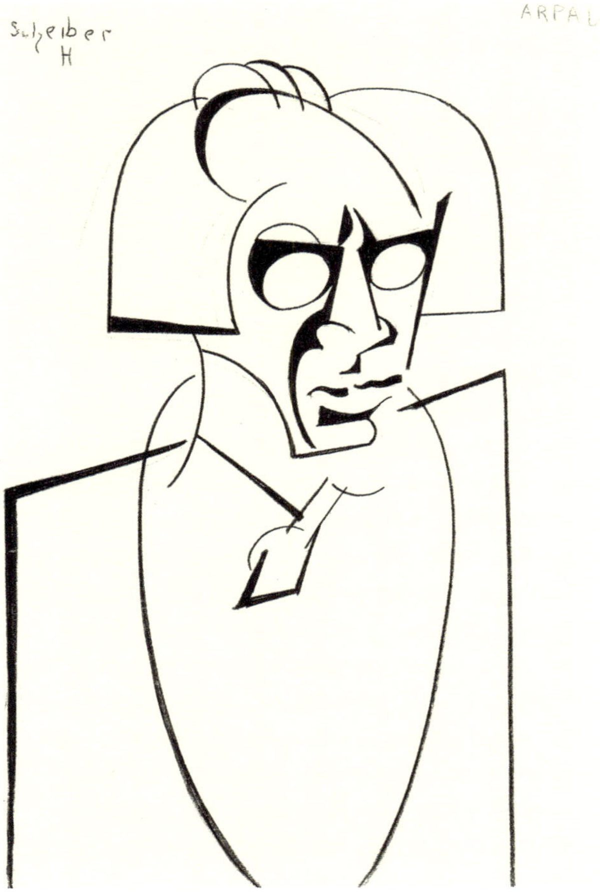

Fig. 7
Hugó Scheiber
Portrait of Herwarth Walden, c. 1925
Collection Ferenc Kiss, Budapest

He had risen from the proletariat and elevated the everyday lives of the downtrodden—people stagnating in poverty, squalor, and contempt—to the highest artistic standards (p. 309) by contrasting it with the arrogance and corruption of society's wealthy classes. At the same time, he captured the empathetic and exalted world of the artist, as well as a sense of shared existence, with extraordinary power and formal command.

Interestingly, many of the artists who had returned from their exile in Vienna and Berlin after a general amnesty was declared in 1926, gradually abandoned their earlier avant-garde mindset and fell in line with expectations in a relatively consolidated Hungary. Bernáth, for instance, renounced his earlier Expressionism and continued in the Post-Impressionist, naturalist tradition, exerting great influence on both his contemporaries and the younger generation. From the mid-1930s, the still-autonomous Berény could not escape this influence, although his works between 1926 and 1932 reveal no presentiment of this development and still sparkle with individuality (pp. 168, 300). He did not adopt the sociocritical approach of an artist like Derkovits, but was interested purely in matters relating to painting, theories of space and composition, and use of color. This is demonstrated by his interiors with figures, infused with skillful spatial illusion, and his still lifes, which merge the influences of Art Déco, the École de Paris, and, to a certain extent, the Bauhaus. His dynamic commercial posters, meanwhile, allowed him the greatest scope to exploit his Expressionist background.

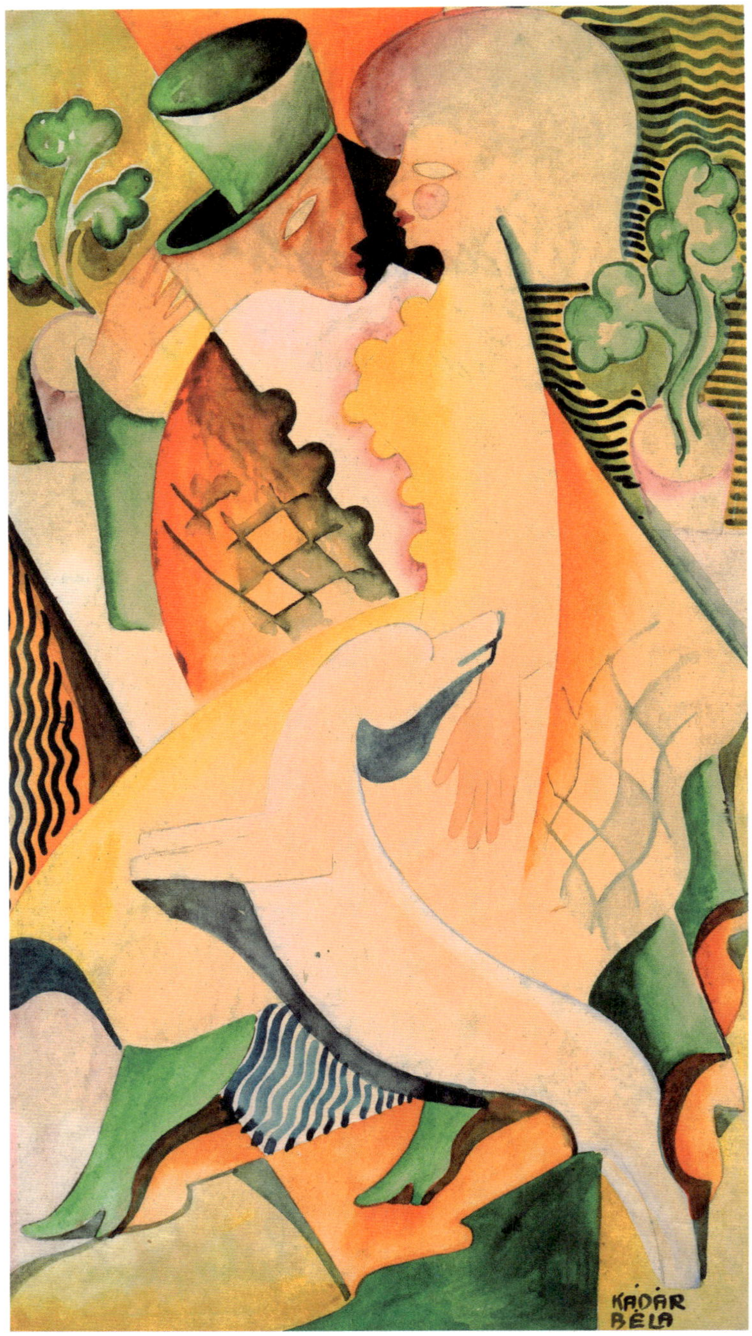

Fig. 8
Béla Kádár
Lovers, 1924
Kunstmuseum Bern, gift from Nell Walden

Members of the youngest generation of artists did not build on their experiences abroad to the same extent but formed their own individual, expressive pictorial world through their quest for local traditions and motifs. At this time, in the small town of Szentendre, a few kilometers from Budapest, a new center emerged, where Lajos Vajda and later Jenő Barcsay (p. 305) ushered in a new language in painting that pointed beyond Expressionism while still exploiting its accomplishments in manifold ways.

1 B. V. (Vilma Balogh), "Im Atelier von Henri Matisse," *Világ*, March 31, 1912, pp. 34–35.
2 Krisztina Passuth, ed., *Hungarian Fauves: From Paris to Nagybánya 1904–1914*, exh. cat. Magyar Nemzeti Galéria, Budapest (Budapest, 2006).
3 Gergely Barki, Evelyn Benesch, and Zoltán Rockenbauer, eds., *Die Acht (A Nyolcak): Ungarns "Highway" in die Moderne*, exh. cat. Bank Austria Kunstforum, Vienna (Vienna, 2012).
4 Zsófia Dénes, "Berény," *Bécsi Magyar Újság*, March 2, 1922, p. 5.
5 Gyula Török, *A porban*, published in instalments in *Magyar Hírlap* in 1912. I should like to thank István Bardoly for drawing my attention to this source.
6 Barbara Schaefer, ed., *1912 Mission Moderne: Die Jahrhundertschau des Sonderbundes*, exh. cat. Wallraf-Richartz-Museum & Fondation Corboud, Cologne (Cologne, 2012).
7 Ernő (Ernst) Kállai, *Neue Malerei in Ungarn* (Leipzig, 1925).
8 Lajos Németh, *Modern magyar művészet* (Budapest, 1968), pp. 91–103.

“Everyone is striving to move on.”[1] The Collapse of the Austro-Hungarian Empire and its Impact on Austrian Expressionism

Stephanie Auer

Almost a decade after the end of World War I, Hans Tietze, in his essay about Vienna's "municipal policies and modern art," made a withering assessment of the situation for the visual arts in the once-flourishing Austro-Hungarian metropolis: "As a city of art, Vienna is the shadow of bygone centuries and does not exist as a vital force. [...] But everyone is striving to move on; to all of them, Vienna has become the center from which they are fleeing. [...] It is no wonder that Kokoschka, such a quintessentially Viennese artist and person, refuses so indignantly to exhibit as an Austrian or even to call himself Austrian. And although Kokoschka is perhaps the most glaring example, he is not the only one."[2]

The loss of creative talent from the crown lands—artists who by migrating to the imperial hub Vienna had provided such an impetus to the development of art in the former multinational empire—resulted in a dramatic hiatus in Austrian art after World War I. As the capital of the new republic, now a rump state, Vienna lost its preeminent role as an artistic magnet to Berlin, Paris, Weimar, and (from the viewpoint of the Austrian provinces) Munich. Artists who wanted to reach a wider public and attain international recognition—Oskar Kokoschka, Frederick Kiesler, Herbert Bayer, Wolfgang Paalen, to cite some examples—had all emigrated long before 1938. As early as 1921, Tietze lamented the city's "supply of fresh air being cut off," but was convinced that it would be possible to reestablish ties with the world's great art movements. "The entire, now calcified art holdings of this rich and poor city need to be infused with new life."[3] Despite the best efforts of artists, critics, and art historians, in interwar Vienna, the avant-garde—based on the international model—remained limited to a few highlights, such as the International Art Exhibition (1924) at the Secession, the *International Exhibition of New Theater Technology* (1924) organized by Frederick Kiesler at Vienna's Konzerthaus, the show *French Contemporary Art* (1926) at the Künstlerhaus, and the aspirations of the young Kinetic artists.

One of the places where the "idea of a cosmopolitan and multicultural Modernism"[4] still defined the exhibition scene, even after the collapse of the Austro-Hungarian Monarchy, was the Hagenbund. Having already advanced to become the "spearhead of Expressionism"[5] before World War I, with startling presentations by Oskar Kokoschka and the artists of the Neukunstgruppe, the role of this art association as a crucible of Austrian Expressionism continued throughout the interwar period. Through its commitment to Central European Modernism and its emphasis on international connections, the Hagenbund remained a bastion of the integrative force and creative potential of the multicultural former Austro-Hungarian Empire.[6] In parallel with attempts

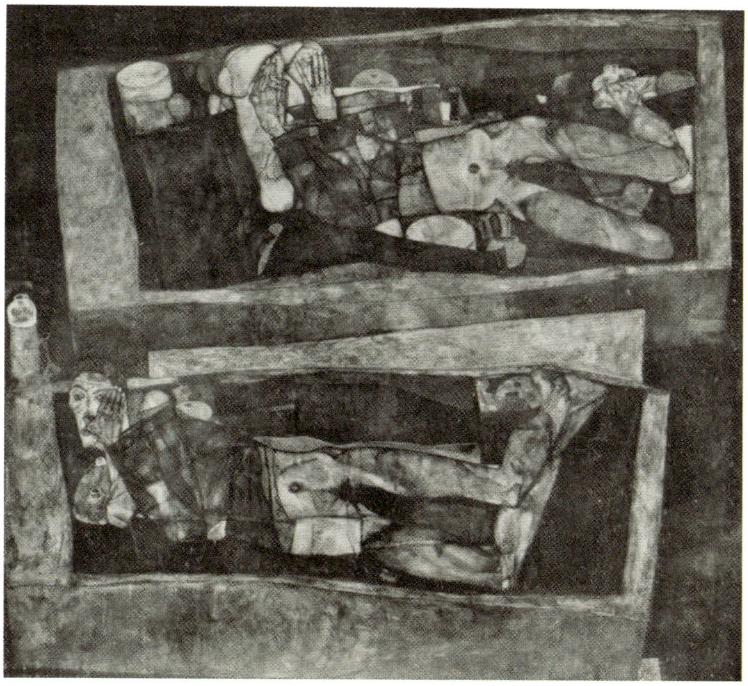

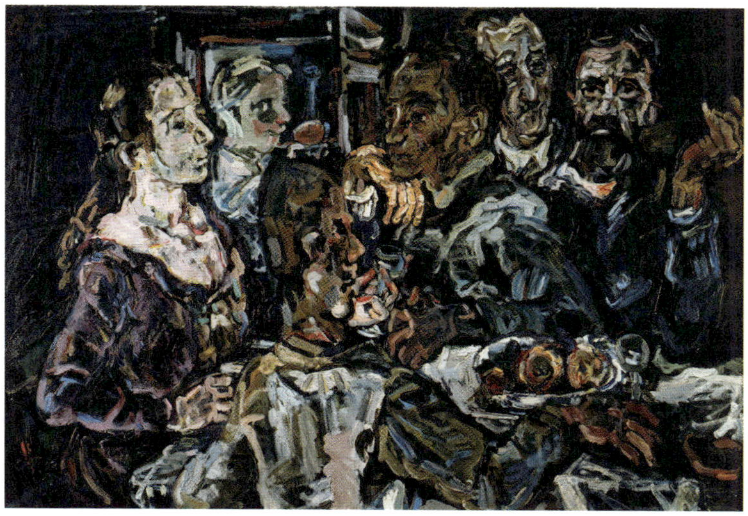

Fig. 1
Egon Schiele
Resurrection (*Resurrection from the Heroes' Graves*), 1913
Whereabouts unknown

Fig. 2
Oskar Kokoschka
The Friends, 1917
LENTOS Kunstmuseum Linz

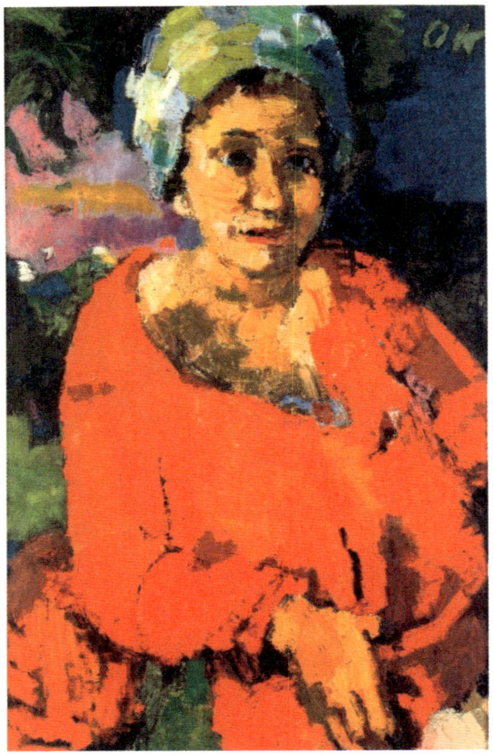

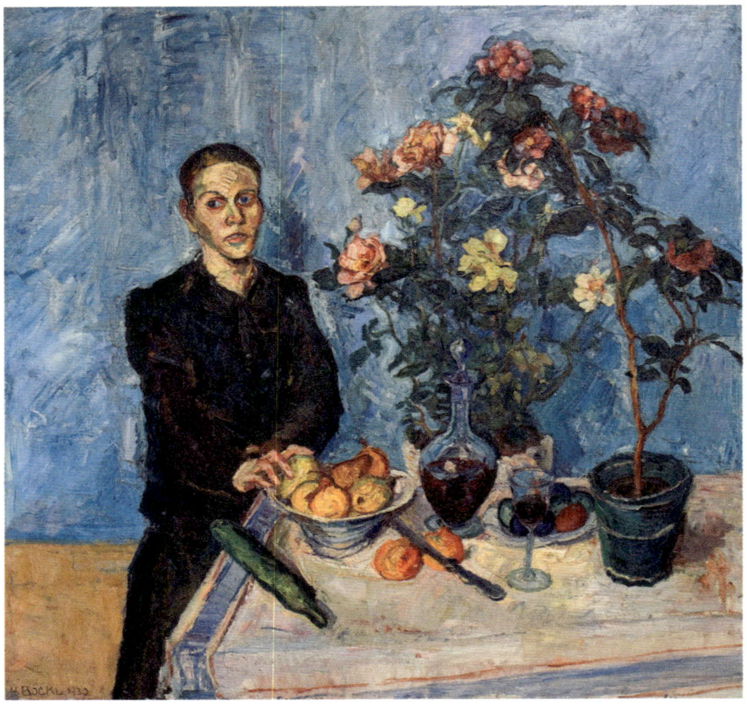

to alleviate Austria's isolation, now a politically, morally, and economically weakened state, and open it up to the foreign avant-garde, art historians and critics also aimed to emphasize the distinctive characteristics of the Austrian contribution to the international avant-garde in order to strengthen the self-confidence and identity of the arts in the young republic.

"I'M THE SUCCESSOR NOW"[7]

A few months before the end of World War I, the Viennese avant-garde was faced with the death of its most prominent exponent: Gustav Klimt. Klimt shaped the art of fin-de-siècle Vienna like no other artist and had crucially influenced the early careers of Oskar Kokoschka and Egon Schiele, who now regarded themselves as his legitimate heirs.[8] "I'm the successor now [...] and I don't feel mature enough to lead this raggle-taggle mob,"[9] Oskar Kokoschka wrote to his mother in February 1918, also confiding that he had wept over the loss. While this self-appointed contender for Klimt's throne was in Dresden in the spring of 1918, Egon Schiele, who had stayed in Vienna, enjoyed a resounding success at the Secession's forty-ninth exhibition in March, prompting Arthur Roessler to see him as the "presumptive successor."[10] A comparison of the exhibited paintings *Resurrection* (fig. 1) and *Family* (*Squatting Couple*; p. 75) clearly demonstrates the artist's development during the war years. Whereas in the composition of 1913, Schiele still subordinated the figures to the formal pictorial structure, rejecting exact anatomical representation, in the painting *Family* he demonstrated a physicality that was entirely new. "For the first time, a human face looks out of Schiele's pictures," remarked Anton Faistauer in 1923. "Who could ever have envisaged lungs or hearts in his earlier pictures? Life has suddenly acquired force here and built a body around itself."[11] Egon Schiele was only able to retain his position as the leading Austrian painter for a brief interlude. He died a few days before the ceasefire between Austria-Hungary, Italy, and the Entente, on November 3, 1918. With his death, Austrian Expressionism lost the artist who had built most on the formal art of Gustav Klimt and the Vienna Secession,[12] only replacing their planar expressive forms with more realistic, sculptural depictions during the war.

1918: THE BREAKTHROUGH OF COLOR

After 1918, the concepts of the "painterly"[13] and of "color,"[14] combined with a reduced emphasis on graphic elements, evolved into the defining characteristic of Expressionist painting. This distinguished it from early Austrian Expressionism with its "agitated, expressive lines and instinctive sense of the subtlest effects of heightened color,"[15] as exemplified in Oskar Kokoschka's and Egon Schiele's work. Influenced by German Expressionism—especially

Fig. 3
Oskar Kokoschka
The Persian, 1922
Leopold-Hoesch-Museum & Papiermuseum Düren

Fig. 4
Herbert Boeckl
Woman by a Table with Flowers, 1930
Province of Carinthia Art Collection / MMKK

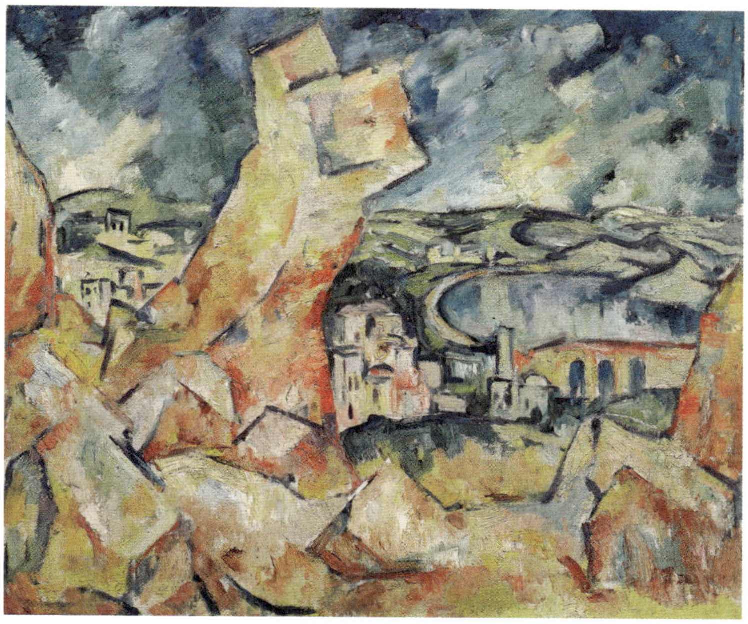

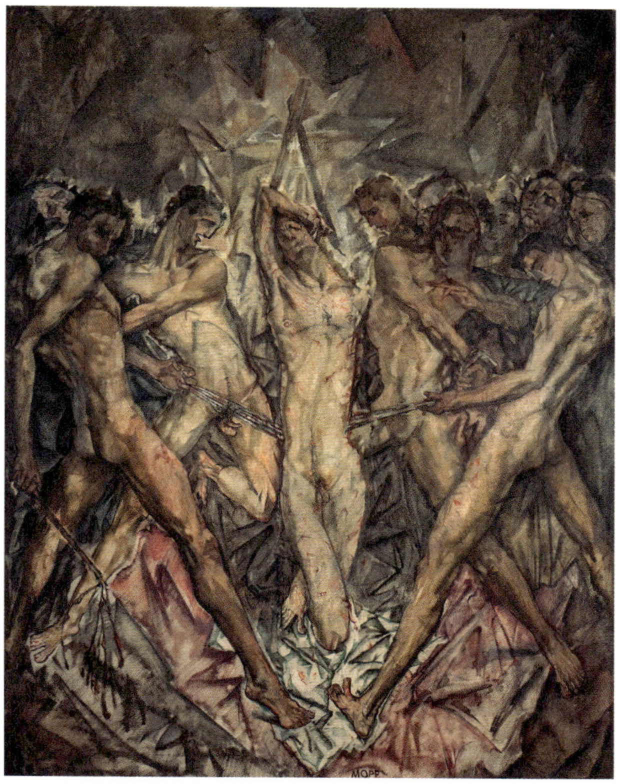

the work of Emil Nolde[16]—Kokoschka's art underwent a dramatic stylistic transformation during his years in Dresden. Instead of separating the colors, an approach still predominant in the portrait of his mother *Romana Kokoschka, the Artist's Mother* (p. 78) or in the group portrait *The Friends* (fig. 2), he introduced a planar effect, "instead of psychological analysis, powerful vitality" and "instead of a deeply felt intimacy, an ecstatic decorative style."[17] This development culminated in his major work *The Power of Music* (p. 79), completed in 1920, in which color finally triumphed over line, which had dominated Kokoschka's early work, and, with its vivid primary contrasts in compact planes of color, became the all-prevailing pictorial theme.

Kokoschka's emigration and Schiele's death led to Herbert Boeckl emerging as Austrian Expressionism's most talented painter after World War I, as well as the leading exponent of a "painterly Expressionism" with the expressive power of elemental and sensual colors at its heart. Following Boeckl's first painterly eruptions in the early 1920s, his impasto so thick that the paint condensed into sculptural bodies (p. 299), from the mid-1920s this "impasto abstraction"[18] was replaced by "precise depiction and lucid three-dimensionality, the immediacy of colorful expression giving way to a considered, comparatively structured style of painting"[19] culminating in a "highly individual, expressive realism"[20] (fig. 4). This toning down of the pictorial devices along with a consolidation of form was related to Boeckl's intensive study of Cézanne's approach to art. Cézanne's influence emerged late in Austria, but became a fundamental feature of Austrian Expressionism between the wars, which few painters were able to ignore. But instead of joining the artist's radical interpreters, who took his fragmentation of reality into patches of color and developed this further to create Cubism, the Austrian Expressionist mainly explored Cézanne's approach to nature, his rules of composition, and his structuring of the picture by subtly modulating hues of color (fig. 5).

Anton Kolig, whose work is characterized by passionately heightened colors and an obsessive concentration on the male nude, is regarded as the most important exponent of Austrian "Color Expressionism" along with Boeckl. His large-scale allegorical male nudes from the early 1920s—*Longing* (1921; p. 297), *Lament* (1920), and *Kneeling Narcissus* (1920; p. 157)—are striking on account of their almost sculptural physical presence and their tectonic "constructedness" and s eem to elevate the human figure from the "uncertainty of the transitory nature of human existence [...] into something universally valid and constant."[21]

In the early 1920s, a variety of Austrian Expressionism emerged that, with its distinctive crystalline approach to form, revealed strong formal parallels with the first

Fig. 5
Josef Floch
Landscape in Palestine, 1923
Belvedere, Vienna

Fig. 6
Max Oppenheimer
Flagellation, 1913
Private collection

responses to Cubism already evident in the pre-war work of Oskar Kokoschka and Max Oppenheimer (fig. 6). Almost a complete opposite to Kolig's sculptural allegories, created in the remote Gailtal valley in Carinthia, is the pulsating, fragmented physicality of *Confession* (1920; p. 156), probably the most famous work by the Viennese painter Fritz Schwarz-Waldegg, who was later murdered in the Shoah. In this self-portrait, the painter points to a gaping wound in his chest—both a pictorial accusation and an echo of the harrowing events of the past war.

THE PROVINCES AND THE METROPOLIS

Whereas before World War I, innovations in Austrian art were centered on Vienna as the capital of the Habsburg Empire, during the interwar period artists from the provinces of the new republic made a vital contribution to defining painting. At the fall exhibition of the Vienna Secession in 1921, Hans Tietze established that now the "young artists from the Alpine provinces were [setting] the tone" reflecting "the greater self-confidence of the provinces in contrast to the weary capital."[22] This hope for art's renewal following the exodus to the provinces was clearly echoed in art criticism at the beginning of the interwar period. The distinct character of Austrian contemporary art was defined in the clash between the center and the periphery in order to distinguish it from German Expressionism, which was seen as the product of metropolitan art, culture, and civilization.[23] Writing about Anton Kolig, Bruno Grimschitz emphasized the two aspects that were later regarded as fundamental to art between the wars and saw these manifested in Kolig's work: the retreat to the rural environment—as demonstrated by the foundation of the Nötsch Circle in the Gailtal valley—as the ideal prerequisite for artistic activity, and a return to the Austrian painting tradition before Gustav Klimt, whose "planar ornamental decoration" Grimschitz regarded as the product of a "metropolitan, decadent" approach to art and as a "tremendous loss of painterly values." "Oskar Kokoschka only became great," Grimschitz claimed, because he "found his way back to earlier painting traditions that gave him a new naturalness and thus his own freedom."[24]

THE "BAROQUE HERITAGE"

No other Expressionist artist between the wars drew on the "Baroque heritage" to the same extent as Oskar Kokoschka, especially during his time in exile in Prague (p. 362) and London. He did this in order to emphasize the specifically "Austrian" and unmistakable character of his art and to distinguish his figurative painting from the non-representational, abstract trends of the time. By harking back to the painting tradition of his homeland he wanted to be seen as the "perpetuator of the great Austrian tradition and as an innovator," not as an "old-fashioned painter who paid no heed to the signs of the times."[25] Based on the understanding of nineteenth-century Neo-Baroque, in the first decades of the twentieth century the concept of the "Baroque heritage" to legitimize an original Austrian tradition evolved into a theme that is frequently cited to this day. After the collapse of the Austro-Hungarian Empire this idea was adopted by art critics as a way of establishing an identity to highlight the distinctive and independent qualities of Austrian art and culture and anchor it in the once-mighty Habsburg Empire.[26] When Hermann Bahr referred to the "Baroque heritage" in 1916 to highlight the "special character" of the Austrian contribution to the international avant-garde, this was surely a response to Fechter's emphasis on the "Gothic soul" of the Germans, reflecting the popular connection made by Worringer between German Expressionism and the Gothic style since the "rediscovery" of Gothic art.[27] After World War I, the Baroque was still used synonymously with an expressive style of art. However, during the time of the *Ständestaat* (Corporate State), the political instrumentalization of the Baroque as the "epitome of past greatness and the successful connection of the Catholic Church and the state" reached its pinnacle.[28] Whereas in 1934 Herbert Boeckl won the Grand Austrian State Prize for the central panel of his triptych *Hymn to Mary* (fig. 7), which was deemed a "continuation of the masters of the Late Gothic and the Baroque,"[29] and still remained at the "heart of public appreciation" in 1938, Oskar Kokoschka was excluded from the cultural debate and increasingly marginalized.[30] Branded a degenerate artist, Kokoschka returned to the Baroque genre of allegory in the late 1930s, while in exile in London, as a way of taking a critical stance toward political events (fig. 8).

"CRISIS OF EXPRESSIONISM. FOLLOWED IN DISCREET BRACKETS BY: THE END OF EXPRESSIONISM"[31]

In his response to Wilhelm Worringer's "Künstlerische Zeitfragen" (Current Questions on Art), in which he pronounced the "end of Expressionism," Hans Tietze already noted in 1921: "The current talking point is the crisis of Expressionism," subsequently adding that "it is not art itself that is dead but a label" that had been imposed upon it.[32] Tietze's critique of pigeonholing art-historical movements is indicative of the times, considering the multifarious strands of expressive painting in the interwar period, which clearly demonstrate that "Austrian Expressionism between the wars" was not a uniform style based around binding ideals and a shared *Kunstwollen* but was, instead, the sum total of individual attitudes.[33] The existential furore characterizing early Austrian Expressionism had already abated before the

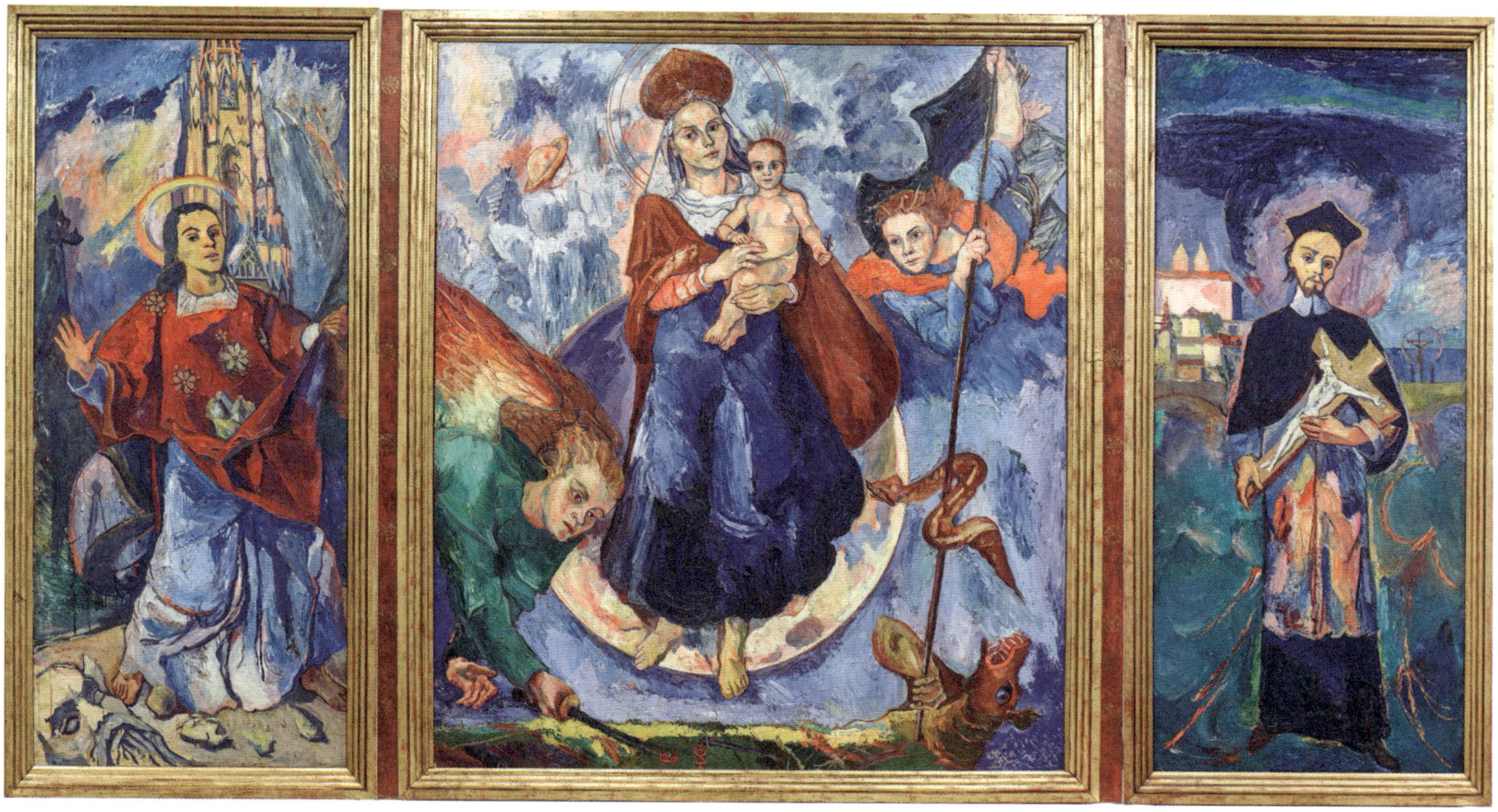

Herbert Boeckl's central panel of this triptych *Hymn to Mary* was deemed a "continuation of the masters of the Late Gothic and the Baroque."

Fig. 7
Herbert Boeckl
Altar *Hymn to Mary*, 1934/43
Property of the Artothek des Bundes, on loan to the parish church Salvator am Wienerfeld, Vienna 10

"It is no wonder that Kokoschka, such a quintessentially Viennese artist and person, refuses so indignantly to exhibit as an Austrian or even to call himself Austrian. And although Kokoschka is perhaps the most glaring example, he is not the only one."

(Hans Tietze)

outbreak of World War I, to be replaced by a expressive style of art in the interwar period in which, during the course of the 1920s, classical tendencies increasingly surfaced, particularly pronounced in the work of Boeckl and Kolig. In retrospect, Arnulf Rohsmann aptly summed up Austrian Expressionism after World War I as follows: "Egon Schiele is dead, Oskar Kokoschka has moved on, Anton Faistauer is in inner exile. By the middle of the decade, Anton Kolig has relinquished proto-existentialist themes. Then he paints 'Flora' and 'French Horn'; [...] Herbert Boeckl paints saints and is appointed professor during the dictatorship of the Corporate State. By strict definition, Boeckl, Faistauer, and Clementschitsch after 1921, Kolig after 1924, and Wiegele after 1926 are no longer modern painters."[34]

Fig. 8
Oskar Kokoschka
Anschluss—Alice in Wonderland, 1942
WIENER STÄDTISCHE Versicherung AG—Vienna Insurance Group

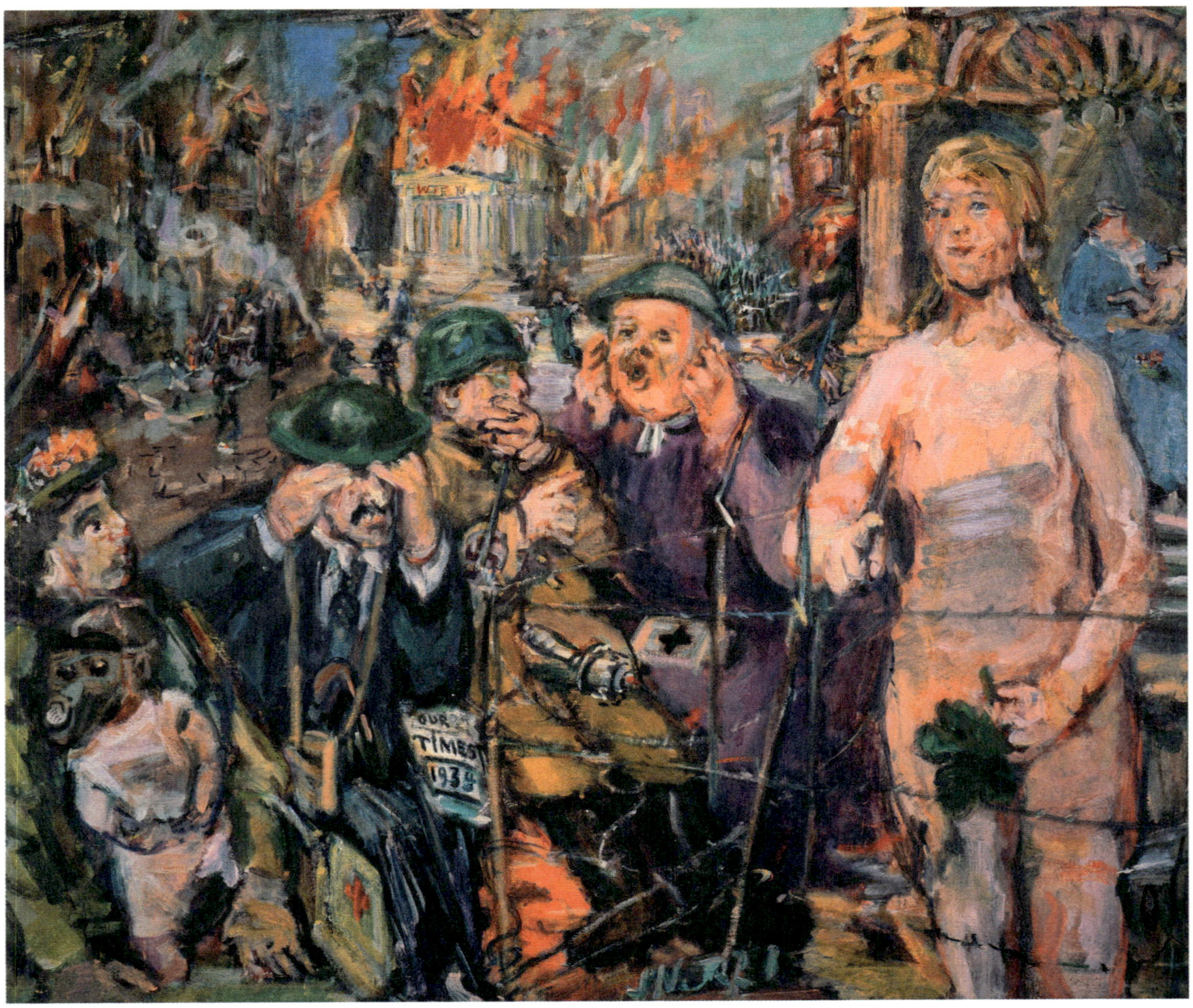

1 Hans Tietze, "Gemeindepolitik und moderne Kunst," *Der Kampf*, 20th yr., no. 8 (Vienna, 1927), p. 375.
2 Tietze 1927 (see note 1), pp. 373, 375.
3 Hans Tietze, "Carl Moll zum 60. Geburtstag," *Die bildenden Künste*, 4th yr. 4. (1921), pp. 123–28.
4 Cornelia Cabuk, "Der Hagenbund als Plattform der Moderne Zentraleuropas in den 20er- und 30er-Jahren," in *Hagenbund: Ein europäisches Netzwerk der Moderne. 1900 bis 1938*, eds. Agnes Husslein-Arco, Matthias Boeckl, and Harald Krejci, exh. cat. Belvedere, Vienna (Vienna, 2014), p. 60.
5 Harald Krejci, "Innere Dynamik und äußere Einflüsse: Das Künstlernetzwerk Hagenbund," in Husslein-Arco, Boeckl, and Krejci 2014 (see note 4), p. 21.
6 Cf. Cabuk 2014 (see note 4), p. 55.
7 Letter from Oskar Kokoschka to Romana Kokoschka, February 11, 1918, quoted from Olda Kokoschka and Heinz Spielmann, *Oskar Kokoschka: Briefe I* (Düsseldorf, 1984), p. 284.
8 See Tobias G. Natter, "'Schnittlauch auf der mageren Suppe.' Anmerkungen zum Verhältnis Kokoschka—Schiele," in *Oskar Kokoschka: Aktuelle Perspektiven*, ed. Hochschule für angewandte Kunst in Wien Archiv und Sammlungen and Oskar Kokoschka-Zentrum (Vienna, 1998), pp. 22–26.
9 Quoted from Kokoschka and Spielmann 1984 (see note 7), p. 284.
10 Arthur Roessler, "Sezession," *Arbeiter-Zeitung*, March 23, 1918, p. 2.
11 Anton Faistauer, *Neue Malerei in Österreich: Betrachtungen eines Malers* (Zurich/Leipzig/Vienna, 1923), pp. 20–21.
12 See Alexander Klee, *Adolf Hölzel und die Wiener Secession* (Munich/Berlin/London, 2006).
13 See Gerhard Schmidt, *Neue Malerei in Österreich* (Vienna, 1956), p. 18.
14 Wieland Schmied, "Die österreichische Malerei in den Zwischenkriegsjahren," in *Österreich 1918–1938: Geschichte der Ersten Republik*, ed. Erika Weinzierl and Kurt Skalnik (Graz/Vienna/Cologne, 1983), vol. 2, p. 691.
15 Schmied 1983 (see note 14), p. 691.
16 Cf. Stephan Koja, "'Ich ging wieder meinen Künstlerweg allein.' Beobachtungen zur Bildkunst Emil Noldes und ihren Reflexen in der österreichischen Malerei," in *Emil Nolde: In Glut und Farbe*, eds. Koja and Agnes Husslein-Arco, exh. cat. Belvedere, Vienna (Vienna, 2013), p. 32.
17 Hans Vollmer, ed., *Allgemeines Lexikon der bildenden Künstler von der Antike bis zur Gegenwart*, vol. 21 (Leipzig, 1992), p. 216.
18 Stephanie Neudorfer (Auer) and Matthias Boeckl, "Phasenverschiebungen: Zäsuren und Brüche im Werk Boeckls, ihr Verlauf, ihre Stellung und ihr Kontext," in *Herbert Boeckl: Retrospektive*, eds. Agnes Husslein-Arco and Matthias Boeckl, exh. cat. Belvedere, Vienna (Vienna, 2009), p. 39.
19 Patrick Werkner, "Verwandlung des Sichtbaren—Expression," in *Der Kunst ihre Freiheit: Wege der österreichischen Malerei von 1880 bis zur Gegenwart*, ed. Kristian Sotriffer (Vienna, 1984), p. 82.
20 Neudorfer and Boeckl 2009 (see note 18), p. 39.
21 Almut Krapf-Weiler, "Die Ethik des Malerischen: Expression und Existenz," *Die uns verließen: Österreichische Maler und Bildhauer der Emigration und Verfolgung*, exh. cat. Österreichische Galerie Belvedere, Vienna (Vienna, 1980), p. 224.
22 Hans Tietze, *Kunstchronik und Kunstmarkt*, 56th yr., new series XXXII (Leipzig, 1921/22), p. 153.
23 Rainer Fuchs, *Apologie und Diffamierung des "österreichischen Expressionismus." Begriffs- und Rezeptionsgeschichte der österreichischen Malerei 1908 bis 1938* (Vienna/Cologne, 1991), p. 155.
24 Bruno Grimschitz, "Anton Kolig," *Die bildenden Künste*, 3rd yr. (1920), pp. 11–18.
25 Almut Krapf-Weiler, "Zur Bedeutung des österreichischen Barock für Oskar Kokoschka," *Wiener Jahrbuch für Kunstgeschichte*, 40th yr. (1987), p. 195.
26 Eva Michel, *Inventing Tradition: Die Rezeption der Alten Meister und das "Barocke" in der österreichischen Malerei des 20. Jahrhunderts: Topos und künstlerische Strategie* (Vienna, 2009), p. 8.
27 See Christian Huemer, "Nuda Veritas im neuen Kleid: Das Expressionismuskonzept von Hermann Bahr," *Belvedere: Zeitschrift für bildende Kunst*, no. 1 (Vienna, 2003), p. 31.
28 Cf. Eva Michel, "Barock von 1918 bis 1938: Katalysator und Legitimation der österreichischen Moderne," in *Barock since 1630*, eds. Agnes Husslein-Arco, Georg Lechner, and Alexander Klee, exh. cat. Belvedere, Vienna (Vienna, 2013), p. 73.
29 Otto Benesch, "Zu Herbert Böckls Stephanuskarton," *Kirchenkunst: Österreichische Zeitschrift für Pflege religiöser Kunst*, 5th yr., no. 1 (1933), p. 14.
30 Cf. Oliver Rathkolb, "Herbert Boeckl—ein Moderner zwischen den Zeiten: Zeithistorische Anmerkungen zu den Wechselwirkungen zwischen Politik und Kunst im 20. Jahrhundert," in Husslein-Arco and Boeckl 2009 (see note 18), p. 216.
31 Wilhelm Worringer, "Künstlerische Zeitfragen" (1921), quoted from Rose-Carol Washton Long, ed., *German Expressionism: Documents from the End of the Wilhelmine Empire to the Rise of National Socialism* (Berkeley/Los Angeles/London, 1995), p. 284.
32 Hans Tietze, "Künstlerische und kunstliterarische Zeitfragen," *Kunstchronik und Kunstmarkt*, 56th yr., new series XXXII (Leipzig, 1920/21), pp. 773, 775.
33 Edwin Lachnit, "'Ausdruck—Leben—Bewegung.' Aspekte des zwischenkriegszeitlichen Expressionismus," in *Die ungewisse Hoffnung: Österreichische Malerei und Graphik zwischen 1918 und 1938*, eds. Christoph Bertsch and Markus Neuwirth (Salzburg/Vienna, 1993), p. 177.
34 Quoted from Erwin Hirtenfelder and Bertram Karl Steiner, *Tatort Kolig-Saal 1929–1999: Ein Kulturskandal* (Klagenfurt, 1999), p. 25.

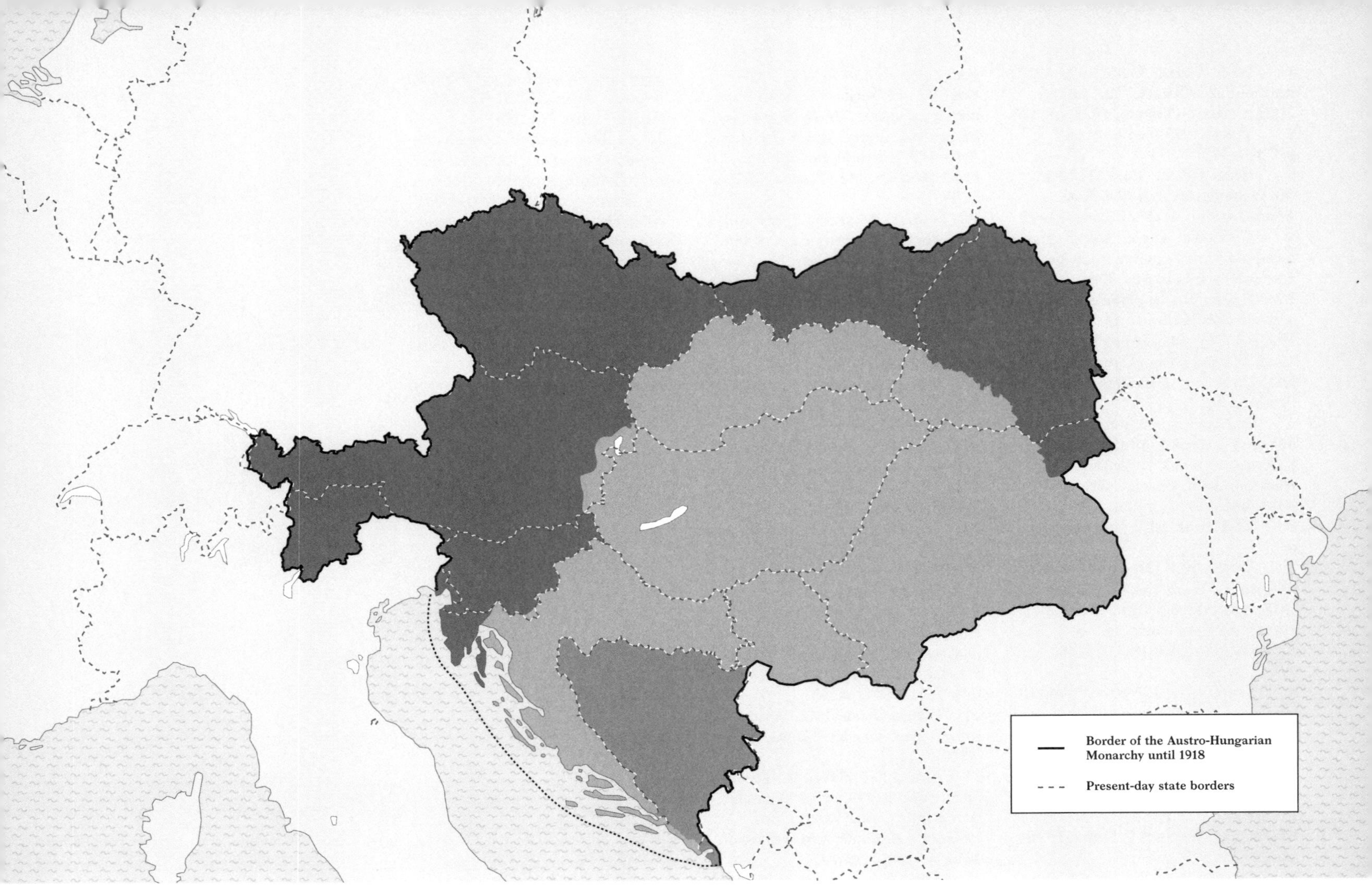

A The Austro-Hungarian Monarchy until 1918 and today's political borders

nation—Nation:

Natiōn (lat., „Völkerschaft“), ein nach Abstammung, Sitte und Sprache zusammengehöriger Teil der Menschheit; Nationalität, die Zugehörigkeit zu ihm. Im französischen und englischen Sprachgebrauch ist N. das Staatsvolk, daher Nationalität Staatsangehörigkeit, dagegen peuple (franz., spr. pöpl) und people (engl., spr. Pīpl) die natürliche Nationalität. Vgl. Volk. Nationalgefühl, das Bewußtsein gemeinsamer Abstammung oder der staatlichen Zusammengehörigkeit; Nationalcharakter, die sittliche Eigenart einer N. Napoleons III. Nationalitätsprinzip besagt, daß jede N. das Recht habe, einen besonderen Staat zu bilden. Vgl. v. Kremer, Die Nationalitätsidee und der Staat (Wien 1885); Treitschke, Politik, Bd. 1 (2. Aufl., Leipz. 1899).

Meyers kleines Konversations-Lexikon, vol. 4 (Leipzig/Vienna, 1907), p. 927

Natiōn (lat.), eine Gesamtheit von Menschen gemeinsamer Abstammung, die dieselbe Sprache sprechen, eine gemeinsame polit. und kulturelle Entwicklung durchgemacht haben und das Bewußtsein der Zusammengehörigkeit besitzen, Nationalität, die Zugehörigkeit zu einer bestimmten N. Nationalitätsprinzip, der polit. Grundsatz, daß jede N. ein Staat und daher Volk werde. Vgl. W. Schücking (1908), F. J. Neumann (1888), Meinecke („Weltbürgertum und Nationalstaat“, 5. Aufl. 1919).

Brockhaus: Handbuch des Wissens in vier Bänden. Sechste gänzlich umgearbeitete und wesentlich vermehrte Auflage von Brockhaus' kleinem Konversations=Lexikon, vol. 3, L–R (Leipzig, 1928), p. 339

German

From Art Nouveau to Expressionism

The seismic changes affecting all parts of European society in the years leading up to the end of the First World War also served as a catalyst for modern art. Artists from the previous generation, such as Alfons Mucha (1860–1939), József Rippl-Rónai (1861–1927), and Gustav Klimt (1862–1918), paved the way for the various Modernist movements emerging in each of the former crown lands of the Austro-Hungarian Empire. These Secession personalities gained cult status, even before their deaths, and successfully reinvented themselves at a time of sweeping changes brought about by war and the collapse of the Habsburg Monarchy. While the work of Mucha, Klimt, and Jan Preisler focused on decorative allegory and a more expressive representation, Rippl-Rónai's works were characterized by an idiosyncratic Post-Impressionist handwriting. Younger artists, such as Anton Kolig, Max Oppenheimer, Egon Schiele, Oskar Kokoschka, and Lájos Tihanyi, engaged in a lively exchange with their older colleagues and developed their own distinctive style of Expressionism, departing from its German counterpart in style and origin. (MH)

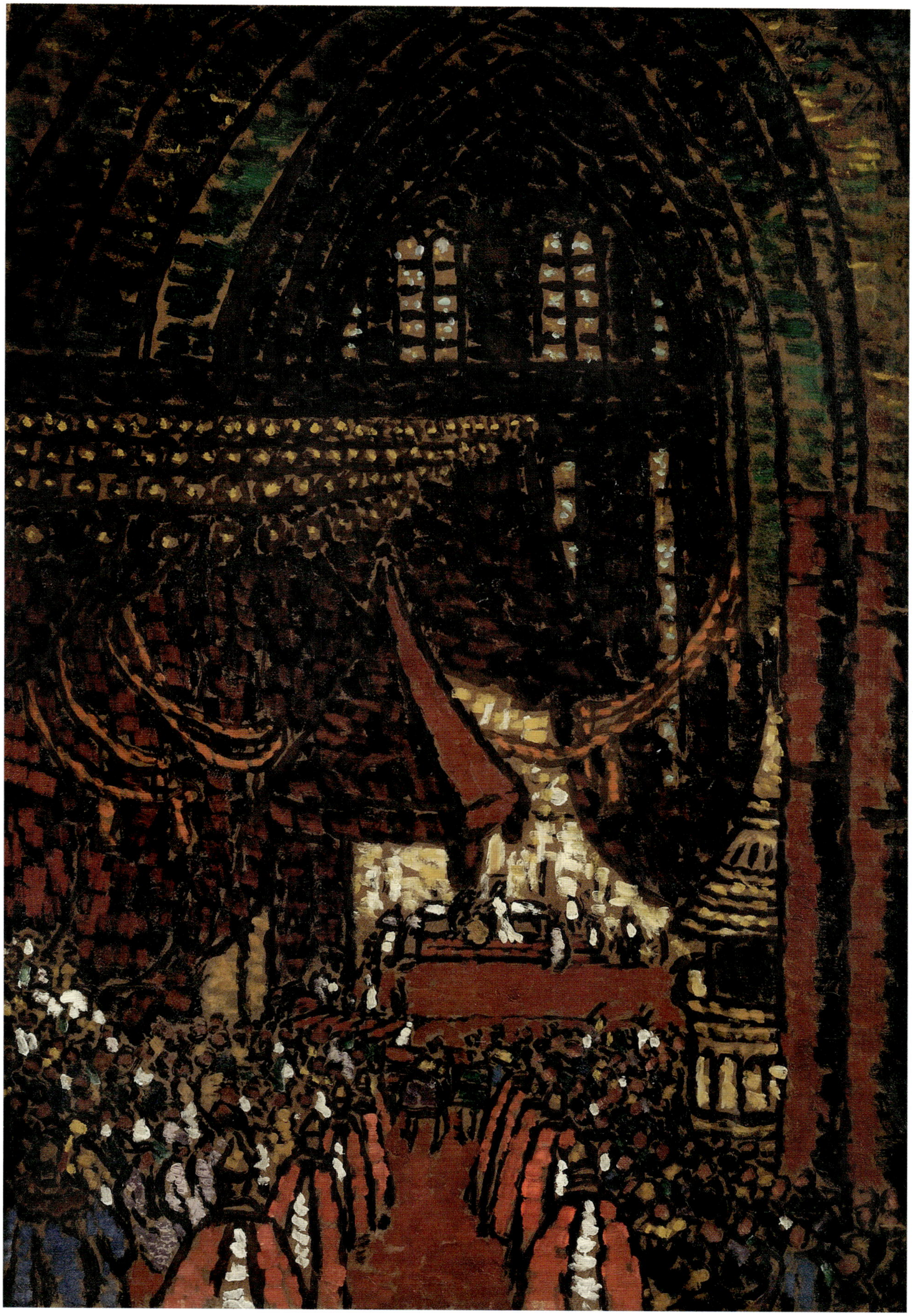

József Rippl-Rónai
The Coronation of Charles IV, 1916
BHM, Museum Kiscell, Municipal Gallery, Budapest, Hungary

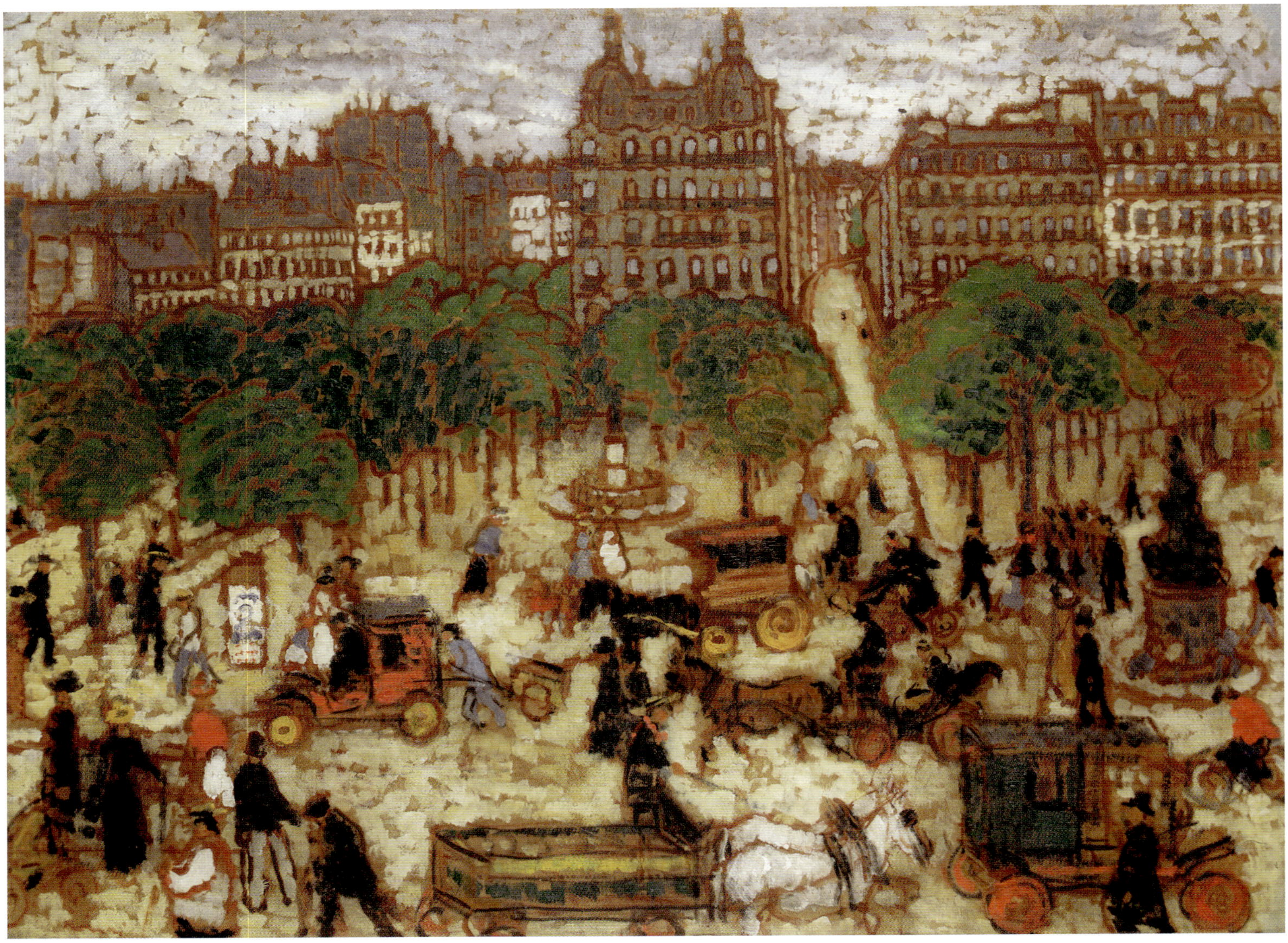

A1

József Rippl-Rónai
Place de l'Observatoire (Parc Monceau), 1914
Museum of Fine Arts—Hungarian National Gallery, Budapest

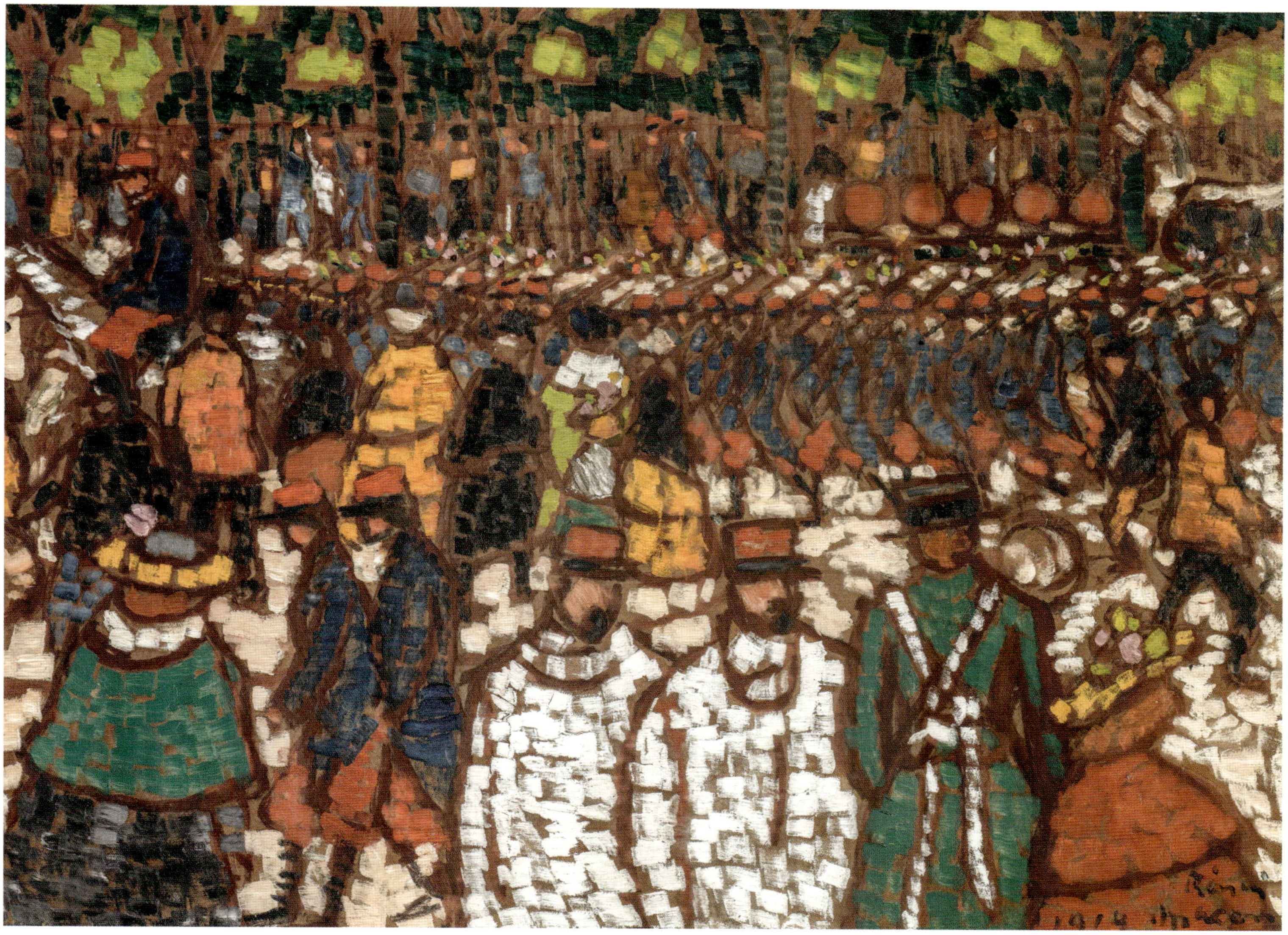

A1 József Rippl-Rónai
French Soldiers Marching, 1914
Musée d'Orsay, Paris

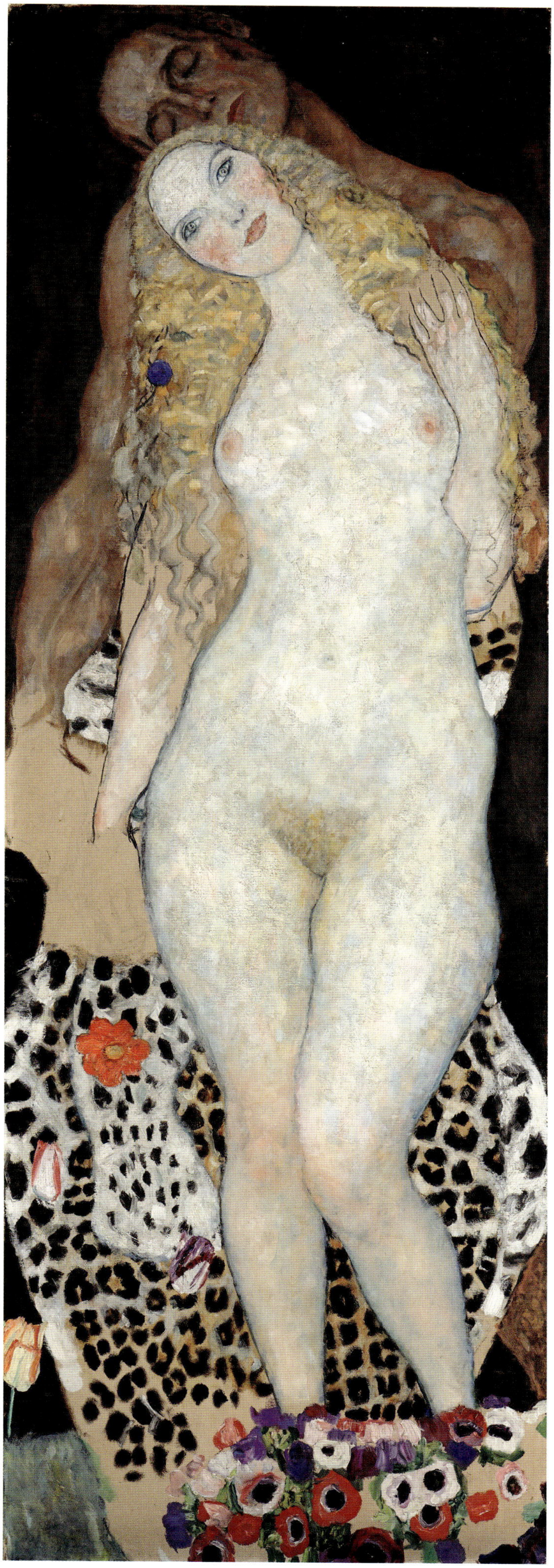

A1

Gustav Klimt
Adam and Eve, 1917/18
Belvedere, Vienna

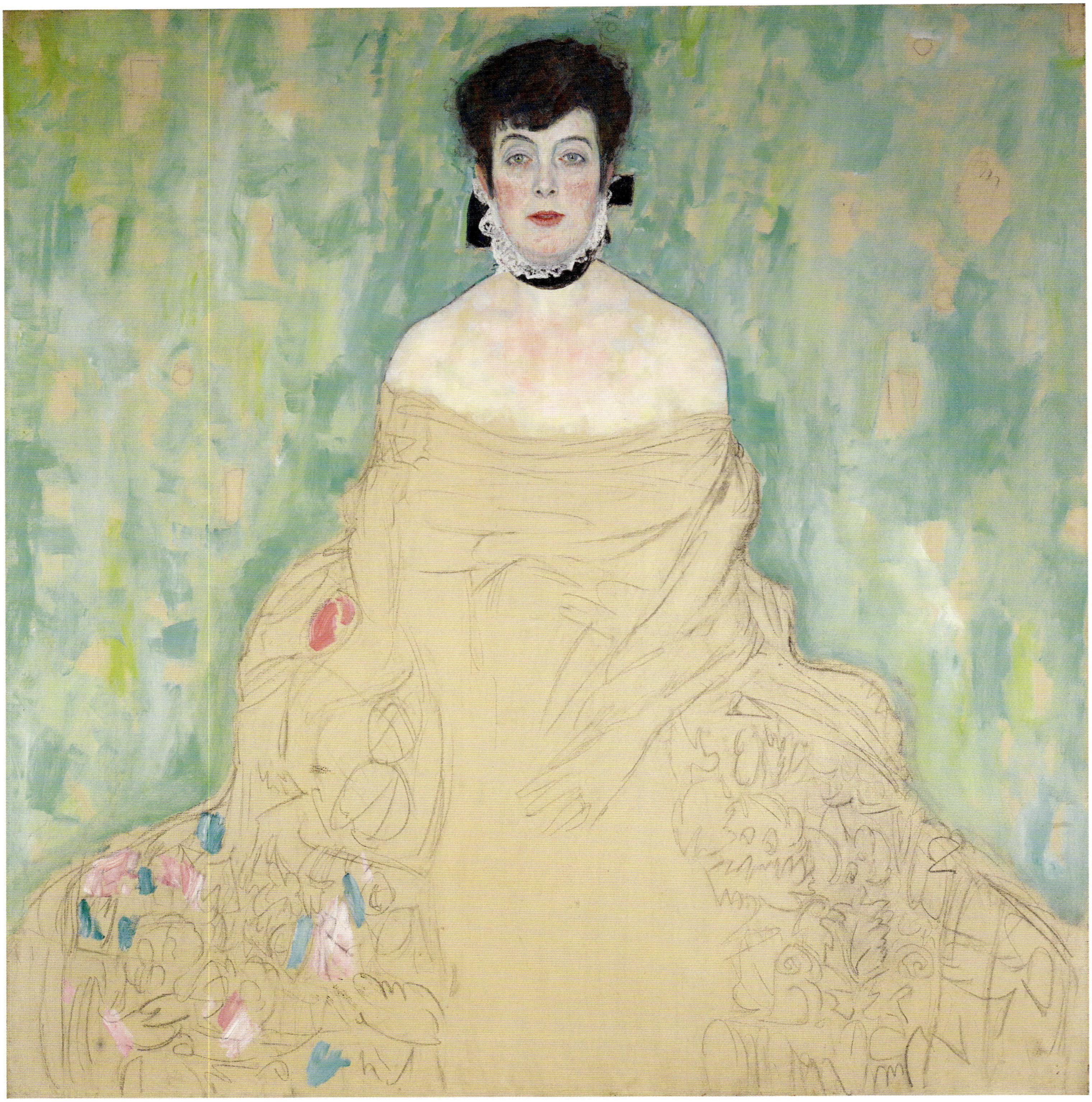

Gustav Klimt
Amalie Zuckerkandl, 1917/18
Belvedere, Vienna, 1988 gift of
Vita and Gustav Künstler

A1

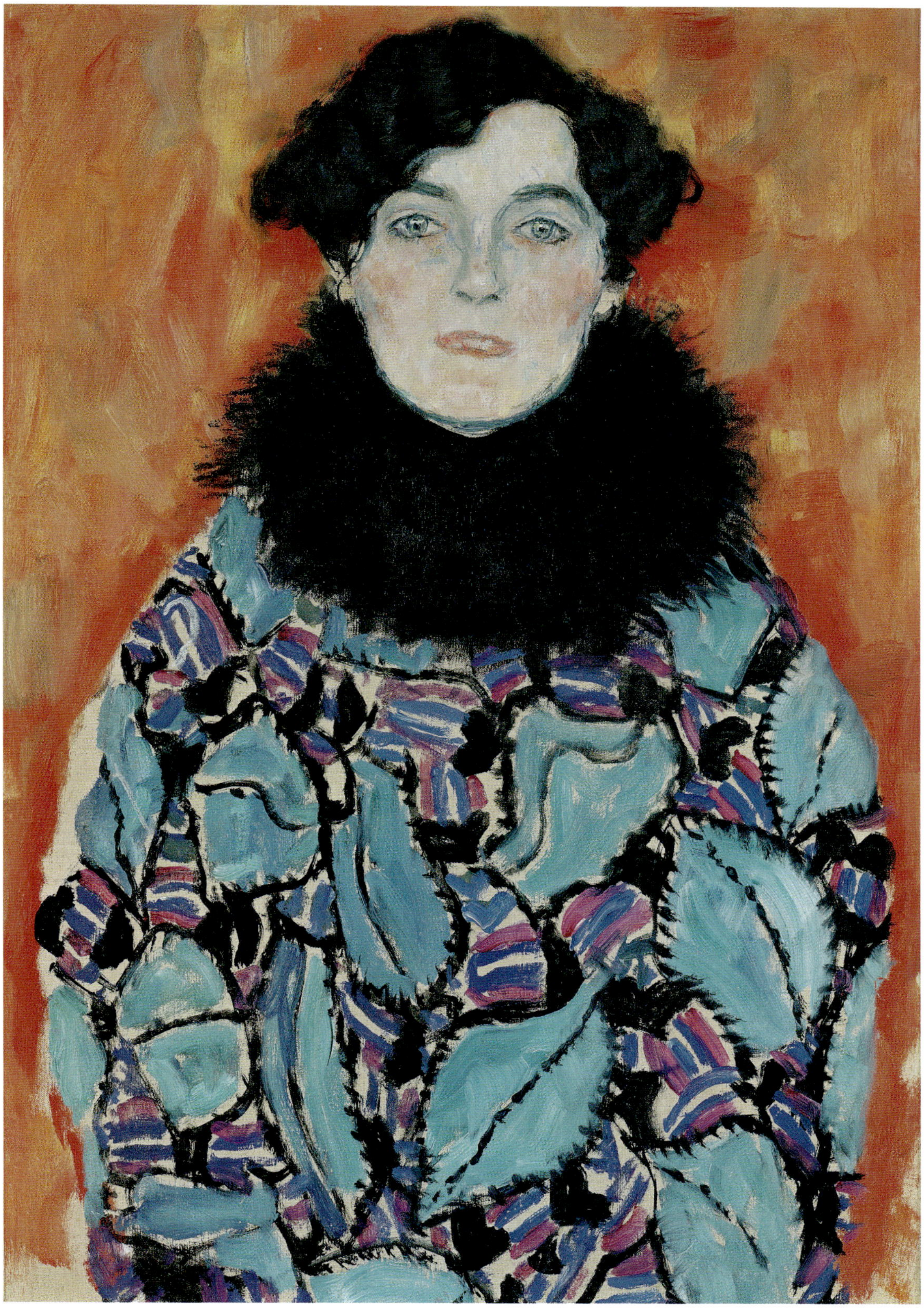

A1

Gustav Klimt
Johanna Staude, 1917/18
Belvedere, Vienna

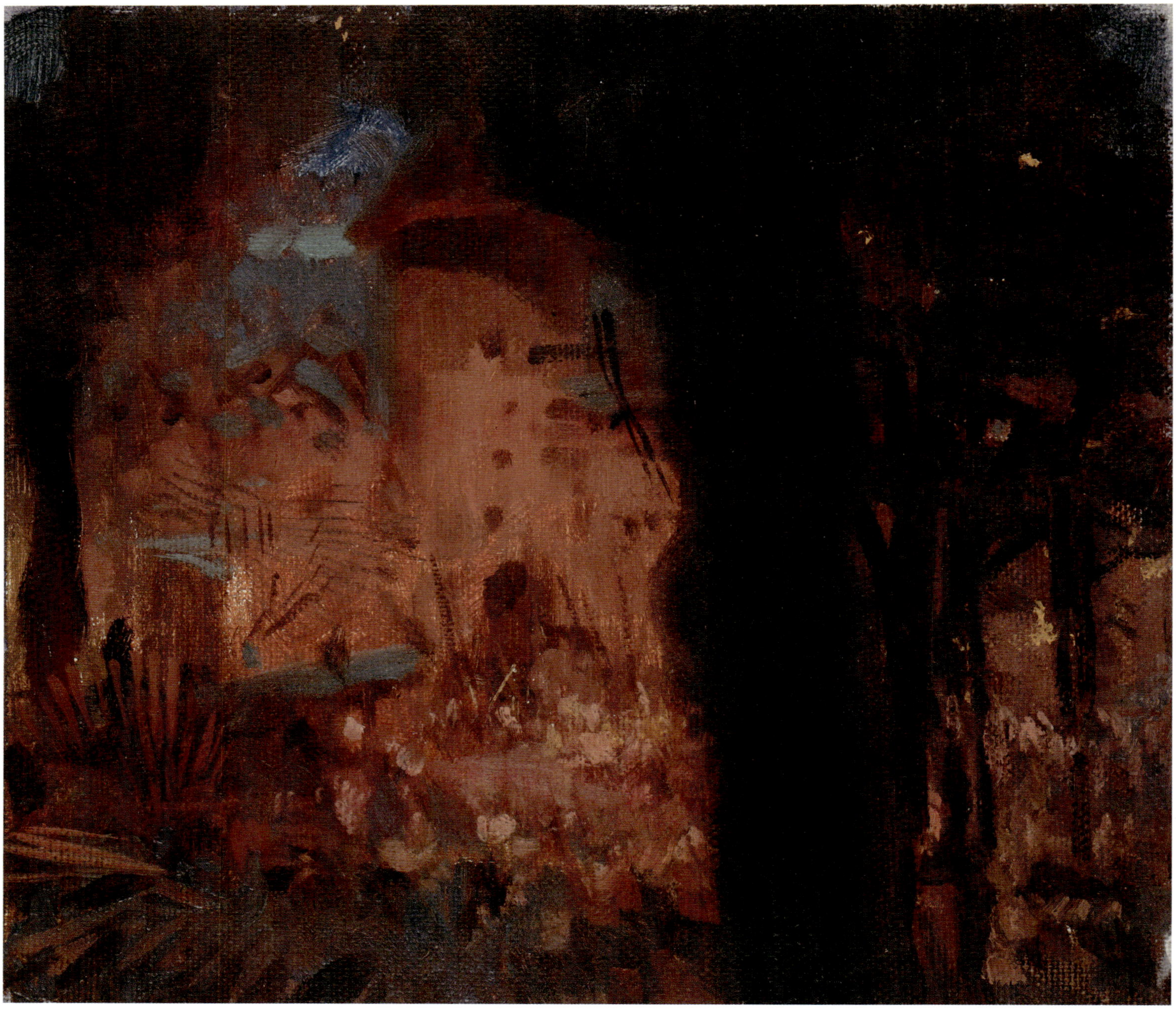

A1

Alfons Mucha
Study for the Slav Epic No. 14: *The Defense of Szigetvár against the Turks by the Ban of Croatia Nikola Šubić Zrinski in 1566*, c. 1913/14
Courtesy of Mucha Trust

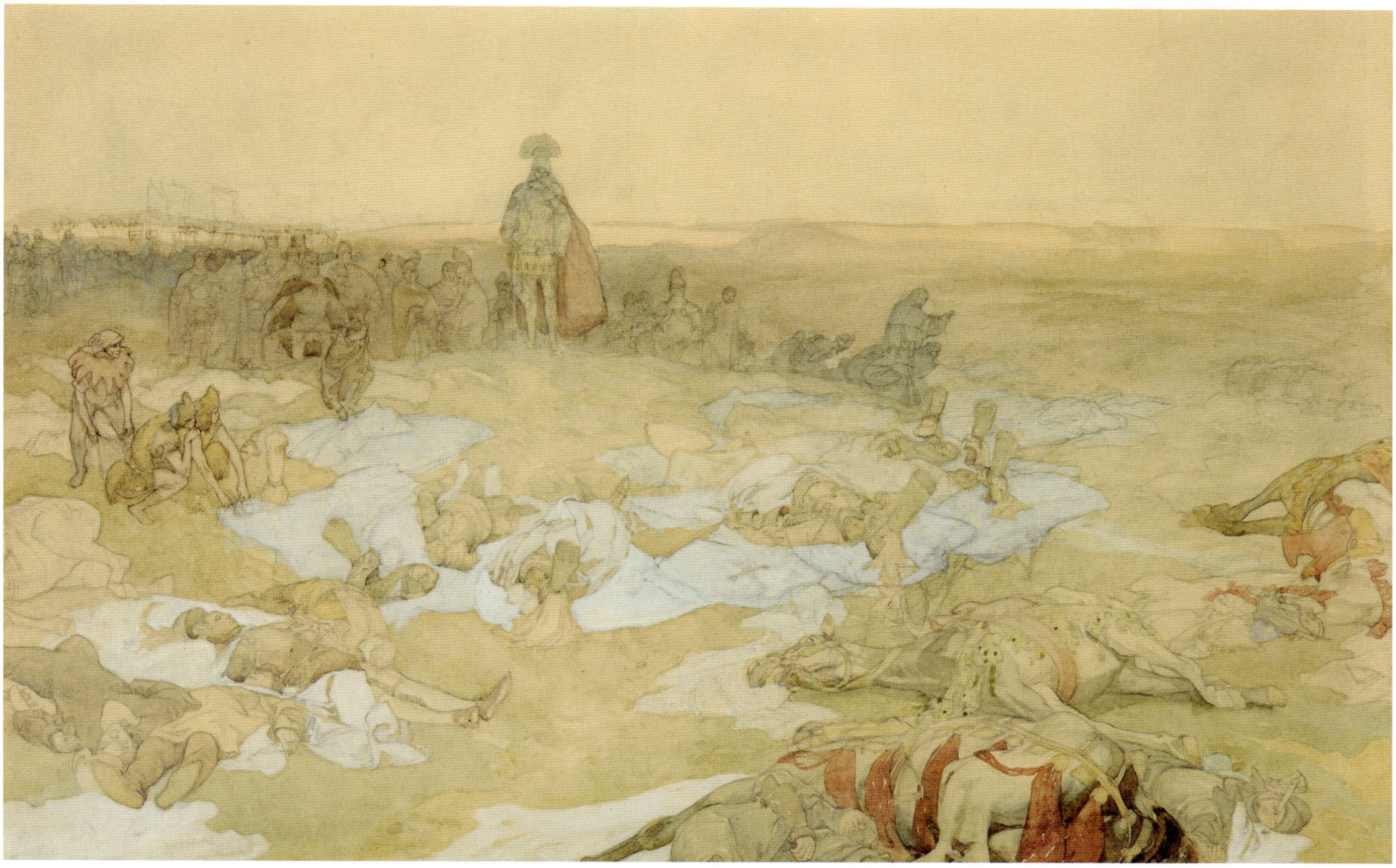

A1

Alfons Mucha
Study for the Slav Epic No. 8:
After the Battle of
Grunwald in 1410, 1923/24
Courtesy of Mucha Trust

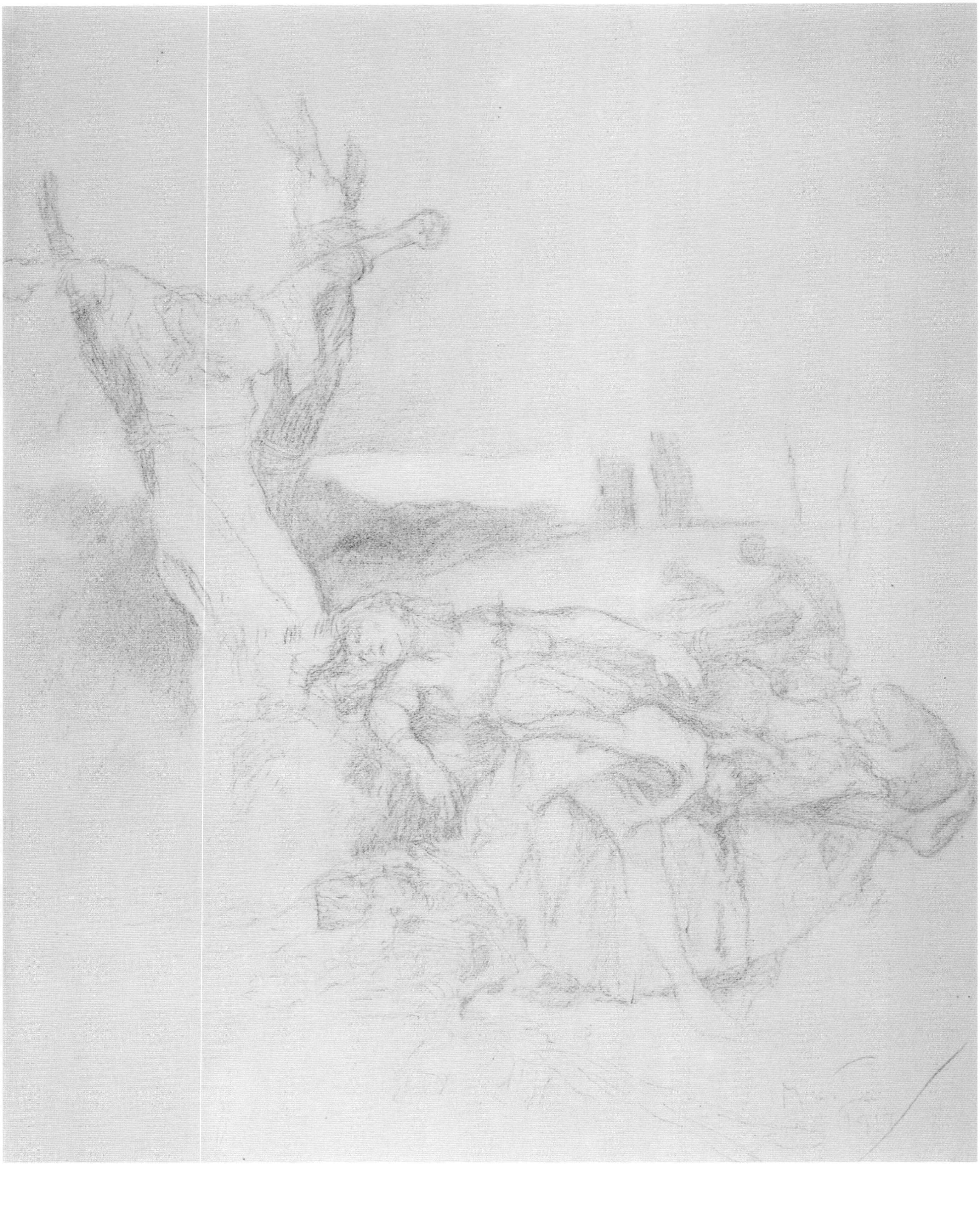

A1

Alfons Mucha
The War, 1917
Courtesy of Mucha Trust

Jan Preisler ▸
The Good Samaritan, 1910–14
The Gallery of West Bohemia in Pilsen

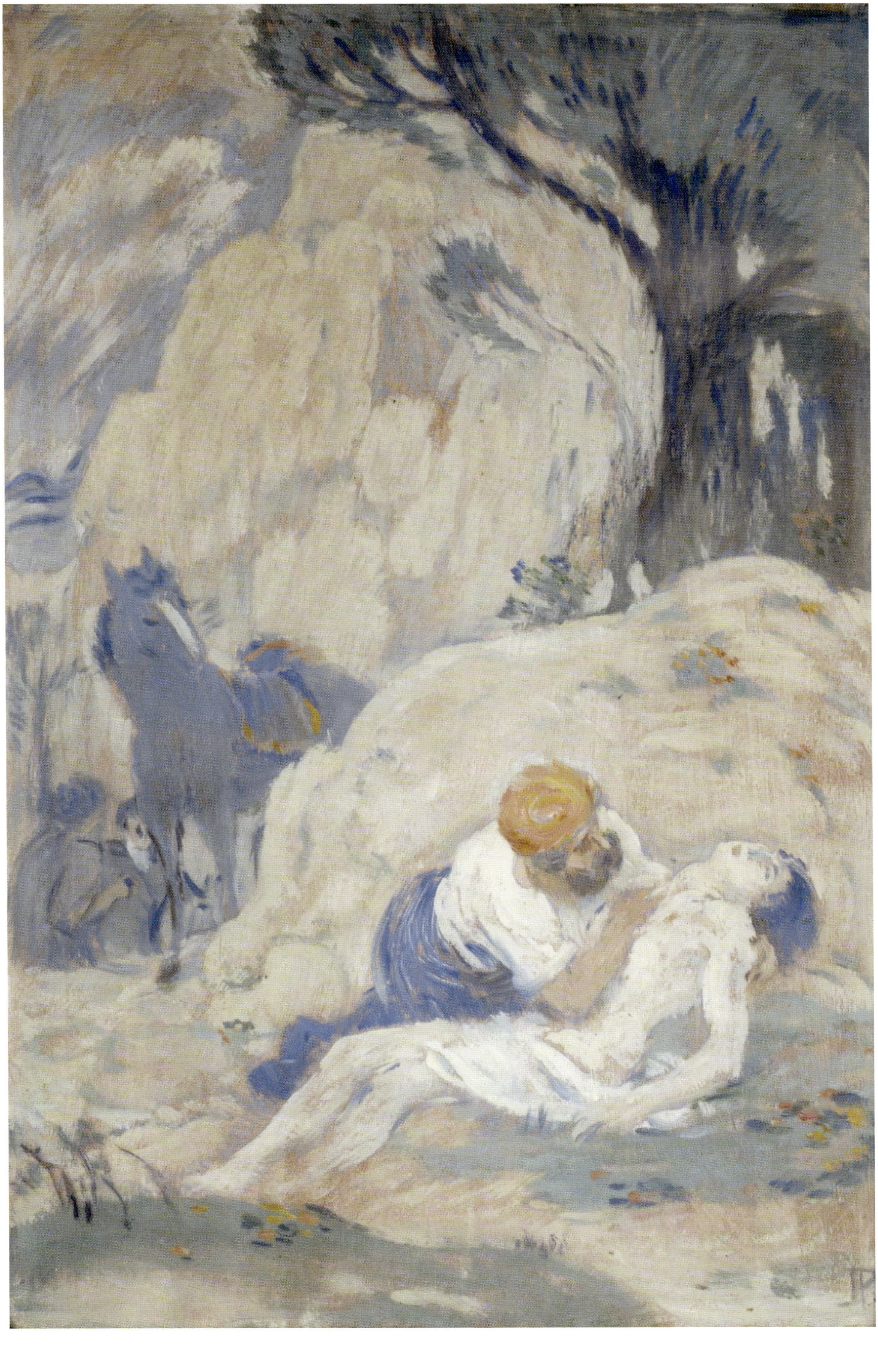

A1

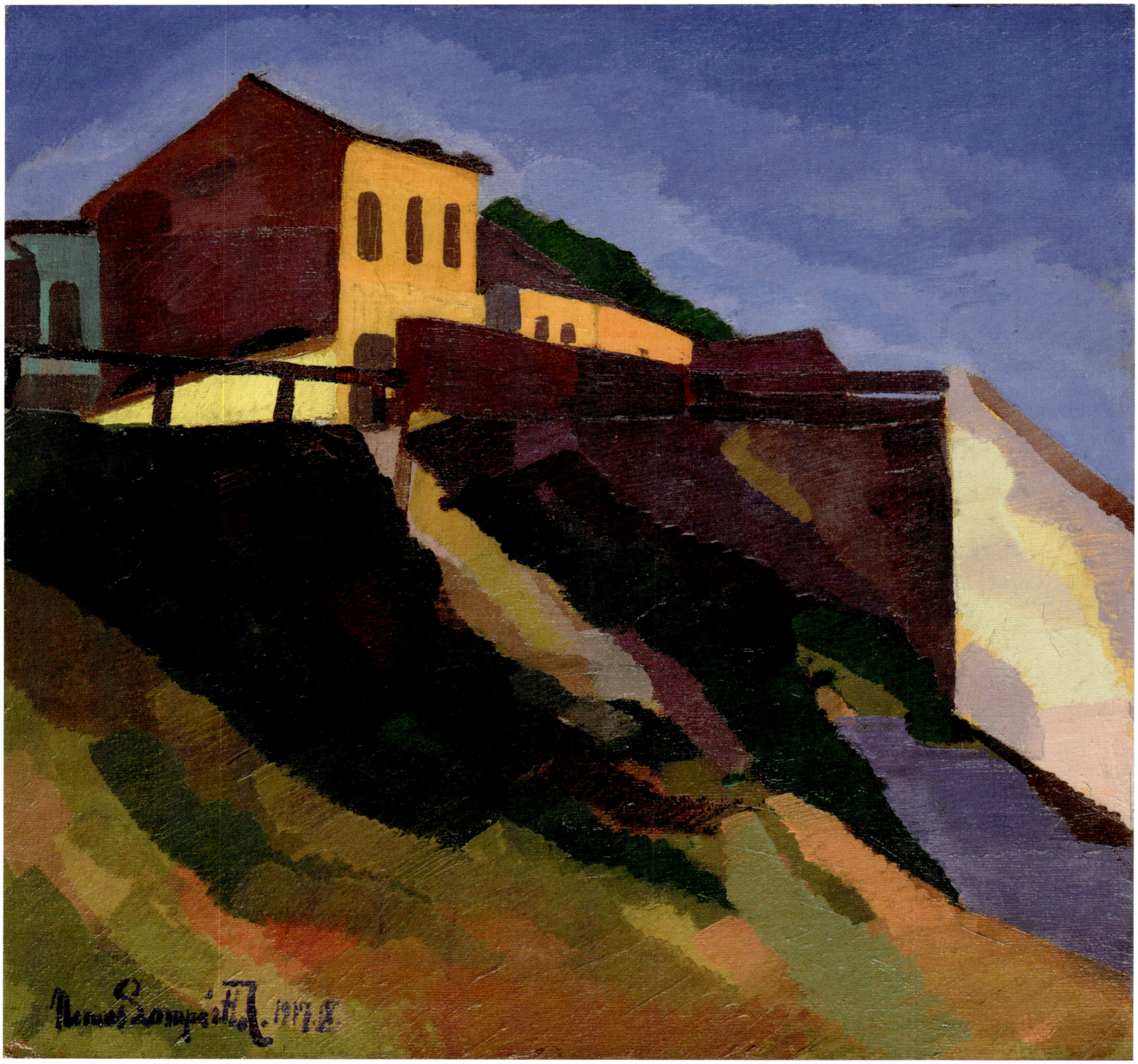

A1

József Nemes-Lampérth
Landscape (with View of Horgony Street), 1917
Museum of Fine Arts—Hungarian National Gallery, Budapest

József Nemes-Lampérth ▸
Standing Female Nude (Frontal View), 1916
Museum of Fine Arts—Hungarian National Gallery, Budapest

A1

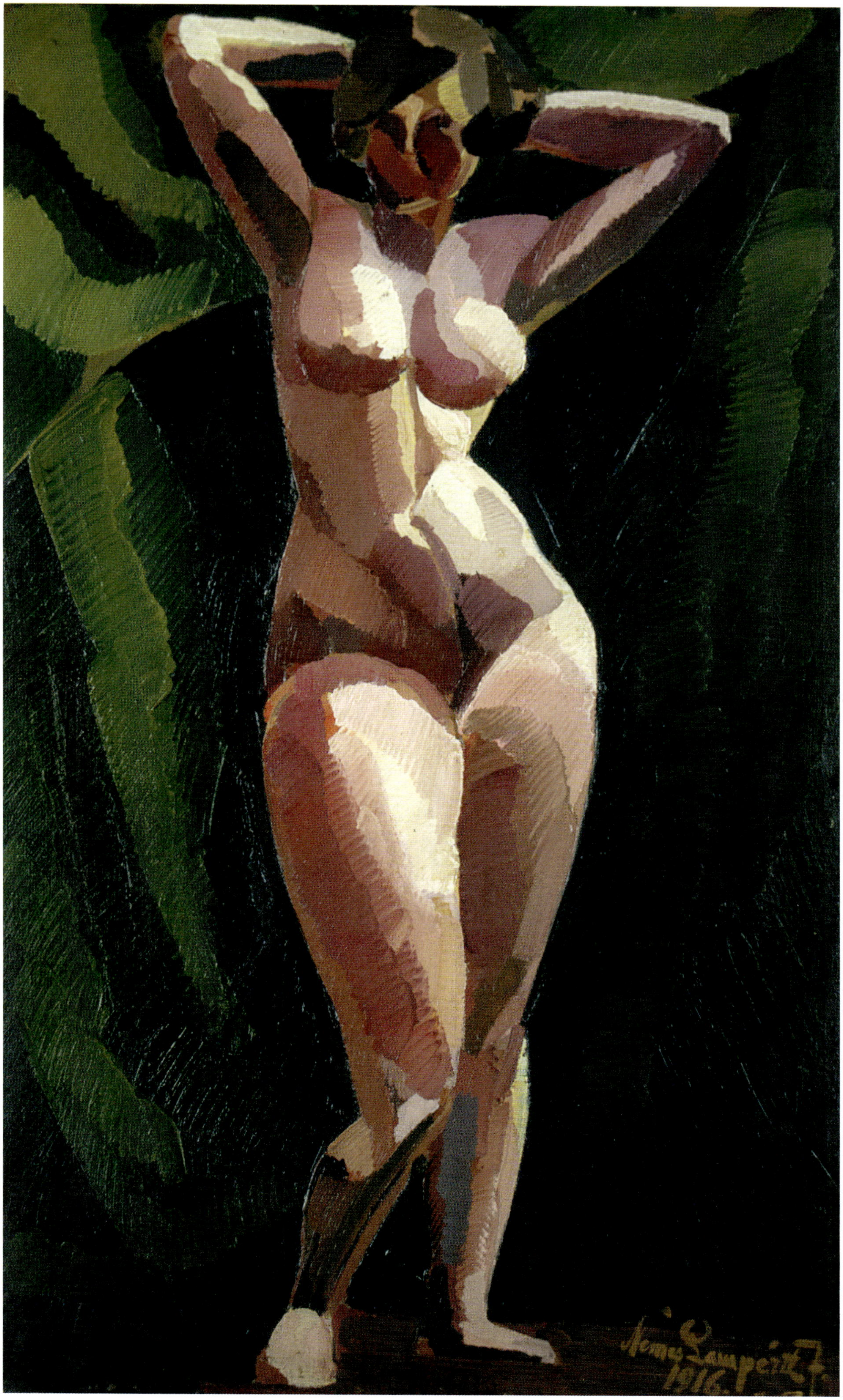

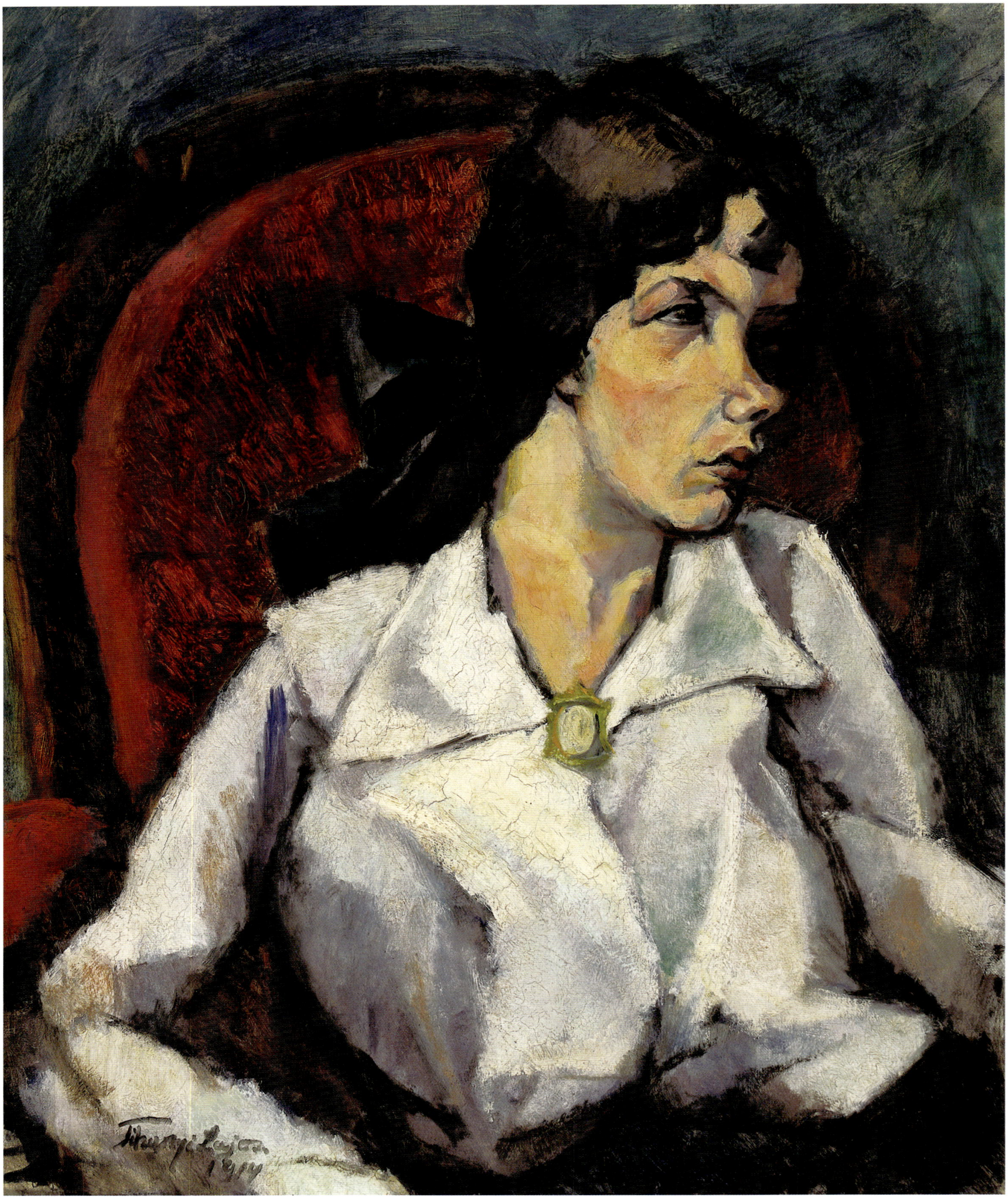

A1

Lajos Tihanyi
Portrait of Magdolna Leopold, 1914
St. Stephen´s King Museum —
Deák Collection, Székesfehérvár

Koloman Moser ▸
Self-Portrait, c. 1916
Belvedere, Vienna

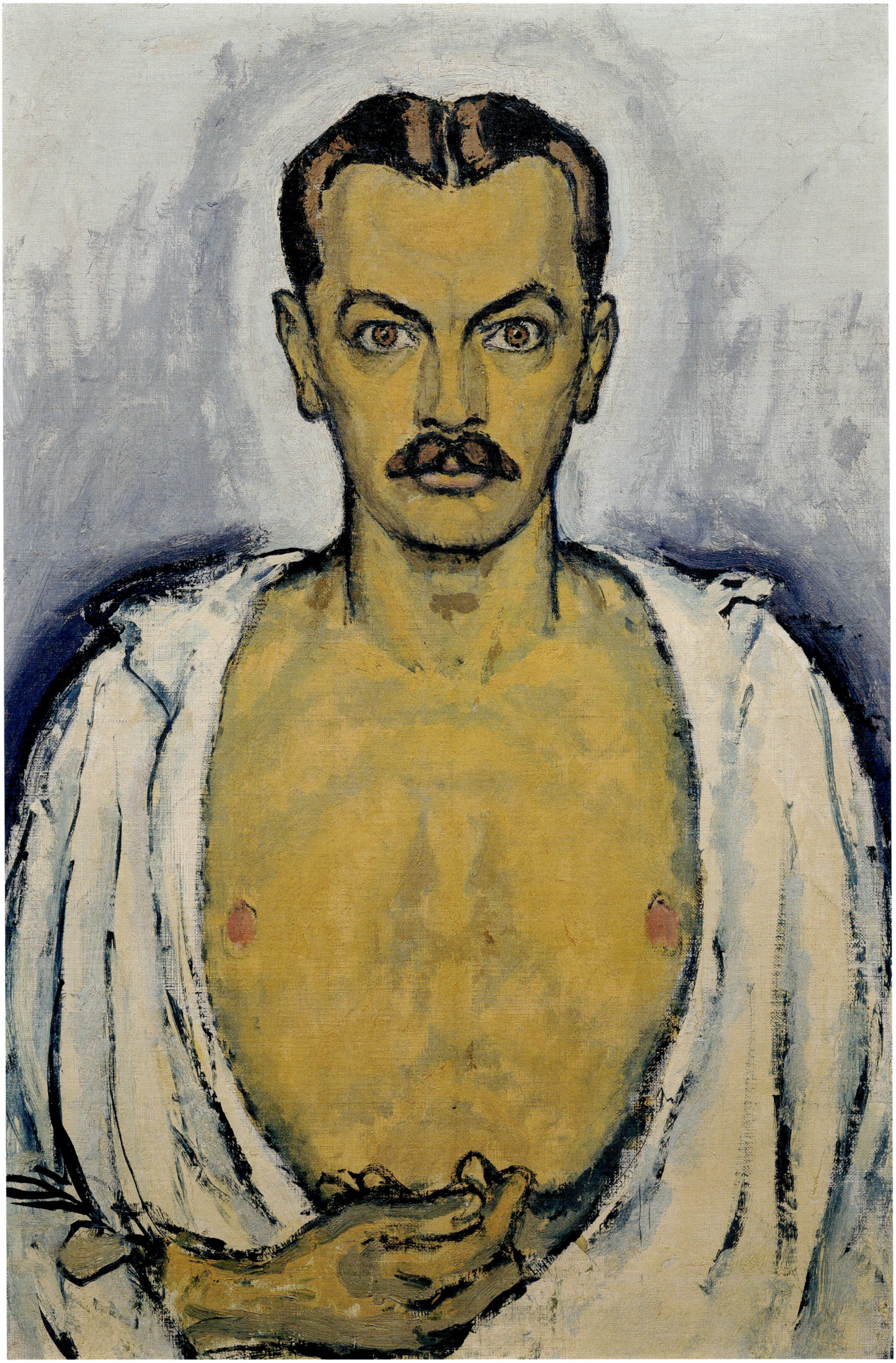

A1

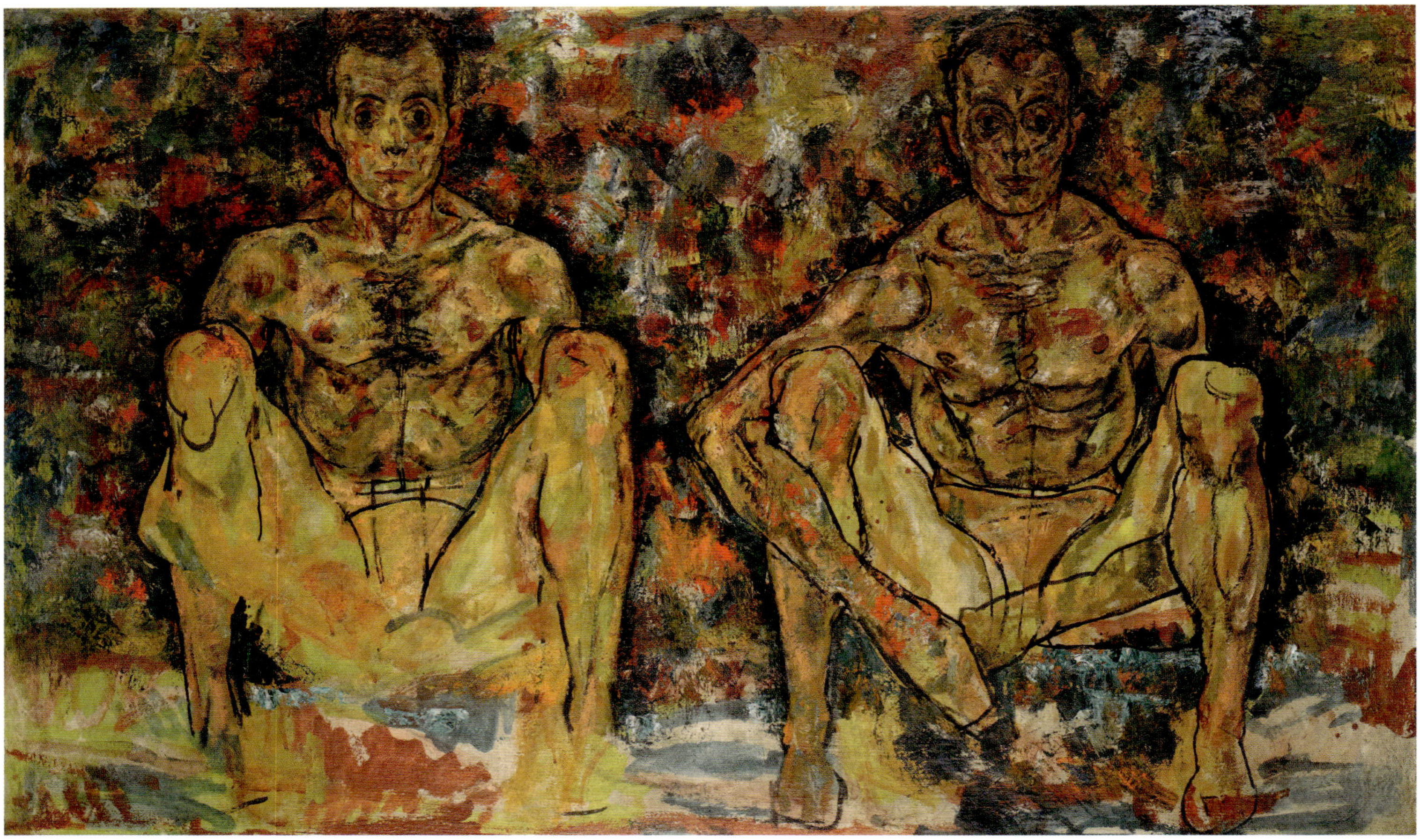

Egon Schiele
Squatting Men (Double Self-Portrait), 1918
(completed by another hand)
Private collection, courtesy of Richard Nagy Ltd., London

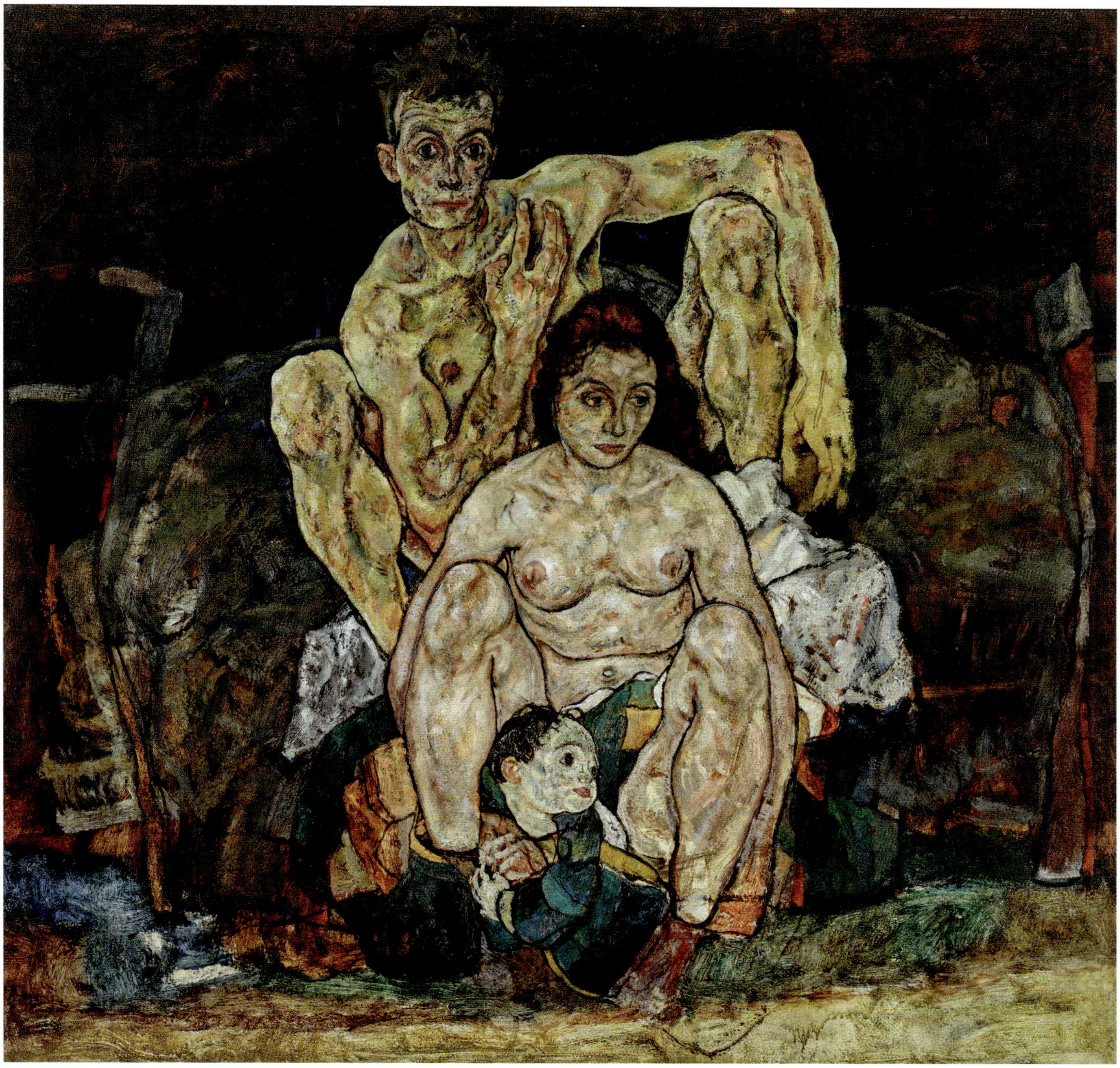

A1

Egon Schiele
The Family (Squatting Couple), 1918
Belvedere, Vienna

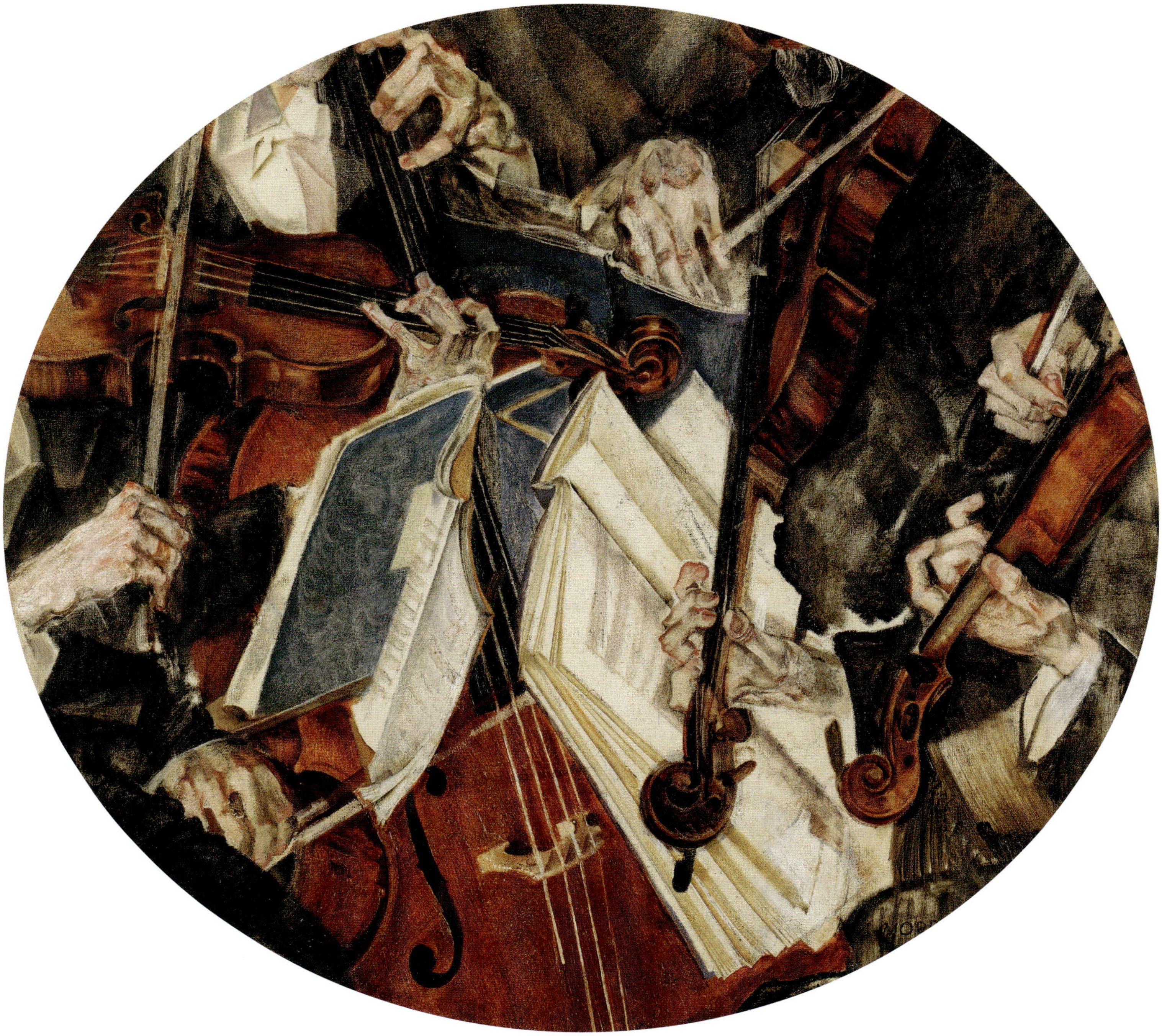

A1

Max Oppenheimer
Klingler Quartet, 1917
Belvedere, Vienna

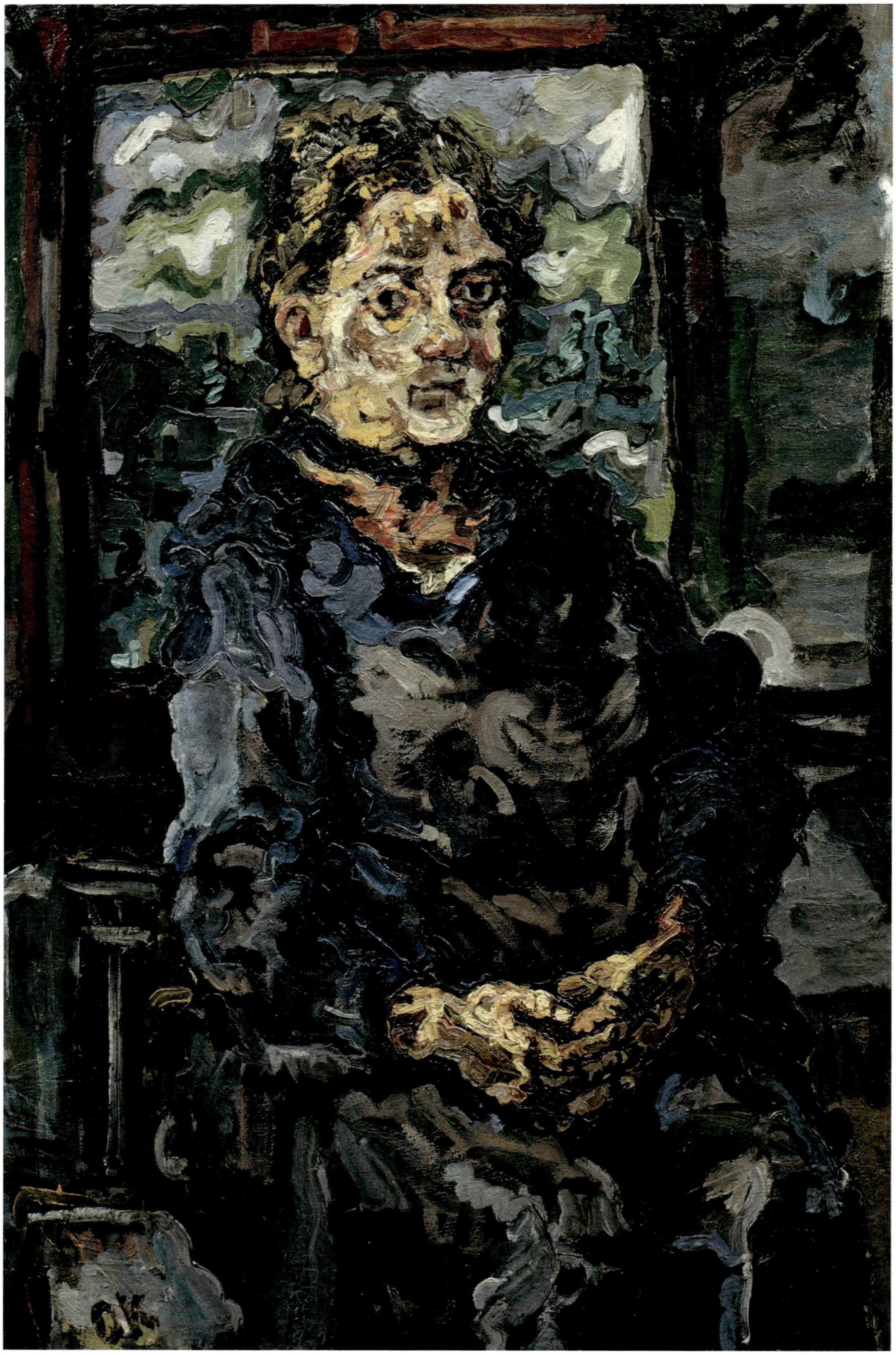

A1

Oskar Kokoschka
Romana Kokoschka, the Artist's Mother, 1917
Belvedere, Vienna

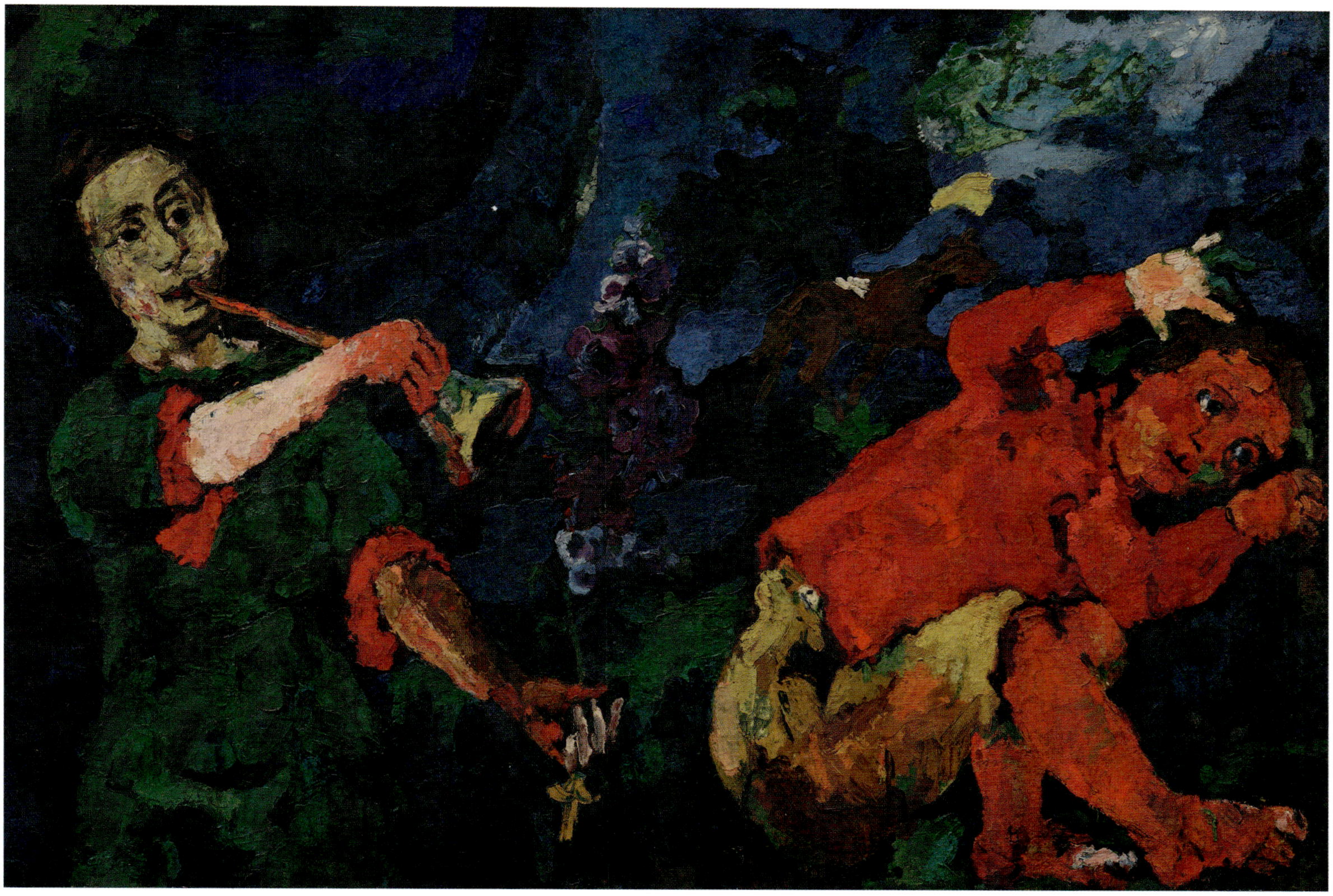

A1 Oskar Kokoschka
The Power of Music, 1918–20
Van Abbemuseum Collection, Eindhoven

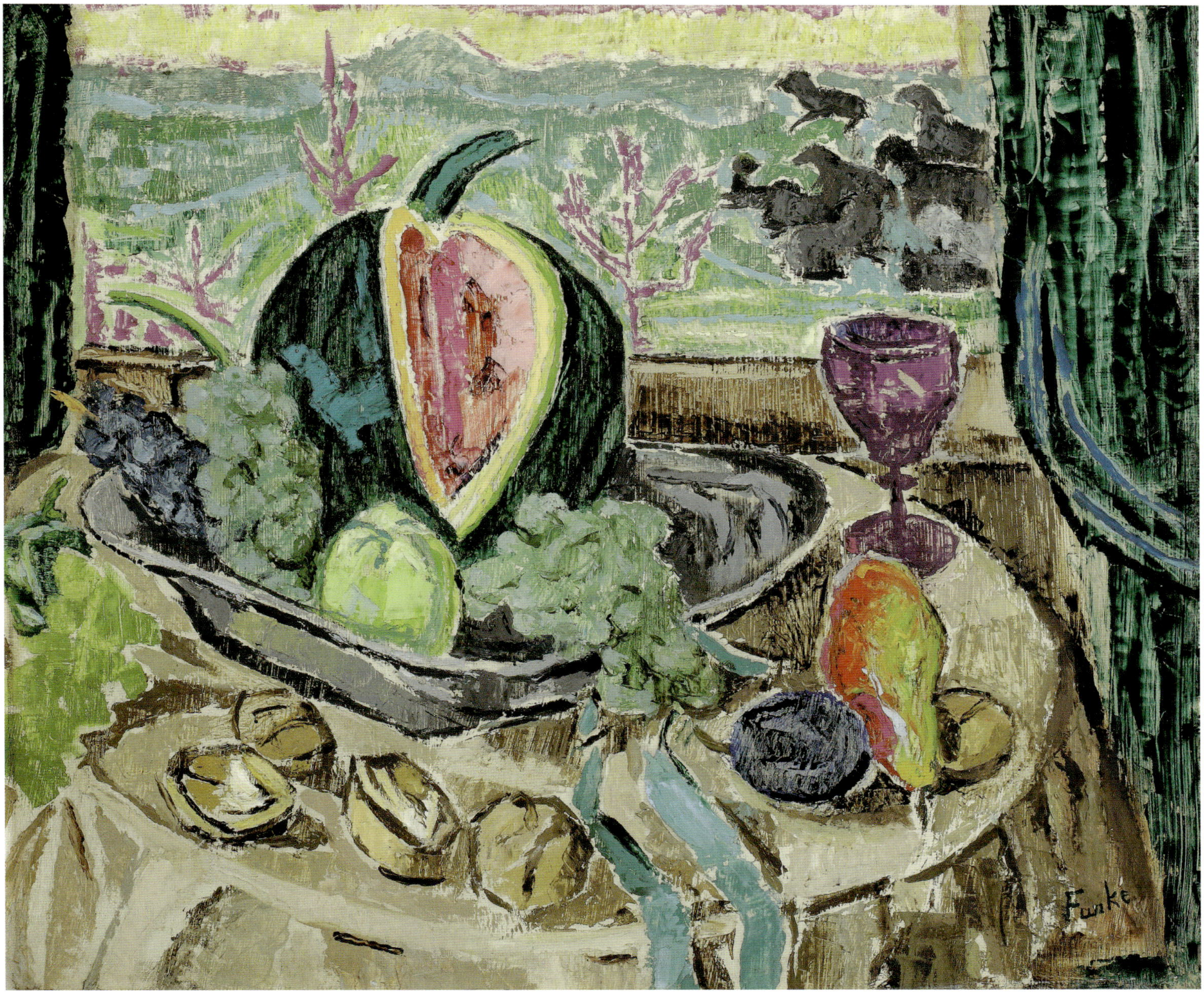

A1

Helene Funke
Still Life with Melon, c. 1918
Courtesy of Kunsthandel Hieke

Form Art and Abstraction

As early as 1910, art education in the Austro-Hungarian Empire was beginning to reflect an aesthetic trend that, as Form Art, was to play a key role in the shaping and establishment of non-representational art, well beyond the Empire's borders. The Czech Cubists—Josef Čapek, Antonín Procházka, Emil Filla, Bohumil Kubišta, and Václav Špála—and other form artists were influenced by a teaching system built upon the pedagogic principles of Johann Friedrich Herbart and practiced in schools of all levels all over the Empire. The negation of object, as promoted by Adolf Hölzel, not only found its full expression in the art of the 1910s, but became an integral part of the artistic agenda. At the same time, experiments in geometric reduction and landscapes suffused with a vibrant, organic rhythm, as in the work of János Mattis-Teutsch, were to reveal elements central to the development of abstract art. (MH)

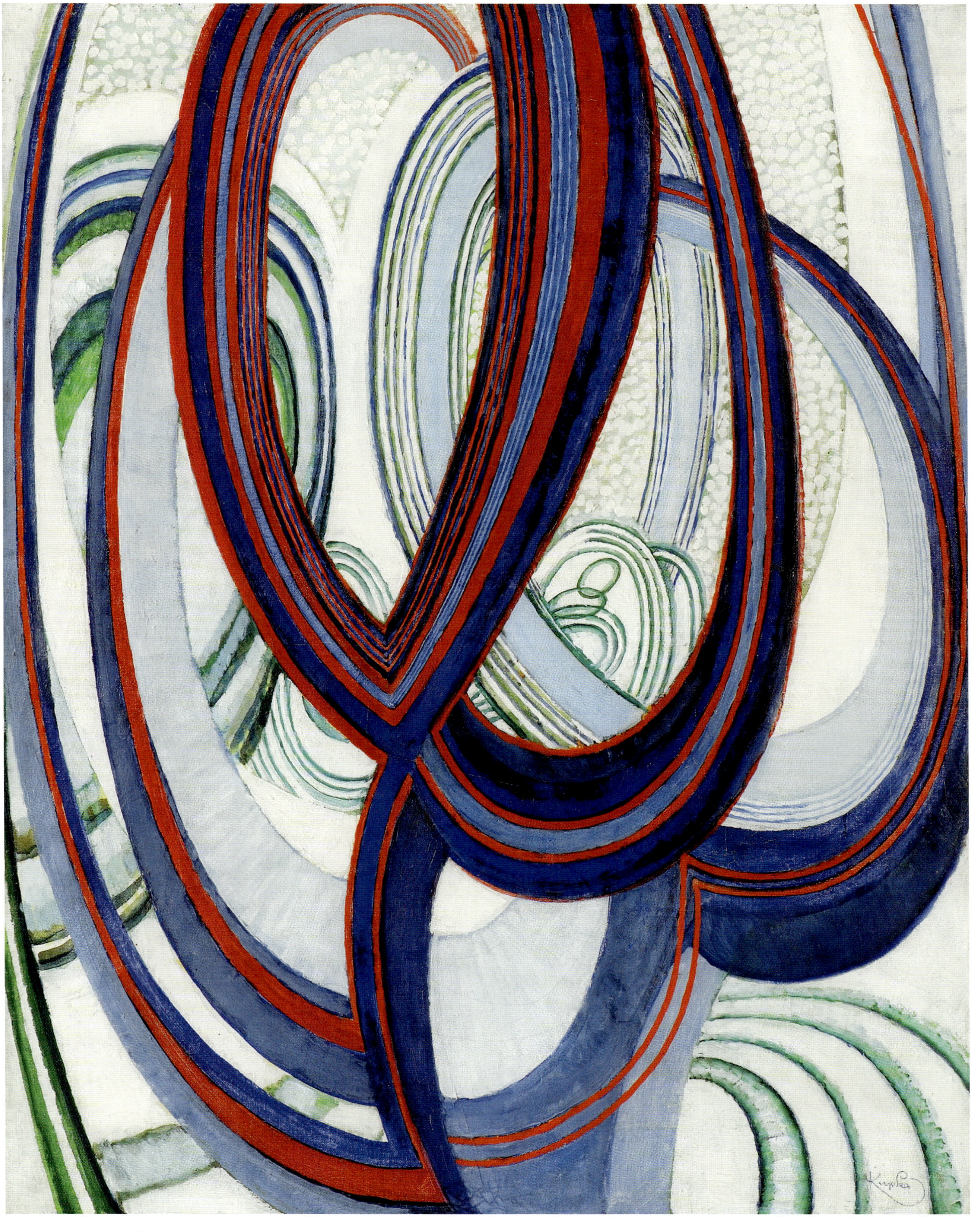

František Kupka
Lines, Planes, Depth, 1911/12
Museum Kampa—The Jan and
Meda Mládek Foundation, Prague

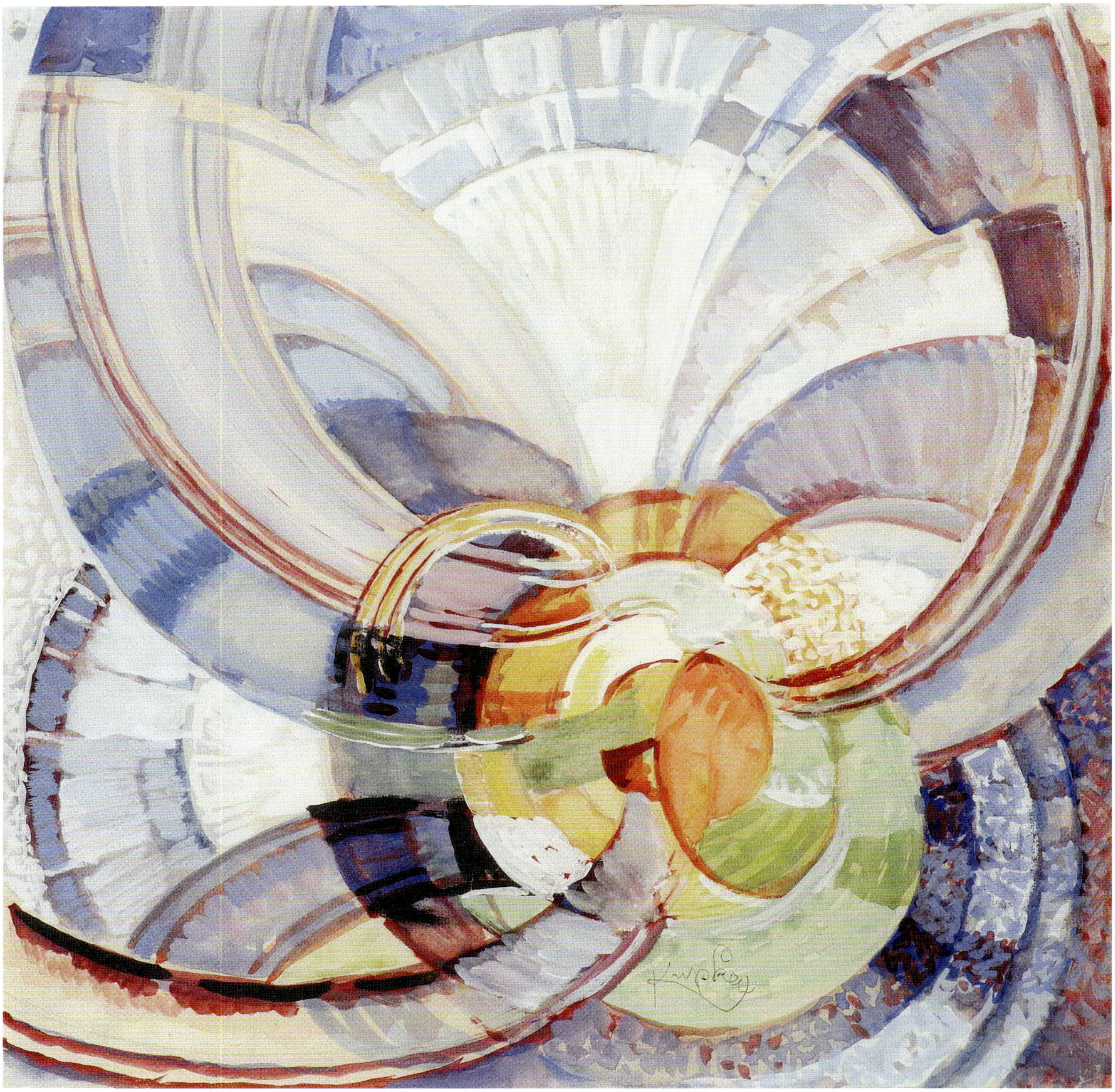

A2

František Kupka
Study for *Around a Point,* 1911–30
Museum Kampa—The Jan and
Meda Mládek Foundation, Prague

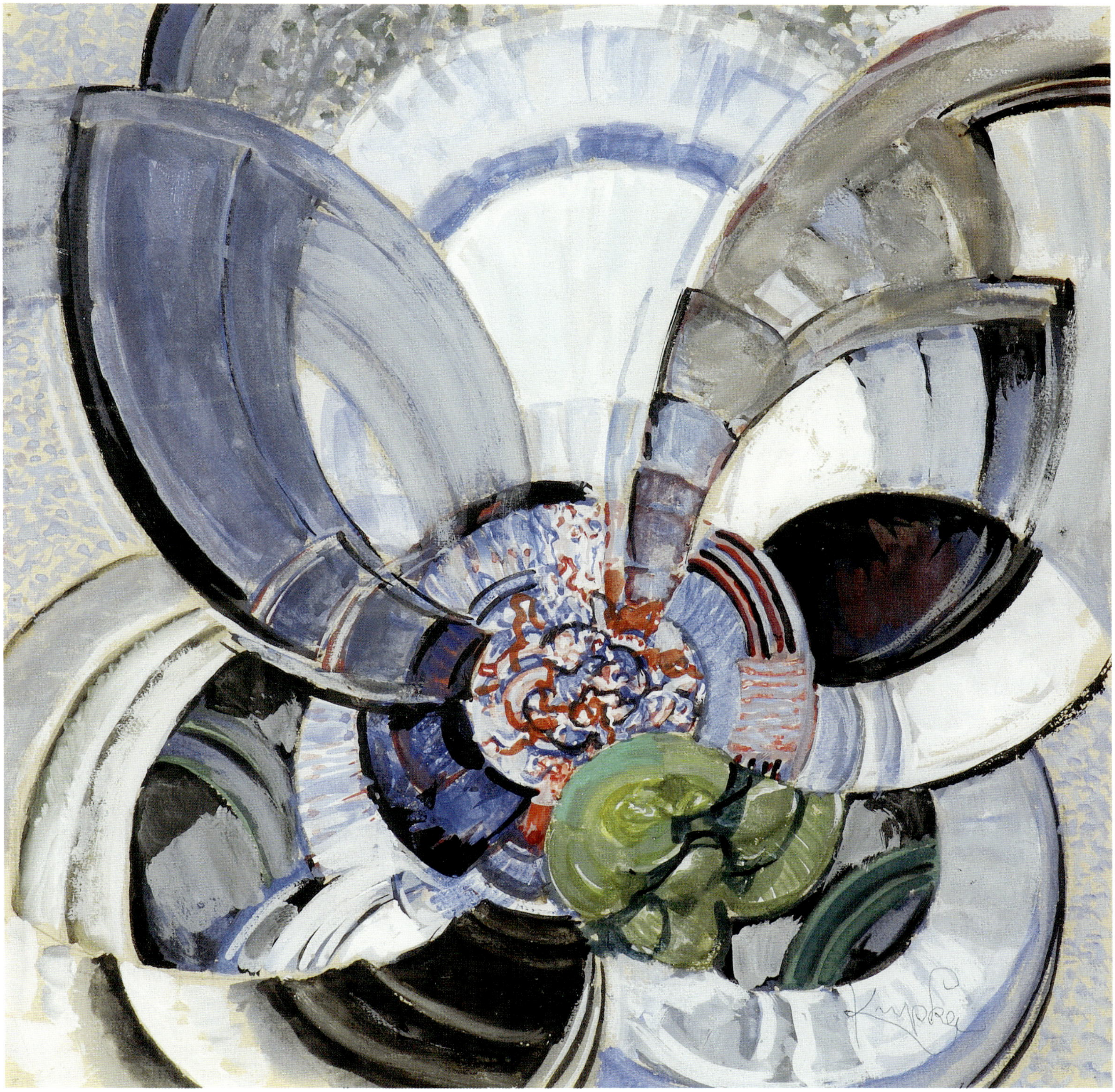

František Kupka
Study for *Around a Point,* 1911–30
Museum Kampa—The Jan and
Meda Mládek Foundation, Prague

A2

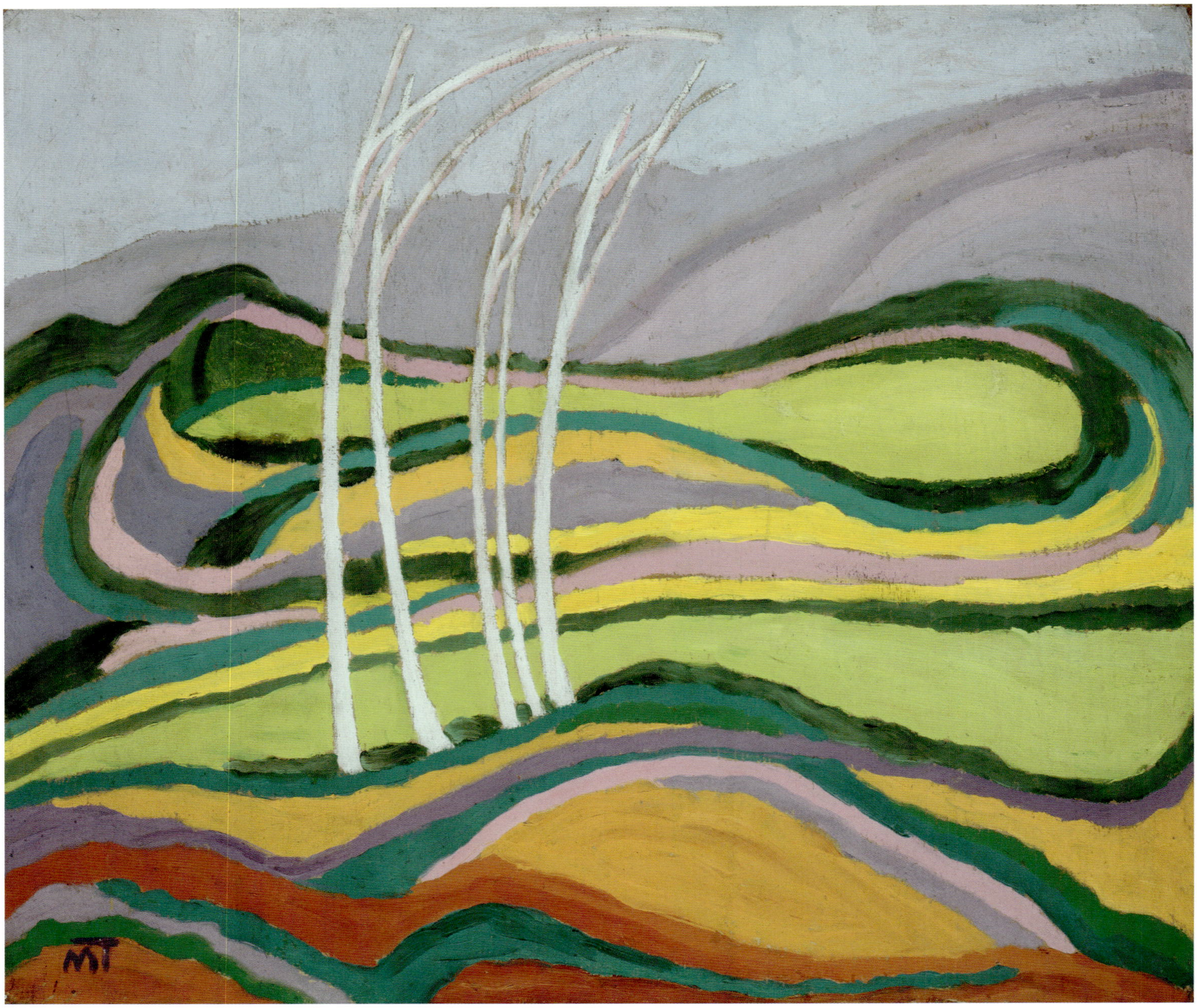

A2

János Mattis-Teutsch
Landscape, c. 1917
Museum of Fine Arts—Hungarian National Gallery, Budapest

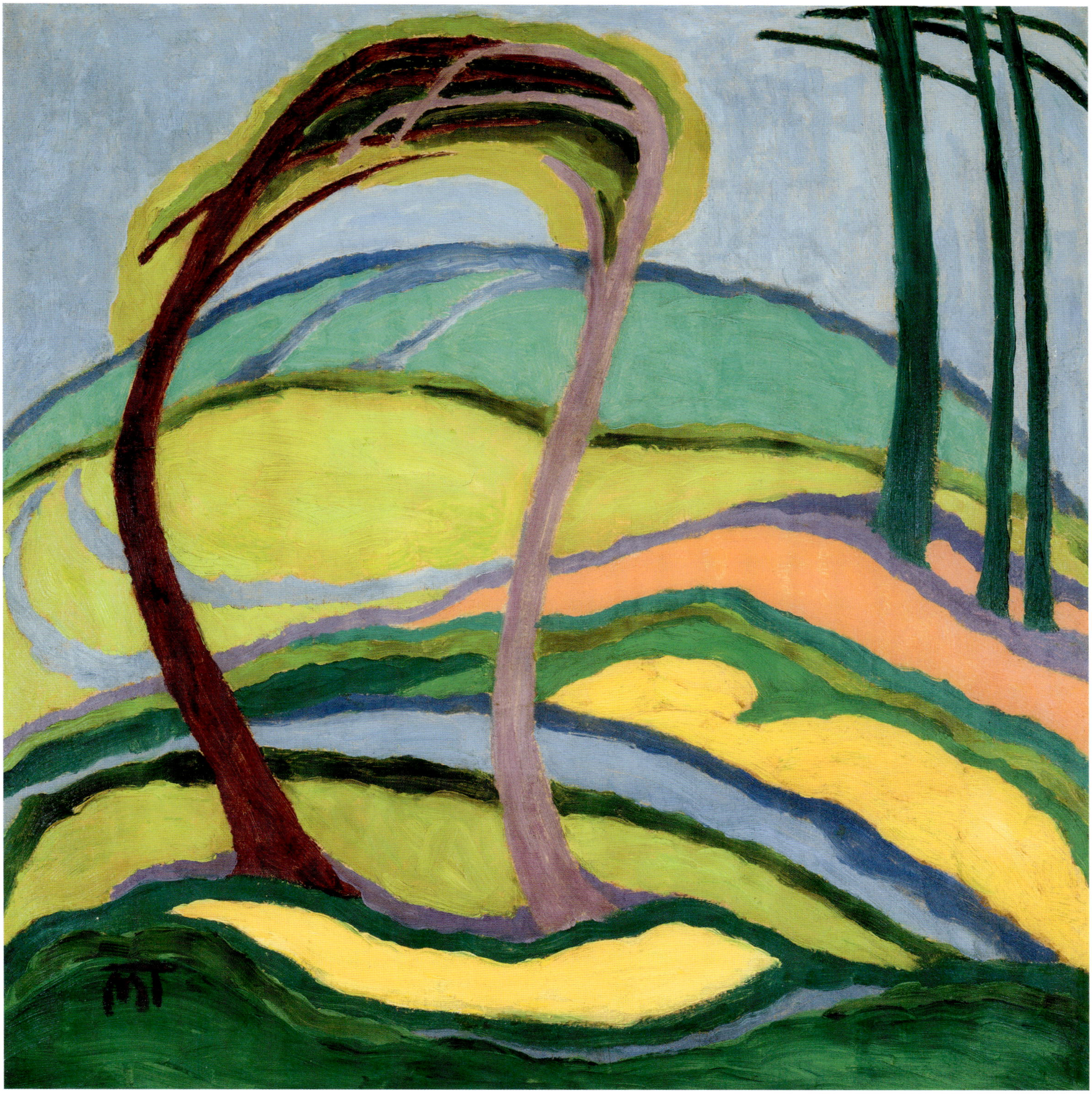

A2

János Mattis-Teutsch
Landscape, c. 1917
Museum of Fine Arts—Hungarian National Gallery, Budapest

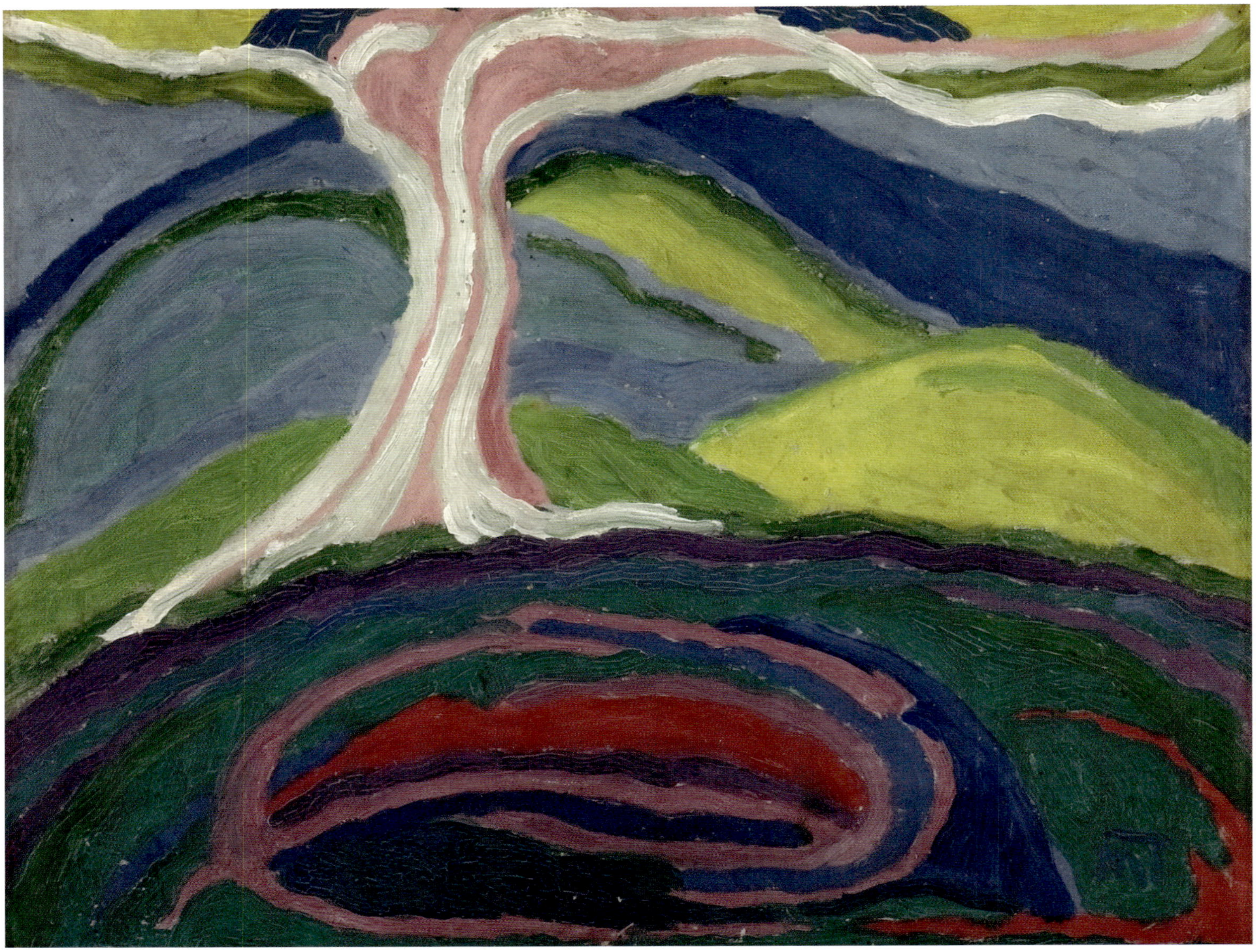

A2

János Mattis-Teutsch
Solitary Tree, c. 1917
Flóris Rómer Museum of Art and History, Győr

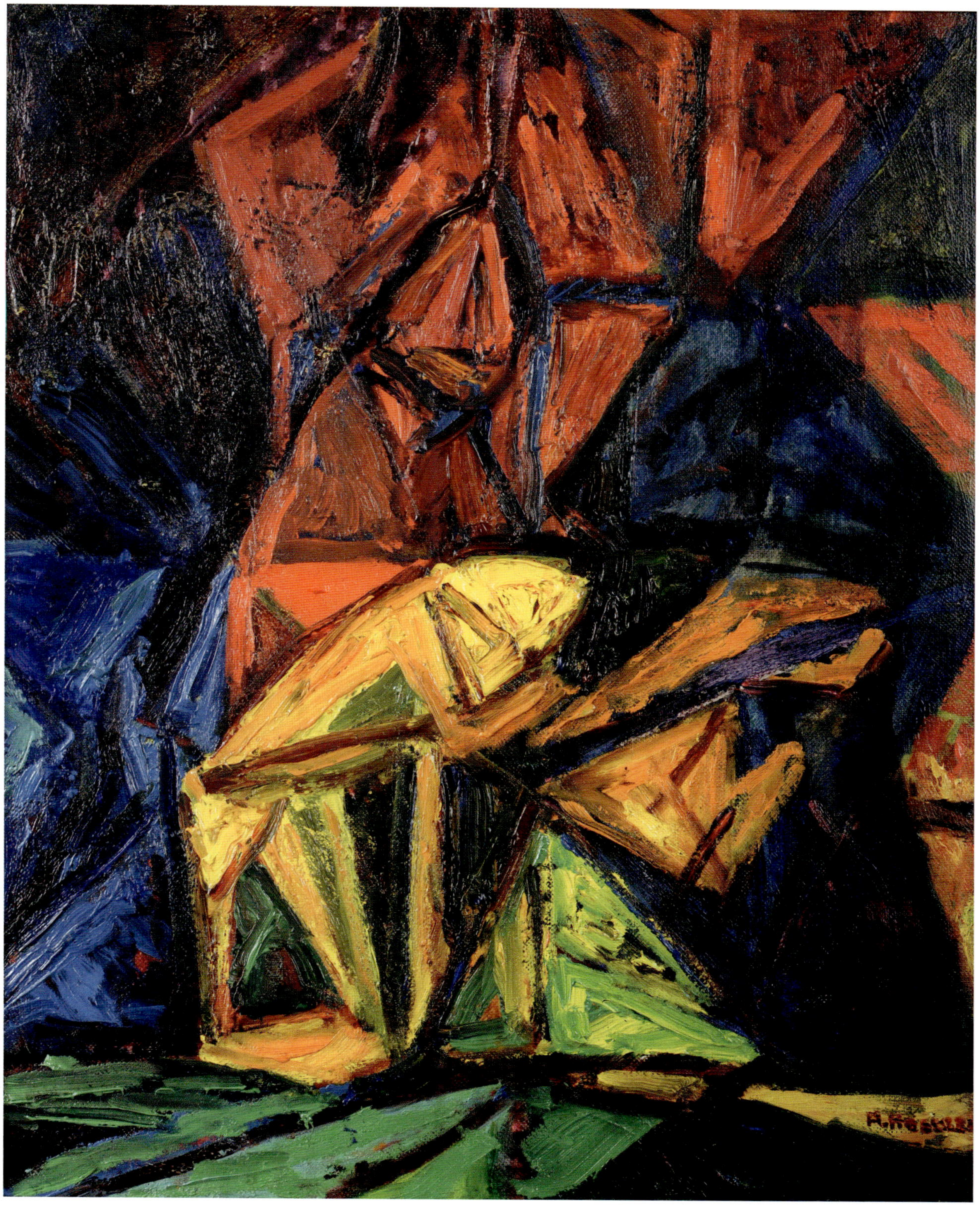

A2

Adolf Hölzel
Abstraction I, c. 1915
Private collection

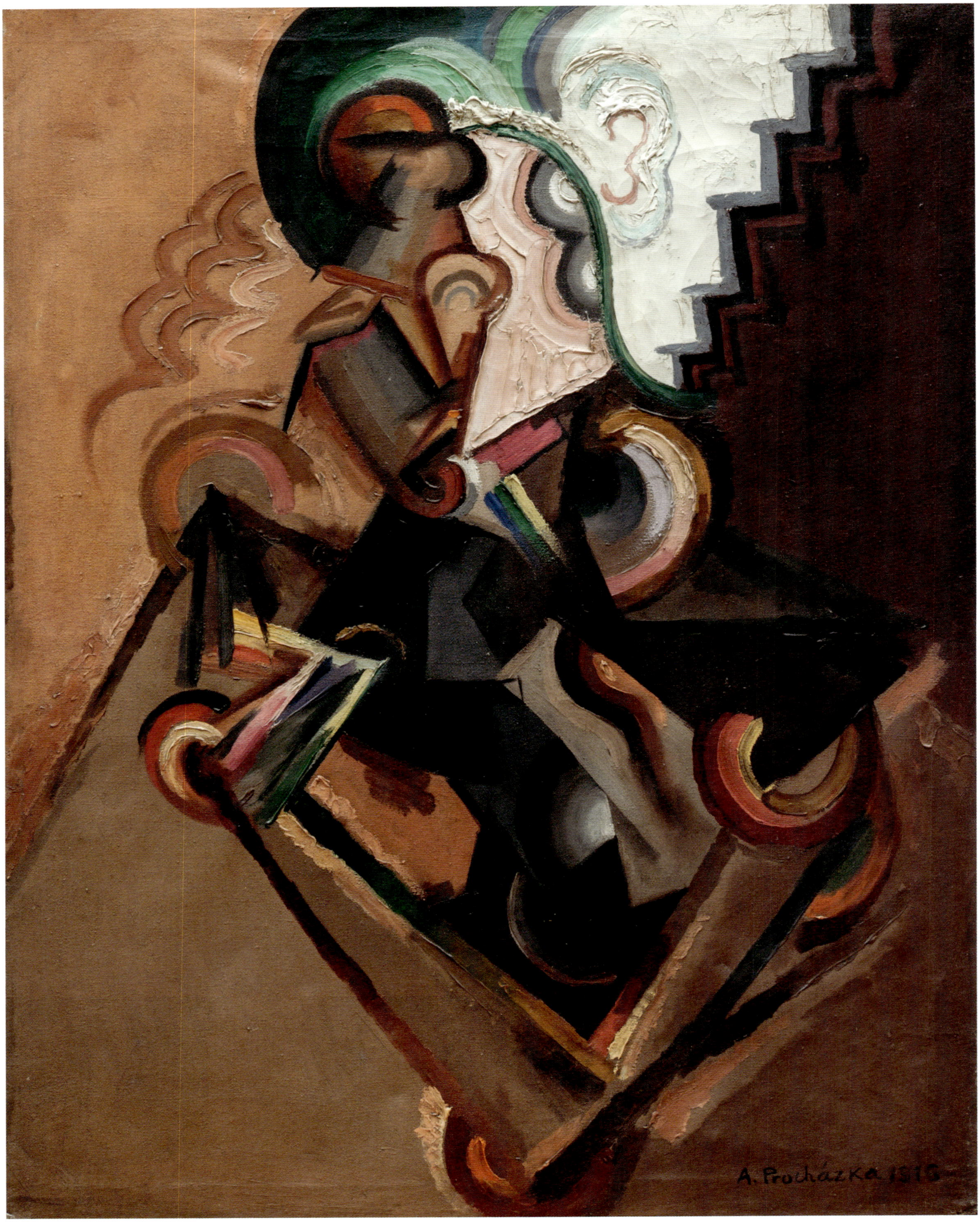

A2 Antonín Procházka
The Singer, 1916
Brno City Museum

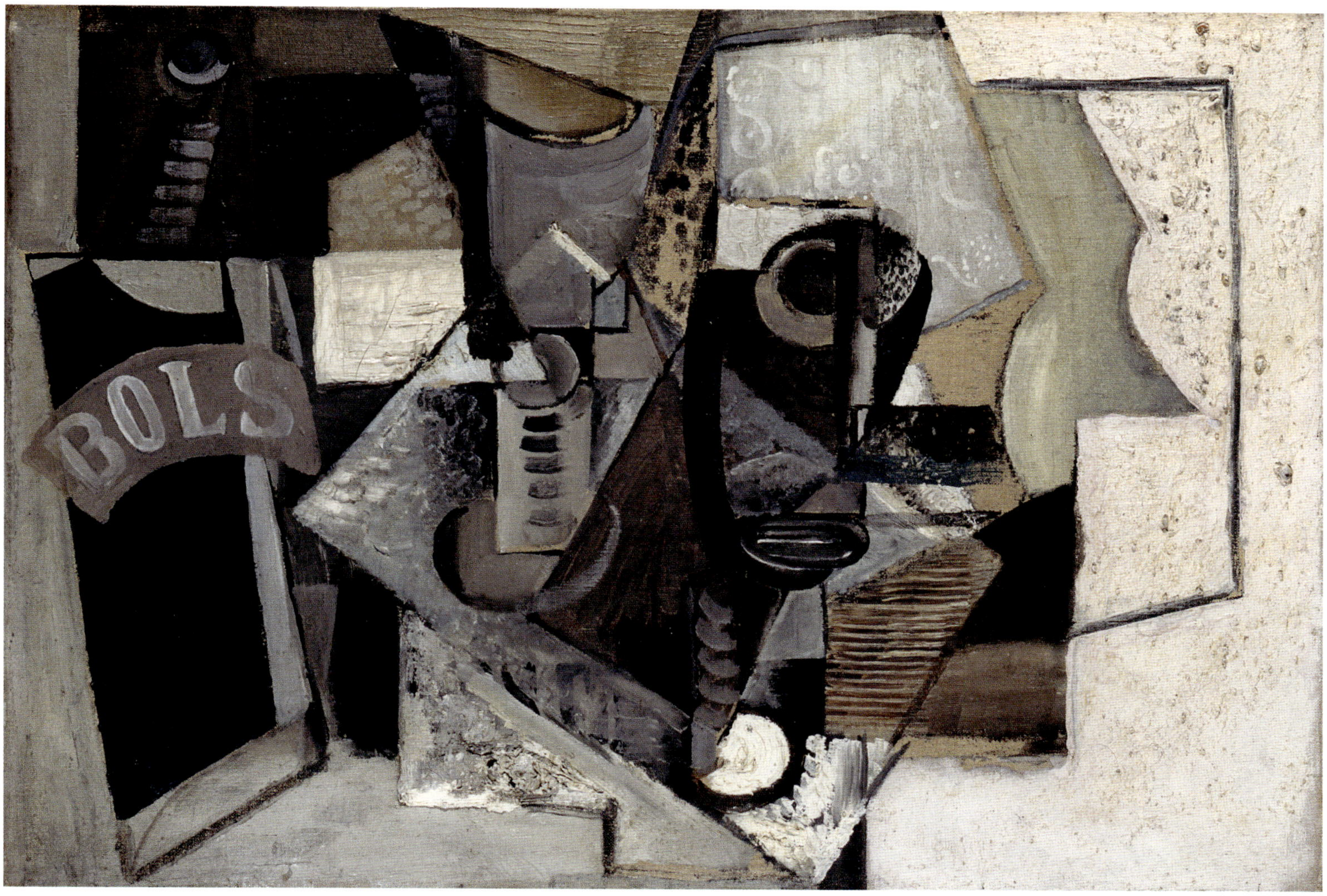

A2

Emil Filla
Still Life Bols, 1914
The Gallery of West Bohemia in Pilsen

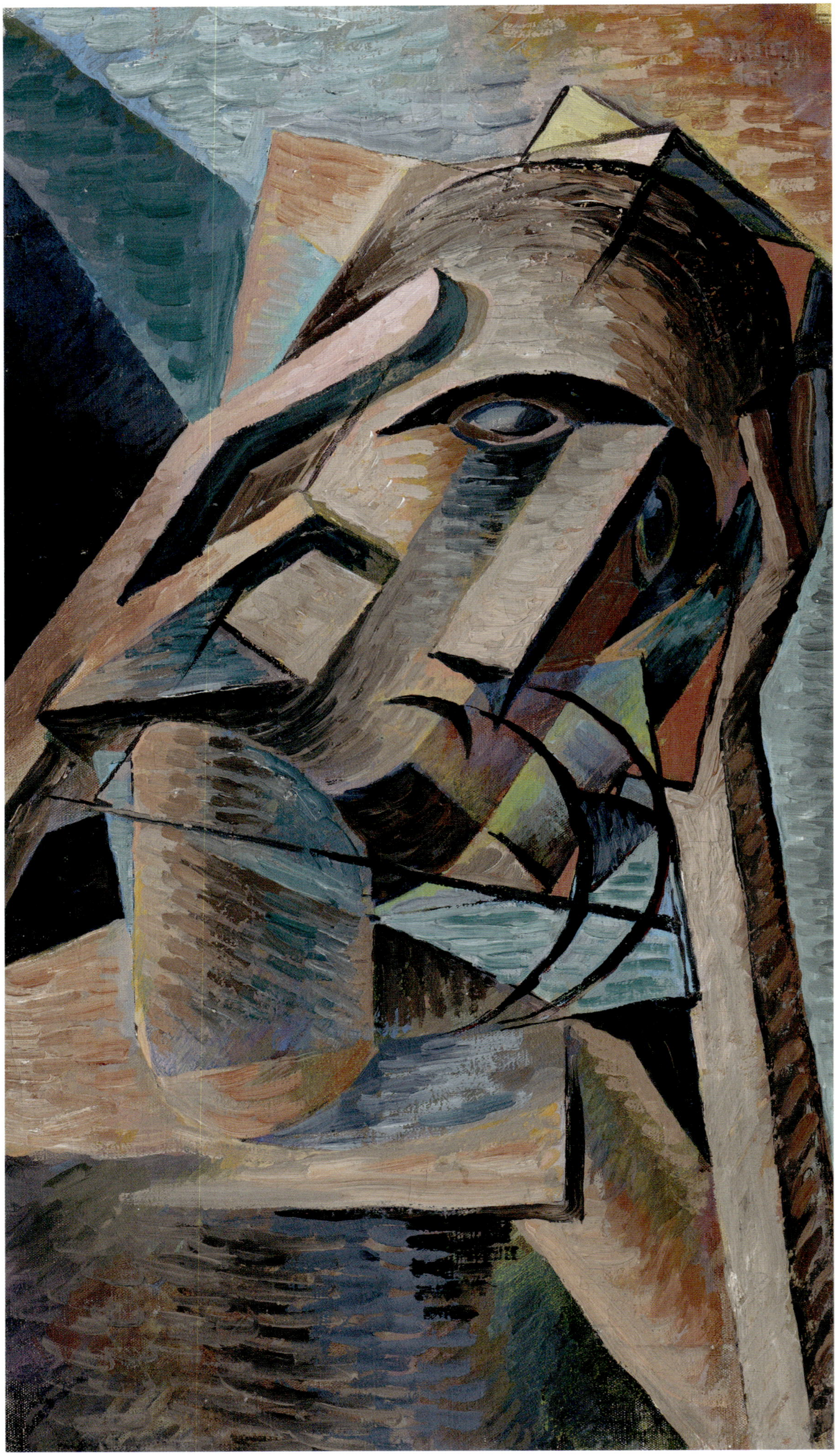

◂
Bohumil Kubišta
Meditation, 1915
National Gallery in Prague
▸
Bohumil Kubišta
Head, 1915
The Gallery of West Bohemia in Pilsen

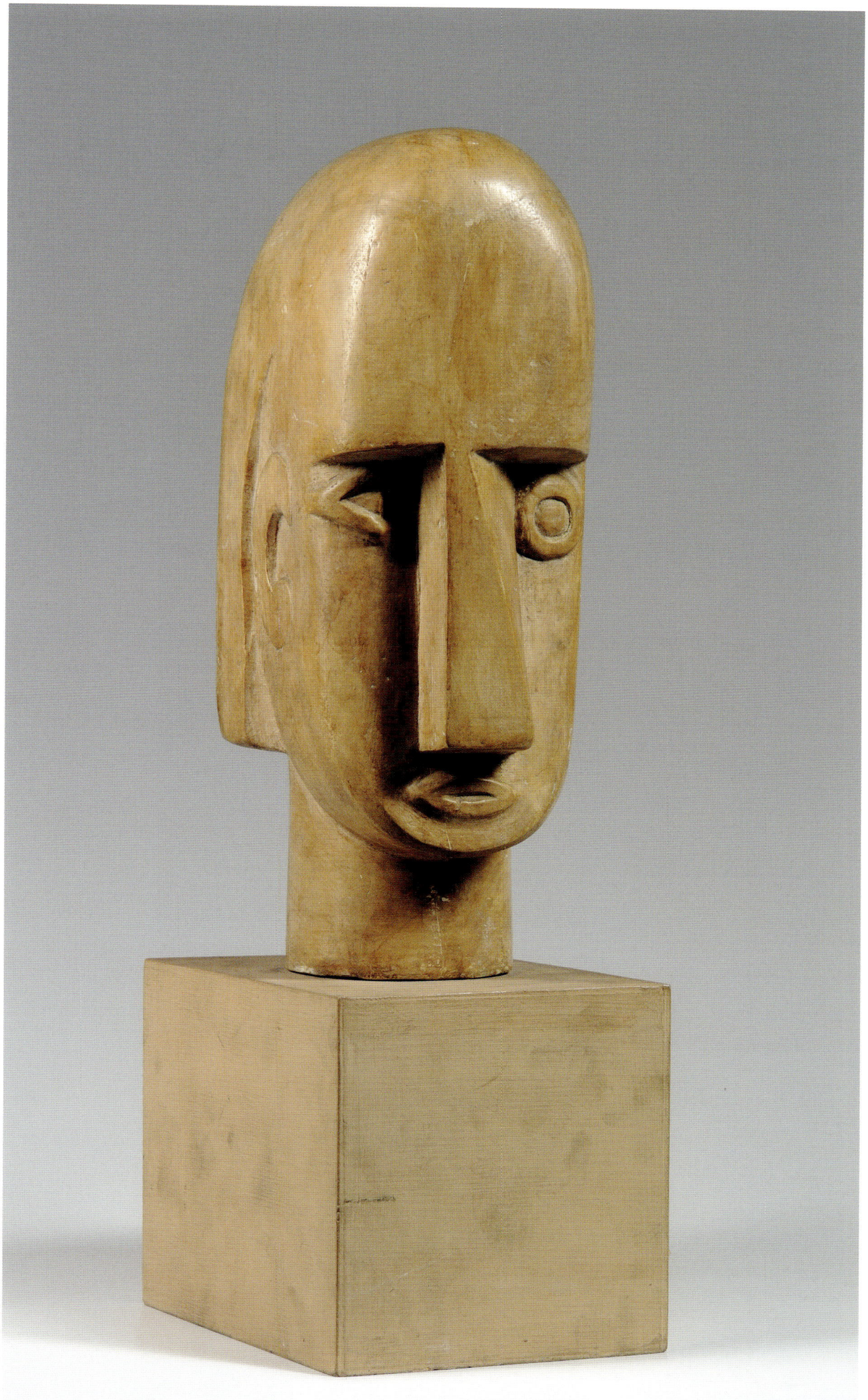

A2

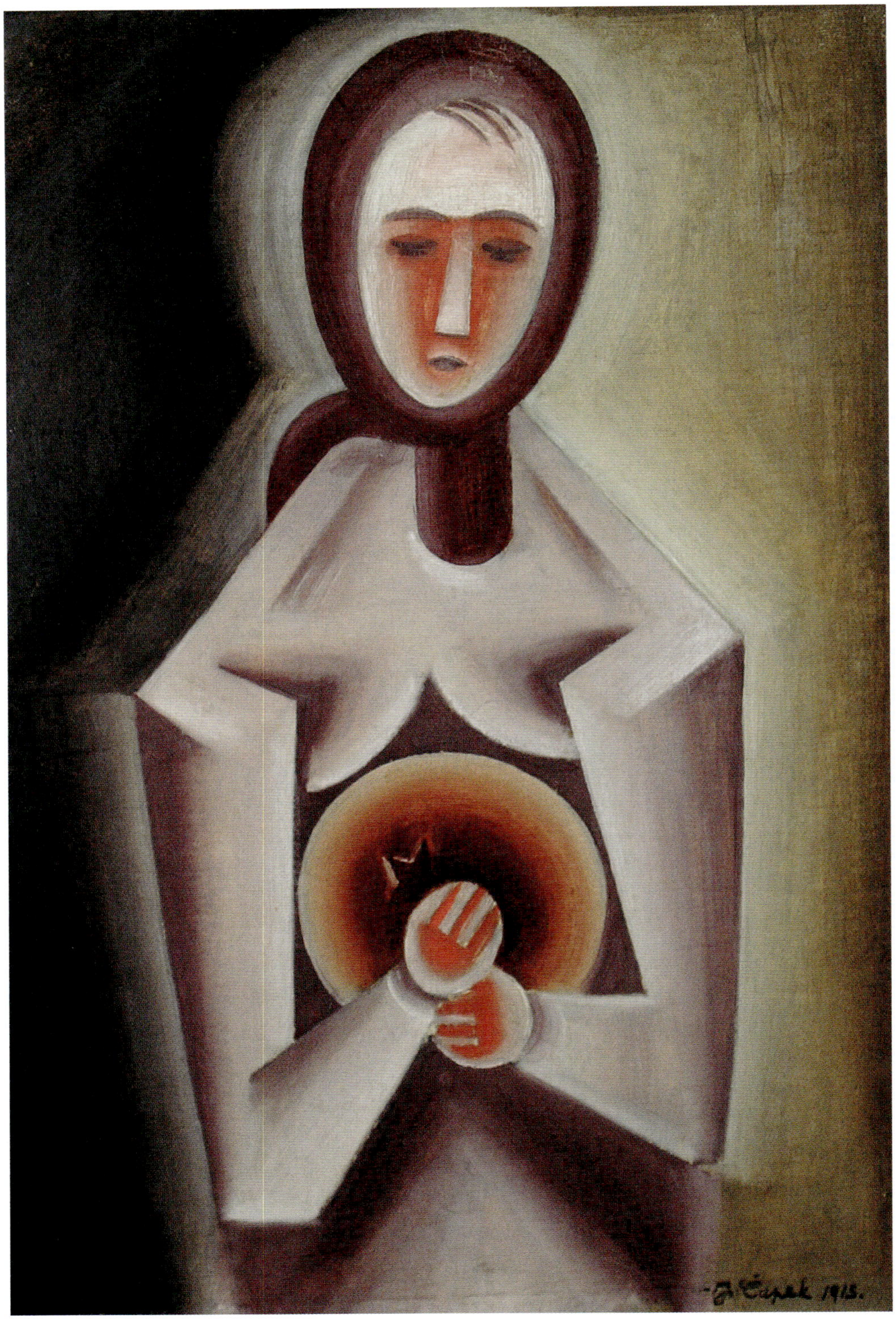

A2

Josef Čapek
Portrait of a Girl, 1915
Private collection

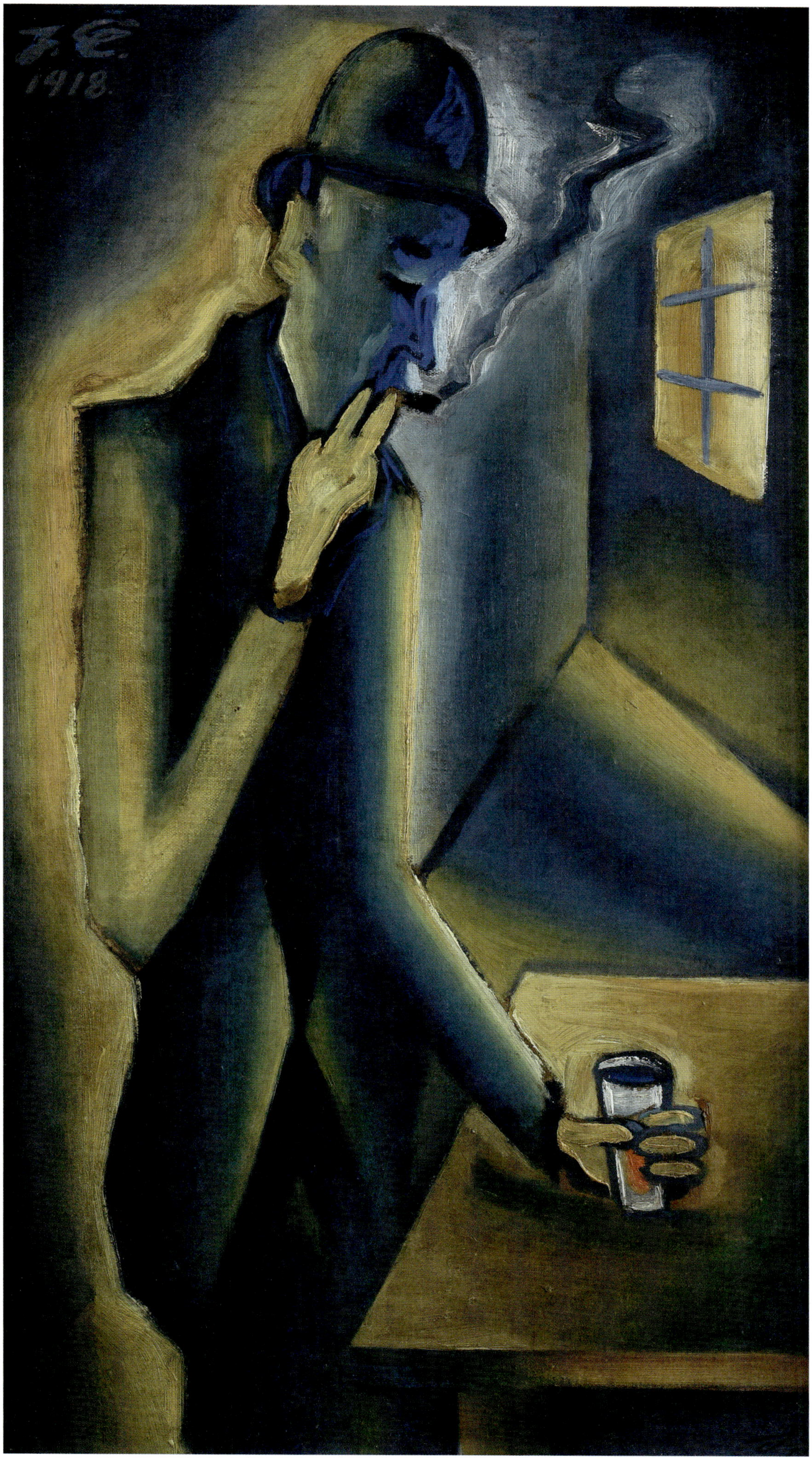

A2

Josef Čapek
The Drinker, 1918/19
Moravian Gallery,
Brno

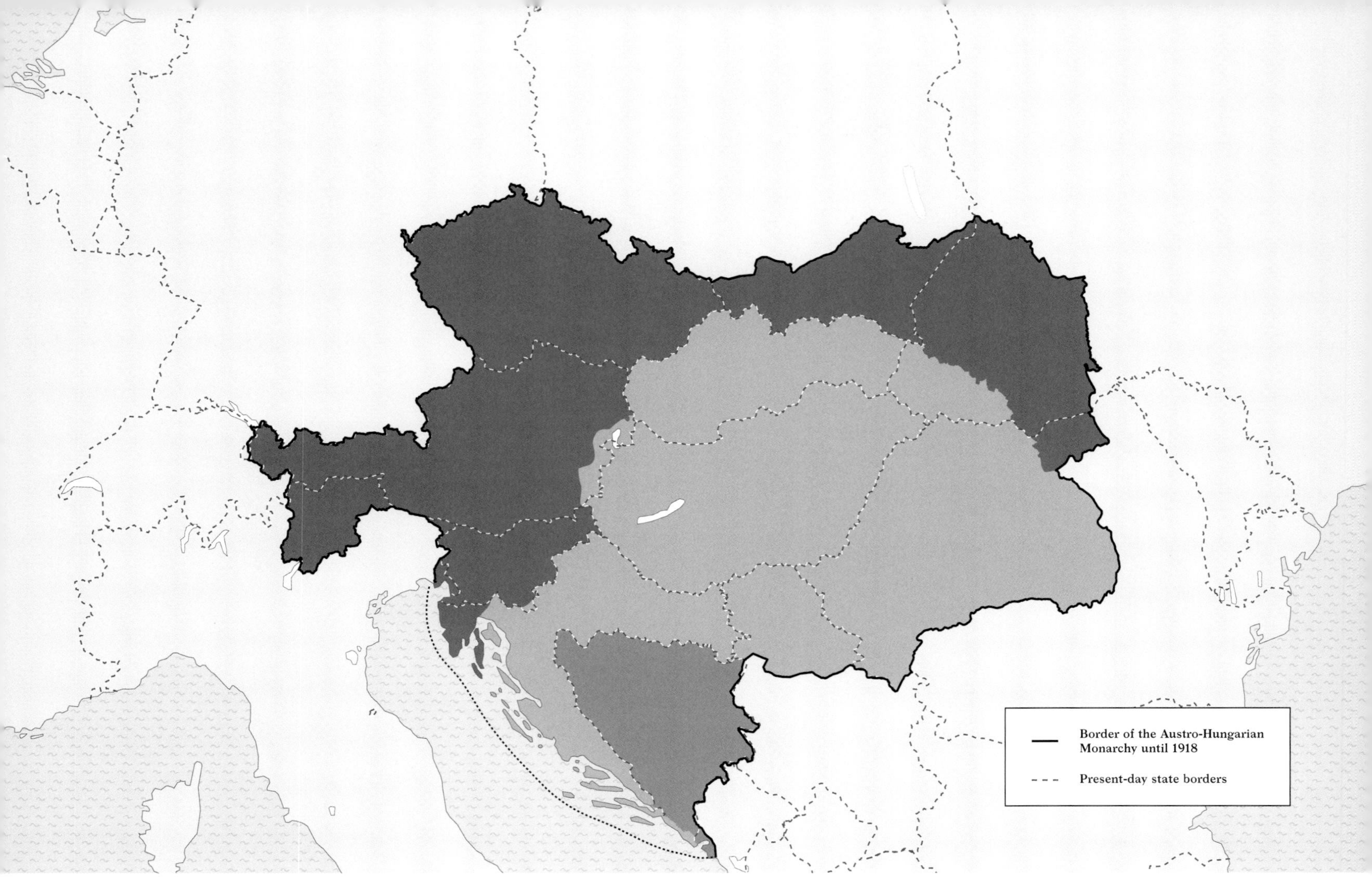

A2 The Austro-Hungarian Monarchy until 1918 and today's political borders

border:

bor´dĕr, *n.* [ME. *border, bordure*; OFr. *bordure*; LL. *bordatura*, border, edging; *bordus*, edge, side.] The outer edge of anything: the extreme part or surrounding line; the confine or exterior limit of a country, or of any region or tract of land; the exterior part or edge of a garment; the rim or brim of a vessel; the exterior part of a garden; the outer edge of an armorial bearing, with a tincture distinct from the field; an overhead piece of scenery in a theater; a limit or boundary; a margin.

bor´dĕr, *a.* Pertaining to that which adjoins, or to outlying districts; as, a *border* ruffian; a desperado of a *border* country or district. *Border states*; a name applied to Maryland, Virginia, Delaware, Kentucky, and Missouri, the five slave states which bordered upon the northern free states.

Noah Webster / Noah Porter, ed., *Webster's Imperial Dictionary of the English Language* (Chicago, 1906), p. 196

´border, 1. n. Edge or part near it, limit; line of division between countries; flower-bed edging garden; band of colour etc. edging material. *The B.*, land near b. between England and Scotland. 2. v.t. & i. Put b. round; be b. to. *B. on,* be almost. -land, n. Sp., anything on the edge of a field of interest etc. (´bɔːdə).

Charles Kay Ogden, ed., *The General Basic English Dictionary* (New York, 1942), p. 40

English

Meditation and the Fantastic

Artists like Richard Teschner and Alfred Kubin combined, each in their own way, perceptible objects and fantastical elements, lending a whole new level of meaning to their figure drawings and melancholy landscapes. Nightmares and fairy tales were summoned into being through dancing beasts, looming forests, or phantasmagoric figures. The works of Ivan Meštrović and Jan Zrzavý, on the other hand, provided ephemeral glimpses into the internal world of the human psyche through intimate, meditative gestures, with both the contemplative poise of Meštrović's *Vestal Virgin* and the auraed radiance of Jan Zrzavý's figures setting a stark contrast to the brutality of the war. While Kubin's gruesome visions reflect humanity's dark side, the corona that surrounds these temperate meditating figures communicates compassion and benevolence. (MH)

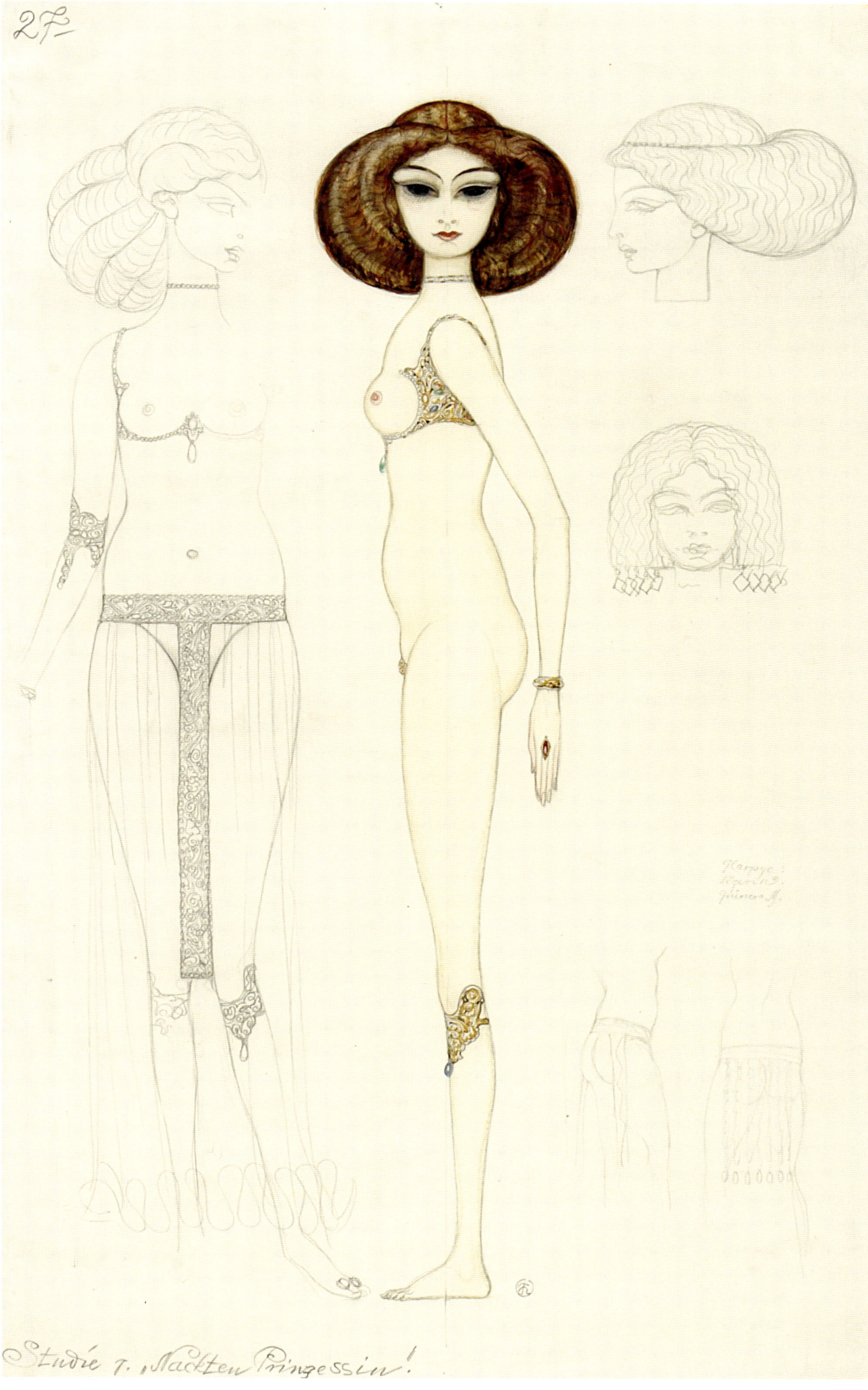

Richard Teschner
Study for the *Nude Princess*, 1913 (?)
Theatermuseum, Vienna

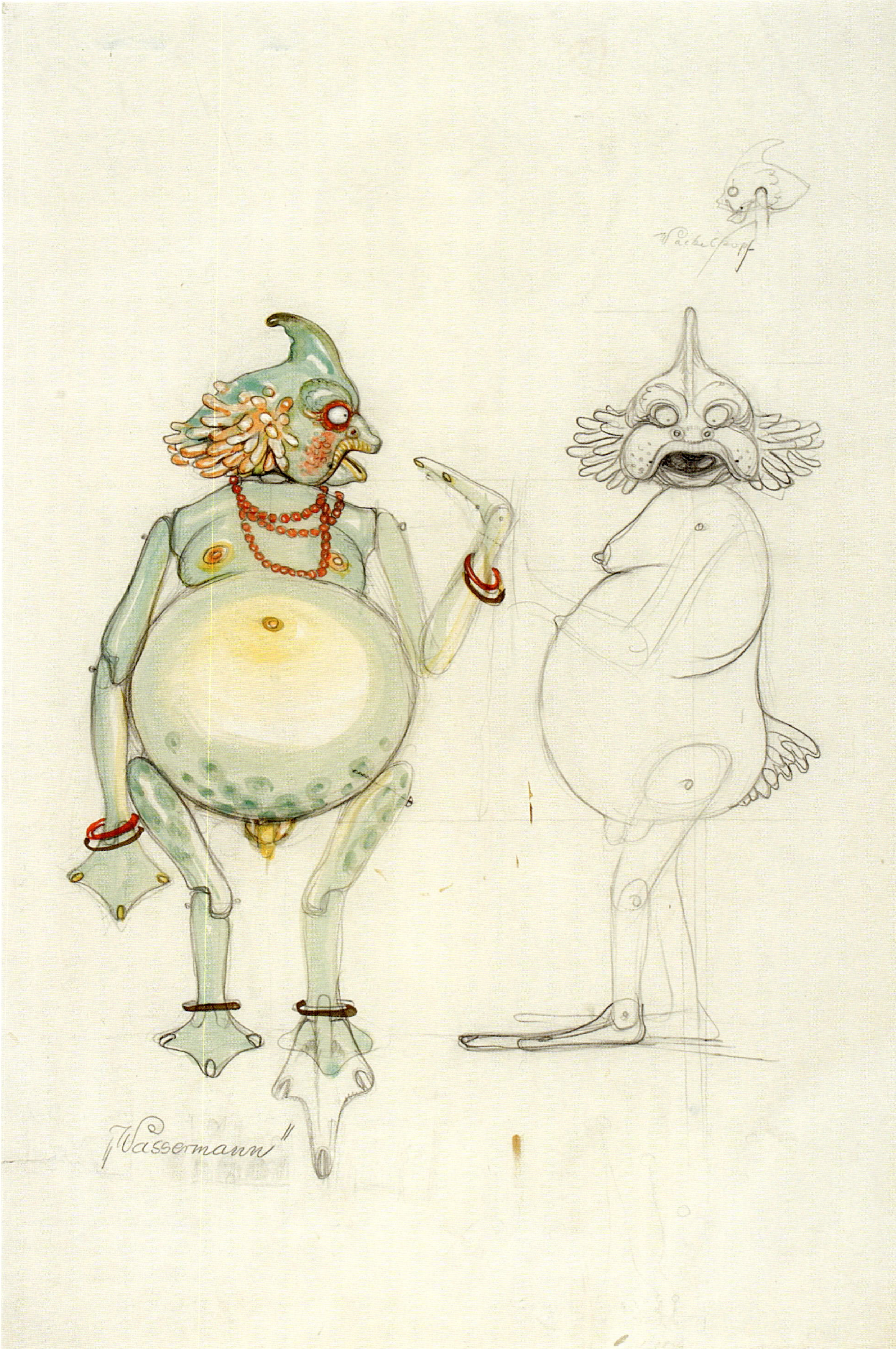

A3 Richard Teschner
Study for the *Wassermann* (Water Elf), 1913 (?)
Theatermuseum, Vienna

100 Richard Teschner ▸
Nawang Wulan rod puppet
from the play *Nawang Wulan*, 1912
Theatermuseum, Vienna

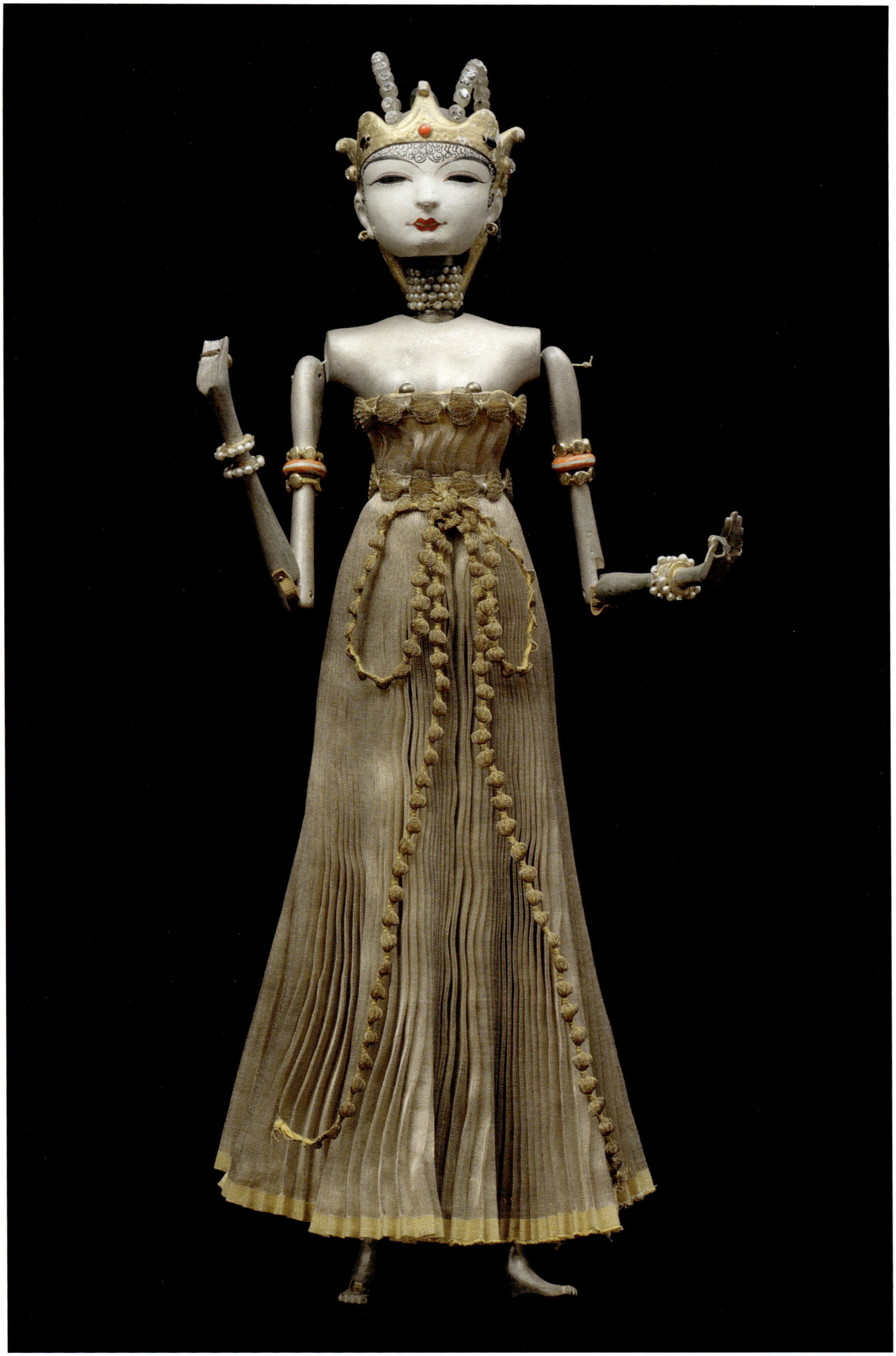

A3

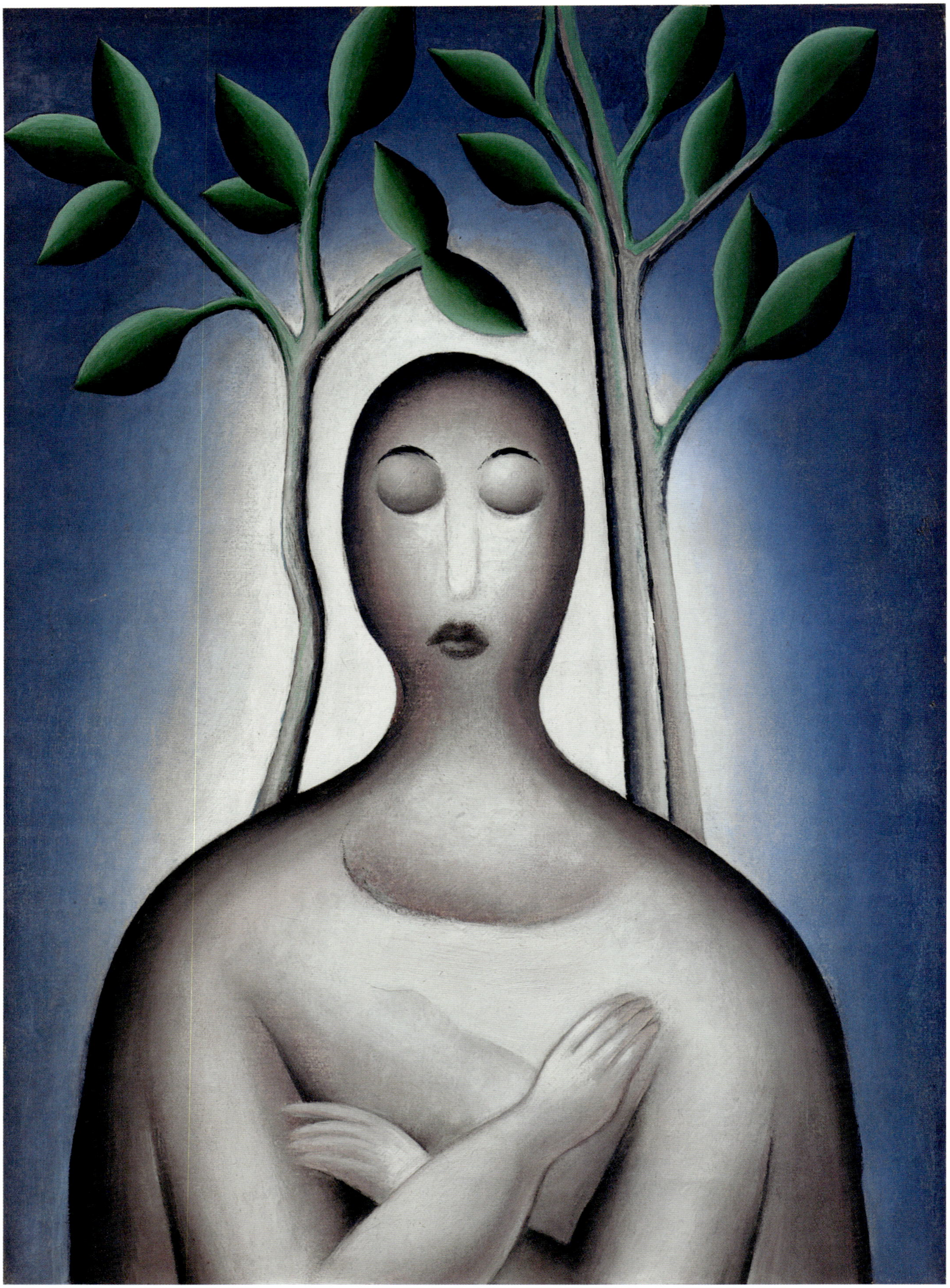

A

Jan Zrzavý
Meditation (Prayer), 1915
National Gallery in Prague

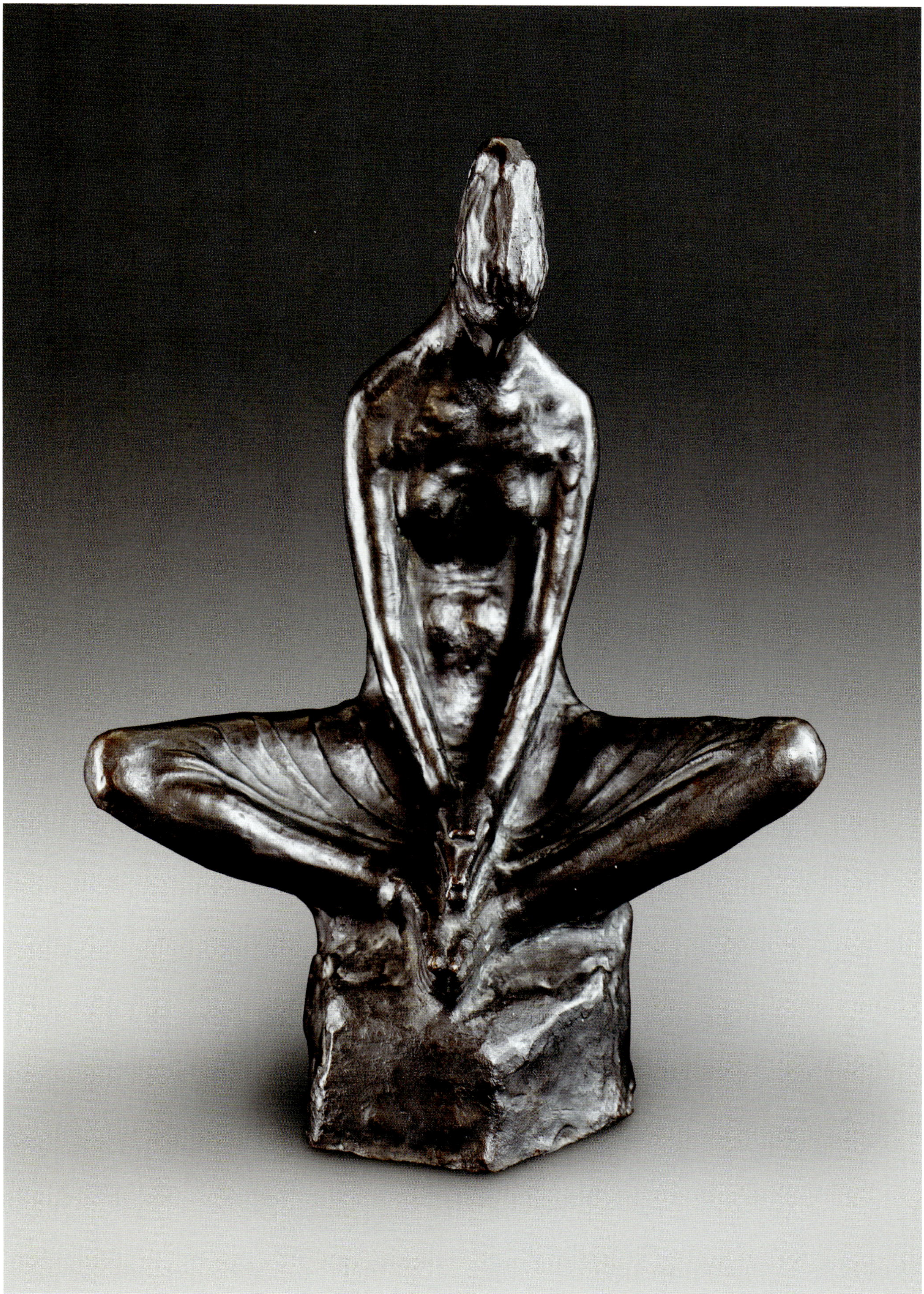

Ivan Meštrović
Vestal Virgin, 1915
The Ivan Meštrović Museums—
Meštrović Atelier, Zagreb

A

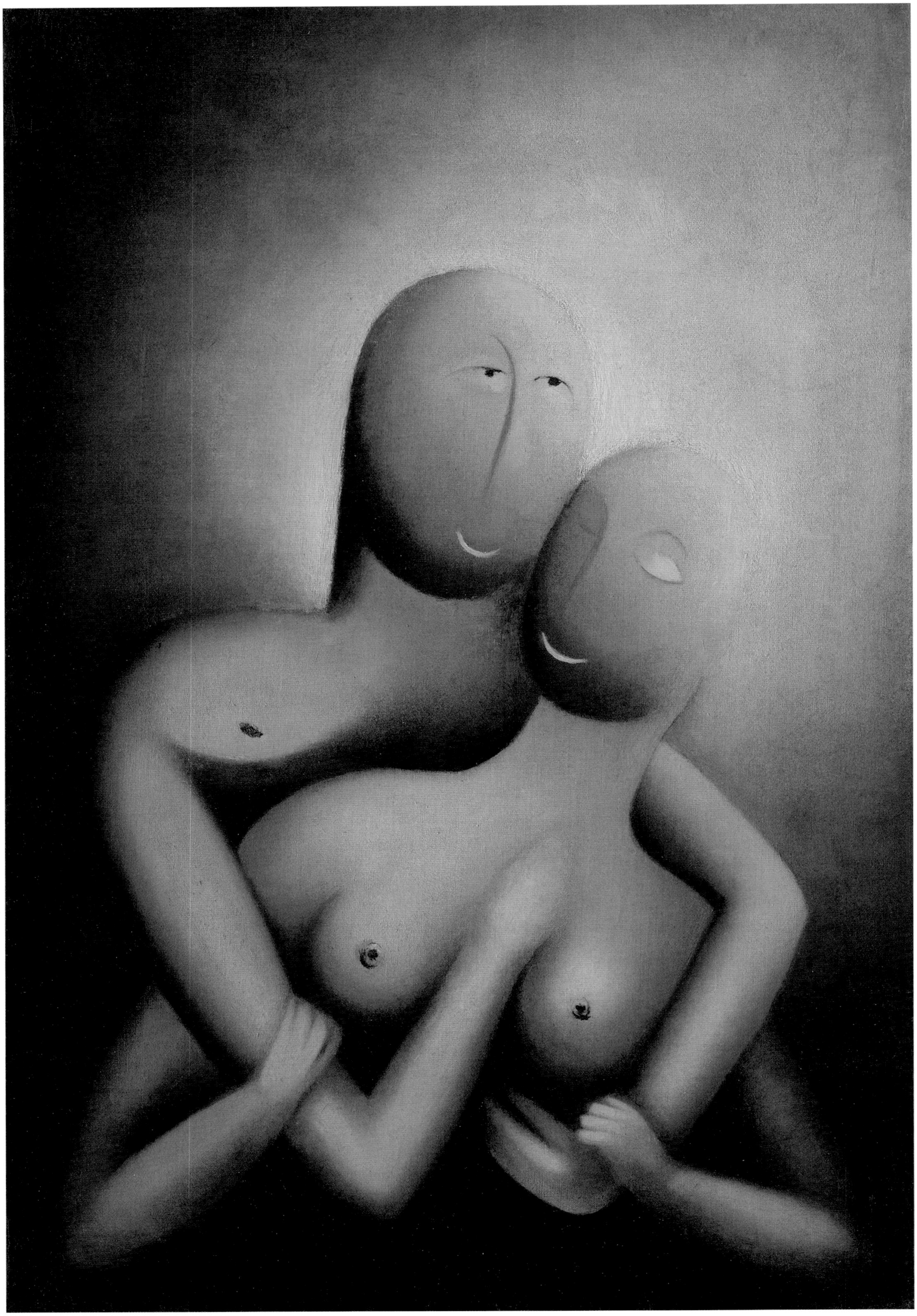

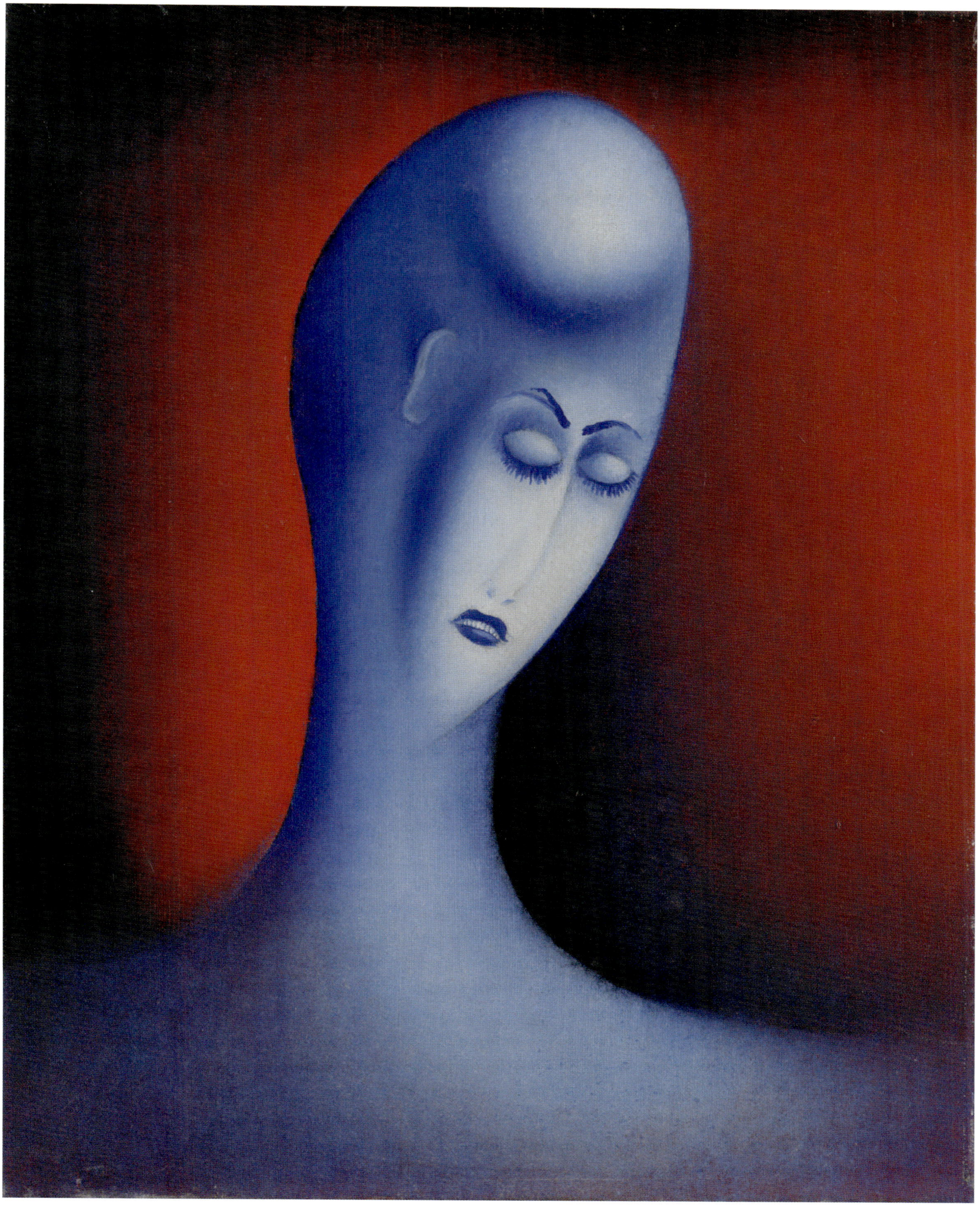

A3

◂ Jan Zrzavý
Obsession (Lovers), 1914
Gallery of Fine Arts in Ostrava

Jan Zrzavý
Suffering, 1916
National Gallery in Prague

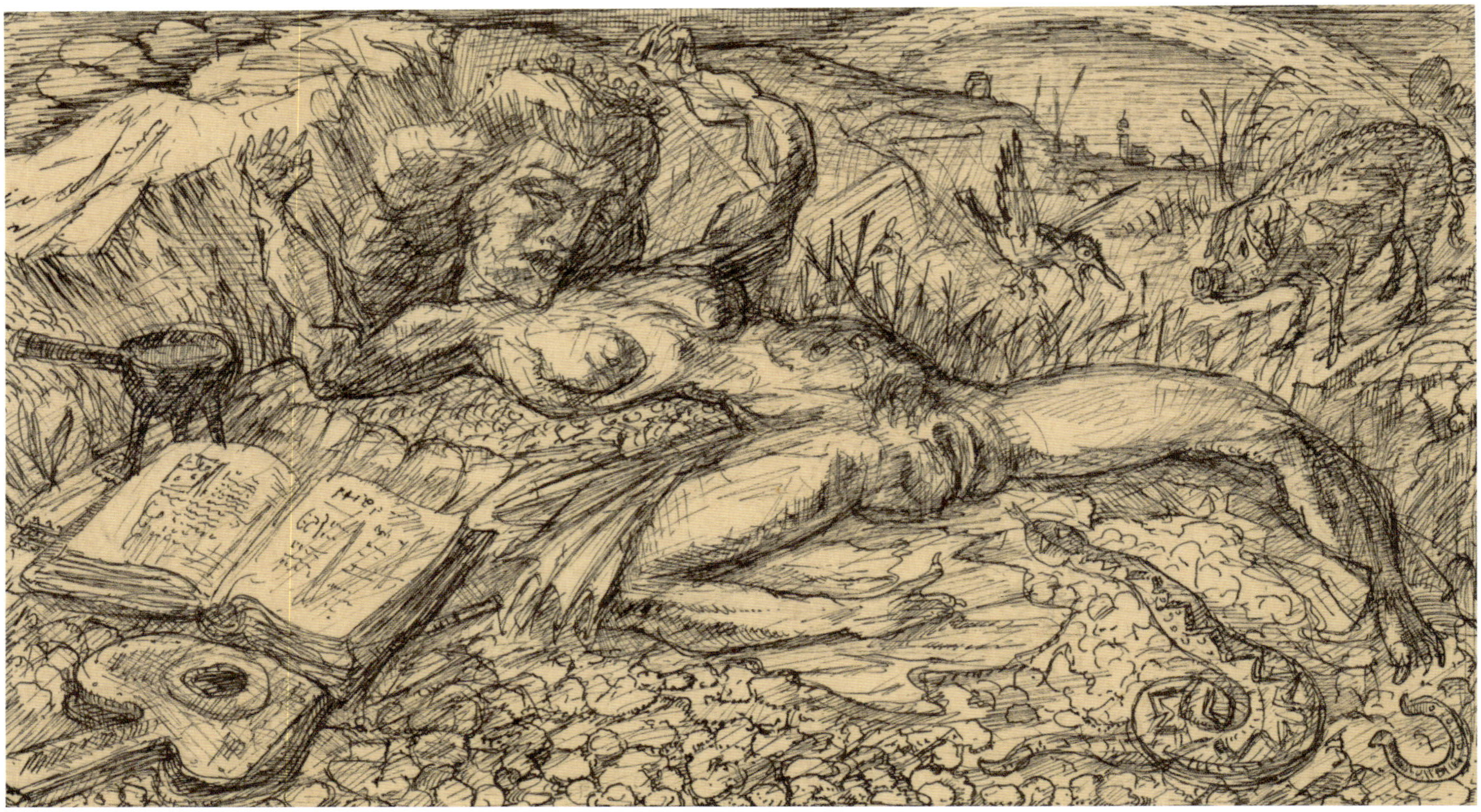

A3

Alfred Kubin
Witch Transforming Herself, c. 1915
Albertina, Vienna

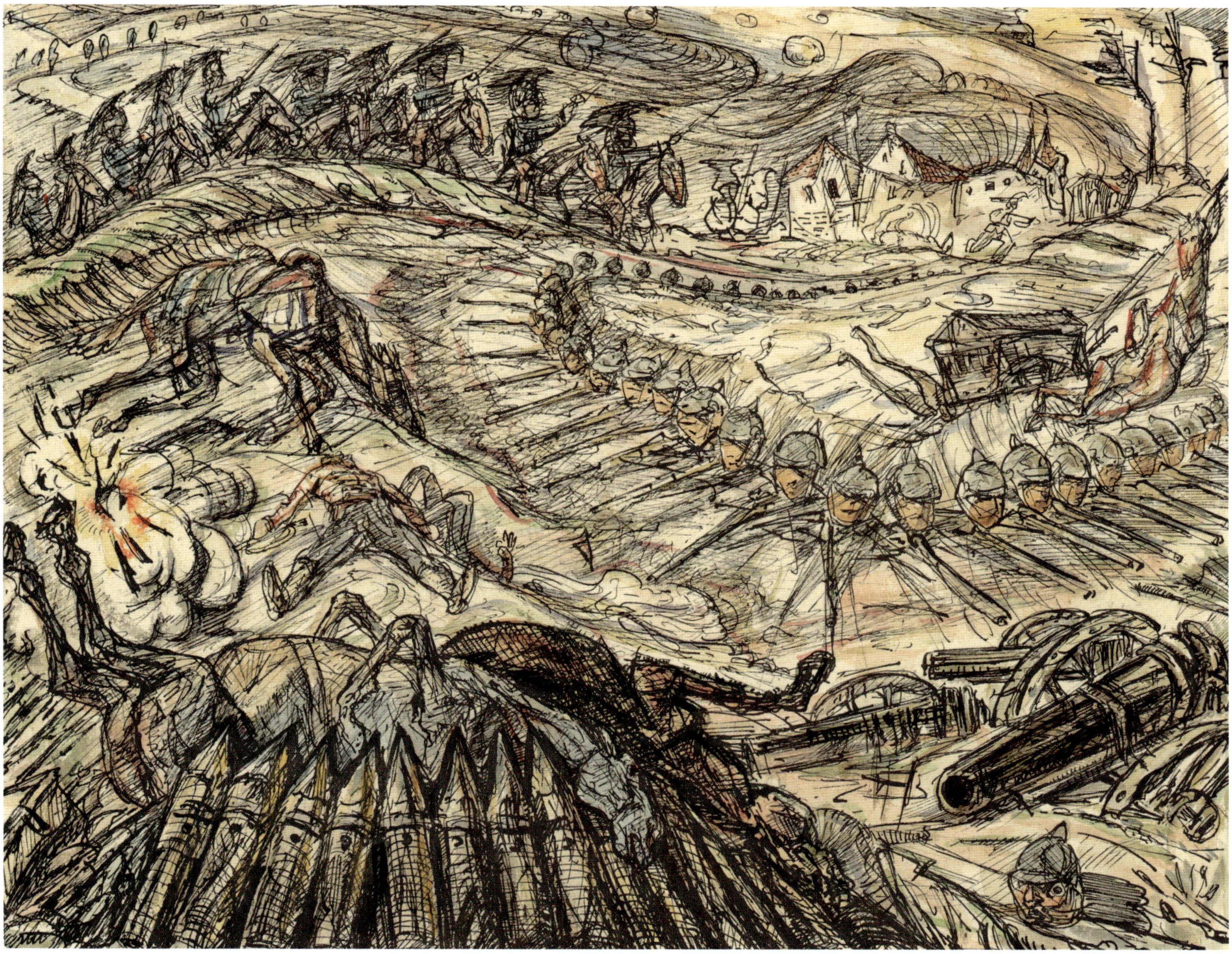

A3

Alfred Kubin
Attack on the Infantry, 1914
Albertina, Vienna

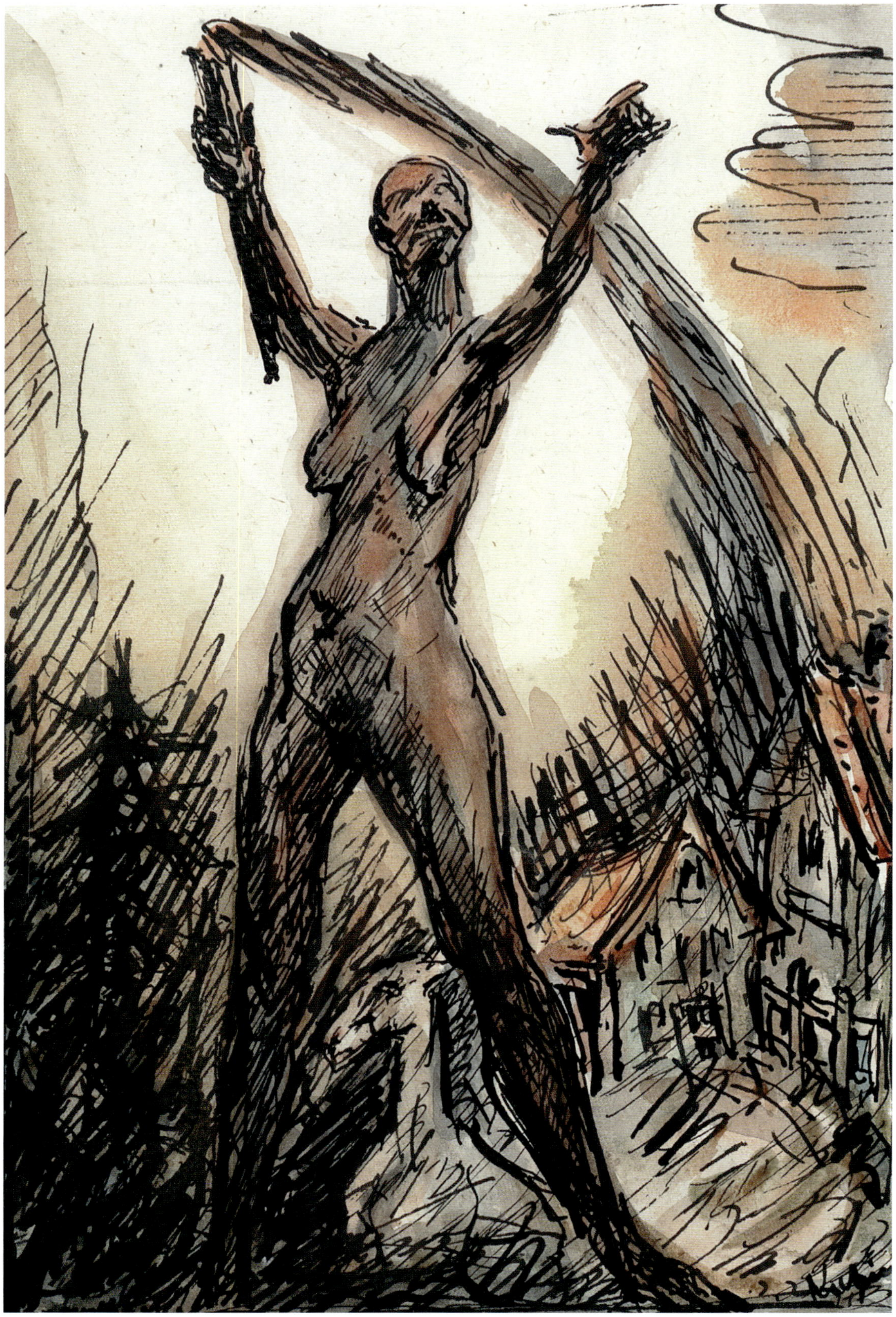

A3

Alfred Kubin
Fury of War with Blazing Torch, c. 1914
Landesgalerie Linz, Graphic Arts Collection

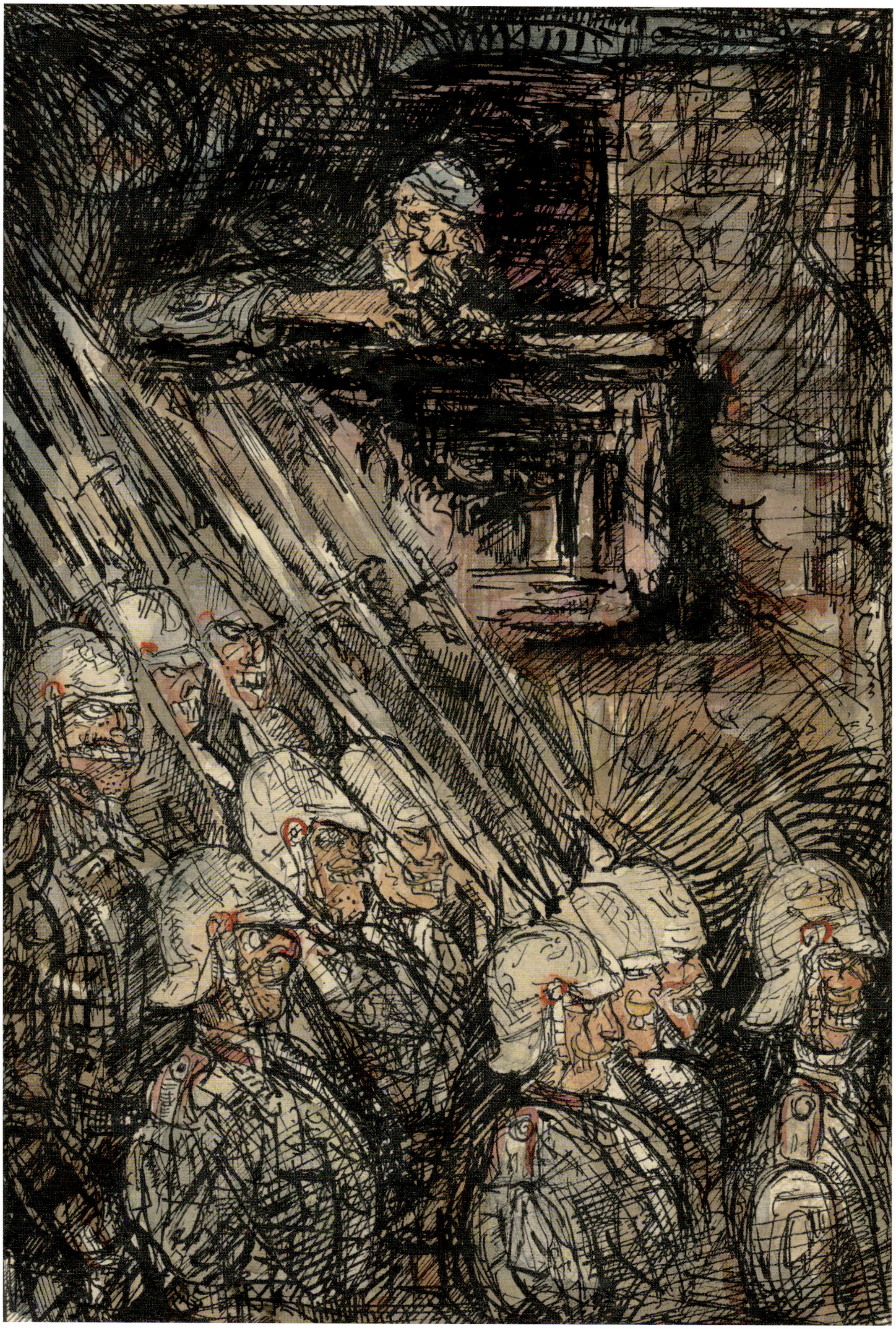

A3

Alfred Kubin
Entering Brussels, 1914
Albertina, Vienna

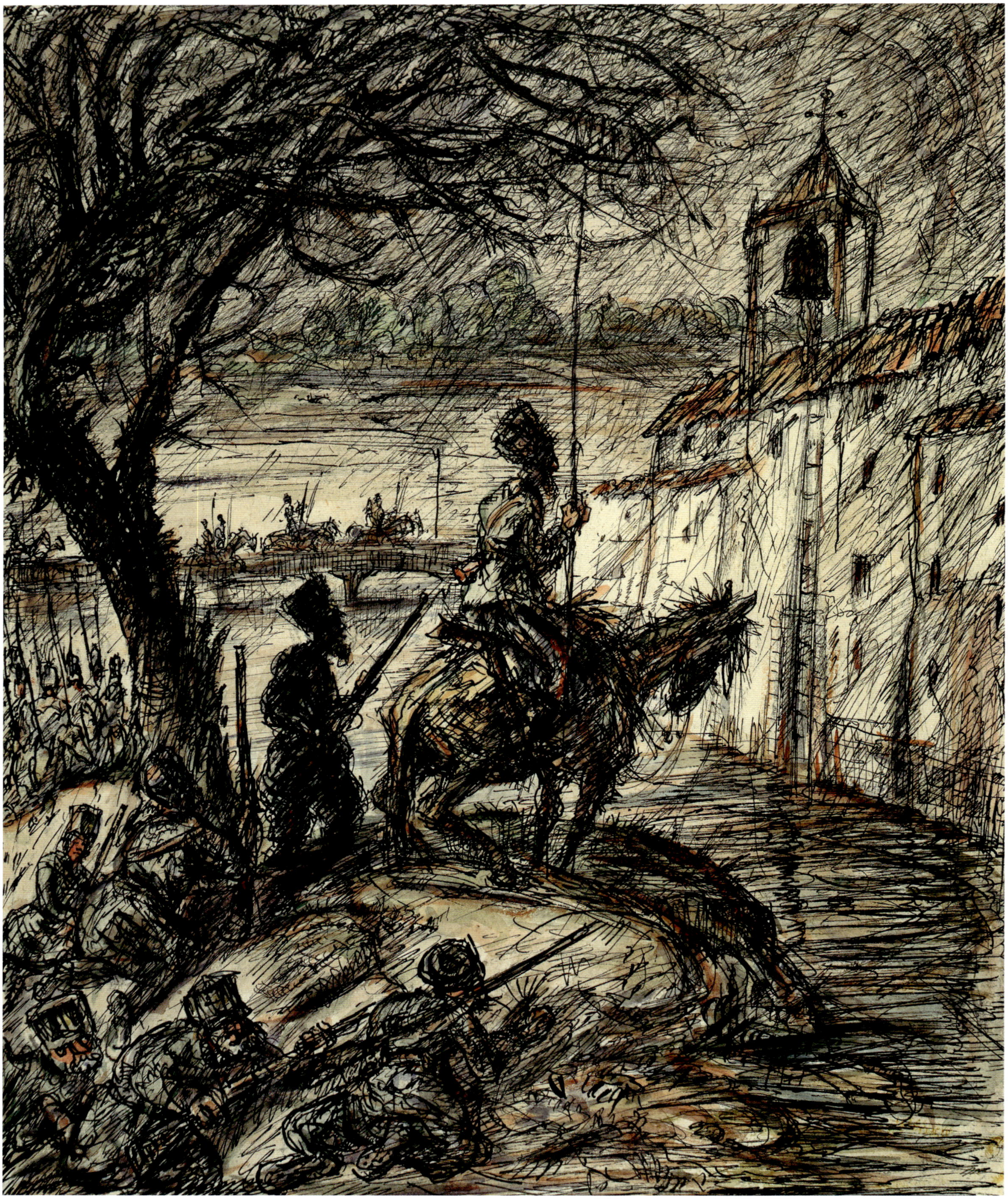

A3

Alfred Kubin
Russian Advance Guard, 1915
Landesgalerie Linz, Graphic Arts Collection, Rombold Collection

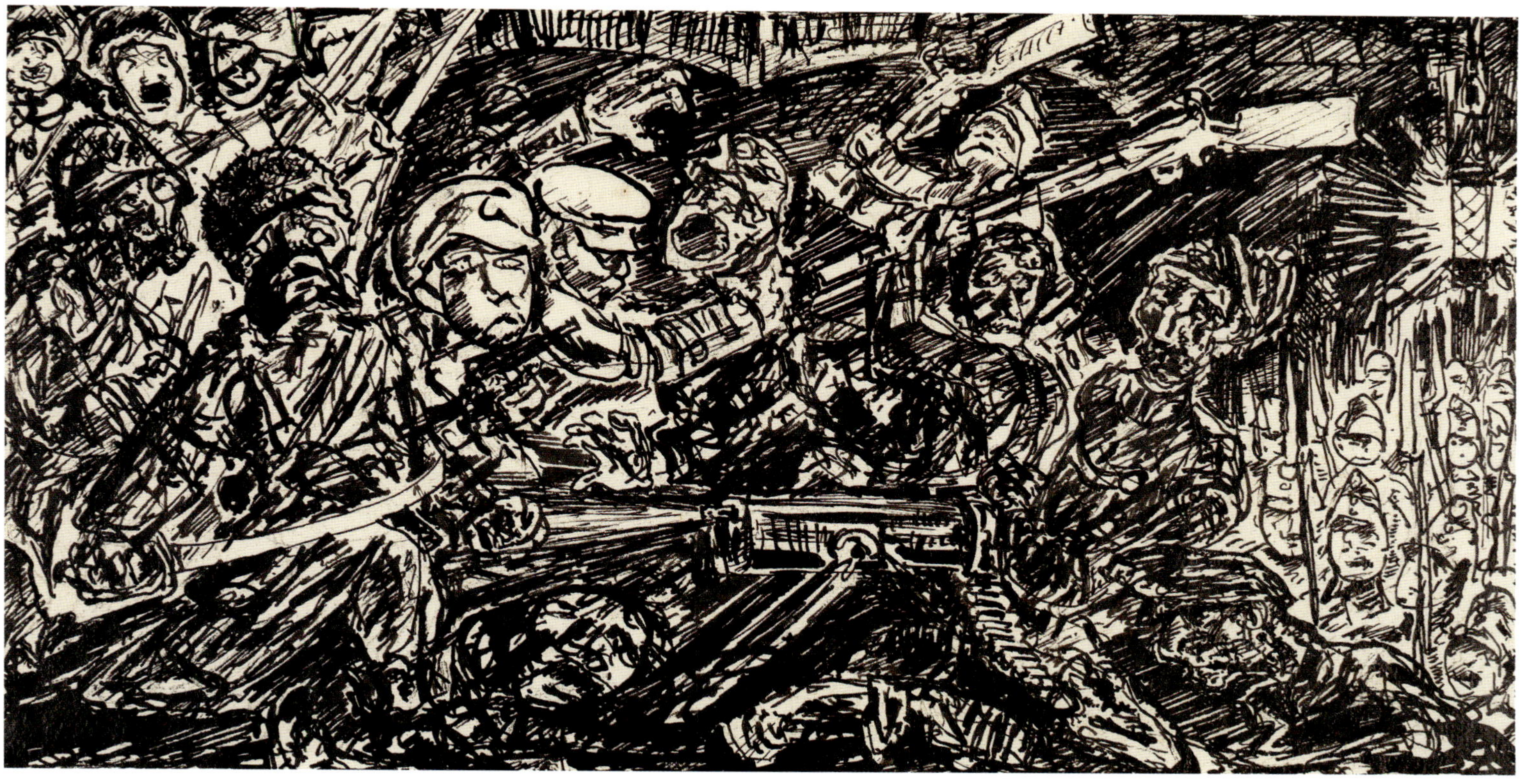

A3

Alfred Kubin
In the Casemates of Przemyśl, c. 1914/15
Landesgalerie Linz, Graphic Arts Collection

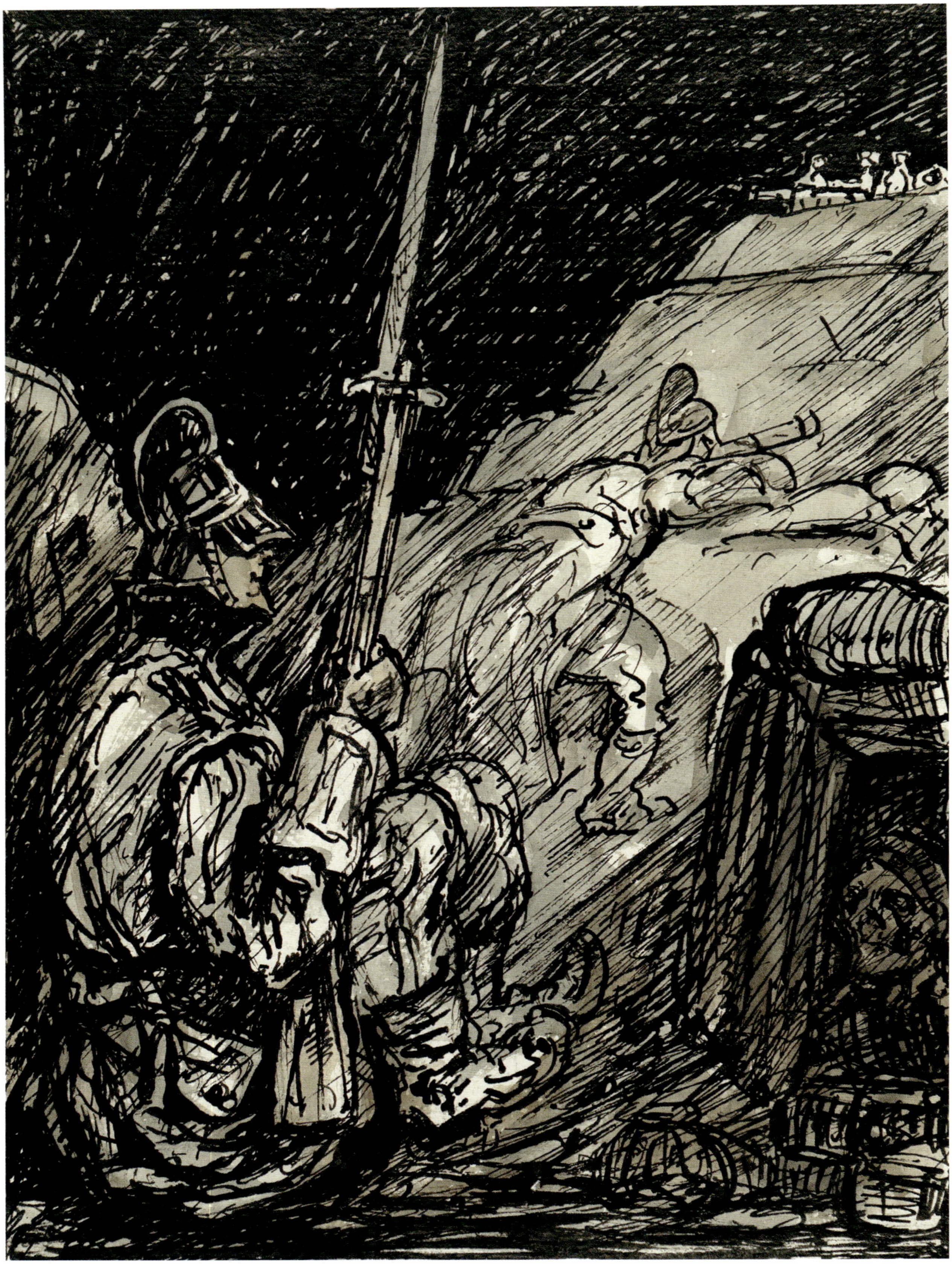

A3

Alfred Kubin
Bavarian Soldiers, c. 1914/15
Landesgalerie Linz, Graphic Arts Collection

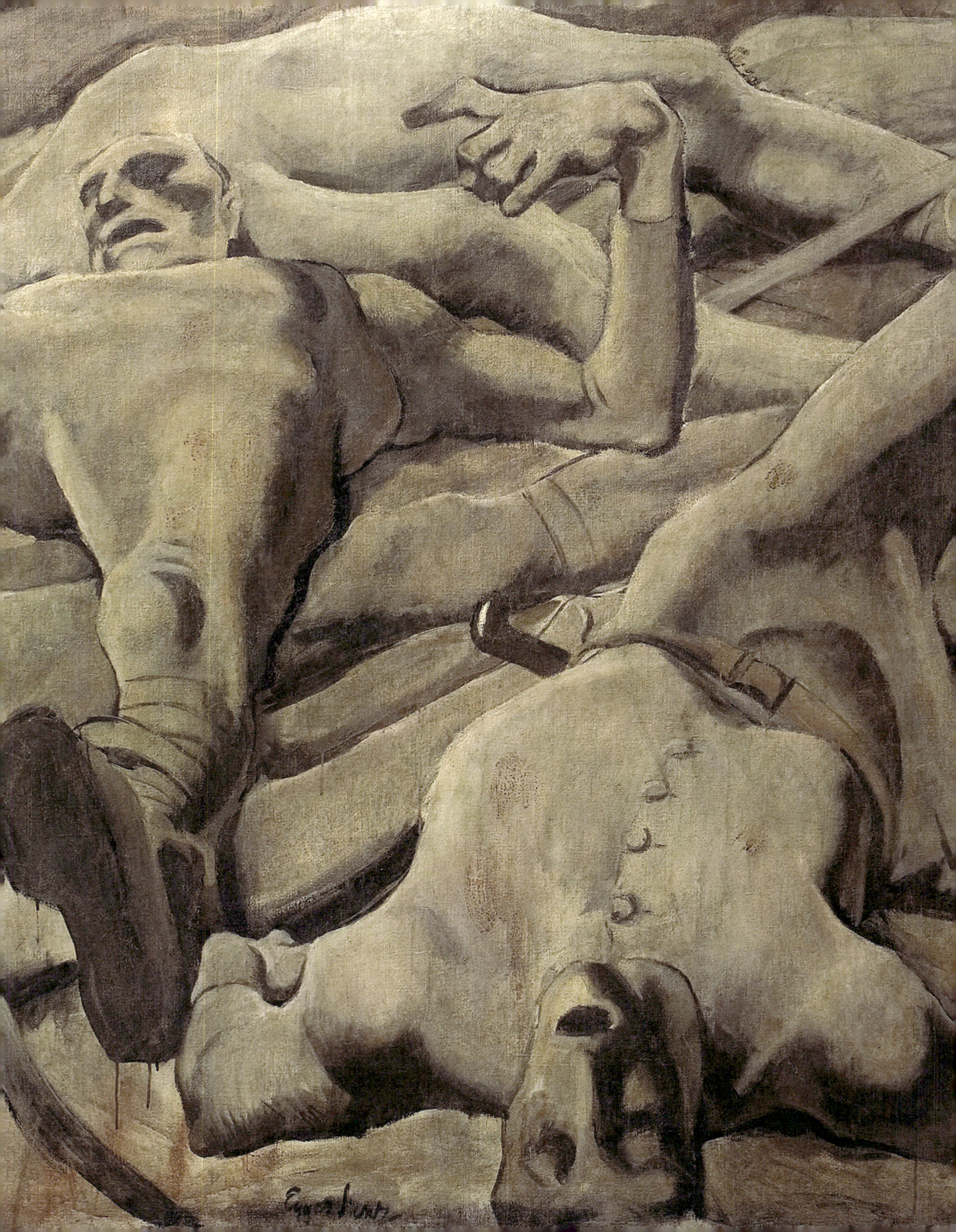

Albin Egger-Lienz, *Finale*, 1918 (detail), Leopold Private Collection

B War and Disillusionment

Documentation and Propaganda: War Painters in the Service of the Habsburg Monarchy

Arnika Groenewald-Schmidt

World War I was the first of its kind in many respects. The use of weapons of mass destruction meant that the traditional form of direct confrontation was replaced by positional warfare, mostly fought from the trenches and leading in a very short time to huge casualty lists. The new form of warfare presented artists engaging with the war, either out of interest or in an official capacity, with the challenge of finding suitable subjects and a new pictorial language.

In order to establish a coherent line in the written and pictorial reporting—and propaganda—of the Austro-Hungarian War Ministry, the War Press Office (KPQ) was established early in the war. The creation of a structure like this had already been presented in 1909 in the "Mobilisierungsinstruktion für das k. u. k. Heer" (Mobilization instruction for the Austro-Hungarian Army).[1] Apart from the censored everyday reporting by journalists, illustrations of noteworthy incidents in the war and impressions of the general mood were to be provided by writers, photographers, filmmakers, and artists. Their reports and depictions were to be used for propaganda purposes and to provide posterity with a lasting impression of what had happened.[2] The "art group" (Kunstgruppe) included both sculptors and painters. They were sent to the front for a few weeks at a time to collect ideas and make sketches. These visits were then followed by a few weeks of work at home to produce final versions. As a rule of thumb for submitting works to the military authorities, "for every week at the front, one sketch suitable for exhibition" and "for every month of work at home, one painting or work of art" should be delivered by the artist.[3] In the "Vorschrift für die bildliche Berichterstattung im Kriege" (Instructions for pictorial war reporting), artists were encouraged to use their own connections with editors and publishing companies to disseminate their works through "reproductions in illustrated newspapers, books, postcards, and the like."[4]

Although care was to be taken in the selection of members to have artists representing both Austrian and Hungarian territories, most of the appointees in fact came from German-Austria.[5] Women could also apply for the KPQ, but few women's names appear in the official lists.[6] Apart from a few idealists like Ludwig Hesshaimer (1872–1956) and László Mednyánszky (1852–1919), who felt called upon to use their art to record the events of war for posterity, for the most part prospective members of the art group applied in order to escape the hazards of fighting on the front.[7] Joining became increasingly difficult, because there were so many casualties of war that men who were fit for military service were called up primarily to bear arms, and already in 1915 many gifted artists—Egon Schiele (1890–1918) was one example—were unable to obtain a transfer to the KPQ. The group was therefore relatively heterogeneous in terms of both quality and style, and the list included not only artists still well known today, such as Ferdinand Andri (1871–1956), Oskar Kokoschka (1886–1980), Anton Kolig (1886–1950), Oskar Laske (1874–1951), and József Rippl-Rónai (1861–1927), but also amateurs.[8]

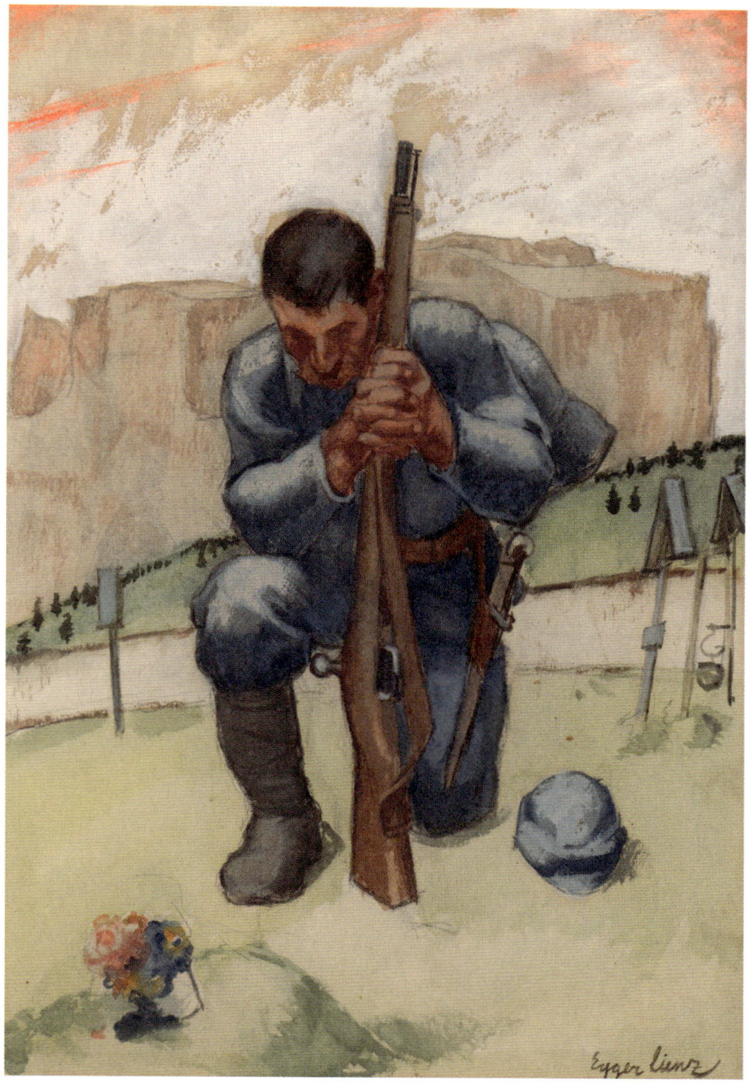

Fig. 1
Albin Egger-Lienz
Parting (Parting of the Landstürmer), 1915
Tyrolean State Museum Ferdinandeum

The profile of the art group is difficult to define as well, because the war picture exhibitions organized by the KPQ also included works by artists who did not belong to the group.[9] Similarly, propaganda posters, newspaper illustrations, and field postcard motifs were designed not only by members of the art group but also by artists in other culture-related military departments or some who produced works as a sideline while on active duty. Whatever their affiliation, all these artists were faced with the challenge posed by modern warfare. Maximilian Ritter von Hoen (1867–1940), until 1917 head of the KPQ and from 1916 also director of the war archive, recognized this and justified the existence of the art group in the foreword to the catalogue for

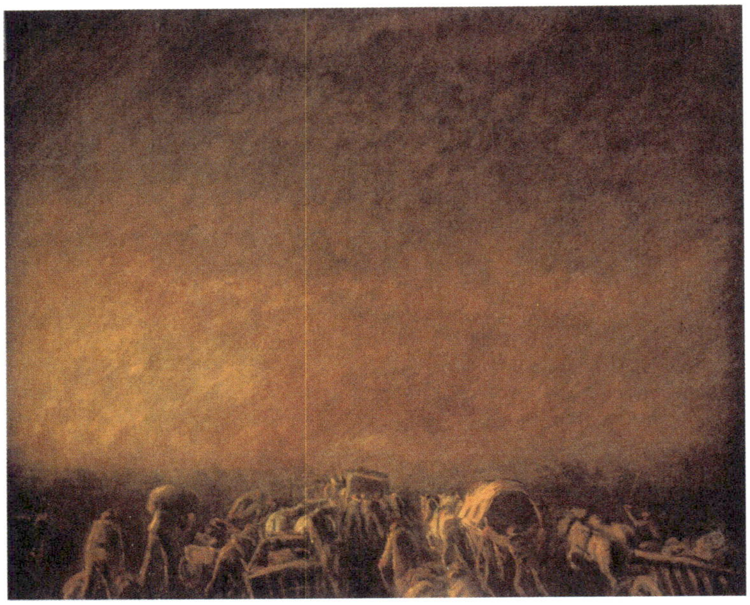

Fig. 2
László Mednyánszky
Refugees, 1914–18
Private collection

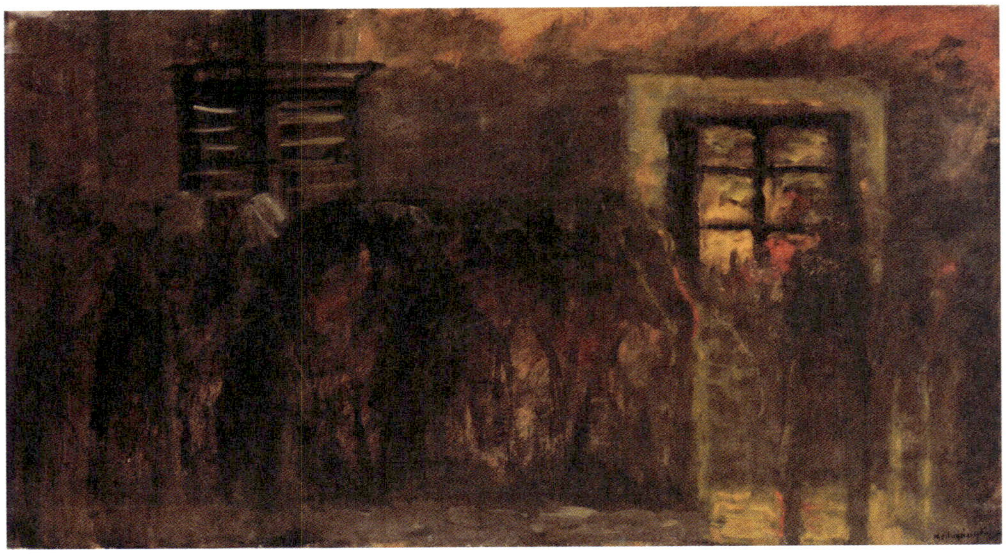

Fig. 3
László Mednyánszky
Queuing for Bread,
1916/17
Damjanich János
Museum, Szolnok

Fig. 4
Albin Egger-Lienz
War, 1915/16
Museum der Stadt
Lienz Schloss Bruck

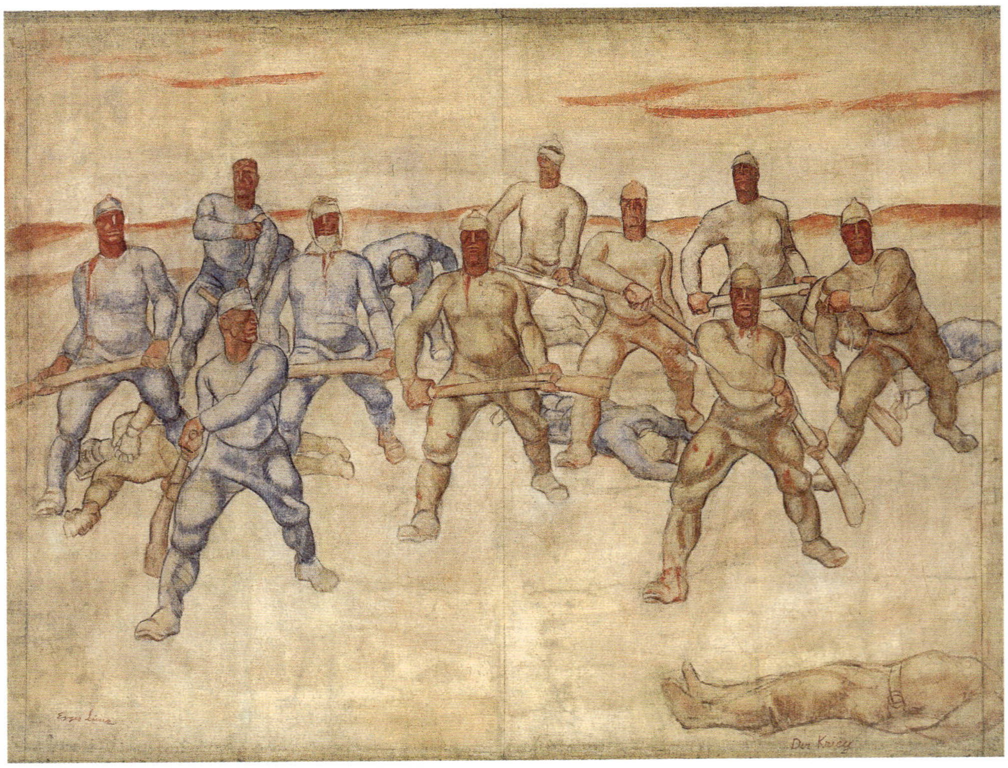

the first war picture exhibition in Vienna in 1915: "A perception trained for a much smaller scale is helpless in the face of the overwhelming impressions flooding in from all sides, searching for forms of expression that will make the impact of the experience comprehensible to the human mind. And what is more suited for this purpose than art?"[10]

The regulations stated that the artists could basically choose subjects at their own discretion, obviously with the exception of anything that was overtly critical of the war.[11] Moreover, the service regulations forbade "any debasement or disparagement of the enemy or exaggeration of their defeats," an attitude also lauded by the press in neutral countries.[12] Most of the works submitted consisted of portraits of high-ranking officers and decorated soldiers,[13] landscapes with or without traces of the war, pictures of modern weapons, and scenes from the everyday life of the troops. The accepted works were sorted and a selection shown in war picture exhibitions in Austria and allied or neutral countries. The idea behind the presentation of these contemporary works was to promote the Habsburg Monarchy as a leading nation in terms of culture and to demonstrate that its artists continued to work at the highest level even during the war, using their art to represent current events. Because of the new type of warfare, the glorified pictures of battles that had been the norm in earlier centuries were extensively absent. Ludwig Hesshaimer's depiction of the situation highlights the problem: "In battle pictures of the past centuries, the artist's main prop was smoke, lots of smoke, with a shako emerging from it here and there, a few gleaming bayonets, and a fallen horse in the foreground. In 1915 there was no smoke or shakos any more, bayonets were out of sight in the trenches, and dead horses were not a feature of trench warfare either. All there was for me to draw was the good old earth with two opposing black lines traced through it [...]."[14]

Apart from many documentary-style works, there were pictures that aimed at reflecting human and emotional elements. This tendency to humanize pictorial accounts of the war can be explained both by the feeling of powerlessness in the face of the atrocities of a war waged with weapons of mass destruction and also by the general development of art and culture in the early twentieth century. The focus of attention changed because of an increasing fascination with the individual and his unconscious, as well as the need for something of general validity at a time of great change. As a result, artists during the war produced not only a mass of conservative and naturalistic representations but also psychological portraits, moody landscapes, and images of mythical universality. The challenge facing the artists in their work here consisted in capturing personal emotions and situations as well as the general human condition. This gave rise to "a transformation from official history pictures to individual artistic interpretations of history, often with a shift from the officially commissioned affirmation of war to a more personal and critical attitude."[15] Time would eventually confirm the approach of those artists who shifted their perspective in this way, because soon after the war, and in some cases even before 1918, it was these symbolic pictures and the earnest, critical approach that became etched in human memory as the defining images of the war.

Typical examples of this are the war and anti-war pictures of Albin Egger-Lienz (1868–1926). Already an established painter when war broke out, his first version of *Dance Macabre* in 1908 informed the style that would produce his iconic World War I pictures, like *To the Nameless of 1914* (1916) and *Finale* (1918; p. 134). After a short period of service in the Tyrolese *Standschützen* in 1915, he was exempted from active military service on account of a weak heart and transferred as an artistic adviser to the war welfare office in Bozen (Bolzano), where he provided subjects for field postcards (fig. 1) and illustrations for the *Tiroler Soldaten-Zeitung*.[16] He was not therefore an official member of the art group but was nevertheless granted permission by the KPQ in early 1916 to paint at the Italian-Austrian front in Folgaria and Trient (Trento) and took part in war picture exhibitions organized by the KPQ.[17] His experiences at the front helped crystallize his idea of a modern battle picture that sought to leave a lasting impression by emphasizing the symbolic character of the representation. *The War 1915/16* (fig. 4) is an early example of how he enhanced the impact of his pictures through the monumentality of the figures and an archaic reduction to the essentials. The message was conveyed not through personal characterization but by depicting soldiers as types in rhythmically arranged groups. He used the same methods some years later to produce *Finale*, an emblematic representation of the horrors of war.

Many other artists were soon to change their position along similar lines. In most cases, their early euphoria quickly gave way to horror at the reality of the war experience, a transformation that was also reflected in their work. Subjects conveying hope and enthusiasm and everyday scenes of army life were gradually replaced by pictures of suffering. Like Egger-Lienz, these artists were less interested in representing the fate of individuals than in depicting the collective suffering of soldiers at the front and of civilians at home. Baron László Mednyánszky, a Hungarian member of the art group, showed shadowy figures standing in line for hours for a loaf of bread (fig. 3), sitting exhausted by the side of the road, or as a faceless mass of refugees on their way to an uncertain future (fig. 2). These dark pictures are a logical continuation of Mednyánszky's pre-war works with their symbol-laden, atmospheric landscapes and expressive characterization of the poor. A fascination with suffering and death combined with an initially glorified idea of war were no doubt the driving forces behind Mednyánszky's desire, in spite of his relatively advanced age, to be posted to the front as a war artist.[18] The experience of war is impressively reflected in his pictures and endows his later work with additional depth.

The artistic positions presented here were not entirely suited for straight-forward propaganda purposes. The main task of the war artists appears increasingly to have been to record their impressions of the war as a legacy for future generations, as an official tribute to the art group in 1918 would suggest: "The art group in the War Press Office had the task during the war of creating a pictorial artistic record of the overwhelming events of this international struggle and of serving patriotic historiography in this way."[19]

The works reflect individual approaches to the challenge of producing an artistic representation of the first "modern" war. Furthermore, they bear witness to a paradigm shift from the glorification of war to a humanizing trend that coincided with the general tendency of modern artists to depict what lies behind the surface rather than merely document visual reality.[20]

1 "Mobilisierungsinstruktion für das k. u. k. Heer. Anhang für das Kriegsattachéquartier und das Kriegspressequartier. Entwurf. Wien: Aus der k. u. k. Hof- und Staatsdruckerei 1909," pp. 53, 67–70, reproduced in, *Musen an die Front! Schriftsteller und Künstler im Dienst der k. u. k. Kriegspropaganda 1914–1918*, ed. Jožo Džambo, exh. cat., Adalbert-Stifter-Verein (Munich, 2003), pp. 5–7.

2 *Dienstordnung für das Kriegspressequartier*, k. k. Hof- und Staatsdruckerei (Vienna, 1917), http://wk1.staatsarchiv.at/propaganda-kuenstler-und-kpq/kriegspressequartier/dienstordnung/#/?a=artefactgroup257 (accessed on July 31, 2017).

3 *Dienstordnung* 1917 (see note 2).

4 Erzherzog Friedrich m. p., Feldmarschall, "Vorschrift für die bildliche Berichterstattung im Kriege," k. u. k. Armeekommando, E. no. 4992 (1916), http://wk1.staatsarchiv.at/propaganda-kuenstler-und-kpq/kriegspressequartier/vorschrift-fuer-die-bildliche-berichterstattung/#/?a=artefactgroup260 (accessed on July 31, 2017); Ludwig Hesshaimer, *Miniaturen aus der Monarchie: Ein k. u. k. Offizier erzählt mit dem Bleistift*, ed. Okky Offerhaus (Vienna, 1992), reproduced in *Musen an die Front!* 2003 (see note 1), p. 70.

5 "Würdigung der Kunstgruppe des Kriegspressequartiers," 1918, KA, FA AOK KPQ KT. 2, p. 1, http://wk1.staatsarchiv.at/propaganda-kuenstler-und-kpq/bedeutung-und-erhaltung-der-kunstgruppe/#/?a=artefactgroup389 (accessed on July 31, 2017); Liselotte Popelka, "Die Musen schweigen nicht," in *Musen an die Front!* 2003 (see note 1), pp. 64–78, esp. p. 66.

6 Ilse Krumpöck, "Suffragetten oder Flintenweiber? Kriegsmalerinnen im Ersten Weltkrieg," in *Viribus unitis: Jahresbericht 1998 des Heeresgeschichtlichen Museums* (Vienna, 1998), pp. 44–53.

7 Popelka 2003 (see note 5), p. 66.

8 For a list of the war painters, see Walter Reichel, *"Pressearbeit ist Propagandaarbeit" – Medienverwaltung 1914–1918: Das Kriegspressequartier (KPQ)* (Vienna, 2016), pp. 178–85.

9 By the end of the war, thirty-nine war picture exhibitions had been organized, Reichel 2016 (see note 8), p. 114.

10 Quoted in https://www.profil.at/gesellschaft/1-weltkrieg-propagandamalerei-schuetzengraben-373278 (accessed on July 31, 2017).

11 "Vorschrift für die bildliche Berichterstattung" 1916 (see note 4), p. 2.

12 Popelka 2003 (see note 5), p. 65.

13 Wilhelm Eisner-Bubna, from 1917 head of the KPQ, gave the instruction that literary and artistic portraits of prominent personalities in the Austro-Hungarian army should be used to "popularize the army," Reichel 2016 (see note 8), p. 91.

14 Ludwig Hesshaimer, "Mit dem Skizzenbuch im Feld," quoted in *Musen an die Front!* 2003 (see note 1), p. 76.

15 Ralph Gleis, "Vom Geschichts- zum Menschenbild: Egger-Lienz und der Wandel der Historienmalerei um die Jahrhundertwende," in *Totentanz: Egger-Lienz und der Krieg*, eds. Agnes Husslein-Arco, Helena Pereña, Stephan Koja, exh. cat., Belvedere, Vienna, Museum der Stadt Lienz Schloss Bruck, Lienz (Vienna, 2014), pp. 33–50, here p. 35.

16 Letter from Albin Egger-Lienz to Maria Egger, Bad Ischl, June 14, 1915, in Wilfried Kirschl, *Albin Egger Lienz, 1868–1926: Das Gesamtwerk*, vol. 1 (Vienna, 1996), p. 268.

17 Kirschl 1996 (see note 16), p. 272.

18 Csilla Markója, "Der Körper ist die Seele von Allem: Ein merkwürdiger Maler aus der Österreichisch-Ungarischen Monarchie: Baron Lászlo Mednyánszky, der 'alte Hund' und moderne 'Bettler-Philosoph,'" in *László Mednyánszky, 1852–1919*, ed. Sabine Grabner, exh. cat. Belvedere, Vienna (Vienna, 2004), pp. 16–51, esp. p. 42.

19 "Würdigung der Kunstgruppe" 1918 (see note 5), p. 1.

20 I should like to thank Walter Kalina from the Museum of Military History, Vienna, for sharing his expertise on art production in World War I.

The initial enthusiasm for the war felt by many artists evaporated rapidly upon their arrival on the front. Many of those mobilized from artistic circles therefore sought to work as war artists for the War Press Office to avoid combat duty and continue producing art. Alongside the commissioned works, many pieces were produced documenting the artists' emotional response to the war and to the fate of soldiers on the frontline. Egon Schiele, for example, painted his portraits of soldiers while serving in a prisoner-of-war camp in Lower Austria and Vienna. László Mednyánszky and János Vaszary produced expressive documentary art of camp life and events on the front. Albin Egger-Lienz and Robert Angerhofer, meanwhile, portrayed traumatic scenes from the war in stylized, symbolic pictures. Yet wartime art also served a mobilizing purpose in the form of propaganda that either legitimized the war—as in the works of Alois Hans Schramm—or promoted the ideal of national uprising and liberation, as in the posters of Vojtěch Preissig. By contrast, Jaroslav Hašek's unforgivingly satirical novel *The Good Soldier Švejk* features the memorable illustrations of Josef Lada, which, in their tragicomic amplification of the military machine, reveal the absurd side of war. (MH)

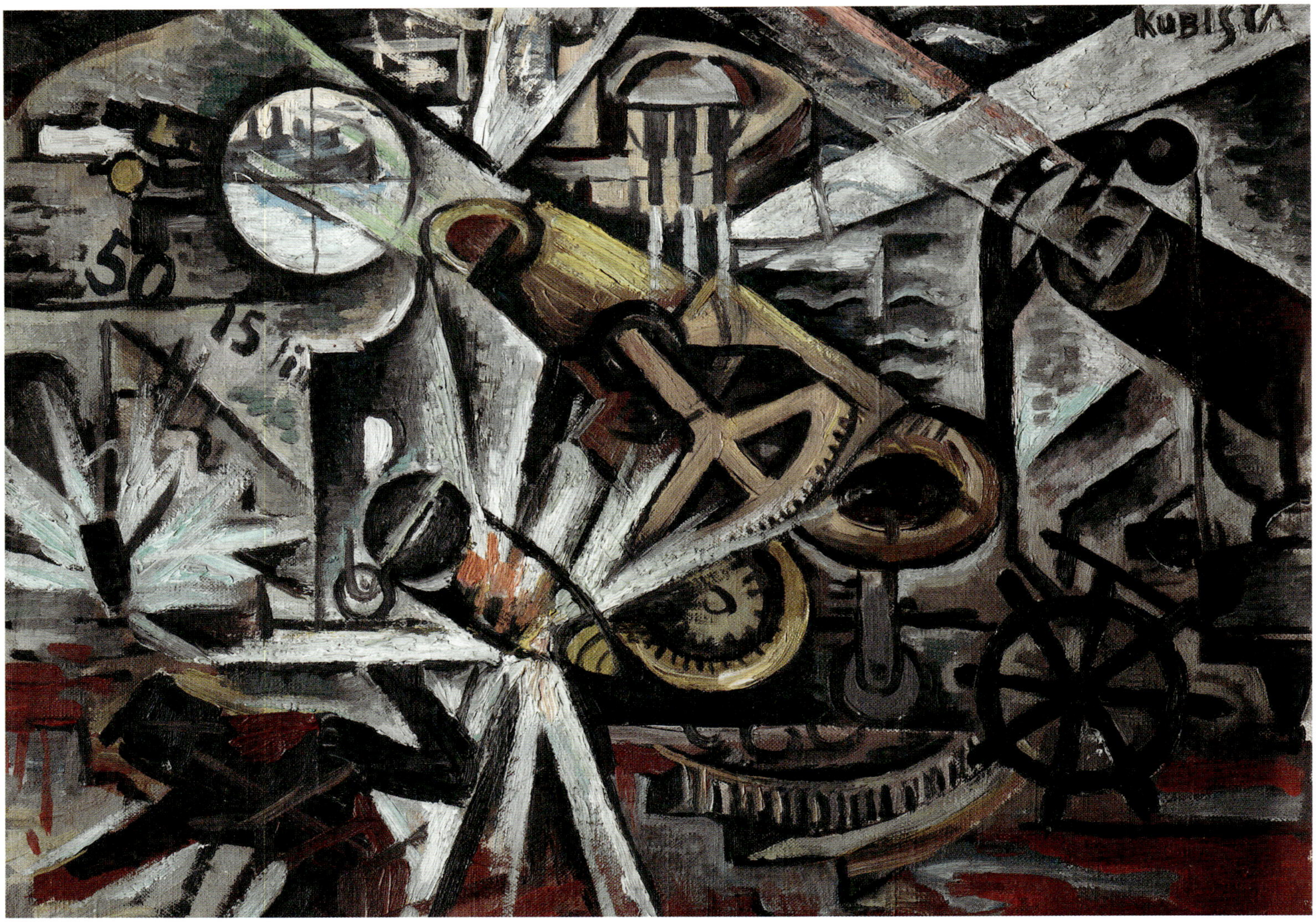

B

Bohumil Kubišta
Coastal Canons Firing Against the Fleet, 1915
National Gallery in Prague

Bohumil Kubišta ▸
Air Raid Attack on Pula, 1915
The Gallery of West Bohemia in Pilsen

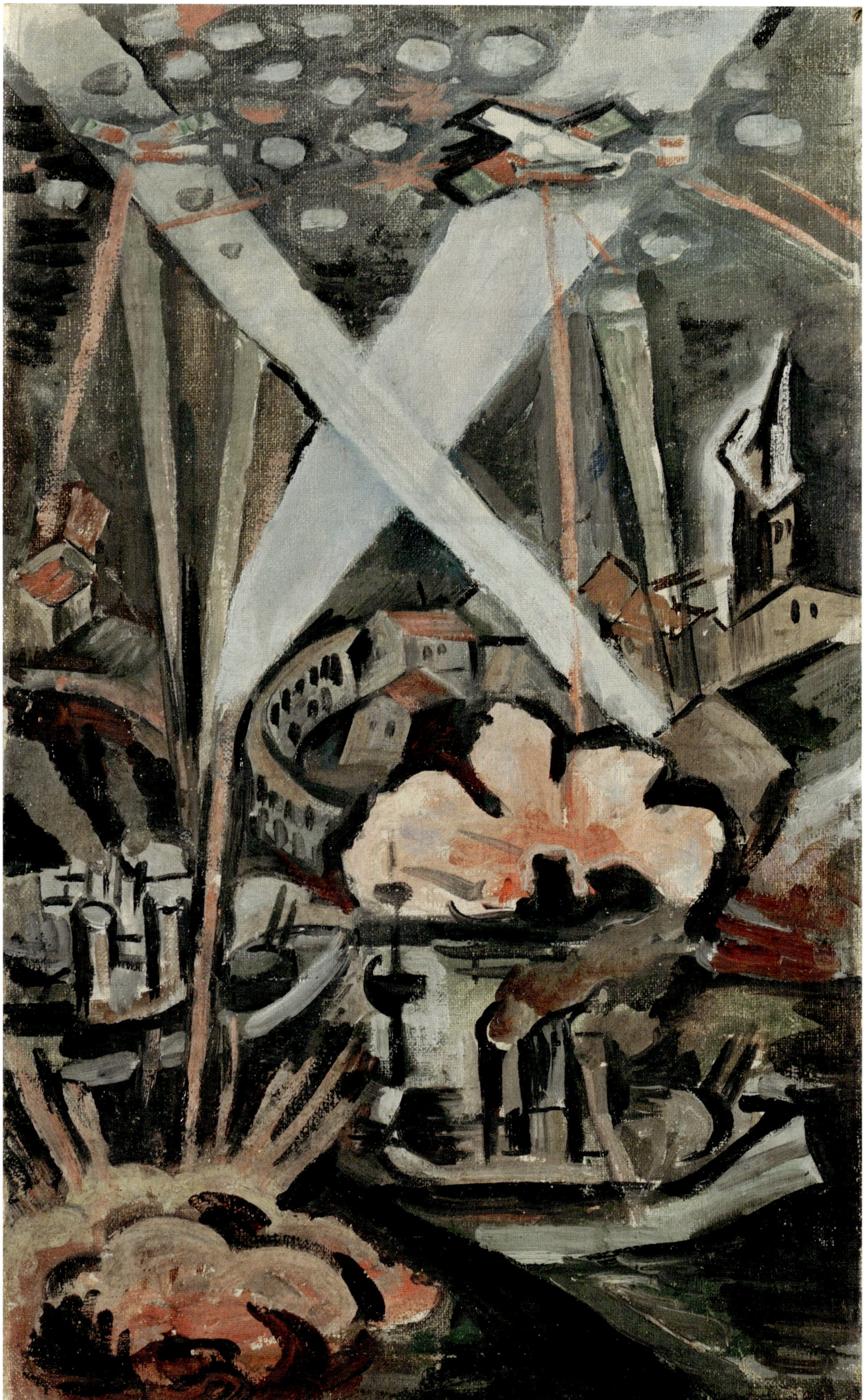

B

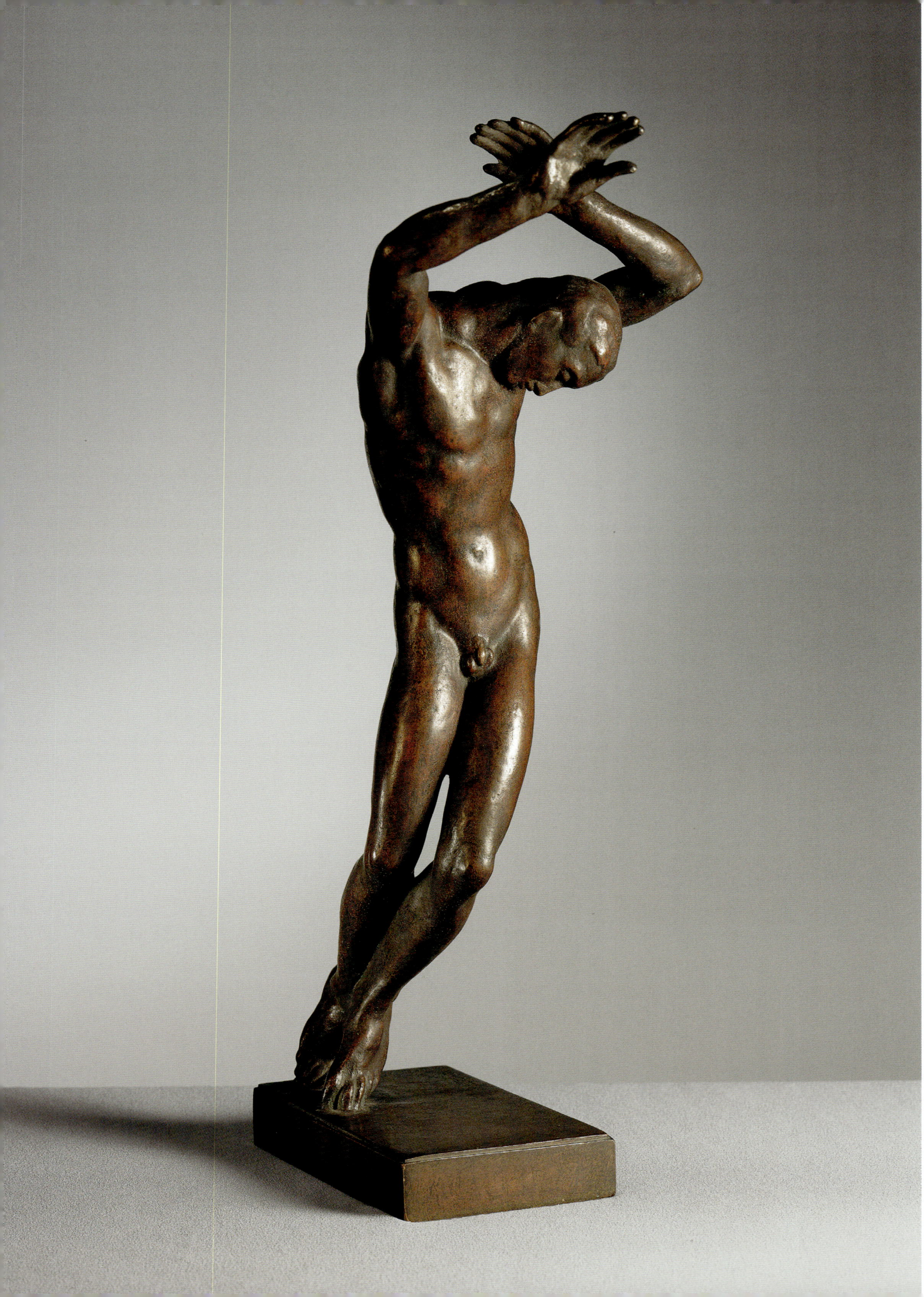

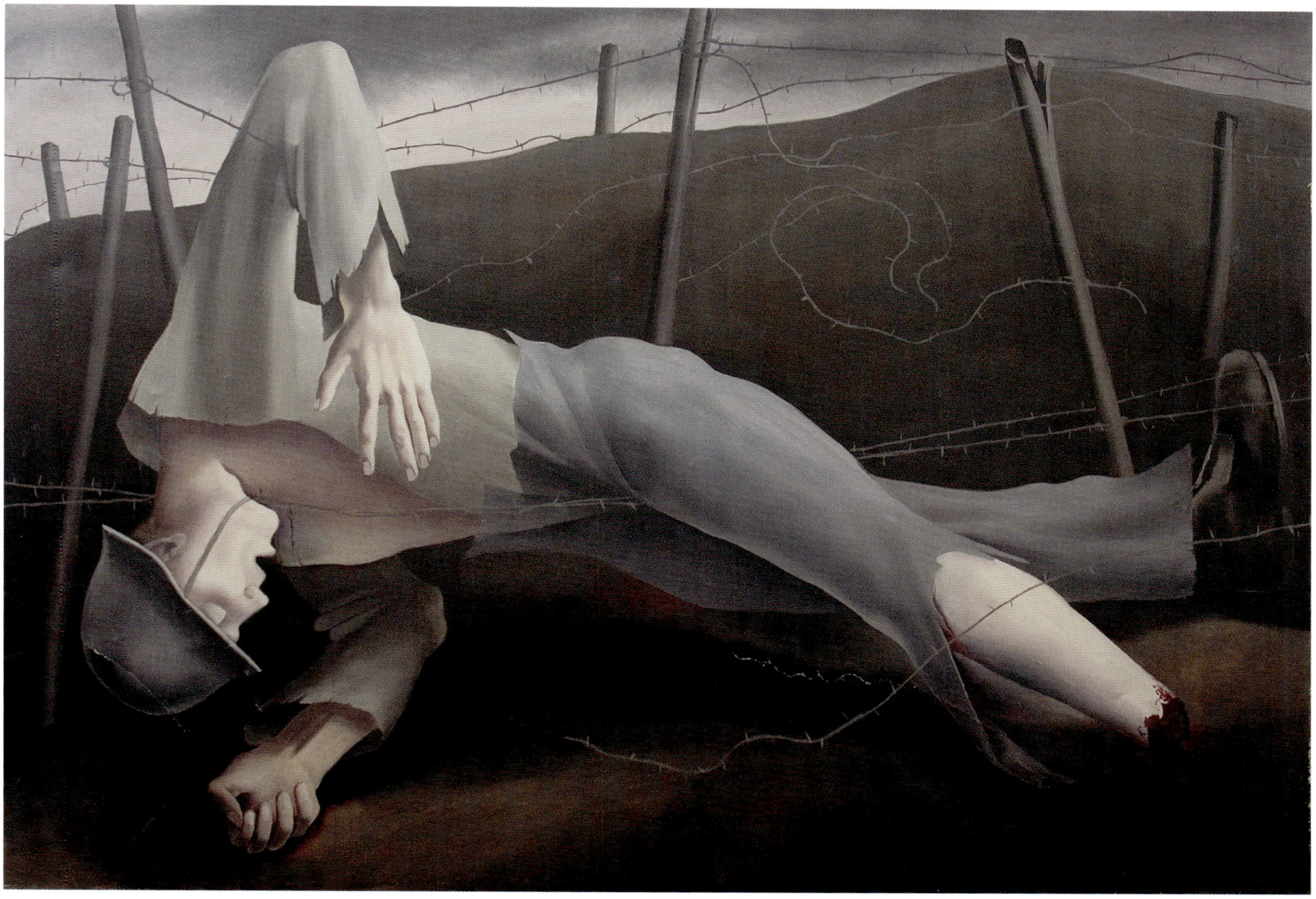

◂ Jan Štursa
Wounded Man, 1916
Belvedere, Vienna

Robert Angerhofer
Dead Soldier in Barbed Wire, c. 1920
NORDICO Stadtmuseum Linz

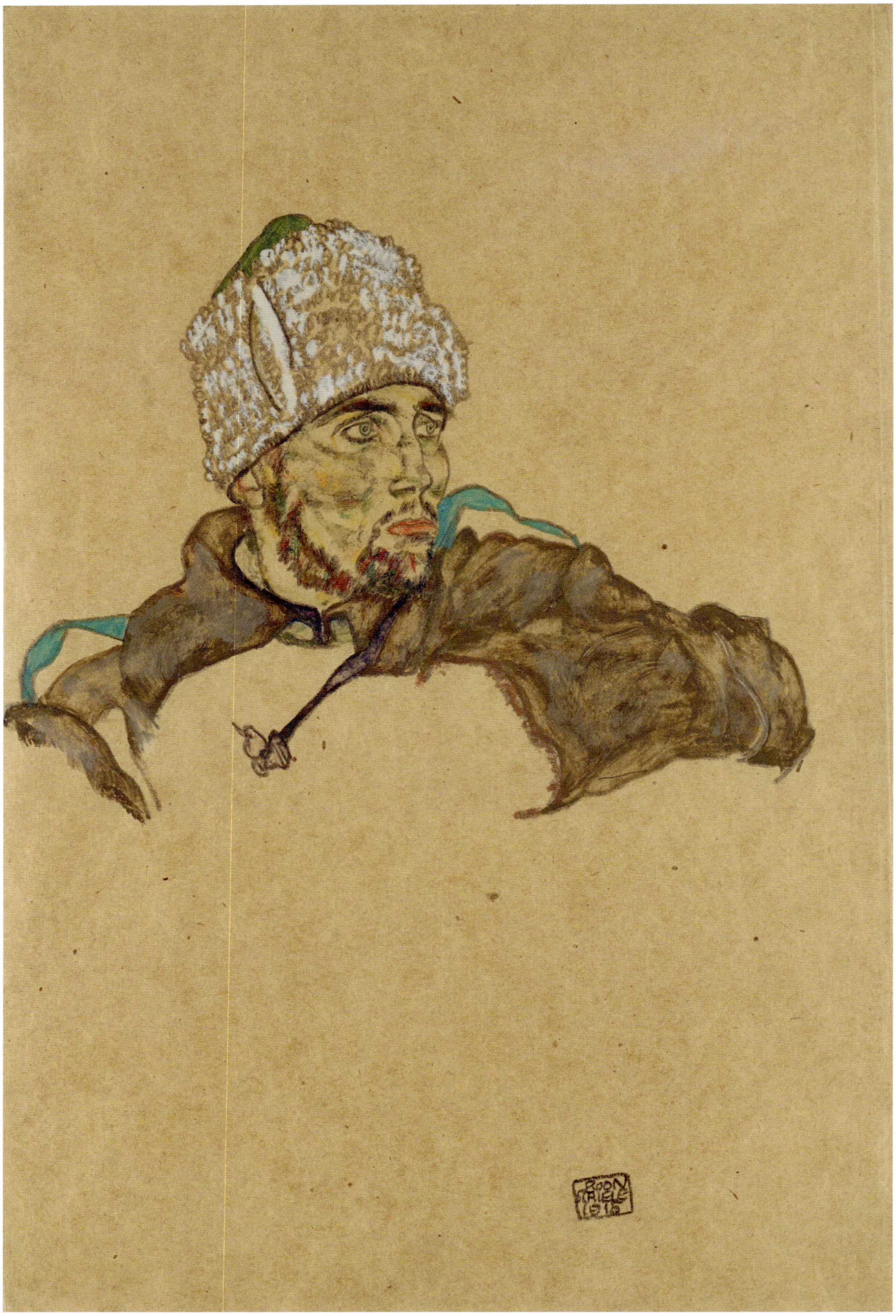

B

Egon Schiele
Russian Prisoner of War, 1915
Belvedere, Vienna

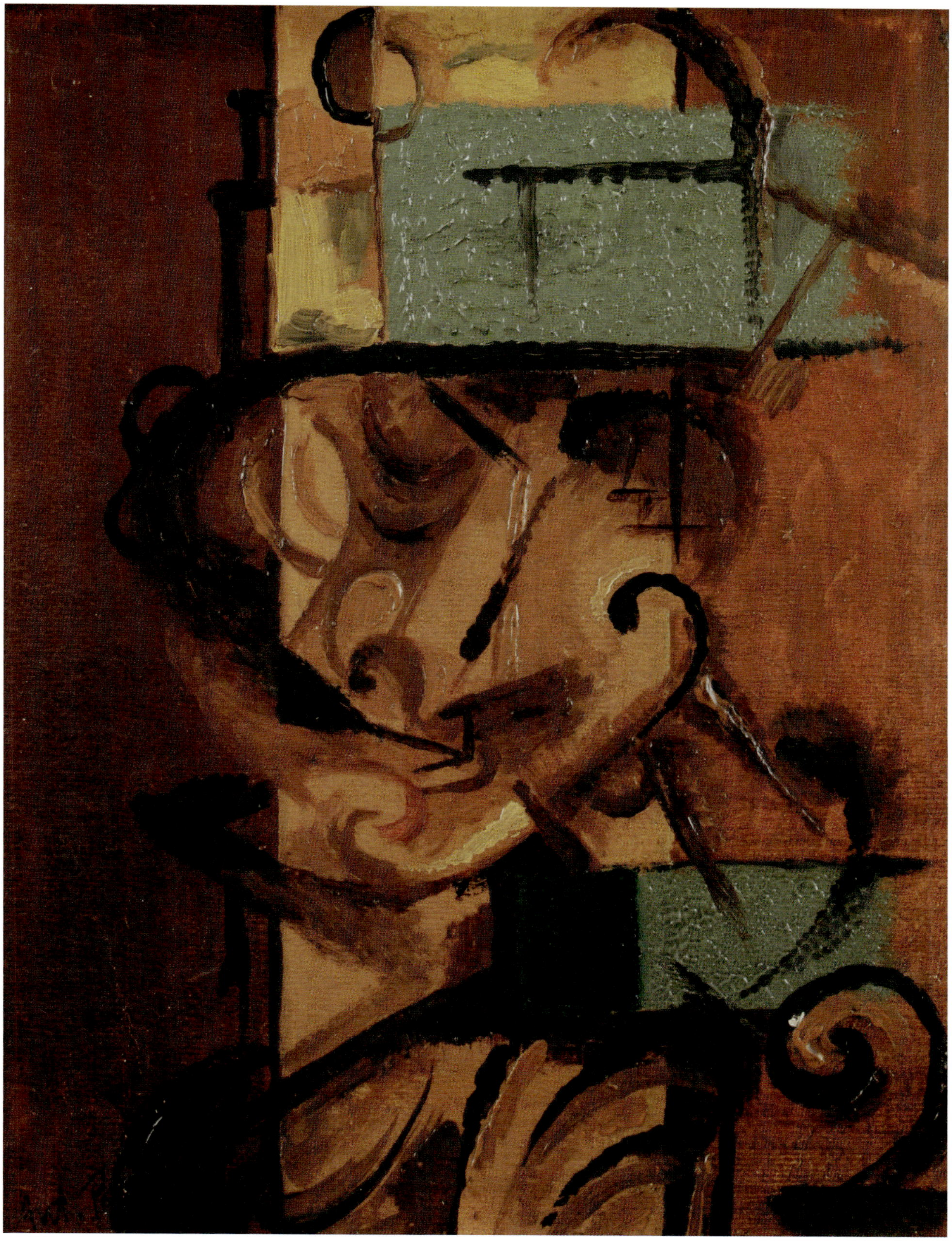

Antonín Procházka
The Soldier, c. 1916
The Regional Art Gallery Liberec

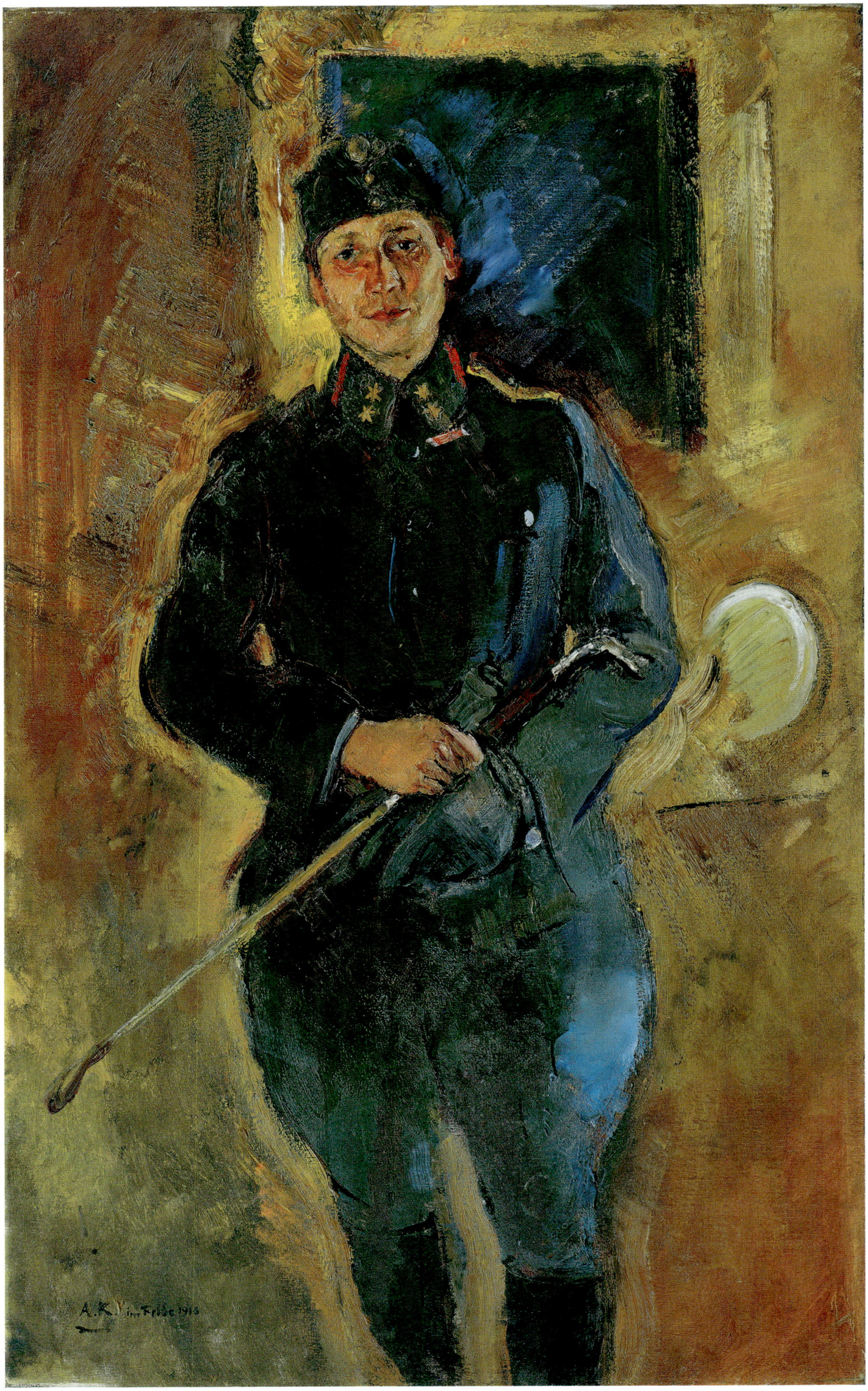
A.K.

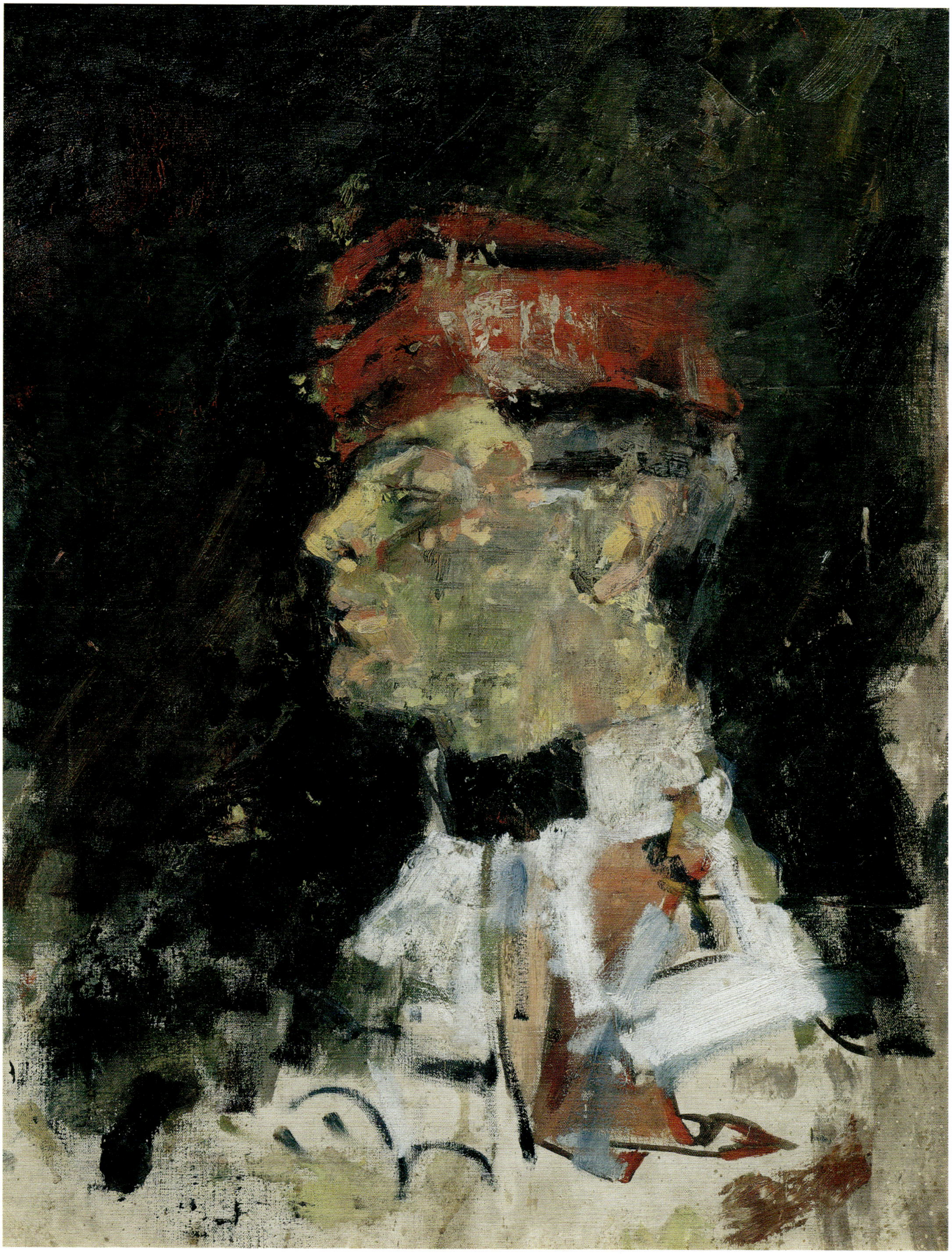

◂ Anton Kolig
Otto von Aichelburg-Zossenegg as First Lieutenant of the Cavalry, 1916
Belvedere, Vienna

Wolfgang Schaukal
Self-Portrait in a Dragoon's Uniform, 1918
Belvedere, Vienna

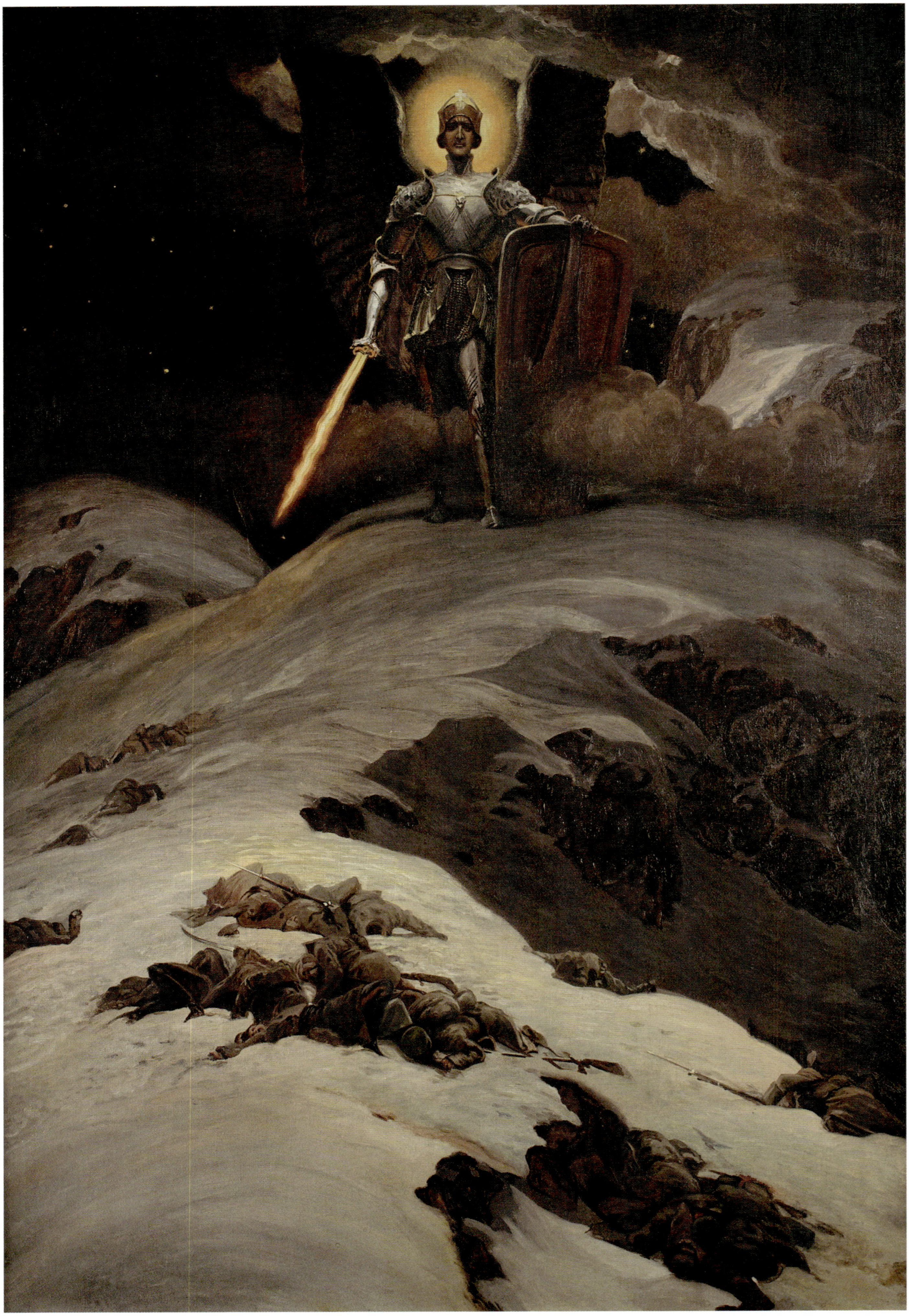

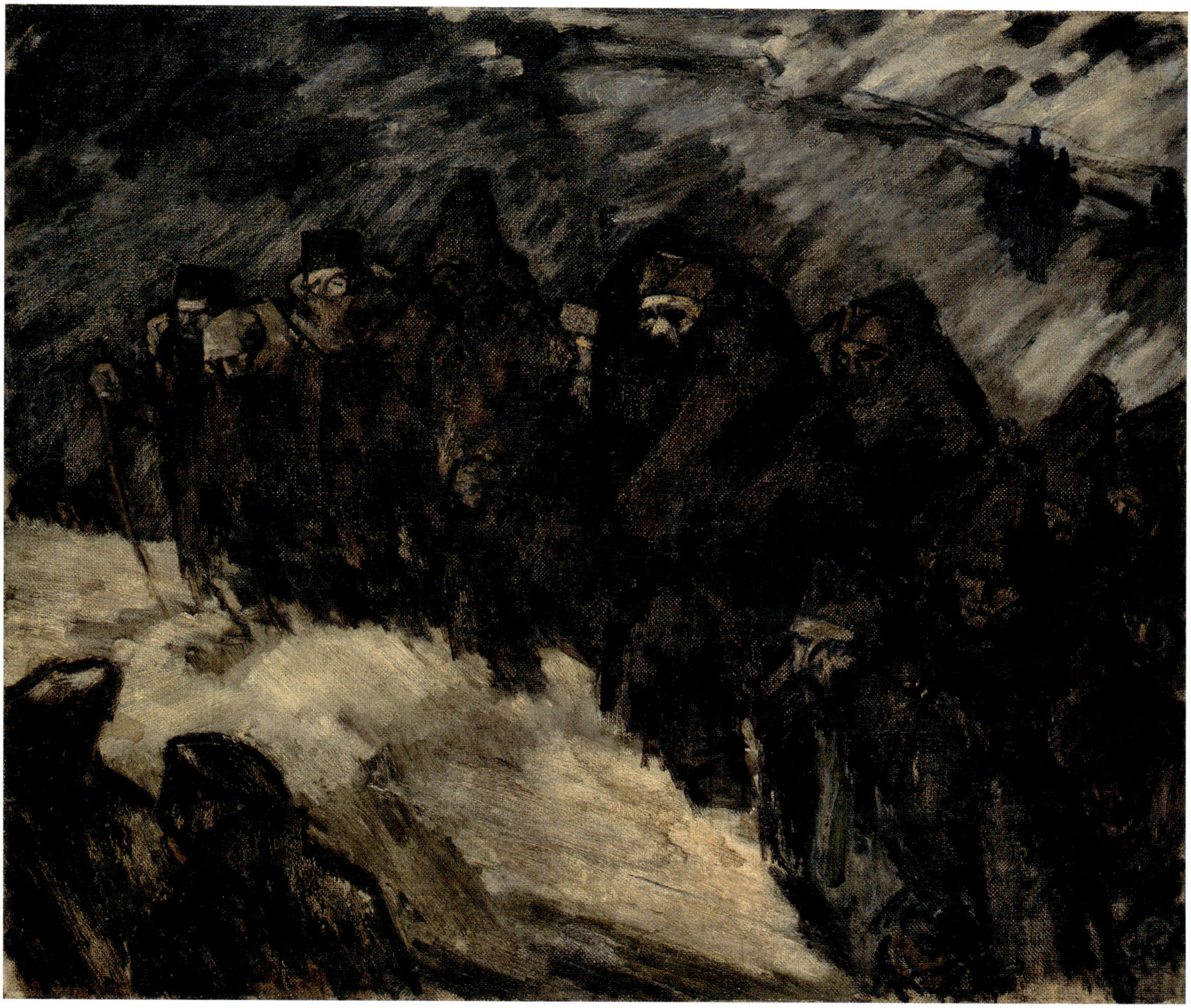

◂ Alois Hans Schramm
Guard of the Carpathians, 1914/15
Belvedere, Vienna

János Vaszary
Soldiers in the Snow, 1916
Museum of Fine Arts—Hungarian
National Gallery, Budapest

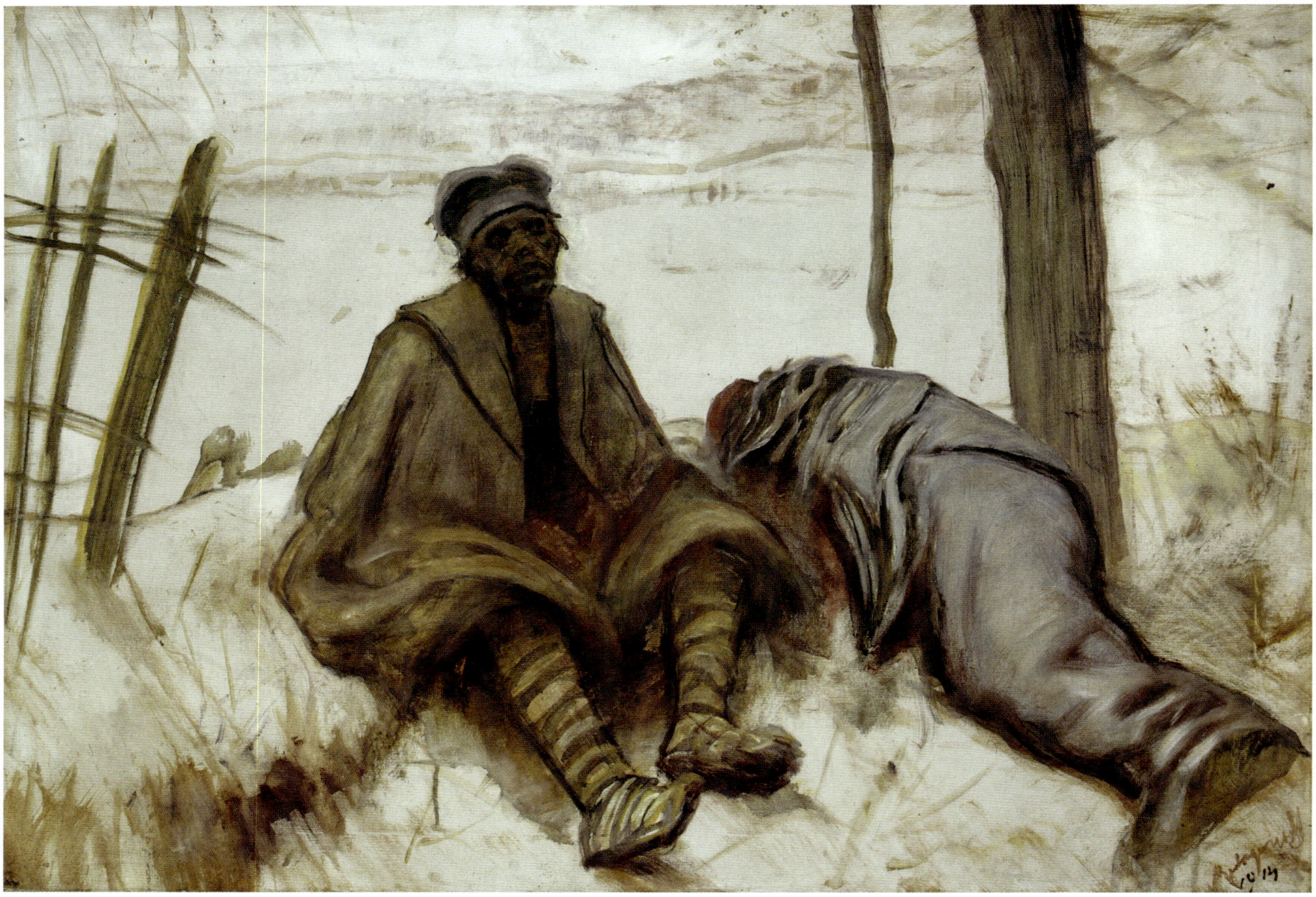

László Mednyánszky
In Serbia, 1914
Museum of Fine Arts—Hungarian
National Gallery, Budapest

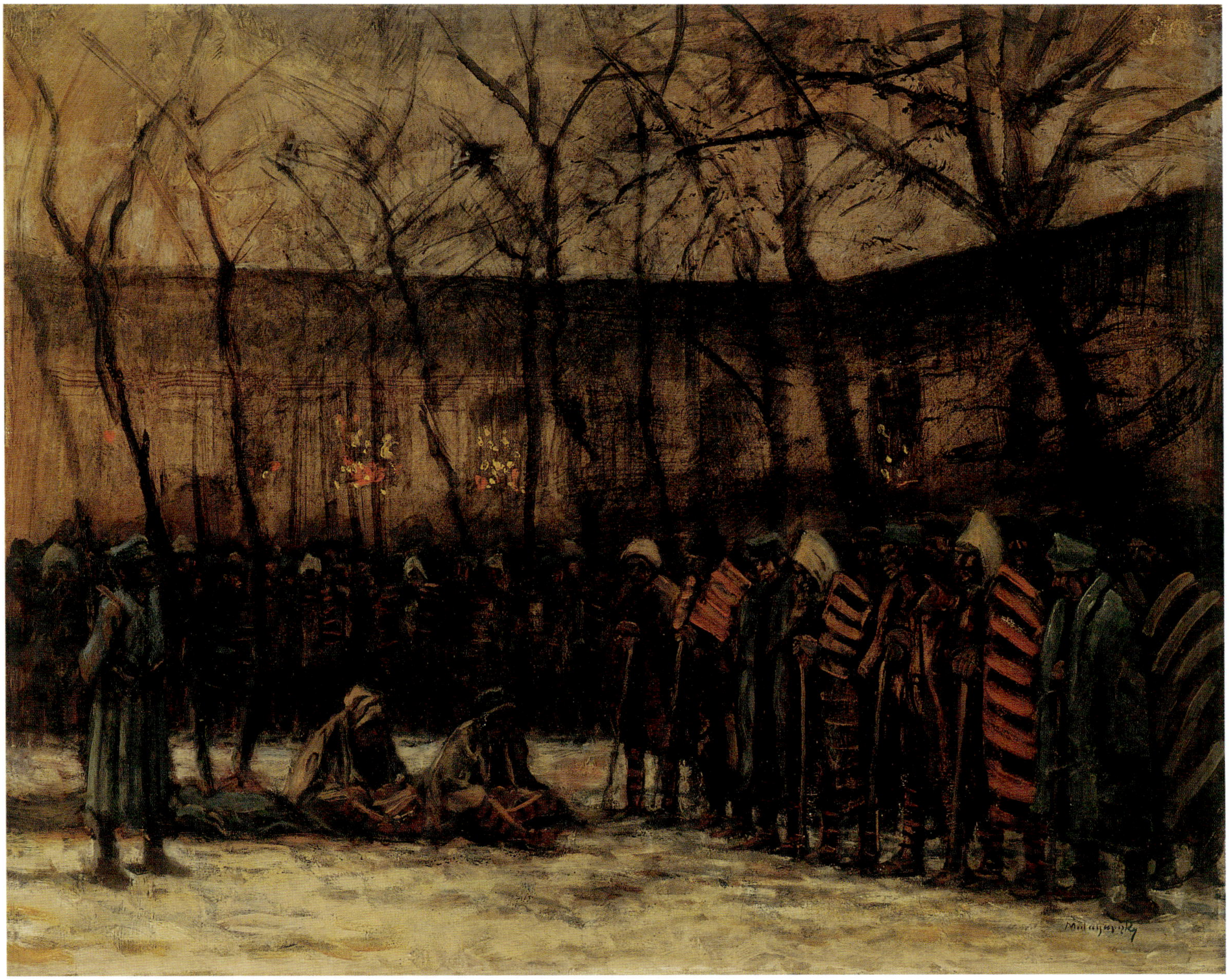

B

László Mednyánszky
Christmas for the Prisoners-of-War, c. 1915
Tamás Kieselbach Collection

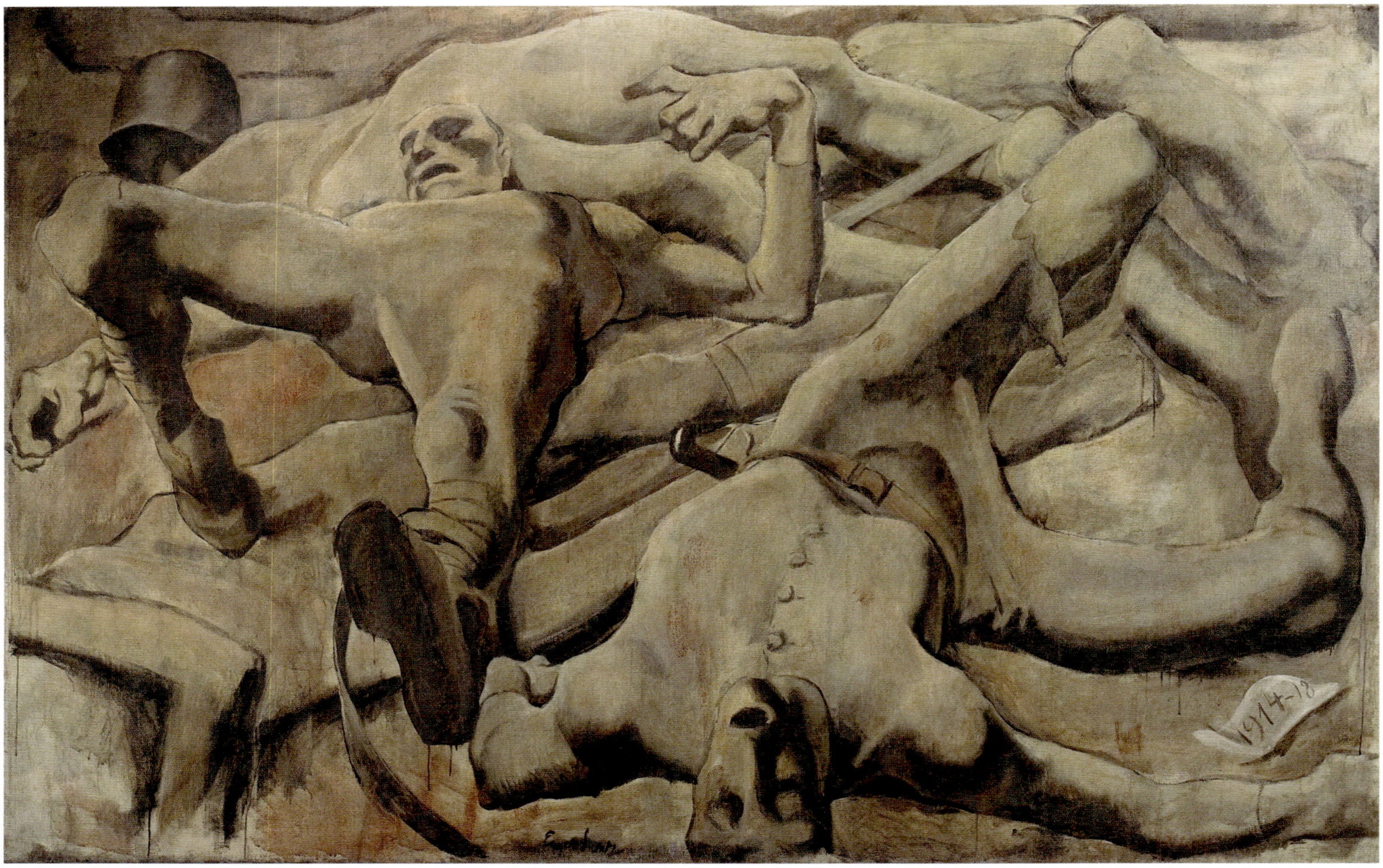

B

Albin Egger-Lienz
Finale, 1918
Leopold Private Collection

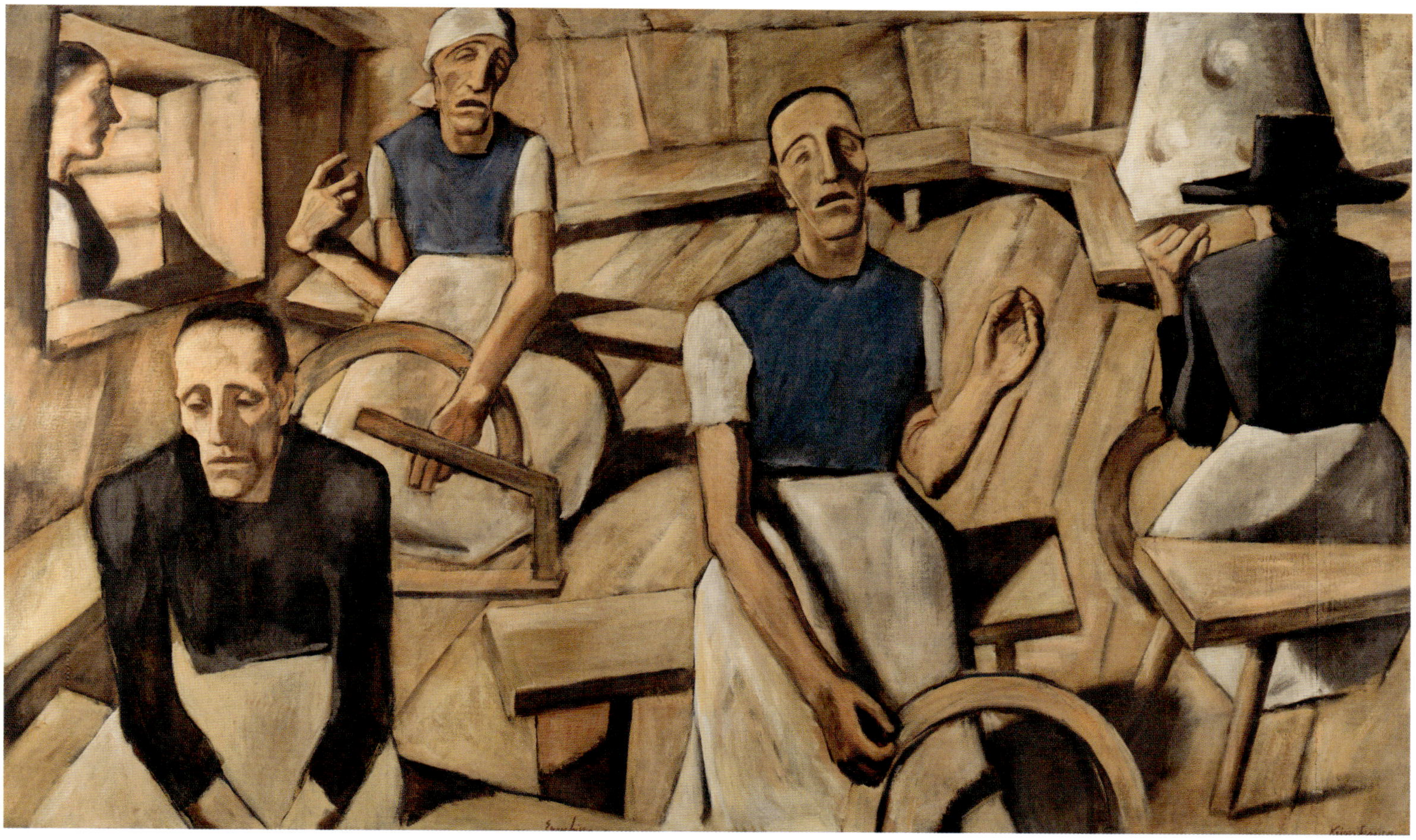

B

Albin Egger-Lienz
Women of War, 1918–22
Museum der Stadt Lienz Schloss Bruck

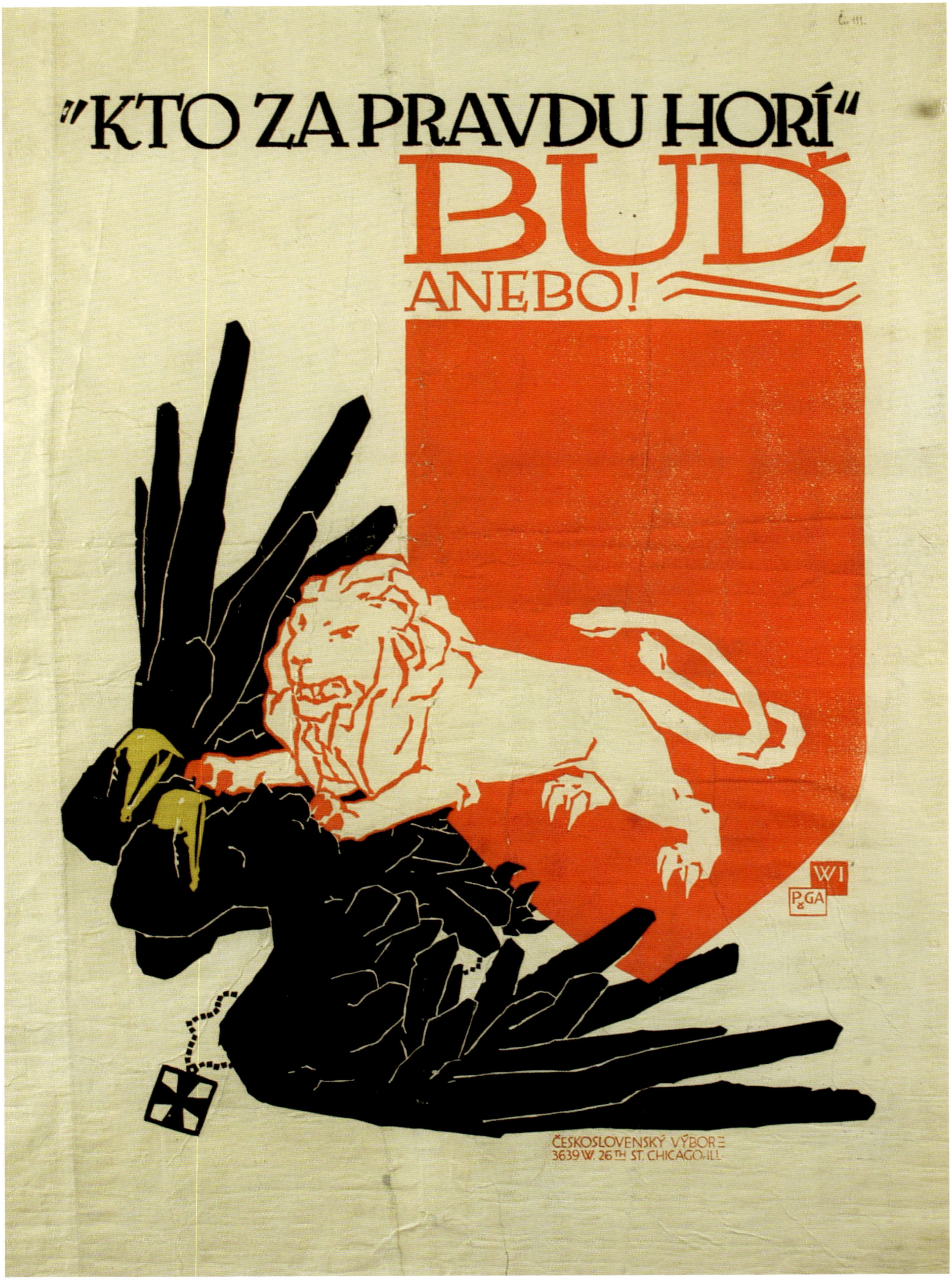

B

Vojtěch Preissig
"Who burns for the truth"—Now or never!, 1916
The Museum of Decorative Arts in Prague

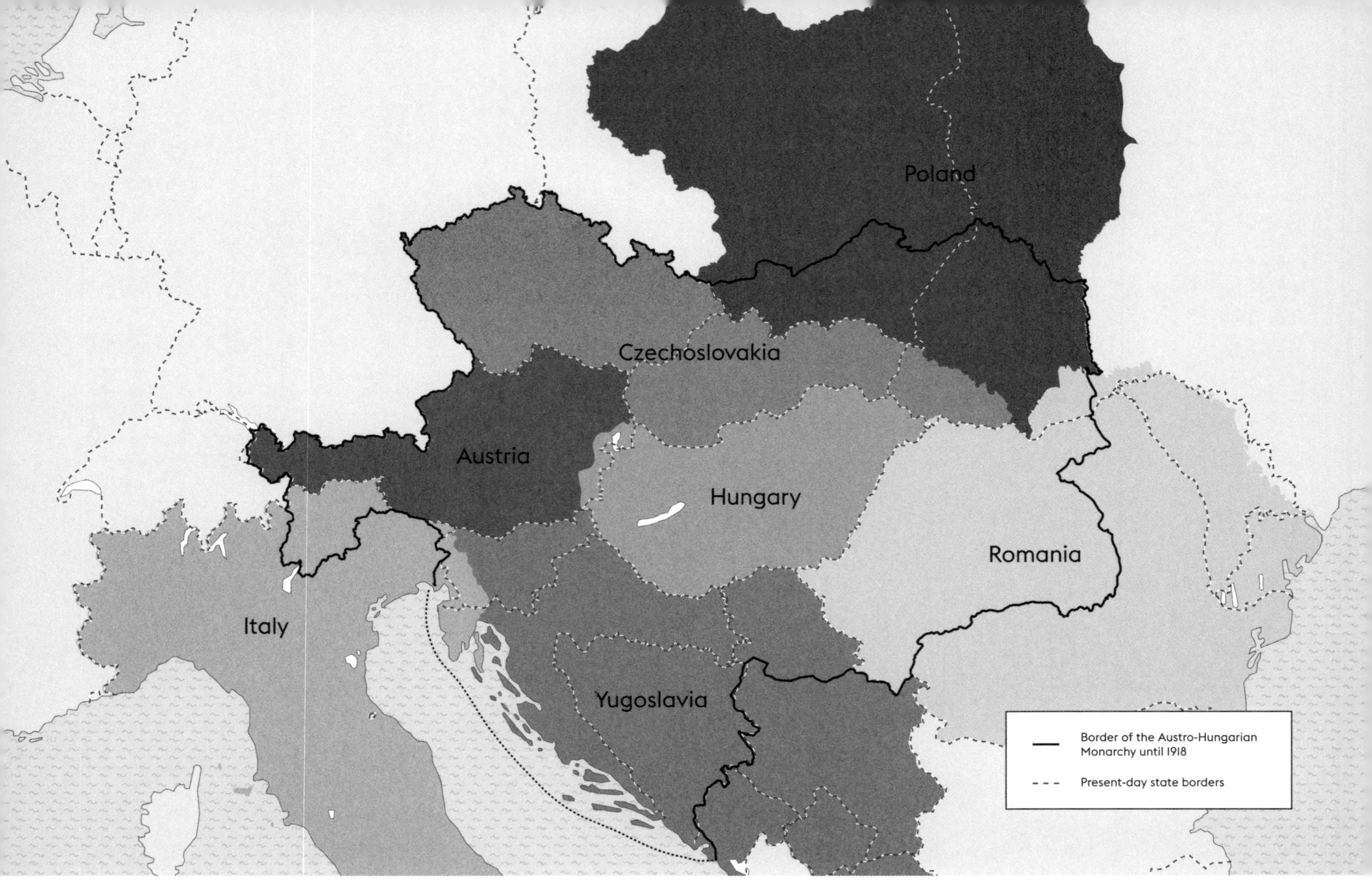

1919 The successor states
of the Austro-Hungarian Empire

nation:

nā´tion, n. [OFr. *nacion, nation*, from L. *natio(-onis)*, birth, a race, people, from *natus*, pp. of *nasci*, to be born.]

1. A body of people inhabiting the same country, or united under the same sovereign or government; as, the French *nation*; the American *nation*. *Nations*, like individuals, are masters of their own destinies. –David G. Ritchie. We have, as an independent people, the confidence of one of the most powerful *nations* on the earth. –President Palma of Cuba.
2. A body of people speaking the same language, or a body that has formerly been under a distinct government, but has been conquered, or incorporated with a larger nation; as, the empire of Russia comprehends many *nations*, as did formerly the Roman and Persian empires.
3. In ethnology, a class of people distinguished by common descent, customs, or language: a linguistic stock; a race.
4. A tribe or community; as, a *nation* of Indians.
5. A great number; as, a *nation* of plants. [Colloq.]
6. Formerly, in some European universities, one of the divisions of students in a classification by nativity.

Noah Webster / Noah Porter, ed., *Webster's Imperial Dictionary of the English Language* (Chicago, 1906), p. 1089

´nation, n Group having common language, history, government. **´-al** (´naʃnl), I. a. Of, common to, a nation. *N. anthem*, special song of a nation. 2 n. Person of certain nation. ´-**alism**, n. Strong feeling for one's nation; desire for national selfgovern-ment. **-´ality** (naʃə´naliti), n. Existence as a nation; being one of a nation (*of F. etc. n.*). ´-**alize**, v.t. Sp., make (land, railways etc.) into national property; make (persons) nationals. (´neiʃn)

Charles Kay Ogden, ed., *The General Basic English Dictionary* (New York, 1942), p. 232

English

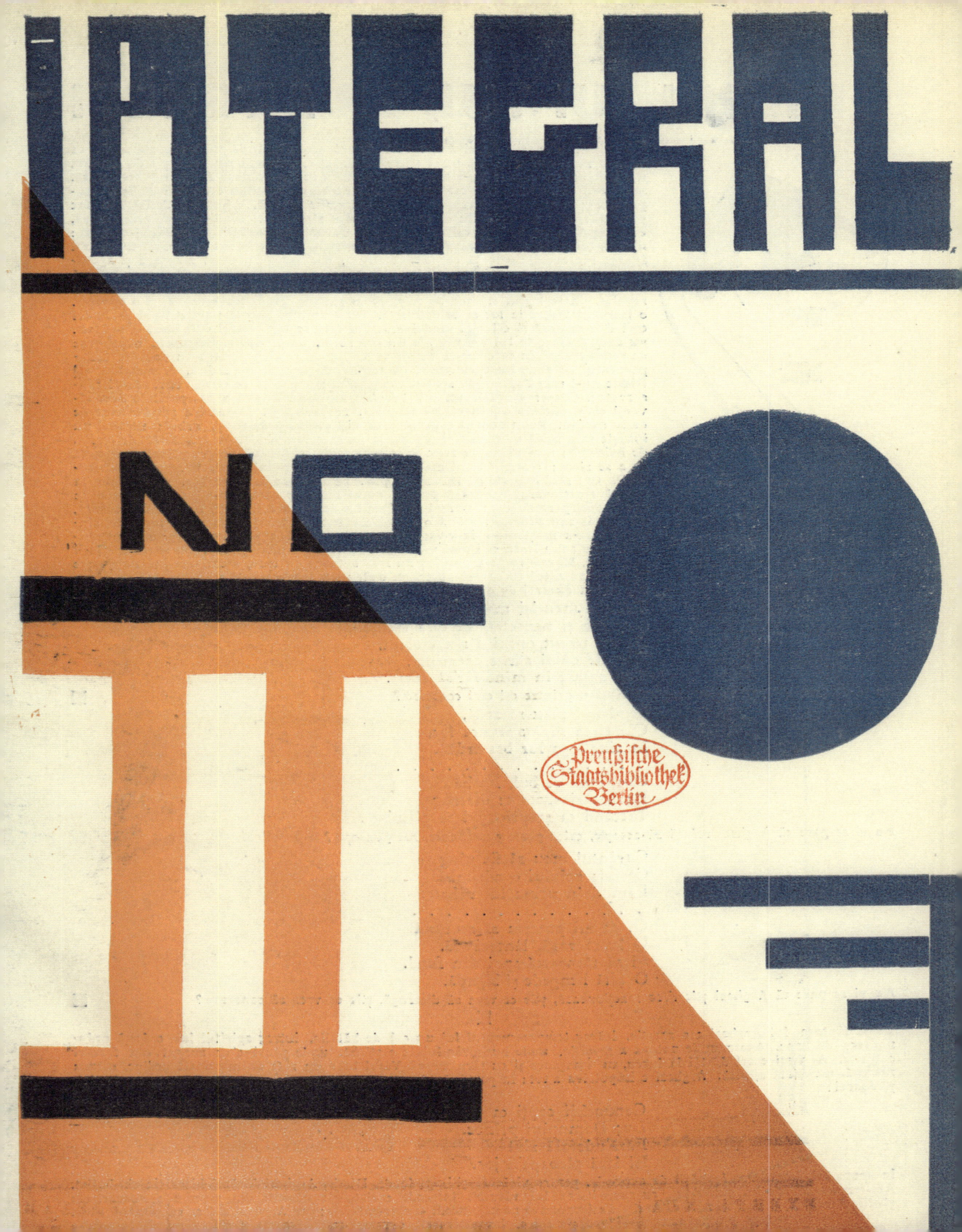
INTEGRAL
NO

Front cover of *Integral* (detail), vol. I, no. 3, Bucharest, 1925

C Psychological Studies — Revolution and Rebirth

“The heart of Austria is not the center, but the periphery”—Avant-Garde Journals in East-Central Europe[1]

Gábor Dobó, Merse Pál Szeredi

"The heart of Austria is not the center, but the periphery. You won't find Austria in the Alps—chamois, yes, and edelweiss and gentians but barely a hint of the double-headed eagle. The substance of Austria is drawn and replenished from the Crown Lands." (Joseph Roth, *The Emperor's Tomb*, 1938, ch. 5)

After the end of the Austro-Hungarian Monarchy, the editors of avant-garde journals in the successor states developed radical concepts that questioned the former function of art and artists. In East-Central Europe, until the end of Communism around 1990, the latter were ascribed a prophetic role inherited from the romantic nationalism of the nineteenth century and carried over into the individual national cultures, which the avant-garde of the time sought to overcome. Artists now regarded themselves as members and parts of an international and collaborative network. Of course, the cultural models of the different regions also had an influence on the avant-garde, and they had a marked effect, for example, as charismatic artists in many genres. Mention might be made here of Ljubomir Micić, Karel Teige, or Lajos Kassák, who were themselves influenced by the Romantic Sándor Petőfi or Adam Mickiewicz. After the disintegration of the Austro-Hungarian Monarchy and in the ensuing complicated geopolitical and cultural situation (called "histoire croisée" by historians, on account of the parallel interconnections that existed[2]), avant-garde artists stepped out of the routine of their accustomed environments in many respects. This enabled them to bring together the diverse Modernist tendencies on the territory of the former Empire within the avant-garde network.[3]

After the collapse of the Monarchy, avant-garde journals played an important role, as they were by definition a collective cultural product in which a group of artists articulated their complex artistic and social program, which in turn contributed to the international discussion of art. The avant-garde journals did not appear out of the blue. Not only the number of "little magazines," as they were called, but also their circulation had been increasing significantly since the 1880s, first in Western Europe and then worldwide.[4] By the end of the nineteenth century, these periodicals had assumed the important role of communicating between European cultures and making cultural trends and their new interpretations more widely known. In another respect as well, the "little magazines" of that time and around the turn of the century resembled the avant-garde journals of the 1920s discussed here: They had a distinctive artistic program, their authors frequently profiled themselves as members of some putative movement, and they often attacked the existing institutional system. The avant-garde editors made exceptionally good use of the "little magazine" strategies so as to formulate their own programs in the successor states of the Austro-Hungarian Monarchy. This essay will look at the strategies by which avant-garde magazines became part of European art discourse, even assuming a trend-defining role within it. Moreover, they gave writers in the countries of the former Monarchy and beyond a platform that enabled them to remain in contact, despite language, ethnic, and national barriers[5] (fig. 1).

The East-Central European avant-garde journals of the 1920s utilized the ground prepared for them by the "little magazines" in what was a crisis-ridden geopolitical context, to say the least. In fact, in his influential work *The Age of Extremes: The Short Twentieth Century*, Eric Hobsbawm interpreted the period from the start of World War I to the end of World War II as a single war.[6] The once multilingual and multinational Monarchy fragmented into individual nation-states, which often closed themselves off and, moreover, in which many millions of people found themselves in a minority situation.[7] The governments of the successor states initiated various modernization programs, including cultural policy concepts, but in general these efforts were not intended to initiate communication between the multinational states of the Carpathian Basin. On the contrary, the neo-national program of Kuno Klebelsberg (1922–31 Minister for Religion and Education in the conservative Horthy system) pushed for comprehensive education reforms that were to present a first step toward restoring the "territorial integrity" of the country, meaning a revision of the peace treaties following World War I.[8]

In the context of this rising nationalism in the successor states, the role of the avant-garde journals, which were published in several languages and distributed internationally, took on increased importance—and not only in Hungary. Their format and the ease with which the "little magazines" could be distributed made them ideal as vehicles for relatively rapid transborder communication, even after several of them had been banned in some countries. Such was the case with *MA* (1916–25) by Lajos Kassák, who in the first half of the 1920s worked as an exile in Vienna. Kassák's colleagues smuggled it under the name of *365* or *Kortárs* from Austria to Hungary, and also distributed it in Czechoslovakia and Romania. An indication of the connecting and integrative role of these avant-garde journals is the fact that their contributors included a strikingly large number of artists who were multilingual and at home in several cultures. Among Kassák's collaborators in *MA* were the painter János Mattis-Teutsch, who worked for the journal in Budapest in the 1910s. In the 1920s he contributed to the periodical *Contimporanul* (1922–32) in Bucharest, although he continued to live in the Transylvanian-Saxon city of Kronstadt (now Brașov, Romania). Róbert Reiter (pseudonym Franz Liebhard/t) began as an avant-garde poet and literary translator, working initially for *MA* in Temeschwar (now Timișoara, Romania) in Hungarian and German. The avant-garde poet Lajos Kudlák was also initially involved in *MA*, becoming known later under the name L'udovit Kudlák as a Slovakian Modernist painter. The Hungarian-born Serbian

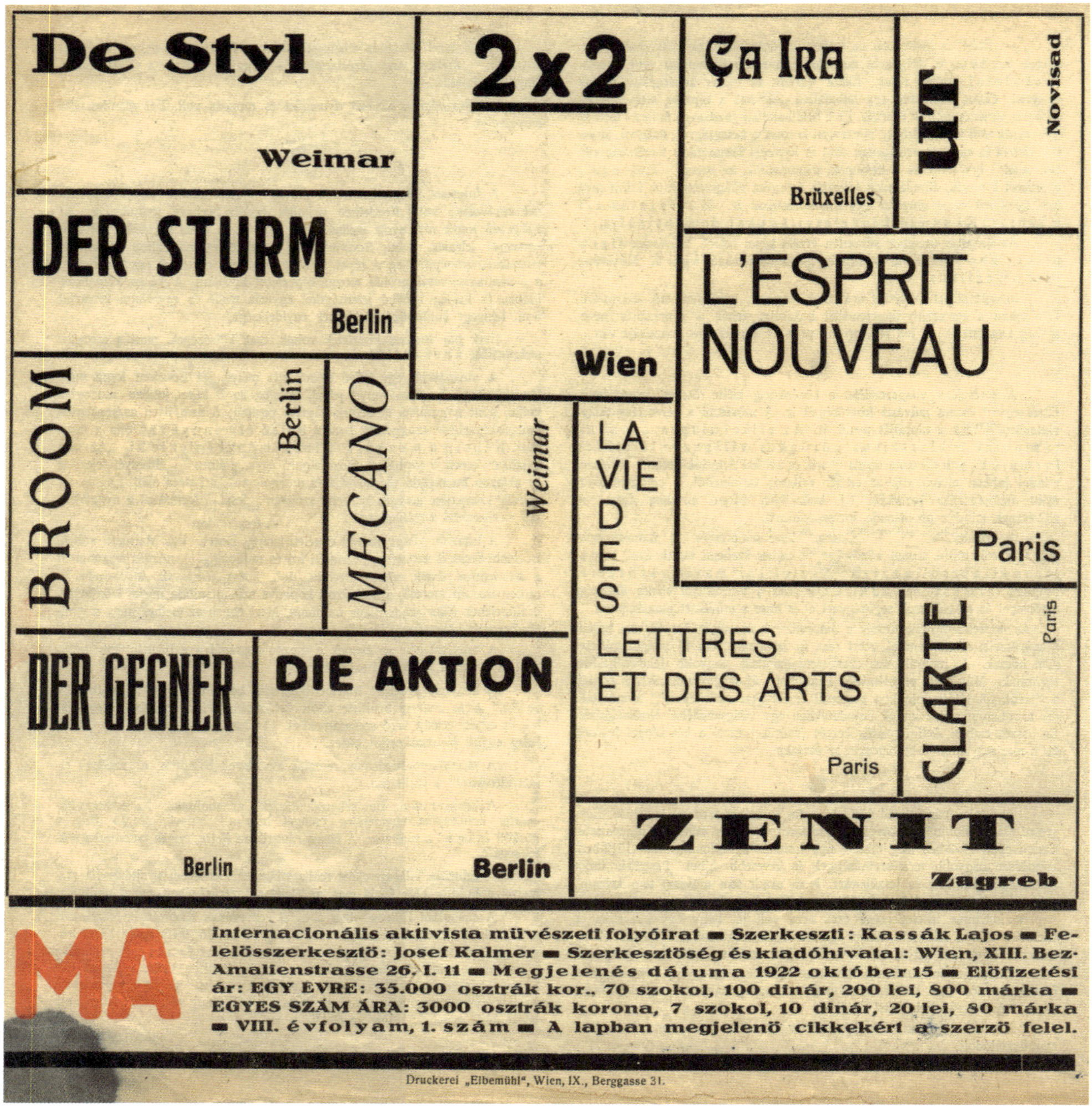

Fig. 1
Advertisement for international avant-garde journals on the back cover of *MA*, vol. 8, no. 1, Vienna, 1922

painter Petar Dobrović / Péter Dobrovits, who also worked for Kassák's journal early on, was later active in the Kingdom of Serbs, Croats, and Slovenes.

The avant-garde journals of the region continued to have a sustained impact during the time of the disintegration of the Austro-Hungarian Monarchy and the associated reduction in the territory of the Kingdom of Hungary. One of the consequences of the new geopolitical situation was the loss of importance, absolutely or relatively, of previous cultural centers. Even Vienna, capital of the former Monarchy, was no exception, losing its significance as an obvious point of reference for the artists of the successor states. For the Eastern European avant-garde journals of the 1920s, however, Vienna retained its important role, albeit for different reasons than before. After the collapse of the Hungarian Republic of Councils, the Social Democrats' "Red Vienna" became the most important emigration destination. It was in this context that the avant-garde émigrés founded their own periodicals, in part because they regarded Kassák's publication *MA* as being insufficiently politically committed. Among these new journals was *Akasztott Ember* (1922), which was influenced by left-wing Berlin Dadaism, *Egység* (1922–24), which advocated the program of the Soviet Proletkult, and *Ék* (1923/24), created out of an amalgamation of the two concepts and editorial boards. Vienna thus still functioned as a catalyst, even though no significant Viennese avant-garde journal was published at the time. Historians explain this with the dominance of the highly institutionalized Modernist trends of the Secession and, later, of Expressionism,[9] while some contemporaries drew attention to the "petty bourgeois" character of the Vienna art scene.[10] At the same time, Vienna retained its importance as one of the meeting places of the avant-garde of the region and of Europe, and major events taking place in the city often provided a basis for friendships, discussions, and later collaborations, as was the case with the *International Theater Exhibition* organized in 1924 by the architect and set designer Frederick Kiesler. The artists saw in theater technology the possibility of creating a "synthesis," a total work of art. Leading international avant-garde artists exhibited at the Konzerthaus, with pieces as diverse as Ferdinand Léger's *Ballet mécanique*, a "dynamic" futuristic play directed by Filippo Tommaso Marinetti and Enrico Prampolini, and Kiesler's revolutionary *Raumbühne* (Space Stage).[11] Many avant-garde journals—*MA*, *Pásmo* in Brno, *Periszkop* and *Contimporanul* in Romania, *Noi* in Rome, and *The Little Review* in the USA—published special issues on the exhibition. It gave rise to feverish activity in the art world, particularly among critics, and sparked lively discourse between European avant-garde journals (fig. 2).

Although Vienna remained a catalyst for the journals of the East-Central European avant-garde, regional avant-garde periodicals no longer regarded the city as a center but saw the network in which they operated as transnational and polycentric.[12] They therefore rejected the idea[13] that the cultural transfer radiated from the "center" to the "periphery,"[14] the center naturally being the "West" and the periphery the "East."[15] The avant-garde periodicals, including the journals published in the successor states to the Monarchy, saw themselves as equal members of a network, unlike the Modernist publications, like *Nouvelle Revue Française* (1909–), *La Ronda* (1919–23), or *The Criterion* (1922–39), which sought to rebuild cultural life in postwar Europe on the basis of the Western cultural canon and rejected the avant-garde.[16] By contrast, the editors of the avant-garde journals believed that statements about the new art could be made from Novi Sad, Bucharest, or Lviv just as well as from Vienna, Paris, or Berlin. These cities remained important but were no longer the absolute points of reference for East-Central European avant-garde journals.[17] The declining importance of earlier cultural centers is illustrated by the fact that avant-garde artists sought their modernization models not in these cities but in the Soviet Union, which they saw as their future reality, in the USA, or even in the Jewish settlements in Palestine (fig. 3).

The journals of the polycentric avant-garde network offered a cultural transfer in several directions. These publications not only had knowledge of innovations in art but also interpreted them and actively shaped contemporary cultural discourse. East-Central European journals like *MA* in Vienna, *Zwrotnica* in Kraków (first series published in 1922/23), *Zenit* (1921–26) in Zagreb and later Belgrade, the journals of the Devětsil Group in Prague and Brno, or *Blok* (1924–26) in Warsaw contributed to international discourse with reproductions of major artworks or original theoretical essays. Through their network, these avant-garde journals were able to establish connections between the successor states of the Austro-Hungarian Monarchy and also between the multilingual cultures within the same country. The East-Central European publications were written not only in the language of the country but also in German and French, both of which served as a *lingua franca*, and often in other local languages as well. This was of particular importance in the successor states created after the 1919 peace treaties, which were fraught with

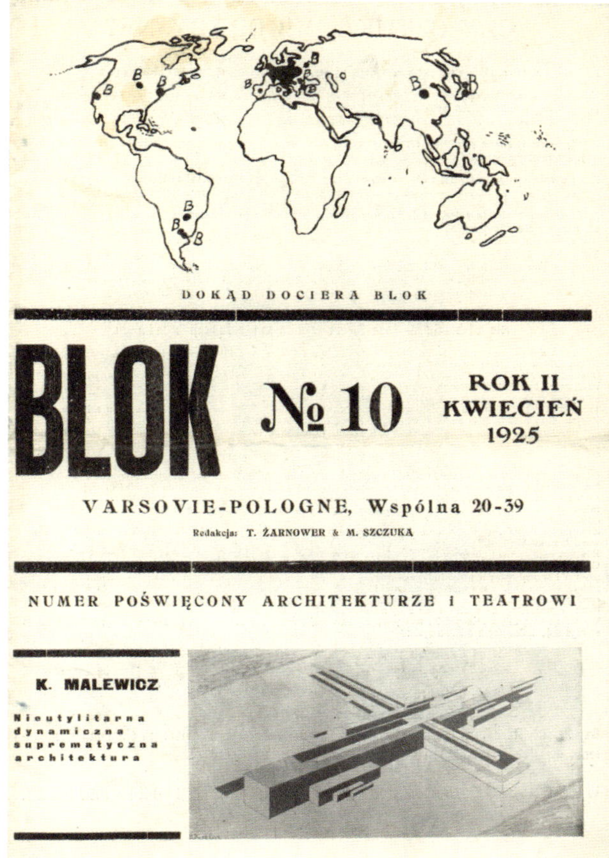

Fig. 2
Front cover of *Blok*, no. 10, Warsaw, 1925

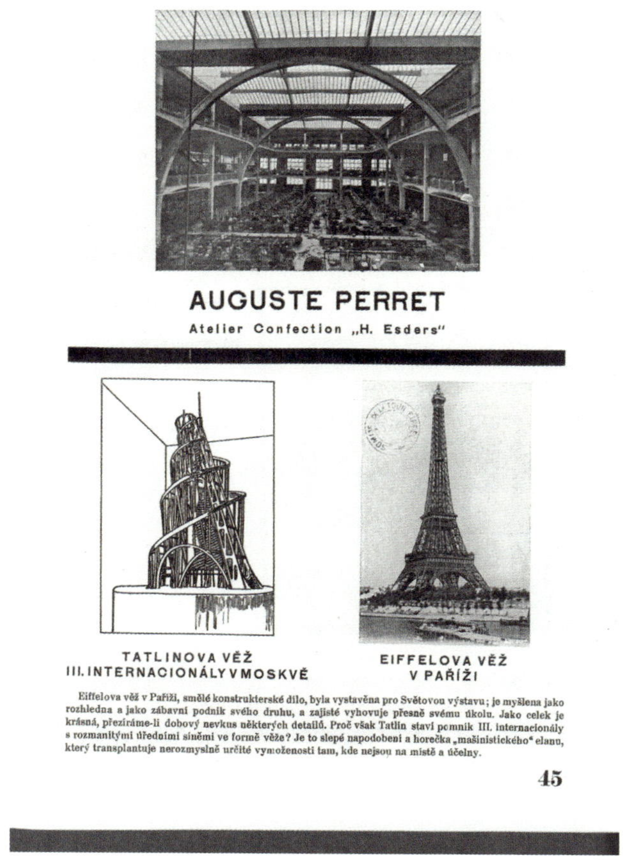

AUGUSTE PERRET

Atelier Confection „H. Esders"

TATLINOVA VĚŽ
III. INTERNACIONÁLY V MOSKVĚ

EIFFELOVA VĚŽ
V PAŘÍŽI

Eiffelova věž v Paříži, smělé konstrukterské dílo, byla vystavěna pro Světovou výstavu; je myšlena jako rozhledna a jako zábavní podnik svého druhu, a zajisté vyhovuje přesně svému úkolu. Jako celek je krásná, přezíráme-li dobový nevkus některých detailů. Proč však Tatlin staví pomník III. internacionály s rozmanitými úředními síněmi ve formě věže? Je to slepé napodobení a horečka „mašinistického" elanu, který transplantuje nerozmyslně určité vymoženosti tam, kde nejsou na místě a účelny.

45

Fig. 3
Page from the almanac *Život 2*, Prague, 1922

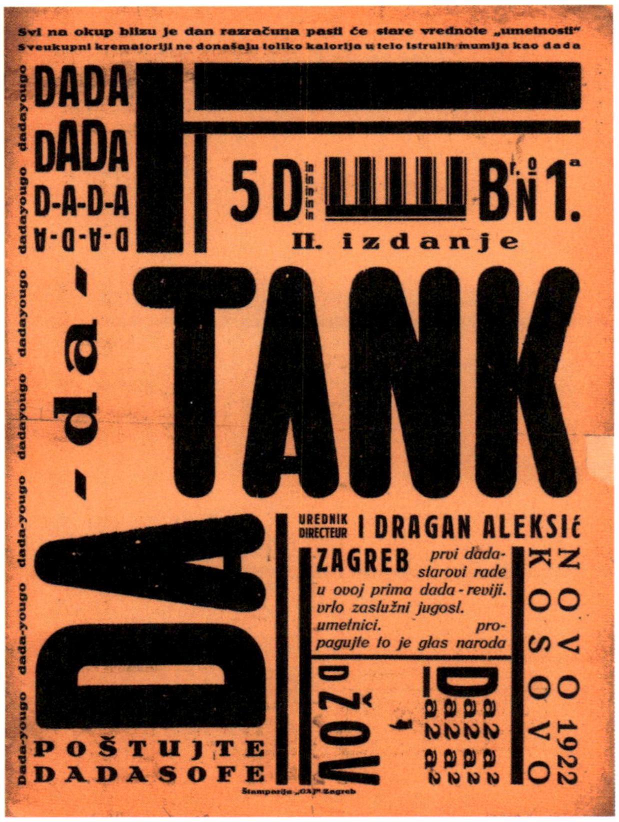

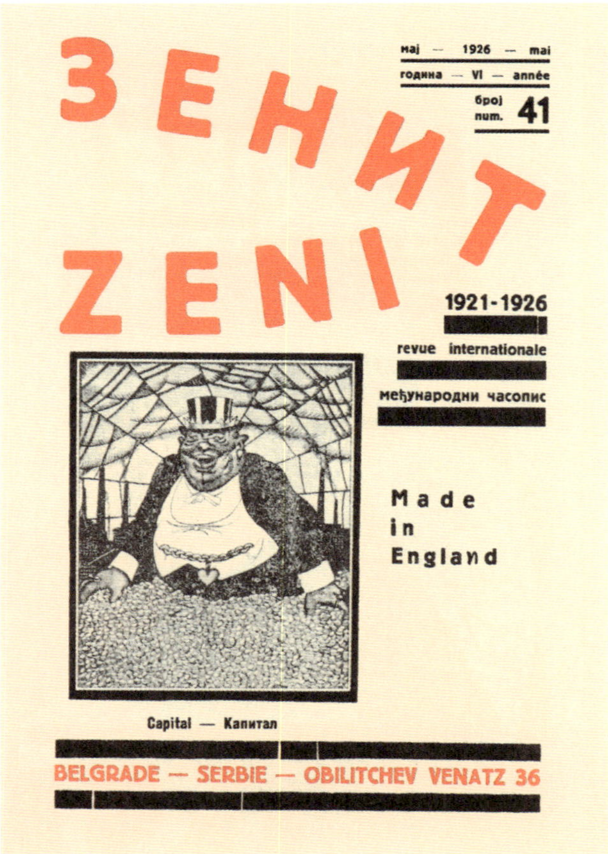

Fig. 4
Front cover of *Dada-Tank*, no. 1, Zagreb, 1922

Fig. 5
Front cover of *Zenit*, no. 41, Belgrade, 1926

nationalist tensions. Thus the Hungarian avant-garde journal *Út* (1922–25) described itself as "Yugoslavian" in Vojvodina and published Hungarian translations of texts by authors from the *Zenit* group. At the same time it also remained in contact with the Vienna and Budapest avant-garde at a time when the majority of intellectuals in Hungary were suffering—in their new situation as a minority—from the "trauma of Trianon," as it was referred to, and did not see the cultural transfer between the new states as a priority (fig. 4).

Apart from articles in Slovenian, French, and German, the periodical *Tank* (1927) in Ljubljana also used Italian, a remarkable gesture given the wartime conflict in the region between the Italian and South Slav inhabitants and the subsequent new border arrangements. The avant-garde journals *Yung-Yidish* (1919) and *Tel-Awiw* (1919–21), published in Yiddish in Poland and Ukraine (previously Galicia, which belonged to the Austro-Hungarian Monarchy), also had a transborder readership, using the avant-garde network and the mediating force of Yiddish to reach readers from Łódź to Poznań, and even as far as New York. With its "Balkanization of Europe" slogan, the magazine *Zenit* vehemently attacked the paradigm that saw cultural transfer in relation to "center" and "periphery," provocatively and (self-)mockingly describing Europe as an "extension of the Balkan peninsula"[18] (fig. 5).

Not only the number of "little magazines," as they were called, but also their circulation had been increasing significantly since the 1880s, first in Western Europe and then worldwide.

The avant-garde journals of the 1920s, including the East-Central European ones, possessed a common code system, "synthetic" editing, as it was called, which investigated connections between contemporary (avant-garde) art, science, and technology, and their communication through different media. Avant-garde artists believed in the potential of synthesis and envisaged its implementation through linking the achievements of contemporary art with those of non-related fields (science, technology, and social sciences).[19] László Moholy-Nagy, a member of Kassák's circle, who had quickly become an important European avant-garde figure, investigated the question of these "synthetic" avant-garde journals as early as 1925. He was a professor at the Bauhaus at the time, but published his study on this subject between 1924

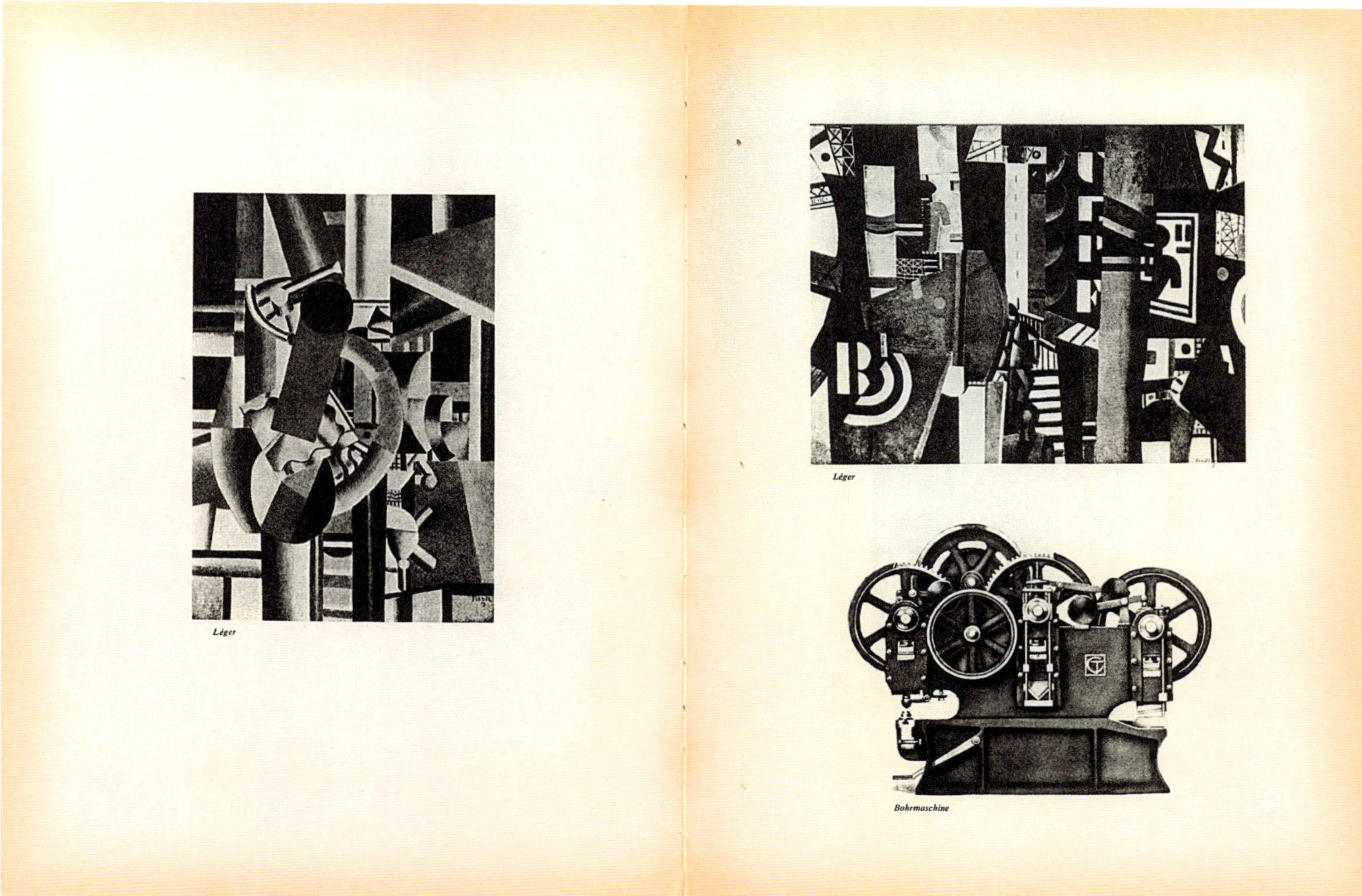

and 1926 in numerous contemporary avant-garde journals, including *Dokumentum* (1926/27) and *Pásmo* (1924–26). The latter was published in Brno, a mid-sized city that had become acclaimed for its Modernist architecture and thus grew into one of the regional centers of Modernism during the 1920s. Moholy-Nagy saw the promotion of the "new lifestyle" and its manifestations as a key feature of the "synthetic" art journals. They therefore included fields that, from a Modernist point of view, promised the most innovations, from architecture to education and typography. The visual appearance of these journals reflected developments in typography and bookmaking that made them recognizable and attracted attention.

One innovation was the fact that the reproductions and photos placed between the text sections not only illustrated the articles but were also items in their own right. The photos showing technological innovations or modern cityscapes, often published without comment, functioned as visual calls to action. Their message was that these beacons of modern life were a true reflection of the time. The "synthetic" journals used multiple resources, providing space for a wide range of creative expression, from architectural sketches to musical scores. They were also multilingual, with articles written in the national languages being summarized in the major European languages, and special issues published on topical subjects.[20]

The synthetic editorial work appeared in its purest form in almanacs and anthologies, because, unlike newspapers, these publications

Fig. 6
Reproductions of artworks by Fernand Léger and a machine, In László Moholy-Nagy, Lajos Kassák, eds., *Buch neuer Künstler*, Vienna, 1922

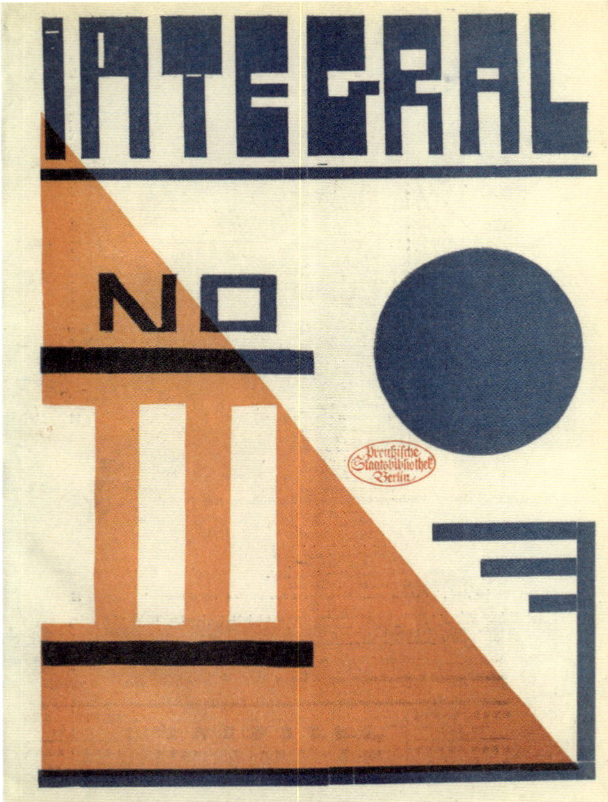

The visual appearance of these journals reflected developments in typography and bookmaking that made them recognizable and attracted attention.

were also typographically consistent. Typical works of this type include Moholy-Nagy's and Kassák's *Buch neuer Künstler* from 1922, the anthology *Revoluční sborník Devětsil*, edited by Jaroslav Seifert and Karel Teige, of the same year, the almanacs by the Polish Futurists in the early 1920s,[21] and *Tisztaság könyve* by Lajos Kassák from 1926 (fig. 6).

The synthetic journals of the East-Central European avant-garde were not at all devoted to the promotion of a single direction but endeavored to present the latest artistic developments in an integrative (eclectic or syncretic) form. The titles alone were an indication of this: *Integral* (1925–28), *Zenit*, *Dokumentum*, *Contimporanul*, *Periszkop* (1925/26), etc. The power of these synthetic journals as a code can be seen from the fact that the Communist periodicals published in the late 1920s, such as *100%* (1927–30) or *ReD* (1927–31), used the same typographical design (fig. 7).

Fig. 7
Front cover of *Integral*, vol. 1, no. 3, Bucharest, 1925

1 This study was written in connection with the research project of the Petőfi Literary Museum–Kassák Museum, financed by the National Research, Development and Innovation Office — NKFIH, project-no. NKFI-K 120779.

2 Michael Werner, Bénédicte Zimmermann, eds., *De la comparaison à l'histoire croisée* (Paris, 2004), pp. 15–49.

3 We use the term "Modernism" to designate cultural movements in the early twentieth century that refer to the era of "modernity"; Peter Brooker, Andrzej Gąsiorek, Deborah Longworth, Andrew Thacker, "Introduction," in ibid., eds., *The Oxford Handbook of Modernisms* (Oxford, 2010), pp. 3–4. "Avant-garde" is used to describe the critical art movements that radically revised modernity and Modernism. There is no sharp boundary between Modernism and avant-garde and there were numerous overlaps.

4 See, e.g., Evanghélia Stead, Hélène Védrine, eds., *L'Europe des revues (1880–1920)* (Paris, 2008).

5 Mica Gherghescu, "Grilles et arborescences: Le rôle des revues dans la construction de l'espace artistique moderne," in *Modernités plurielles, 1905–1970*, ed. Catherine Grenier, exh. cat., Centre Pompidou, Paris (Paris, 2013), pp. 39–45.

6 Eric J. Hobsbawm, *Age of Extremes: The Short Twentieth Century, 1914–1991* (London, 1994).

7 One illustrative example is the title of the monograph about the Yugoslav avant-garde: Dubravka Djurić, Miško Šuvaković, *Impossible Histories: Historic Avant-Gardes, Neo-Avant-Gardes, and Post-Avant-Gardes in Yugoslavia, 1918–1991* (Cambridge, 2003).

8 Kuno Klebelsberg, "Neonacionalizmus," *Nemzeti* Újság, January 29, 1928.

9 Christian Weikop, "Introduction: Germany, Austria, Switzerland," in Christian Weikop, Peter Brooker, Sascha Bru, Andrew Thacker, eds., *The Oxford Critical and Cultural History of Modernist Magazines: Volume III: Europe 1880–1940* (Oxford, 2013), pp. 693–708.

10 On the Vienna experience of avant-garde artists, see, e.g., the introduction by the pro-Bauhaus reviewer Ernő Kállai to Lajos Kassák's 1924 exhibition at Galerie Der Sturm: Ernst Kállai, "Ludwig Kassák," in *Der Sturm, 131. Ausstellung: Ludwig Kassák und Nikolaus Braun*, exh. cat., Galerie Der Sturm, Berlin (Berlin, 1924), p. 3.

11 More about the exhibition in Merse Pál Szeredi, "Budapest — Berlin — Budapest: magyar művészek Berlinben az 1920-as években," in *Berlin — Budapest 1919–1933: Képzőművészeti kapcsolatok Berlin* és *Budapest között, kiállítási katalógus*, exh. cat., Virág Judit Galéria, Budapest (Budapest, 2016), p. 11–147.

12 Béatrice Joyeux-Prunel, "Weimar, Berlin, New York, Varsovie, São Paulo, Mexico ... Une géographie polycentrique," in ibid., *Les avant-gardes artistiques (1918–1945): Une histoire transnationale* (Paris, 2017), pp. 113–18.

13 Per Bäckström, Benedikt Hjartarson, eds., *Decentring the Avant-Garde* (Amsterdam/New York, 2014).

14 We placed "center" and "periphery" in quote marks to indicate that ideological and historical constructions are implied. This issue is also picked up on in the history of East-Central European avant-garde magazines. For historiographic questions of "center" and "periphery," see, most recently, Piotr Piotrowski, *In the Shadow of Yalta: Art and the Avant-Garde in Eastern Europe, 1945–1989* (London, 2011).

15 Similarly, "East" and "West" are not neutral terms, as history has shown; see Larry Wolff, *Inventing Eastern Europe: The Map of Civilization on the Mind of the Enlightenment* (Stanford, 1994).

16 Anne-Rachel Hermetet, *Pour sortir du chaos: Trois revues européennes des années vingt* (Rennes, 2009).

17 Béatrice Joyeux-Prunel, "Provincializing Paris: The Center-Periphery Narrative of Modern Art in Light of Quantitative and Transnational Approaches," in *Artl@s Bulletin*, vol. 4, no. 1, 2015, art. 4.

18 Ljubomir Micić, "Nova Umetnost" (New Art), in *Zenit*, vol. 4, no. 34, 1924, n.p.

19 The term was used for the first time by Jean Cocteau in *Le rappel à l'ordre* (Paris, 1926); see also Jean Laude, *Le retour à l'ordre dans les arts plastiques et l'architecture, 1919–1925* (Saint-Étienne, 1986); Jennifer Ruth Bethke, *From Futurism To Neoclassicism: Temporality In Italian Modernism, 1916–1925* (Berkeley, 2005).

20 László Moholy-Nagy, "Richtlinien für eine Synthetische Zeitschrift," in *Pásmo*, vol. 1, nos. 7–8, 1925, p. 5; for further discussion, see Jindřich Toman, "Permanent Synthesis: László Moholy-Nagy's Idea of a Synthetic Journal," in Gábor Dobó, Merse Pál Szeredi, eds., *Local Contexts/International Networks: Avant-Garde Journals in East-Central Europe* (*The Avant-Garde and Its Journals* 2), proceedings of the International Conference held in the Kassák Museum, September 17-19, 2015 (Budapest, 2018) (forthcoming).

21 Krisztina Passuth, *Les avant-gardes de l'Europe Centrale: 1907–1927* (Paris, 1988), p. 77.

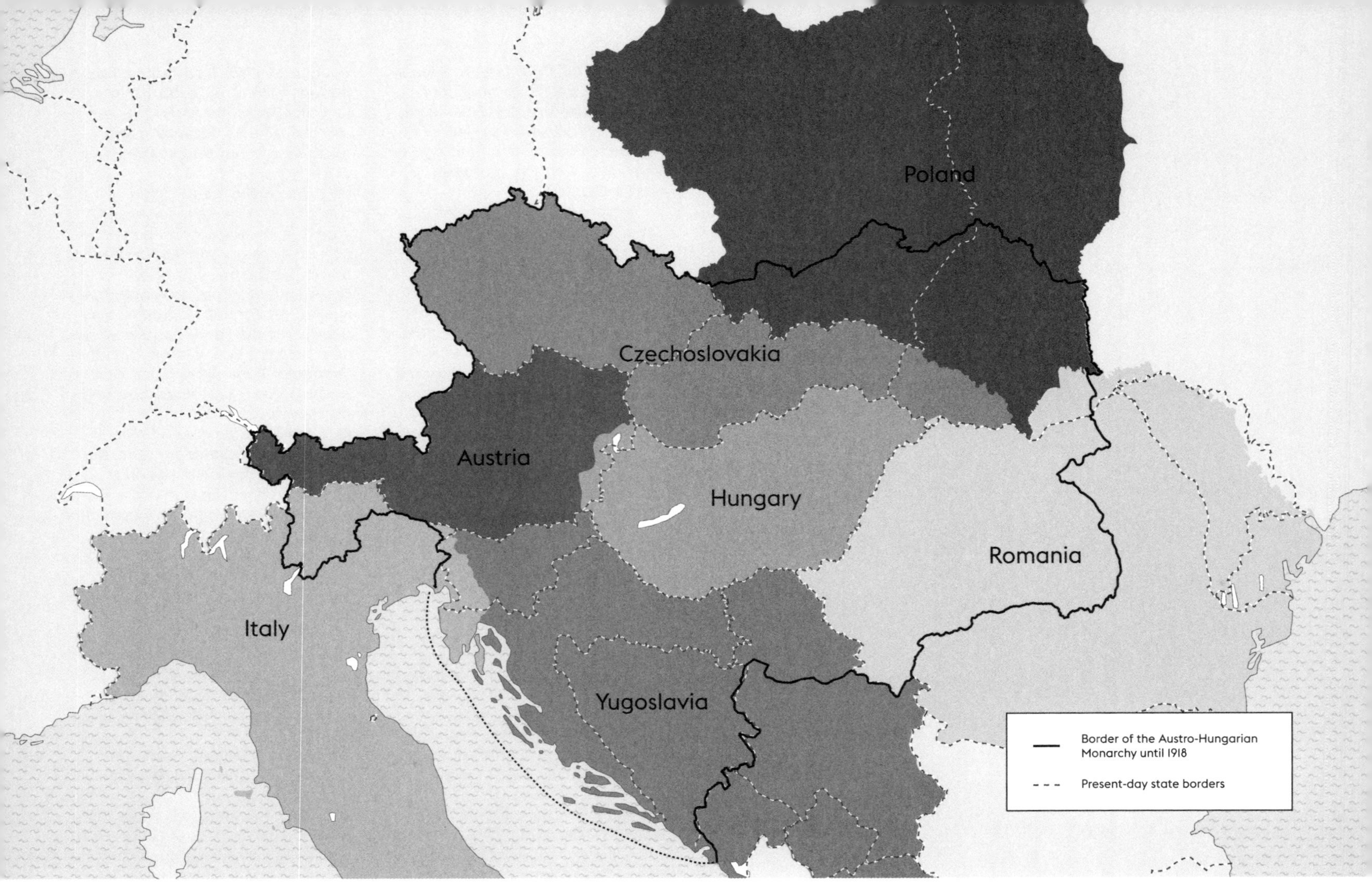

C 1919 The successor states of the Austro-Hungarian Empire

border—gránica:

GRÀNICA, f. finis, confinium, terminus, *mjesto dokle se proteže ńešto prostrano (naj češće zemļa, država), pa po tome i mjesto gdje se onakovo što dotiče s drugijem čim; uprav bi bila linija bez debeline, ali se gdjegdje ovako zove i dio (zemļe, države) koji je pri (pravoj) granici. — isporedi* međa, kraj krajina. — *Akc. se mijeńa u gen. pl.* grànîcâ. — *Riječ je praslavenska, isporedi stslov., rus., poļ.* granica, *češ.* hranice. — *Po svoj prilici postaje od* гранъ (*vidi kod* 1. grana) *nastavkom* ica (*ńem.* grenze *uzeto je iz slavenskoga jezika*). ...

P. Budmani, *Rječnik hrvatskoga ili srpskoga jezika* (Zagreb, 1891), p. 386

border—meja:

meja: 1. rob, kraj, konec česa; hrepenenje brez mej; — 2. njegova označba; mejo staviti, potegniti; živa meja: zasajena z grmovjem, nav. z gabrovjem; črez mejo orati, pobegniti; — 3. mera; to pravilo velja samo do neke meje.

Jožа Glonar, *Slovar slovenskega jezika* (Ljubljana, 1936), p. 206

Croatian
Slovenian

Psychological Studies

The challenge of the postwar period lay not just in the geopolitical restructuring of Europe, but also in the fundamental question concerning the identity of Austria-Hungary's newly formed successor states. The art world reacted to the social instability of the time by painting a psychological portrait of a continent stretched to its limits by war. The works of Fritz Schwarz-Waldegg, Anton Kolig, Alfred Wickenburg, Anton Hanak, and the expressive statue by Jan Štursa, all contain themes in which the crisis of the individual is articulated. Templates from antiquity *(Kneeling Narcissus* and *Narcissus)* were revisited and adapted, as were iconographies of Christian martyrdom *(Ecce Homo, The Confession, Wounded Man,* and *The Last Judgment).* The cultural traditions that had the deepest impact on Europe's humanist self-image were thus reincorporated, albeit indirectly, into the continent's postwar art. (MH)

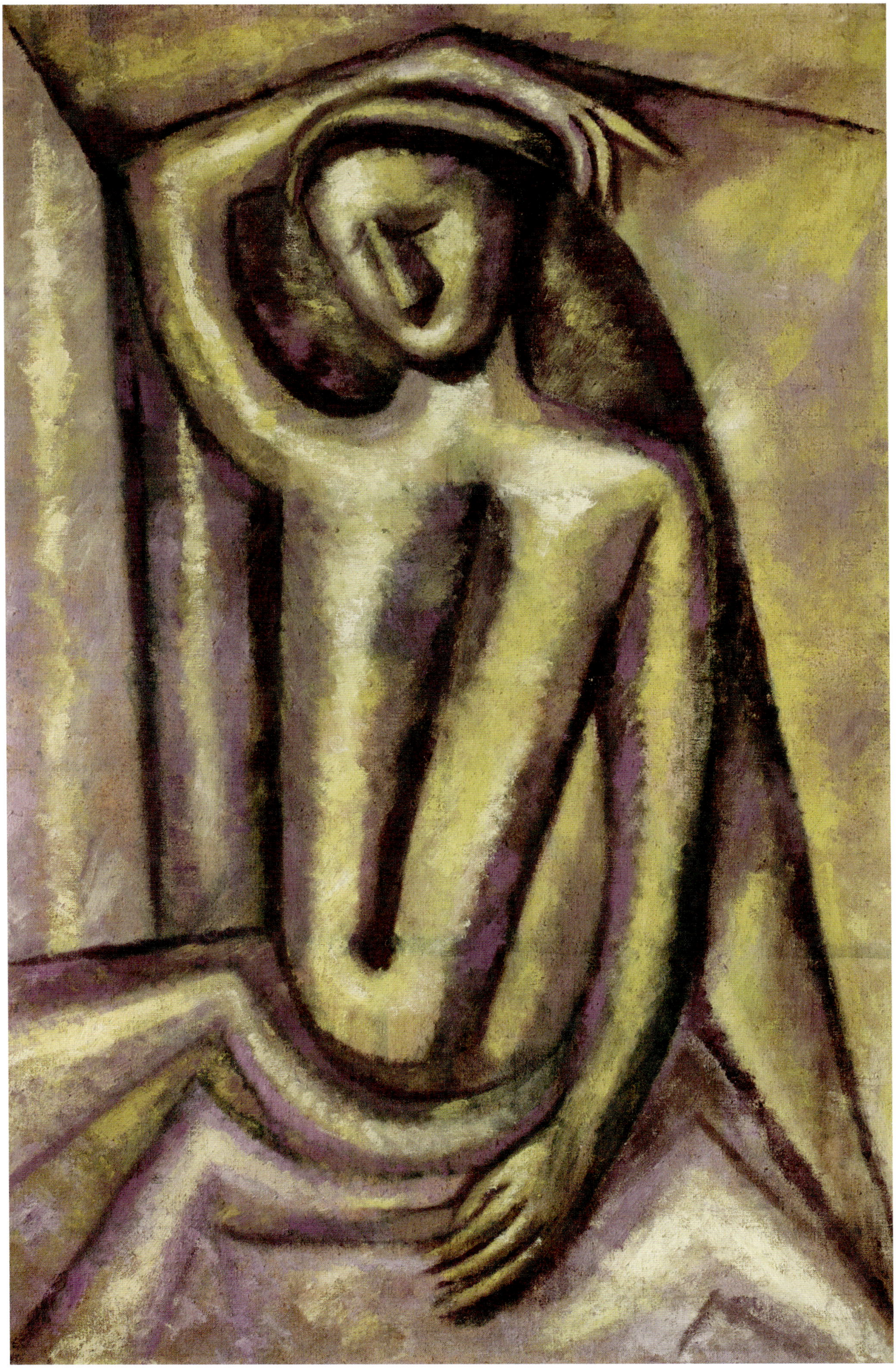

Alfred Wickenburg
Narcissus, 1922
Private collection

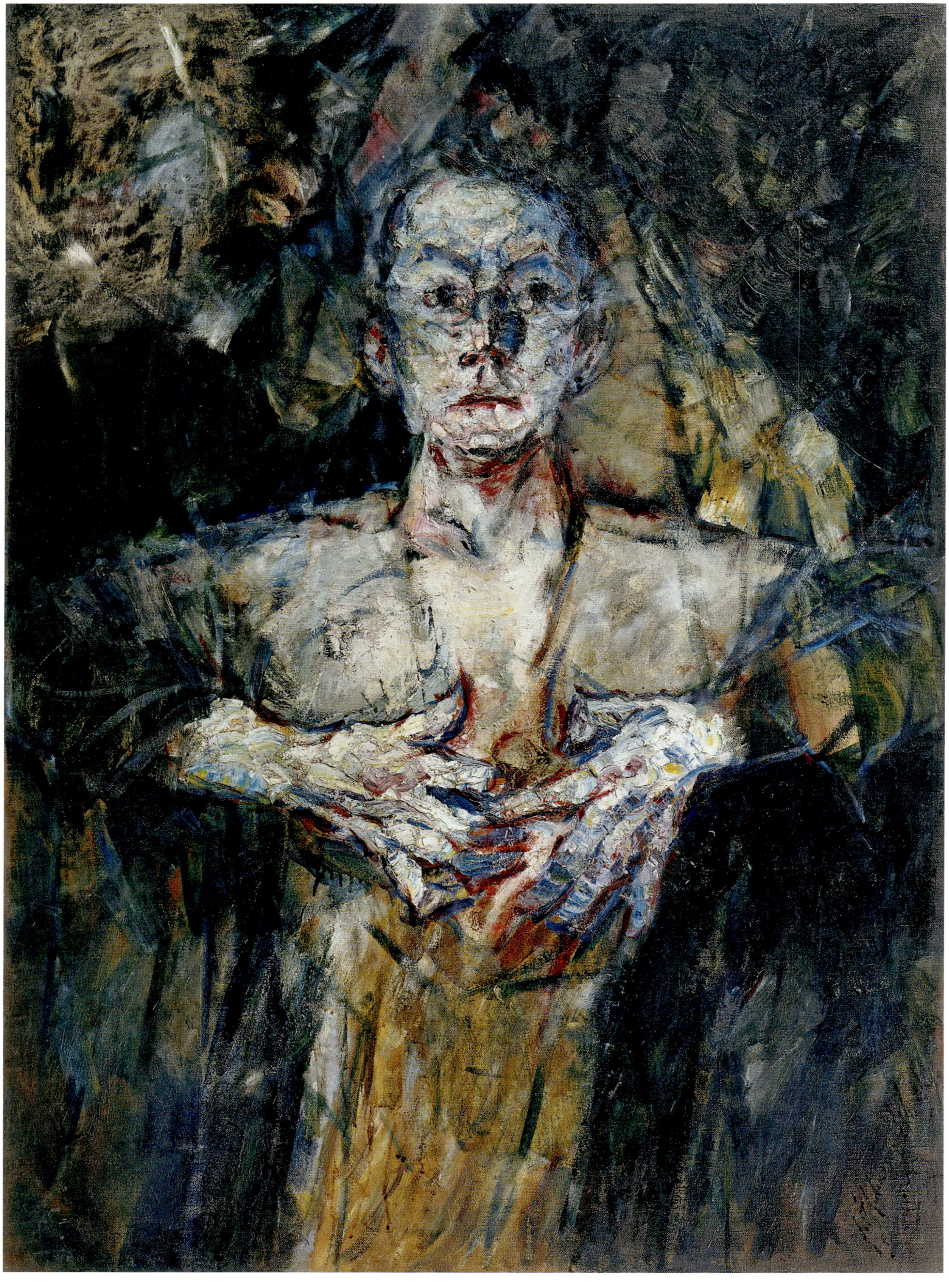

C1

Fritz Schwarz-Waldegg
Confession, 1920
Belvedere, Vienna

Anton Kolig ▸
Kneeling Narcissus, 1920
Belvedere, Vienna

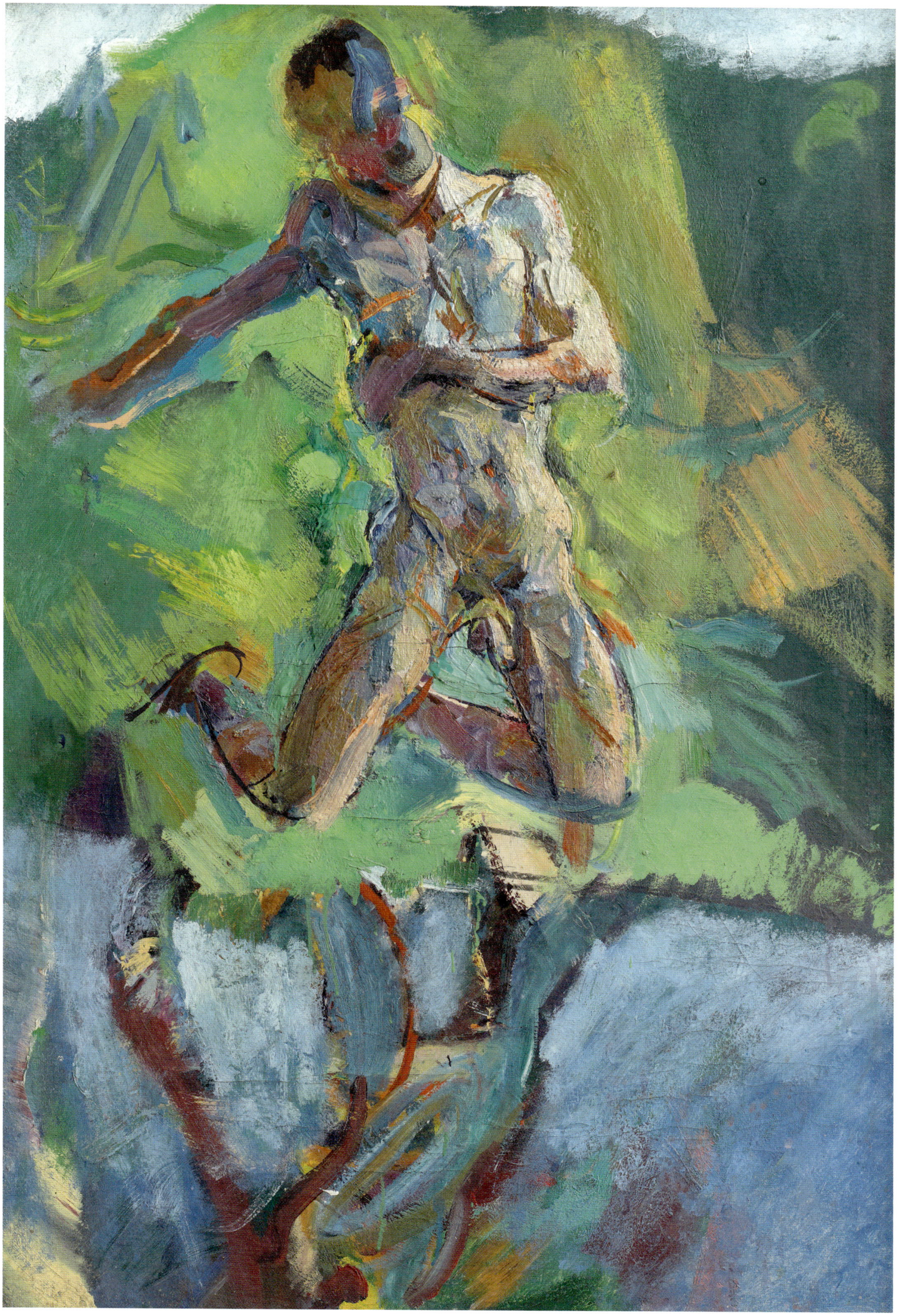

C1

Franz Metzner
Breakdown, 1919
Kunstforum Ostdeutsche
Galerie Regensburg

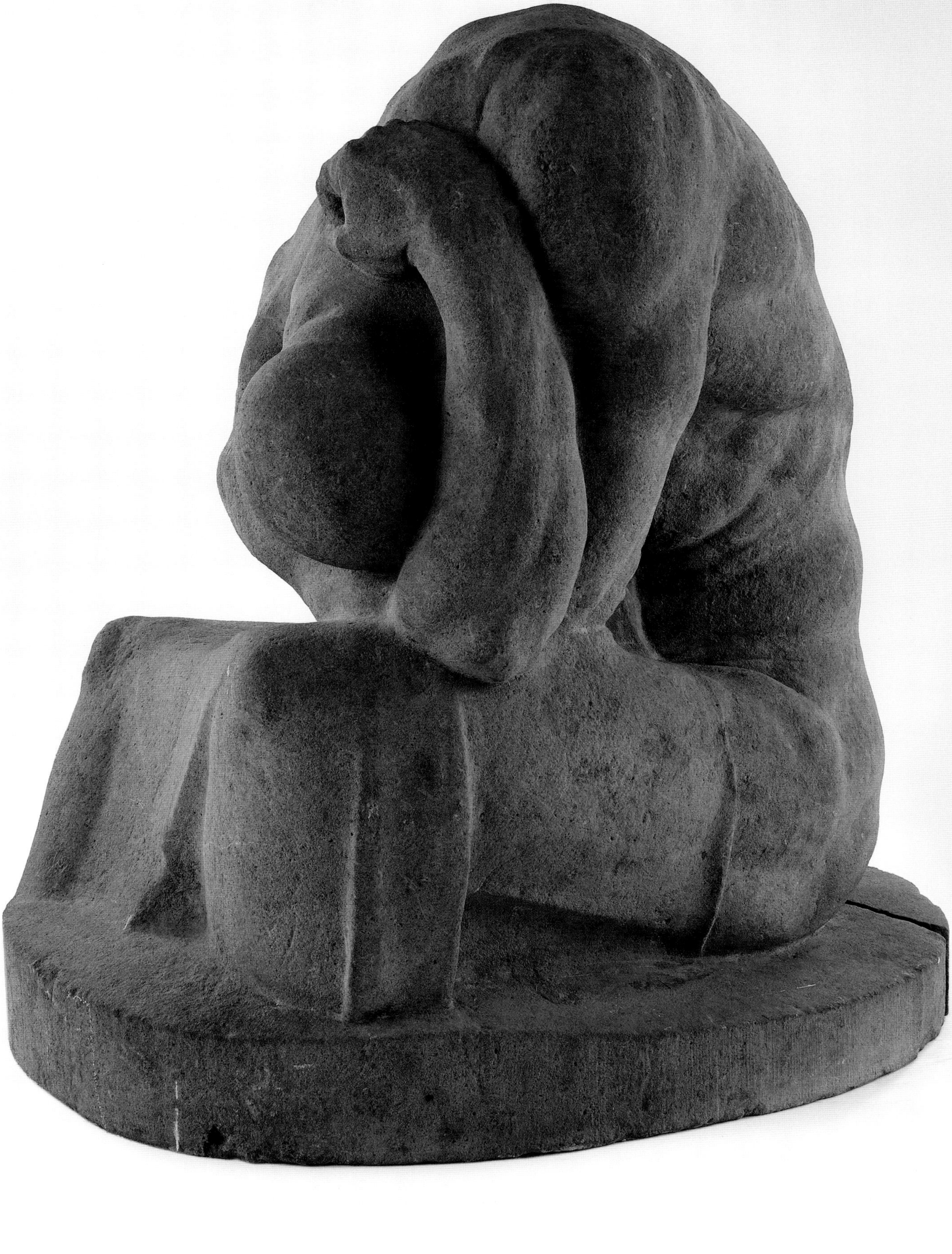

Anton Hanak
The Last Human (Ecce Homo), 1917–24
Belvedere, Vienna

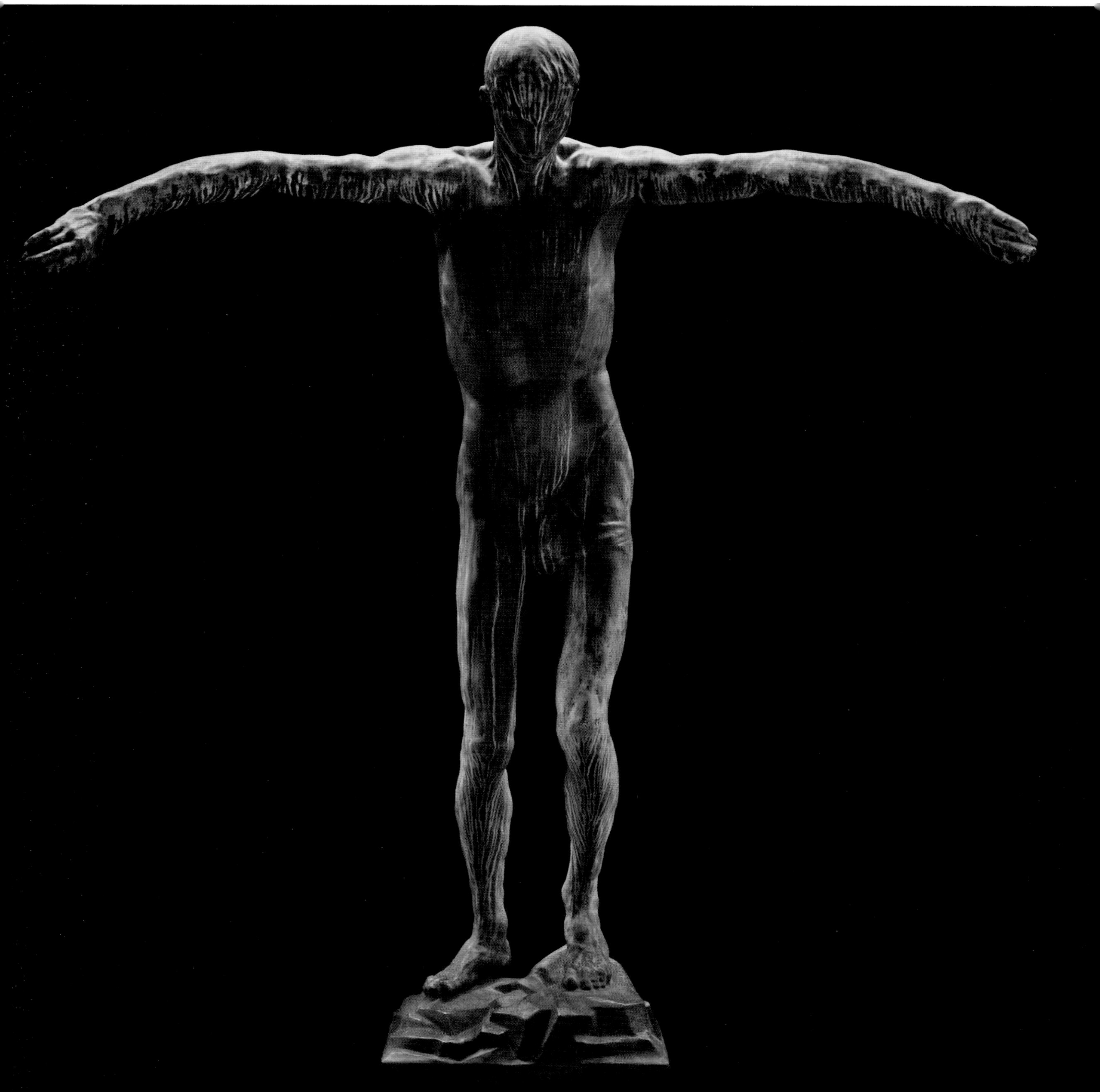

C1

Revolution and Rebirth

During the interwar years, avant-garde journals became active, dynamic platforms of art, placing all aspects of public and cultural life under scrutiny. They also functioned as international networks for artistic exchange. Journals like Austria's *MA,* Hungary's *Akasztott Ember, Egység,* and *Ék,* Romania's *Periszkop, Contimpuranul,* and *Integral,* Serbia's *Zenit* and *Út,* Slovenia's *Tank,* the Czech journals *Pásmo, Styl,* and *RED,* and Slovakia's *DAV* were produced in transnational collaboration by left-wing intellectuals such as Lajos Kassák, László Moholy-Nagy, Jaroslav Seifert, and Karel Teige. This kind of politically motivated artistic production, which is also reflected in poster designs of the time, documents the spirit of euphoria and revolution that dominated the various artistic circles of the 1920s. (MH)

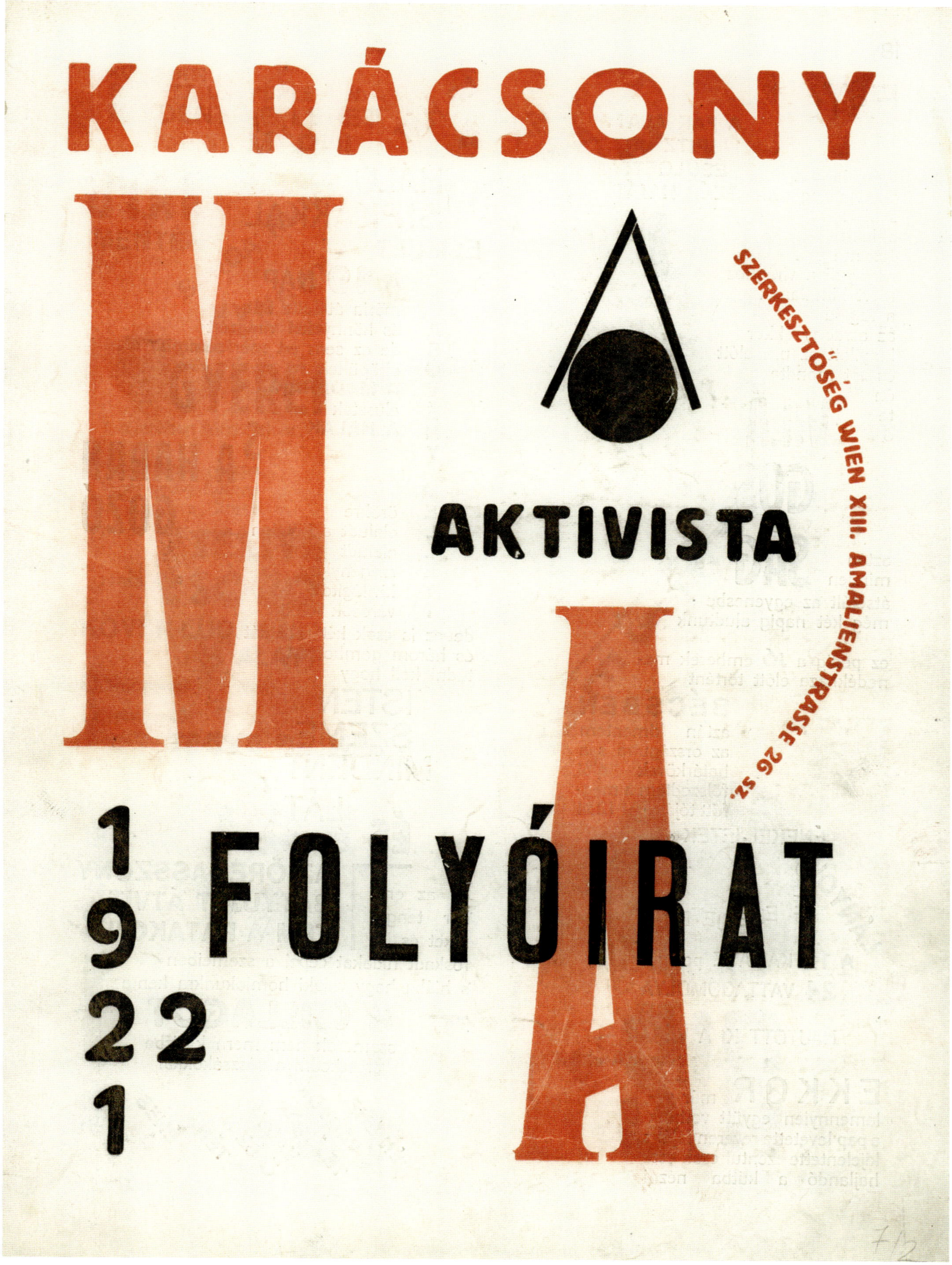

C2

Lajos Kassák (ed.)
MA, yr. 7, no. 2, Vienna, 1922
Petőfi Literary Museum—Kassák Museum, Budapest

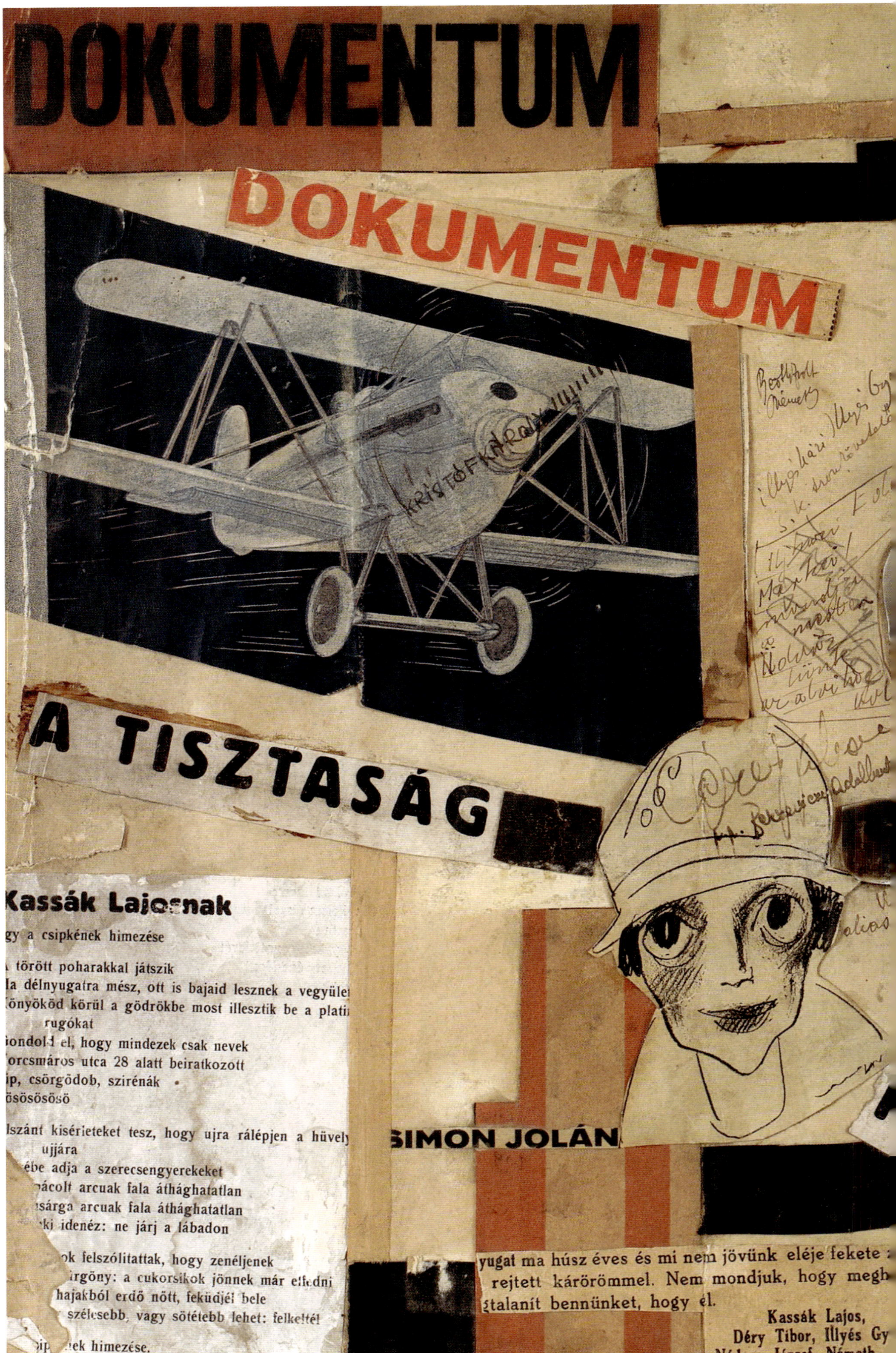

C2

Lajos Kassák
Fortieth Anniversary, 1927
Petőfi Literary Museum—Kassák Museum, Budapest

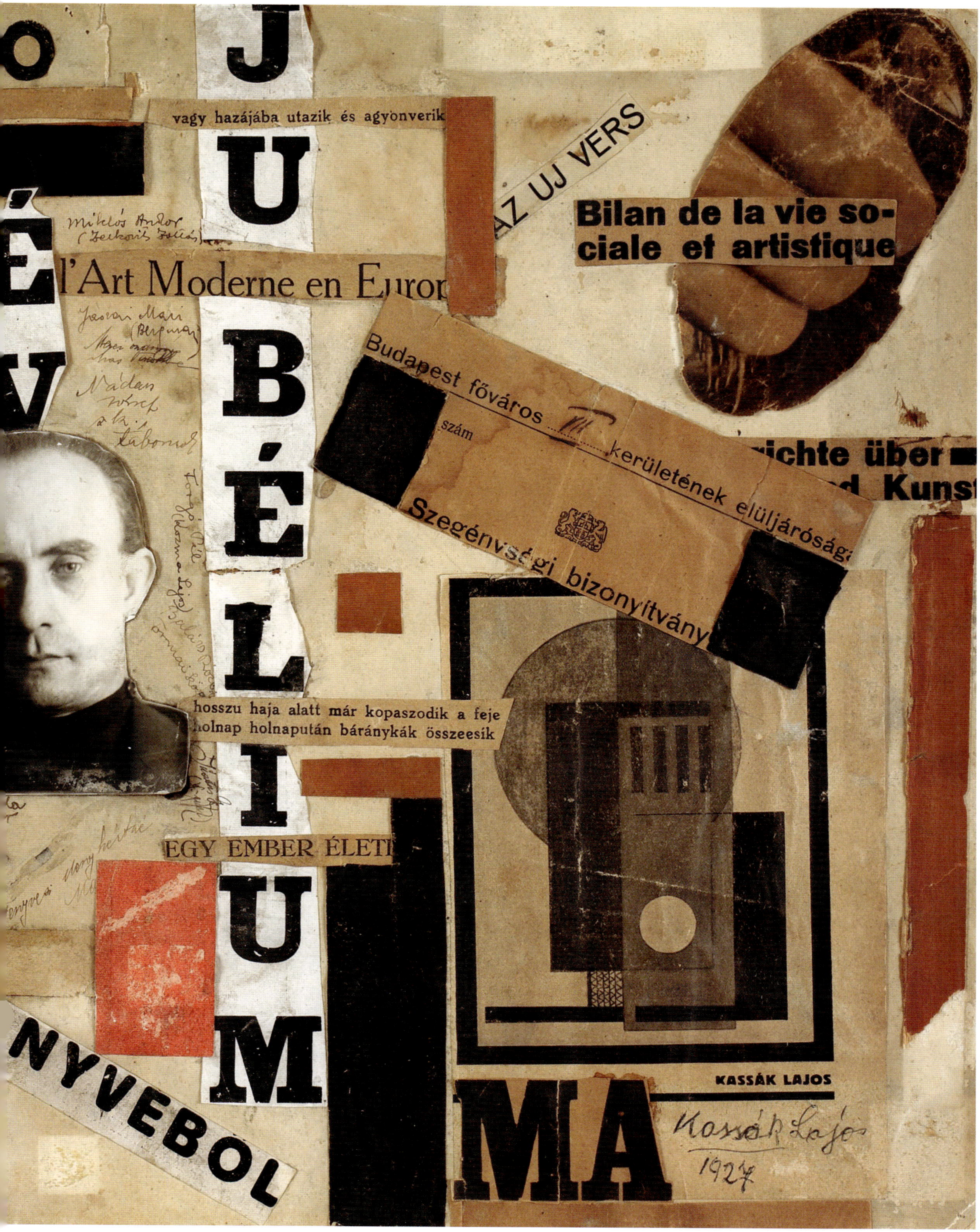
JUBÉLIUM
vagy hazájába utazik és agyonverik
AZ UJ VERS
Bilan de la vie sociale et artistique
l'Art Moderne en Europ
Budapest főváros
szám
kerületének elüljárósága
Szegénységi bizonyítvány
richte über
hosszu haja alatt már kopaszodik a feje
holnap holnapután báránykák összeesik
EGY EMBER ÉLETI
NYVEBOL
KASSÁK LAJOS
MA
Kassák Lajos
1927

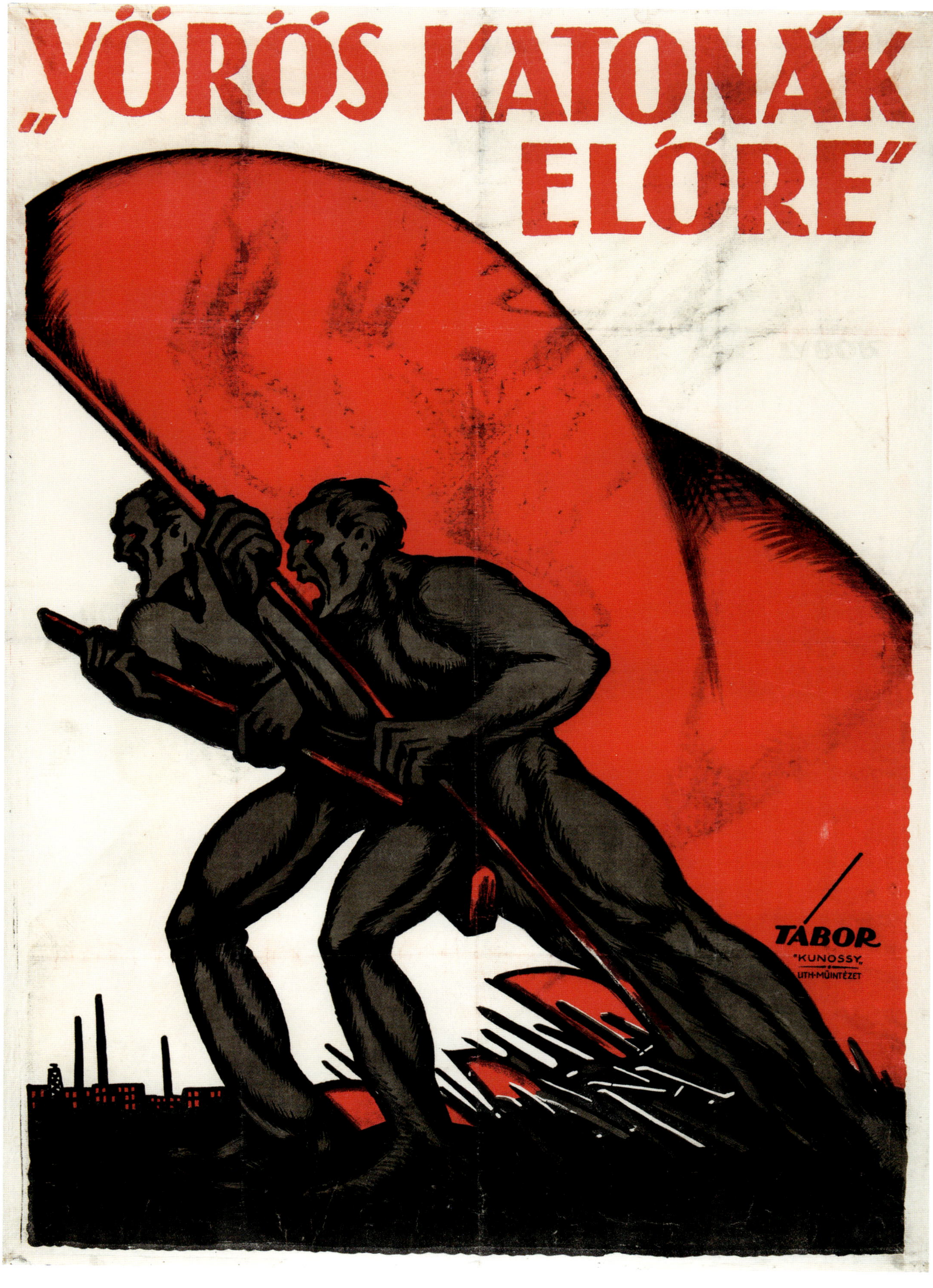

János Tábor
Red Soldiers Advance!, 1919
Museum of Fine Arts—
Hungarian National Gallery, Budapest

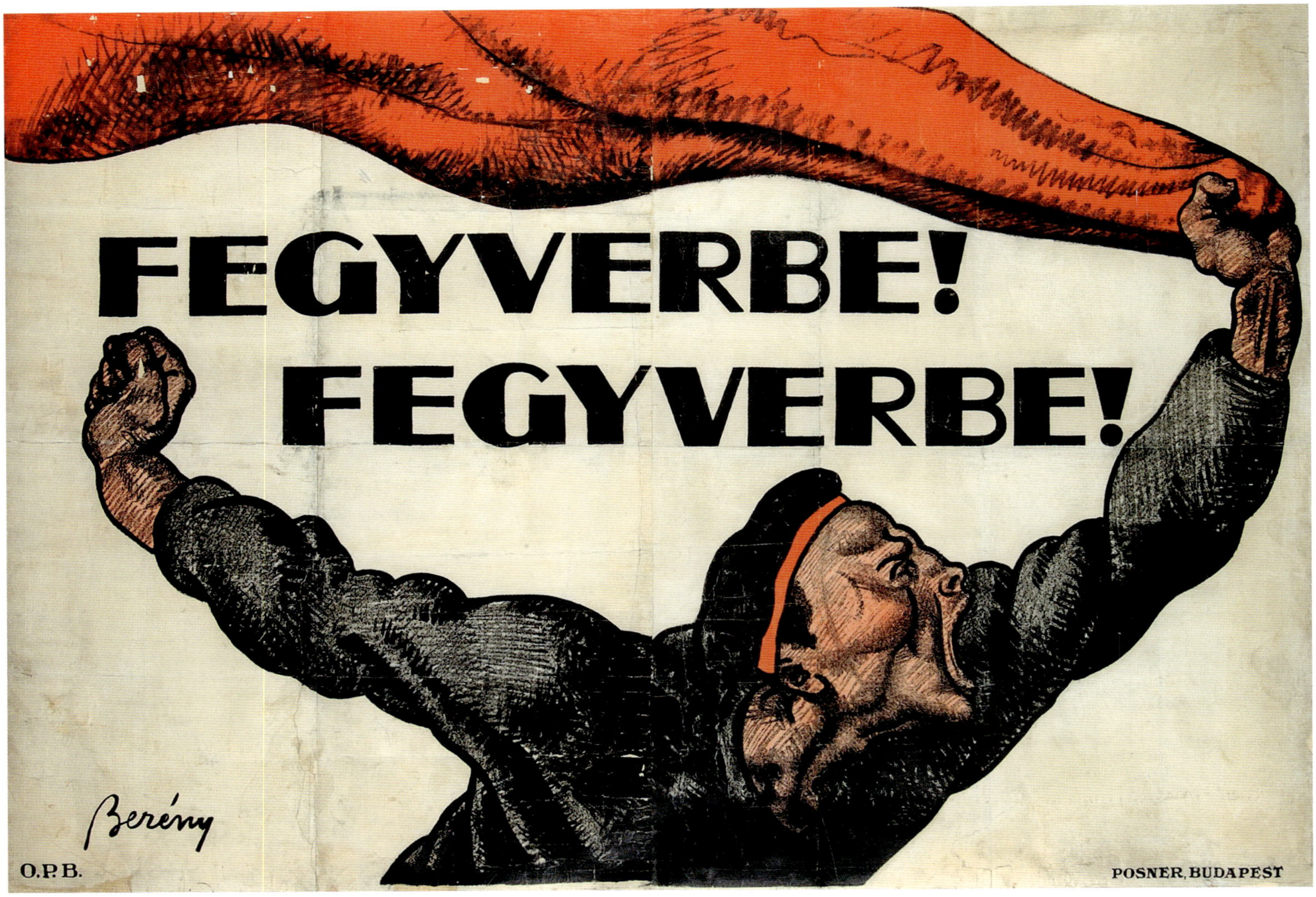

C2

Róbert Berény
To Arms! To Arms!, 1919
Museum of Fine Arts—
Hungarian National Gallery, Budapest

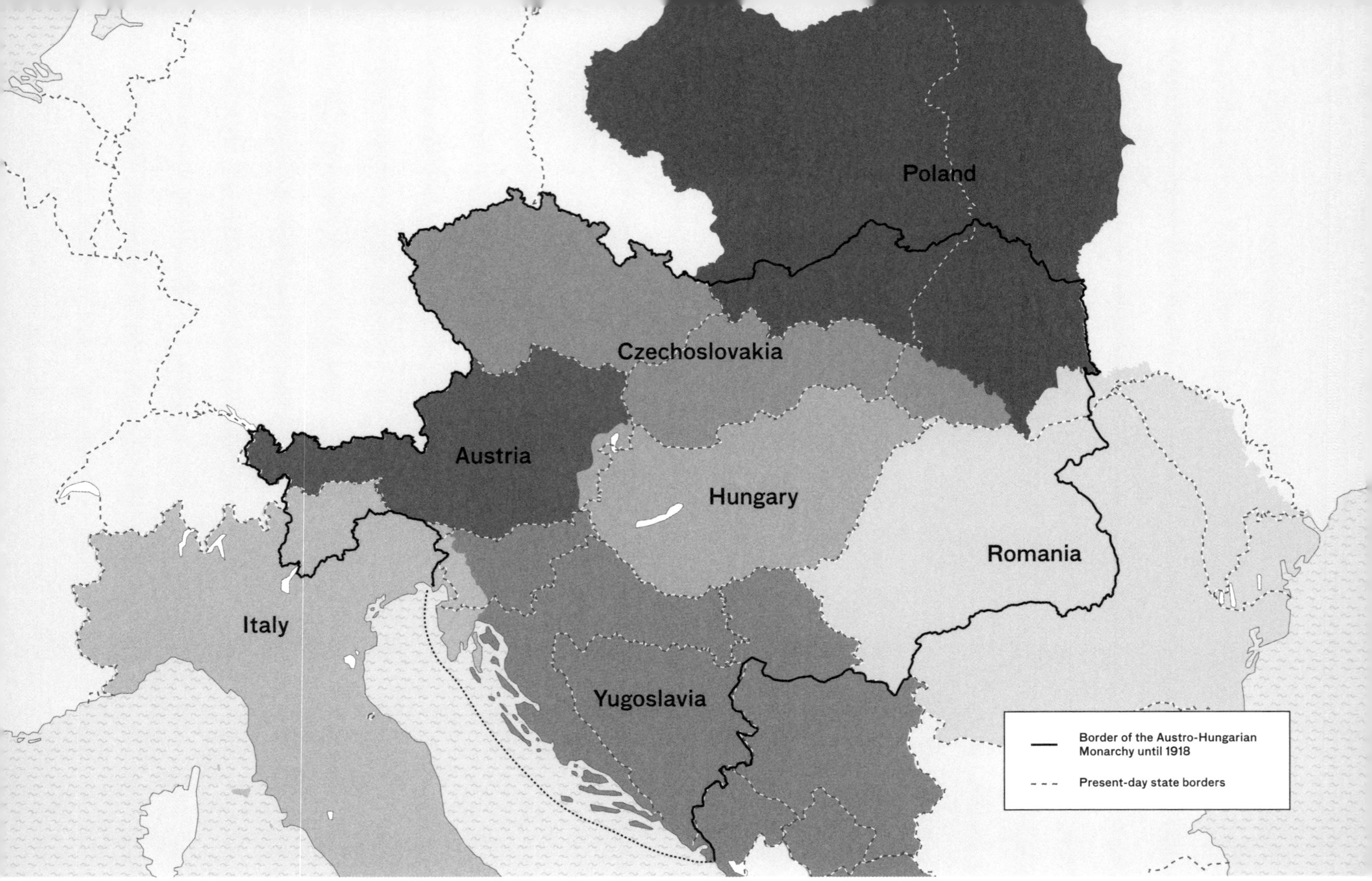

1919 The successor states
of the Austro-Hungarian Empire

nation—národ:

NÁROD, *m.* progenies, homines, populus, genus. ... *Riječ je upravo nom. act. prema glag. naroditi i znači ono, što se narodilo, a nalazi se i u drugim slav. jezicima, na pr. staroslov. i rus.* НАРОДЪ, češ. národ, *poļ.* narod. ...
d. narod *u političkom smislu, t.j. veliko mnoštvo ļudi istoga postańa i jezika. ...*

P. Budmani, *Rječnik hrvatskoga ili srpskoga jezika*, (Zagreb, 1891), p. 386–89.

nation—narod:

narod: 1. rod; ljudje istega rodu; svoj narod zatajiti; iz naroda za narod; gl. izrod; — 2. po novejšem: skupina ljudi, ki jih veže isto poreklo, isti jezik, ista kulturna in politična preteklost in usoda ter zavest te skupnosti; — gl. ljudstvo

Joža Glonar, *Slovar slovenskega jezika*, (Ljubljana, 1936), pp. 231–32

Croatian
Slovenian

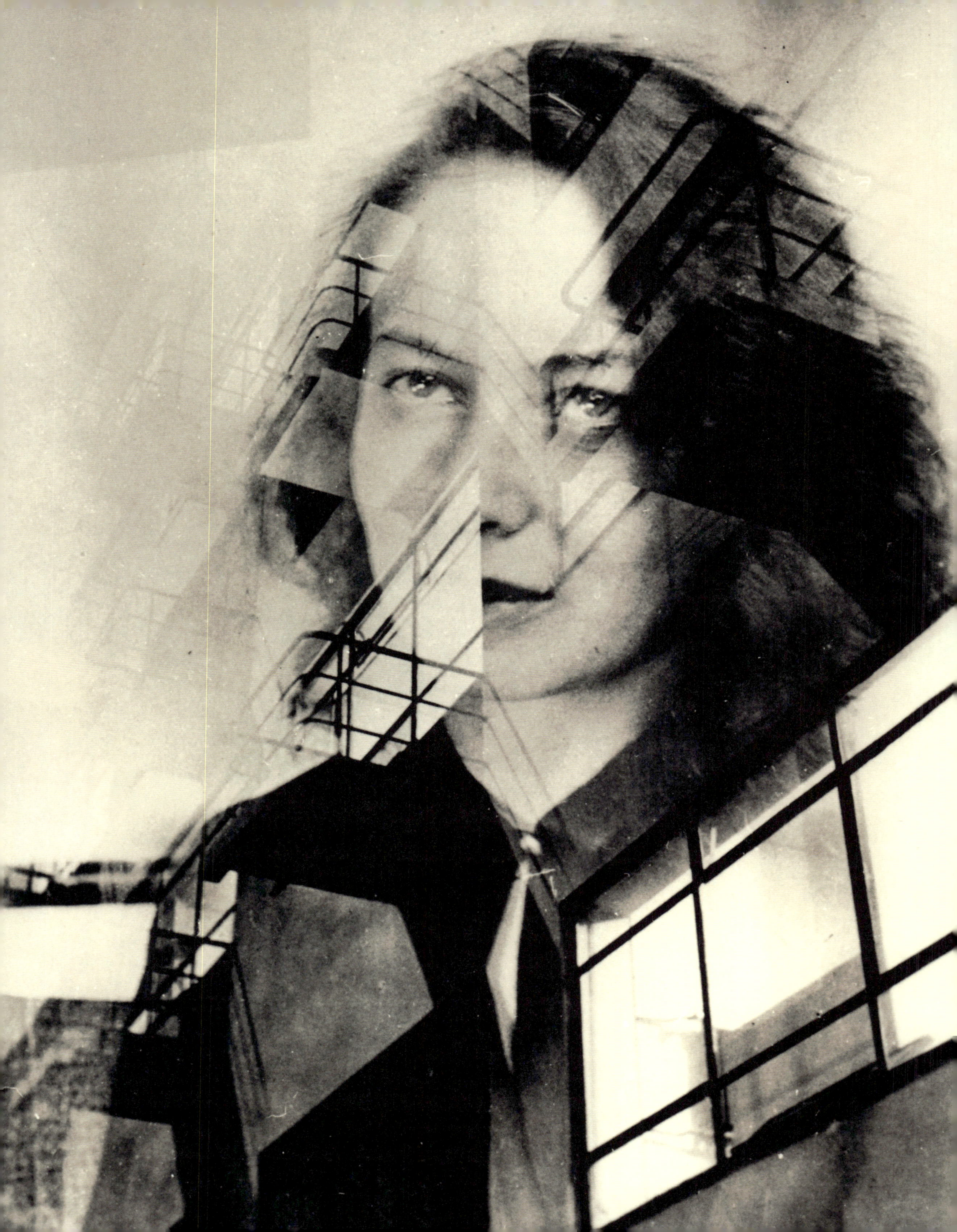

D Internationalist Art

Judit Káráz, *Otti Berger with the Bauhaus building in Dessau*, 1931 (detail), Private collection, Budapest, from the artist's estate

To the Bauhaus!

Éva Bajkay

The Bauhaus school (1919–1933) recruited talented young people from the neighboring countries through flyers, newspaper articles, and word of mouth. It subsequently became a magnet for young people from these industrially underdeveloped, politically "backward" countries. No longer content with traditional academic education, budding artists from the four nation-states that now constituted the former Austro-Hungarian Monarchy left for Weimar. Their common language was German and, as was usually the case in the Monarchy, their national identity was often mixed: they came from Hungarian, Danube-Swabian, South Slavic, and Jewish families. Most of them were born in the historic territory of Hungary, a country that had disintegrated into a series of small states after the First World War and, following the turmoil of the revolution, was now isolating itself. The Hungarian students at the Bauhaus were not political emigrants, like the left-wing intellectuals who had left Hungary for Vienna, Berlin, or Paris, but young people hoping for a more modern education abroad. In one of history's curious twists of fate, following a resolution by the Entente, Serbian troops occupied parts of the southern Hungarian county of Baranya from 1918 to 1921, causing six students from the region's Modernist "enclave" of Pécs to move on to the Bauhaus.[1]

In 1919, Walter Gropius, director of the Bauhaus and one of the pioneers of twentieth-century architecture, picked up the Jugendstil ideal of uniting arts and crafts and established a new, democratic school to match Germany's new democracy. He made it clear that, for him, all students—male and female—were equal, regardless of their nationality or religion. Compared with other institutions of higher education in Germany, the Bauhaus was more open to accepting teachers and students from abroad and, from an economic perspective, it was also more affordable. Poorer students were offered opportunities to earn their keep in the workshops, and the most talented students received scholarships (from Pécs, these were Marcel Breuer, Farkas Molnár, and Andor Weininger).

In this essay, I will focus primarily on teaching at the Bauhaus, the connections between the Bauhaus and Vienna, and the innovations by the Hungarians.

Throughout the nineteenth century, in the absence of suitable educational institutions at home, students from East-Central Europe continued to be attracted to the traditional academies in Vienna and Munich. In the early twentieth century, however, these academies came to be seen as outmoded. Moreover, with the dissolution of the Austro-Hungarian Monarchy, Vienna became a foreign city for graduates of schools from the successor states. Those eager for new experiences soon moved on to Weimar. The first group came to the Bauhaus from Vienna. New research is making it increasingly clear that the cosmopolitan, mathematics- and geometry-based art education that dominated in Vienna from the latter half of the nineteenth century had its roots in educational reforms, in particular relating to the teaching of drawing, that were inspired by Johann Friedrich Herbart's pedagogical theories.[2] The progressive education movement also found fertile ground in Vienna. The Galician Eugenie Schwarzwald, who had earned her doctorate in Zurich, was an advocate of a free and diverse approach to artistic practice, combined with activities that promoted personal development. Her school, the Schwarzwaldschule, opened in 1911 and its teachers included Adolf Loos, Oskar Kokoschka, and Arnold Schönberg. Gropius, too, was aware of the Schwarzwald School, which was receptive to the latest innovations in art.

The development of creativity was similarly promoted at the rhythm- and movement-focused art classes for children run by the Czech Franz Cizek, which were later continued by the Vienna School of Applied Arts. Here, at around 1920, this innovative approach to art education combined with a liberal use of the products of various "-isms" gave rise to Austrian Kineticism, which first and foremost operated as a new approach to art rather than an avant-garde movement. The most talented representatives of Kinetic art, Erika Giovanna Klien and My Ullmann, found success as teachers and in abstract painting, design, and theater.

The efforts of KURI's members contributed to major changes that marked a turning point in the history of the Bauhaus and the start of its second period, in which the unity of art and technology was promoted and Gropius turned away from Itten, appointing Moholy-Nagy in his stead, who understood the school's new ambitions and was able to drive them forward.

The abstract painter Johannes Itten ran a private art school in Vienna along similar lines. Whether Itten had any contact with the School of Applied Arts—and, if so, in what form—remains unknown. In any case, Gropius is likely to have become acquainted with the fruits of Cizek's teaching in the 1910s at his students' graduation shows. Nevertheless, in 1919, he opted for Itten, appointing him to the

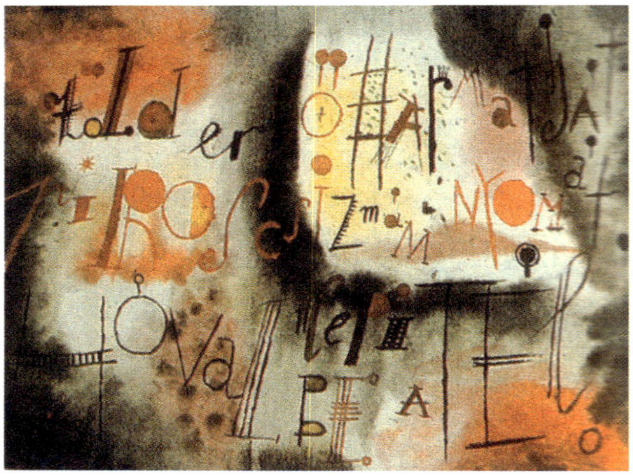

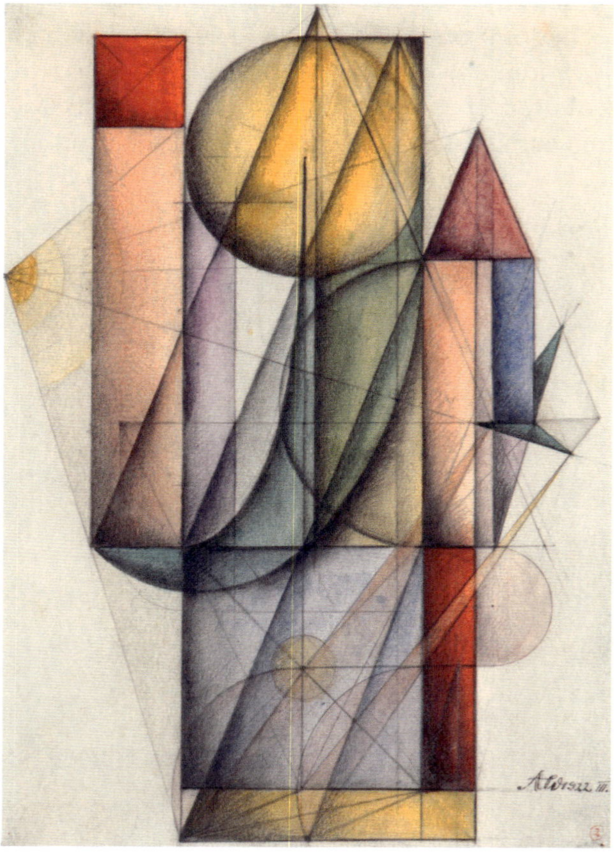

Fig. 1
Marcel Breuer
"Zöld erdő harmatja" (Dew of the Green Forest), From *Staatliches Bauhaus in Weimar 1919–1923*, Weimar/ Munich, 1923

Fig. 2
Andor Weininger
Kuri 2, 1922
Museum Ulm

Bauhaus. Until 1923, the foundations of the Bauhaus approach to education were therefore determined by Itten's progressive education theories.[3]

At his private art school in Vienna, which he ran from 1916 until 1919, Itten advocated the unity of intellectual, aesthetic, practical, and physical education and the free development of inherent talents. His teaching was largely based on his own training in Stuttgart under the Moravian Adolf Hölzel, a member of the Viennese Secession and the Klimt Group. Gropius knew Itten well, having met him at the salon of the composer Gustav Mahler's widow, Alma Mahler, whom Gropius went on to marry in 1915. He was therefore quite familiar with the protagonists of Viennese Modernism. He would not only have attended Itten's exhibitions at Galerie Der Sturm in Berlin—where he met most of the Bauhaus teachers, including Lyonel Feininger and Paul Klee—he also knew him from Vienna, where, in May 1919, the modern Austrian architect Adolf Loos organized the first exhibition of Itten's non-figurative works in the rooms of the Freie Bewegung artists' association. Afterwards, Gropius invited Itten to lead the Bauhaus preliminary course and run the majority of its workshops as Master of Form.

The free development of the students' inherent talents was encouraged through experimentation with elementary colors and forms, materials, textures, movement, dynamics, and contrasts, interfused with the teachings of the biocentric Mazdaznan movement, which based its eccentric philosophy on what was claimed to be ancient wisdom from Persia. Not many of the Hungarians studying at the Bauhaus followed the ideas of the Mazdaznan sect, perhaps with the exception of Gyula Pap, but the spontaneous expression of emotions was evident in most of the students' works displayed at the 1922 end-of-term exhibition. At this show, the Hungarian students, headed by Breuer with his formidable furniture and masterful, multihued watercolors (fig. 1), contributed some of the best works.[4] Breuer had initially enrolled at the Vienna Academy of Fine Arts. Yet, following the advice of the Pécs architect Alfréd Forbát, he swiftly moved on to Weimar, where Forbát was working for Gropius. Once there, the two were able to attract other Pécs-based artists to the Bauhaus, such as Farkas Molnár, Henrik Stefán, Hugo Johan, and Andor Weininger, all of whom had already exhibited successfully in Pécs.

Consequently, the cradle of the Bauhaus was in Vienna, as it was from here that twenty students of various nationalities followed Itten to Weimar. Among them we find the Hungarian Margit Téry from Transylvania, who went on to marry the Austrian writer and aesthete Bruno Adler, editor of the publication *Utopia: Dokumente der Wirklichkeit*, which is associated with the early Bauhaus. Téry worked as a graphic designer for the series, as did Friedl Dicker, who had started her career under Cizek and

Itten.[5] The students followed in Itten's footsteps and became educators themselves: Margit Téry taught from 1923 to 1926 in Carlsbad, Gyula Pap from 1927 to 1933 at the Itten School in Berlin, and Dicker from 1934 to 1938 in Prague. Later, she gave drawing lessons to children in the Theresienstadt ghetto. When Itten left the Bauhaus in 1923, many of his students left too. From 1926 to 1931, Dicker and Franz Singer continued the course set at the Bauhaus in the architecture, interiors, furniture designs, paintings, and applied arts they produced at their studio in Vienna. The Austrian graphic artist and set designer Georg Teltscher, who had studied under Cizek in Vienna and from 1921 under Itten at the Bauhaus, had an eventful life that took him from Germany to Nigeria and London. In 1922 he was a member of the Constructivist KURI group in Weimar; in 1923 he returned to Vienna to work in avant-garde theater and graphic art.

Another Austrian, Herbert Bayer, achieved global fame as a graphic designer, typographer, painter, and "art director for advertising in the interwar years."[6] He and his Hungarian friend Marcel Breuer,[7] renowned for his furniture designs at the Bauhaus and, later, as an

The Hungarians were a driving force behind many of the Bauhaus innovations. In 1924, Molnár, Breuer, and Muche emerged as campaigners for an architecture department.

architect in the USA, count among Itten's most high-profile students in Weimar. From 1925, both played vital roles as junior Bauhaus Masters in helping to modernize teaching methods to bring them in line with the times and by procuring orders from big industry for the Bauhaus, which by then had moved to Dessau. Under Breuer's leadership, the Bauhaus furniture workshop developed tubular steel furniture in a groundbreaking new design suitable for mass production. Bayer, meanwhile, as head of printing and advertising, introduced innovations in typography, such as all-lowercase typefaces, and the adoption of the German DIN standard.

In the early days, one of the defining characteristics of the Bauhaus—the combination of artistic and practical education—was shown to its best advantage in the graphic printing workshop, where Hungarian artists produced a number of significant works, from Breuer's expressive woodcuts on biblical themes to Moholy-Nagy's constructive linocuts. The first portfolio to be printed there, entitled *Italia 921*, was designed by the Hungarian students Farkas Molnár and Henrik Stefán. Based on drawings from their study trip to Italy, they developed a series of expressive, Cubism-inspired lithographs, in which they departed from the geometric compositions of their workshop leader Feininger and by the German artists, who had also traveled to Italy.

Discussions aimed at changing Itten's Bauhaus program had already begun in 1922 and received considerable support from the foreign parties. The renowned Dutch Constructivist Theo van Doesburg had moved to Weimar in spring 1921 to establish an international De Stijl network.[8] While there, he continued to publish the journal *De Stijl* and held public lectures and seminars on De Stijl in his apartment. His reductive, universal, objective, cosmopolitan approach, predominantly based on primary colors and rectangular (black) lines, was worlds away from Itten's mystical subjectivism. Doesburg's Constructivist endeavors proved attractive to many members of the Bauhaus. Among his followers, alongside the first German De Stijl group, was an informal, multinational circle that went by the name of KURI, led by the Hungarians from Pécs. The group's rationalism drew its members toward Doesburg rather than Itten. Sándor Bortnyik's arrival further expanded the circle of Hungarians in Weimar. An independent painter and graphic artist, Bortnyik followed developments at the Bauhaus with a certain ironic detachment (*The New Adam, The New Eve*), although he later continued its ideas at his own private art school in Budapest.

Farkas Molnár had likewise come to Weimar via Vienna. He contributed to the Hungarian journal *MA*, then being published in Vienna, and played an important role as mediator between Gropius and Doesburg. It was Molnár who established the international KURI group from the undersigners of the "Constructive, Utilitarian, Rational, International" manifesto. Topping the list of signatures were his friends from Pécs: Henrik Stefán, Hugó Johann, and Andor Weininger, followed by Kurt Schmidt, Otto Umbehr, Paul Häberer, Walter Menzel, Walter Herzger, Franz Frahm-Hessler, and Peter Keler from Germany; Heinrich Koch and R. Kossnik from Czechoslovakia; Georg Teltscher from Austria; Rudolf Paris from Estonia; Semih (Sefai Temel) Rüstem from Turkey; and the Croatian architect Lajos Cacinovic (Tarai), who had remained in Pécs. Most of them were students in the Bauhaus mural painting workshop, but they also attended Doesburg's seminars, where Weininger worked as an assistant. Weininger's works were at their most beautiful in the 1920s—and later, in the 1960s infused with nostalgia for De Stijl—enriched with soft watercolors and form variations (fig. 2).[9]

The members of the international KURI group took a universal, rationalistic approach that went beyond Doesburg's theories, i.e. after the analysis of historical form

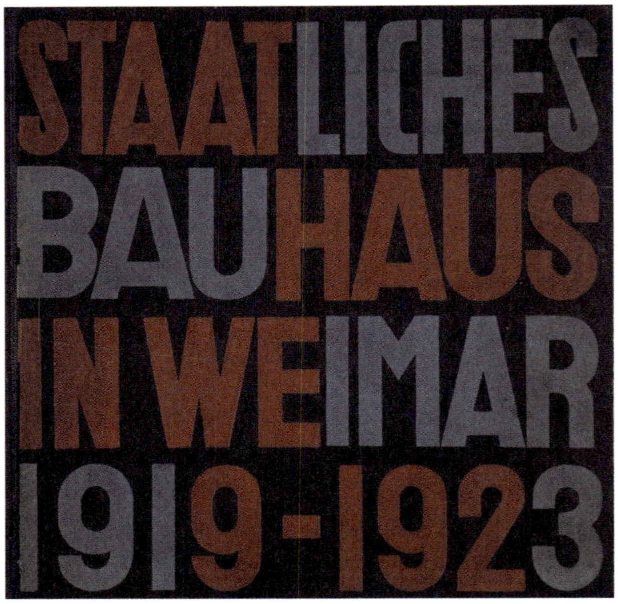

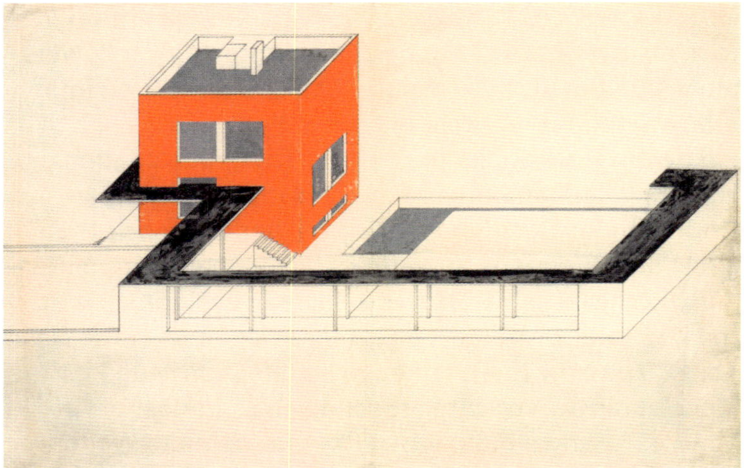

they didn't stop to dwell on the basic principles that built on geometric pictorial structure. They declared the "-isms" outmoded and, in place of analysis, they proclaimed a new synthesis of the arts under the primacy of architecture. In late 1922, they proposed an evolution of the 1919 *Bauhaus Manifesto* along constructive lines and sought to create order from chaos through the utopian vision of building a new world, as was fashionable at the time. They stepped from the two-dimensional plane into three-dimensional space, from individual paintings to international architecture.[10] Following the example of the Russian and Dutch Constructivists, they sought to unite the achievements of art and technology, as was proposed at the Congress of International Progressive Artists in Düsseldorf in May 1922 and the Congress of the Constructivists and Dadaists in September in Weimar under Doesburg and El Lissitzky. Also in attendance at the Weimar congress was the Hungarian László Moholy-Nagy, who had risen to fame in Berlin, and his wife, the Prague photographer and editor Lucia Schulz.

The efforts of KURI's members contributed to major changes that marked a turning point in the history of the Bauhaus and the start of its second period, in which the unity of art and technology was promoted and Gropius turned away from Itten, appointing Moholy-Nagy in his stead, who understood the school's new ambitions and was able to drive them forward. Moholy-Nagy had published his manifesto *The Dynamic-Constructive System of Forces* in December 1922 in the magazine *Der Sturm*. In February 1923, he once again exhibited at the Galerie Der Sturm, where he was able to demonstrate the impressive results of this theoretical approach as a painter, graphic artist, and constructor. Moholy-Nagy, together with Josef Albers, used his rational, ideology-free formal ideas to reorganize the experimentation with material and space that formed part of the Bauhaus preliminary course.

A further sore point was the teaching of architecture, which was still missing even after the third year of the Bauhaus school's existence. Only the architectural studio run by Gropius and Adolf Meyer was actively practicing in this field and was also counting some Hungarians among its staff. In 1920, these were joined by Alfréd Forbát, who had completed his studies in Budapest and Munich. He was instrumental in the innovative design of the Bauhaus Siedlung, a housing development consisting of a flexible modular system based on cubic components. Through Forbát, Farkas Molnár also joined Gropius's studio (1922–1924). The two Hungarians wanted to take this concept further and looked to Doesburg for inspiration. Showing great foresight, Gropius encouraged them to put their ideas into practice and to integrate the De Stijl elements into the Bauhaus, rather than risking a rift; in recognition of their achievements he displayed their work at the architectural exhibition in Weimar in 1922.

Fig. 3
Herbert Bayer
Front cover of the *Staatliches Bauhaus in Weimar 1919–1923* catalogue, Weimar/Munich, 1923

Fig. 4
Farkas Molnár
Design for the *Red Cube*, 1922/23
German Architecture Museum, Frankfurt am Main

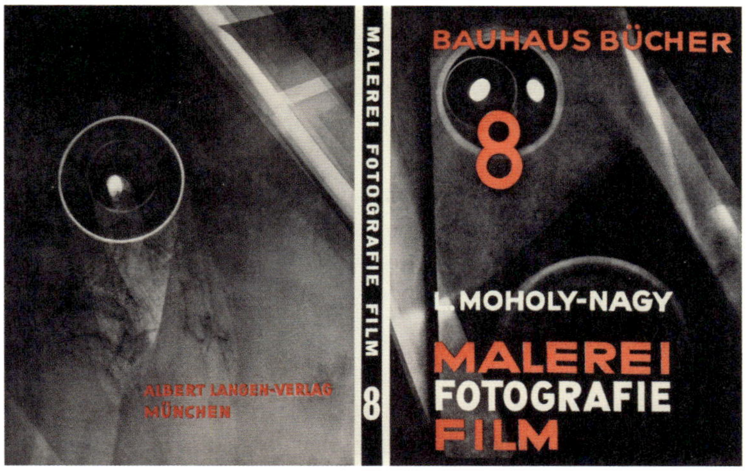

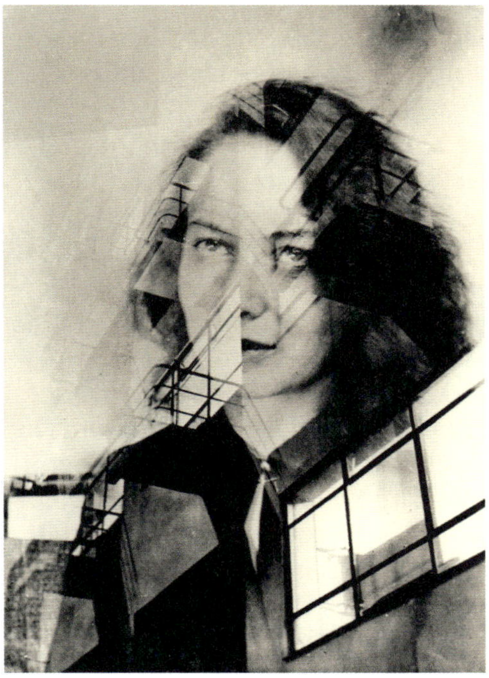

Fig. 5
Front cover of *Malerei, Fotografie, Film (Painting, Photography, Film)* by László Moholy-Nagy, Bauhaus Books Vol. 8, Munich, 1925

Fig. 6
Judit Kárász
Otti Berger with the Bauhaus building in Dessau, 1931
Private collection, Budapest, from the artist's estate

The Hungarians were represented in even greater force at the first major Bauhaus exhibition in 1923, which this time was co-organized by the innovative, multitalented Moholy-Nagy, who was referred to as the "minister president" of the Bauhaus.[11] He created the layout for the exhibition catalogue, which came in a unique square format with a new typography and included many works by Hungarian students. The cover design, featuring large capital letters in blue and red, was the work of Herbert Bayer (fig. 3). The preparations for the exhibition were overseen by Georg Muche. Although a painter, he drew up the designs for the functionalist Haus Am Horn prototype family home, which was built for the exhibition. The interior in three of its rooms bore Marcel Breuer's handwriting, and the house was managed by Molnár as a live-in caretaker. The Hungarians played a major role in both the art and the architectural exhibition, even though in the latter the majority of participants were Czech. Also on show was Molnár's alternative design for the prototype home, known as the *Red Cube,* which he described as "the universal KURI" (fig. 4). This was reflected in the asymmetrical rhythm of the windows as well as the design of the building's surroundings in a practical continuation of De Stijl principles, combined with Bauhaus practice. On a postcard in 1923, Weininger depicted the Bauhaus school in the shape of the red cube, which had become a symbol of its Constructivist reform, while underscoring the institution's international character by adding the flags of the various different nations.

Part of the *Gesamtkunstwerk* presentation of 1923 was a theatrical performance by the students, entitled the *Mechanical Cabaret*. The Germans Kurt Schmidt and Friedrich Wilhelm Bogler and the Austrian Georg Teltscher presented an abstract synthesis of form and color, the *Mechanical Ballet*—with geometrical figures as "dancers"—which they and other artists, including Fernand Léger and Moholy-Nagy, were then also invited to show at the *International Exhibition of New Theater Technology* in Vienna in 1924.[12] Presumably in connection with this, from 1923 onwards, Weininger began to develop a utopian play entitled *Mechanical Stage Revue (Phase I–III)*, using "moving surfaces, rotating scenery, horizontal and vertical stripes. Rotating circles. Puppets, flashing lights + noise music" (p. 239). His aim was to create the moving mechanical image the KURI group aspired to in the form of a mechanized performance with abstract moving objects rather than actors.

The foreigners also made their mark in organizing the international collective. The Bauhaus orchestra, led by Weininger, consisted mainly of KURI members. From 1924 onwards, the Estonian Rudolf Paris, the Czech Heinrich Koch, and the German Hans Hoffmann had great success with their improvised musical blend of folk music from various nations and the popular jazz sounds of 1920s urban culture. Gropius valued Weininger's skill at fostering team spirit and, in 1925, called him to Dessau to offer him a full-time position.

The Hungarians were therefore a driving force behind many of the Bauhaus innovations. In 1924, Molnár, Breuer, and Muche emerged as campaigners for an architecture department,[13] Breuer calling their proposal a "palace revolution." However, the Bauhaus leadership dismissed it as little more than a bold plan put together by inexperienced youngsters. The protesters developed designs for utopian townhouses and functionalist apartment buildings, declaring that: "The current financial weakness of Central European states can only pose a temporary obstacle to us; it cannot destroy the actuality of constructive ideas. Implementation and dissemination of our thoughts, incidentally, runs parallel to the same efforts in the West."[14] The two Hungarians left Weimar in 1925. Molnár returned to Hungary, studied architecture in Budapest and went on to design residential houses for the country's new intellectual class. He joined the International Congress of Modern Architecture (CIAM) as an outlet for his ideas and writings. Breuer initially went to Paris before returning to the Bauhaus, by then in Dessau, to teach as a junior Master. In addition to his innovative designs for tubular steel furniture, he also launched an architectural career, which reached its peak in the USA in 1941 with the founding of his own architectural practice.

Between 1923 and 1928, the painter and constructor László Moholy-Nagy was the most influential of the Hungarians, not just as head of the preliminary course and the metal workshop, but also in everything from typography to theater, from writing topical articles to his editorial activities. He also presented his experiments in photography and film long before either was being taught at the Bauhaus.[15] He and Gropius worked together on the famous Bauhaus book series, in which they—in characteristic openness to new ideas—also published the theories of Theo van Doesburg, Piet Mondrian, and Kazimir Malevich, as well as works by their students, but above all by the Bauhaus Masters, including two volumes by Moholy-Nagy: *Malerei, Fotografie, Film (Painting, Photography, Film)* (1925, fig. 5) and *Von Material zur Architektur (The New Vision: From Material to Architecture)* (1929), outlining his pedagogical creed, which remains relevant to this day. Having risen up the Bauhaus ranks to become Masters, Moholy-Nagy, Marcel Breuer, Andor Weininger, Herbert Bayer, and others left the school in 1928, coinciding with the end of the Gropius era. Moholy-Nagy continued his teaching activities in Chicago from 1937.

Another Hungarian, Ernő (Ernst) Kállai, took over the role of editor and teacher of theory at the Bauhaus in 1928. From 1920, he had worked as a journalist in Berlin, and the new Bauhaus director Hannes Meyer appointed him editor-in-chief of the *Bauhaus Zeitschrift für Gestaltung* (Bauhaus Journal for Design), his remit being to showcase Bauhaus products and technological innovations (e.g. by Bayer, Moholy-Nagy, Breuer, Weininger, and others) aimed at satisfying the demands of modern society and the new industrial age.

During the economic crisis, the number of women at the Bauhaus dropped to one third of its previous level; the number of women from abroad decreased to one quarter. Otti Berger from the Hungarian region of Southern Baranya was one of them, receiving her Bauhaus Diploma at the weaving workshop in 1930. She filed patents for her handwoven patterns and textiles made from experimental materials, produced pattern books, wrote articles, and taught at the weaving workshop in 1931 and 1932. From 1932, she worked in Berlin and then in London. Later she returned to her home country, which by then was already part of Yugoslavia. Her innovative, still little-known career tragically ended in Auschwitz.

The number of Hungarian women in the photography class, which was finally established in 1929, was remarkable: Etel Fodor came from Pécs, Judit Kárász from Szeged, Irén Blüh from Vágbeszterce (now Považská Bystrica in Slovakia and at the time already part of Czechoslovakia). Initially, they took photographs of life at the Bauhaus, informed by the "New Vision" principles championed by Moholy-Nagy, or produced portraits (fig. 6) and photos of materials and textures in line with the new, objective approach of the workshop leader Walter Peterhans. The increasing left-wing politicization of the students gave rise to a new social sensitivity; their snapshots of life in Berlin or in their home countries are remarkable in their adventurous framing and surprising details.

The Bauhaus teaching continued to exert an influence in the countries of the former Austro-Hungarian Empire. Some of the most successful examples were Bortnyik's private school for advertising design in Budapest (1928–1938)—known as *műhely* (workshop) or *magyar bauhaus* (the Hungarian Bauhaus), where Victor Vasarely was a student—and the Bratislava School of Arts and Crafts (ŠUR, 1928–1938). The latter became affiliated with the Bauhaus Dessau at the invitation of Moholy-Nagy, Kállai, Hannes Meyer, Karel Teige from Prague, and others. The Slovak school followed the tradition of Cizek in Vienna by offering art classes for children, designed to foster their inherent talent.

1 Cf. *Von Kunst zu Leben. Die Ungarn am Bauhaus*, ed. Eva Bajkay, exh. cat., Janus Pannonius Múzeum, Pécs; Bauhaus-Archiv Berlin (Pécs, 2010); *Das Bauhaus im Osten: Slowakische und tschechische Avantgarde 1928–1939*, ed. Susanne Anna, exh. cat., Museum Morsbroich, Morsbroich Castle; Städtisches Museum Zwickau; Bauhaus Dessau Foundation (Stuttgart, 1997).
2 Cf. *Klimt, Kupka, Picasso and Others: Cubism—Constructivism—Form Art*, eds. Agnes Husslein-Arco and Alexander Klee, exh. cat., Belvedere, Vienna (Munich/London/New York, 2016).
3 Rainer Wick, "Ästhetische Erziehung als Ganzheitserziehung," in *Johannes Itten*, eds. Hans Christoph von Tavel/Josef Helfenstein, exh. cat., Kunstmuseum Bern (Bern, 1984) pp. 105–28.
4 *Pécsi Lapok*, July 23, 1922.
5 *Bauhaus in Wien. Franz Singer. Friedl Dicker*, eds. Georg Schrom and Stefanie Trauttmansdorff, exh. cat., University of Applied Arts Vienna (Vienna, 1988).
6 *Ahoi Herbert! Bayer und die Moderne*, eds. Elisabeth Novak-Thaller and Bernhard Widder, exh. cat., Lentos Kunstmuseum, Linz (Linz, 2009).
7 *Marcel Breuer. Design und Architektur*, ed. Matthias Remmele, exh. cat., Vitra Design Museum, Weil am Rhein (Weil am Rhein, 2003).
8 Cf. Mariann Gergely, "De Stijl kontra Bauhaus und die Rolle der Ungarn in der konstruktivistischen Wende des Bauhauses," in Bajkay 2010 (see note 1), pp. 174–89.
9 *Andor Weininger: Von Weimar nach New York*, ed. Michael Siebenbrodt, exh. cat., Kunstsammlungen zu Weimar (Weimar, 2000).
10 The *KURI Manifesto* was published in *ÚT*, a magazine based in Újvidék/Novi Sad, in April 1923.
11 Éva Bajkay, "Das Bauhaus und die Ungarn—eine besondere Chronologie," in ibid. 2010 (see note 1), p. 42.
12 Cf. the essay by Barbara Lesák in this catalogue.
13 Annemarie Jaeggi, "Ein Bauhaus, das nicht bauen kann, ist kein Bauhaus," in Bajkay 2010 (see note 1), pp. 97–113.
14 Sándor Bortnyik, Marcel Breuer, Farkas Molnár, and Andor Weininger, "The Demands of the Age," in *Beyond Art: A Third Culture: A Comparative Study in Cultures, Art, and Science in 20th Century Austria and Hungary*, ed. Peter Weibel (Vienna/New York, 2005), p. 550.
15 Krisztina Passuth, *László Moholy-Nagy*, Budapest 1982 (German 1987); *László Moholy-Nagy*, ed. Catherine David, exh. cat., Museum Fridericianum, Kassel (Kassel, 1991); *Moholy-Nagy: Future Present*, ed. Matthew S. Witkovsky, Carol S. Eliel, and Karole P. B. Vail, exh. cat., The Art Institute of Chicago; Los Angeles County Museum of Art; Solomon R. Guggenheim Museum (New Haven/London, 2016).

Artists from the Successor States of the Austro-Hungarian Monarchy and the Group Abstraction-Création in 1930s France

Flóra Mészáros

During the interwar years, Paris became the multicultural capital of an immigrant community. The city's cosmopolitan character was conducive to the artistic scene of the time and led to the flourishing of supranational non-figurative art organizations. A field that still remains largely unexplored (with some exceptions) is the role of the Central European arrivals—specifically artists coming from the former Austro-Hungarian Monarchy—in Modernism and non-figurative art within this cultural and historical context.

The immigrant population of France increased in the aftermath of the First World War, and, by 1931, was approximately three million,[1] making France the second largest immigrant country in the world.[2] The French government was acutely aware of this particular situation and, during the 1920s, began to consciously direct immigration, especially as the United States' 1928 Immigration Act prevented artists from choosing America. France was an exception within Europe in that it welcomed foreigners.[3] Furthermore, new legislation abroad, which outlawed certain ideologies, led to an increase in internationalism in France.[4] For example, after the fall of the Hungarian Republic of Councils, the short-lived Communist state of 1919, many left-leaning artists left Hungary as they had either sympathized with or participated in the revolution. Some of them were arrested for their activism, and most of them had also been members of the Republic's art directorate, including Étienne Béothy, who was unhappy with the new situation in Hungary and left the country in 1926, or Lajos Tihanyi and László Moholy-Nagy, who were part of Lajos Kassák's circle in Vienna before becoming involved in the artistic world of Paris. All three of them were later to become members of Abstraction-Création. Apart from political reasons, another important reason behind the arrival in Paris of these non-figurative artists from the former Austro-Hungarian Monarchy was the city's sheer attractiveness. In addition to being a center of Modernism—at least after 1928, when it took over from Berlin—Paris already had a long-standing reputation as a capital of the arts. The French capital and its international cultural life encouraged and gave free rein to various non-figurative trends. Yet, at the same time, government art institutions were attempting to censor foreign works of art and gave artists working in Neoclassicist styles priority over non-figurative ones.[5]

Nevertheless, several exhibitions, galleries, and avant-garde journals during that period could be perceived as consciously promoting non-figurative artistic groups, among them the Paris World's Fair and *Art d'Aujourd'hui* (both 1925), journals such as *l'Esprit nouveau* (1920–1924) or *Cahiers d'Art* (from 1926), and some exhibition venues, such as the Galerie de l'Effort Moderne. Moreover, the artistic and political reasons that had prompted the existence of an international non-figurative art scene in Paris—combined with the need felt by many artists to stem the tide of Surrealism, which was flourishing at the time—meant that the moment seemed right to synthesize the non-figurative ideas of artists who found themselves living in the same city. This was further facilitated by the presence of a young, dynamic generation of artists whose hunger for action was palpable from 1930 onward.[6] This large group then, including young and old artists alike, began to form abstract art associations in that same year.

Two groups were formed in 1930 that paved the way for the furtherance of non-figurative art: Art Concret, led by Theo van Doesburg, and Cercle et Carré, under Michel Seuphor and Joaquín Torres-García. However, for ideological and financial reasons, these short-lived forerunners ceased to operate in the same year they were initiated. Yet even within this short space of time, the first journal of non-figurative art in Paris, *Cercle et Carré*, was able to publish three issues over the course of just six months. The group Cercle et Carré concentrated exclusively on geometric abstraction, omitting all forms of organic abstraction. In April 1930, they held an exhibition at Galerie 23, introducing forty artists in what was the first exhibition in Paris to focus on abstract art only. The Hungarian painter Vilmos Huszár and the Czechs František Kupka and František Foltyn participated in this show. Meanwhile, Art Concret also focused on geometrical abstraction, but narrowed down their scope even further: on Neoplasticism. Because of this special focus, the number of participants was smaller—only four artists, in addition to Theo van Doesburg. No Eastern European artists took part in this group.

These two early groups represent a milestone in the history of non-figurative art, and some sources suggest that these two different directions were united in Abstraction-Création.[7] Gladys Fabre described the group's birth thus: "It rose from the ashes of Cercle et Carré and Art Concret."[8] This assertion seems to be close to the truth, although, in my opinion, these groups can only be considered as forerunners of Abstraction-Création in that they instigated the vision of creating a permanent forum for non-figurative art. Although many former members of either group were to be found in Abstraction-Création, the groups' theoretical basis, their relation to Surrealism and even the organizational structure of the two earlier associations were very different from Abstraction-Création, which was an altogether freer, looser association.

Abstraction-Création, the most significant and largest supranational non-figurative artists association of the time, indeed, of the twentieth century, was founded at the beginning of 1931. Among the participants in the inaugural negotiations was one of the earliest abstract artists, the Czech František Kupka (pp. 83–85, 224–26, 228–29),[9] who was also one of the official directors of the group in 1931.[10] During its five years of operation, well-known artists such as Auguste Herbin (the group's president), Jean

Arp, Jean Hélion, Alexander Calder, Robert Delaunay, Paule Vézelay, Otto Freundlich, and many others took part in the group's activities. Also among its hundred or so participants were artists from the former Austro-Hungarian Monarchy, including the Hungarians Étienne Béothy, Alfred Reth, Lajos Tihanyi, and Ferenc Martyn, the aforementioned Kupka, the Czech František Foltyn, and the Austrian Wolfgang Paalen; László Moholy-Nagy was granted membership even though he was not living in Paris. Thus, five Hungarians participated, a relatively large number compared to other Central European artists and those from other nationalities. There were also a few Anglophone artists, while only eleven French artists were members of this France-based group. Despite their large numbers, the Central European artists did not form their own sub-group, nor did they represent a specific artistic direction within the group.

These artists joined the group for the opportunities it offered and for its non-figurative focus. It is worth mentioning, however, that there were other Central European non-figurative artists living in Paris at the time (including some from the former Habsburg Monarchy) who did not join the association. These included the Czech Josef Šima, the Hungarians Victor Vasarely, Anton Prinner, Henri Nouveau, and others. The Hungarian painter Vilmos Huszár, who lived in the Netherlands, joined Cercle et Carré, but had no connection with Abstraction-Création.

A decision was taken from the outset that a non-figurative approach was the only condition required for any artist wishing to participate in the group's activities. Nevertheless, the word "non-figurative" was omitted from its official name. Interestingly, Kupka later revealed that the name of the association had been extensively debated among members and in the end Abstraction-Création was chosen as a compromise.[11] Abstraction-Création went further than the two previous organizations in that it attempted to combine a new and an already-in-use term that together could be applied to all existing abstract artistic trends—including non-figurative works. It thus opened the doors for artists who represented "abstraction" as a new common definition for "organic" abstraction, as well as for artists who understood "création" as the use of exclusively geometric elements in composition. The concept of "non-figurative art" could thus be taken as the broadest definition for gathering together artists representing different abstract trends. In addition, the aspect of "création" as understood in Abstraction-Création was also present in both Art Concret and Cercle et Carré, while abstraction was not. This is a further reason why the group cannot be considered as a mere amalgamation of its two forerunners.

Originally, Abstraction-Création was intended as an exclusive group, as the plan was for a much more theoretically based organization for the promotion of non-figurative art.

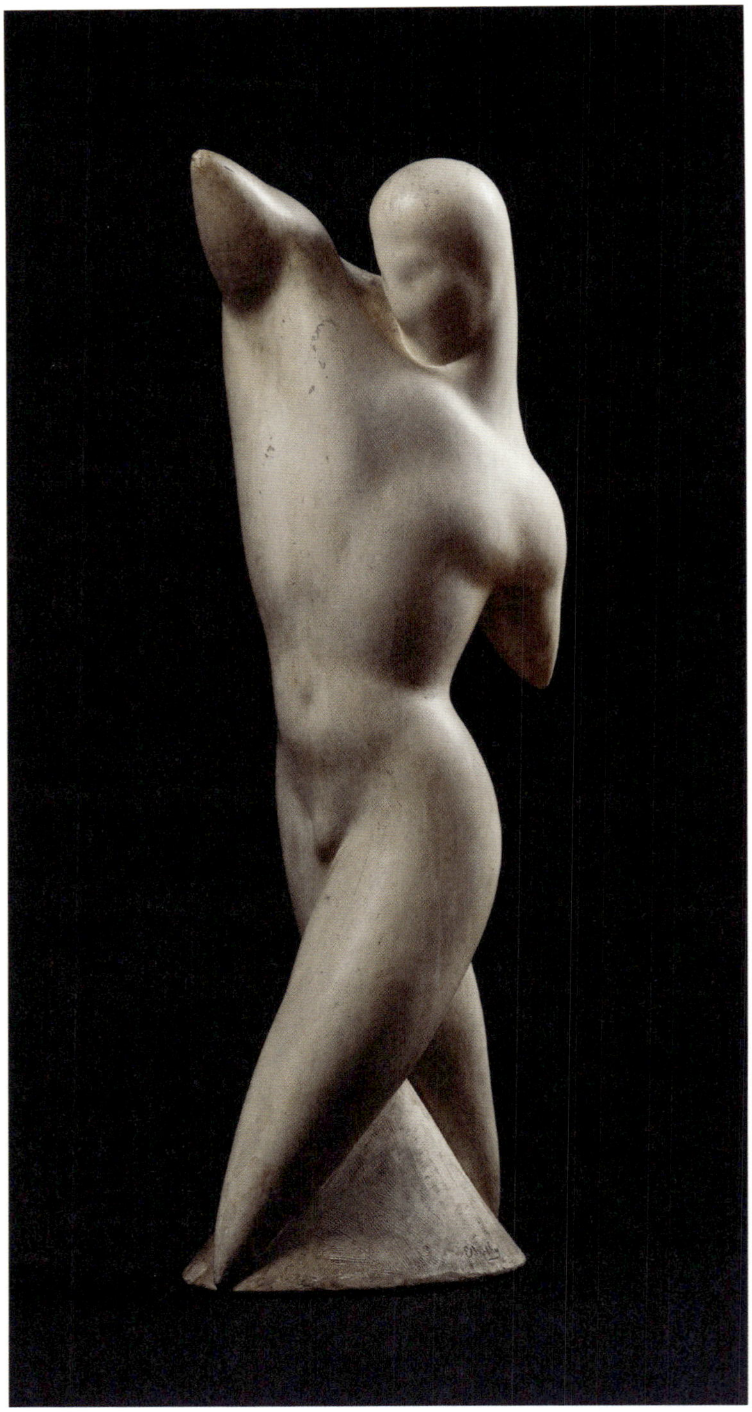

Fig. 1
Étienne Beothy
Heros, Action directe (Op. 19), 1927
Emmanuelle & Jérôme de Noirmont Collection, Paris

However, due to the group's struggle—from the very beginning—for financial survival, it had to open its doors to far more abstract artists, including many who were not widely known.[12] This explains why the Central European artists, with the exception of Kupka and Moholy-Nagy, needed an existing group member to support their application for membership. Thus, Étienne Béothy, who replaced Michel Seuphor as secretary in 1932[13] and who, along with Kupka, took a leading role in the association, was able to endorse the memberships of Ferenc Martyn, Alfred Reth, and Lajos Tihanyi.[14] Or, since Kupka was Foltyn's teacher in Paris, he probably also helped him to join the association in its early days. (Foltyn was a member until he left Paris in 1934.)

During their application period, artists were under strict instruction to exhibit only non-figurative works. So, although they might still be producing figurative works of art during that time, these were not to be publicly shown until membership had been granted. For example, the first Hungarian artist who joined Abstraction-Création in 1931, Étienne Béothy, probably presented his newest works from the same year, the "rythme — plastique" series, in his application. Nevertheless, he was also still creating semi-figurative works in sculpture around this time, works such as *Danse Cosaques (op. 45)* (p. 252) from 1930. Béothy only experimented with abstraction in 1927 and 1928, while living in Paris, for example, in his 1927 work *Heros*, *Action directe (op. 19), 1927* (fig. 1), in which he played with the reduction of the human figure and the concave forms of the torso, thereby edging toward non-figuration. It is therefore likely that he wanted to join a group where he could work entirely as a non-figurative artist.[15] The motivations of the other Central European artists already mentioned varied. Most importantly, they all followed their painterly or sculptural ambitions; presumably only František Foltyn, Alfred Reth, and Béothy were attracted primarily by the group's purist agenda.

Martyn and Tihanyi were hoping to obtain financial support and artistic recognition through exhibiting and/or publishing.[16] Abstraction-Création provided a dedicated forum for non-figurative art, organizing individual and collective exhibitions, and even running its own gallery for one year. Indeed, the original ambition in establishing the association was to organize exclusively non-figurative exhibitions.[17] From 1932 to 1936, the group published an annual journal entitled *abstraction-création art non-figuratif* (fig. 2). Moreover, it offered a forum for its members to discuss their non-figurative work in official meetings as well as informal café gatherings. The Central European artists benefited in particular from this—with the exception of Tihanyi and Martyn. Rather than participating in the group, the former concentrated above all on a written monograph; from 1934 he produced half-geometric and half-organic abstract paintings in which he avoided any focus on dimensionality (p. 213), culminating, in 1937, in *Composition* (p. 212), which he completed one year after the end of Abstraction-Création.

Returning to the opportunities offered by the group's gallery and journal, and, in particular their impact on the Central European artists, it is worth highlighting Moholy-Nagy's dominant role in these platforms too. For example, he was the only member of the group to have a solo exhibition. Although the organization's focus on painting suited him well,[18] he only exhibited his early canvases, made between 1924 and 1928. Moreover, he published work in every issue of the magazine, with reproductions as well as artist's statements. Moholy-Nagy was much appreciated by Abstraction-Création, not only for his extensive artistic and theoretical output, but also for initiating new trends and his teaching work at the Bauhaus. In 1932, the Hungarian Béothy became a member of the group's editorial board and was chief editor in 1935 and 1936, where he was able to contribute his own ideas and preferences.[19]

It thus opened the doors for artists who represented "abstraction" as a new common definition for "organic" abstraction, as well as for artists who understood "création" as the use of exclusively geometric elements in composition.

For the other artists discussed here, being able to develop their abstract ideas was probably the main reason for joining the group. Alfred Reth was interested above all in the relationship between color and line, and drew inspiration from Robert Delaunay's research and Herbin's line-centric paintings of the time. Moreover, Reth was exploring the big question of the time, three-dimensionality, in his *Découpages* series, in which he made attempts to produce three-dimensional paintings analogous to the works in relief made around the same time by Cesare Domela.[20]

Kupka also played with three-dimensional effects in his compositions, especially in the series *Abstractions* (1930–33), mainly by emphasizing the contrast of white backgrounds with black or blue lines and circles. His way of thinking came closer to the Neo-plasticist ideas of the time,[21] thereby taking the route of more geometric abstraction ("création"). Nevertheless, his importance

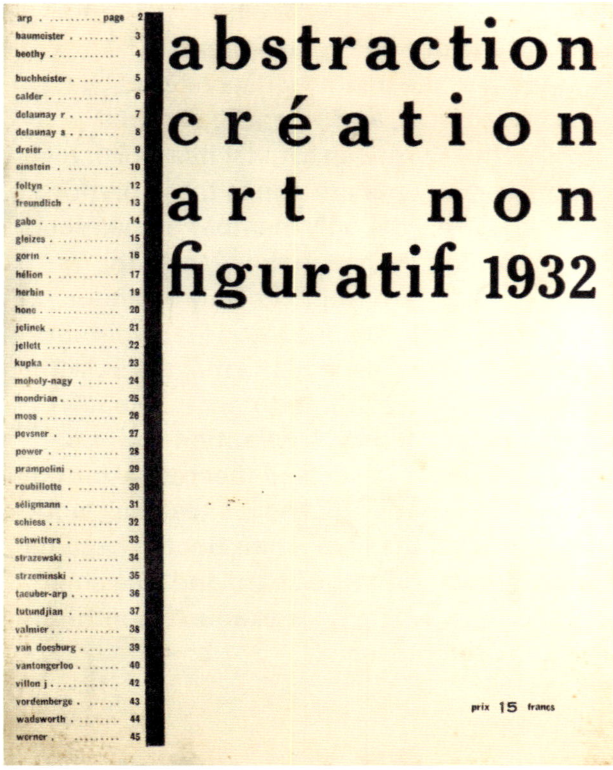

arp . . . . page 2
baumeister 3
beothy 4
buchheister 5
calder 6
delaunay r 7
delaunay s 8
dreier 9
einstein 10
foltyn 12
freundlich 13
gabo 14
gleizes 15
gorin 16
hélion 17
herbin 19
hone 20
jelinek 21
jellett 22
kupka 23
moholy-nagy 24
mondrian 25
moss 26
pevsner 27
power 28
prampolini 29
roubillotte 30
séligmann 31
schiess 32
schwitters 33
strazewski 34
strzeminski 35
taeuber-arp 36
tutundjian 37
valmier 38
van doesburg 39
vantongerloo 40
villon j 42
vordemberge 43
wadsworth 44
werner 45

abstraction
création
art non
figuratif 1932

prix 15 francs

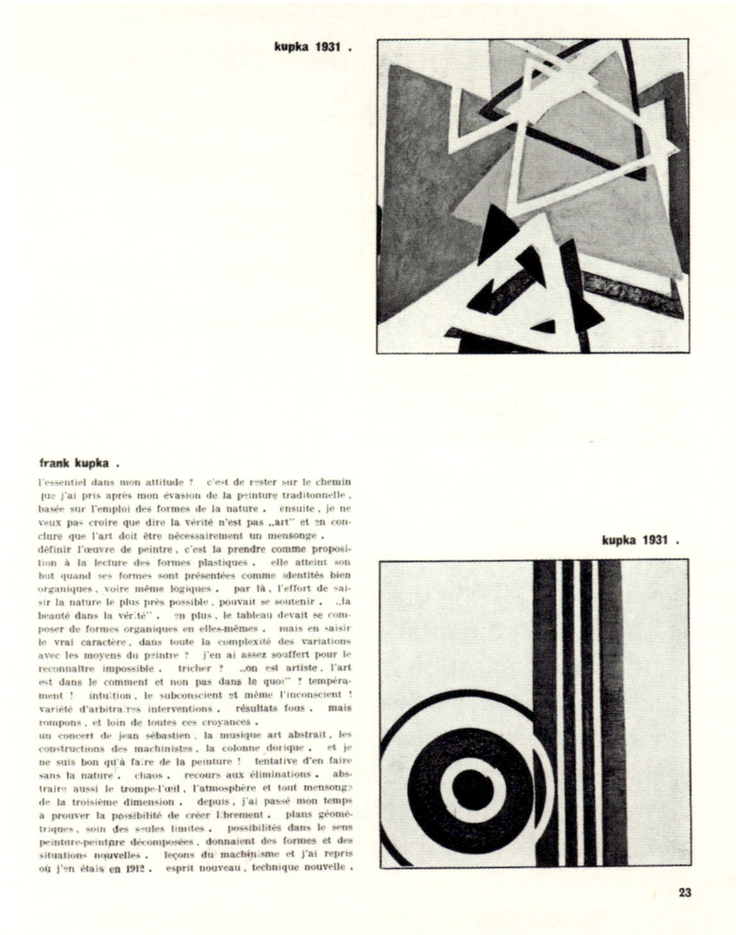

kupka 1931 .

frank kupka .

l'essentiel dans mon attitude ? c'est de rester sur le chemin que j'ai pris après mon évasion de la peinture traditonnelle, basée sur l'emploi des formes de la nature. ensuite, je ne veux pas croire que dire la vérité n'est pas „art" et en conclure que l'art doit être nécessairement un mensonge.
définir l'œuvre de peintre, c'est la prendre comme proposition à la lecture des formes plastiques. elle atteint son but quand ses formes sont présentées comme identités bien organiques, voire même logiques. par là, l'effort de saisir la nature le plus près possible, pouvait se soutenir. „la beauté dans la vérité". en plus, le tableau devait se composer de formes organiques en elles-mêmes. mais en saisir le vrai caractère, dans toute la complexité des variations avec les moyens du peintre ? j'en ai assez souffert pour le reconnaître impossible. tricher ? „on est artiste, l'art est dans le comment et non pas dans le quoi" ? tempérament ! intuition, le subconscient et même l'inconscient ! variété d'arbitraires interventions. résultats fous. mais rompons, et loin de toutes ces croyances.
un concert de jean sébastien, la musique art abstrait, les constructions des machinistes, la colonne dorique. et je ne suis bon qu'à faire de la peinture ! tentative d'en faire sans la nature. chaos. recours aux éliminations. abstraire aussi le trompe-l'œil, l'atmosphère et tout mensonge de la troisième dimension. depuis, j'ai passé mon temps à prouver la possibilité de créer librement. plans géométriques, soin des seules limites. possibilités dans le sens peinture-peintpre décomposées, donnaient des formes et des situations nouvelles. leçons du machinisme et j'ai repris où j'en étais en 1912. esprit nouveau, technique nouvelle.

kupka 1931 .

23

Fig. 2
Front cover of *abstraction-création art non-figuratif*, no. 1, Paris, 1932

Fig. 3
František Kupka
Composition, 1931
From *abstraction-création art non-figuratif*, no. 1, Paris, 1932

is evident in his influence on the work of other members, including Central European artists like Béothy. His oil painting *Composition* (1932, fig. 3), reproduced in the first cahier of the group, influenced not only Béothy's sculptural work but also his later graphic works, as can be seen in the cover design for his 1939 theoretical volume *Le problème de la Création* (The problem of creating, fig. 4).[22]

By the end of Abstraction-Création's existence, the rise of Surrealism was the main artistic and operational challenge for the group. Cercle et Carré had openly attacked Surrealism,[23] as did Art Concret in its journal.[24] Abstraction-Création was also unsupportive of this movement, yet out of the three non-figurative associations it was still the most permissive toward Surrealism. During the last years of its existence (1934–36), worn down by financial struggles as a result of the worldwide economic crisis (which hit France with a slight delay from 1934), Abstraction-Création was starting to lose hold of its original ambitions, such as maintaining its own gallery. In an attempt to weather the storm, the group began to show more forbearance toward new members who financially supported the association, even accepting representatives of Surrealism. Their political agenda, namely the participation of adherents of both styles in the Communist Association d' Écrivains et d'Artistes Révolutionnaires, provided some common ground between them.[25]

Artistically, three different Surrealist-Abstract directions were now represented in the group. Firstly, there were artists from the Surrealist circle, such as Arhile Gorky, Léon Tutundjian, or, from Central Europe, the Austrian Wolfgang Paalen, who experimented with non-objective elements in his Surrealist landscapes. Secondly, there were artists who discovered Surrealism while already members of Abstraction-Création, such as Alexander Calder. Thirdly, there were artists like the Hungarian Ferenc Martyn, who had affiliations with both directions: he rediscovered Surrealism in 1936 (having already displayed tendencies toward it in the late 1920s).[26] He created unique oil paintings with coastal and ornithological themes combined with organic abstraction, while adopting a Surrealist treatment of space. Interestingly, his work may be compared with some of František Foltyn's 1932–34 paintings, described as "biomorphic abstract" works.

The year 1936 spelled the end of Abstraction-Création. By now the group had become fractured as a result of conflicts over theory and other internal squabbles, as well as its ongoing unsuccessful battle against the economic crisis. Among the members discussed here, Foltyn and Martyn were the only ones to return to their home country. Foltyn abandoned non-figuration, while Martyn delved deeply into the world of organic abstraction, mixing it with Surrealist approaches. His work had a great influence on Hungarian art. The other artists hailing from the former Austro-Hungarian Empire either remained in France or settled in other countries, where they continued their artistic careers with the benefit of the experience gained as members of Abstraction-Création.

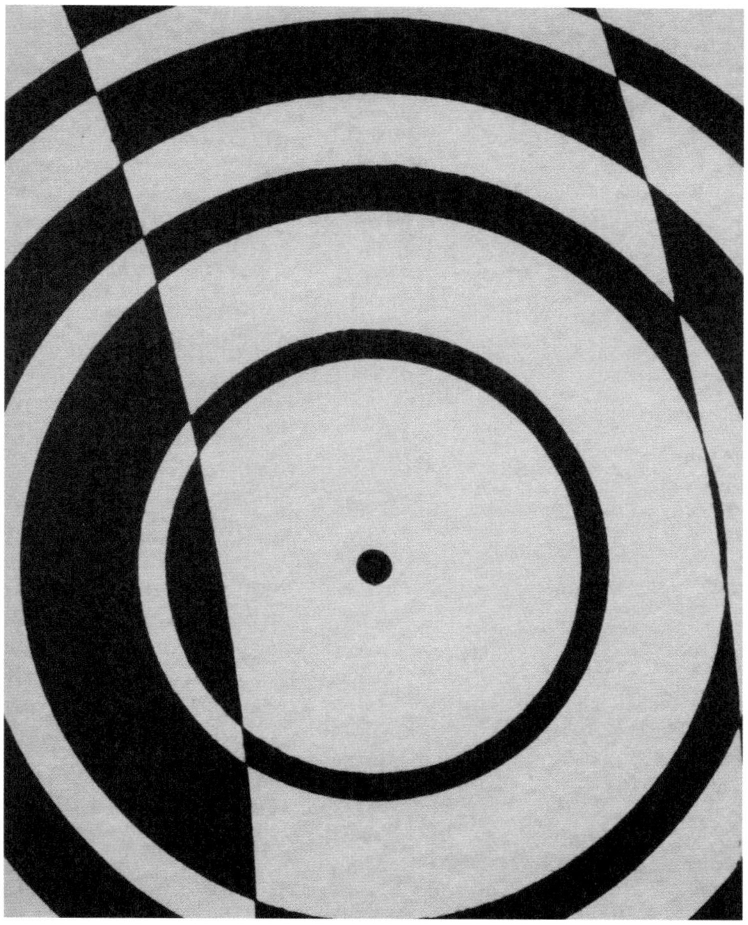

Fig. 4
Étienne Beothy
Front cover of
Le Problème de la Création, Paris, 1939

1 Ralph Schor, *l'Opinion française et les étrangers en France, 1919–1939* (Paris, 1985), p. 27.
2 Margaret Sanger, *Proceedings of the World Population Conference* (London, 1927), p. 295.
3 Duncan H. Gerald, *Immigration and Assimilation* (Boston/New York, 1933), p. 145.
4 Gerald 1933 (see note 3), p. 145.
5 Gladys Fabre, "L'Art d'Années 30," in *Années 30 en Europe: Le temps menaçant 1929–1939*, ed. Suzanne Pagé and Aline Vidal, exh.cat., Musée d'Art moderne de la Ville de Paris (Paris, 1997), p.65.
6 Dora Vallier, *L'art abstrait* (Paris, 1967), p. 223.
7 See, e.g., Marie-Aline Prat, *Cercle et Carré: Peinture et Avant-garde au seuil des années 30* (Lausanne, 1984), p. 15.
8 Gladys Fabre, "Abstraction-Création 1931–1936," in A.D.S. Donaldson and Ann Stephen, eds., *J.W. Power: Abstraction-Création, Paris 1934* (Sydney, 2013), p. 93. This text is the English translation by Antonia Fredman and extended version, reviewed by Gladys Fabre, of the catalogue *abstraction-création 1931–1936*, ed. Gladys Fabre, exh.cat., Westfälisches Museum, Münster/Musée d'Art moderne de la Ville de Paris (Münster/Paris, 1978).
9 Jean Hélion, *Journal d'un peintre: carnets 1929-1984, vol. I* (Paris, 1992), p. 357.
10 Listed in the journal of Abstraction-Création every year until 1936.
11 Fabre 2013 (see note 8), p. 93.
12 Flóra Mészáros, "Hungarian Artists in Abstraction-Création in the Context of Art," in Mészáros Flóra, ed., *Modern Art and Internationalism: Lives in Motion. A Festschrift in Honor of Krisztina Passuth* (Pécs, 2017), p. 48.
13 Krisztina Passuth, *Étienne Beothy: Le Sculpteur de la Série d'Or* (Paris/Budapest, 2011), p. 95.
14 Flóra Mészáros, "Vonzások és választások: Magyar művészek és az Abstraction-Création csoport," in *Új Művészet* 2014/15, p. 9.
15 Passuth 2011 (see note 13), p. 95.
16 Mészáros 2014 (see note 14), p. 9.
17 Letter from Jean Hélion to Otto Freundlich, March 13, 1931, Paris, in *Fonds Freundlich*, IMEC, FRN 10.15. 303479
18 Krisztina Passuth, *Moholy-Nagy* (English version) (London, 1985), p.66.
19 The names of its editors are given in the published issues of *abstraction-création art non-figuratif* (Paris, 1932–36).
20 Mészáros 2017 (see note 12), p. 54.
21 See Arnauld Pierre, *Frank Kupka in Black and White* (Liverpool, 1998).
22 Passuth 2011 (see note 13), p. 103.
23 Cf. for example, Michel Seuphor, *Cercle et Carré* ed. Jean-Michel Place (Paris, 1977), p. 11; or Torres-García, *circulo y cuadrado 5*, Montevideo, (May 1936). Cited in Marie-Aline Prat 1984 (see note 7), p.32.
24 Theo van Doesburg, "Vers la Peinture Blanche," in *Art Concret*, no. 1, April 1930. p.1.
25 Anna Moszynska, *Abstract art (World of Art)* (London, 1990), p. 96.
26 Mészáros 2017 (see note 12), pp. 59–60.

The Rise and Fall of Avant-Garde Theater in the Countries of the Former Austro-Hungarian Empire

Barbara Lesák

TRADITION AND INNOVATION IN THE THEATER OF THE AUSTRO-HUNGARIAN EMPIRE

Even as late as the early twentieth century, a clear symptom of the absolute dominance of the Austrian Imperial Court Theater—the largest and most highly regarded "theatrical machine" of the Habsburg Empire—was its ongoing replication even in the farthermost reaches of the Empire's many crown lands. The Vienna-based architect's practice Fellner & Helmer, who specialized in theater design, created more than sixty new theaters in almost every major provincial capital, to satisfy the exaggerated craving for status of a strengthened, culture- and theater-obsessed bourgeoisie. From 1905, Czernowitz (Chernivtsi), the capital of Bukovina, too, was served by one of these theaters from the drawing boards of Ferdinand Fellner and Hermann Helmer. It was this provincial theater, as the embodiment of precariously outmoded theatrical traditions, that so incensed the revolutionary stage designer Frederick Kiesler, who grew up in Czernowitz. All his fantasies of destruction, which, in 1924, culminated in the revenge-fueled text *Debacle des Theaters*,[1] may well have been directed squarely at the Czernowitz Municipal Theater, where outdated practices such as empty declamation and stencil-like, illusionistic scenery continued to thrive.

Post-1918, a new cultural landscape was burgeoning in many of the Austro-Hungarian Empire's successor states. The driving force for this development were often artists from Hungary and Czechoslovakia, although, in the case of Hungary, the push for modernity came from its exiled artists, who only found fertile ground for their creative drive outside of their home country's borders. And, against all odds, in Austria—however small and seemingly insignificant it had now become—a cultural scene emerged that not merely rehearsed the break from outdated traditions, but actually implemented it. In this optimistic, re-energized cultural climate, theater took on a very special role, as it gave all those visionaries—who were experiencing a boom of their own at the time—an opportunity to try their hand at redesigning the world within the small, clearly defined universe of the stage.

Only a small number of these visionaries came from the world of professional theater, where the vogue was very much for incremental reform in small steps. Flying the flag for a much more radical departure from all theatrical conventions were, above all, the visual artists and architects of the avant-garde. For the very first time, female theater artists were also able to make inroads into this traditionally male-dominated arena. A key figure in Austria was Erika Giovanna Klien, whose designs for a *Kinetic Puppet Theater* (fig. 1), produced between 1924 and 1926, made a significant contribution to theatrical renewal.[2] Klien breathed new life into the old tradition

D

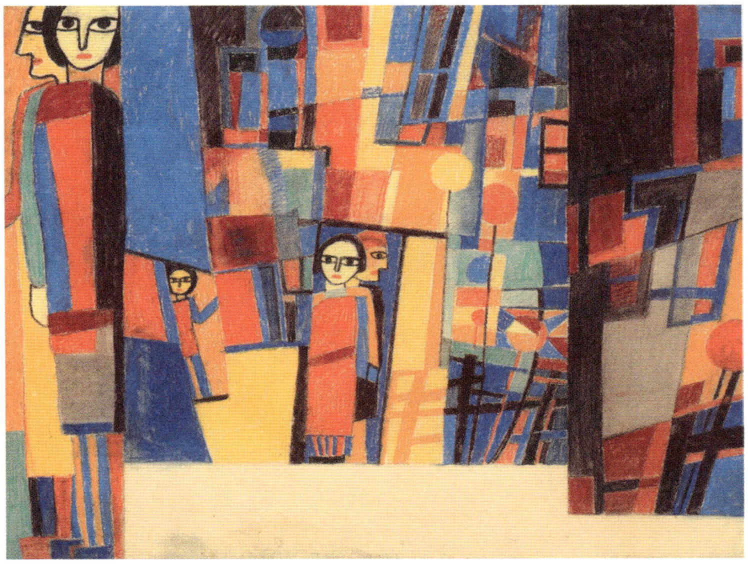

Fig. 1
Erika Giovanna Klien
Design for a *Kinetic Puppet Theater*, 1926
Theater Museum, Vienna

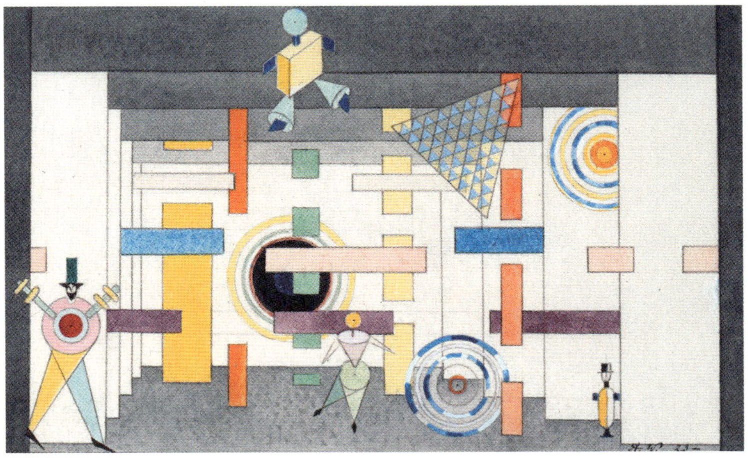

Fig. 2
Andor Weininger
Design for an *Abstract Revue (Mechanical Theater)*, after 1923
Museum of Fine Arts — Hungarian National Gallery, Budapest

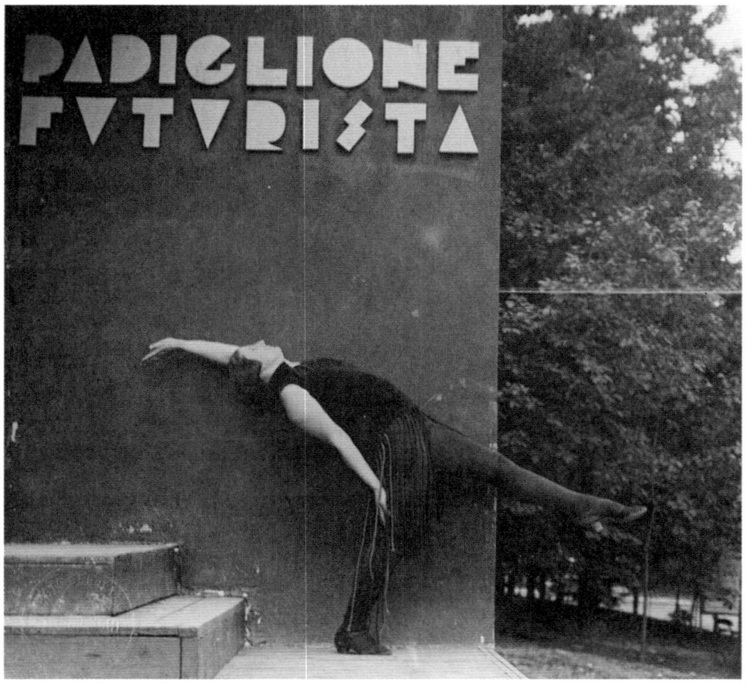

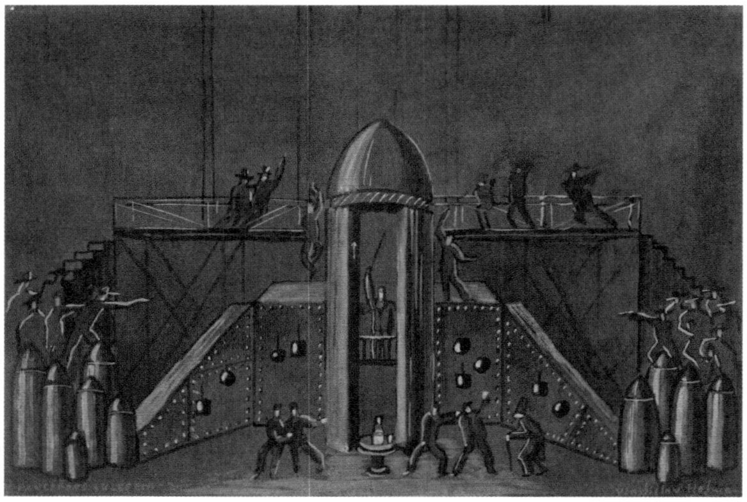

Fig. 3
Silvio Ottolenghi
The dancer Zdenka Podhajská in costume for *Vortice* (*Whirling Dance*) in front of the Futurist Pavilion in Turin, 1928

Fig. 4
Vlastislav Hofman
Set design for *The Man Who Was Thursday* by G. K. Chesterton, Prague National Theater, 1927
Theater Museum, Vienna

of puppet theater—which by then was no more than a form of children's entertainment—using a mechanized system to transform abstract decorative elements and figures into kinetic sequences of wild, whirling images. These were to represent the narrative of the big city, which Klien not only idealized as a magical beacon of modernity but also suitably demonized. Klien's ingenuity with mechanized puppets finds comparison with works created by Russian artists a few years previously in the early days of the Soviet Union.

THE POST-WAR ERA: RADICAL MODERNITY

Different sociopolitical and cultural forces were at work in Hungary, Czechoslovakia, and Austria respectively, which served to either fuel or suppress the new theater art. Artists of the progressive Left from the circle around Lajos Kassák and his journal *MA* (Today), left Hungary in their droves after the demise of the Communist Hungarian Republic of Councils in 1919 and the establishment of Miklós Horthy's reactionary regime. Most of them initially followed Kassák to Vienna, while others, such as Andor Weininger, Marcel Breuer, László Moholy-Nagy, and Farkas Molnár traveled to Germany, where they went on to either study or teach at the Bauhaus in Weimar and, later, Dessau. In social democratic Vienna—cripplingly poor after the war, yet brimming with new ideas—innovative thinkers were demonstrating how the future could be built upon modern principles to the benefit of humanity (the city was given the nickname "Red Vienna" in the 1920s). This dynamic atmosphere, however, was contrasted with a tremendous nostalgia for the city's former splendor and greatness, as well as an overwhelming desire to emulate the German Reich.

In the fall of 1924, despite widespread destabilizing inflation, Vienna played host to a major event in the avant-garde world, the *International Exhibition of New Theater Technology,* held at Vienna's Konzerthaus. Contrary to the nationalist tendencies emerging in the political arena,[3] theater artists from almost every nation in Europe were united here by an artistic language that crossed borders. An important linking element in this proved to be abstraction (whether based on Constructivism, metaphysics, or esoterics). Under its umbrella came a variety of things: the cult of the machine, optimistic faith in progress, and an infatuation with technology and speed.

In Vienna, Kassák—poet, theoretician, activist, Constructivist painter, and the editor of *MA* all at once—became embroiled in the theoretical debate about the new theater. For him, the future of theater lay in a new form of theatrical entertainment that was on the rise during the 1920s: the revue—as long as it could be placed on a more serious footing.[4] Revue theater had freed itself from literary theater's centuries-long dominance and, like a well-oiled machine, was producing an endless stream of entertainment. Speed, titillation, precision, artistry, humor, and jazz music were the ingredients that made this style of theater so unceasingly popular with modern urbanites. The revue style was thus adopted with equal enthusiasm by the revolutionary theater of Soviet Russia as it was in Bauhaus theater, whose artists and architects, such as the Hungarian exiles Móholy-Nagy, Molnár, Weininger, and Breuer, transformed the medium into an abstract mechanical art form (fig. 2).

In contrast to their Hungarian peers, Czech theater artists were an almost fully integrated part of a modern, democratic, young nation. On achieving their independence, Bohemia and Moravia—which had been the most industrially advanced regions of the Austro-Hungarian Empire—experienced an even more pronounced push toward modernity. One may speculate whether this could have been at the root of Karel and Josef Čapek's highly successful science fiction plays. Although virtually unknown today, Karel Čapek's 1921 "utopian collective drama" *R.U.R.* was a global success at the time. In 1922, even before premiering in Berlin in 1923, the futuristic play (which brought the term "robot" into everyday speech) was already staged in New York. The Berlin premiere was a huge success, thanks to Frederick Kiesler's stage set, which only survives in the form of three photographs (pp. 234–35). In Čapek's futuristic drama, robots rise up against their brutal exploitation by global industrial trusts, their revolt ultimately leading to the destruction of humanity. However, Čapek was an optimist and champion of humanity and thus provided a happy ending for the play: a scientist named Dr. Gall creates a robot couple with the ability to love and reproduce, ensuring humanity's rebirth, albeit in the form of robots. For this science fiction play, Kiesler devised a suitably cold, glittering wall of apparatus and machinery that filled the entire back of the stage. As Kiesler describes in his article "De la nature morte vivante," the machinery was operating visually and acoustically in sync with the play: "The projector lense opens slowly: the film projector whirrs [...] The seismograph (in the center) gradually jerks forward [...] The turbine control (lower center) spins [...] Work sirens whine."[5]

Prague in the 1920s and early 1930s was defined by a climate of openness in which the new zeitgeist was embraced with absolute optimism. This spirit of modernity also permeated Prague's experimental theater scene—so much so that the Futurists, including Filippo Tommaso Marinetti and Enrico Prampolini, established a temporary branch of Futurist theater in Prague.[6] On December 15, 1921, Marinetti took to the stage at the Švandovo divadlo (Švanda Theater) and declaimed the Manifestos of Futurism. To give a taster of the new Futurist dramaturgy, which advocated the rejection of logical syntax, several "syntheses," e.g., by Emilio Settimelli and Bruno Corra, were presented using costumes and stage décor by Prampolini. Futurism also attracted a few female Czech artists

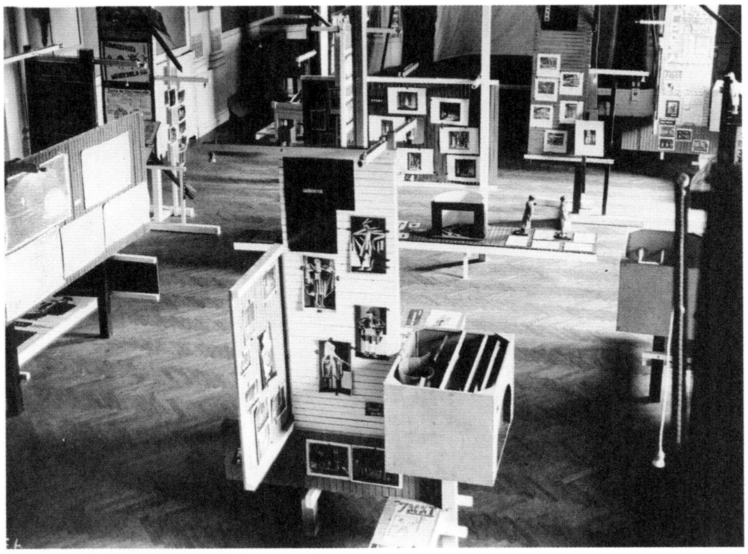

Fig. 5
Frederick Kiesler
International Exhibition of New Theater Technology, interior view of the exhibition, 1924

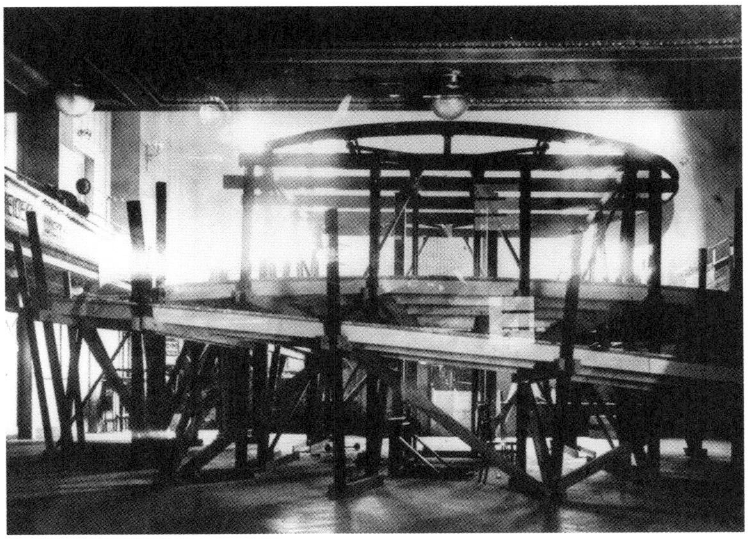

Fig. 6
Frederick Kiesler
The *Space Stage* (during construction or disassembly) at the *International Exhibition of New Theater Technology* in the Vienna Konzerthaus (middle hall—now the Mozartsaal), 1924

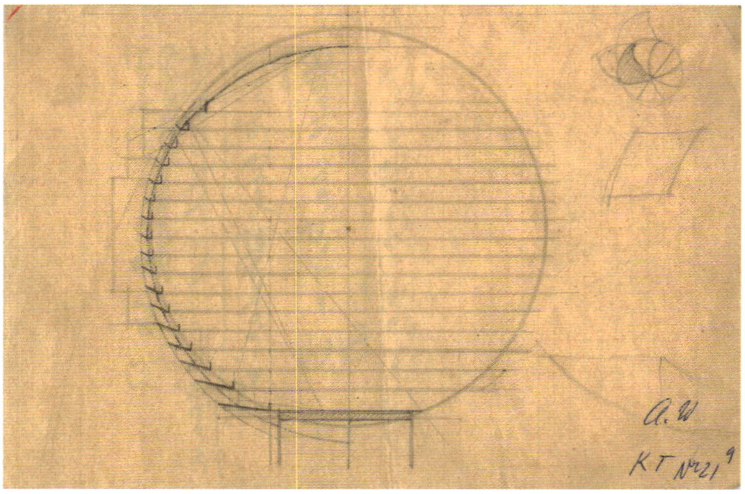

Fig. 7
Andor Weininger
Design for a *Spherical Theater*, 1926/27, Theater Collection, University of Cologne

By the mid-1920s, avant-garde theater had already reaped a rich harvest, and it was to be Vienna—in its diminished political importance—that provided the ideal platform for the latest innovations in theater, reuniting artists from the successor states of the Austro-Hungarian Empire, but also from Germany, France, Italy, Poland, Finland, and the Soviet Union.

to its ranks, such as the dancer Zdenka Podhajská.[7] Between 1926 and 1928, she was an ensemble member of the Théâtre de la pantomime futuriste (fig. 3), which, under the direction of dancer Maria Ricotti and set designer Prampolini, gave several guest performances at the Théâtre de la Madeleine in Paris and, from 1928, in Italy. The Futurists wanted to imbue traditional Italian pantomime with a new futuristic spirit, which was expressed, among other things, by idealizing sports. This aspect in particular was received by the emerging mass audiences with an almost frenetic enthusiasm. For example, Prampolini devised sports-themed pantomime scenarios, such as the tennis- and football-inspired *Danze sportive* or the *Danza dell'elica* (Propeller Dance), an ode to aeronautics, performed by Podhajská wearing a propeller costume he had designed.

Another prominent Czech stage design innovator, whose work brought an ultra-modern spirit to such traditional theaters as the Prague National Theater, was the Cubist architect and stage set designer Vlastislav Hofman.[8] Hofman was an expert in drawing up technologized worlds that were in tune with those created by the Čapek Brothers or the British author G. K. Chesterton, whose novel *The Man Who Was Thursday*—a satire about the British anarchist movement and Scotland Yard—was published in 1908. A highly successful stage adaptation followed in 1926. Hofman's set design for this featured a transparent house in which an elevator transported people into the mysterious anarchist underworld, where an arsenal of high-tech weapons was awaiting its use against the state (fig. 4).

AVANT-GARDE THEATER IN FREDERICK KIESLER'S *INTERNATIONAL EXHIBITION OF NEW THEATER TECHNOLOGY IN VIENNA*

In October 1924, the main protagonists of Europe's avant-garde theater scene came together in spectacular fashion at the *International Exhibition of New Theater Technology*, an event that was remarkable in every sense.[9] Invited to organize the event was the artist Frederick Kiesler,[10] who, while still virtually unknown in Vienna, was already celebrating great success in Berlin. The innovative body responsible for the commission was the Sozialdemokratische Kunststelle, Vienna's social-democratic arts council, an organization which, earlier that year, had played a key role in organizing the city's first Music and Theater Festival, celebrating the achievements of modernity. By the mid-1920s, avant-garde theater had already reaped a rich harvest, and it was to be Vienna—in its diminished political importance—that provided the ideal platform for the latest innovations in theater, reuniting artists from the successor states of the Austro-Hungarian Empire, but also from Germany, France, Italy, Poland, Finland, and the Soviet Union. And it was Kiesler who gave the exhibition its Constructivist appearance (fig. 5), created its ultra-modern logo and catalogue design, and—most importantly—designed the utopian object at its center, the *Space Stage*. He also ensured the highly charged climate of innovation that attracted names such as Filippo Tommaso Marinetti, Theo van Doesburg, Fernand Léger, and many others. Unsurprisingly, this cauldron of innovation also led to the odd explosion, and the accusations of plagiarism directed at Kiesler by the future guru of psychodrama, Jacob Levy-Moreno, were an expression of this charged atmosphere.

The uniqueness of the *Space Stage* (fig. 6) lay in the fact that this futuristic stage design was actually realized and used for performances during the exhibition. Kiesler's *Space Stage,* a round, two-story tower comprising stages at different levels, connected via spiral ramps, staircases, ladders, and an electric elevator (as a symbol of modern high-speed acceleration), was a radical departure from the traditional picture-frame stage. The *Space Stage* was erected in the middle hall of the Konzerthaus (now the Mozartsaal), with the audience seated around the stage on a U-shaped raised balcony. Like many others, Kiesler was interested in overcoming the separation between audience and stage. His dynamic architecture created a powerful current that swept actors and spectators together into a single whole. Kiesler's *Space Stage* was met with ridicule and scorn, but also with much enthusiasm, especially when it was put to the test as to its suitability for staging a theater play. *Im Dunkel* was the name of a three-person Expressionist play by Paul Frischauer that was performed on the *Space Stage*, although it was much less suited as a test piece than the dance performances that were later staged on it with great success. The most apt comment about the *Space Stage* may have been by Karl Kraus who, although of an older generation and therefore rather more skeptical of the avant-garde, nevertheless had some well-meaning words to contribute: "The *Space Stage* may be much better suited [...] to plays that actually require a space stage."[11]

Even more cutting edge than Kiesler's *Space Stage* was Móhóly-Nagy's *Sketch for a Score for a Mechanized Eccentric*. It never progressed beyond the conceptual stage, however, and was displayed at the exhibition in the form of two sheets with "scores" for abstract, kinetic, and color experiences, set to mechanical noise and assigned to different stage-like platforms. Like Kiesler, Móhóly-Nagy had gained practical experience in stage design at the Kroll Opera House in Berlin and, like him, had expended much thought on the modernization of theater through the integration of technological innovations, such as film, photography, and radio.[12] The bold theater designs produced by other Hungarian exiles working at the Bauhaus, such as Andor Weininger's 1927 *Spherical Theater*[13] (fig. 7) or Farkas Molnár's 1925 *U-Theater*[14] (featured in *Die Bühne im Bauhaus* in 1925) were not yet ready to be shown in 1924.

All these theatrical experiments would soon come to an abrupt end, however. Kiesler—whose roots were in Chernowitz's Jewish community—was already called to New York in 1926, where he was able to further develop his visions for an *Endless Theater*. Others were forced to follow him into emigration by the National Socialist terror regime. Many more died in the concentration camps. Across large swathes of Europe, including the Soviet Union, where avant-garde theater was suppressed by the Stalinist regime, the great surge of the avant-garde movement was to come to a standstill.

1 Friedrich Kiesler, "Debacle des Theaters: Die Gesetze der G.-K.-Bühne," in *Internationale Ausstellung neuer Theatertechnik*, ed. Friedrich Kiesler (Vienna, 1975, reprint of the 1924 first edition), pp. 43–58.

2 See Barbara Lesák, "Der Wiener Theaterkinetismus," in *Kinetismus: Wien entdeckt die Avantgarde*, eds. Monika Platzer and Ursula Storch, exh. cat., Wien Museum (Vienna, 2006), pp. 138–53.

3 An example of nationalist agitation is the campaign launched against a Czech play, such as Karel Čapek's *R.U.R.* (*W.U.R.* in German), being performed in Budapest. See "W.U.R. in Budapest," *Der Tag*, February 2, 1924, p. 12.

4 Ludwig Kassák, "Für die neue Theaterkunst," *Die Bühne*, no. 106 (Vienna, 1926), pp. 13–14.

5 Friedrich Kiesler, "De la nature morte vivante," in Kiesler 1975 (see note 1), pp. 20–21.

6 For more about the Futurists in Prague, see Giovanni Lista, *La scène futuriste* (Paris, 1989), pp. 362–67.

7 Part of her estate is housed in Vienna's Theatermuseum.

8 For more on Vlastislav Hofman, see Miroslav Rutte and František Bartoš, *Die moderne tschechische Szene* (Prague, 1938), pp. 13–14.

9 For more on the *Internationalen Ausstellung neuer Theatertechnik* and the *Space Stage*, see Barbara Lesák, *Die Kulisse explodiert: Friedrich Kieslers Theaterexperimente und Architekturprojekte 1923–1925* (Vienna, 1988), pp. 99–160.

10 Frederick J. Kiesler (1890–1965), the Austrian-American architect, theater innovator, set designer, designer, and theoretician, lived in Vienna as a relatively unsuccessful painter until 1923. This changed after the success of his set for Karel Čapek's play *R.U.R.* in Berlin. For more on his life and work, see *Friedrich Kiesler 1890–1965*, ed. Dieter Bogner (Vienna, 1988), pp. 9–208; and Barbara Lesák, "Die Theaterbiographie des Frederick J. Kiesler: Stationen eines Theatervisionärs: Czernowitz, Wien, Berlin, Paris und New York," in *Frederick Kiesler — Architect and Visionary Theater Designer*, eds. Barbara Lesák and Thomas Trabitsch, exh. cat., Theatermuseum Vienna (Vienna, 2012), pp. 19–121.

11 Karl Kraus, "Serpentinengedankengänge," *Die Fackel*, no. 668–75, December, 1924, p. 39.

12 Laszlo Móhóly-Nagy, "Theater, Zirkus, Varieté," in *Die Bühne im Bauhaus*, ed. Hans M. Wingler (Berlin, 2003), pp. 45–56.

13 Katherine Michaelsen, "Andor Weiningers Bühnenprojekte am Bauhaus," in *Wechselwirkungen: Ungarische Avantgarde in der Weimarer Republik*, ed. Hubertus Gaßner, exh. cat., New Gallery, Kassel (Marburg, 1986), p. 430.

14 Farkas Molnár, "U-Theater," in Wingler 2003 (see note 12), pp. 57–58.

Not Master in His Own House—Topologies of Surrealism and Freud's Legacy

Judith Elisabeth Weiss

VISIT TO VIENNA—A PRIMAL SCENE

When André Breton arrived in Vienna on an October day in 1921, he had a clear destination: Berggasse 19, then the home and office of the founder of psychoanalysis (now the Sigmund Freud Museum). The leading Surrealist had high expectations, but the visit is known to have been a bitter disappointment. The conversation between colleagues, which Breton, as a former student of medicine and military psychiatrist, had sought with a view to discussing his artistic Surrealism project, did not turn out as he had hoped. Having been dismissed with a few courtesies, he must have returned to Paris with his pride deflated. In a feature essay entitled "Interview du Professeur Freud à Vienne" (Interview with Professor Freud in Vienna, 1922), published after a significant period of reflection, he describes polemically how, after the "famous padded door" opened, he was confronted by a "nondescript little old man," who received him "in the shabby consulting room of a local doctor" (figs. 1, 2).[1] Instead of the revered visionary who had discovered the pathological components of the everyday rituals of a bourgeois world, was a conservative middle-class figure whose very offices epitomized this abhorred world. It was not until more than ten years later that Freud was to make a "confession" in a letter to Breton: He had been unable to understand what Surrealism actually was and, as someone for whom art was so alien, he himself had perhaps no need to understand it.[2]

By linking Surrealism and psychoanalysis, Breton hoped to give scientific credentials to his artistic program, which had begun with the publication of the "first purely Surrealist work" *Les champs magnetiques* (*The Magnetic Fields,* 1919) and the *écriture automatique* (automatic writing) developed in it. "Prisoners of drops of water, we are only perpetual animals. We run through noiseless cities, and the enchanted posters no longer touch us," is the enigmatic opening to the book. Language is constructed here as an uninhibited stream of consciousness in which words are presented seemingly without conscious control and hence with unexpected breaks in the logic of the statements. Poetry of this type was in the anti-literary tradition of Lautréamont and his much quoted aphorism about the "chance encounter of a sewing machine and an umbrella on a dissecting table." The liberation of thought from censorship and the confines of logical consequence—even more, the unshackling of the arts from rational control—was to be the guiding principle of Surrealism, analogous to Freud's technique of free association.

While it is true that Freud's concept of the unconscious was part of the canon of Surrealist paradigms from the outset and that *The Interpretation of Dreams* (1900) had a great influence on artistic practice, there was agreement very early on in the movement that Surrealism was not merely the artistic equivalent of psychoanalysis. Its

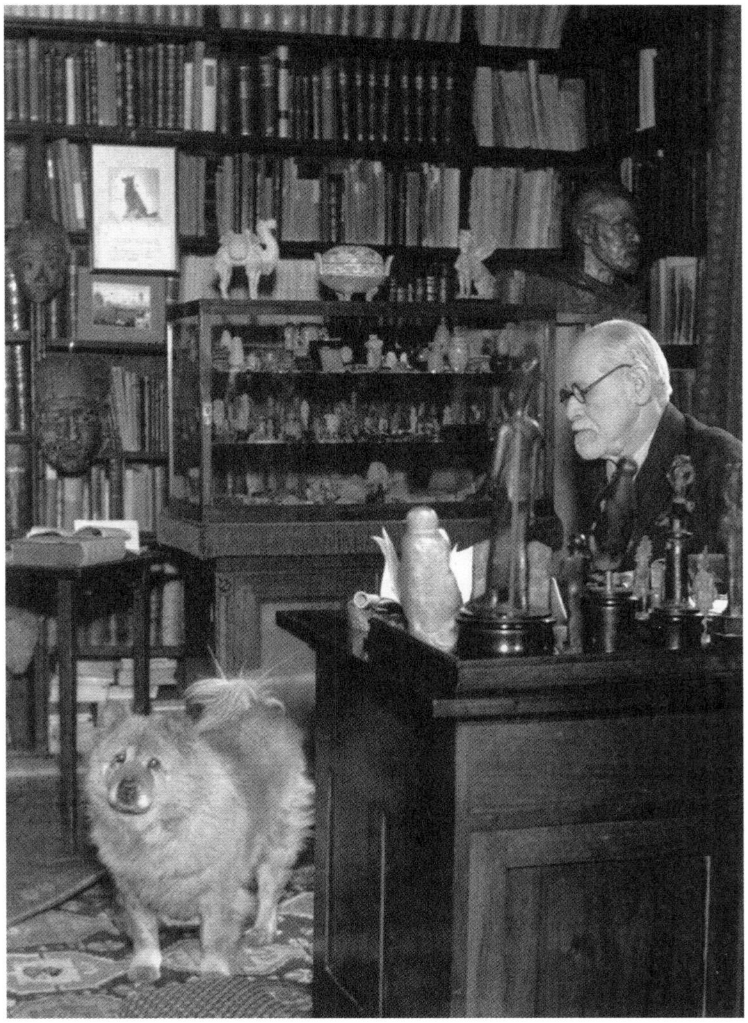

Fig. 1
Sigmund Freud with his dog in his office at Berggasse 19, Vienna, 1936

apologists were not in the least interested in therapeutic intentions or in critical analysis as a methodology aiming at normalization. They practiced their art rather as "pioneers in search of complete denormalization."[3] They were more intent on systematically borrowing metaphors and concepts from Freud's writings, such as Oedipus, Narcissus, Gradiva, censorship, dreams, and other figures and concepts whose suggestive potential could be utilized in Surrealist creativity. The unedifying encounter between Breton and Freud might ultimately be symptomatic of the numerous misinterpretations and misunderstandings that existed between Surrealist and psychoanalytic practice, highlighting the fact that psychoanalysis and Surrealism are parallel paradigms. And yet, even if the motivation was different in each case, there was common ground, namely the hidden terrain of the human psyche. In his first "Surrealist Manifesto" (1924) Breton explicitly states that Surrealism "must give thanks to the discoveries of Sigmund Freud."[4] The entry on Freud in José Pierre's *Dictionary of Surrealism* (1973) is prefaced by a quote from Breton: "'Surrealism has been led to attach a particular importance to the psychology of the dream mechanism in Freud and—in a general way, in the work of this author—to any elucidation of the unconscious based on clinical explorations' (A. Breton, 1935)."[5]

"DÉPAYSEMENT" AND "INTERNAL FOREIGN TERRITORY": ALIENATION AS A RESOURCE

In order to visualize unspoken and repressed images and to document the frailty of man's mastery of himself, the Surrealists developed new imaging processes and design principles, producing pictures that were partly controlled and partly fortuitous. From 1925, Max Ernst used *frottage* (rubbing) and *grattage* (scraping) techniques and modified the *collage technique* invented by Picasso in 1912. Óscar Domínguez developed *decalcomania* (transfer), and Wolfgang Paalen experimented with candle smoke to produce images using the *fumage* (smoking) technique.

With the thematic investigation of the unreal, macabre, and libidinous, with the rhetoric of madness and the paranoiac-critical method of fragmentation and deformation, artists turned their attention to the extreme, the marginalized, and the unfamiliar, in short the alien. Here they found a vast reservoir of material, enabling them to escape from the confines of conventional speaking, thinking, and designing—with the intention not of transforming the alien into the familiar, but of going beyond the bounds of familiarity. Themes representing strangeness and alienation could be in the form of an urban topos, nature, femininity, emotional life—or cartography. Yves Tanguy's Surrealist map of the world was published in 1929 in the Belgian magazine *Variétés* under the title *Le monde au temps des surréalistes* (literally: "The world in the time of the Surrealists," fig. 3). The map looks authentic enough but presents the world with new coordinates and shifted borders, enlarging some countries and making others disappear. Among the privileged locations within a topography in which the familiar contours have been removed are the Soviet Union and China as political spaces standing for revolutionary renewal and non-Western culture, which, in contrast to Euro-Atlantic cartographic convention, were put at the center of the map. In a considerably shrunken Europe, only Paris, as the birthplace of Surrealism, and Germany, as the source of intellectual traditions linked with Surrealism, were shown. Austria-Hungary, which in reality no longer existed, also occupied a tiny place on the map, perhaps as a warning against failed nation-building along nationalist lines in Eastern and Southern Europe after the end of the Habsburg Empire, but also to mark the country where psychoanalysis was born. The redimensioning of the continents and the recentering of the map exposed the myth of Europe as the embodiment of civilization and represented a harsh criticism of the hegemonial mapping of the world.[6] In his interpretation of the Surrealist topography, Patrick Waldberg refers to Breton's concept of *dépaysement*, the removal of objects from their normal context, as an act of displacement and deformation. The topographical denationalization on the aesthetic map and the inversion of a codified social and cultural normality relate thus to the Surrealist practice of taking politically and culturally localized items from their customary place and giving them a new context in an unexpected setting.[7] Moreover, the map of the world is a document revealing an interest in a comprehensive physical, aesthetic, and mental transcendence of boundaries.

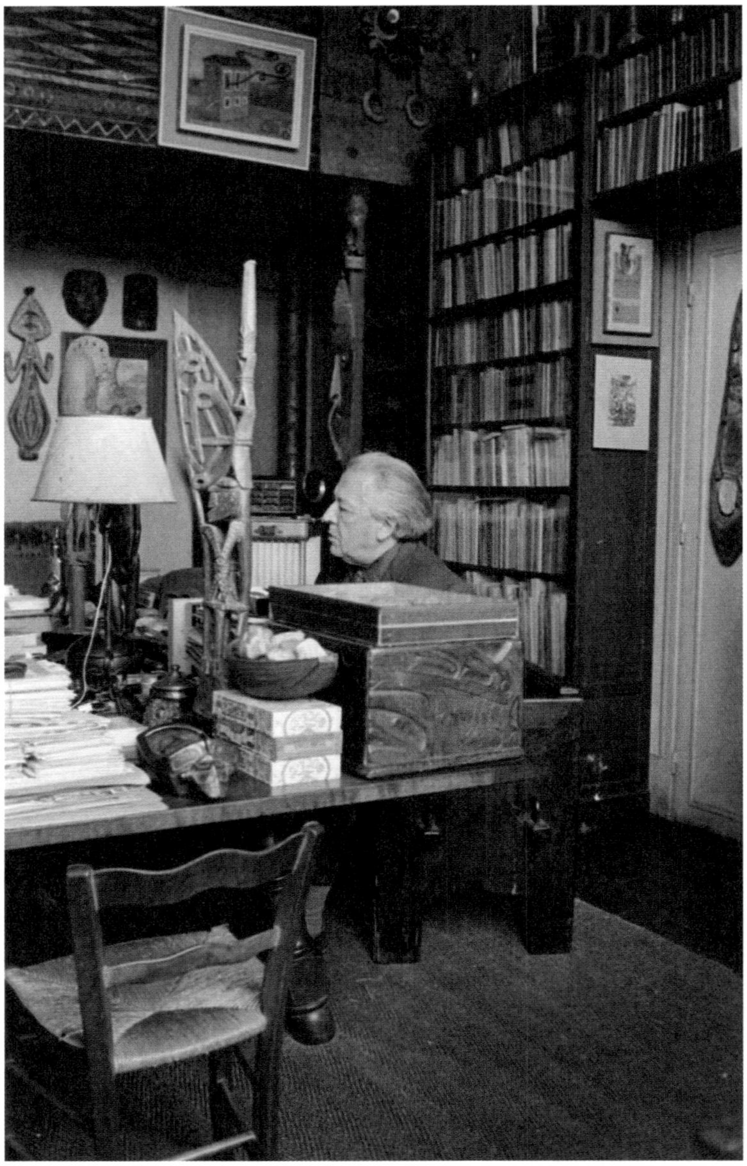

Fig. 2
André Breton in his studio, Paris, 1966

By rejecting any national characteristics and through the vast amount of travel by its protagonists, the globally active Surrealism was effectively able—in spite of ideological theorizing, quarrels, and exclusions—to bring together a highly diverse group of artists with individual, disparate, and conflicting creative methods and to unify stark contrasts. The movement knew no international boundaries: Along with Salvador Dalí, Pablo Picasso, and Luis Buñuel, Surrealism attracted many Spanish artists, such as Alberto Sánchez, Óscar Domínguez, and Luis Fernández, into its direct sphere of influence. Also closely orbiting the Surrealists were Jean Arp from Alsace, Man Ray from the USA, Max Ernst, Hans Bellmer, and Unica Zürn from Germany, Meret Oppenheim from Switzerland, Victor Brauner from Romania, Frederick Kiesler, Wolfgang Paalen, and Herbert Bayer from

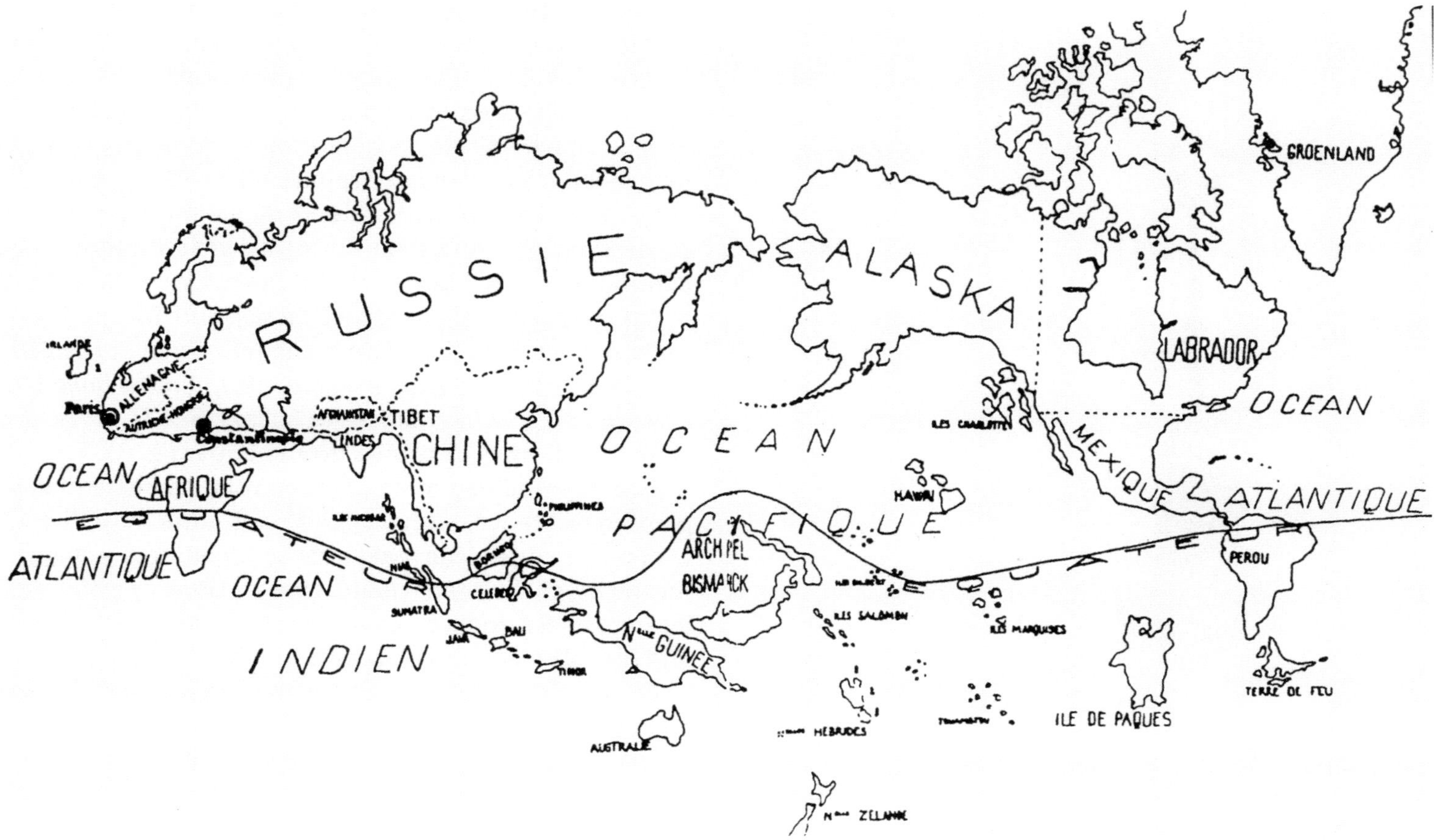

Fig. 3
Surrealist map of the world *Le monde au temps des surréalistes* In *Variétés: Revue mensuelle illustrée de l'esprit contemporain*, Brussels, 1929

Austria, Wilhelm Freddie from Denmark, Aldo Pellegrini from Argentina, César Moro from Peru, Octavio Paz from Mexico, and many others. Josef Šima, member of *Devetšil* (Butterbur), the Czech avant-garde association and forerunner of Surrealism, who settled permanently in Paris in 1921, was without doubt the most important intermediary between the art scenes in Paris and Prague. Radiating from Paris, the Surrealist movement soon comprised an international network of writers and artists, who, in an intensive interdisciplinary exchange, investigated the traces of psychic exaltation and the limits and shattering of taboos.

> **"A specter is haunting Europe—the specter of fascism."**
>
> (Manifesto of the Group of Surrealists in the ČSR)

When considering a poetic topology that combined the complexities of the external world with interior domains, the work of Wolfgang Paalen deserves particular attention. During a stay in Paris in 1935, the Viennese artist came into contact with Breton and other members of the Surrealist movement, who revealed to him the idea of a holistic synthesis of life and poetry, politics, and art. He was interested in "removing internal barriers, without which no external barrier can be fully removed," as he was later to formulate it when already living in Mexico.[8] The subject of works like *Pays interdit* (*Forbidden Land*, 1937), his first oil painting using the fumage technique, or *Les Étrangers* (*The Foreigners*, 1937) dealt with the recognition of Paalen's own alienation from himself. The removal of all narrative elements and the impossibility of precisely defining what was being presented, the chimera-like beings, which José Pierre described as "nightmarish totems," "clawed monsters," and "finely veined tissue" reminiscent of spiders' webs and bats' wings,[9] placed the work within the realm of uncertainty. The foreignness of *Les Étrangers* appears as a "basic figure of perceptual horror"[10] designed to shock the observer, since it was only through internal involvement, Paalen claimed, that an alienated life could be perceived in the first place.

The fact that the alien and strange come from the interior corresponds to the mapping of the mind by Freud, who also resorted to spatial metaphors and spoke of the ego, id, and superego as the three "realms, regions, provinces," into which the mental apparatus was divided.[11] It is the unconscious, paraphrased by Freud elegantly as the "internal foreign territory,"[12] that invalidates a person's autonomy: "The ego is not master in its own house."[13] In his allusive object *Le Moi et le Soi* (*The Ego and the Id*, 1937; fig. 4) Paalen combines these relationships between consciousness and instinct, authority and sanctioning,

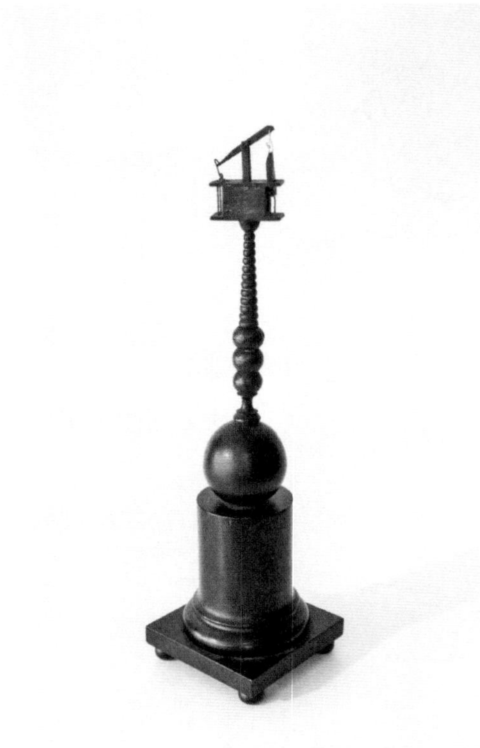

Fig. 4
Wolfgang Paalen
Le Moi et le Soi
(*The Ego and the Id*),
1937, Collection
Museum Franz Mayer,
Mexico City

in an idiosyncratic interpretation. The work shows an open mousetrap containing a cube balanced on a tapered turned-wood base. If the cube, the instrument of fate, is touched, not only will the mousetrap snap shut but the entire structure will become unbalanced and collapse. The human psyche is presented as a fragile structure whose contradictions and randomness seem impossible to control. Their underlying mechanisms, however, can be visualized through art.

THE "MAGICAL CAPITAL OF EUROPE"

The "magical capital of Europe," as Breton dubbed Prague so enthusiastically, is not to be found on the Surrealist map.[14] In José Pierre's *Dictionary of Surrealism,* however, the significance of the city for Surrealism is documented, since "Surrealism never awakened deeper and more lasting echoes than in Czechoslovakia."[15] The *Group of Surrealists in the ČSR* (Skupina surrealistů v ČSR) was founded in March 1934 with a manifesto whose opening sentence paraphrased the introduction to the *Communist Manifesto* by Karl Marx and Friedrich Engels: "A specter is haunting Europe—the specter of fascism."[16] It was a warning of what was to come. Caught between Stalinist authority and occupation by Hitler's fascist Germany, the Czech Surrealists were banned from working and exhibiting from 1939 onward, and threatened with persecution. Their works were thus created separately and in complete isolation, without any public feedback, while the reality became an unabashed "sur-reality." In Toyen's cycle *Schovej se, válko!* (*Conceal Yourself, War!,* 1944) the extermination had reached its highpoint and the disaster was evident for all to see (fig. 5). Many artists later pointed out that everyday life during the war produced more disturbing scenes than were ever to be depicted in the pictures by the Surrealists. The idea that man was not master in his own house now took on a bitter and all too real, political dimension.

The artistic solidarity between Paris and Prague was confirmed a year after the founding of the Surrealist group through Breton's visit to Prague in early 1935, together with Paul Éluard and the painter Josef Šima. Breton's talks during his visit attracted enormous public interest, as did the return visit to Paris by Vítězslav Nezval, Jindřich Štyrský, and Toyen. The exchange resulted in a joint, bilingual edition of the *Bulletin international du surréalisme / Mezinarodní bulletin surrealismu,* in which Štyrský's collage *Sen / Le rêve* (*The Dream*, 1935) featured prominently (fig. 6). The frequently modified motif of the sewing machine makes pointed reference, with a nod to Lautréamont, to the irrational and to a Surrealist *ars combinatoria*, hoping for the much vaunted "poetic spark." Štyrský's lifelong interest in dreams was something he shared with Breton and his followers and also with psychoanalysis. But, unlike the French Surrealists, who were interested above all in an aesthetic transformation using the tools of irony, Štyrský sought an iterative appropriation of his own dreams and the frequently investigated problem of their media reproduction. Max Ernst's dream protocols, meanwhile, are based on the pattern of Freud's and simulate an etiology of neurosis. They contain classic primal scenes of a sexual nature, defective memories, and profound interconnected condensations. Self-pathologization is a calculated instrument, however, counteracted through humor with a view to disrupting the senses.[17] While dreams originate here from the practice of simulation, for Štyrský they are a source of aesthetic stimulation. This may have to do with a fundamentally different historical perception of psychoanalysis. Freud's great significance for Surrealism also applies to the Czech context, but on a different basis, since the Czech translation of *The Interpretation of Dreams* was not published until 1938, whereas it was available in French from 1926. In Prague, psychoanalysis was not initially seen as a therapeutic method for treating neurotic disorders. In his article "Čím je surrealismu Sigmund Freud" (What is the significance of Sigmund Freud for Surrealism?, 1936), Vítězslav Nezval, one of the leading lights in Czech Surrealism, described psychoanalysis more as a cultural theory, and it was in this capacity that it was of significance for Surrealism.[18]

With Freud's comment that "past, present, and future are strung together, as it were, on the thread of the wish that runs through them,"[19] the conjunction of dream and the Surrealist concept of the city becomes evident. The "magical capital" was seen as the setting for the interleaving of an external spatial topography with an internal topology of memories and imagination, a place for layering the different temporal levels. It offered opportunities for poetic excess and was at the same time a place for surreal

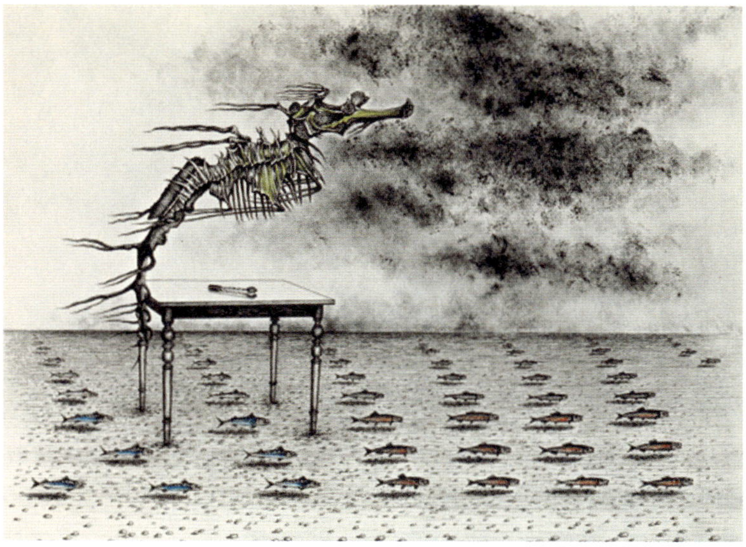

illumination, where bizarre window displays could be dramatized to become "two cut-off hands in a bidet." Prague—like Paris—has frequently been used as a topos in literature and art: a turn-of-the-century coffeehouse city, a mystical, Cabbalistic, German-Czech-Jewish world, a sacred place in which reality seems overlaid with a world of intellect and ideas—the "dream city" of Europe. The Surrealist concept of perambulation—of wandering aimlessly through the city—and of chance encounters is intended to present an altered view of one's own city, to be blind to the familiar and deaf to one's own language in order to perceive a different reality.[20] Petr Král says of the "magical capital of Europe": "Prague is real and at the same time disembodied to the point of being a mere idea."[21]

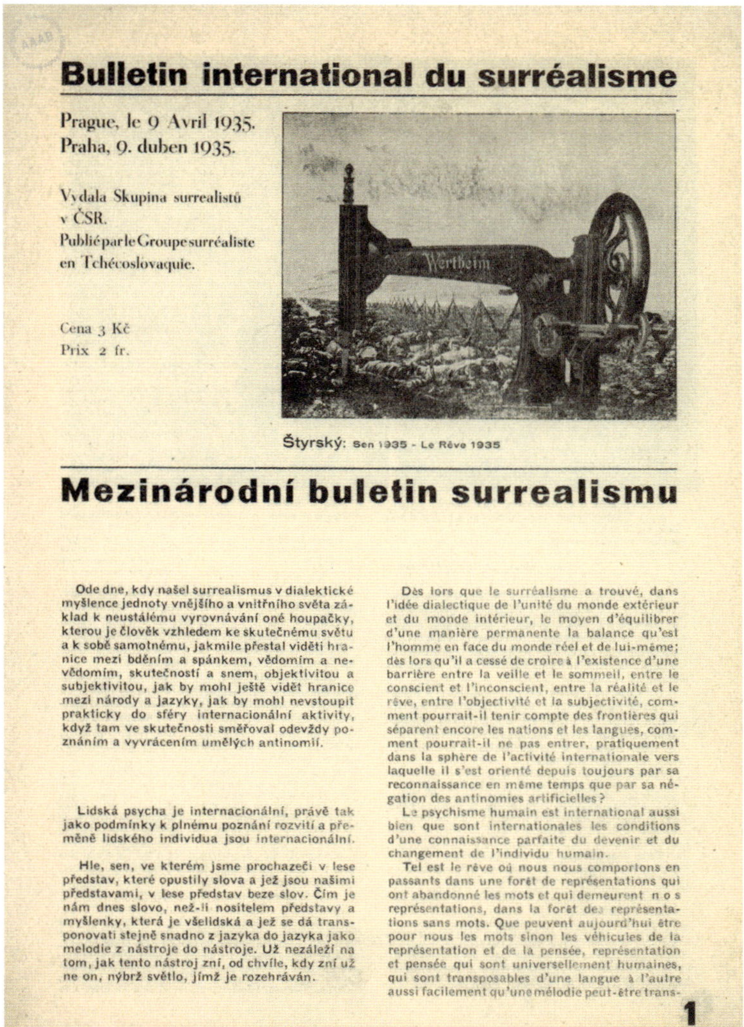

Bulletin international du surréalisme

Prague, le 9 Avril 1935.
Praha, 9. duben 1935.

Vydala Skupina surrealistů v ČSR.
Publié par le Groupe surréaliste en Tchécoslovaquie.

Cena 3 Kč
Prix 2 fr.

Štyrský: Sen 1935 - Le Rêve 1935

Mezinárodní buletin surrealismu

Ode dne, kdy našel surrealismus v dialektické myšlence jednoty vnějšího a vnitřního světa základ k neustálému vyrovnávání oné houpačky, kterou je člověk vzhledem ke skutečnému světu a k sobě samotnému, jakmile přestal viděti hranice mezi bděním a spánkem, vědomím a nevědomím, skutečností a snem, objektivitou a subjektivitou, jak by mohl ještě vidět hranice mezi národy a jazyky, jak by mohl nevstoupit prakticky do sféry internacionální aktivity, když tam ve skutečnosti směřoval odevždy poznáním a vyvrácením umělých antinomií.

Lidská psycha je internacionální, právě tak jako podmínky k plnému poznání rozvití a přeměně lidského individua jsou internacionální.

Hle, sen, ve kterém jsme prochazeči v lese představ, které opustily slova a jež jsou našimi představami, v lese představ beze slov. Čím je nám dnes slovo, než-li nositelem představy a myšlenky, která je všelidská a jež se dá transponovati stejně snadno z jazyka do jazyka jako melodie z nástroje do nástroje. Už nezáleží na tom, jak tento nástroj zní, od chvíle, kdy zní už ne on, nýbrž světlo, jímž je rozehráván.

Dès lors que le surréalisme a trouvé, dans l'idée dialectique de l'unité du monde extérieur et du monde intérieur, le moyen d'équilibrer d'une manière permanente la balance qu'est l'homme en face du monde réel et de lui-même; dès lors qu'il a cessé de croire à l'existence d'une barrière entre la veille et le sommeil, entre le conscient et l'inconscient, entre la réalité et le rêve, entre l'objectivité et la subjectivité, comment pourrait-il tenir compte des frontières qui séparent encore les nations et les langues, comment pourrait-il ne pas entrer, pratiquement dans la sphère de l'activité internationale vers laquelle il s'est orienté depuis toujours par sa reconnaissance en même temps que par sa négation des antinomies artificielles?

Le psychisme humain est international aussi bien que sont internationales les conditions d'une connaissance parfaite du devenir et du changement de l'individu humain.

Tel est le rêve où nous nous comportons en passants dans une forêt de représentations qui ont abandonné les mots et qui demeurent nos représentations, dans la forêt des représentations sans mots. Que peuvent aujourd'hui être pour nous les mots sinon les véhicules de la représentation et de la pensée, représentation et pensée qui sont universellement humaines, qui sont transposables d'une langue à l'autre aussi facilement qu'une mélodie peut-être trans-

1

Fig. 5
Toyen
From the series *Schovej se, válko!* (*Conceal Yourself, War!*), 1944

Fig. 6
Bulletin International du Surréalisme / Mezinarodní bulletin surrealismu with a collage by Jindřich Štyrský, April 1935

1 On Breton's visit to Freud and their correspondence, see Renate Schlesier, "Drei Visiten: Aus der Geschichte des Verhältnisses von Surrealismus und Psychoanalyse," in Ortrud Gutjahr, ed., *Kulturtheorie: Freiburger literaturpsychologische Gespräche—Jahrbuch für Literatur und Psychoanalyse*, vol. 24 (Würzburg, 2005), pp. 185–216, here pp. 185–86.
2 Schlesier 2005 (see note 1), p. 207.
3 Jürgen Link, "Zur erotischen Faszination durch die nicht normale *passante* in und nach dem Surrealismus," in Nanette Rissler-Pipka, Michael Lommel, and Justyna Cempel, eds., *Der Surrealismus in der Mediengesellschaft: Zwischen Kunst und Kommerz* (Bielefeld, 2010), pp. 33–48, here p. 38.
4 André Breton, "Manifesto of Surrealism," in ibid., *Manifestoes of Surrealism*, transl. by Richard Seaver and Helen R. Lane (Ann Arbor, 1972), pp. 1–47, here p. 10.
5 José Pierre, *A Dictionary of Surrealism*, (London, 1974), p. 73.
6 On Surrealist cartography, see Christian Semler, "Weltentwurf: Die Kartografie der Surrealisten," in ibid., *Kein Kommunismus ist auch keine Lösung—Texte und Essays*, Stefan Reinecke and Mathias Bröckers, eds. (Berlin, 2013), n.p.
7 See Patrick Waldberg, *Surrealism* (London, 1965), pp. 23–25; see also Judith Elisabeth Weiss, "Surrealismus zwischen Subversion und Ordnung: Deutsche Nachkriegsmoderne und Ausstellungspraxis nach 1945," in Karina Schuller and Isabel Fischer, eds., *Der Surrealismus in Deutschland (?)* (Münster, 2016), pp. 177–95, here pp. 177–79.
8 Foreword to Paalen's magazine *DYN*, no. 4/5, 1943; see also Andreas Neufert, *Wolfgang Paalen: Im Inneren des Wals* (Vienna/New York, 1999), p. 145.
9 Pierre 1974 (see note 5), p. 130.
10 Neufert 1999 (see note 8), p. 129.
11 Sigmund Freud, "The Dissection of the Psychical Personality," in *The Standard Edition of the Complete Psychological Works of Sigmund Freud*, ed. and transl. by James Strachey in collaboration with Anna Freud, assisted by Alix Strachey, Alan Tyson, and Angela Richards (London, 2001), vol. XXII, pp. 57–80, here p. 72.
12 Freud 2001 (see note 11), p. 57.
13 Sigmund Freud, "A Difficulty in Psycho-Analysis," in Strachey 2001 (see note 11), vol. XVII, pp. 135–144, here p. 143.
14 André Breton, "Introduction à l'œuvre de Toyen," in ibid., Jindřich Heisler and Benjamin Péret, eds., *Toyen* (Paris, 1953), p. 11.
15 Pierre 1974 (see note 5), p. 43.
16 Quoted in Karel Srp and Lenka Bydžovska, "Hinter den Augen," in *Gegen jede Vernunft: Surrealismus Paris — Prag*, exh. cat., Wilhelm-Hack-Museum, Ludwigshafen, Kunstverein Ludwigshafen am Rhein (Stuttgart, 2009), pp. 33–62, here p. 54.
17 Max Ernst, "Visions de demi-sommeil," in *La revolution surréaliste*, no. 9/10, 1927, p. 7; see also Max Ernst, *Écriture* (Paris, 1970), p. 237.
18 On the reception of psychoanalysis, see Anja Tippner, *Die permanente Avantgarde? Surrealismus in Prag* (Cologne/Weimar/Vienna, 2009), pp. 81–92.
19 Sigmund Freud, "Writers and Day-Dreaming," in Strachey 2001 (see note 11), vol. IX, pp. 141–154, here p. 148.
20 Tippner 2009, p. 154 (see note 18).
21 Petr Král, *Praha* (Prague, 2000), p. 7.

From Cubism to Constructivism

Cubism didn't end with the secession of Braque and Picasso or the folding of the Prague-based periodical *Umělecký měsíčník* (Art Monthly) in 1914. Non-representational art continued to develop in the new states of Europe, for example in the guise of Constructivism or—in the case of Austria—Kinetic Art, associated with the artists Erika Giovanna Klien and Friedl Dicker-Brandeis. In postwar Czechoslovakia, Synthetic Cubism was advanced by the artists Otto Gutfreund, Emil Filla, and Antonín Procházka. Constructivist art in Hungary was based on compositions of pure geometric forms, proletarian Cubo-Futurism (Béla Uitz), and innovations in metaphysical painting (Sándor Bortnyik). Highly unusual were the "organic" compositions of Anton Jasusch, whose formal language evokes comparisons with János Mattis-Teutsch's early work. (MH)

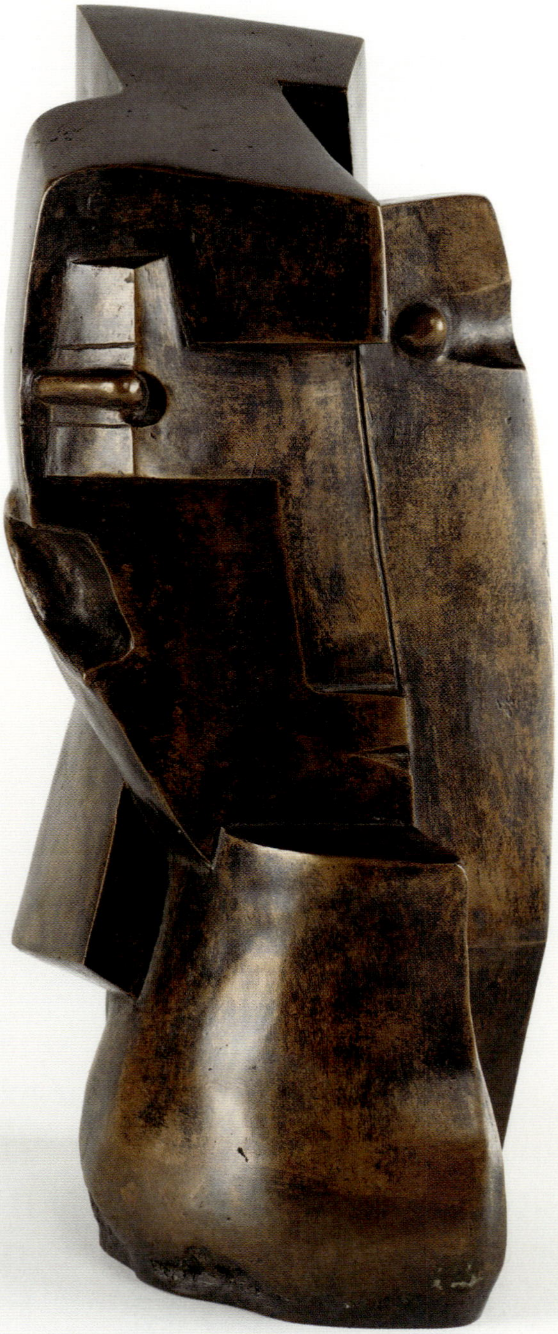

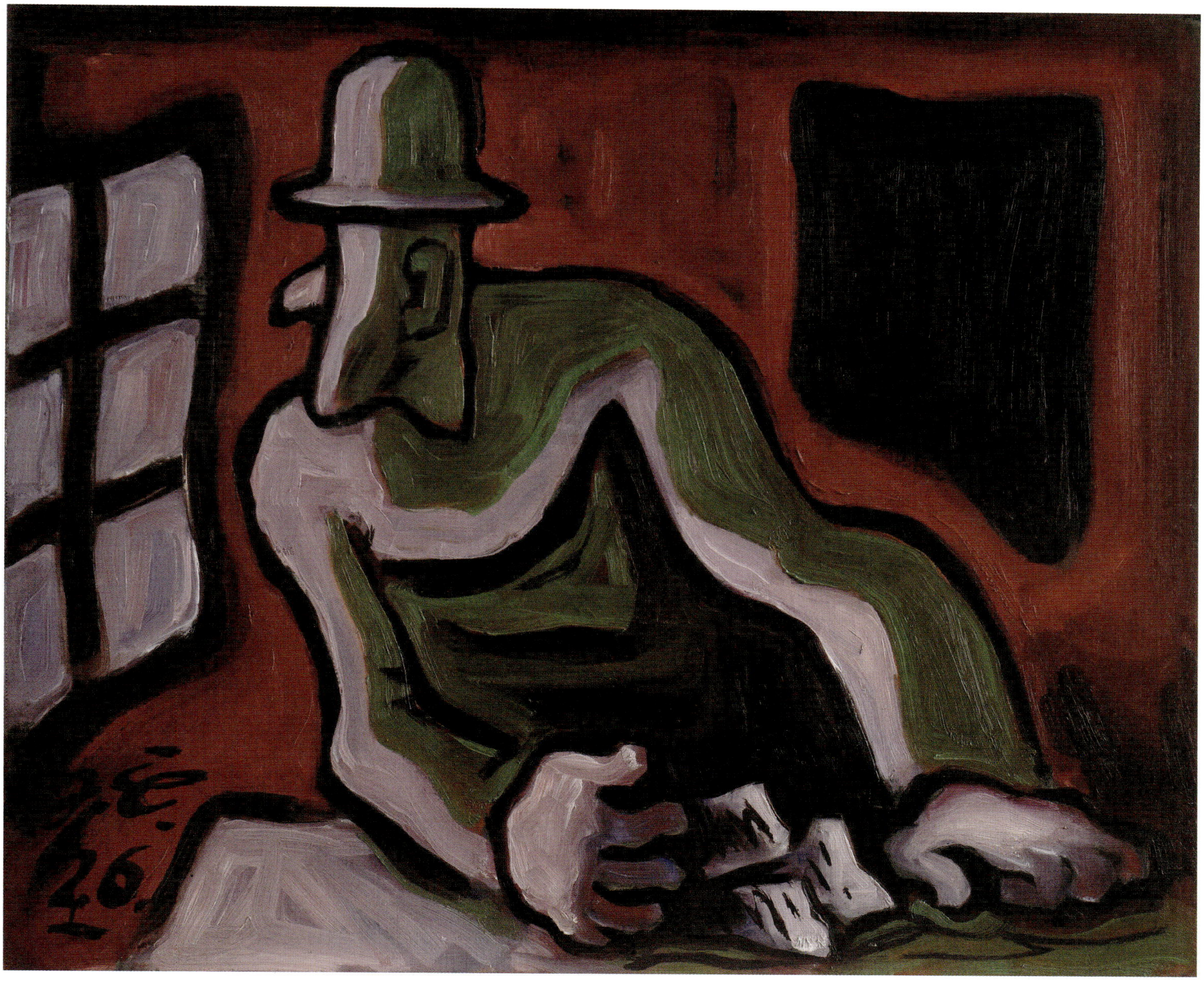

◂ Otto Gutfreund
Head II, 1919
Belvedere, Vienna, on permanent loan from the Rotter Collection

Josef Čapek
Guilty Conscience, 1926
Moravian Gallery, Brno

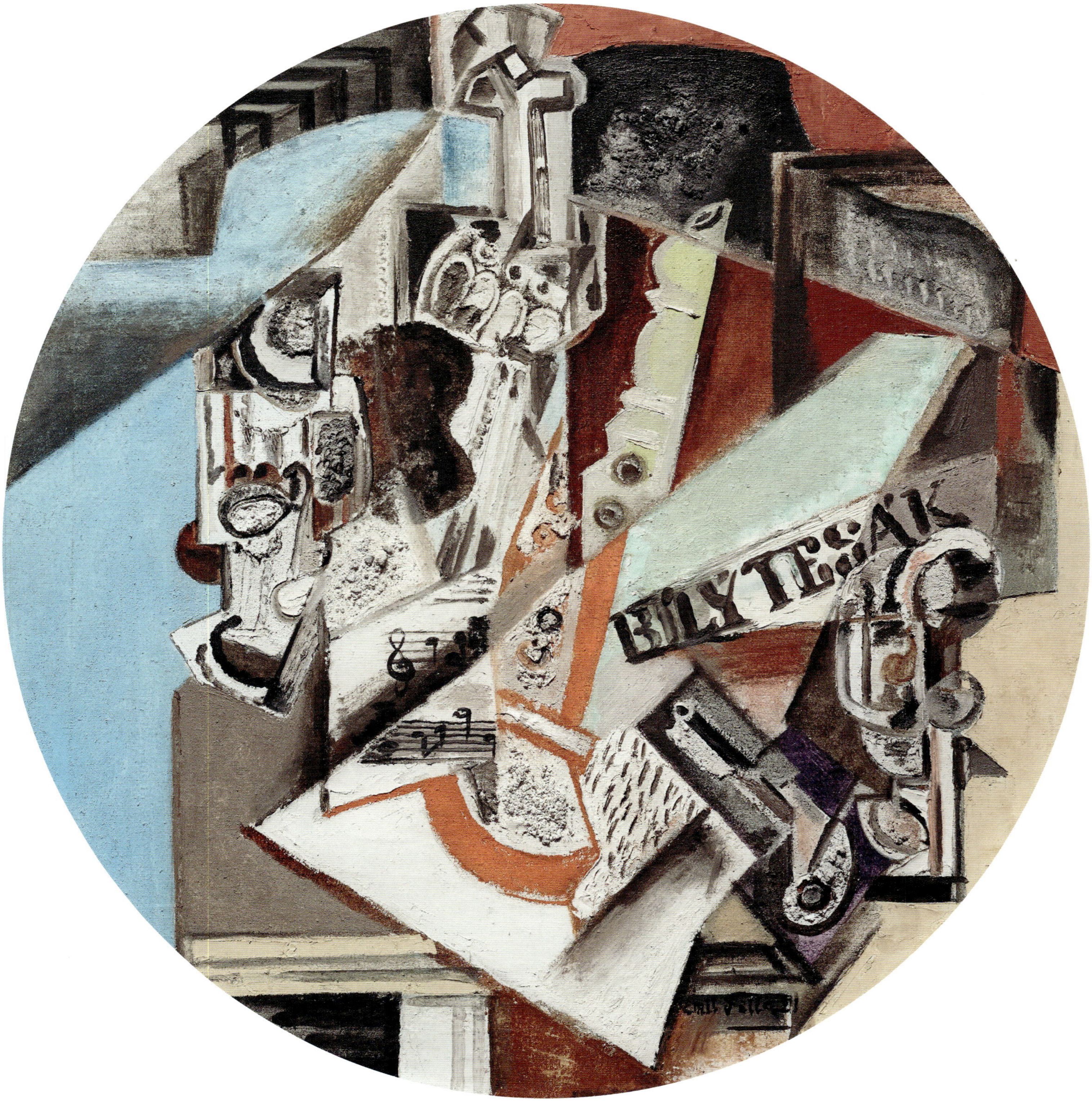

Emil Filla
Still Life with Book
(Jack London, The Son of the Wolf*)*, 1921
Belvedere, Vienna, on permanent loan
from the Rotter Collection

Antonín Procházka ▸
Still Life with Kerosene Lamp, 1921
Belvedere, Vienna,
on permanent loan from
the Rotter Collection

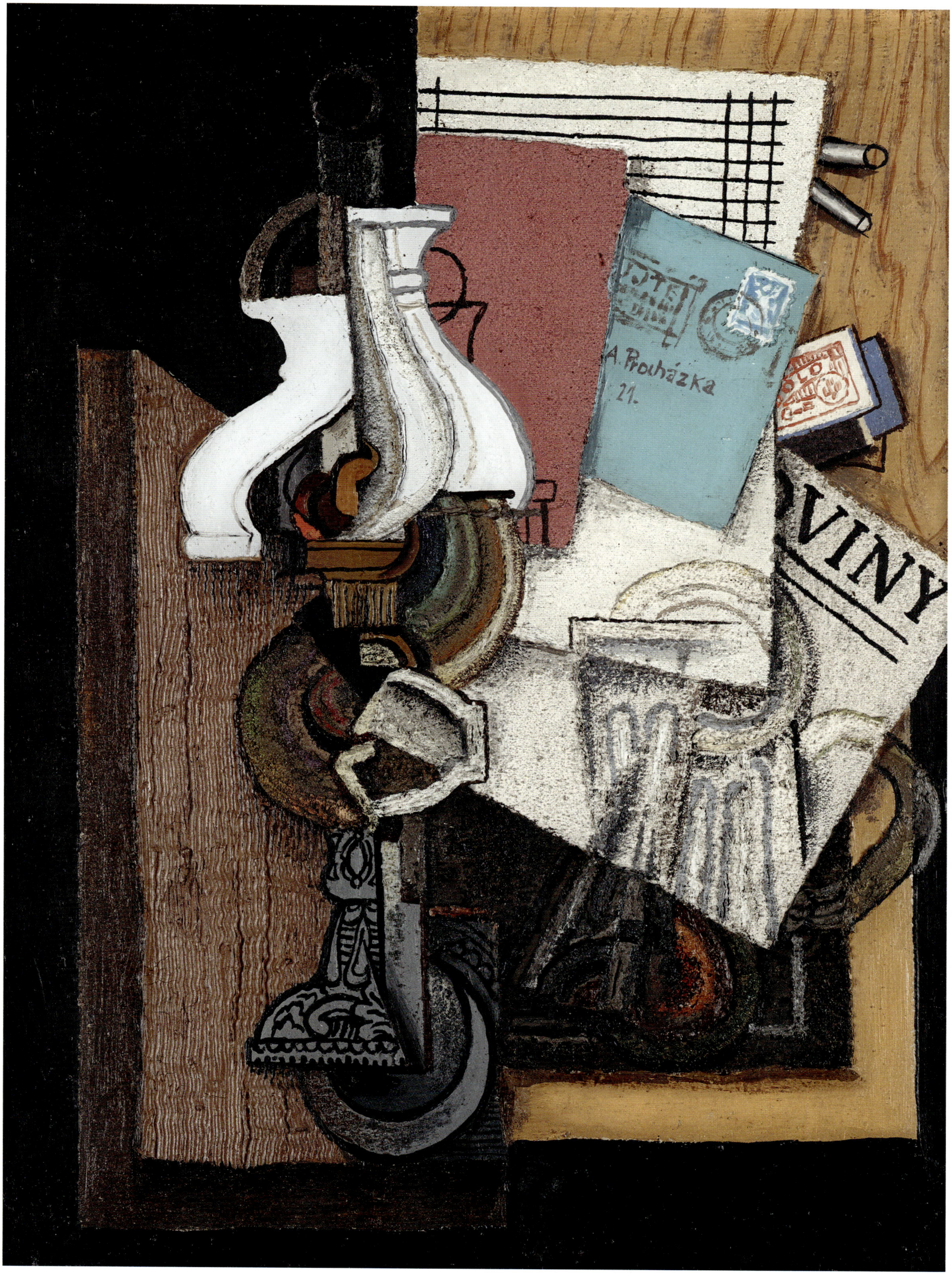
A. Procházka
21.
VINY

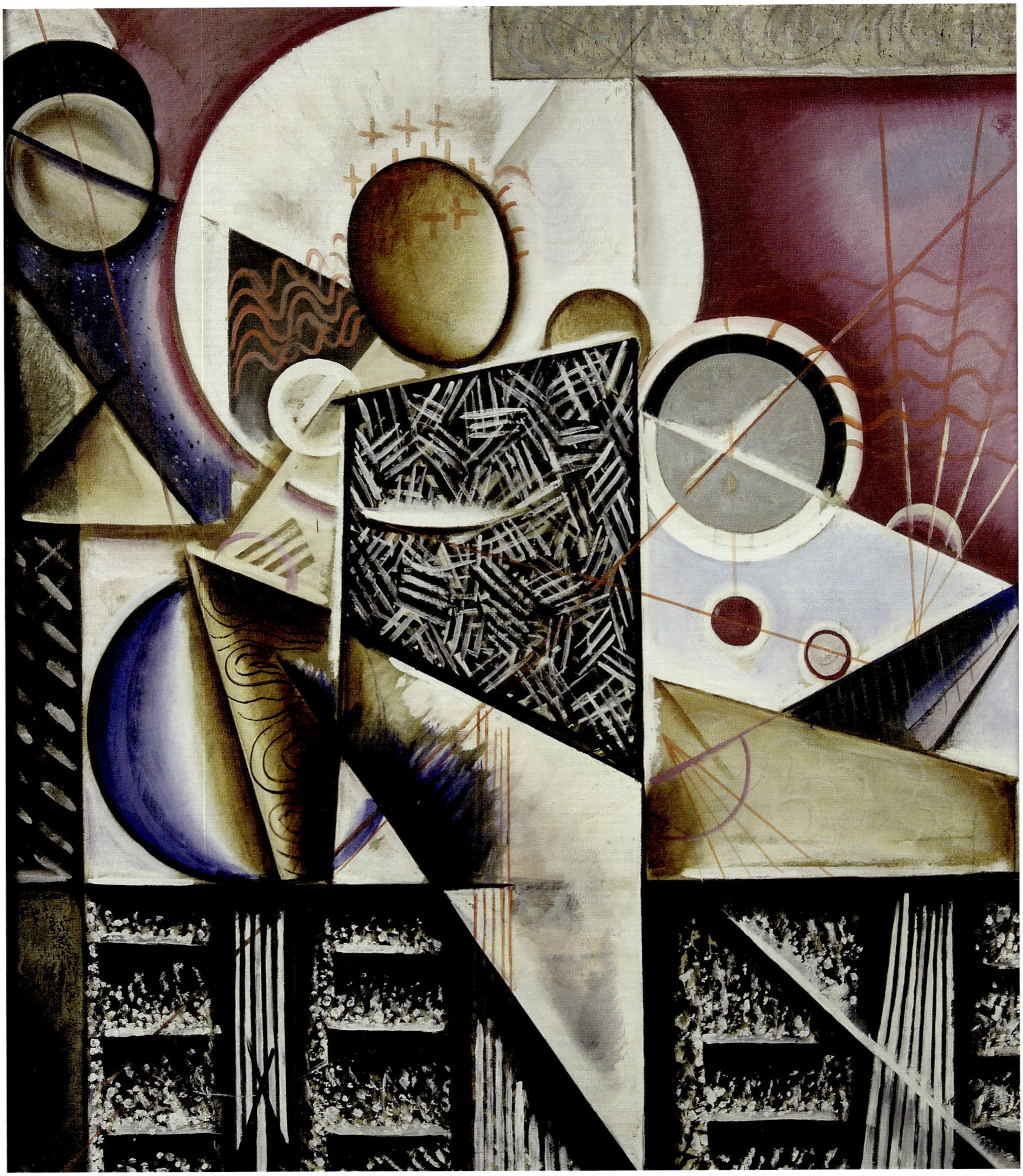

Béla Uitz
Icon Analysis on a Purple Background, 1922
Museum of Fine Arts—Hungarian
National Gallery, Budapest

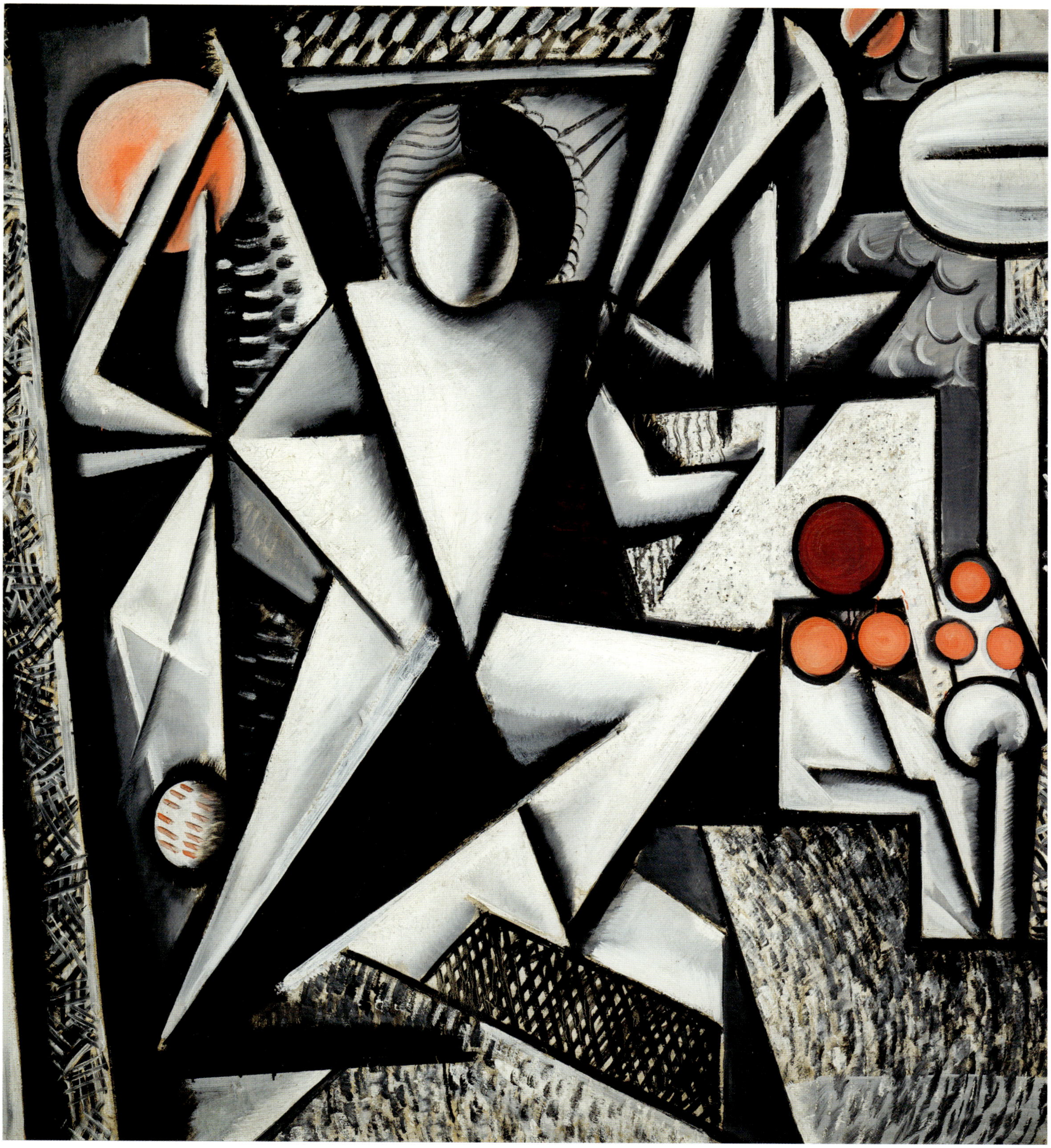

Béla Uitz
Fight, 1922
Museum of Fine Arts—Hungarian National Gallery, Budapest

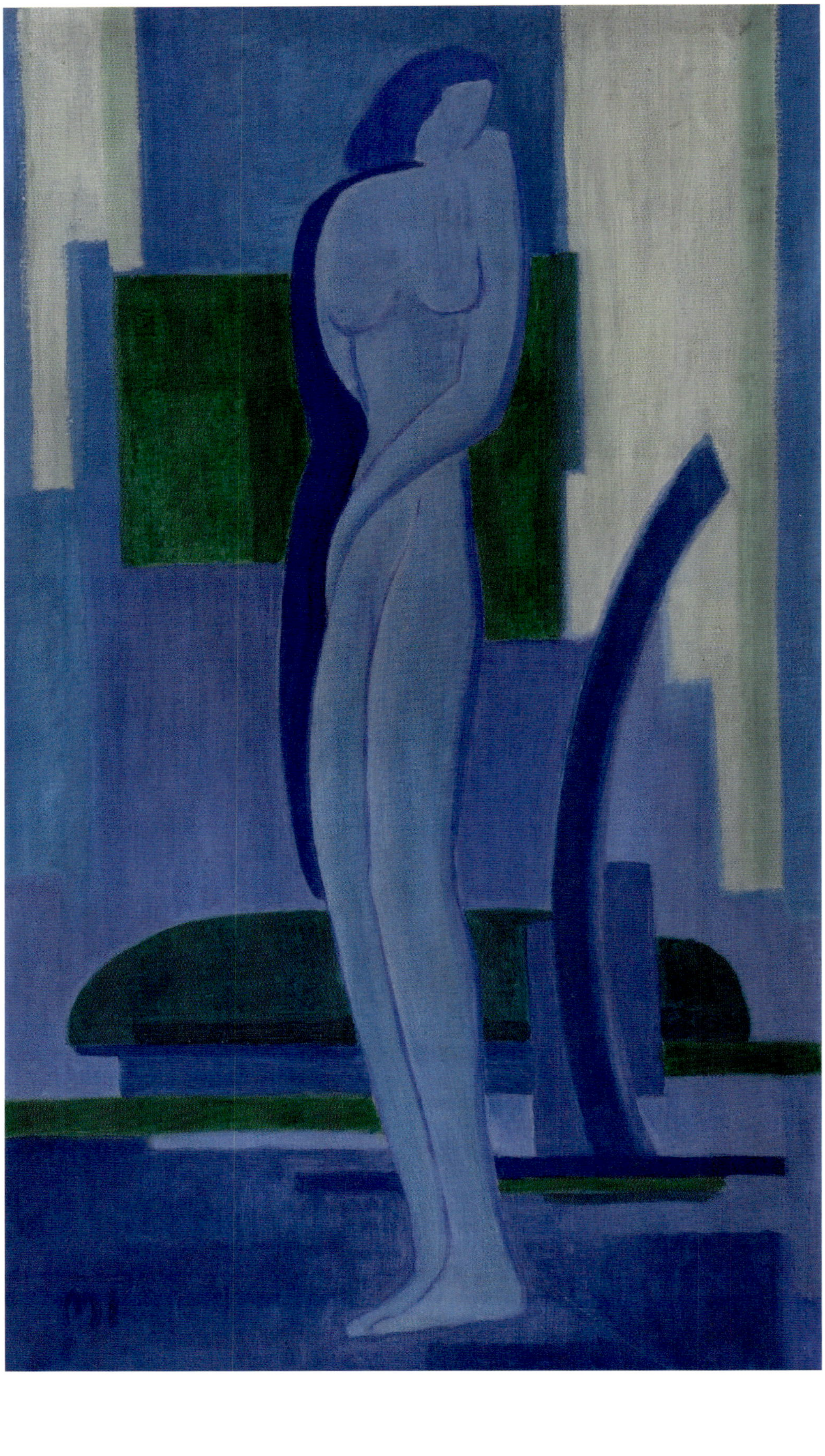

D1

János Mattis-Teutsch
Calling, 1928
Rechnitzer Collection Hungary, Győr

János Mattis-Teutsch ▸
Symmetry, 1927
Rechnitzer Collection Hungary, Győr

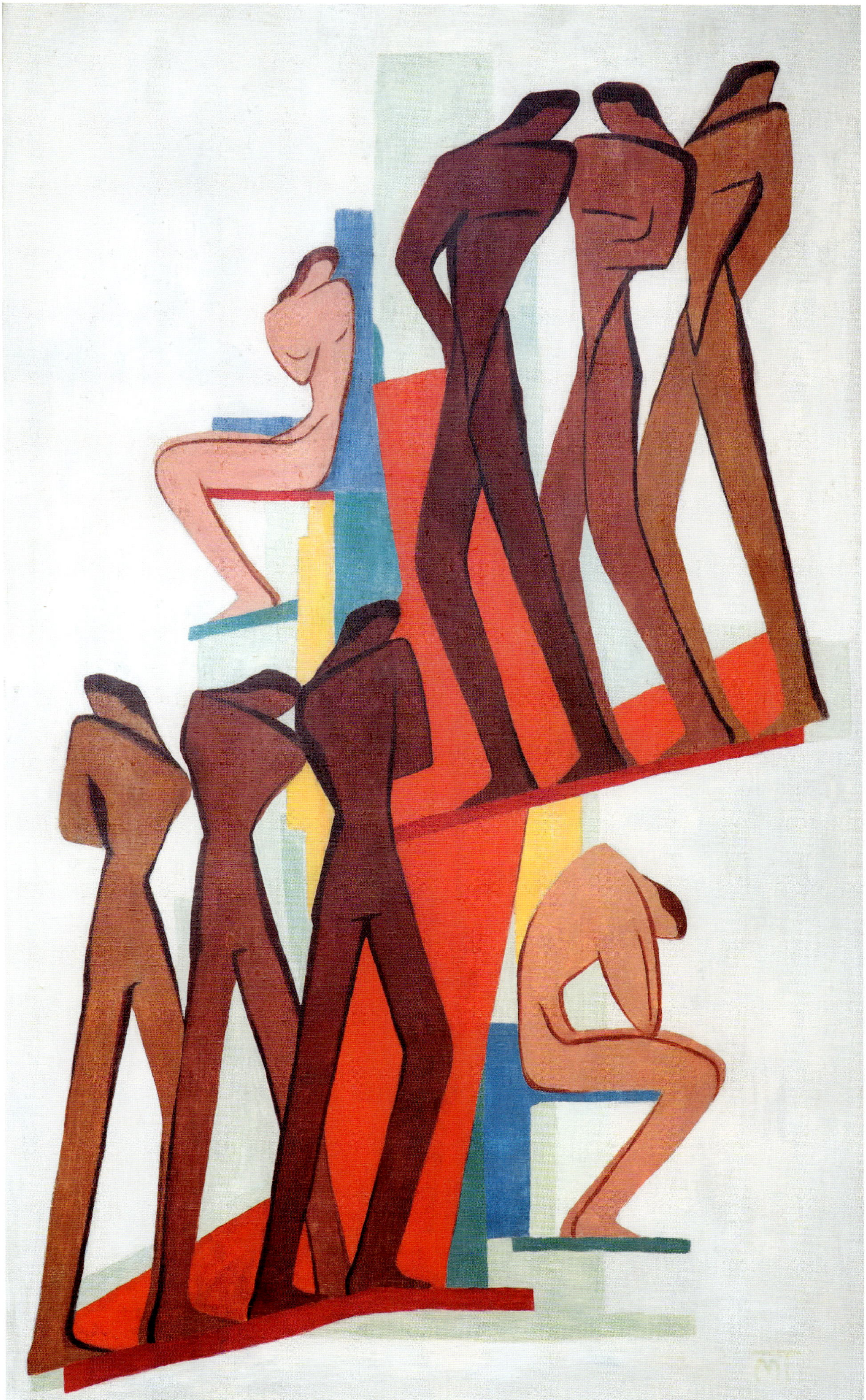

D1

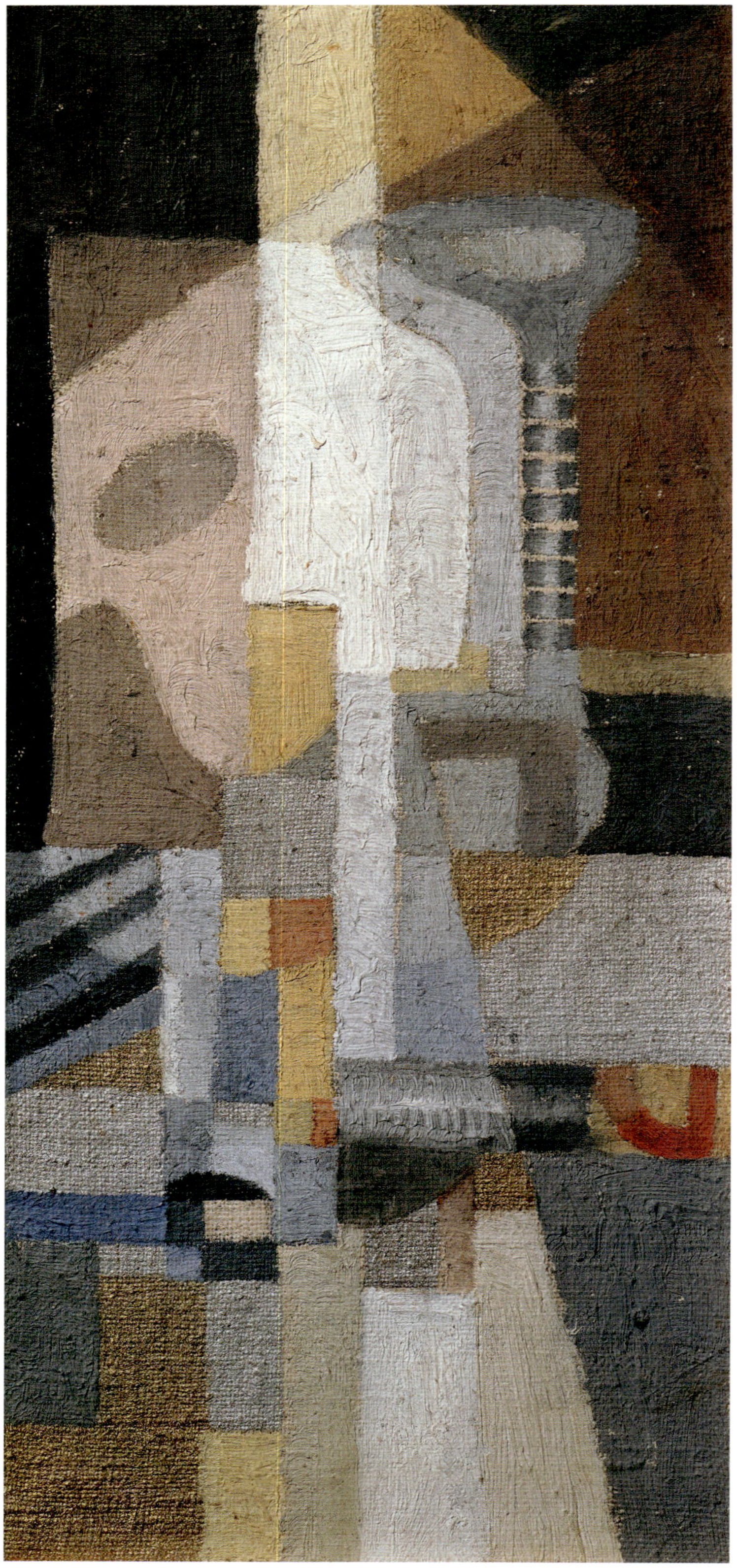

D1

Erika Giovanna Klien
Composition with
String Instruments, 1923/24
Belvedere, Vienna

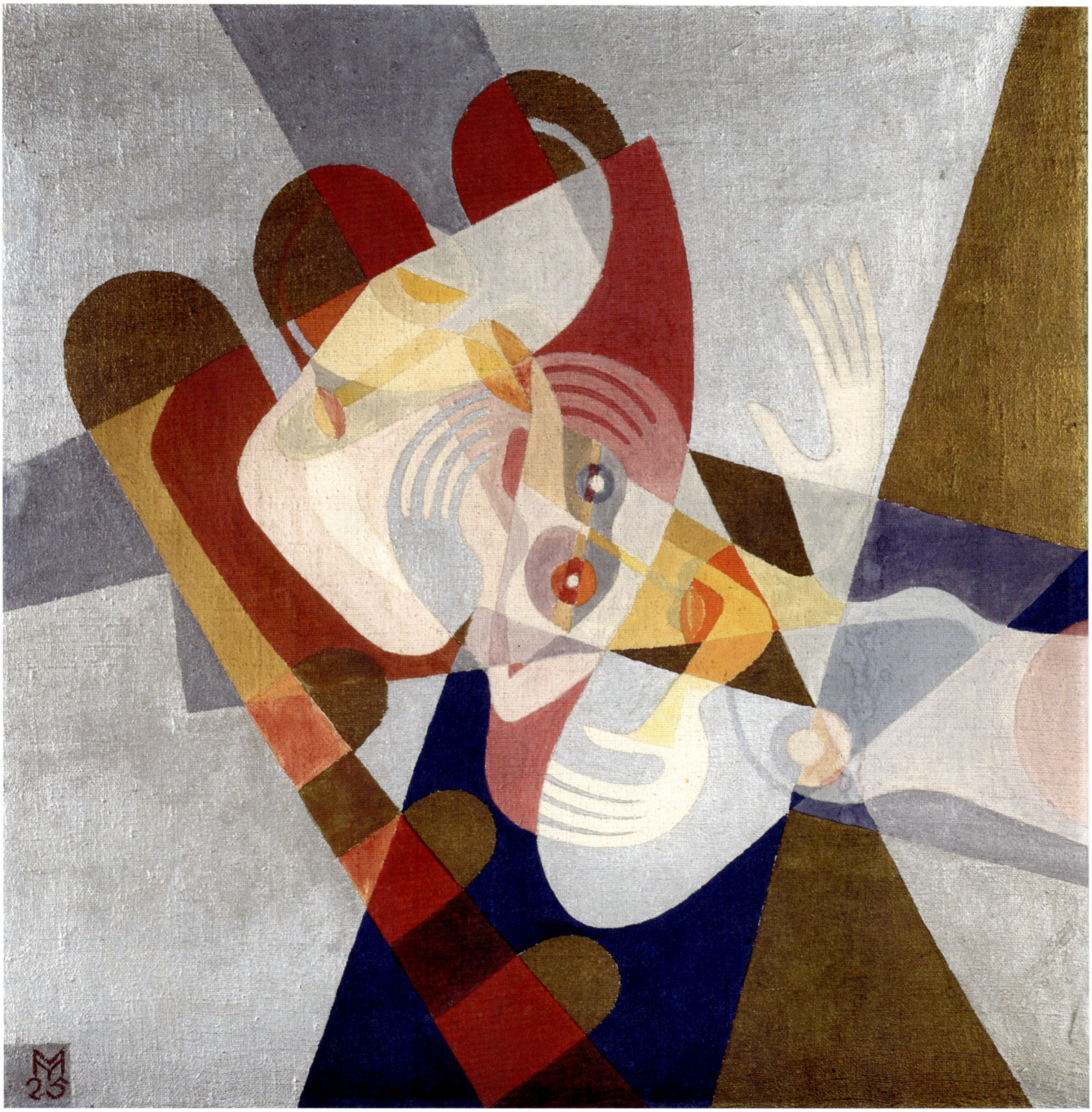

Marianne (My) Ullmann
Modest, 1925
University of Applied Arts Vienna,
Collection and Archive

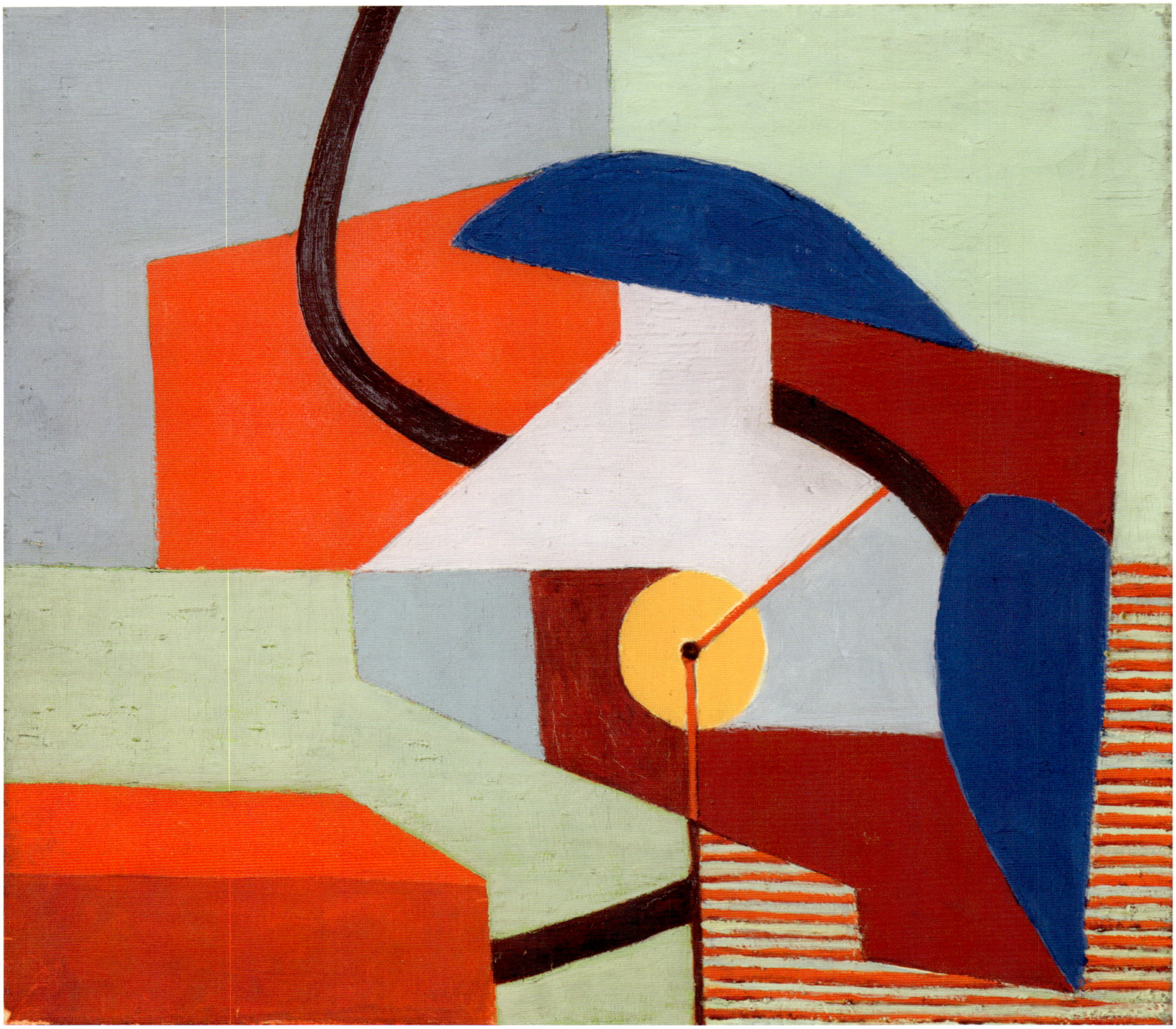

D1

Lajos Tihanyi
Composition, 1937
Museum of Fine Arts—Hungarian
National Gallery, Budapest

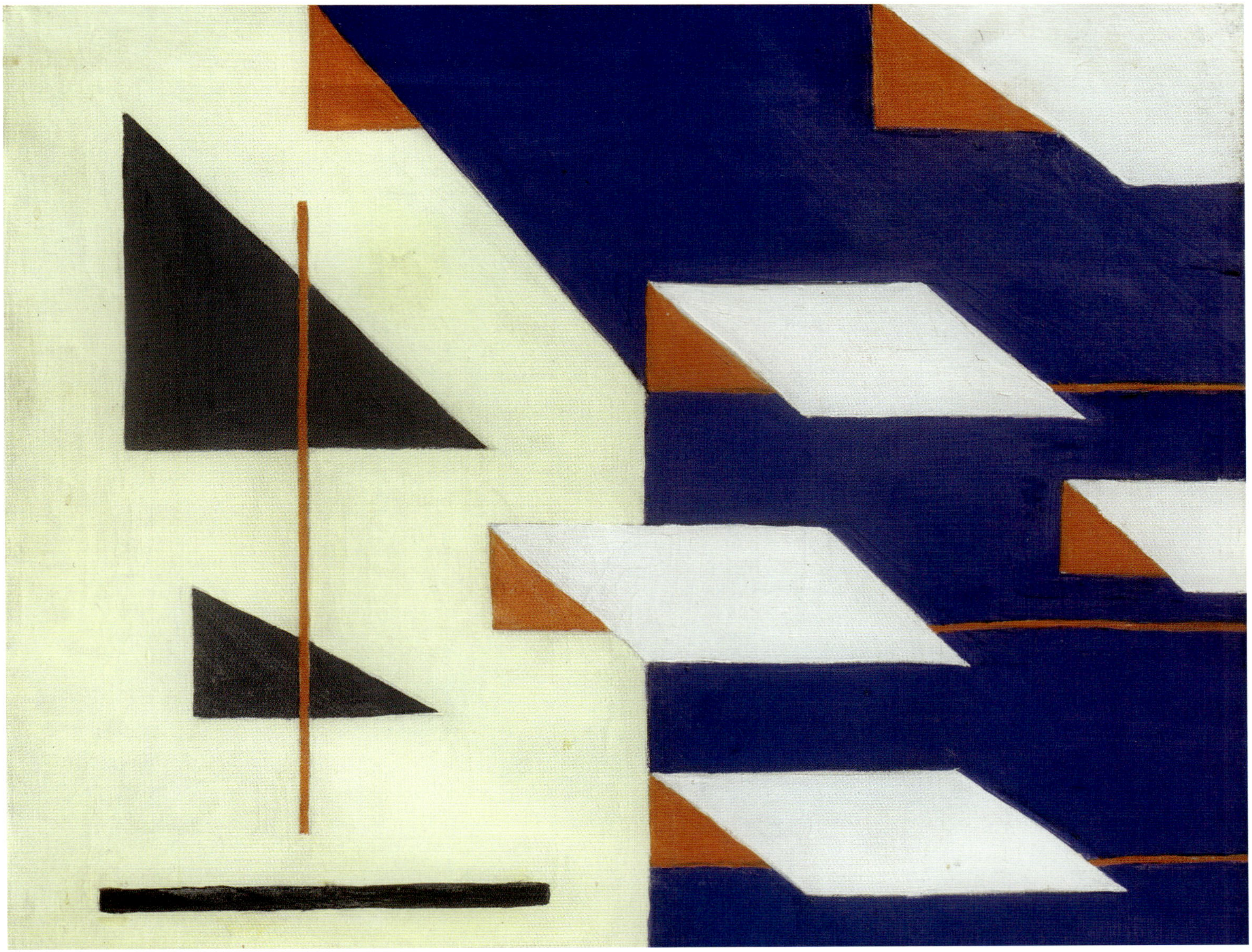

Lajos Tihanyi
Composition in Blue and Yellow, 1934
Museum of Fine Arts—Hungarian
National Gallery, Budapest

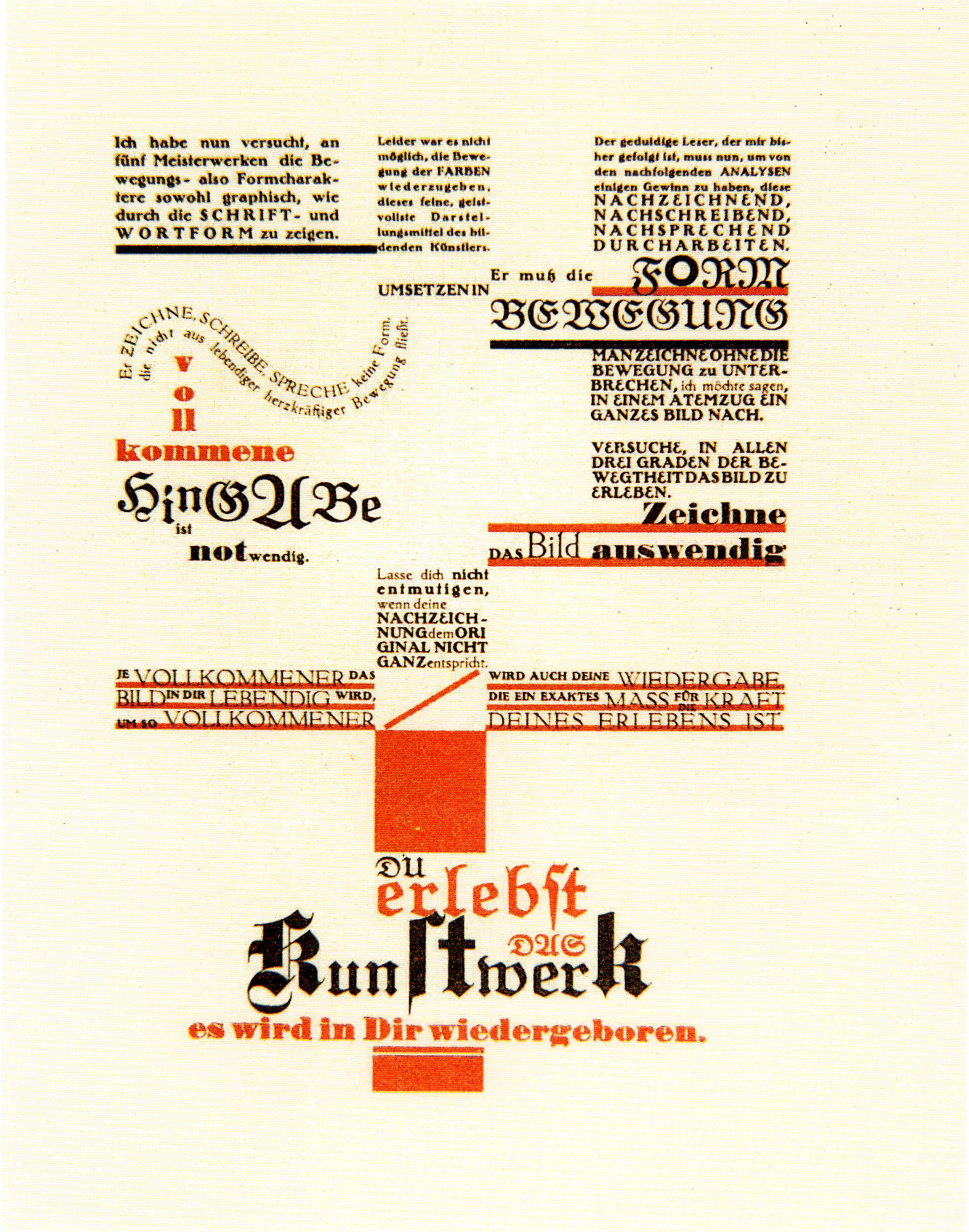

Friedl Dicker-Brandeis
From *Utopia: Dokumente der Wirklichkeit*,
Weimar, 1921
Georg Schrom, Vienna

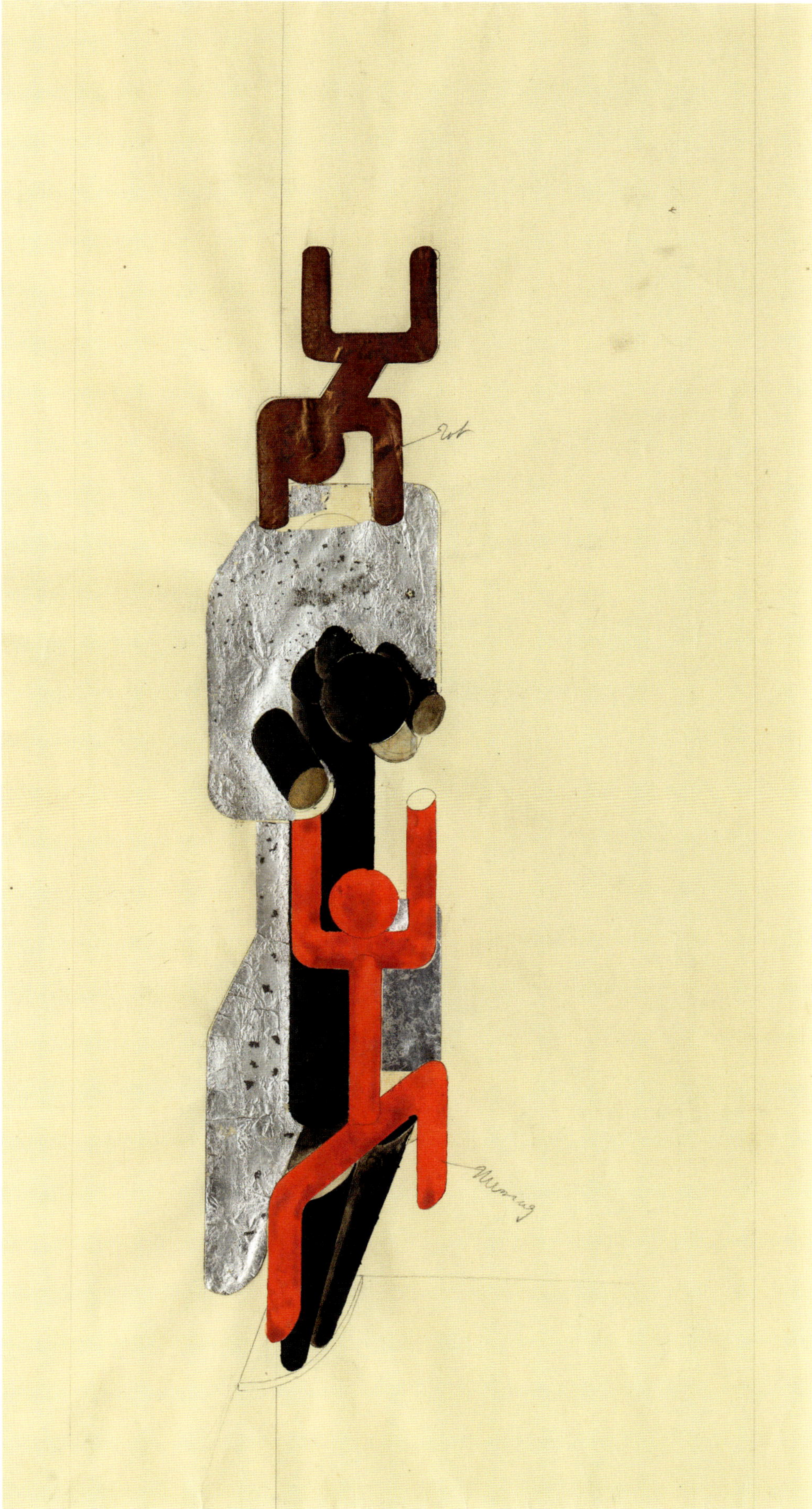

Friedl Dicker-Brandeis
Virgin and Child with Saint Anne, 1915–25
University of Applied Arts Vienna,
Collection and Archive

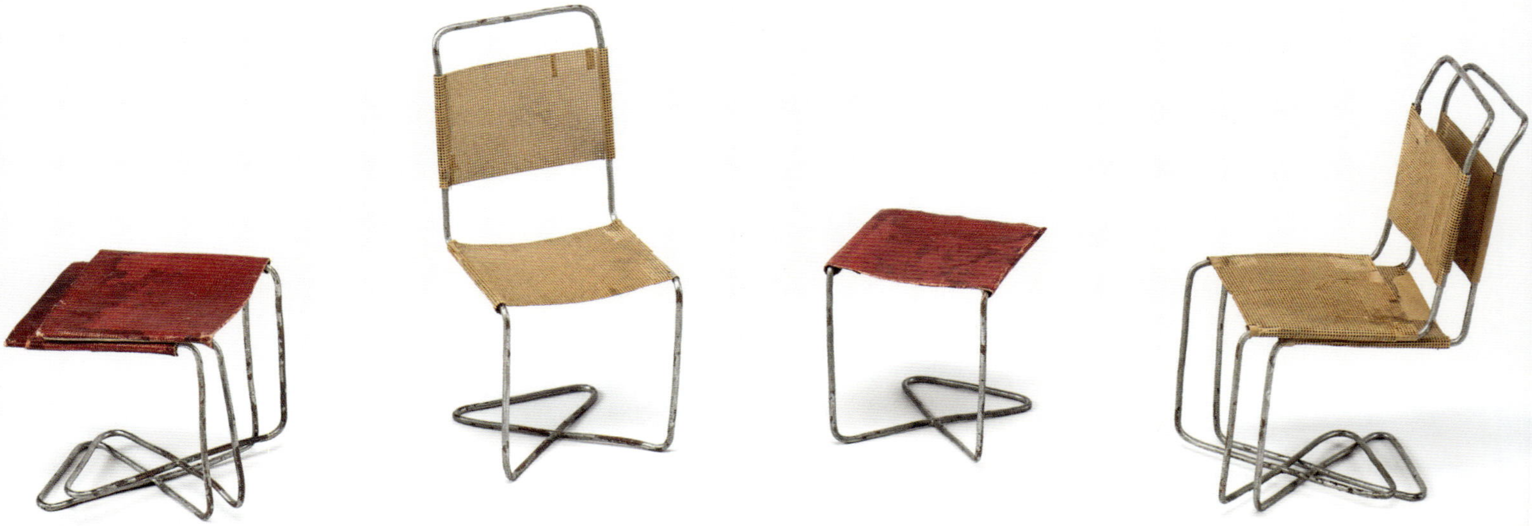

D1

Friedl Dicker-Brandeis, Franz Singer
Models for Two Chairs and for Stools, c. 1932–34
Georg Schrom, Vienna

Marcel Breuer, Anton Lorenz ▸
Cantilever chair, model no. 317 (B34); produced by: J. A. Talos, Vienna, 1928, MAK — Austrian Museum of Applied Arts / Contemporary Art, Vienna

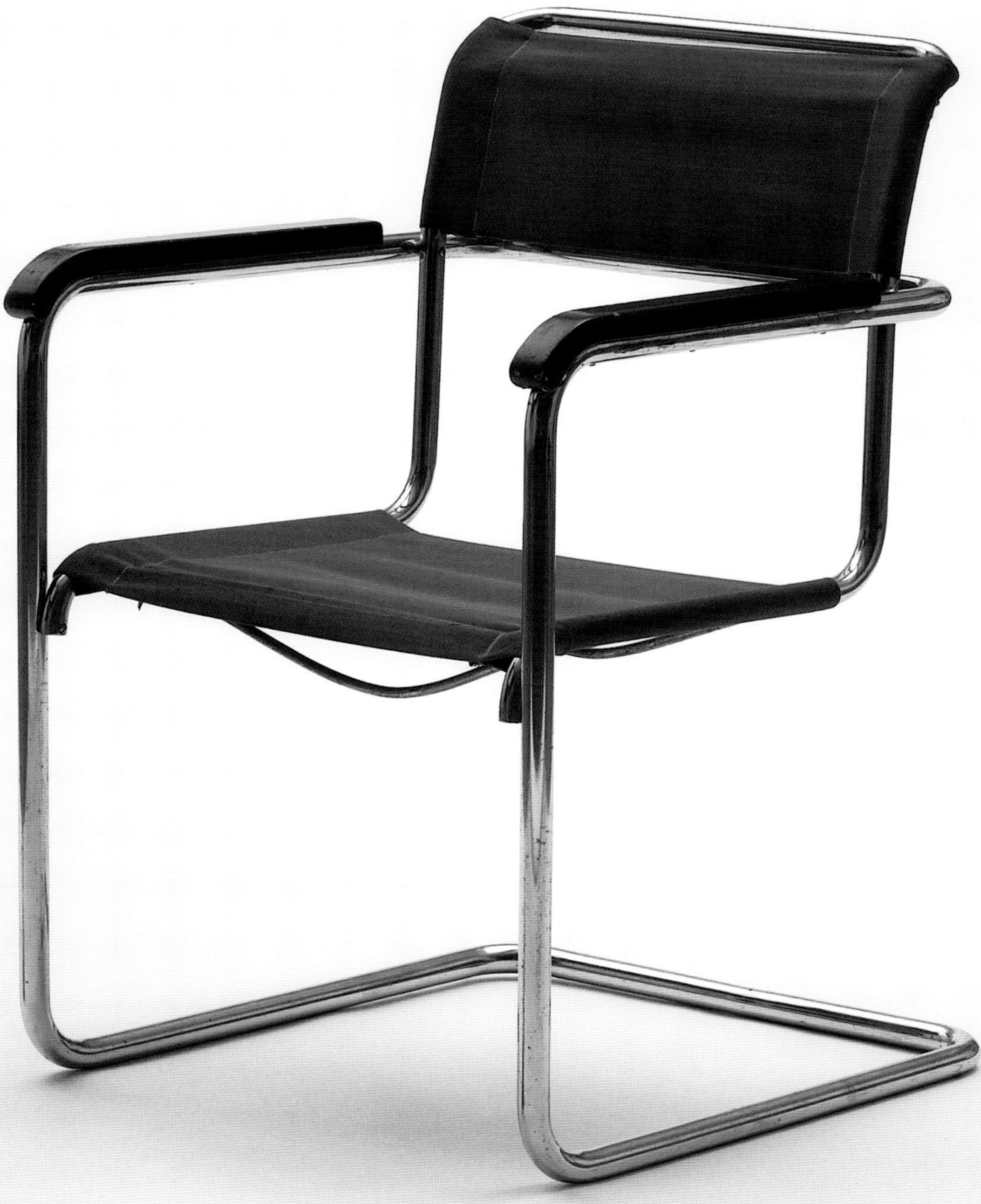

D1

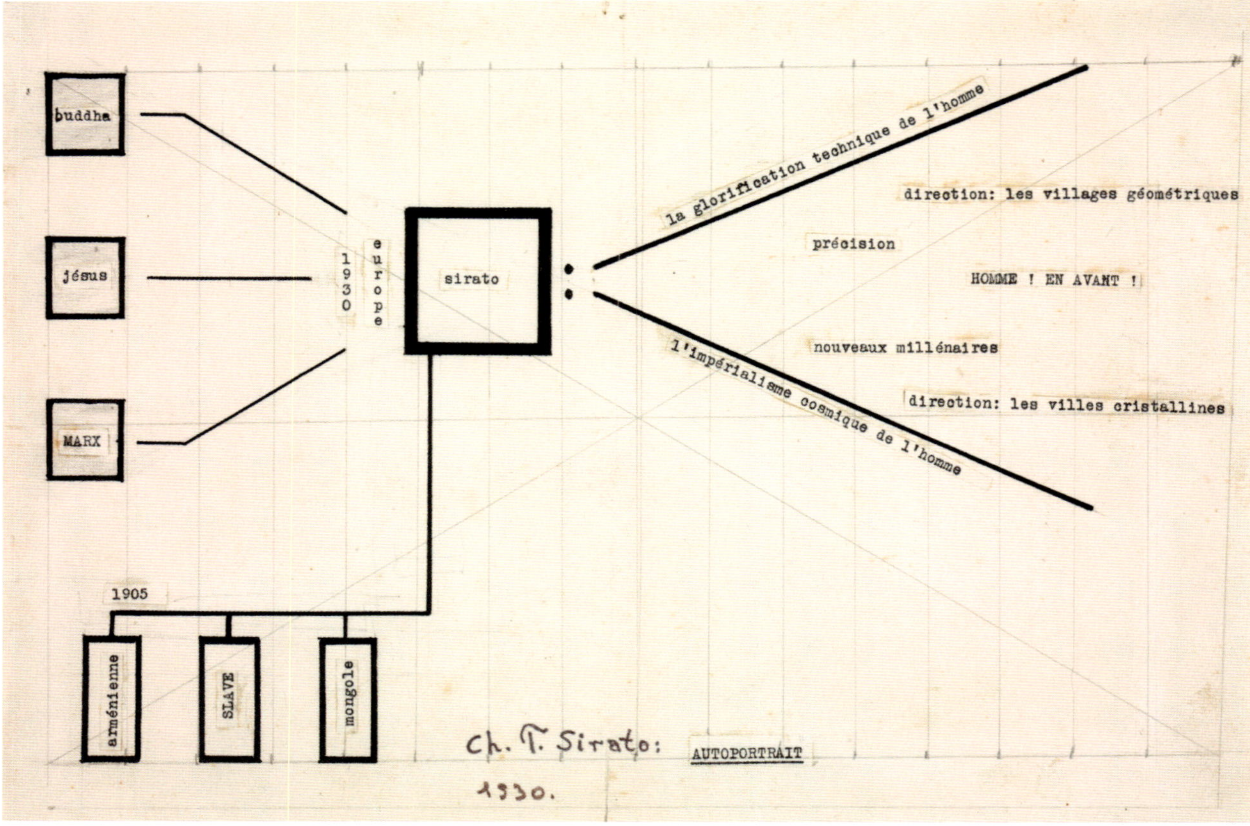

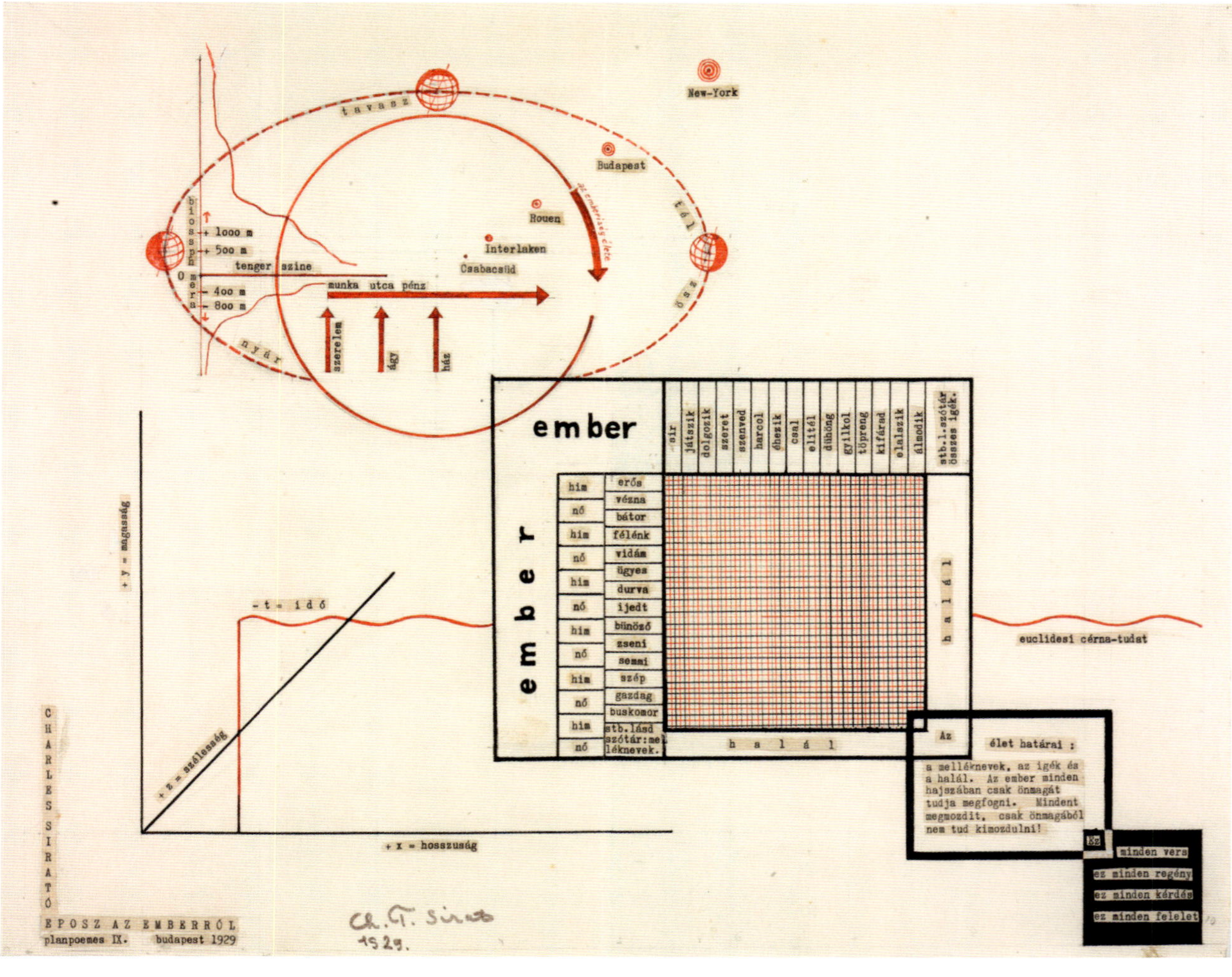

Károlý Tamkó Sirató
Self-Portrait, 1930
Private collection, Switzerland

Károlý Tamkó Sirató
Epic about Humanity, "Planpoemes IX," 1929
Private collection, Switzerland

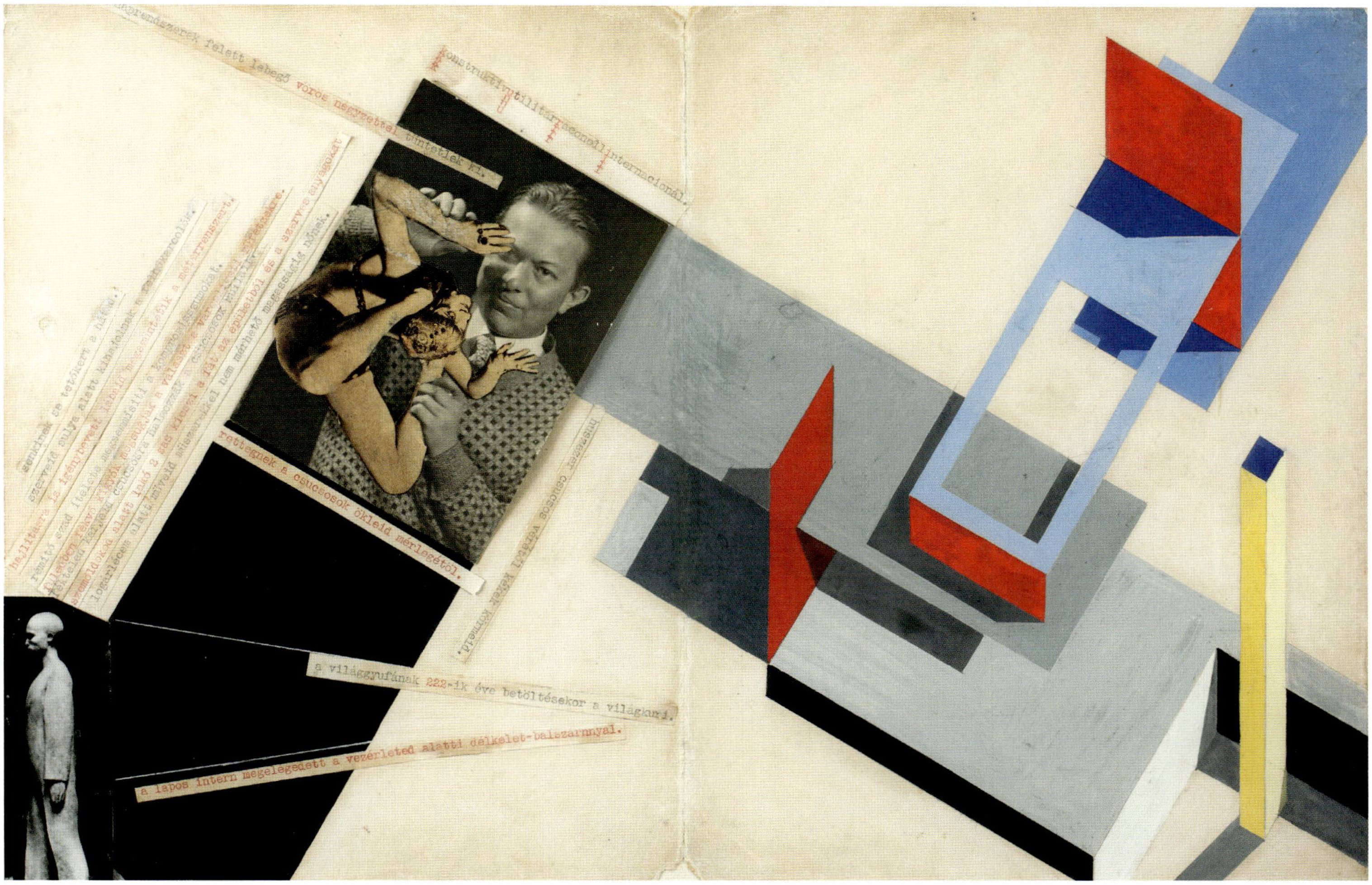

Farkas Molnár
KURI Collage with Self-Portrait, 1929
Petőfi Literary Museum—
Kassák Museum, Budapest

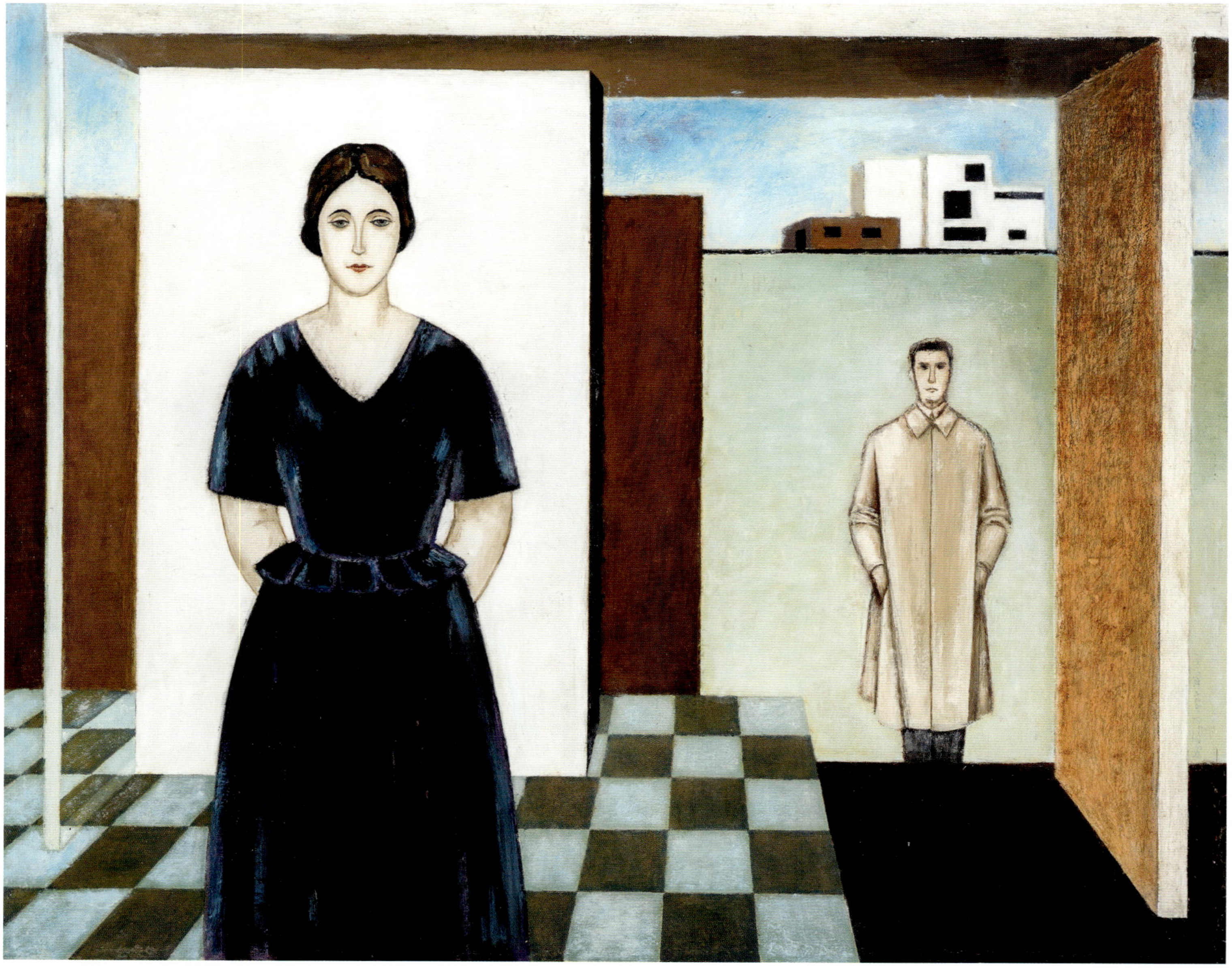

Sándor Bortnyik
The Architect Alfréd Forbát and his Wife, 1924
Museum of Fine Arts—Hungarian
National Gallery, Budapest

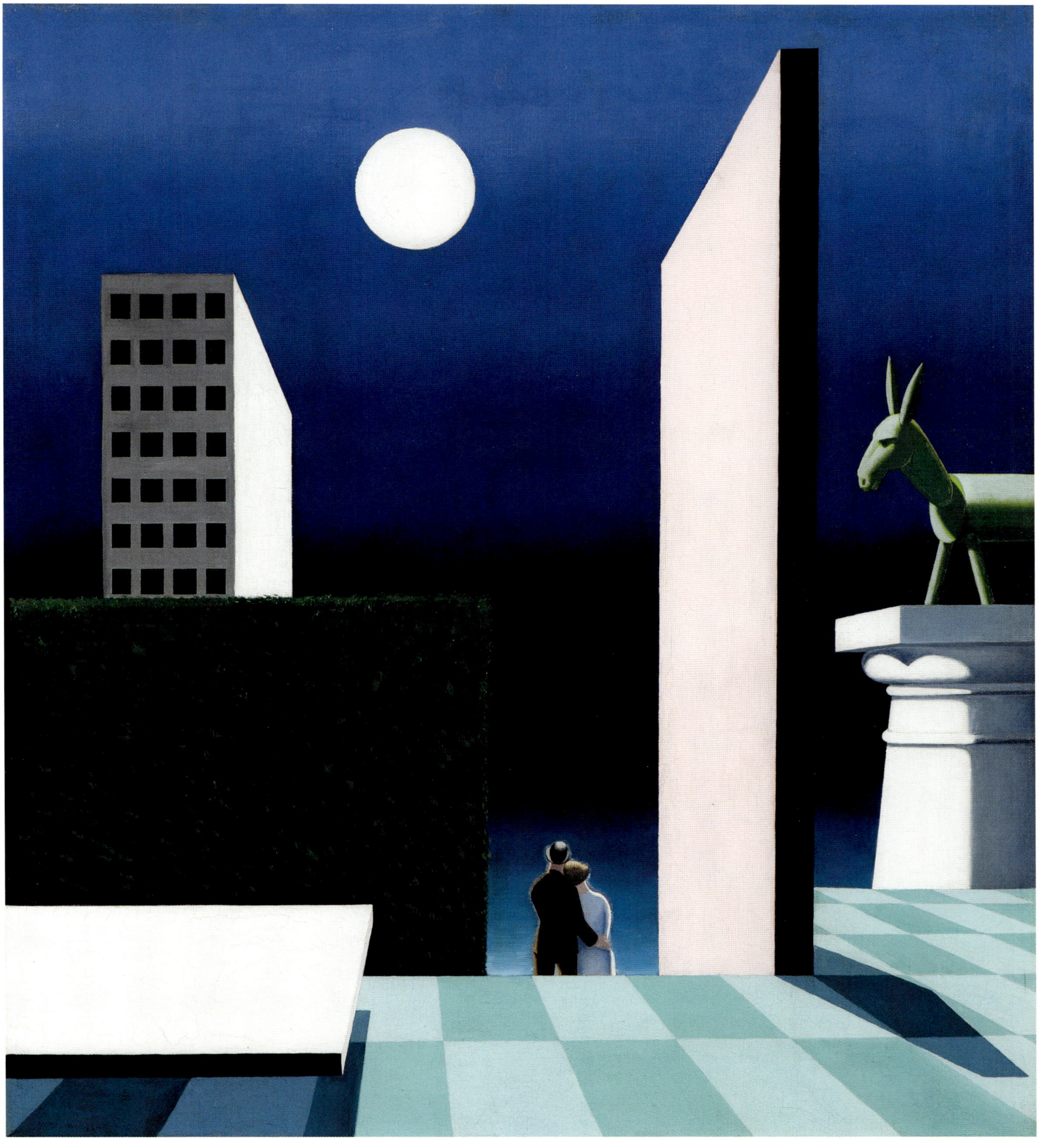

Sándor Bortnyik
Green Donkey, 1924
Museum of Fine Arts—Hungarian
National Gallery, Budapest

Sándor Bortnyik
The New Adam, 1924
Museum of Fine Arts—Hungarian
National Gallery, Budapest

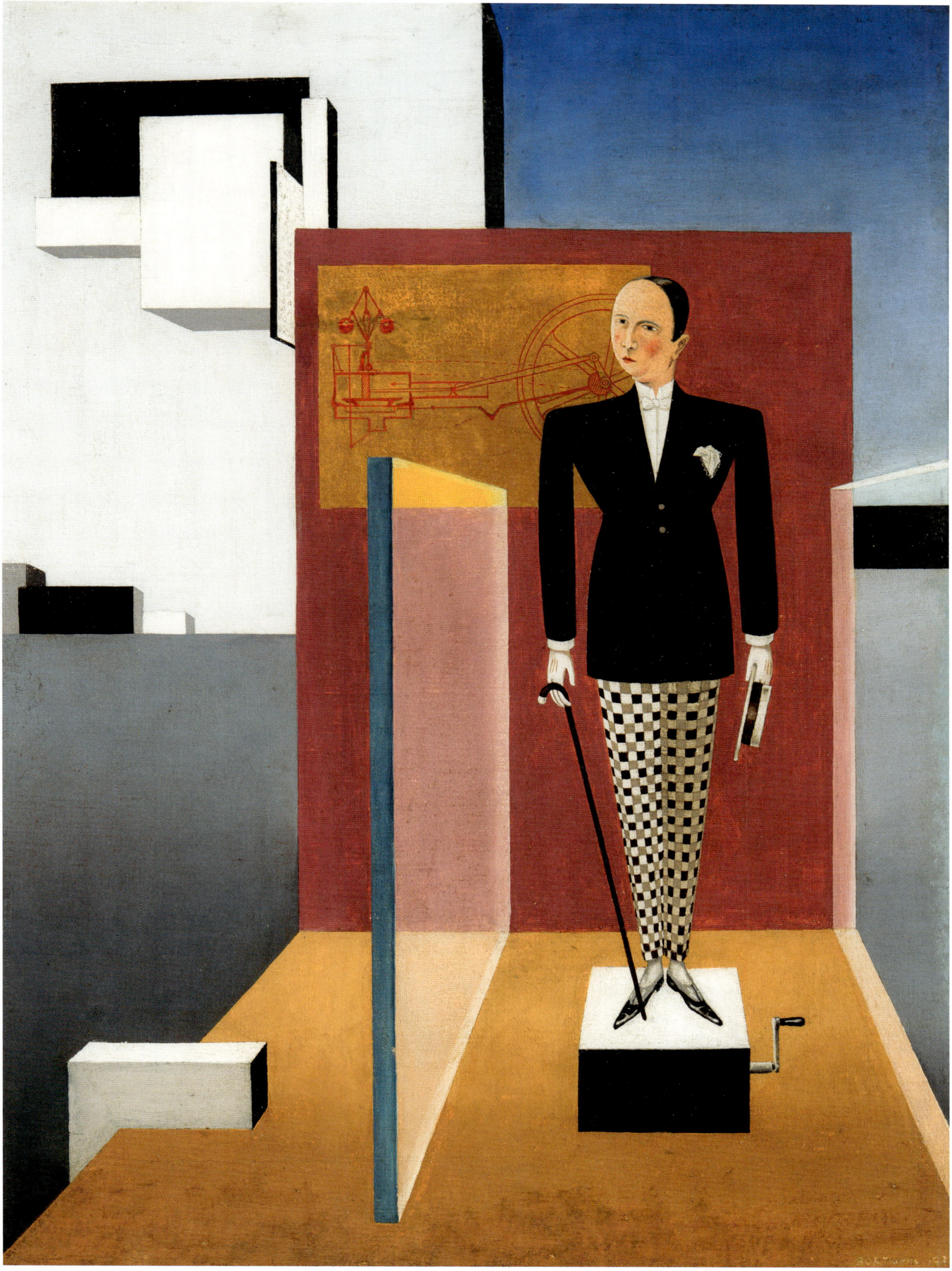

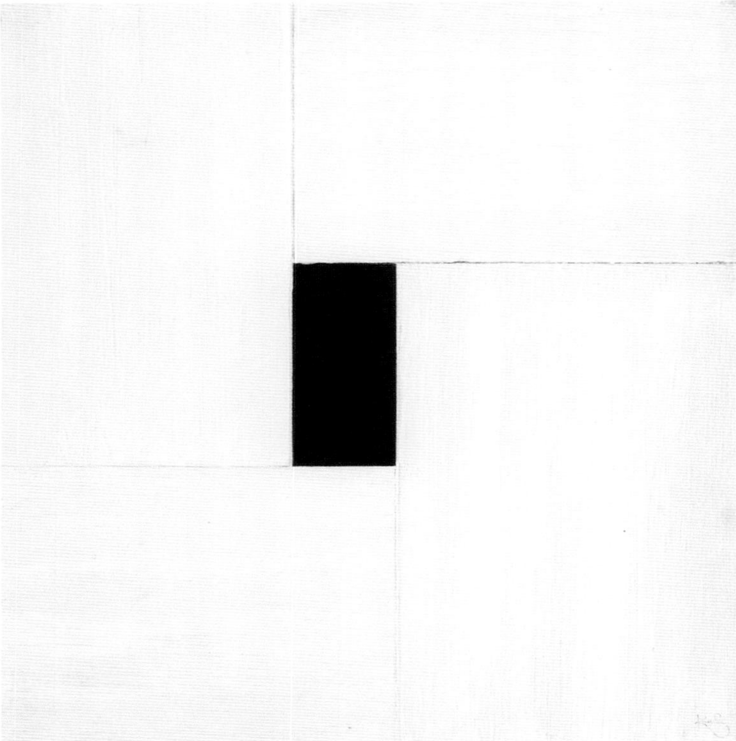

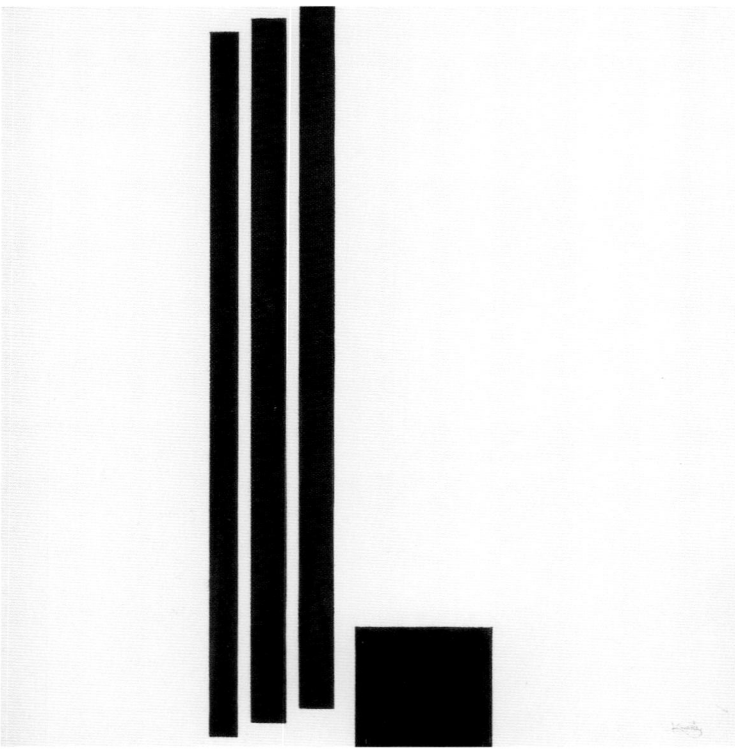

(top)
František Kupka
Abstraction, c. 1931
Museum Kampa—
The Jan and Meda Mládek
Foundation, Prague

(below)
František Kupka
Abstraction, c. 1933
Museum Kampa—
The Jan and Meda Mládek
Foundation, Prague

(top)
František Kupka
Abstraction, c. 1930
Museum Kampa—
The Jan and Meda Mládek
Foundation, Prague

(below)
František Kupka
Abstraction, c. 1935
Museum Kampa—
The Jan and Meda Mládek
Foundation, Prague

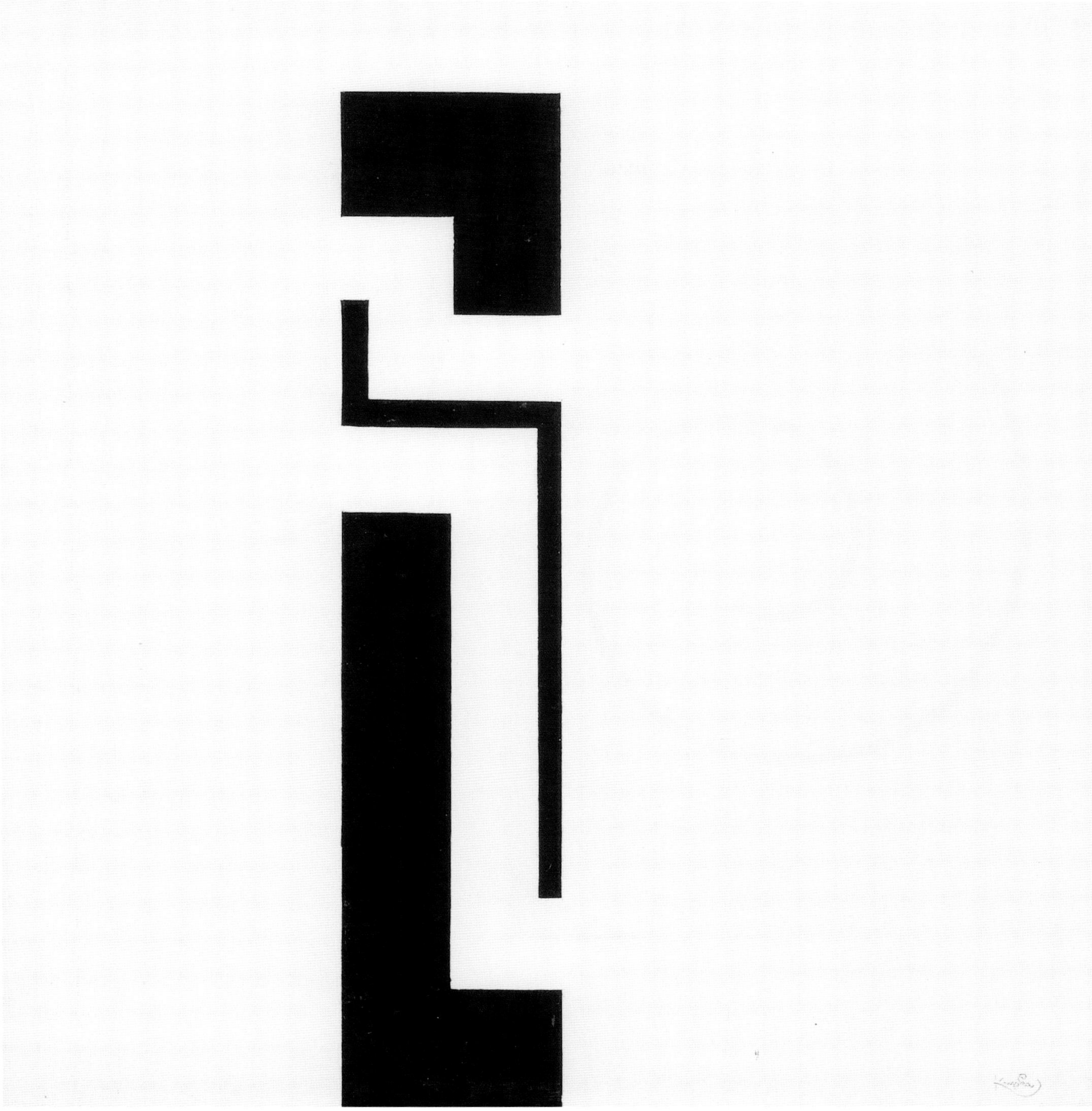

František Kupka
Abstraction, c. 1932
Museum Kampa—
The Jan and Meda Mládek
Foundation, Prague

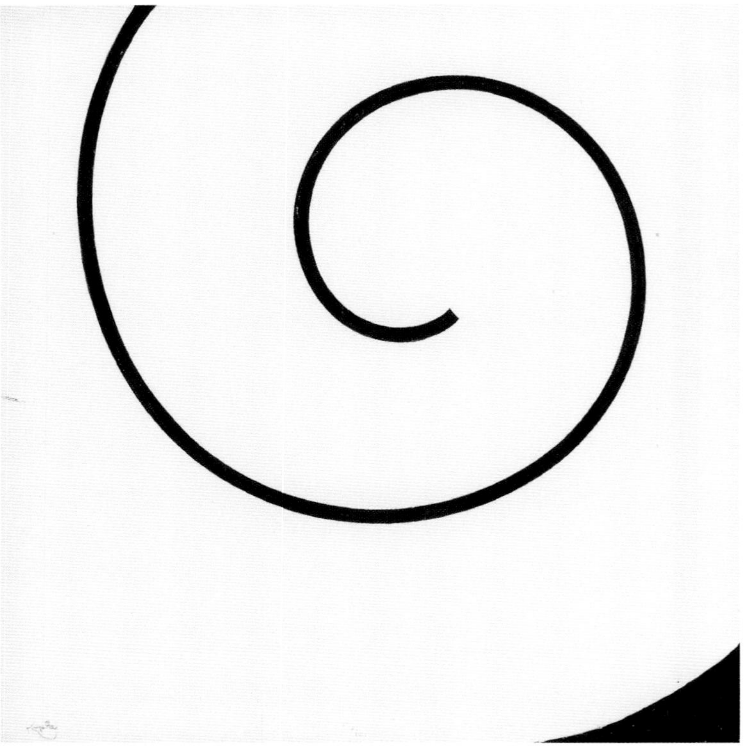

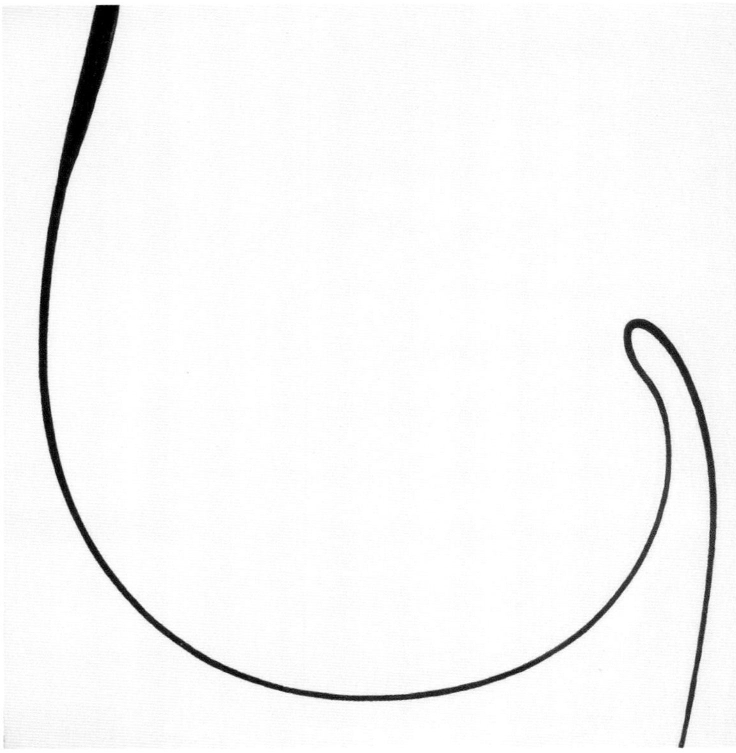

František Kupka
Abstraction, c. 1936
Museum Kampa—
The Jan and Meda Mládek
Foundation, Prague

František Kupka
Abstraction, c. 1934
Museum Kampa—
The Jan and Meda Mládek
Foundation, Prague

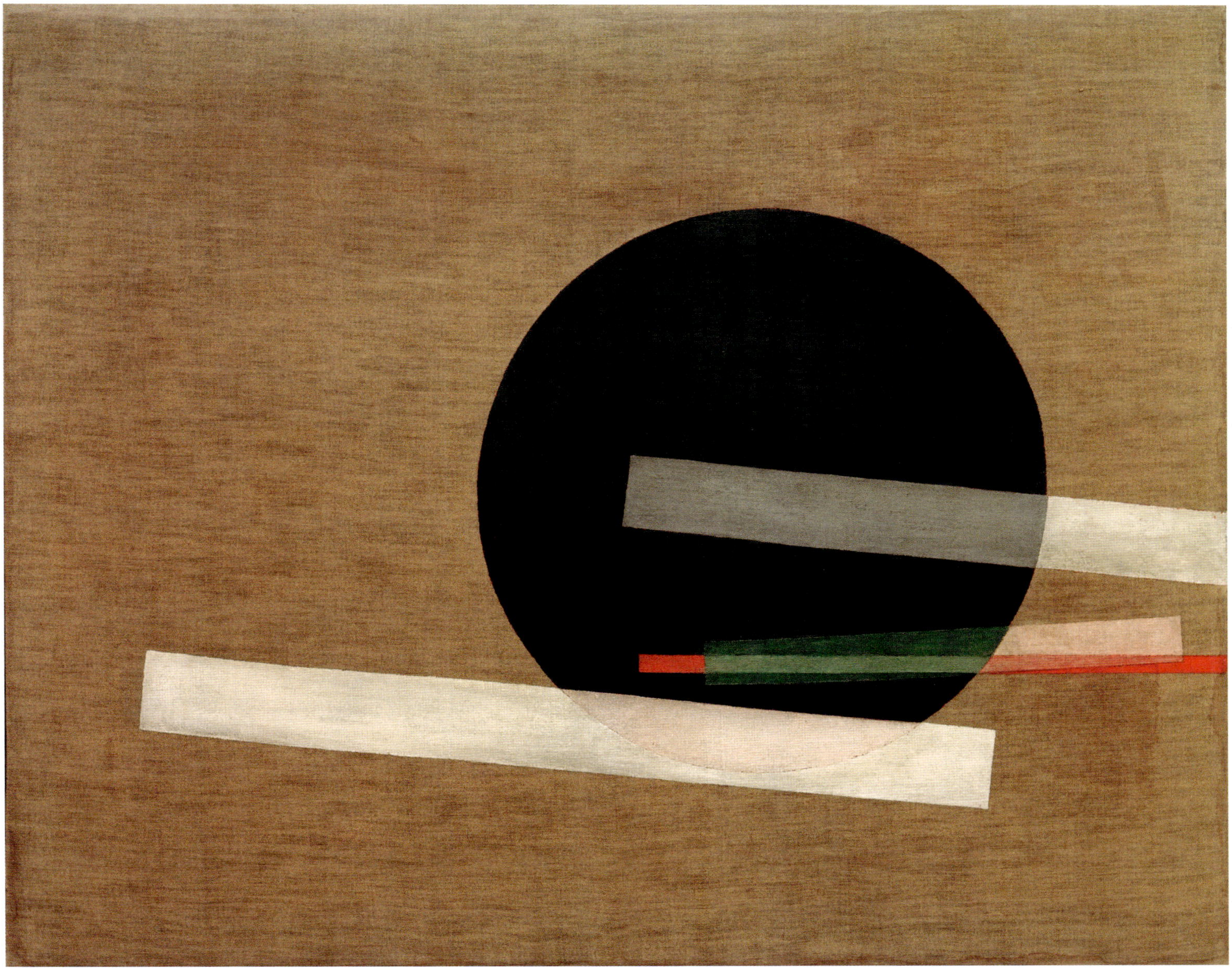

D1

László Moholy-Nagy
Composition A 17, 1927
Kunstmuseum Gelsenkirchen

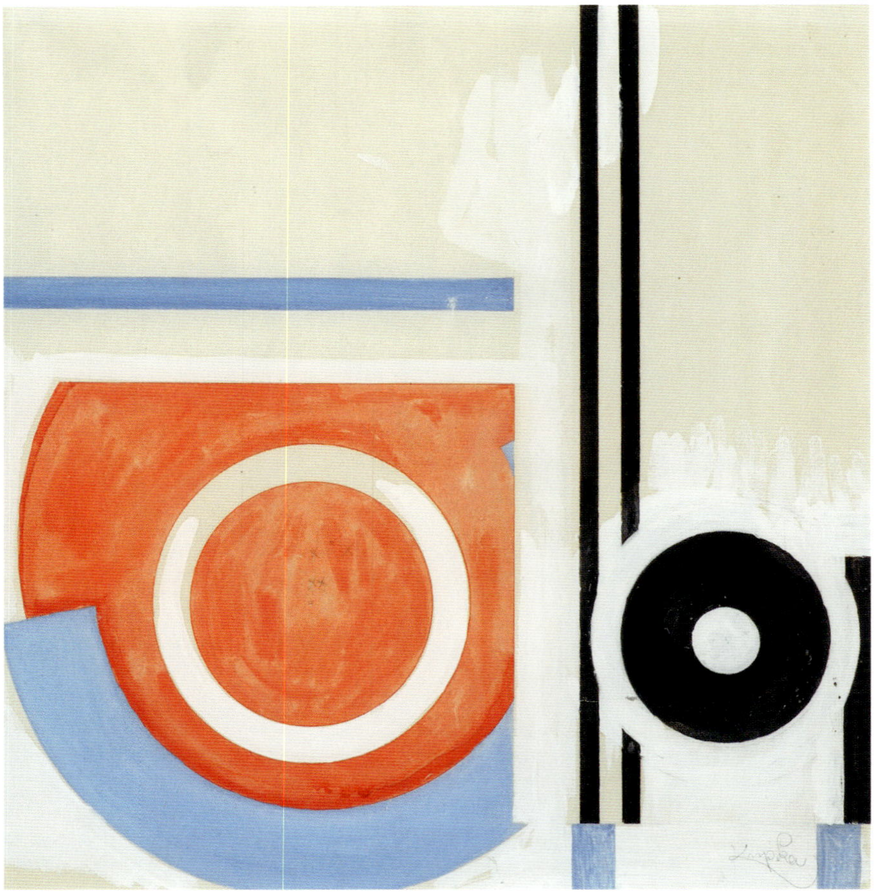

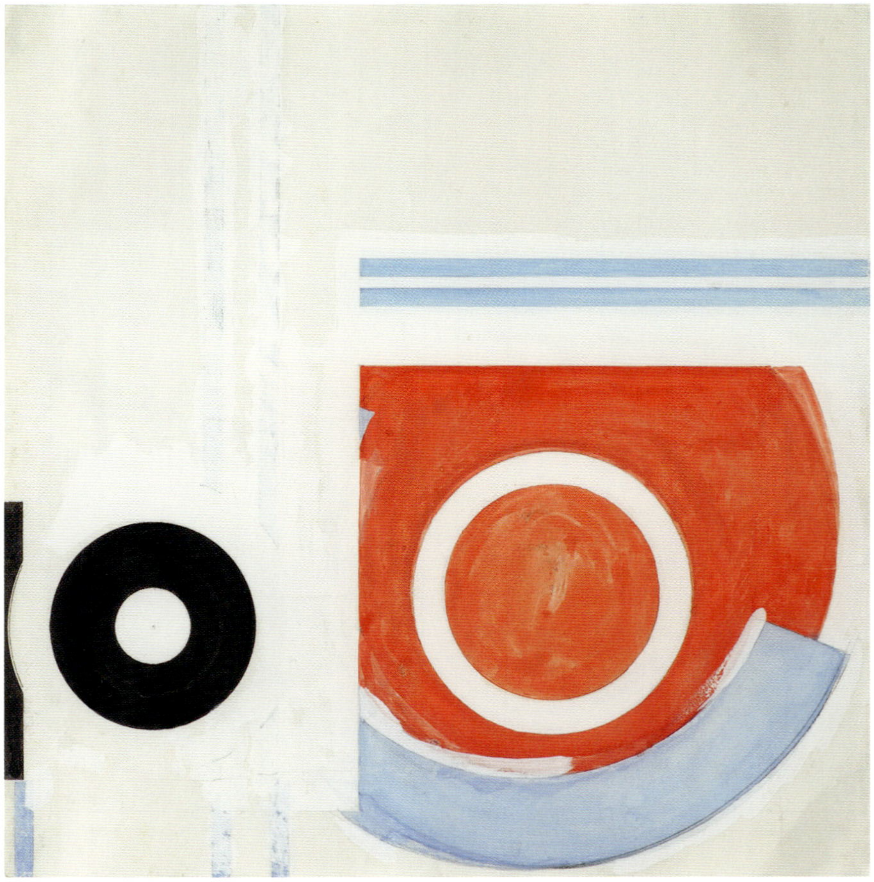

František Kupka
Study for *Circles and Straight Lines,* 1928–30
Museum Kampa—The Jan and
Meda Mládek Foundation, Prague

František Kupka
Study for *Circles and Straight Lines,* 1928–30
Museum Kampa—The Jan and
Meda Mládek Foundation, Prague

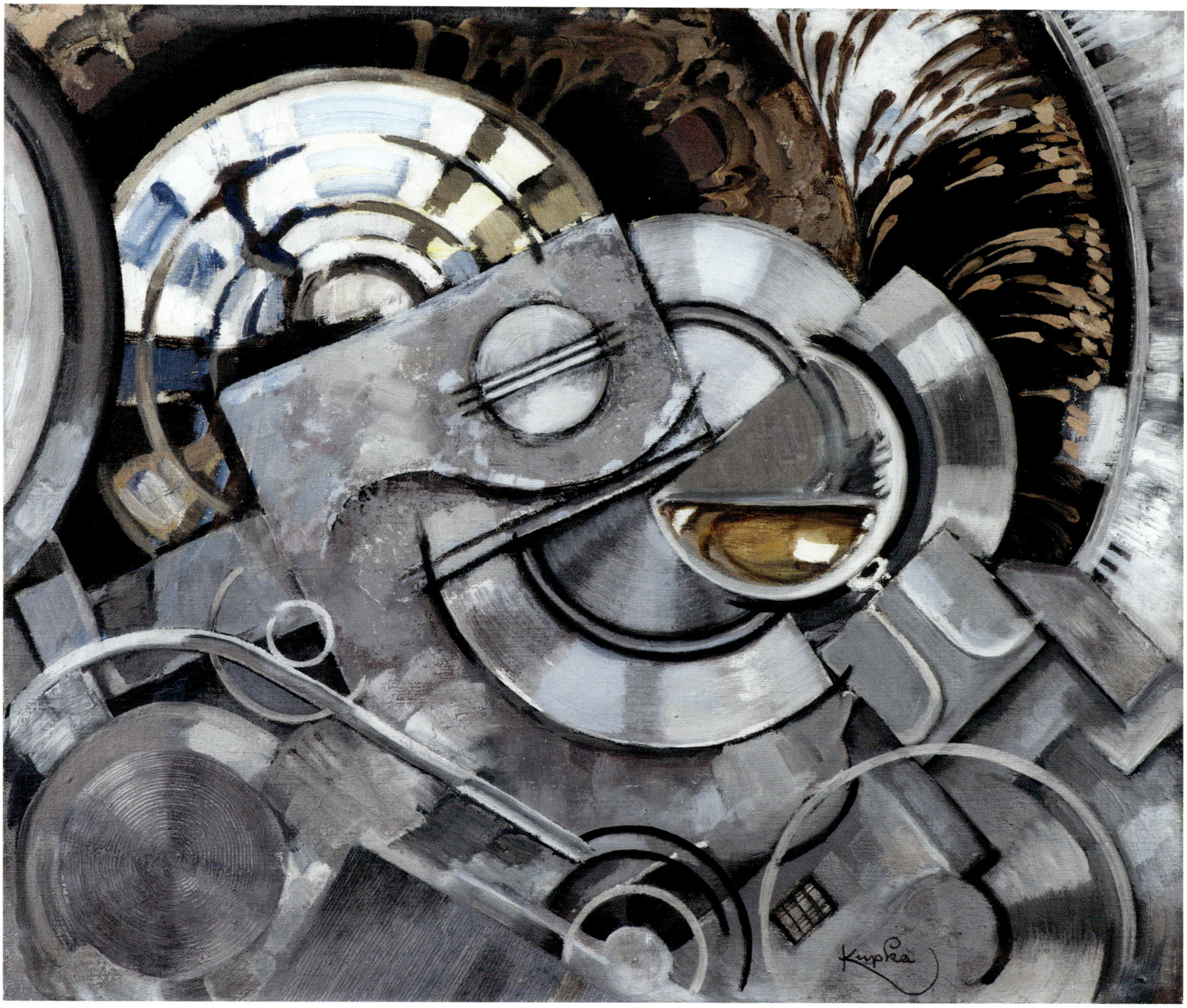

D1

František Kupka
L'Acier boit (Drinking Steel), 1927
Private collection, Prague

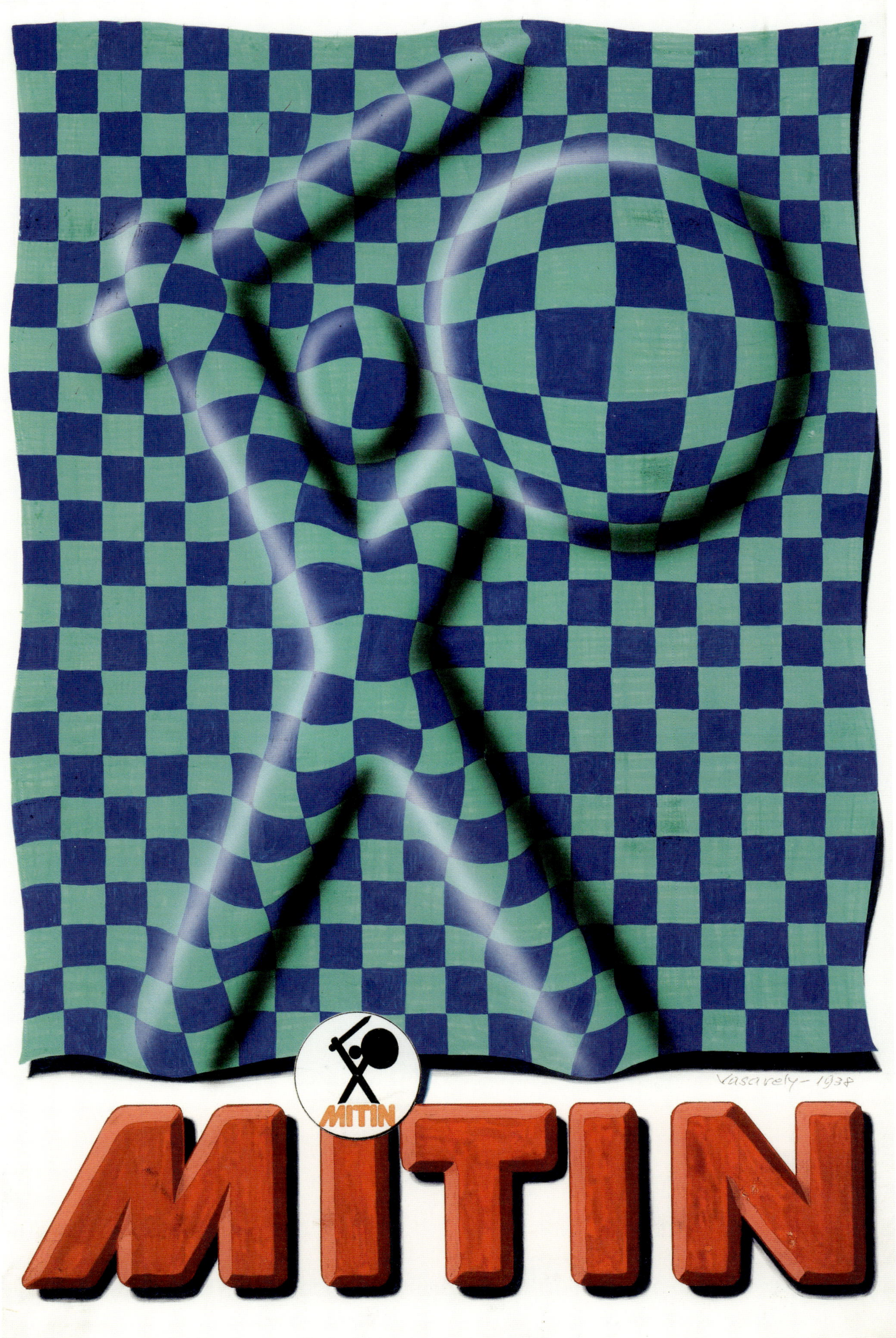

Victor Vasarely
Mitín, 1938
Museum of Fine Arts—Vasarely Museum, Budapest

The International Exhibition of New Theater Technology

The *International Exhibition of New Theater Technology* was held in the fall of 1924 at Vienna's Konzerthaus, opening not just a new chapter in the history of theater, but of other art forms as well. With its skillful dramaturgy, innovative exhibition concept, and Frederick Kiesler's graphic designs, the event transformed the city of Vienna into a magnet for the world of avant-garde theater. Presented alongside Kiesler's imposing *Space Stage* were recent sketches and studies by Franz Singer, Friedl Dicker-Brandeis, Josef Čapek, and László Moholy-Nagy. This emphasized the cross-pollination of styles and media that was occurring across different branches of the visual and performing arts: Whether painting, sculpture, photography, or scenography, Constructivist, Kinetic, Dadaist, or Futurist, the art of the inter-war period took its inspiration from this synthesis of genres. (MH)

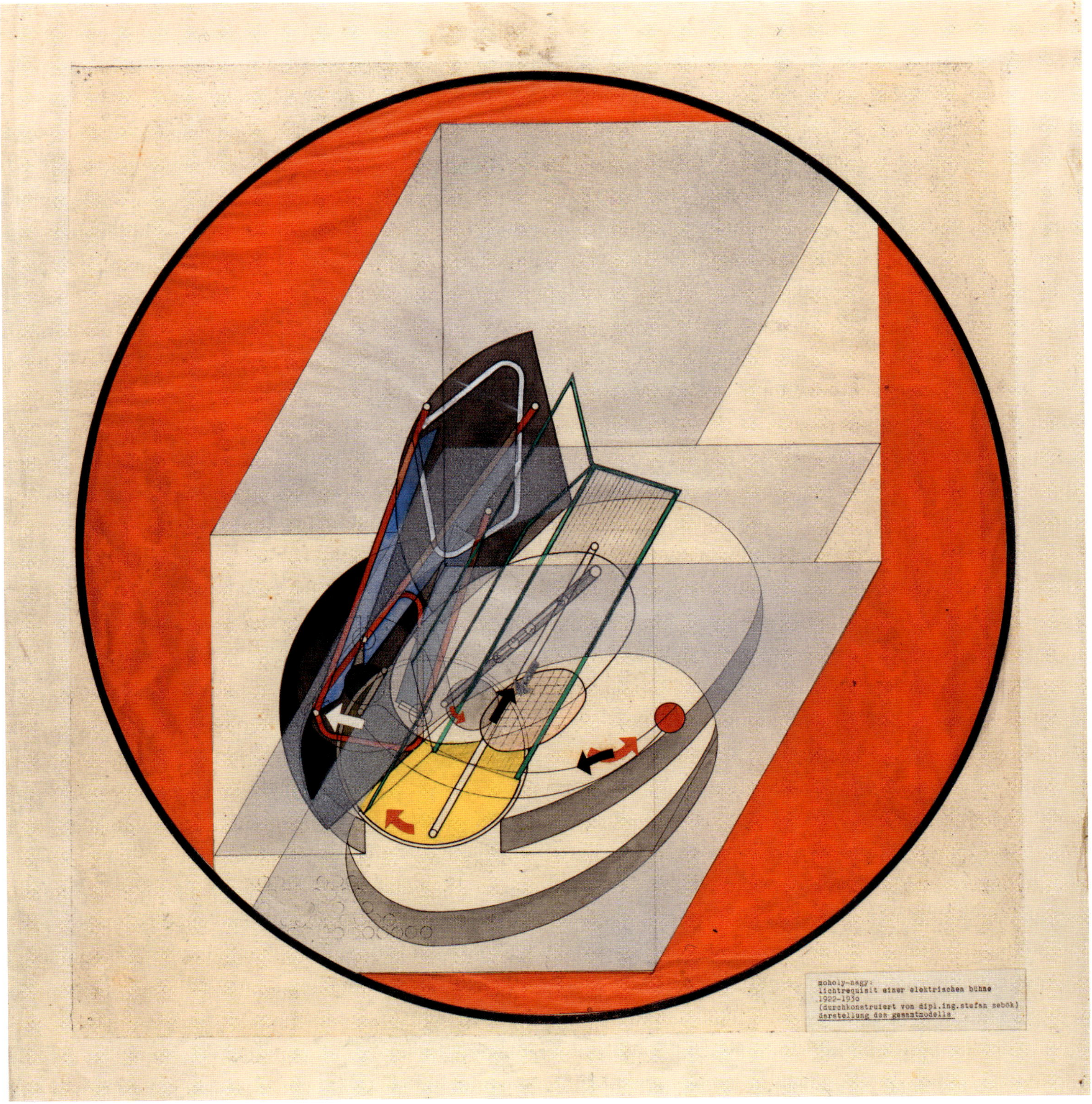

D2

László Moholy-Nagy
Electrical Stage Lighting, 1922–30
Theater Collection, University of Cologne

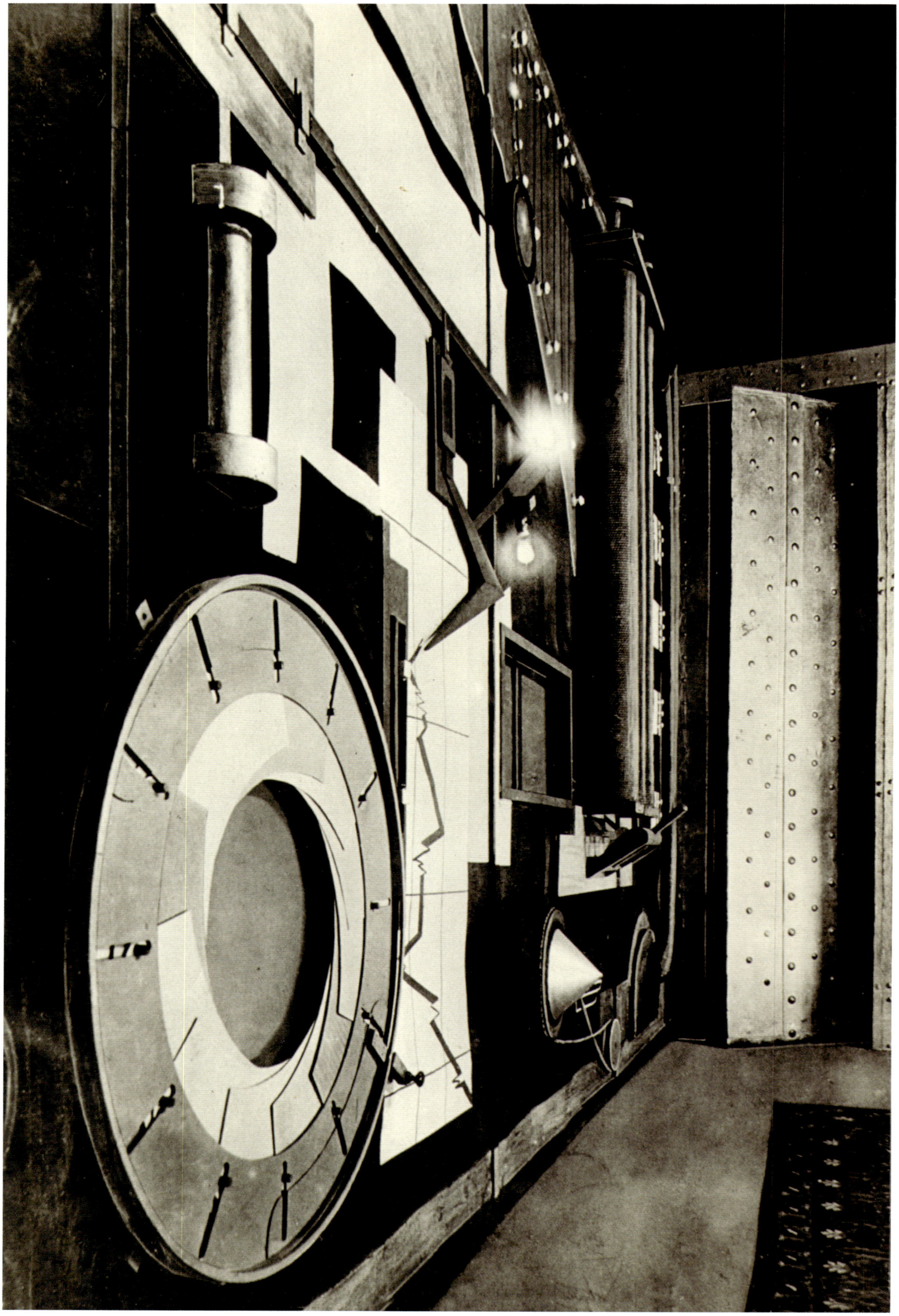

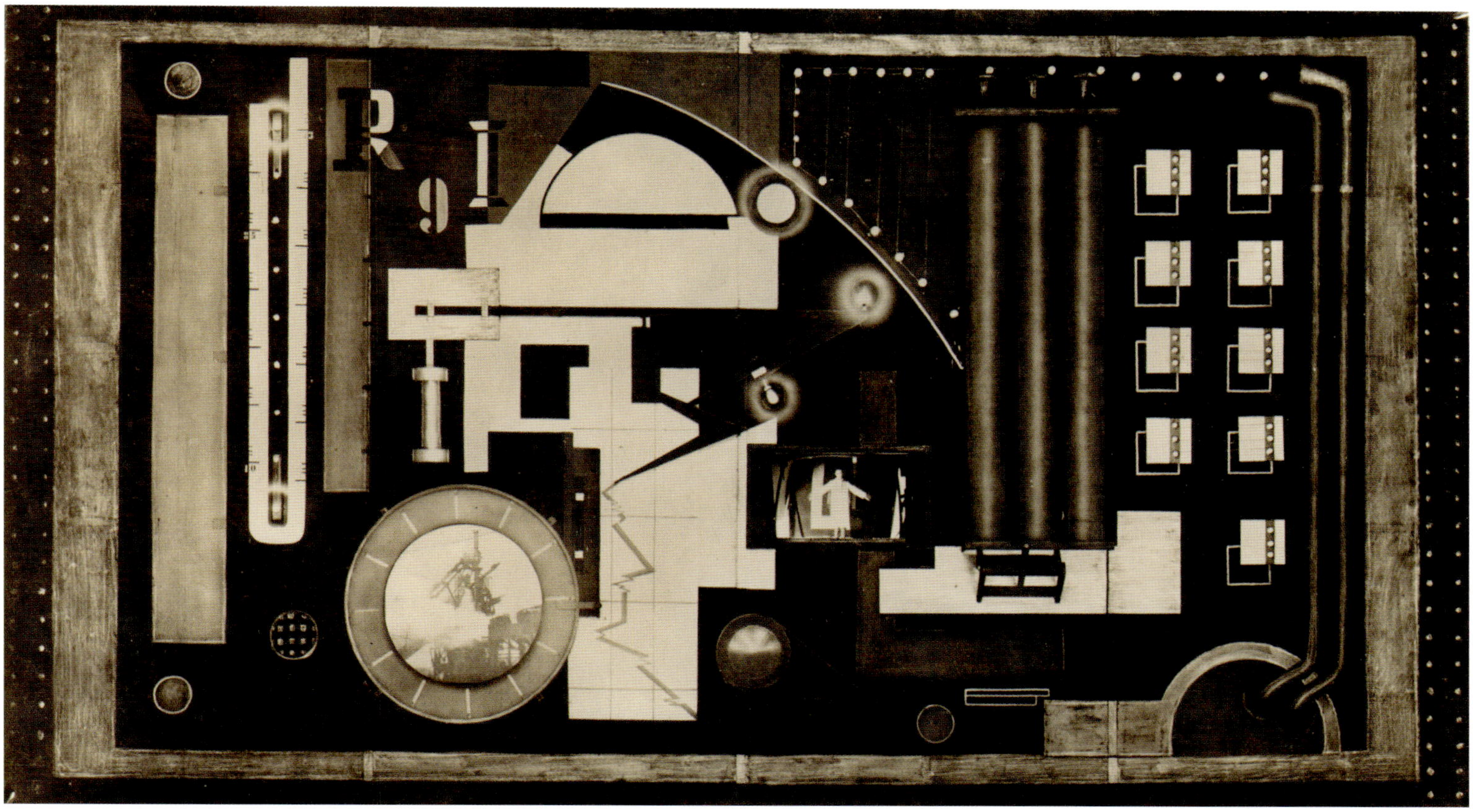

◂ Frederick Kiesler
Side view of the *Electro-Mechanical Set* for *R.U.R.*, 1923
Play: Karel Čapek, production: John Gottwort,
set: Frederick Kiesler, Theater am Kurfürstendamm,
backdrop for the final act, Austrian Friedrich and
Lillian Kiesler Private Foundation, Vienna

Frederick Kiesler
R.U.R. (Rossum's Universal Robots), 1923
Play: Karel Čapek, production: John Gottwort,
set: Frederick Kiesler, Theater am Kurfürstendamm,
backdrop for the final act, Austrian Friedrich and
Lillian Kiesler Private Foundation, Vienna

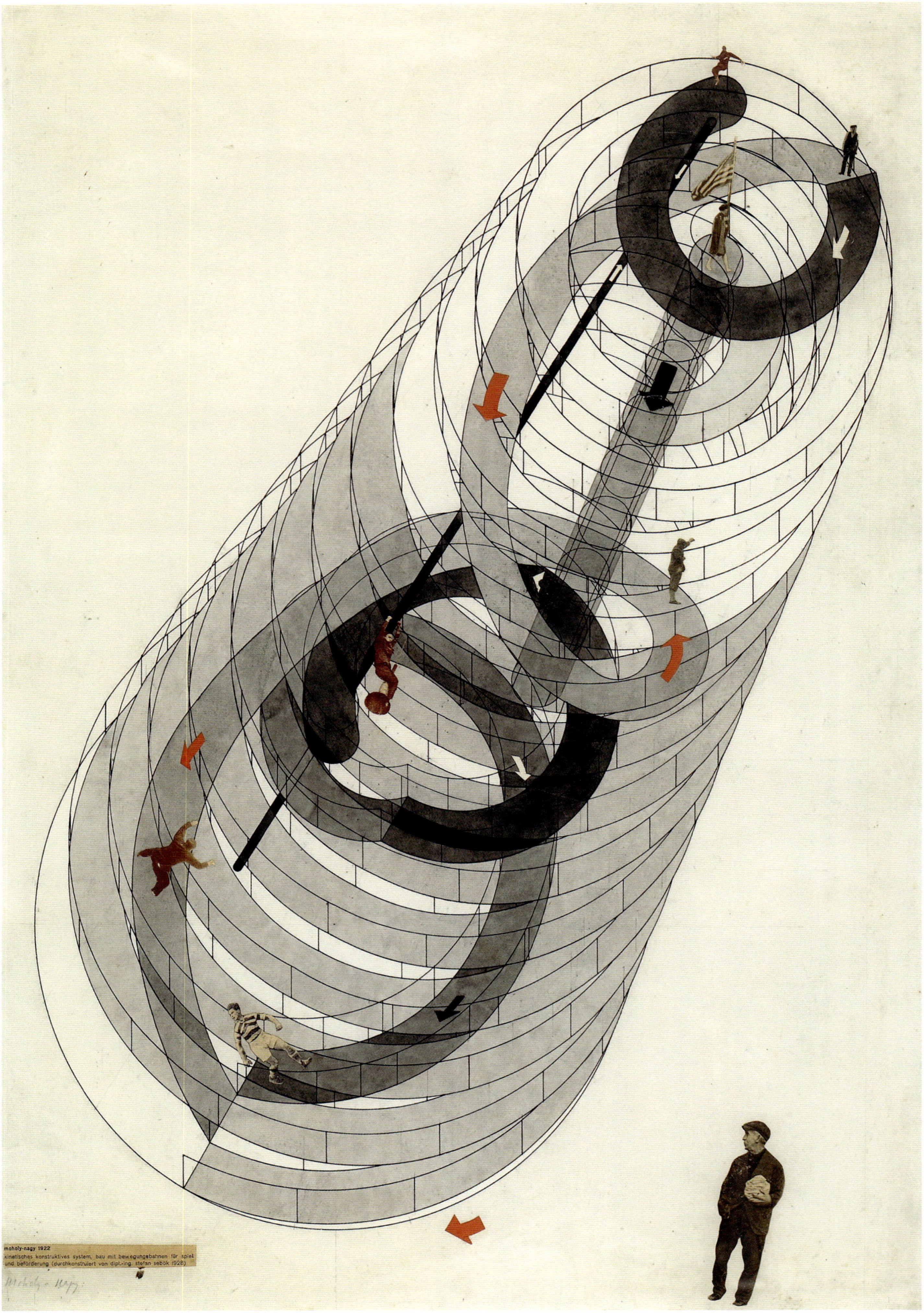
moholy-nagy 1922
kinetisches konstruktives system, bau mit bewegungsbahnen für spiel und beförderung (durchkonstruiert von dipl.-ing. stefan sebök 1928)

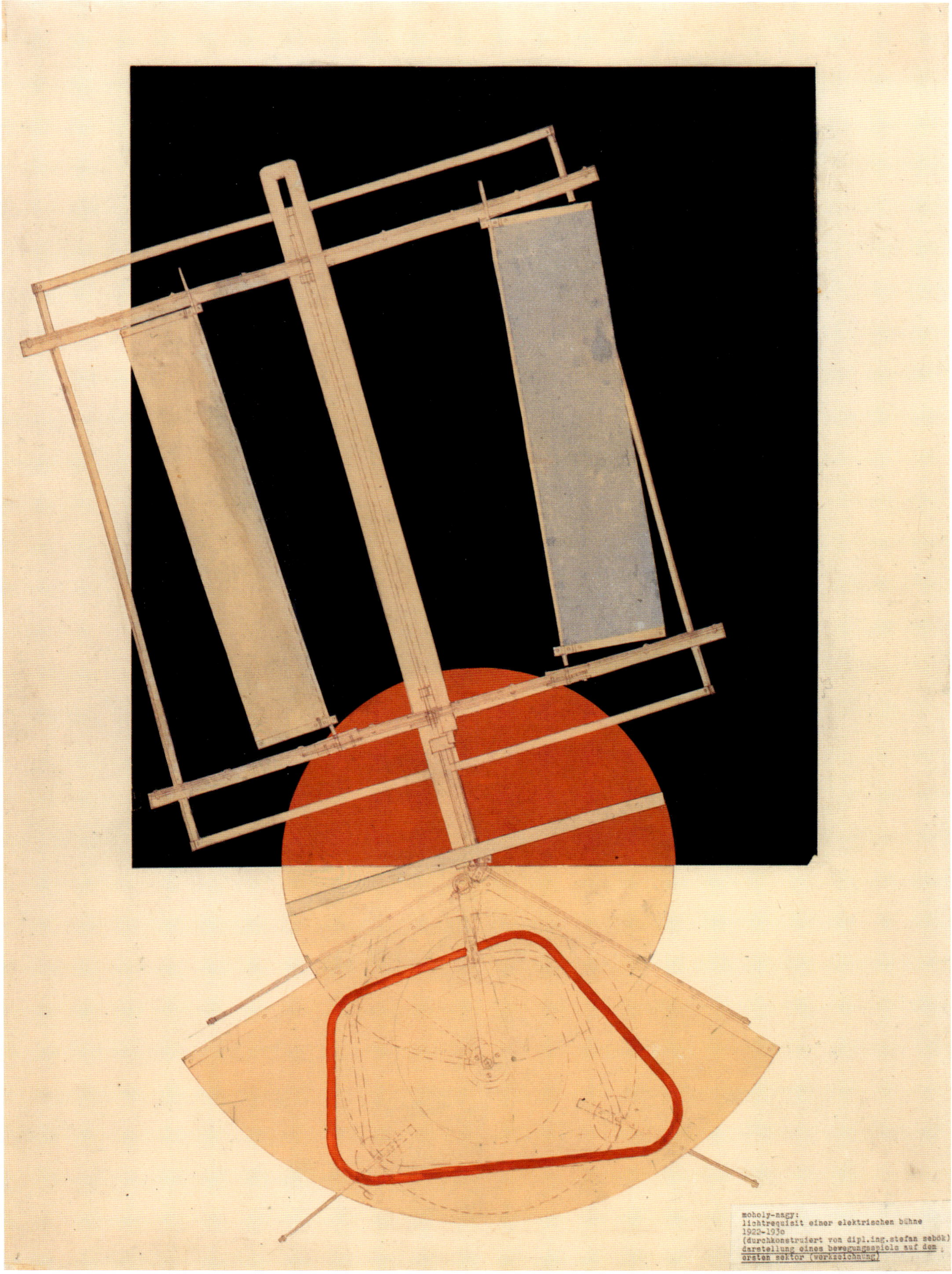

◂ László Moholy-Nagy
Kinetic Constructive System (Structure for Moving Parts for Play and Movement), 1922–28
Theater Collection, University of Cologne

László Moholy-Nagy, István Sebök
Electrical Stage Lighting, 1922–30
Theater Collection,
University of Cologne

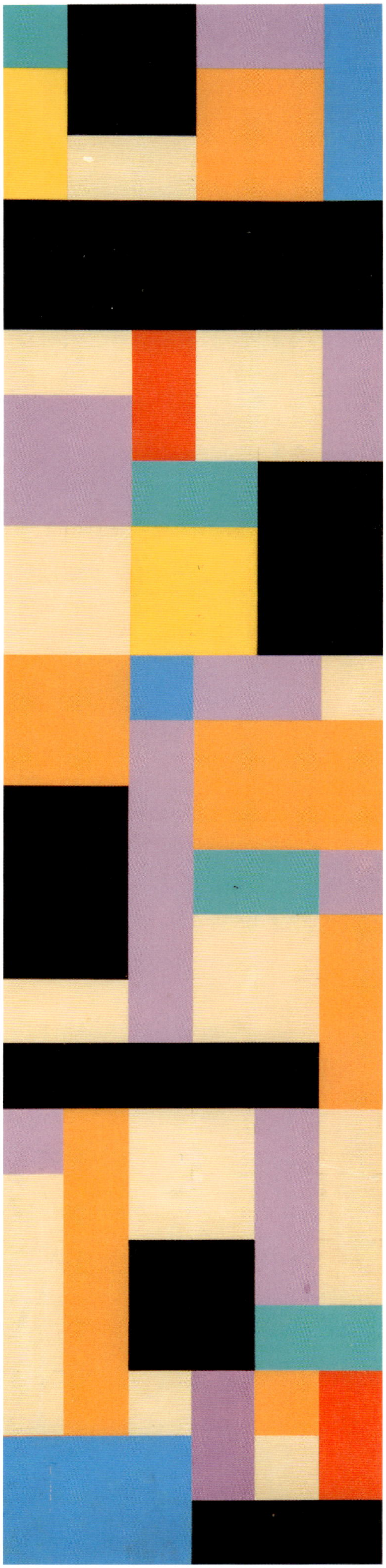

D2

Andor Weininger
De-Stijl Composition, 1922/62
Museum of Fine Arts—Hungarian
National Gallery, Budapest

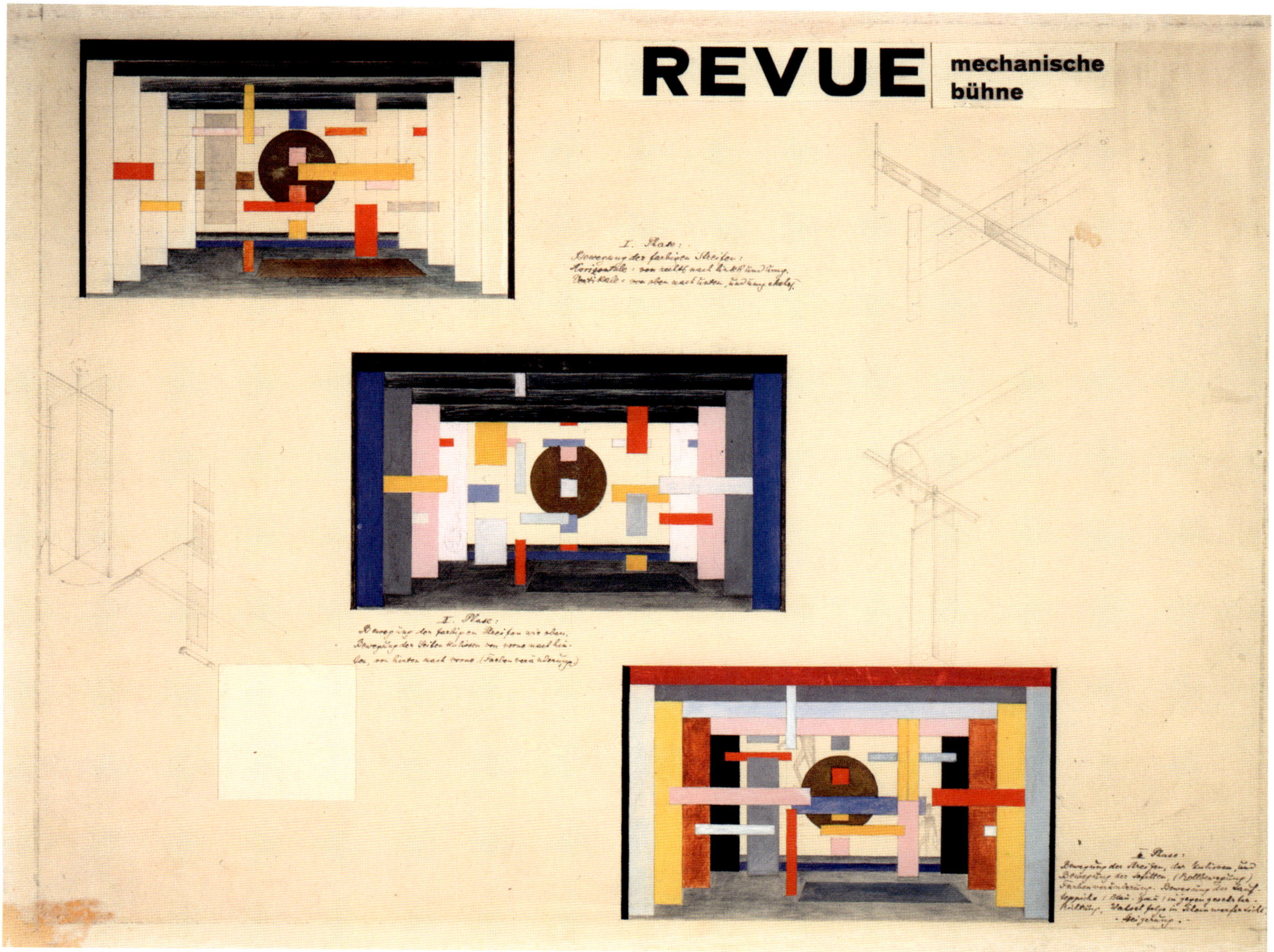

D2

Andor Weininger
Mechanical Stage Revue, phase I–III, n.d. (Dessau)
Theater Collection, University of Cologne

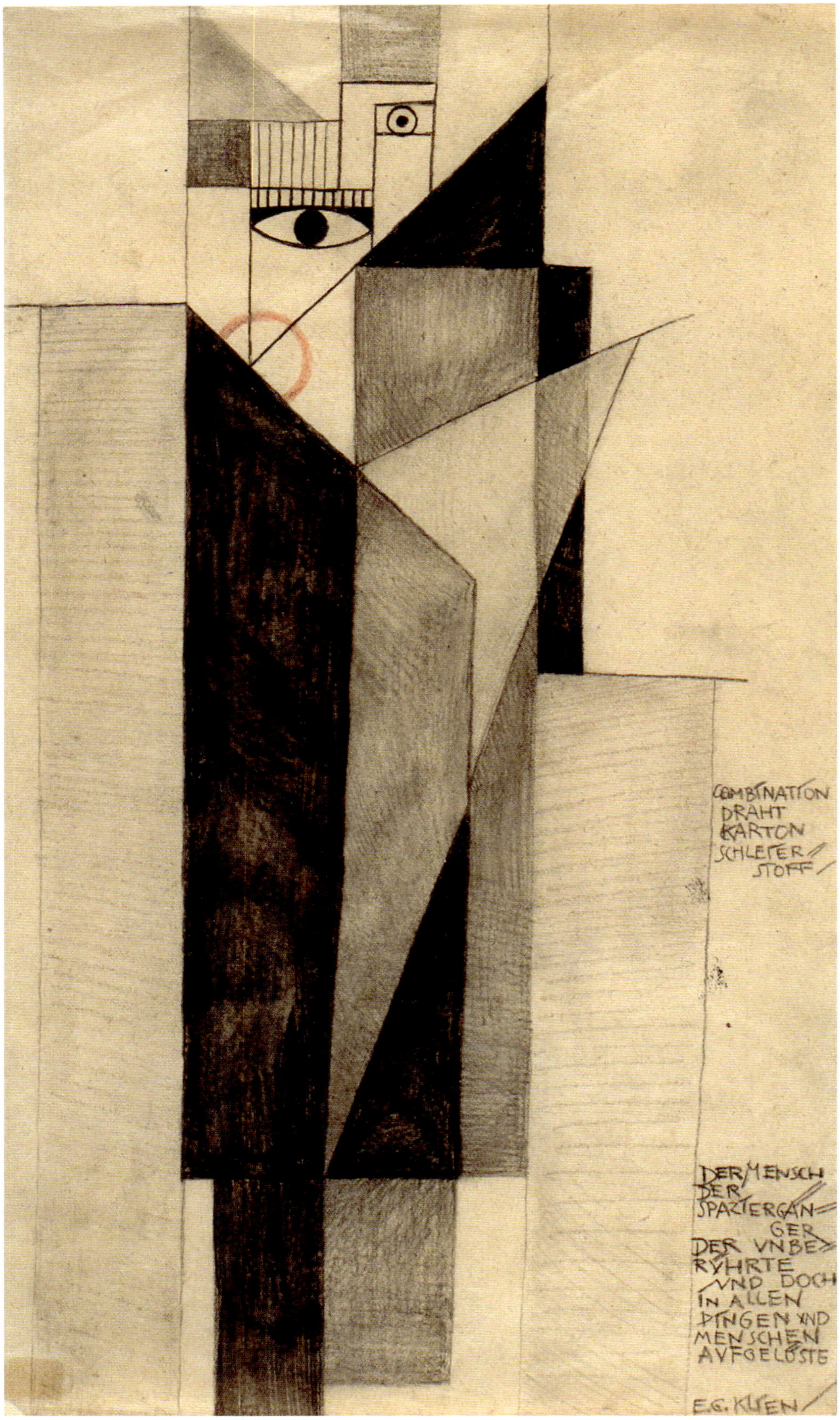

Erika Giovanna Klien
Figurine *The Human Being, the Walker*, c. 1924
University of Applied Arts Vienna, Collection and Archive

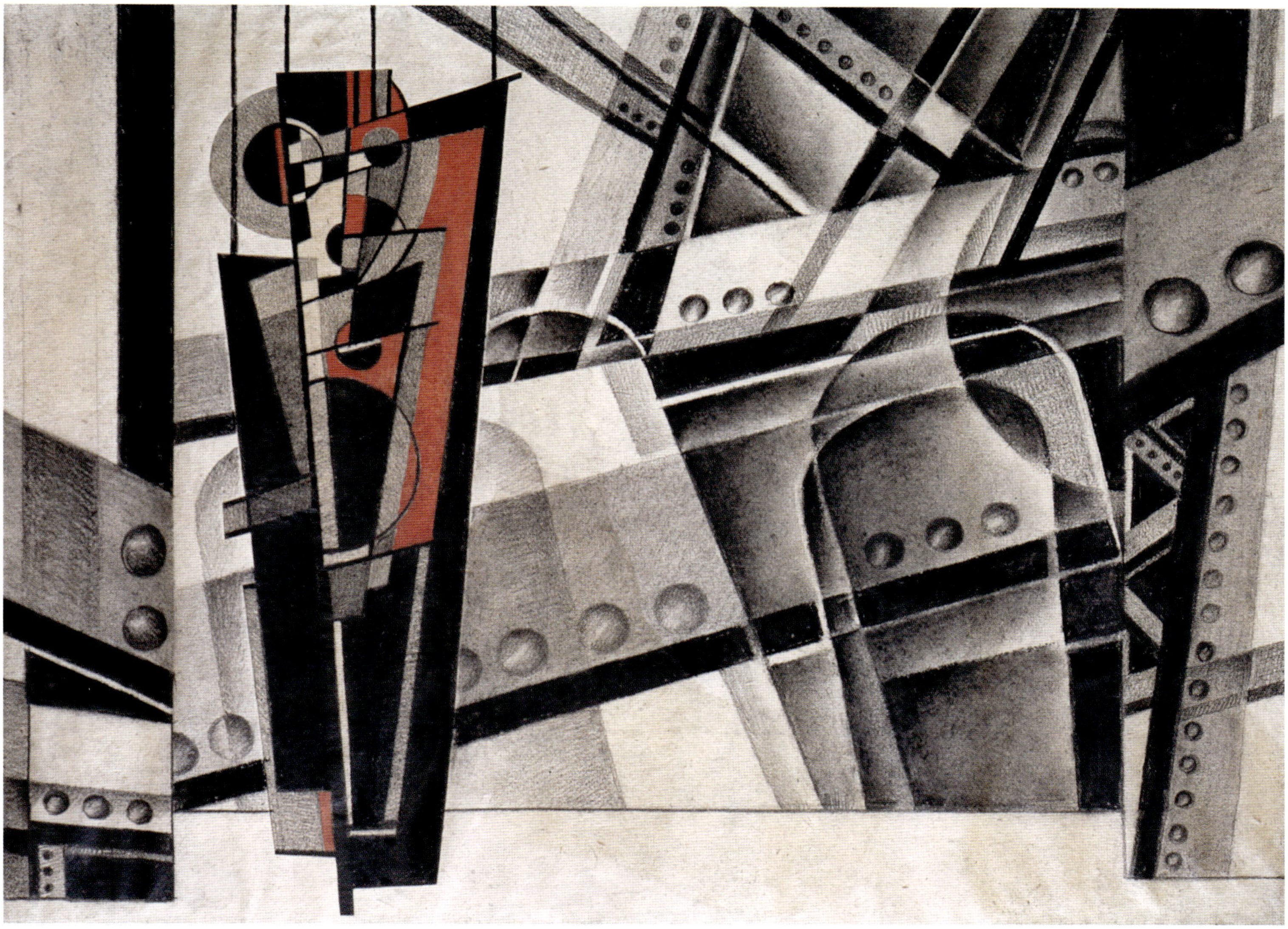

D2

Erika Giovanna Klien
Kinetic Puppet Theater, 1926
Private collection, Vienna

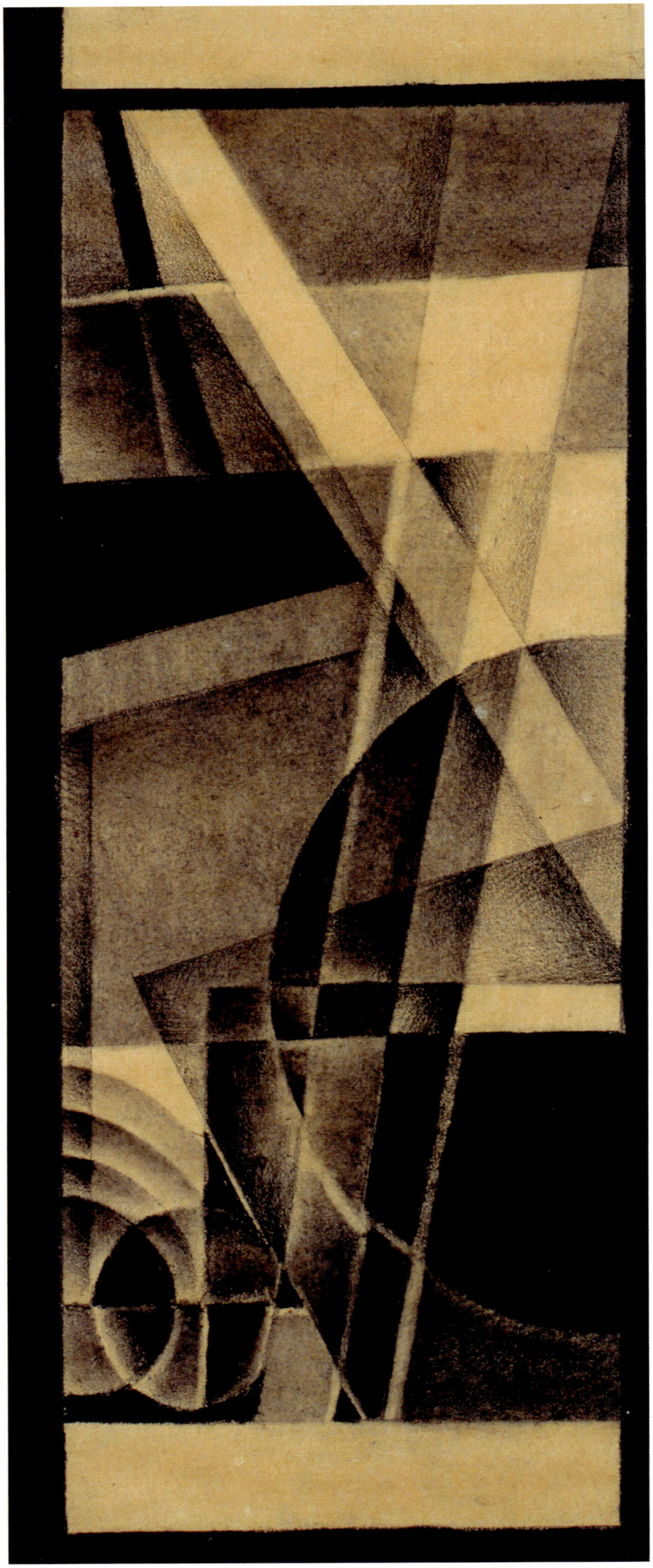

◂
Erika Giovanna Klien
Kinetic Puppet Theater, 1926
University of Applied Arts Vienna, Collection and Archive
▸
Erika Giovanna Klien
Kinetic Puppet Theater, 1926
Private collection, Vienna

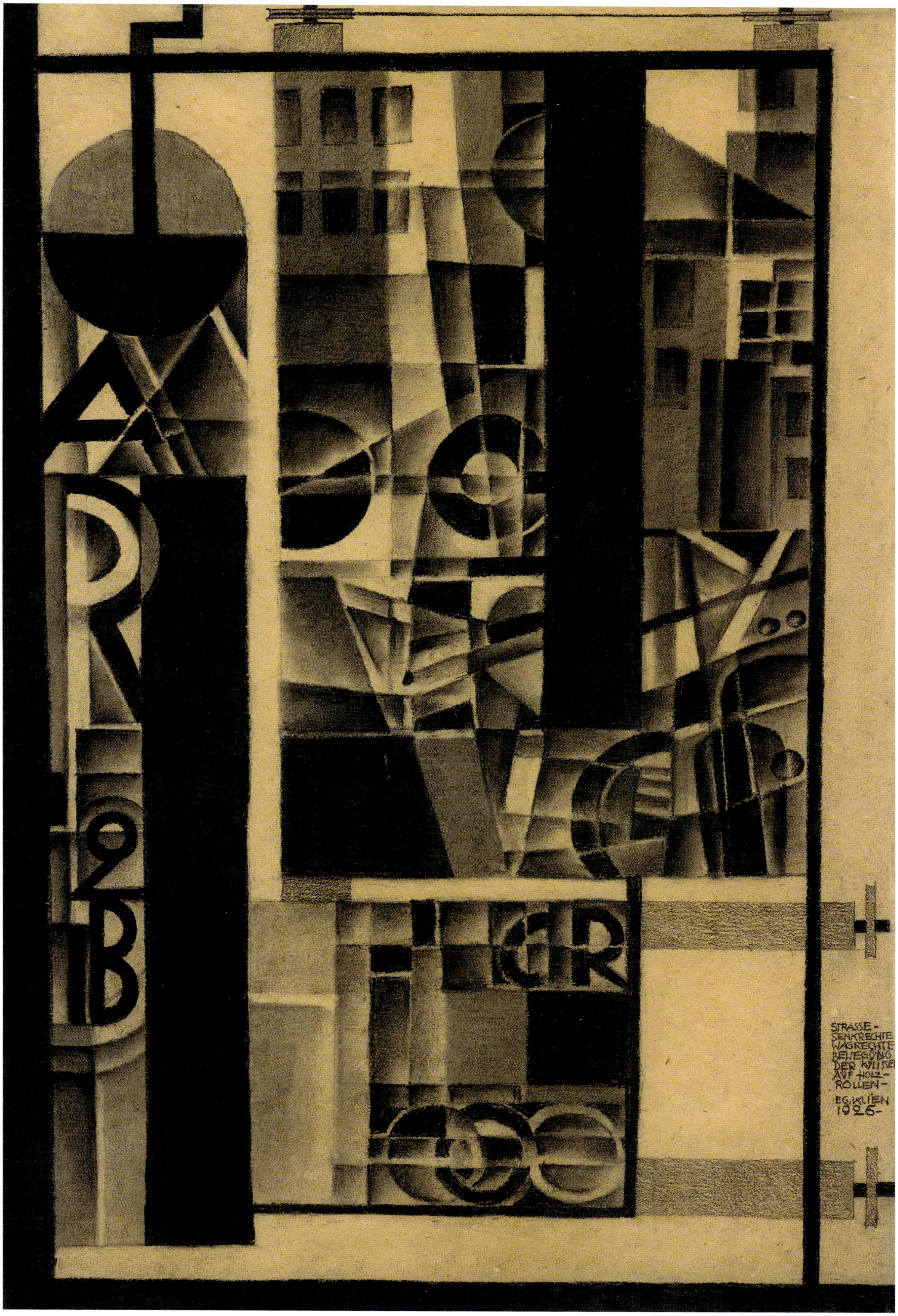
STRASSE-
SENKRECHTE
WAGRECHTE
BEWEGUNG
DER KULISSEN
AUF HOLZ-
ROLLEN-
E.G. KLIEN
1926-

D2

Surrealism / Abstraction-Création: Transnational Movements

A simmering cauldron of influences, ideas, and movements, Europe after the First World War became the stage for radical political change. The Surrealist response to the confusion caused by the clash of “old order nostalgia” and “new system zeal” was an art that focused on the human subconscious and the irrationality of dreams. Although the Surrealist agenda received no official endorsement from Sigmund Freud, psychoanalysis was clearly a source of inspiration for these artists. The large number of artists from the former Austro-Hungarian Empire, especially Czechoslovakia, who became involved in and shaped the Surrealist movement is notable. Despite the political and social pressures facing them, artists such as Jindřich Štyrský, Toyen, and František Foltýn, or the Austrian artists Wolfgang Paalen and Herbert Bayer, developed groundbreaking artistic concepts, securing the Austro-Hungarian successor states’ position on the Surrealists’ imaginary map of the world. (MH)

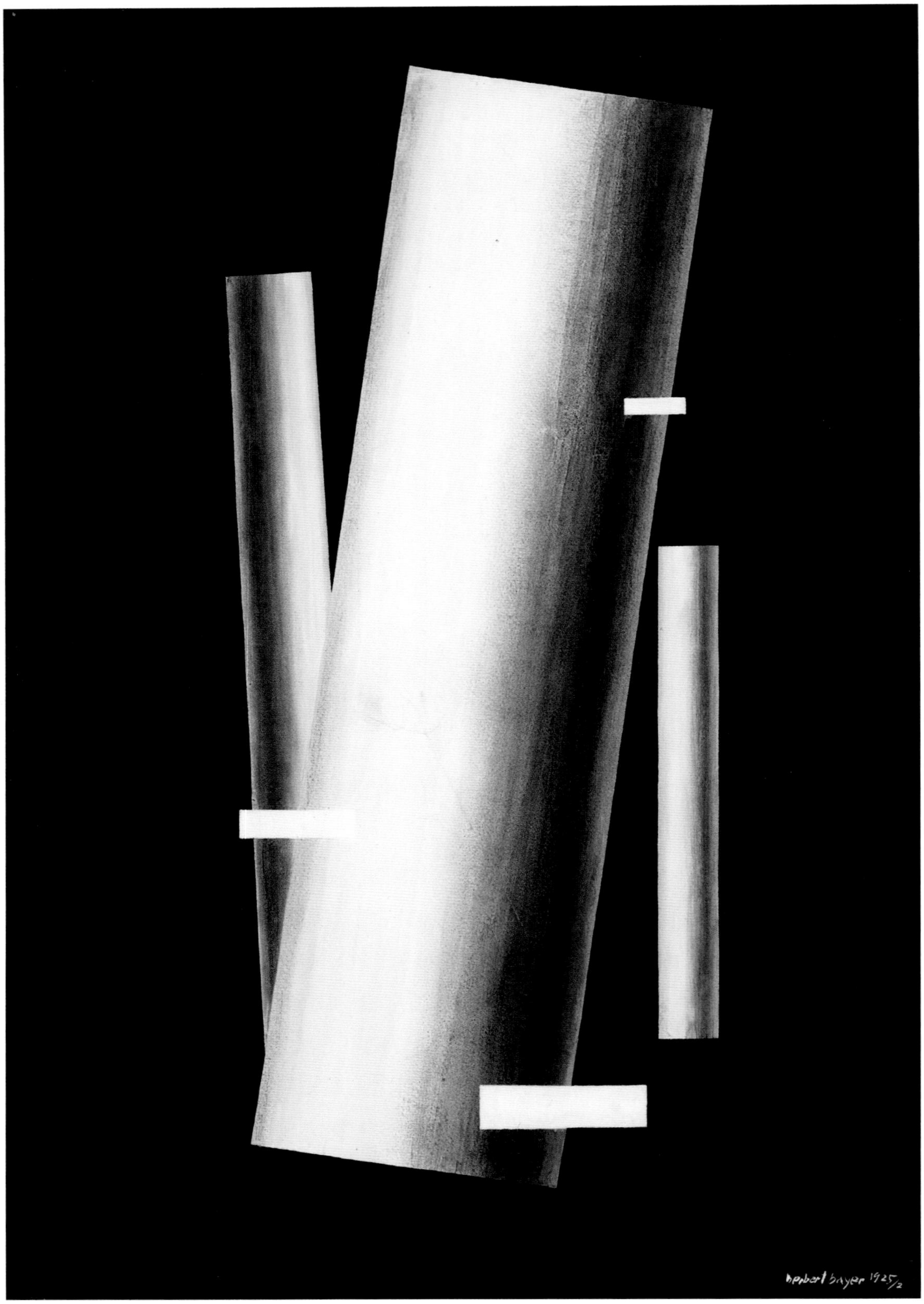

D3

Herbert Bayer
Floating Architecture, 1926
mumok—Museum moderner Kunst Stiftung Ludwig Wien

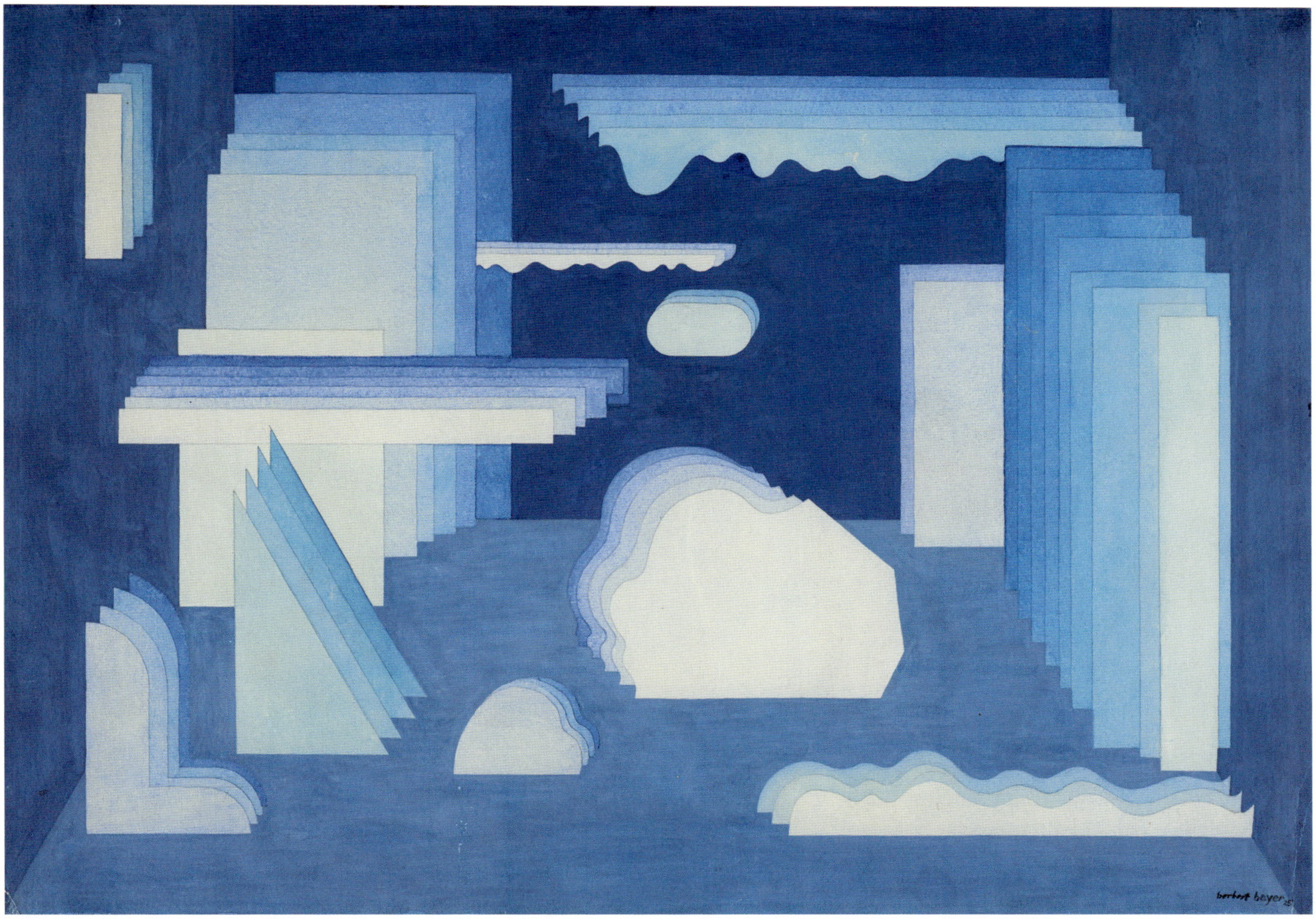

D3

Herbert Bayer
Backdrops, 1925
LENTOS Kunstmuseum Linz

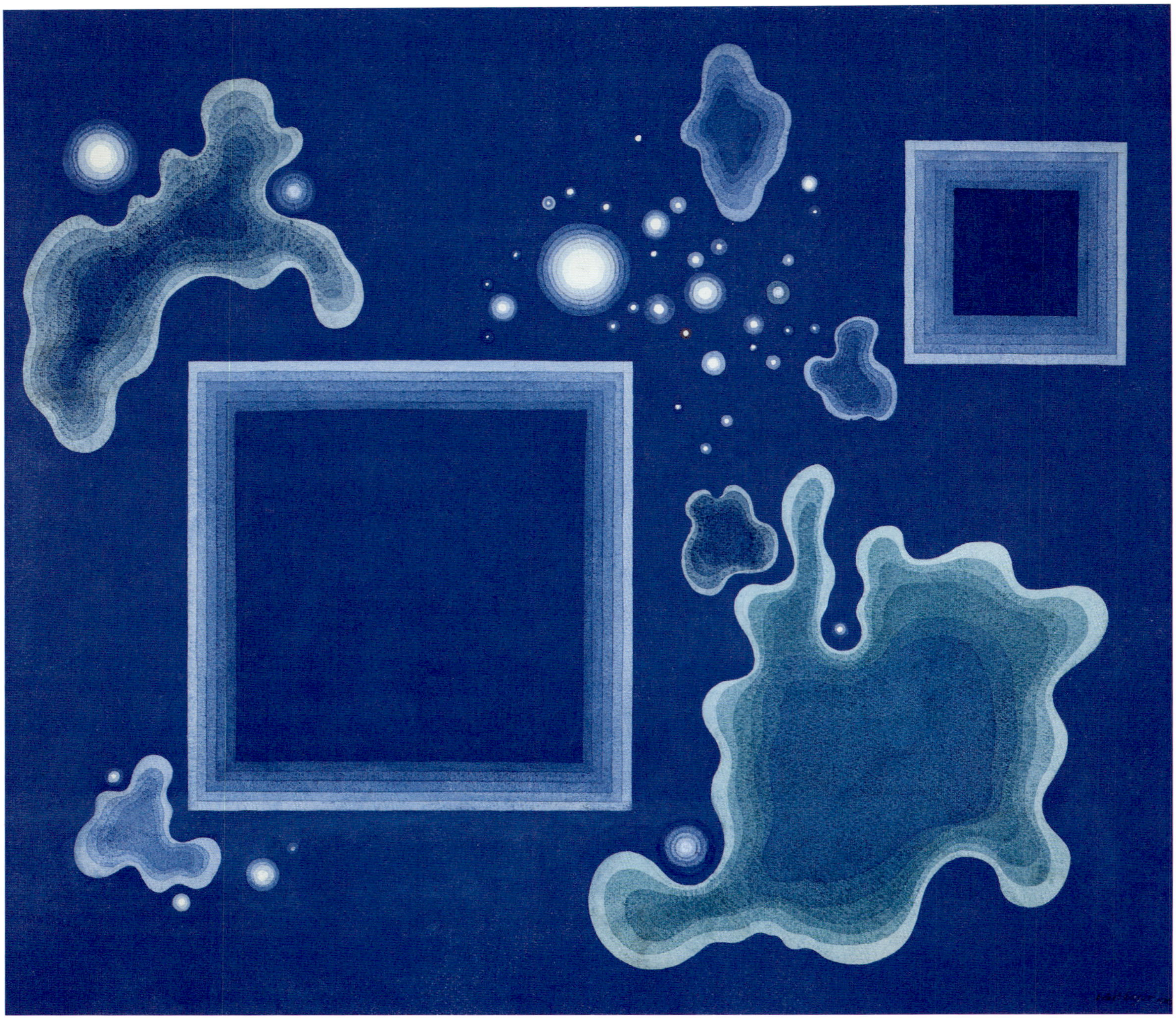

Herbert Bayer
Blue 1926/II, 1926
mumok—Museum moderner Kunst Stiftung Ludwig Wien

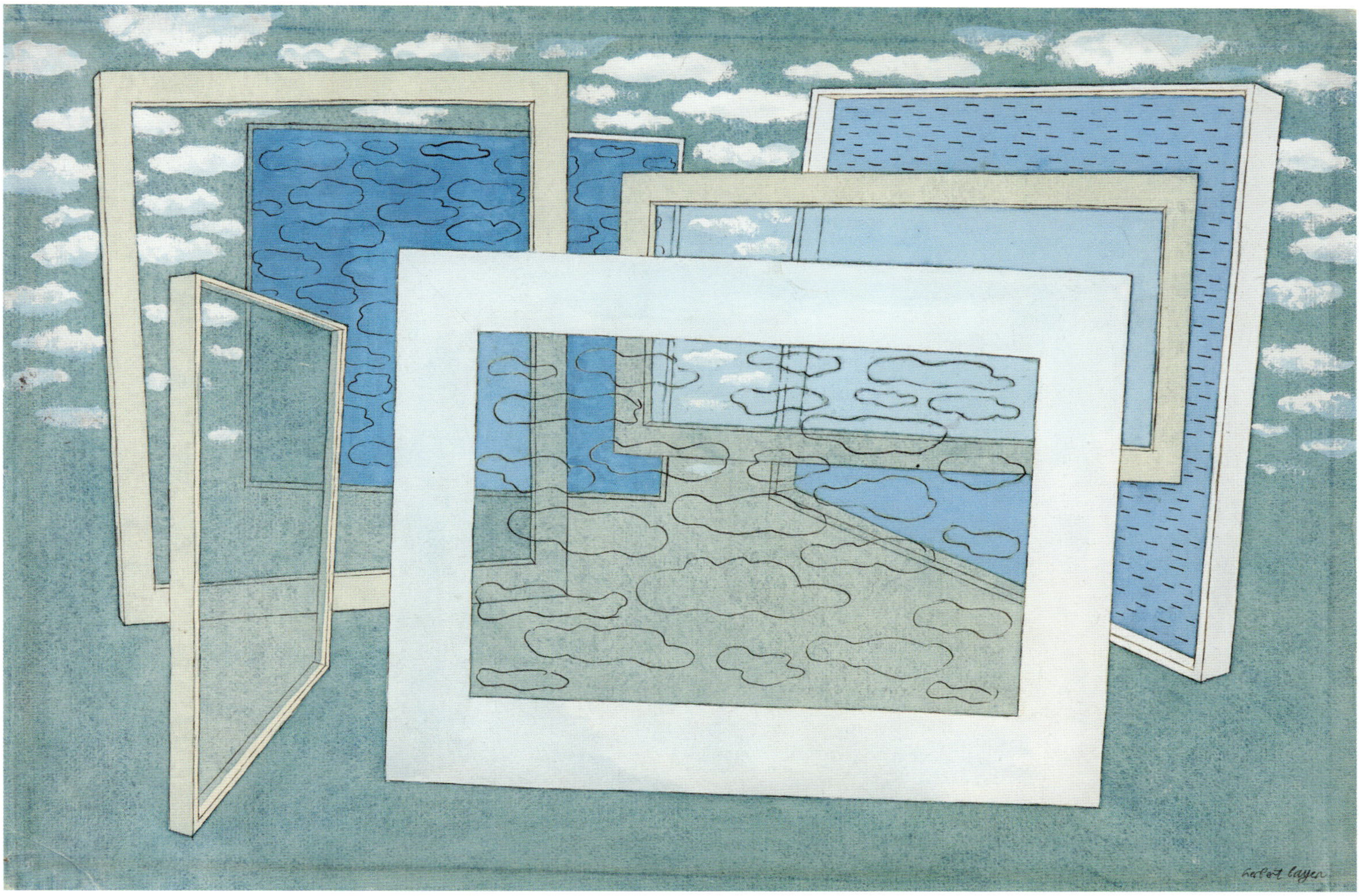

D3

Herbert Bayer
Composition in Space, 1928
LENTOS Kunstmuseum Linz

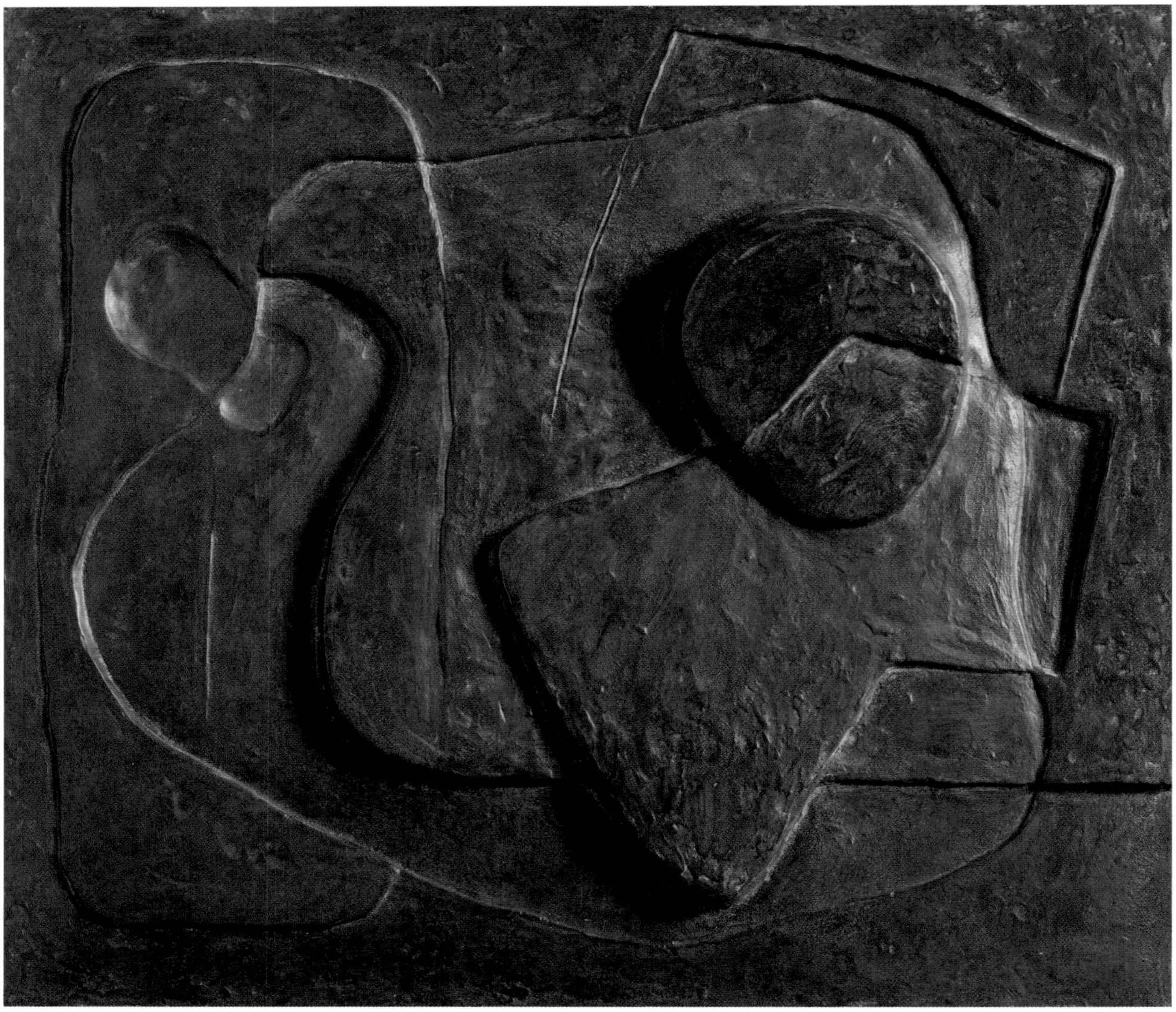

Zdeněk Dvořák
Plastron, c. 1935
National Gallery in Prague

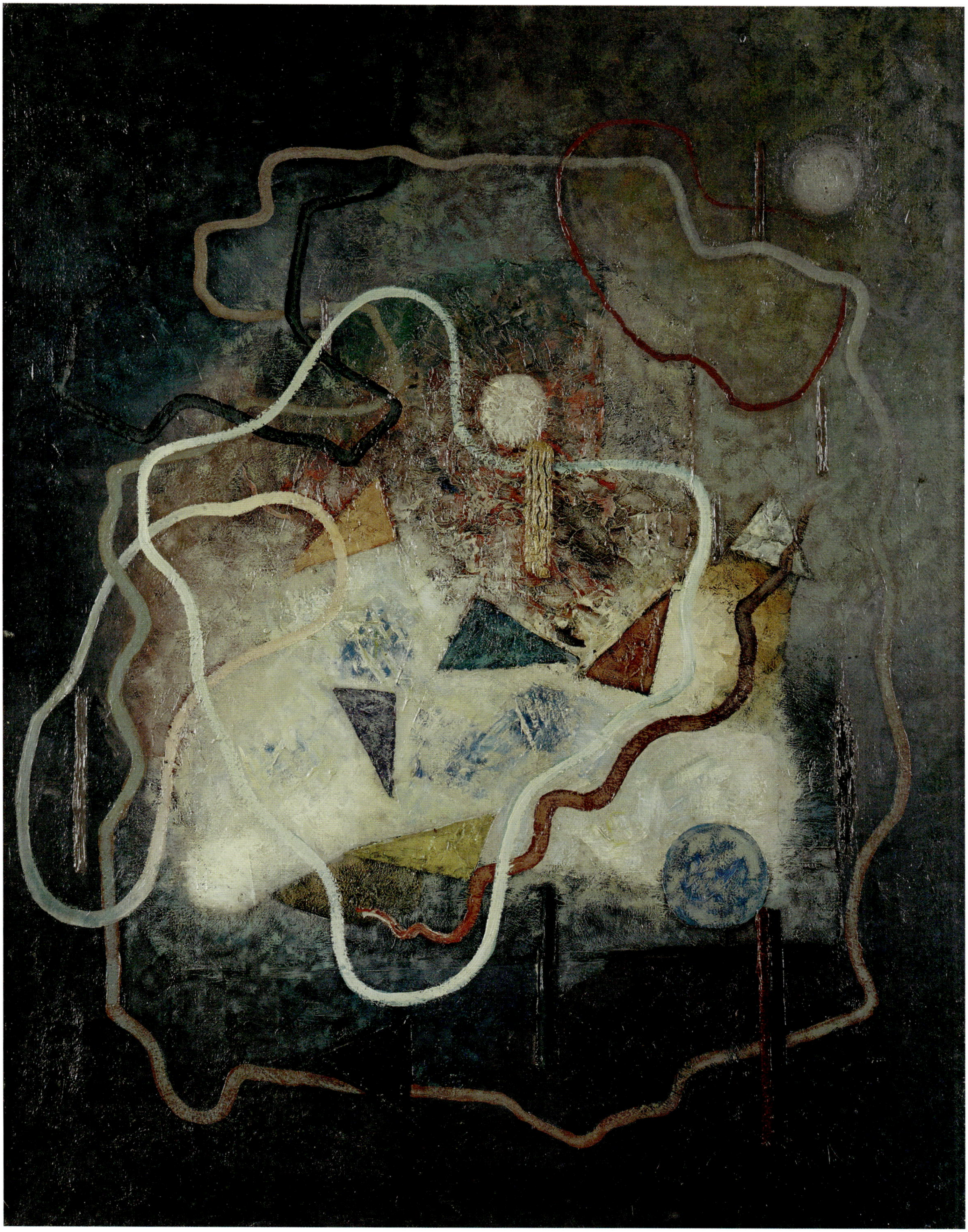

D3

František Foltýn
Composition, 1928, Belvedere, Vienna,
on permanent loan from the Rotter Collection

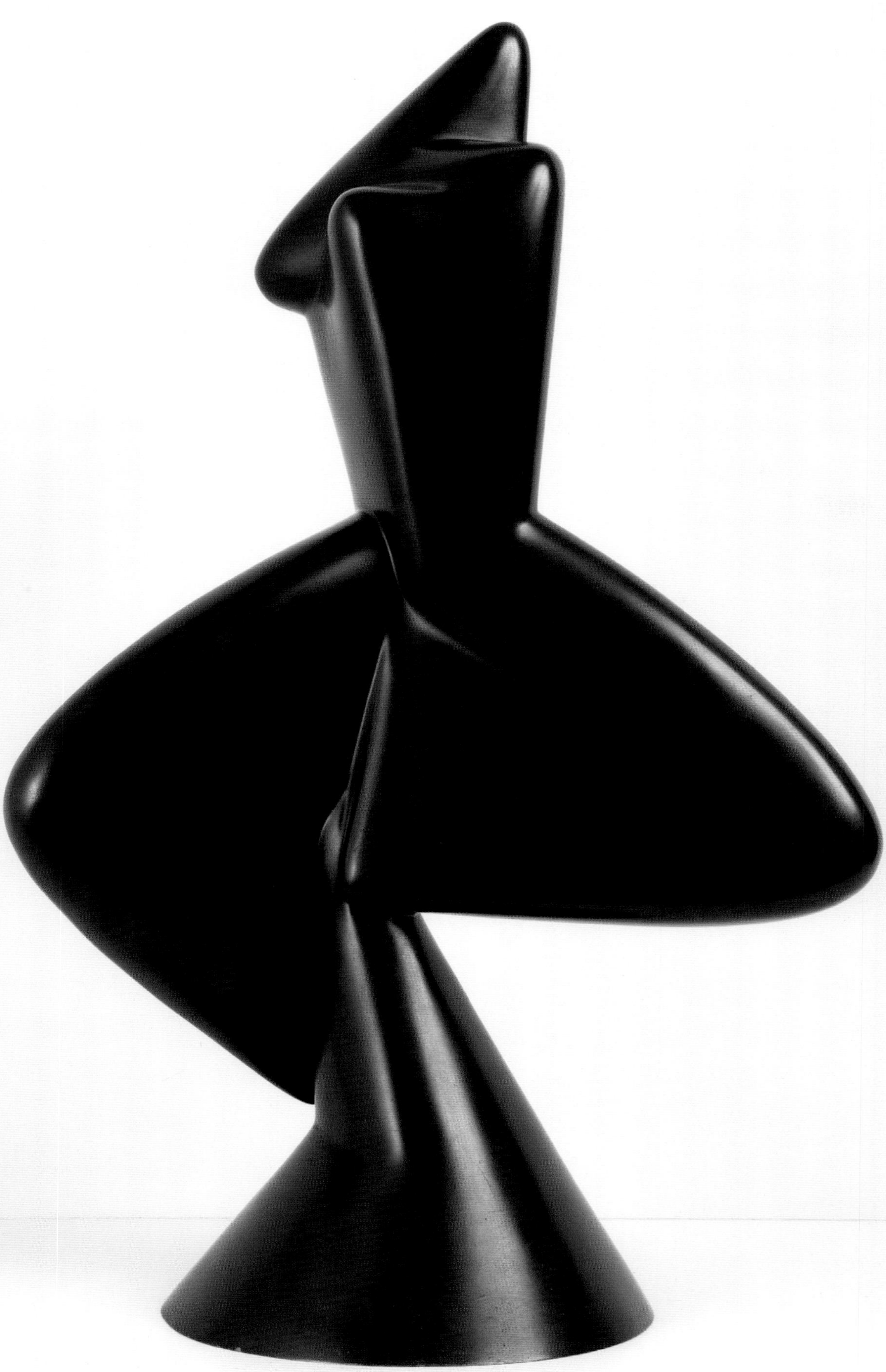

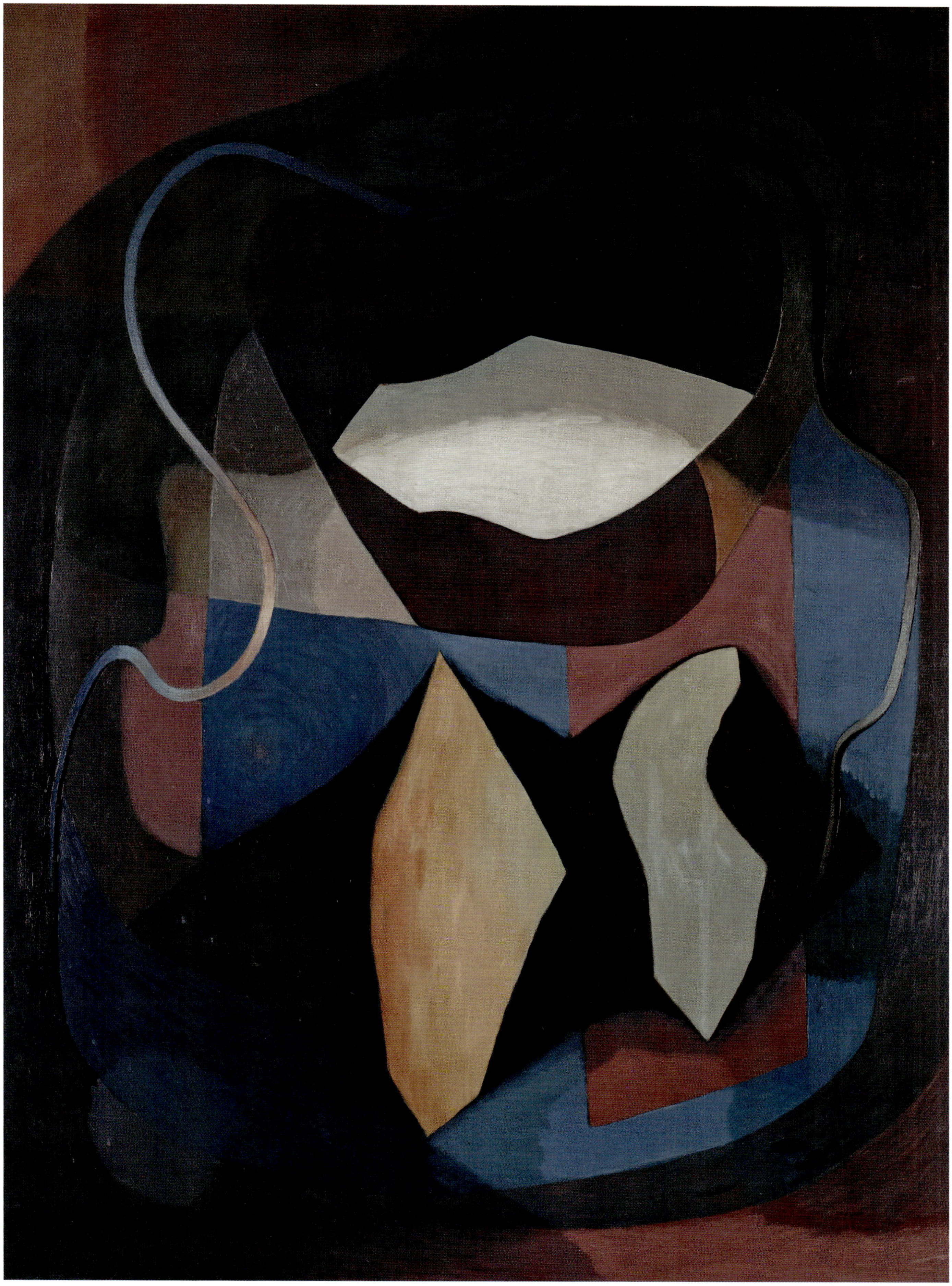

◂ Étienne Beothy
Danse Cosaque
(Danse Russe, Paraboles, Op. 45), 1930
Courtesy of Galerie Le Minotaure

František Foltýn
Abstract Composition, 1936/37
Belvedere, Vienna, on permanent loan from the Rotter Collection

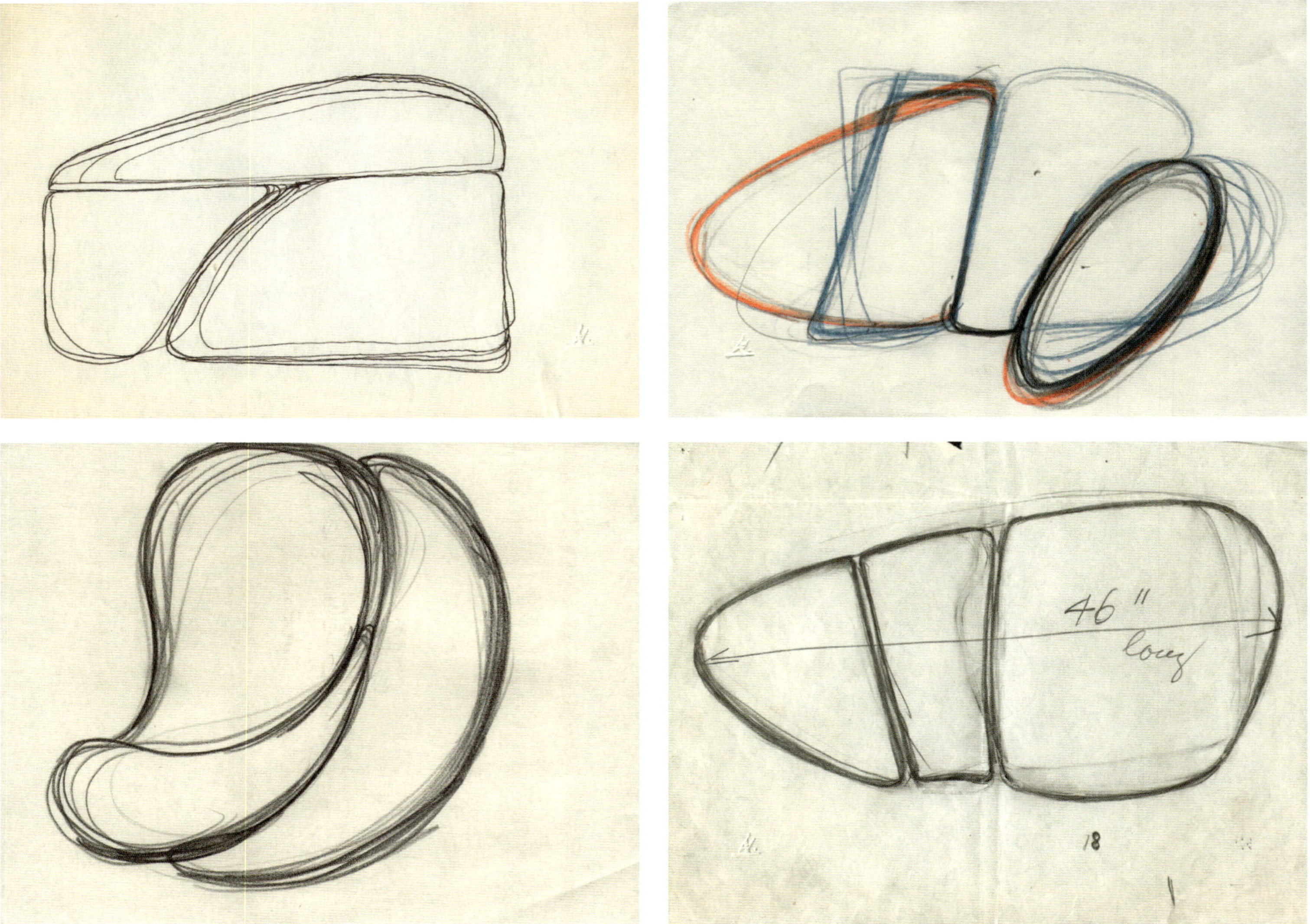

Frederick Kiesler
Sketches for a Table, 1935
Austrian Friedrich and Lillian Kiesler
Private Foundation

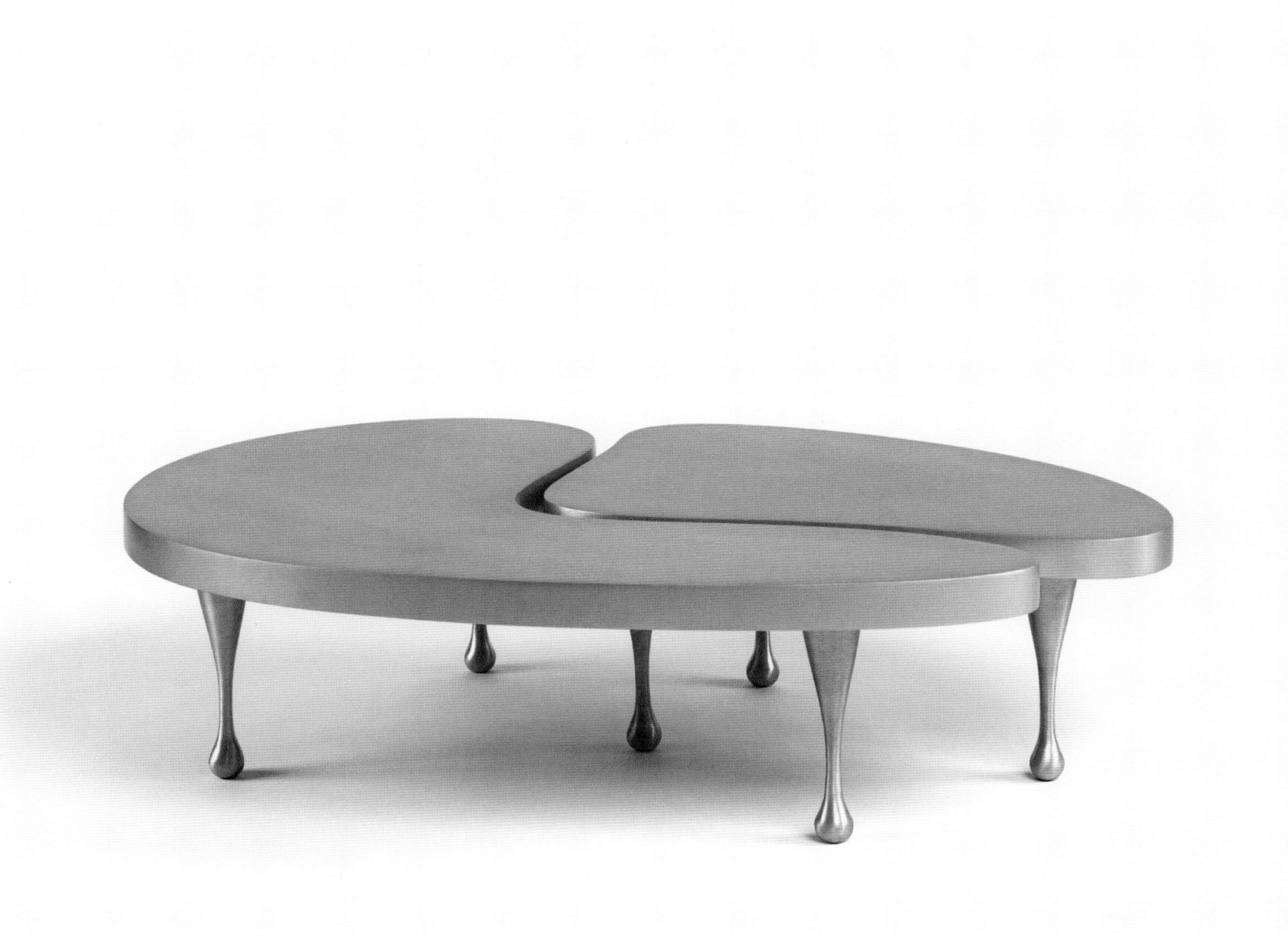

Frederick Kiesler
Two-Part Occasional Table, 1935–38
Part of an installation by Plamen Dejanov & Swetlana Heger, Belvedere, Vienna

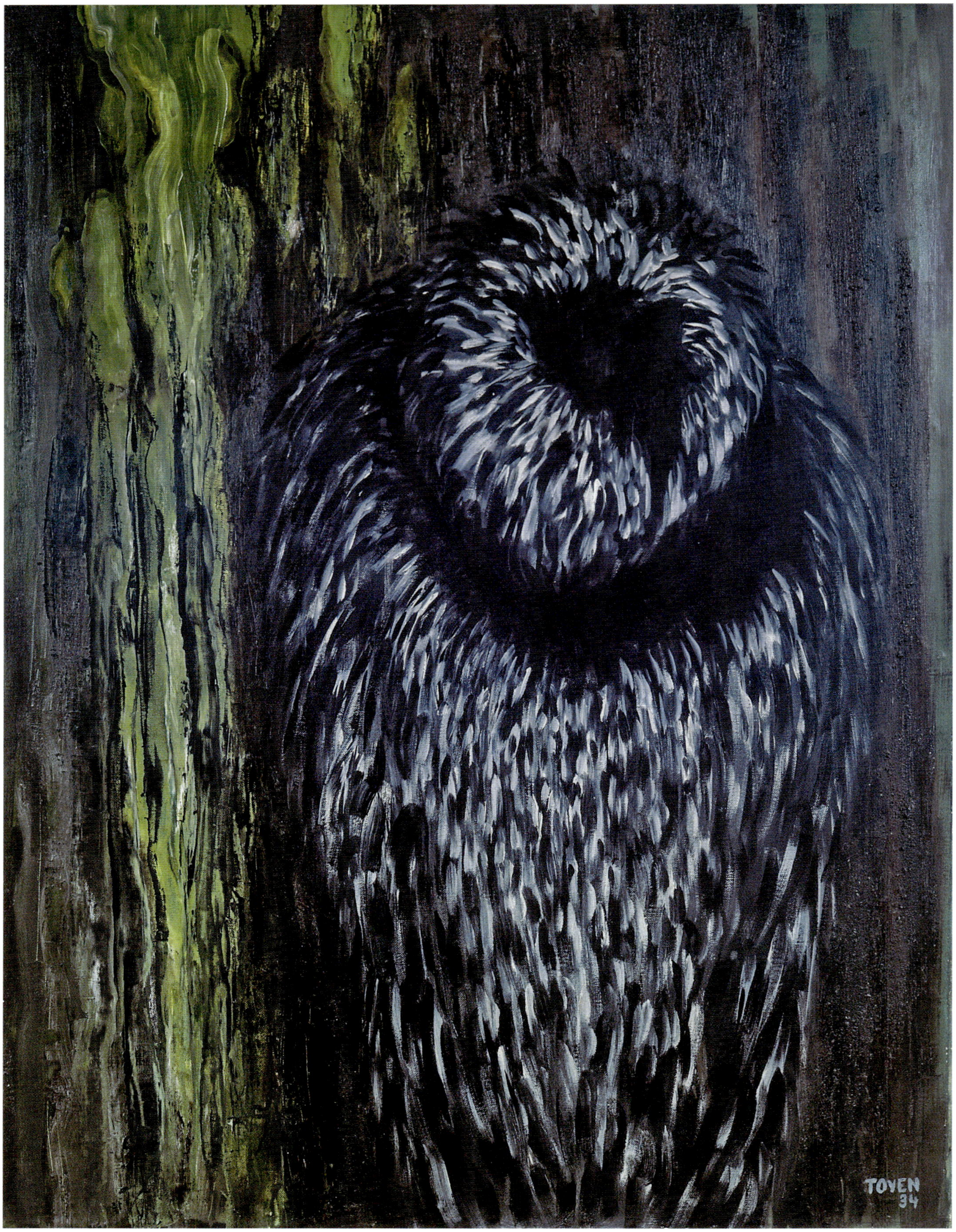

D3

Toyen
Voice of the Forest, 1934
Moravian Gallery, Brno

Toyen ▸
Abandoned Cave, 1937
Gallery of Fine Arts in Cheb

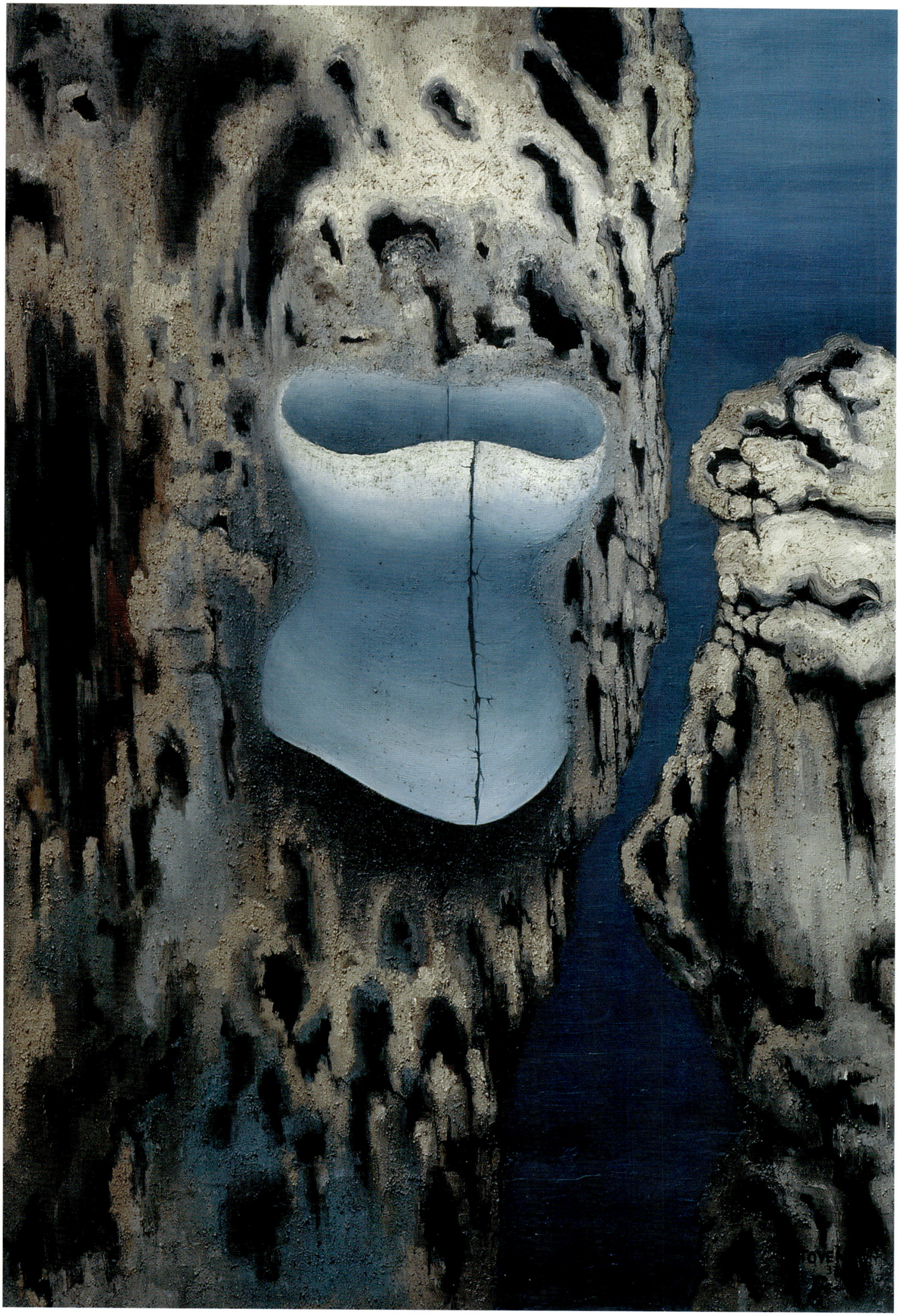

D3

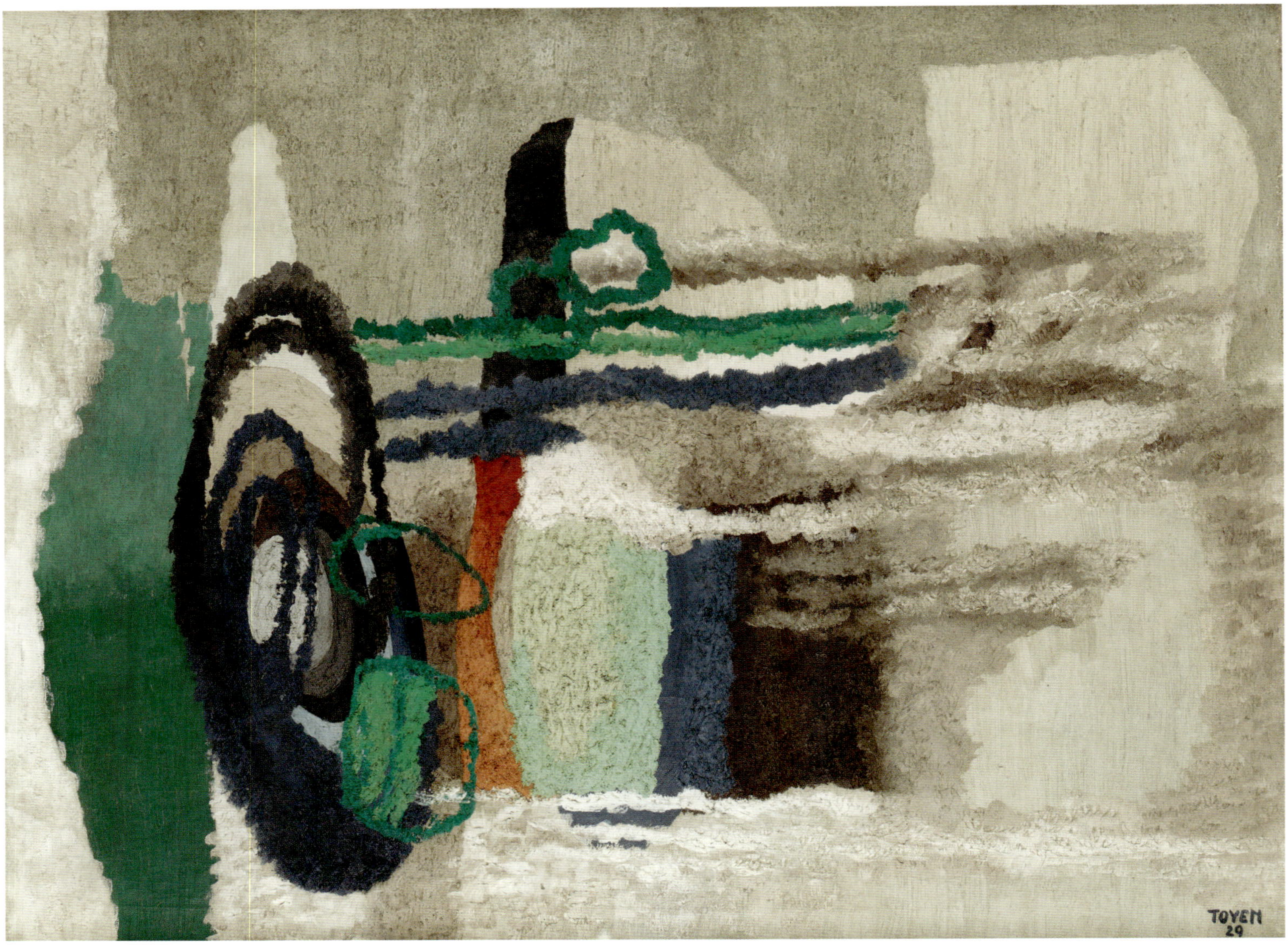

Toyen
Painting, 1929
Belvedere, Vienna, on permanent loan from the Rotter Collection

D3

Wolfgang Paalen ▸
Paysage totémique, 1938
Private collection

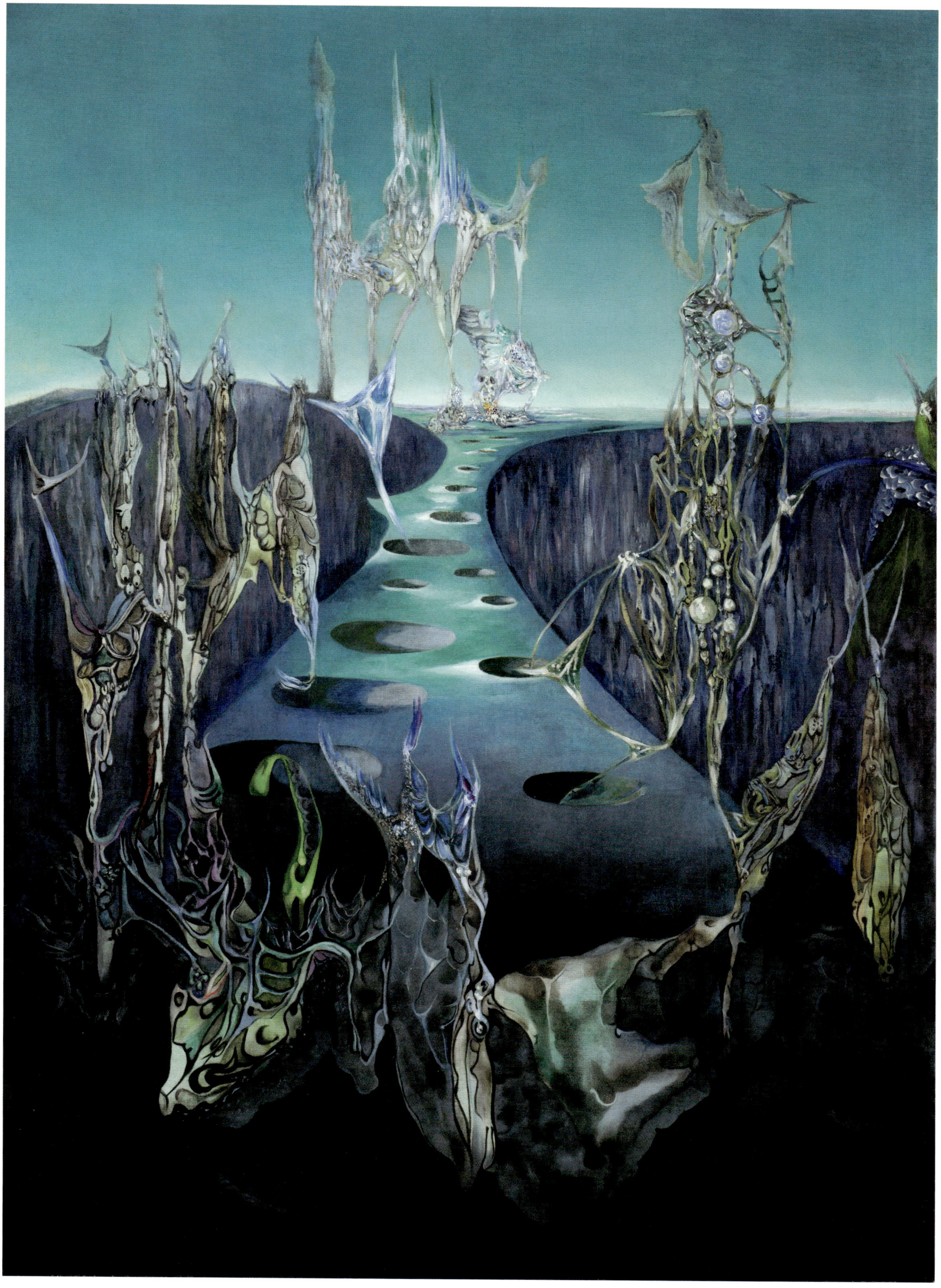

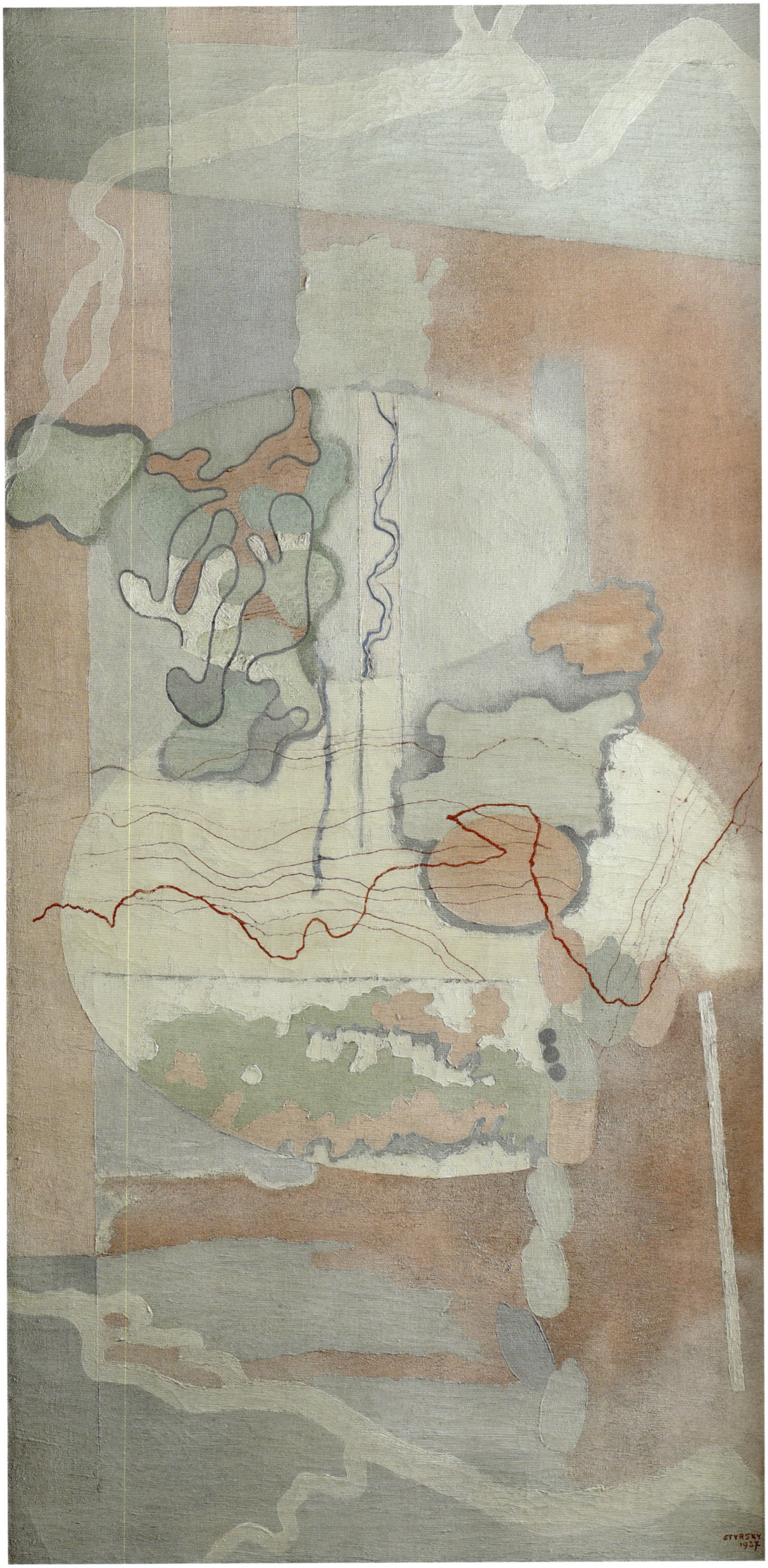

D3

Jindřich Štyrský
Flood, 1927
Moravian Gallery, Brno

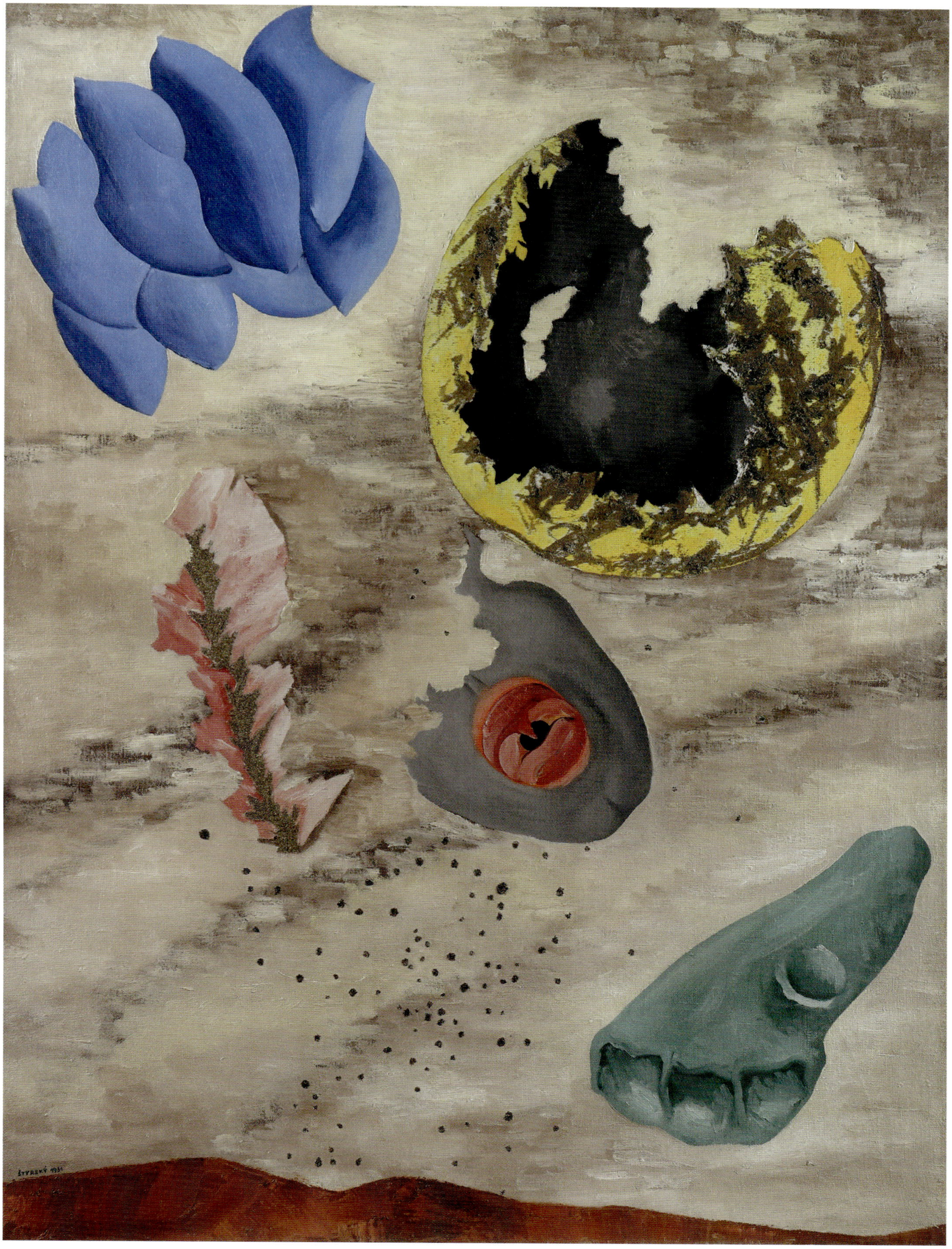

D3

Jindřich Štyrský
Palmette, 1931
Moravian Gallery, Brno

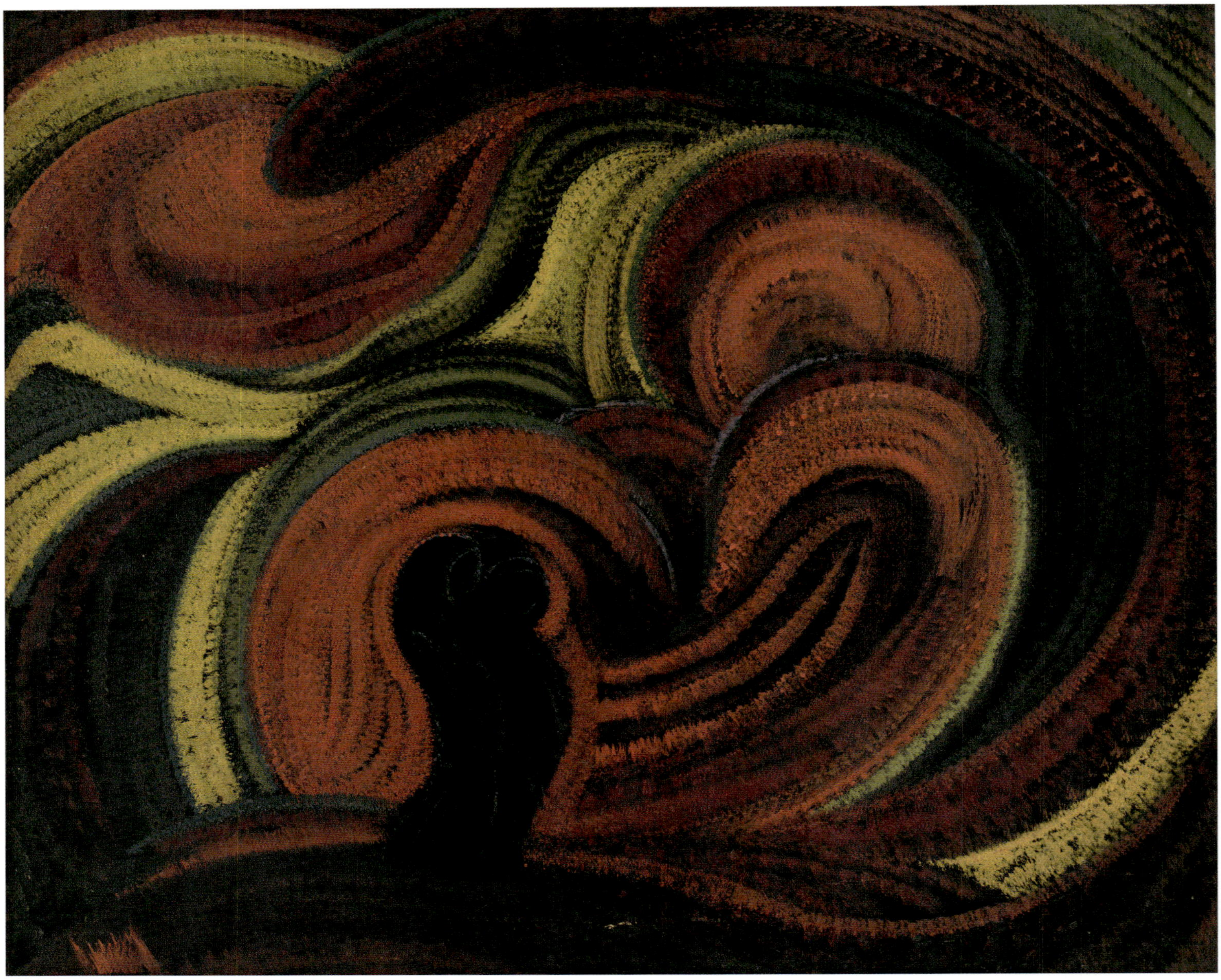

D3

Anton Jasusch
The Symphony, 1922
Slovak National Gallery, Bratislava

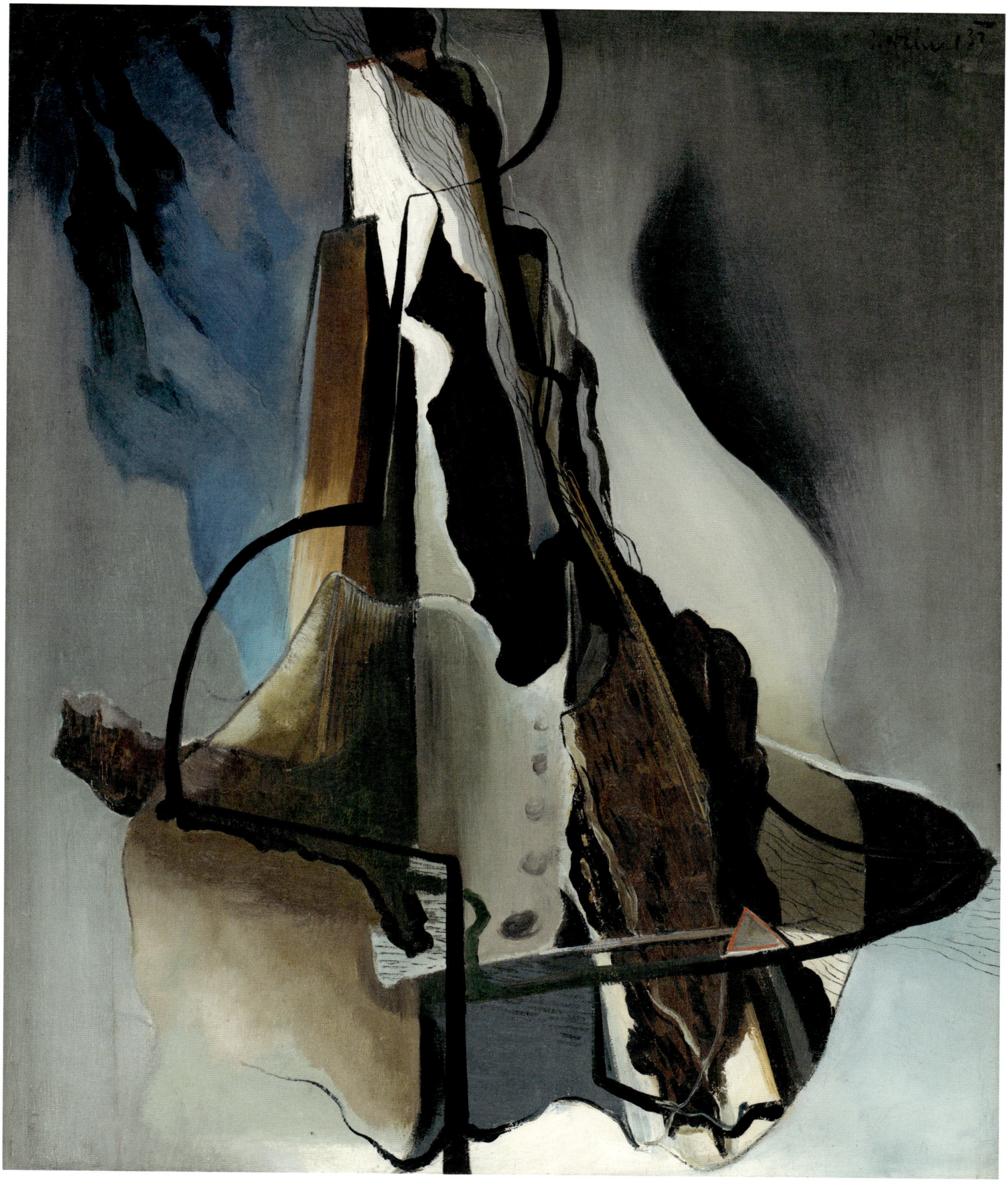

D3

Imrich Weiner-Kráľ
Tatra, 1933
Slovak National Gallery, Bratislava

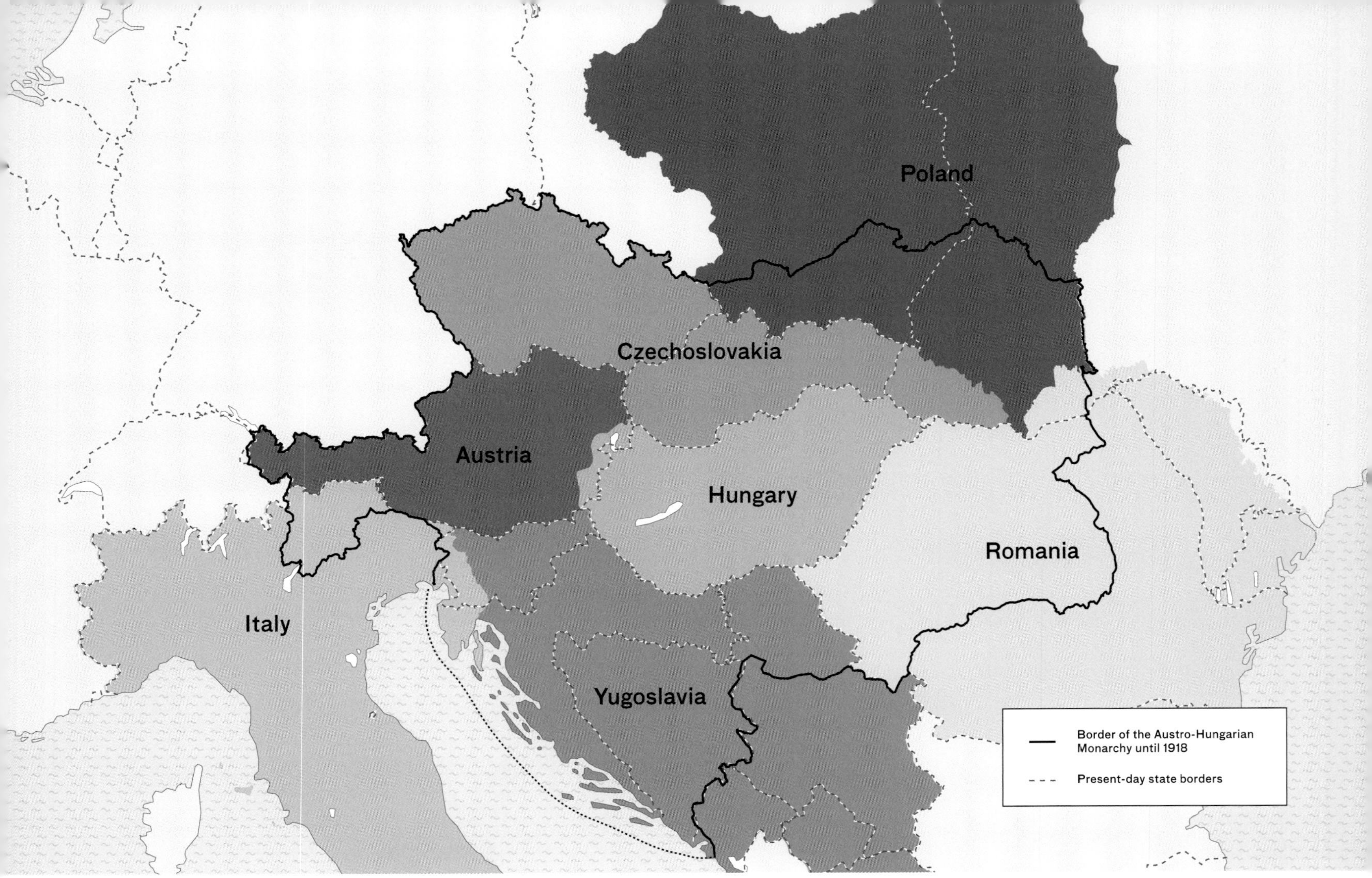
Poland
Czechoslovakia
Austria
Hungary
Romania
Italy
Yugoslavia
Border of the Austro-Hungarian Monarchy until 1918
Present-day state borders

border—hranica:

hranica *(vsl.)* *b* m. *hranice* (pl.; **hraničiar** *b* hraničář (*Cz.*); **hraničište** pohranič. místo.

Mir. Kálal, *Slovenský slovník z literatúry aj nárečí: Slovensko-Český slovník a Český ukazovateľ* (Banská Bystrica, 1924), p. 182

hranica, -e: Na hranici krajinskej býva. — Vojenská hranica.

Peter Tvrdý, ed., *Slovenský frazeologický slovník* (Prague/Prešov, 1933), p. 158

border—frontieră, graniţă, hotar:

frontieră f. graniţă, hotar.

Lazăr Şaineanu, *Dicţionar universal al Limbei Române*, (Bucharest, 1929), p. 260

graniţă f. hotarul unei ţări. [Slav. GRANIŢA]

Lazăr Şaineanu, *Dicţionar universal al Limbei Române*, Române (Bucharest, 1929), pp. 260, 281

hotar n. **1.** semn servind a despărţi două mosii; **2.** limită (şi *fig.*): *mânia grădinarului trecu orice hotar; o iale fără margini, un dor fără hotar* AL.; **3.** marginale unei ţări, graniţă: *hotarele României;* **4.** (poetic) margine *în genere: să străng în brate vieaţa-mi pe a zilelor hotare* AL. [Ung. HATÁR].

Lazăr Şaineanu, *Dicţionar universal al Limbei Române*, (Bucharest, 1929), pp. 260, 297

Slovakian
Romanian

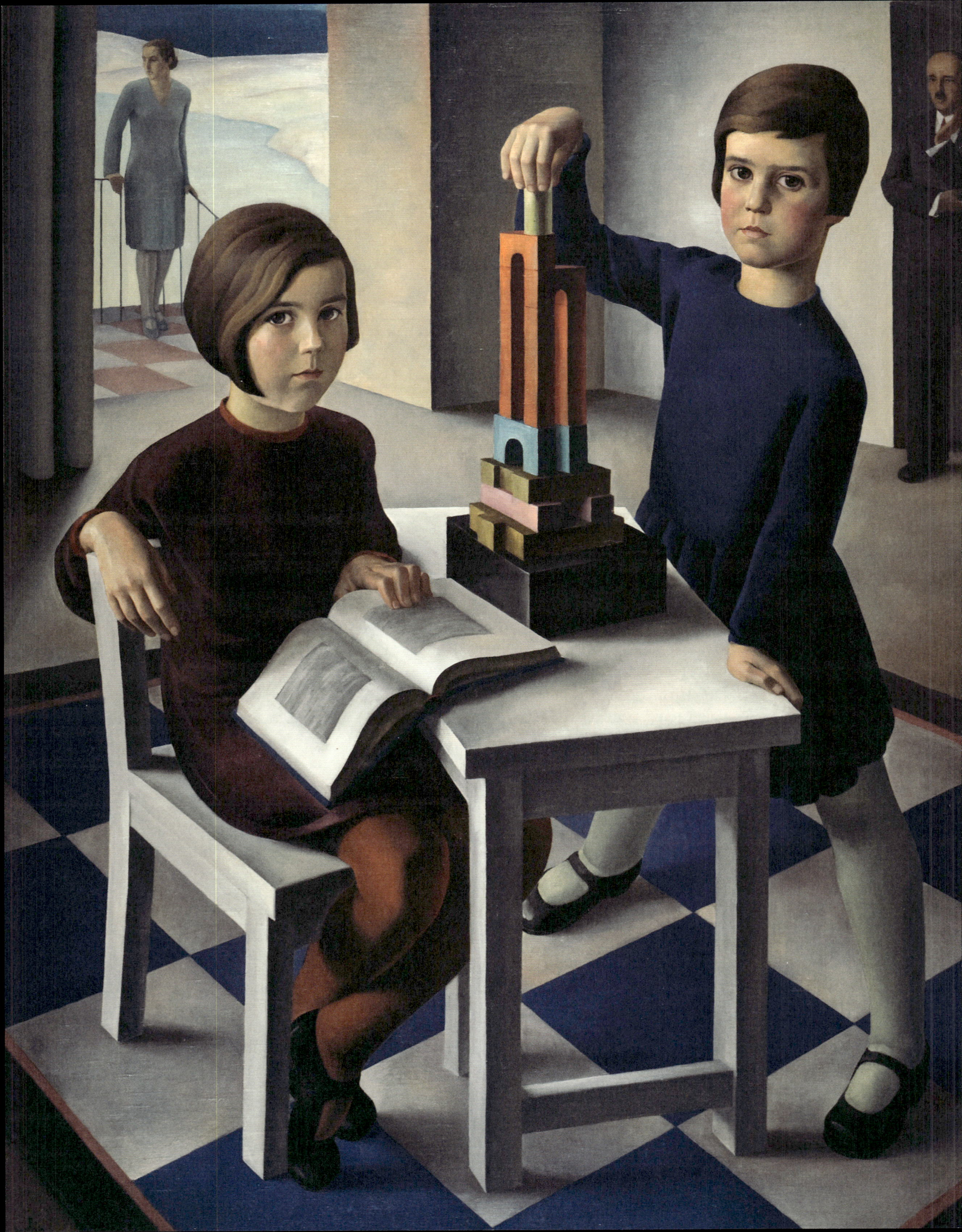

E Variations on the Figurative

Ernst Nepo, *Family Portrait*, 1929 (detail), Tyrolean State Museum Ferdinandeum

Magical Hideaways: Fantastic Trends in Austrian Art Between the Wars

Gabriele Spindler

Across the eras, artists of various stylistic affiliations have employed fantastic modes of expression, and, consequently, the Fantastic in art could never be regarded as a "style" in the sense of an art-historical classification. And it is not only in the visual arts that the Fantastic is difficult to define and often cannot be clearly distinguished from related manifestations.[1] The following two definitions are examples offering a glimpse of the various research approaches.

In the view of Hans Holländer, "the Fantastic is constructed, certainly not irrational, but the result of an astute and precise combination and a technique of realization that gives the improbable the strong semblance of the probable. For only when it appears probable can the Fantastic indeed be perceived as improbable. This always calls for a high degree of realism. The Fantastic could not be expressed in abstract painting."[2] Therefore, in its formal appearance, fantastic art is not only associated with a realistic style of representation but this can also intensify its effect.

By contrast, Wieland Schmied, another scholar of the Fantastic, highlights repressed, irrational, and magical elements as the essential engine behind the creation of fantastic art: "It only seems possible to see the real world as rationally ordered because we have grown accustomed to repressing or deliberately blocking out many elements of our existence. Putting these repressed elements into words or expressing them in images is the role of a type of art we perceive as fantastic, i.e. alien and unsettling. It shows how much of human existence has remained an enigma and can probably never be explained. It recalls the mysterious character of the world."[3]

Despite their evident contradiction, both of these approaches are mirrored in the fantastic trends in Austrian art between the wars. Moreover, within this outlined spectrum of the Fantastic, each artist demonstrates a highly individual mode of expression. If we wish to do justice to this individualism, each artist needs to be considered in their own right, with all their idiosyncrasies and independent qualities. This essay introduces Klemens Brosch, Franz Sedlacek, Richard Teschner, Alfred Kubin, and Rudolf Wacker, as a selection of artists grouped under the heading "fantastic trends" in the exhibition *Beyond Klimt: New Horizons in Central Europe*. Reflecting a key theme of the project, the discussion will focus on their experience of World War I and artistic development between the wars.

KLEMENS BROSCH—THE GENIUS DRAFTSMAN

Before World War I, the young Linz-based artist Klemens Brosch (1894–1926) seemed poised for a promising artistic career. After his exceptional artistic talent was recognized at school, together with several colleagues he founded the Linz

E

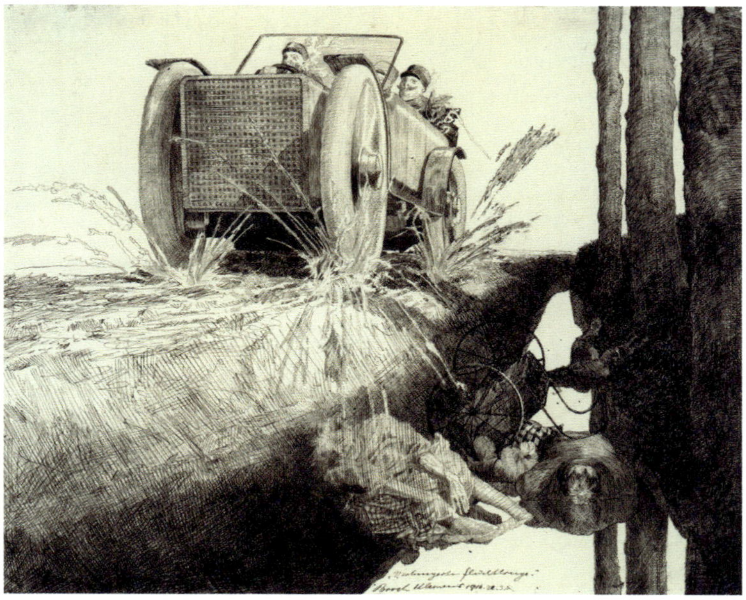

Fig. 1
Klemens Brosch
Starved Refugees, 1916
Landesgalerie Linz,
Graphic Arts Collection

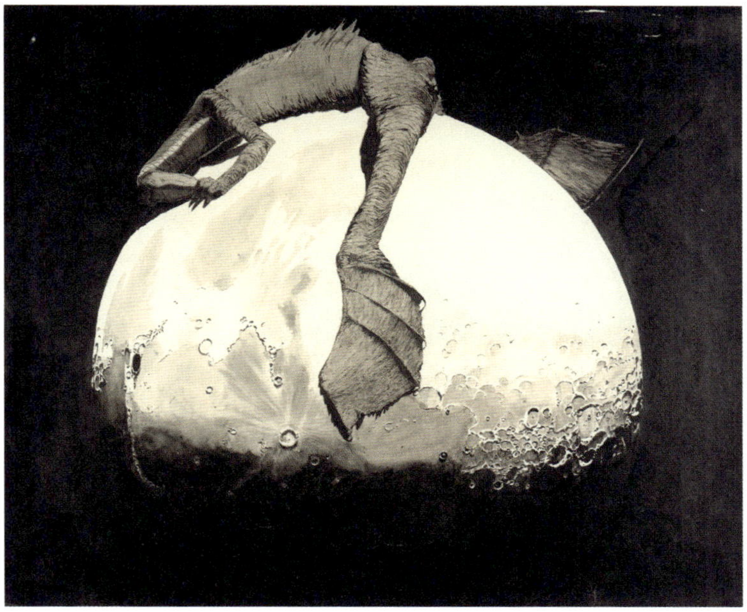

Fig. 2
Klemens Brosch
Crocodile on the Moon, c. 1912
Landesgalerie Linz,
Graphic Arts Collection

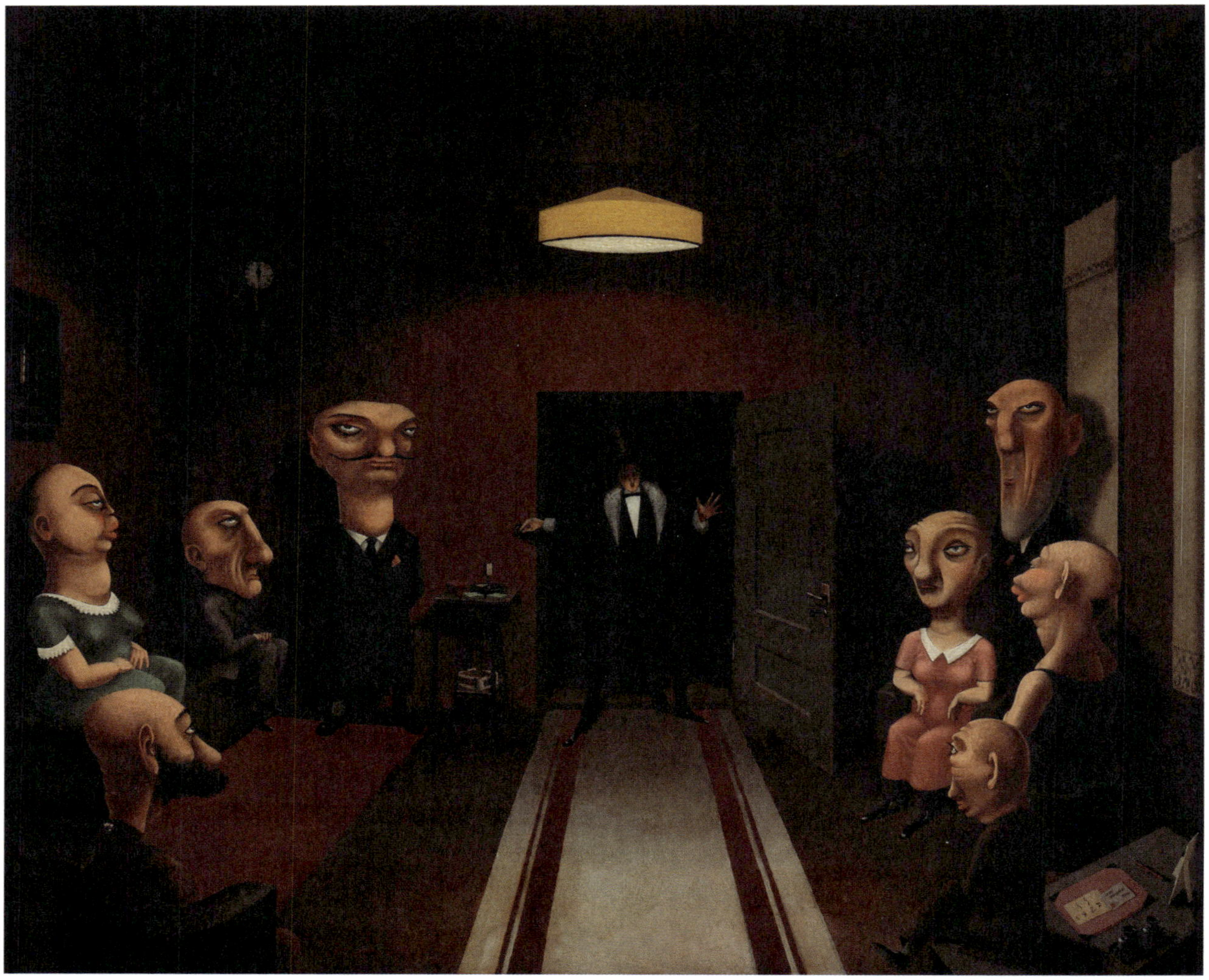

Fig. 3
Franz Sedlacek
Nocturnal Homecoming, 1927
Landesgalerie Linz, Oberösterreichisches Landesmuseum

artist association MAERZ in the spring of 1913, the first attempt to form a Secessionist artistic movement in Upper Austria. The inaugural presentation of the new association received an enthusiastic response from public and critics alike. Immediately following his Linz exhibition debut, Brosch started studying at the Vienna Academy of Fine Arts where he enjoyed considerable successes in his first year.[4]

These remarkable beginnings to his artistic career were abruptly interrupted by the outbreak of World War I and Brosch's conscription into the army. The war was a dramatic watershed in Brosch's life and his subsequent artistic development, affecting him more profoundly than any of the other artists discussed here. Although spending no more than seven weeks at the front, the experience plunged him into a physical and mental breakdown from which Brosch never fully recovered. To make matters worse, an army doctor prescribed morphine for pain relief, triggering a lifelong dependency on drugs (fig. 1).

Between 1914 and 1916, in an attempt to process the horrors he had experienced on the battlefields, Brosch produced countless drawings of the war. They depict harrowing scenes of wartime violence with a realism that is hard to surpass. One of his most haunting images shows starved refugees, thus shifting the focus to the impact of war on civilians. Brosch adopts the perspective of the victims and points an accusing finger, a message underpinned in the composition by depicting the military vehicle from an extremely low viewpoint.

Brosch's work is not only characterized by a meticulous, sometimes unsparing realism but also by his strong leanings to the Fantastic. Even before World War I, major works by the artist point in this direction, an outstanding example being the large image *Crocodile on the Moon* (c. 1912, fig. 2). After the war, under the influence of his escalating drug addiction, he created dark, unsettling visions resonant with deep despair and a longing for death. Stylistically, the artist's work evolved from his meticulously detailed early pencil drawings to the expressive, dynamic brushstrokes of his works in ink of the 1920s.

FRANZ SEDLACEK—THE PAINTING CHEMIST

Franz Sedlacek (1891–1945), also from Linz, was one of the founders of MAERZ along with Klemens Brosch. In 1911, he had begun a chemistry degree at Vienna Technical University but was forced to interrupt his studies when he was enlisted as a soldier in World War I. He had contributed caricature drawings to an exhibition in 1912 at the Oberösterreichischer Kunstverein (Upper Austrian Art Society) in Linz, but, following his father's wishes, he chose to study a science instead. On returning from the war, he completed his studies and was employed as a chemist at

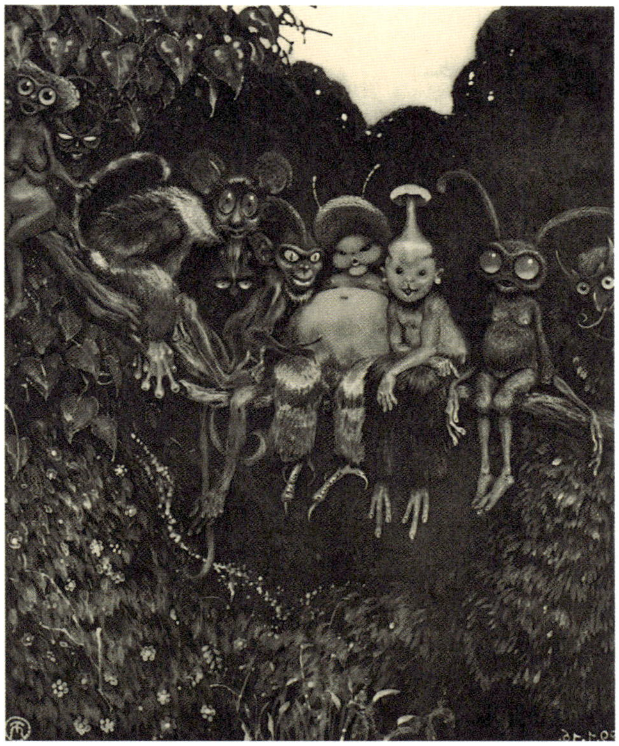

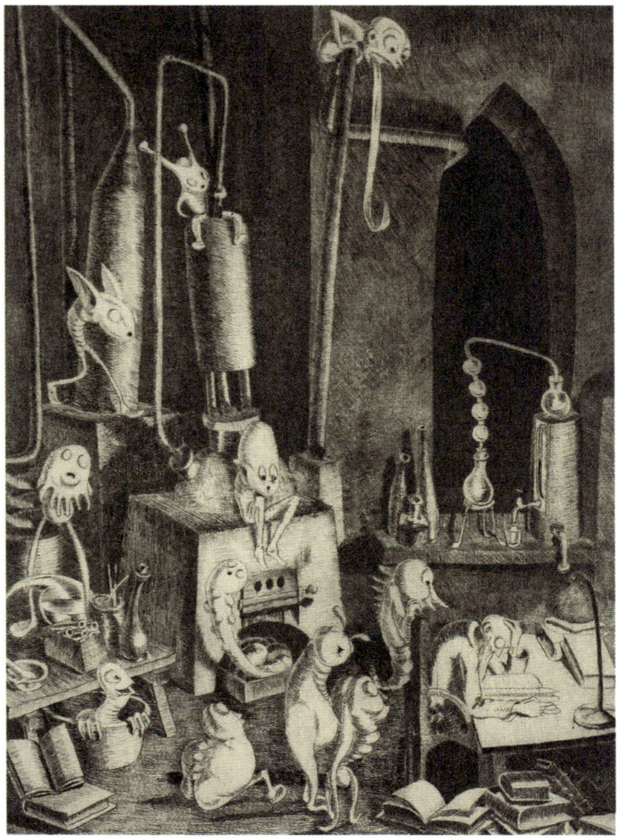

Fig. 4
Richard Teschner
Indifferent Spectators, 1916, Theater Museum, Vienna

Fig. 5
Franz Sedlacek
The Chemist, 1923
NORDICO Stadtmuseum Linz

Vienna's Technical Museum. His life as a civil servant was ordered and bourgeois, defined by conformity and a sense of duty.

His true passion, however, was for art. In 1920, he started teaching himself to paint and experimented with different colors and pigments. By studying the Old Masters at the Kunsthistorisches Museum, Sedlacek developed his own meticulous painting technique, reminiscent of New Objectivity. His subjects, however, were usually drawn from the realms of the Fantastic and ranged from imbuing his paintings with magical, uncanny moods to populating his imagery with ghosts, deformed figures, and grotesquely bizarre hybrid creatures in the tradition of Hieronymus Bosch (fig. 3).

That being said, Franz Sedlacek's approach to the Fantastic was entirely rational, as he himself emphasized: "How little it takes to cause horror. Painters of uncanny beings, however fantastic their creations may appear, essentially employ simple means. They use natural organ forms and only go beyond nature inasmuch as they distort or exchange these forms, allow them to proliferate or wither."[5] During the 1920s and 1930s, this artistic strategy resulted in national and international success for the painter-chemist.[6]

RICHARD TESCHNER—THE FANTASTIC PUPPETEER

Richard Teschner (1879–1948) also aspired throughout his life to create an artistic world beyond everyday realities and "to storm into the immeasurable realms of the imagination,"[7] as he once said himself. Originally from Bohemia, Teschner studied in Prague, moving in 1909 to Vienna, where he devoted himself to his life's work: the puppet theater. He was influenced and fascinated by the Indonesian rod puppets called *wayang golek*. Teschner based his first plays on Javanese legends; from 1913 he created his own storylines with a fantastical, fairytale cast of figures. Deemed unfit for service, he was spared from fighting during World War I and could instead devote the war years to developing his puppet theater. Entitled *Figurenspiegel* (Figure Mirror), its first public performance took place in 1920.

As with Sedlacek, Teschner's artistic beginnings were in graphic art, particularly in the field of caricature and satirical drawings. His works appeared in the magazine *Der liebe Augustin*, published by Gustav Meyrink, while Sedlacek initially drew for the satirical weeklies *Simplicissimus* and *Muskete*. The two artists' similarities in style and subject matter are especially apparent in their approach to the grotesque and in depictions of bizarre hybrid creatures (figs. 4, 5).

In the 1920s, Richard Teschner finally established his puppet theater at his studio in Gersthof in Vienna's eighteenth district. Franz Sedlacek could sometimes be found in the audience and his figures later revealed the obvious influence of Teschner's *Figurenspiegel* puppets.

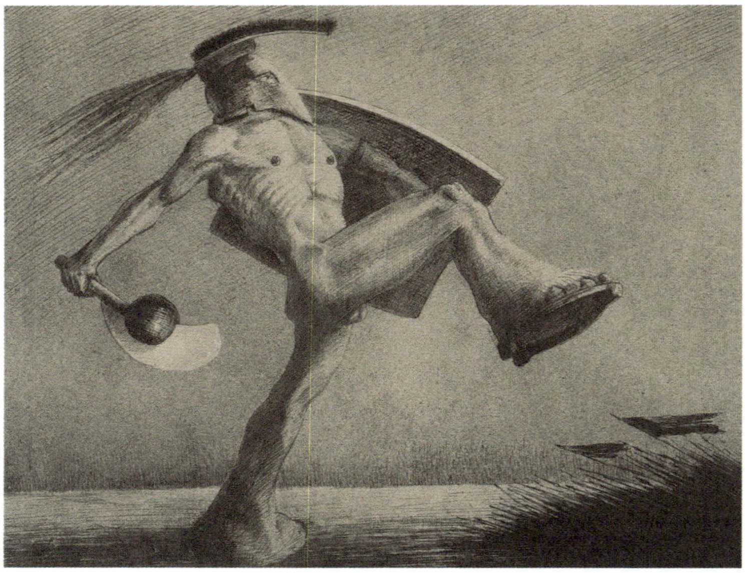

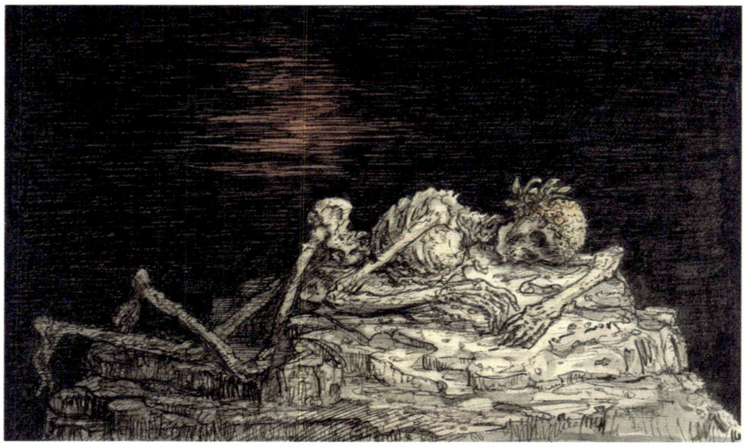

ALFRED KUBIN—THE WIZARD OF ZWICKLEDT

"Everywhere on earth it's burning. Inhabitants of other stars watching this spectacle will be strangely moved.—I have made several 'war sheets' for *Simplicissimus* and pamphlets.—Also, I once again drew my 'famous' 'War' (Weber portfolio). [...] Hopefully this disgrace for humanity will soon be over,"[8] Alfred Kubin (1877–1959) wrote to his friend, the writer Fritz von Herzmanovsky-Orlando, in November 1914. What is remarkable about this quote is Kubin's reference to extraterrestrial beings and their impressions of the earthly "spectacle," as it reveals the complete merging of the real and fantastic in the artist's imagination, also a defining trait of his art (fig. 6).

It also mentions Kubin's graphic work *War* (1903), one of his most important early sheets: A monstrous figure strides forth with giant steps across the

"It only seems possible to see the real world as rationally ordered because we have grown accustomed to repressing or deliberately blocking out many elements of our existence." (Wieland Schmied)

land, menacing and unstoppable, defying the tempestuous wind. The hybrid figure is naked, but armed with a monumental helmet, sickle, and shield, his colossal feet shod with horseshoes. Whether this is a visionary premonition of World War I or the sheet is merely "a generalized visual image of Kubin's personal state of mind, which at the time was marked by fears and paranoia,"[9] has already been discussed at length by Kubin scholars. What we do know is that "Kubin's early drawings would be horrifically confirmed by history [...]"[10] and this sheet can be seen as a timeless, haunting metaphor against the violence of war (fig. 7).

For Alfred Kubin, the watershed in his artistic development was not triggered by the war. His turning point had occurred years before, when he, after his brilliant early work in Munich—created between 1899 and 1904—spiraled into a creative crisis. At its height, the artist switched medium and wrote his only novel *Die andere Seite* (The Other Side), which is still considered a masterpiece of fantastic literature. After this, Kubin shifted his focus to an expressive style of ink drawing, sometimes adding color. He regularly worked as an illustrator; his themes developed a stronger narrative and occasionally had a folkloric touch. The only noticeable change during

Fig. 6
Alfred Kubin
War (sheet 15 from the Hans von Weber portfolio), 1903
Landesgalerie Linz, Graphic Arts Collection

Fig. 7
Alfred Kubin
The End of the War, 1918
Landesgalerie Linz, Graphic Arts Collection, Rombold Collection

World War I was his drawing style, which moved toward clearer outlines and a calmer style of detailing inside the figures.[11] Particularly in the 1920s and 1930s, Kubin looked to the rural environment of his chosen home Wernstein am Inn for his subject matter, both to the landscape and the people with their myths and legends. Kubin had moved from Munich to Zwickledt near Wernstein in 1906, thus also distancing himself physically from the city that had been so inspirational for his early work.

Across all turning points and crises, however, it was Kubin's passion for grotesque, enigmatic, and fantastic subject matter that consistently shaped his work, a passion that grew out of his constant questioning of supposed reality and its manifestations. "From the beginning I had a natural tendency toward exaggeration and fantasy: a cow with four horns always seemed to me more interesting than one with two,"[12] the artist noted in 1926, also disclosing the significance of memorable childhood experiences in his artistic development.

RUDOLF WACKER—THE MYSTERIOUS REALIST
Rudolf Wacker (1893–1939) was studying at the acclaimed Weimar University of Fine Arts under Walther Klemm and Albin Egger-Lienz until just before the outbreak of World War I. In 1914, he reluctantly joined the army: "I feel how ill-suited I am to military service; my organism is built differently [...] in the night I find myself and every morning feels like a suicide."[13] In 1916, he was taken prisoner by the Russian army, only returning to his native city of Bregenz four years later. A stay in Berlin after his release helped him recover from his wartime experiences and captivity and reintroduced him to the contemporary art scene. Even years later, whenever faced with difficult existential situations in life, Wacker drew from his resilience as a prisoner of war: "I must retain my Siberian faith, the unequivocal belief in the spirit and the essential!"[14]

In the early 1920s, Rudolf Wacker was stylistically influenced, above all, by the German Expressionism of the Brücke artists. Around the middle of the decade he turned toward realism, although, at least in his drawings, an Expressionist undertone remained. The objects the painter henceforth combined in his still lifes seem isolated, almost removed from reality with their exaggerated realism and surfaces so smooth that, as far as possible, every trace of the brush has been eradicated. Yet despite this smoothness, it is a damaged, a fragmented world Wacker preferred to present in his works.

Seen in the context of the realist art movements in German-speaking countries during the 1920s, Rudolf Wacker seems to fit most with the style of Magic Realism. Art critic Franz Roh, who coined the term in 1924, emphasized: "'Magic' [...] should indicate that the mystery does not enter the depicted world, but hovers behind it."[15] Several years

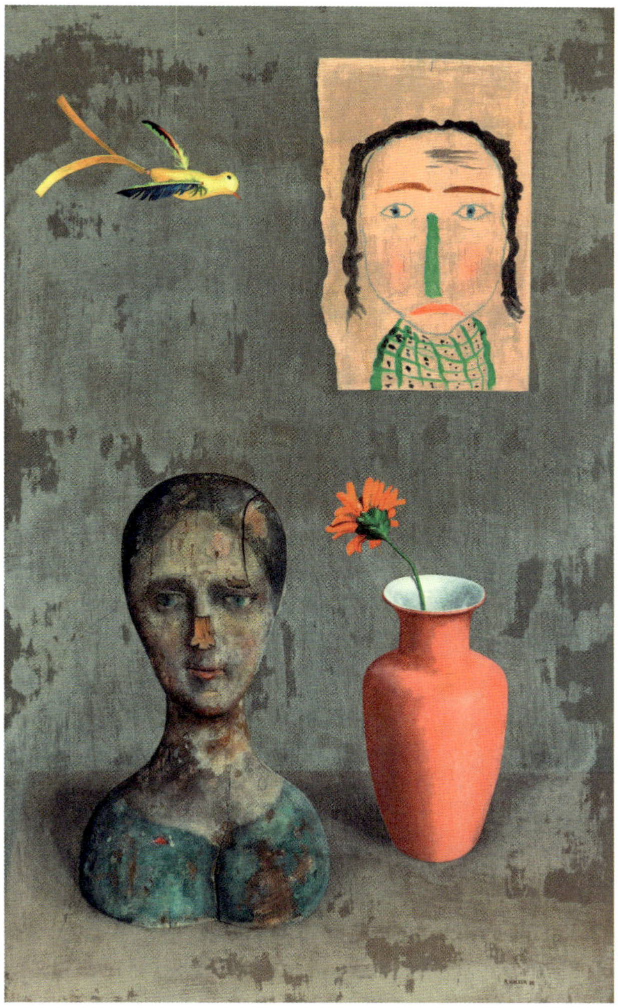

Fig. 8
Rudolf Wacker
Two Heads, 1936
Belvedere, Vienna

earlier, Wacker had described his artistic intention along similar lines: "My art is nothing other than a means, an endeavor, to probe the mysteries hidden beneath the skin of the visible by depicting life."[16] He later wrote in his diaries that, in his view, the simplest object was more fantastic than all invention and there was mystery enough in the naked reality of things.[17] This view of the world is directly expressed in the enigmatic atmosphere of his works (fig. 8).

Whether these artists were in quest of the enigmatic and mysterious hidden beneath reality's surface or introducing the Fantastic into the realm of their images by way of rational construction, the fantastic trends of the interwar years certainly seem to have been a form of escapism. Remarkably, this flight from reality does indeed appear to reflect the spirit of the time. When, in 1930, the art historian Hans Tietze compiled an exhibition of contemporary art, *Die Kunst in unserer Zeit*, the section entitled "Supernatural" showed art that "seeks humanity's insatiable longing within the darkness of mysteries."[18] In doing so, he emphasized as a special contemporary quality of this art that it was aimed at seekers who "behind the material world that oppressed them sensed another realm for which they yearned."[19]

1 See Christine Ivanović, Jürgen Lehmann, and Markus May, eds., *Phantastik—Kult oder Kultur? Aspekte eines Phänomens in Kunst, Literatur und Film* (Stuttgart/Weimar, 2003).

2 Hans Holländer, "Wunderbare und seltsame Sachen: Antonius und die Versuchungen der Malerei," in Ivanović, Lehmann, and May 2003 (see note 1), p. 91.

3 Quoted from Peter Assmann, "Gespräch mit Wieland Schmied zum Thema Phantastik," in *Andererseits: Die Phantastik. Imaginäre Welten in Kunst und Alltagskultur*, ed. ibid., exh. cat. Oberösterreichische Landesmuseen, Linz (Linz, 2003), p. 63.

4 Brosch's biographer Elisabeth Nowak-Thaller refers to over fifty mentions in the media in the first year of his studies as well as numerous scholarships and prizes: *Klemens Brosch: Kunst und Sucht des Zeichengenies*, ed. Elisabeth Nowak-Thaller, exh. cat. Nordico Stadtmuseum Linz, Landesgalerie Linz des Oberösterreichischen Landesmuseums (Salzburg, 2016), p. 79.

5 "Wiener Maler," *Die Bühne*, no. 386, 2nd October issue 1934, p. 23.

6 A success that also continued during the Nazi era. See Gabriele Spindler, "Erfolg und Vergessen: Zur Rezeption von Franz Sedlaceks Œuvre," in *Franz Sedlacek 1891–1945: Monografie mit Verzeichnis der Gemälde*, eds. Gabriele Spindler and Andreas Strohhammer (Vienna, 2011), pp. 133–47.

7 Letter from Richard Teschner to Karl Wilfert the Younger, quoted from *Mit diesen meinen zwei Händen … Die Bühnen des Richard Teschner*, ed. Kurt Ifkovits, exh. cat. Österreichisches Theatermuseum, Vienna (Vienna, 2013), p. 9.

8 Letter from Alfred Kubin to Fritz von Herzmanovsky-Orlando of November 6, 1914, quoted from Michael Klein, ed., *Fritz von Herzmanovsky-Orlando: Briefwechsel mit Alfred Kubin 1903 bis 1952* (Salzburg/Vienna, 1983), p. 85.

9 Christoph Brockhaus, quoted from Wieland Schmied, "Heimsuchung oder Prophetie: Konflikte in Kubins Frühwerk," in *Nach Klimt: Schriften zur Kunst in Österreich* (Salzburg, 1979), p. 46.

10 Schmied 1979 (see note 9), p. 46.

11 See Annegret Hoberg, "Das Selbstverständnis des späten Kubin," in *Alfred Kubin (1877–1959): Mit einem Werkverzeichnis des Bestandes im Oberösterreichischen Landesmuseum*, ed. Peter Assmann (Linz, 1995), p. 14.

12 Alfred Kubin, *Dämonen und Nachtgesichte* (Dresden, 1926), p. 7. English translation quoted from *The Life and Art of Alfred Kubin* (New York, 2017), p. 4.

13 Rudolf Wacker, quoted from Max Haller, *Der Maler Rudolf Wacker 1893–1939* (Lustenau, 1971), n.p.

14 Rudolf Wacker, diary entry from November 1924, quoted from Haller 1971 (see note 13), n.p.

15 Franz Roh, quoted from Wieland Schmied, *Neue Sachlichkeit und Magischer Realismus in Deutschland 1918–1933* (Hannover, 1969), p. 8.

16 Rudolf Wacker, diary entry from the year 1919, quoted from Haller 1971 (see note 13), n.p.

17 Rudolf Wacker, diary entry from December 1928, quoted from Haller 1971 (see note 13), n.p.

18 Gesellschaft zur Förderung moderner Kunst in Wien, ed., *Die Kunst in unserer Zeit* (Vienna, 1930), p. 74.

19 Gesellschaft zur Förderung moderner Kunst in Wien 1930 (see note 18), p. 75.

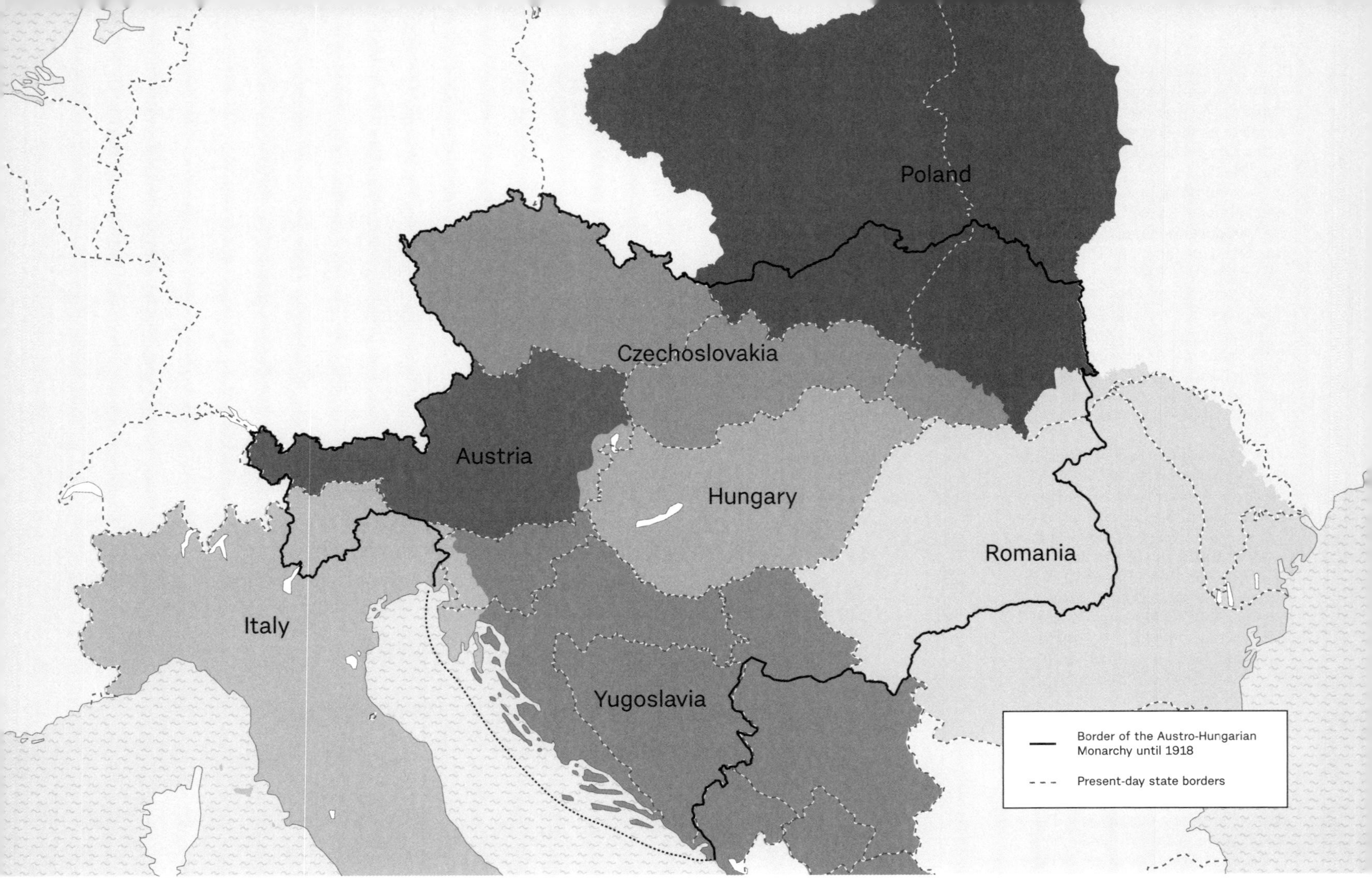

1919 The successor states of the Austro-Hungarian Empire

nation—národ:

národ 1) *bt* národ *(vsl.)*, 2) *bt* lid *(vsl) (tam bolo národa)*, 3) *(vsl) narod* m. *narod(z) enie* narození *(t. mor.) (prežili dva národy* dvě pokolení, K. X.); **narodeniatko** *b* v. **narodzenča** *b* novorozeně *(Phľd.)*; **narodiť sa** 1) naroditi se, 2 uroditi se *(Koll.)*; **narodovčiť** *b* býti, dělati národovce; **národniar** *bt* príslušník národní strany [odv. sr. *K.* VI., VIII.]

Mir. Kálal, *Slovenský slovník z literatúry aj nárečí. Slovensko-Český slovník a Český ukazovateľ*, (Banská Bystrica, 1924), p. 182

národ, -a, národ je celok pokolení, ktorého hlavnou známkou je spoločný jazyk: Hlas národa, hlas boží. — Proti svojej krvi bojuje, kto svoj národ nemiluje. — Národ slovenský, kňazstvo a staršina naša, kroz nás ti, slávny cáre, svoj pozdrav prináša. (Samo Chalúpka.) — Lež večná meno toho nech ovenčí sláva, kto seba v obeť svätú za svoj národ dáva. (Samo Chalúpka).

Peter Tvrdý, ed., *Slovenský frazeologický slovník*, (Prague/Prešov, 1933), p. 311

nation—naţiune:

naţi(un)e f. totalitatea locuitorilor din aceeaş ţară, trăind sub acelaş guvern.

Lazăr Şaineanu, *Dicţionar universal al Limbei Române*, (Bucharest, 1929), pp. 260, 420

Slovakian
Romanian

New Objectivity or New Realisms? Trends in the Successor States of Austria-Hungary, with a Special Focus on Czechoslovakia

Ivo Habán

The New Objectivity (Neue Sachlichkeit) of the Weimar Republic, commonly seen as lasting from 1919 to 1933, has been extensively researched. However, this does not necessarily apply to the Austro-Hungarian successor states on either side of the Danube.[1] Here, the influence of German centers of artistic production and a German-speaking population continued to play a significant role. Throughout the 1920s—alongside the prevailing Modernist styles of Expressionism and Post-Expressionism and (abstract and Constructivist) avant-garde influences—we also find Modern Realisms that were associated with the German production centers. Grouped together under the term "New Objectivity" are a vast array of intriguing, often conflicting, iterations of Modern Realism. In 1931, the Dutch painter, poet, and art critic Albert Plasschaert recognized the term as "a German export product" and rejected it in favor of the term "New Realisms,"[2] as had the Czech-German cultural philosopher Emil Utitz a few years earlier, in 1927.[3]

In contrast to its importance in Germany, the New Objectivity phenomenon had not been paid much attention in interwar Czechoslovakia and its fellow Austro-Hungarian successor states.[4] This was due—to some extent—to the complexities of the term's formal definition and terminological differentiation. National notions of art history had thus far stood in the way of attempts to acknowledge New Objectivity influences in the successor states and, in the case of Czechoslovakia, this had led to the marginalization and suppression of the German- and Hungarian-speaking artists who provided New Objectivity with its momentum. It was viewed as the product of a German cultural milieu, and as such was considered an unwanted addition to the country's art-historical account. In their search for a new identity and a place within the redrawn map of Europe, the countries of the Little Entente (Czechoslovakia, Romania, and Yugoslavia) looked to France for direction.[5] Czechoslovakia in particular rejected any form of nostalgia for the Habsburg Monarchy—from which the young republic was eager to distance itself in the early 1920s. An in-depth exploration of the various expressions of New Objectivity in Czechoslovakia, Austria, and Hungary could be a topic for an interdisciplinary international research project and, as such, goes beyond the scope of this essay.

Attempts have been made in several recent major exhibitions and research projects to redefine the boundaries of the ever-slippery term "New Objectivity" and to identify possible connections and overlaps.[6] These projects revealed roots stretching back to Italy, something that Franz Roh and Gustav Friedrich Hartlaub[7] were already acutely aware of prior to the mid-1920s.[8] Furthermore, successive research is gradually uncovering interterritorial and interdisciplinary connections that—as Klaus Beekman and Ralf Grüttemeier have recently noted—

E

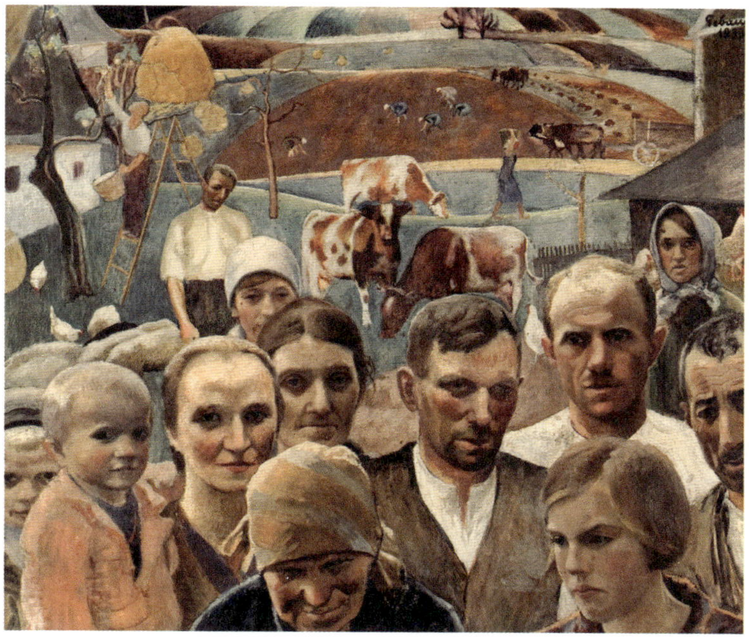

We are thus left in a quandary between the occasionally misunderstood, yet—from our present perspective—ultra-modern statements of the artistic forebears of Hyperrealism and their uncompromising left-wing social criticism

Fig. 1
Paul Gebauer
My Silesian Village, 1933,
Collection of Slezské zemské museum / Silesian Museum, Opava

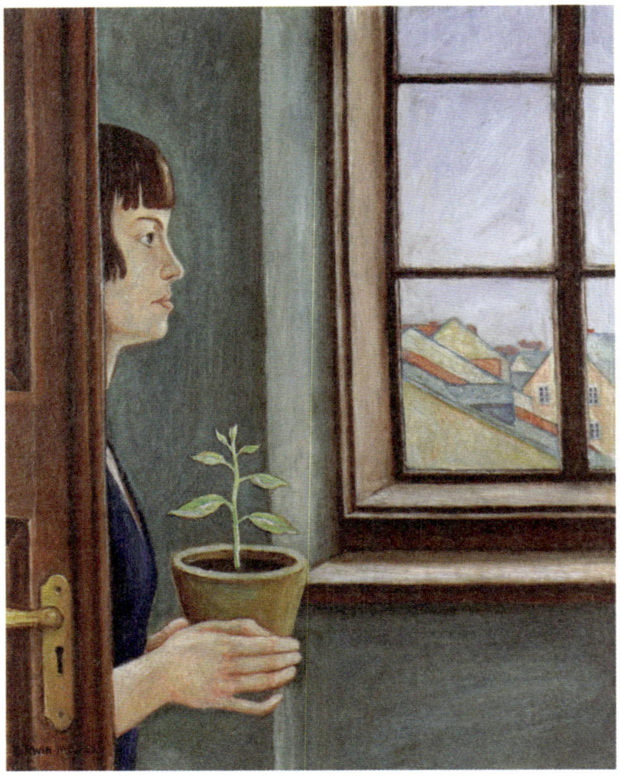

Fig. 2
Erwin Müller
Girl in the Studio, c. 1928
Private collection

appear to lead back to the Netherlands.[9] It is likely that further parallels could also be found in the Precisionist painting of the USA.[10]

Over recent years, the various expressions of New Objectivity have been the subject of extensive scrutiny across the disciplines, since it also has close ties with photography, typography, literature,[11] film, theater, and music, as well as affecting design, advertising, and lifestyle.[12] Aspects of New Objectivity can further be found in a variety of architectural styles, including Functionalism, Neues Bauen, and International Style, although different terminological conventions have become established here. The result of these comprehensive studies investigating the use and perception of the term "New Objectivity" is two-fold: firstly, they have enabled a clearer definition of the areas of the visual arts that can be subsumed under the term. Secondly, they have demonstrated that neither Gustav Friedrich Hartlaub's formal categories of a right (Classicist) and a left (Verist) wing, nor a political definition according to content as right- or left-wing art are consistently applicable—and this concerns visual art as much as literature.[13] Franz Roh's approach seems to be more practical here—and not just in the context of interwar Czechoslovakia. Roh used more fluid criteria to identify an inner and outer circle of contemporary artists working in a New Realist style, whereby he used the term "Post-Expressionism," and also included foreign artists working in more far-flung corners of Europe in this definition.

Just as complex as the definition of New Objectivity is the essence of objectivity itself. For instance, does it center on the object—i.e. the human being as such—its psychological state, relationships, and status in the world? Or does the specific perception of reality associated with New Objectivity lead to a depersonalized representation of reality, mechanically repeating established artistic templates? Here, late-1920s metropolitan optimism meets left-wing utopia and criticism of consumer society. In the works of the New Objectivity artists, faith in technological progress and euphoria for the modern world—embodied by Americanism—mixes with the negative aspects of radical social liberation, economic boom, and the ruthless dictate of market forces, which are threatening to enslave humanity and to undermine the value of the individual.

We are thus left in a quandary between the occasionally misunderstood, yet—from our present perspective—ultramodern statements of the artistic forebears of Hyperrealism and their uncompromising left-wing social criticism,[14] which compared New Objectivity's artistic output with production line aesthetics[15]—although its main protagonists were at pains to distance themselves from the accusation of commercialism. Sociological and anthropological approaches, meanwhile, have thus far

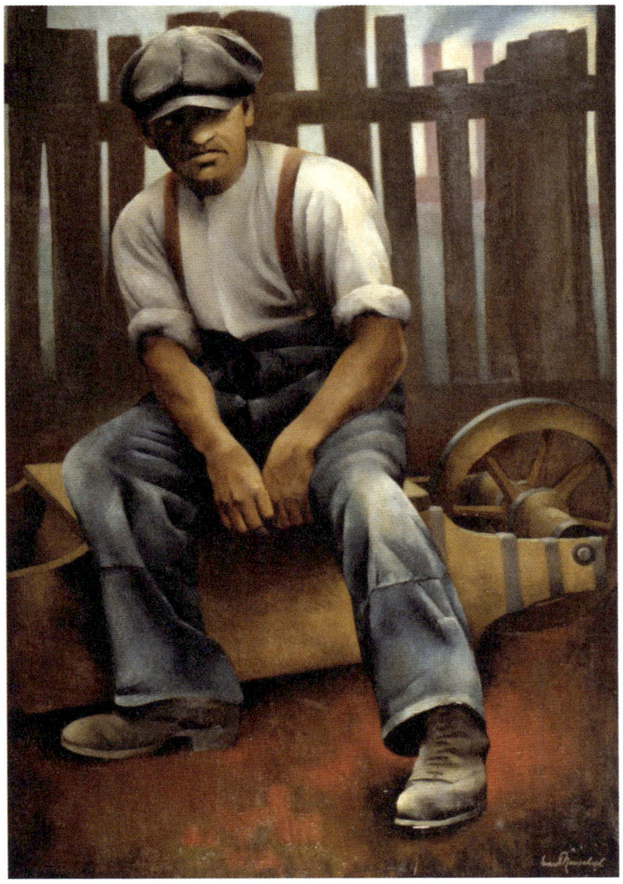

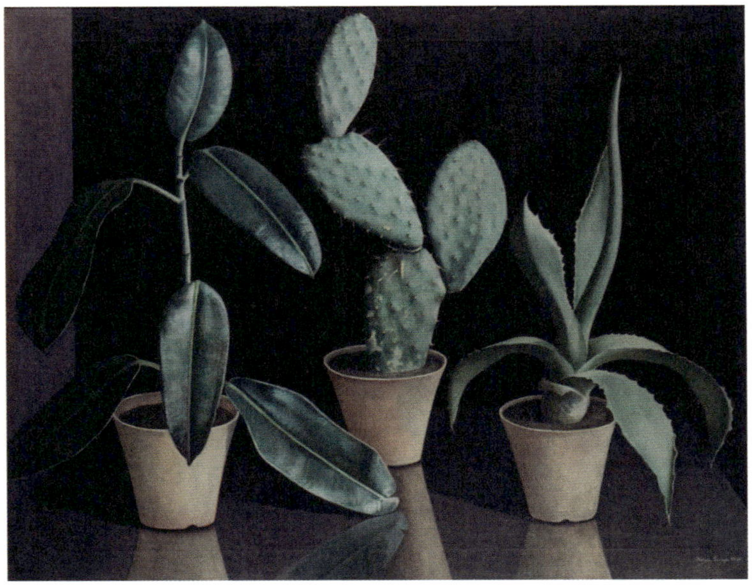

Fig. 3
Ernst Neuschul
Rest, 1928
Municipal Museum of Ústí nad Labem

Fig. 4
Ilona Singer
Still Life with Cacti, 1930
Jewish Museum in Prague

focused primarily on the specific conditions of the German New Objectivity scene and its particular social and political constellation.[16] A highly complex question in its own right, albeit outside the scope of this essay, is the reception and misuse of New Objectivity by totalitarian regimes, i.e., for the purposes of National Socialist and Communist propaganda.[17]

Recent research undertaken jointly by Germany and the USA reveals a number of different approaches to New Objectivity: along territorial lines, drawn according to the prevailing direction of travel in individual centers of production,[18] or based on formal criteria or political content. While making it easier to define a group of characteristic works, these models also make it necessary to cast to one side unclassifiable or isolated works that fall outside the prescribed schema.[19]

In the Austro-Hungarian successor states of the 1920s, the artists whose work is on a par with the iconic examples of German New Objectivity painters, such as Heinrich Maria Davringhausen, Otto Dix, George Grosz, Alexander Kanoldt, and Georg Schrimpf, were largely speakers of German or Hungarian. If we want to refer to New Objectivity as a phenomenon of the German-speaking world, we must at least briefly set out what the term means within the context of the visual arts. In the case of the newly formed state of Czechoslovakia—and, by extension, the other successor states—it refers to the New Realisms that emerged prior to the mid-1920s, after the decline of Expressionism. Their main common denominator was their modernity: the inseparable interrelationship between content and form.

An objective consideration of Czechoslovakia's New Realisms of the interwar period is hindered, above all, by the traditionally impermeable national categorization. Only by overcoming this will we be able to examine the New Realisms of Czechoslovakia with the kind of objective detachment that permits the absorption of forgotten artists into the art-historical canon and the free comparison of the style's various representatives. As suggested above, the task of compiling a list of New Objectivity artists is complicated by terminology and the challenge of finding a definitive classification for the works considered. This situation is even more complex in Czechoslovakia, where the blending of different artistic traditions is a common phenomenon. The key here is to find precise definitions for terms such as "Neoclassicism," "Social Realism," and, most importantly, "Primitivism," inspired, above all, by Henri Rousseau, who found adherents among both avant-garde[20] and more traditionally minded artists. The Modern Realism of Slovakia, for instance, often contains a folkloric element or lies on the boundary to Expressionism or Surrealism.[21]

When searching for examples of New Objectivity in Czechoslovakia, a multicultural

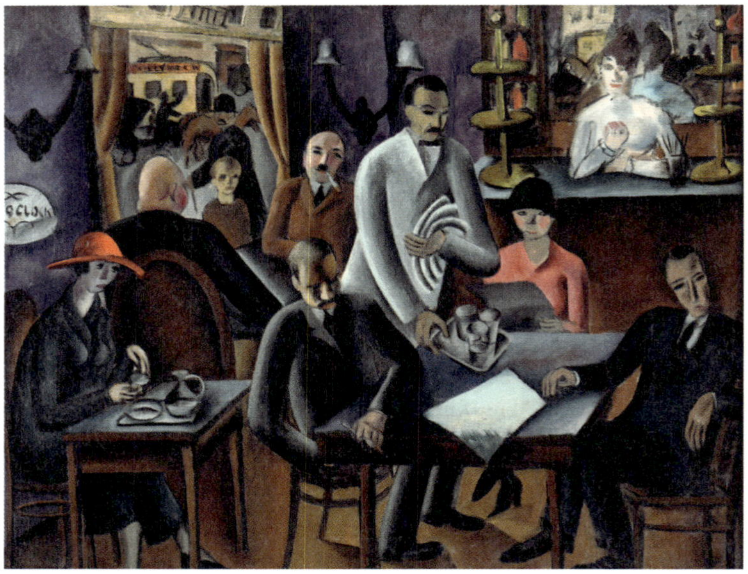

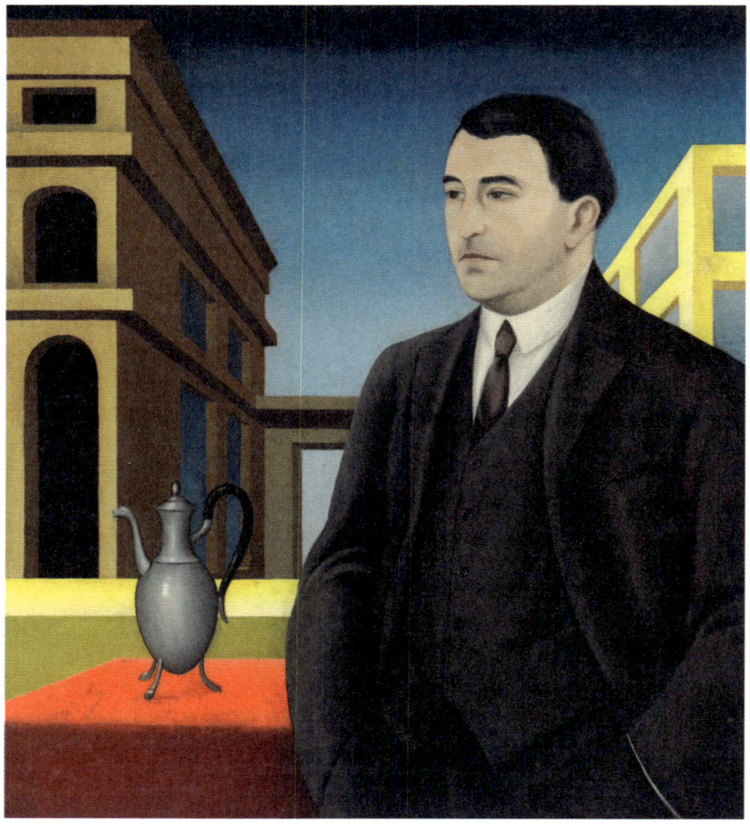

successor state of the former Habsburg Empire, we find two perspectives available to us. The first is to look for New Objectivity in its strictest definition, while the second is to put forward the broader model of New Realism, as was already proposed by contemporary scholars.[22] If works are defined strictly according to the description of New Objectivity as presented in the Weimar canon of literature, the definition applies to around two dozen Czech artists, mostly male painters, but also some female painters as well as several sculptors and photographers, all of them with links to academies in Dresden, Berlin, Breslau (Wrocław), Cologne, and Vienna.

The term "New Realisms," on the other hand, enables comparisons to be drawn across a wider spectrum of artists from each ethnic group, not in order to identify their differences, but to find common characteristics resulting from a common historical and cultural identity based on territorial commonality. A synthesis of this kind can be achieved by applying general criteria of Modernism rather than the strictly formal definition of New Objectivity based on one of its theoretical postulates (static, calm, cool, etc.), while still excluding any form of Expressionism, Post-Impressionism, or descriptive Realisms. Criteria established in this way can be used to examine works produced concurrently within a state entity spanning several thousand kilometers, as they were exhibited at contemporary national and international shows, such as the Venice Biennale, the International Exhibition in Dresden in 1926, the Exhibition of German-Bohemian Art in Vienna in 1927, or the Exhibition of Contemporary Culture in Czechoslovakia in Brno/Brünn in 1928.[23]

In the search for New Realisms in Bohemia, Moravia, and Silesia it is necessary to look at the interfusion of segments of the qualitatively separate German-speaking artists with the output of Czech post-war Neoclassicism, the Sociální skupina Ho-Ho-Ko-Ko group, the female Modernist artists who were plugged into the German art scene, and isolated provincial artists who had only temporarily flirted with New Objectivity. This definition then includes the painters Anton Bruder, Gottfried Erben, Hans Frohne, Paul Gebauer (fig. 1; p. 314), Karel Holan, Miloslav Holý, Pravoslav Kotík, August Walter Müller, Erwin Müller (fig. 2), Milada Marešová, Ernest Neuschul (fig. 3), Grete Passer, Viktor Planckh, Artur Ressel, Herbert Seemann, Richard Schrötter, Vlasta Vostřebalová Fišerová, and Ilona Singer-Weinberger (fig. 4), the sculptors Karel Kotrba, Jost Pietsch, and Karl Vogel, and the photographers Jaromír Funke, Grete Popper, and Franz Fiedler. Surprisingly close links to the German scene can also be found in Modernist Czech typography. However, rather than being clear evidence of a New Objectivity trend, the work of these artists should be viewed as the assertion of personal preference and individual style. In fact, Czechoslovakia had neither a clear center of

Fig. 5
Gejza Schiller
In the Coffee House, 1924
Collection of Východoslovenská galéria / East Slovak Gallery, Košice

Fig. 6
Sándor Bortnyik
Portrait of Dr. J. Polák, Director of the East Slovak Museum in Košice, 1924,
Collection of Východoslovenská galéria / East Slovak Gallery, Košice

New Realisms nor a distinct group of artists working in the style. The group most closely associated with New Objectivity was the October Group in Liberec, which was active from 1922 to 1927, but dissolved of its own accord with the end of the 1920s economic boom before being able to have an impact on the wider national context.[24]

In mid-1920s Slovakia, the city of Košice emerged as a center of Modernism, with Bratislava only later assuming a more active role in the Modernist scene. The city's New Objectivity artists included Konštantín Bauer, Gejza Schiller (fig. 5), and the Constructivist painter Sándor (Alexander) Bortnyik (fig. 6), who, when viewed through the lens of nationality, tends to be placed within a Hungarian context. The Slovak scene, too, is characterized by further, formally similar, Modernist iterations of Realism, as well as discrete works in transitional styles.

If we were to look at an imaginary map of New Objectivity in Central Europe, Austria would be home to around five influential names, whose fame on the international stage has so far eclipsed that of German Bohemian artists. These names include Herbert

> The range of receptions of New Objectivist influences that came out of Weimar Germany was extensive and was transported by individuals, many of whom were to remain misunderstood at home.

Ploberger (fig. 7), Rudolf Wacker, Sergius Pauser, Franz Sedlacek, and Ernst Nepo (fig. 8), whose sole tie to the lands of Bohemia was his birthplace of Dauba (today Dubá, CZ). In Austria, too, alongside today's figureheads of New Objectivity, we find another, wider circle of artists, whose members had weaker connections with the movement or were partially inspired by it during a particular phase of their career. These include Franz Lerch and Wilhelm Traeger.

In the context of interwar Hungary, Budapest—known during the 1920s as "America on the Danube"[25]—was the country's principal center and home to several influential personalities whose Modern Realist style was closely associated with potential German models. Nevertheless, Budapest's predominant artistic connection was with

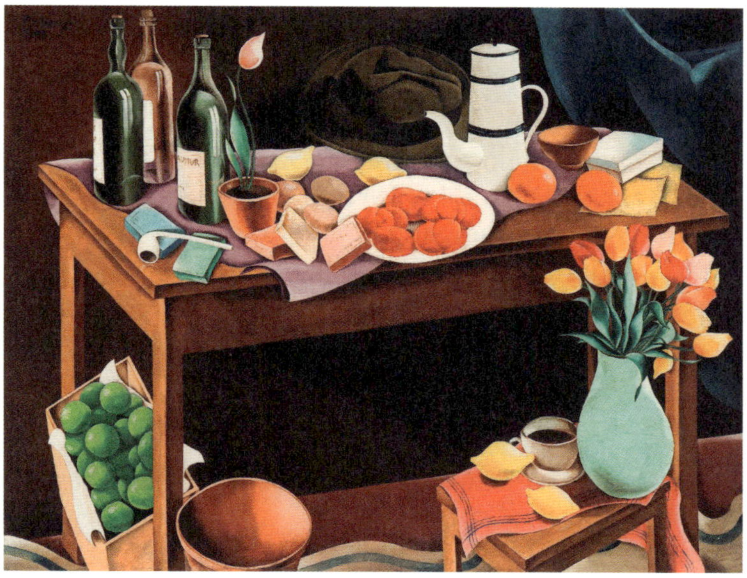

Fig. 7
Herbert Ploberger
Still Life (On the Table, Under the Table), 1925
Kunsthandel Widder, Vienna

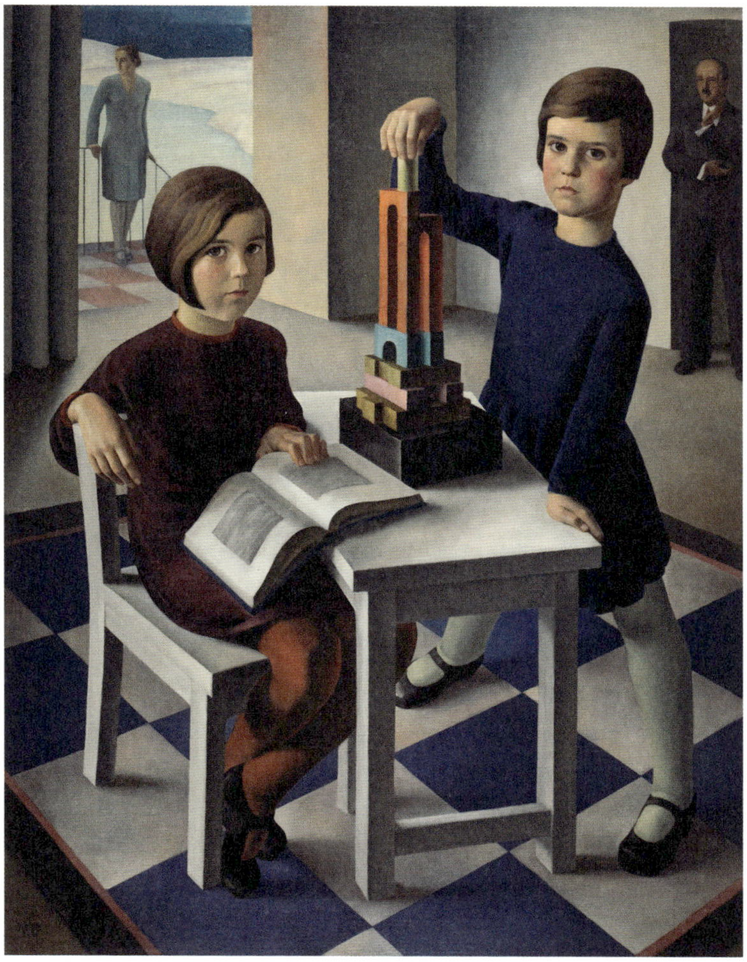

Fig. 8
Ernst Nepo
Family Portrait, 1929
Tyrolean State Museum Ferdinandeum

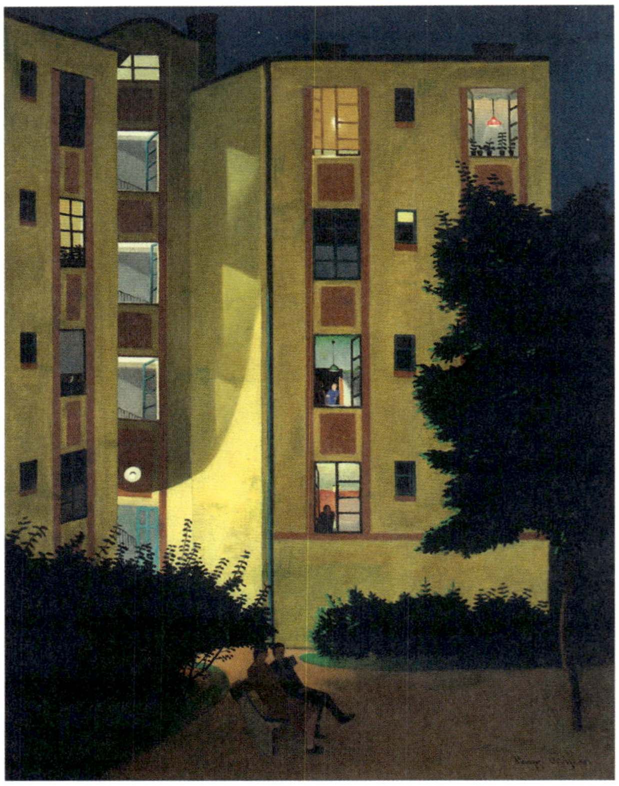

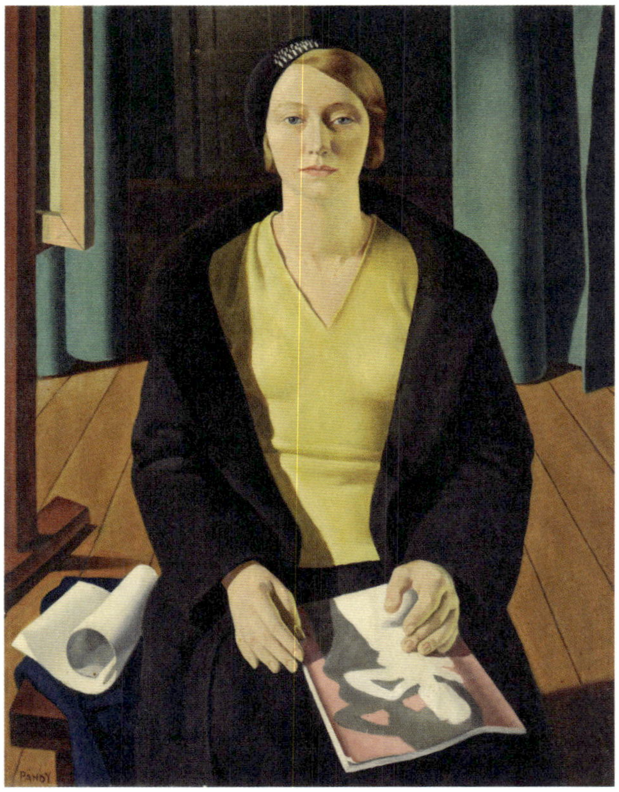

Constructivism and the Bauhaus aesthetic, while the term "New Objectivity" remained restricted to the field of literature.[26] Franz Roh gives Sándor Bortnyik as an example of New Objectivity in Hungary, with further obvious examples including Ödön Vaszkó (fig. 9), György Rauscher, and Lajos Pándy (fig. 10).

Modern Hungarian photography also played a vital role in the context of New Realisms. Alongside the Paris-based Hungarian photographer Gyula Halász or "Brassaï"—a pseudonym based on the name of his birthplace, Brașov/Brassó—1920s and 30s Hungary also laid claim to a number of notable New Objectivity photographers, such as György Kepes, Éva Besnyö, Imre Kinsky, André Kertész, István Kerny, and Martin Munkácsi.[27]

Today, state and private institutions in Hungary are committed to boosting the profile of New Objectivity. Austria, too, takes pains to cultivate its "own" New Objectivity artists. The situation in the Czech Republic is rather different, however, since here New Objectivity is still viewed as a potentially foreign phenomenon and as such is excluded from the country's traditional art-historical canon.

The search for New Objectivity in Slovakia, as in Bohemia, is characterized by the existence of two ethnolinguistic groups. Here, New Objectivist tendencies can be seen in the circles of the Košická moderna (Košice Modernism), where Slovak- and Hungarian-speaking artists were mingling in the urban, cosmopolitan atmosphere of the 1920s.

The collapse of Austria-Hungary into a series of successor states redrew the political map of Central Europe. Yet, despite the new borders, the lasting cultural impact of the German Reich on countries previously under Habsburg rule prevailed, and the region's cultural and social interrelationships were not severed completely; certain common features persisted. It may seem somewhat forcibly construed, but New Objectivity still clearly had validity in these regions and its proponents could also be found among artists whose everyday language of communication was not German—although merely accepting this idea as a possibility continues to have political connotations, even to this day. The numerous manifestations of New Objectivity make a definitive classification impossible. The range of receptions of New Objectivist influences that came out of Weimar Germany was extensive and was transported by individuals, many of whom were to remain misunderstood at home. I will therefore close this essay by briefly outlining three examples of artists whose careers started in the Danube region, and who clearly illustrate the artistic links between each successor state and the overall framework of New Objectivity in those countries.

One of Prague's pioneering New Objectivity painters at the turn of the 1920s

Fig. 9
Ödön Vaszkó
Evening (In the Park), 1932
Private collection

Fig. 10
Lajos Pándy
Portrait of a Woman, 1932
Museum of Fine Arts — Hungarian National Gallery, Budapest

and 30s was Ilona Singer-Weinberger (1905–1944). Born in Budapest to a middle-class, German-speaking family of Jewish descent, she went on to study in Berlin and then became one of the first women to be associated with the Prague Secession. She settled in Hodonín, but left no trace of her life there. Tragically, she was murdered in Auschwitz.[28]

Among Hungary's painters of New Realisms, Béla Kontuly (1904–1983) stands out in particular. On graduating from the Royal Catholic school in his native city of Miskolc, he enrolled in the first year of the General School at the Academy of Fine Arts in Prague, where he studied under Josef Loukota. His studies lasted no more than a year—from 1921 to 1922. Thereafter his artistic direction came under the influence of the Novecento Italiano and New Objectivity.

Even Moravia's conservative urban population had occasional encounters with the Austrian interpretation of New Objectivity, as several exhibitions of Modernist European art were held at the House of Arts in Brno/Brünn during the interwar period. Names such as László Moholy-Nagy and the renowned Austrian painter Sergius Pauser were present here. Pauser's portraits, commissioned by the family of Brno radiologist Gustav Prochaska, had a lasting impact on potential art buyers from the wealthy, intellectual classes and added their own flavor of Modernism to Czechoslovakia's New Realisms.[29]

1 Stephanie Barron and Sabine Eckmann, *New Objectivity: Modern German Art in the Weimar Republic 1919–1933*, exh. cat., Los Angeles County Museum of Art; Museo Correr, Venice (Munich/London/New York, 2015); Ralf Grüttemeier, Klaus Beekman, and Ben Rebel, *Neue Sachlichkeit and Avant-Garde* (Amsterdam, 2013); Steve Plumb, *Neue Sachlichkeit 1918–33: Unity and Diversity of an Art Movement* (Amsterdam/New York, 2006).
2 Klaus Beekman, "The Term New Objectivity and Nieuwe Zakelijkheid in Art Criticism" in Grüttemeier, Beekman, and Rebel 2013 (see note 1), pp. 171–84, here p. 174.
3 Emil Utitz, "Der neue Realismus," in *Zeitschrift für Ästhetik und allgemeine Kunstwissenschaft*, no. 2, 1927, pp. 179–80.
4 František Šmejkal, "Nové tendence v českém malířství první poloviny 20. let," in *Výtvarné umění*, yr. 12, 1962, pp. 250–64, 289–303.
5 Milena Bartlová et al., *Co bylo* Československo? *Kulturní konstrukce státní identity* (Prague, 2017); Milena Bartlová et al., *Budování státu: reprezentace* Československa *v umění, architektuře a designu* (Prague, 2015); Vendula Hnídková and Jindřich Vybíral, *Národní styl, kultura a politika* (Prague, 2013).
6 See note 1, as well as *Messerscharf und detailverliebt: Werke der Neuen Sachlichkeit*, ed. Agnes Tieze, exh. cat., Kunstforum Ostdeutsche Galerie Regensburg (Regensburg, 2015); *Das Auge der Welt: Otto Dix und die Neue Sachlichkeit*, exh. cat., Kunstmuseum Stuttgart (Stuttgart, 2012–13); *Neue Sachlichkeit in Dresden*, ed. Birgit Dalbajewa, exh. cat., Staatliche Kunstsammlungen Dresden (Dresden, 2011)
7 Gustav Hartlaub was an art historian and director of the Mannheim Kunsthalle. He coined the term "New Objectivity" in 1924. The art critic Franz Roh proposed "Magic Realism" as a competing term for the same artistic style.
8 Franz Roh, *Nach-Expressionismus: Magischer Realismus—Probleme der neuesten europäischen Malerei* (Leipzig, 1925).
9 Grüttemeier, Beekman, and Rebel 2013 (see note 1).
10 Andrew Hemingway, *The Mysticism of Money* (Pittsburgh/New York 2013), p. 1.
11 Sabina Becker, *Neue Sachlichkeit, vol. 1: Die Ästhetik der neusachlichen Literatur (1920–1933)*, vol. 2: *Quellen und Dokumente* (Cologne, 2000); Gabriella Hima, *Dunkle Archive der Seele in hellen Gebärden des Körpers: Die Anthropologie der neusachlichen Prosa* (Frankfurt, 1999); Elena Supprian, *"Perfect lovers" oder nur "two alien bodies"? Zur Konzeption von Liebe in ausgewählten Beispielen der Literatur der Neuen Sachlichkeit und der Pop-Literatur* (Hamburg, 2015).
12 *Berlin Metropolis 1918–1933*, ed. Olaf Peters, exh. cat., Neue Galerie, New York (Munich/London/New York, 2015; Markéta Svobodová, *Bauhaus a* Československo *1919–1938: studenti, koncepty, kontakty* (Prague, 2016).
13 See also Wolfgang Fähnders, *Avantgarde und Moderne 1890–1933* (Stuttgart/Weimar, 2010), p. 244, quote from Grüttemeier, Beekman, and Rebel 2013 (see note 1), p. 9: "[…] if one takes *Neue Sachlichkeit* as a style, the relation to the different ideological positions under the same label is hard to cope with; and if one defines *Neue Sachlichkeit* politically, then not all of the antagonistic writers following this flag can be dealt with."
14 Gyorgy Lukács, "L'Art pour l'art und proletarische Dichtung," in *Die Tat*, yr. 18, no. 3, 1926, pp. 220–23.
15 Béla Balázs, "Sachlichkeit und Sozialismus," in *Die neue Weltbühne*, yr. 24, no. 51, 1928, p. 916.
16 Helmut Lethen, *Neue Sachlichkeit 1924–1932: Studien zur Literatur des "Weißen Sozialismus,"* (Stuttgart, 1970).
17 Silke von Berswordt-Wallrabe, *Artige Kunst: Kunst und Politik im Nationalsozialismus*, exh. cat., Kunstsammlungen der Ruhr-Universität Bochum, Kunsthalle Rostock, Kunstforum Ostdeutsche Galerie Regensburg (Regensburg/Bielefeld, 2016).
18 Sergiusz Michalski, *Neue Sachlichkeit: Malerei, Graphik und Photographie in Deutschland 1919–1933* (Cologne, 1992).
19 Plumb 2006 (see note 1); Sabine Eckmann, "A Lack of Empathy on New Realisms of New Objectivity" in Barron and Eckmann 2015 (see note 1), pp. 26–39.
20 Karel Teige, "Umění přítomnosti," in Život, yr. 2, 1922, pp. 119–42.
21 *Košická moderna. Umenie Košíc v dvadsiatych rokoch 20. storočia*, eds. Lena Lešková and Zsófia Kiss-Szemán, exh. cat., Východoslovenská galéria, Košice (Košice, 2012).
22 Šmejkal 1962 (see note 1); Hana Rousová, Český *neoklasicismus dvacátých let,* část *1. Malba — kresba*, exh. cat., Prague City Gallery (Prague, 1985); Hana Rousová, *Český neoklasicismus dvacátých let,* část *2., Mezi klasickým* řádem *a selankou: malba — kresba*, exh. cat., Galerie hlavního města Prahy (Prague, 1989); Vojtěch Lahoda, "Civilismus, primitivismus a sociální tendence v malířství dvacátých a třicátých let," in *Dějiny českého výtvarného umění IV/2,* eds. Vojtěch Lahoda, Mahulena Nešlehová, and Marie Platovská (Prague, 1998), pp. 61–99; Vojtěch Lahoda, "Proměny realismu a kubismu v malířství dvacátých a třicátých let," in ibid., pp. 101–46.
23 *Internationale Kunst-Ausstellung Dresden 1926: Juni–September: Jahresschau deutscher Arbeit: amtlicher Führer und Katalog durch die Ausstellung*, exh. cat. (Dresden, 1926); *Große Kunstausstellung 1927*, exh. cat., Vienna Künstlerhaus (Vienna, 1927); *Moderne deutsche Kunst in der Tschechoslowakischen Republik. Československé výtvarné umění 1918–1928, výstava soudobé kultury v Brně*, exh. cat. (Brno, 1928); Anna Habánová, "Neue Sachlichkeit," in *Junge Löwen im Käfig. Künstlergruppen der deutschsprachigen bildenden Künstler aus Böhmen, Mähren und Schlesien in der Zwischenkriegszeit*, ed. Anna Habánová, exh. cat., Oblastní galerie v Liberci (Řevnice/Liberec, 2013), pp. 278–91.
24 Anna Habánová, *Erwin Müller (1893–1978)*, exh. cat., Oblastní galerie v Liberci, (Liberec, 2014).
25 Balázs Sipos, "Worldviews, Cultural Registers and the Presence of America in the Horthy Era: On Ways to Adapt the Exploration of Transnational and Relationship History," in: Zoltán Ripp, ed. *Influences, Pressures Pro and Con, and Opportunities: Studies on Political Interactions in and Involving Hungary in the Twentieth Century*, (Budapest, 2014).
26 Hima 1999 (see note 11) contains a reflection on New Objectivist prose in Hungarian literature in the context of Germany and Austria.
27 Péter Baki, "Hungary Between the Wars: A Photographic Portrait," in *Object: Photo. Modern Photographs: The Thomas Walther Collection 1909–1949*, eds. Mitra Abbaspour, Lee Ann Daffner, and Maria Morris Hambourg. An online project of The Museum of Modern Art, New York, The Museum of Modern Art 2014, http://www.moma.org/interactives/objectphoto/assets/essays/Baki.pdf (accessed on November 6, 2017).
28 Michaela Sidenberg, "Ilona Singer," in Habánová, 2013 (see note 23), p. 366.
29 This study formed part of project 17-06031S, *New Realisms in the Czech Visual Arts 1918–1945*, which was sponsored by the Czech Science Foundation and developed under the supervision of the National Memorial Institute's regional office in Liberec.

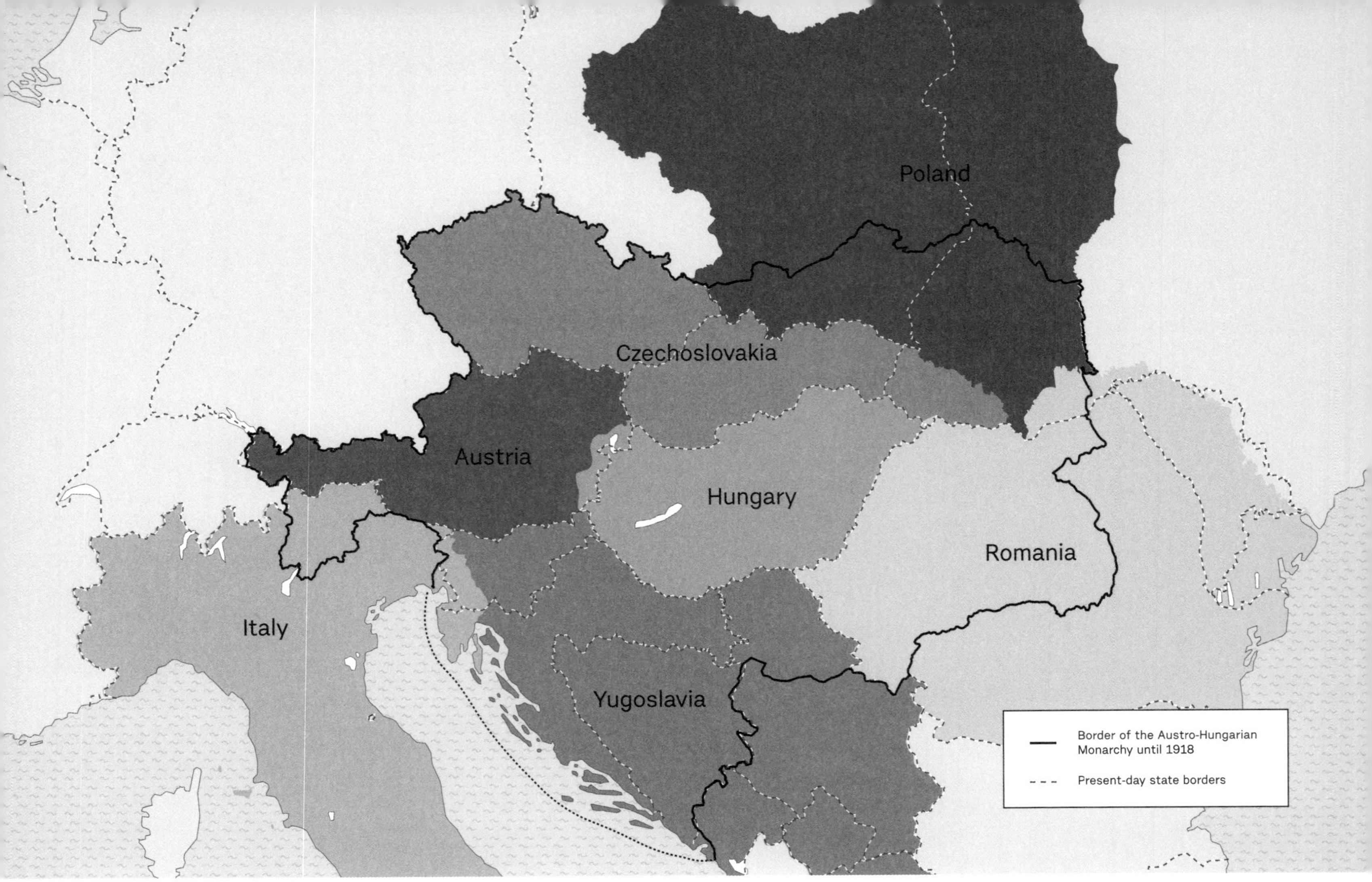

E

1919 The successor states of the Austro-Hungarian Empire

border—hranice:

Hranice, čára n. pruh dělící dvě sousední držby, v širším smyslu celé území podél hraniční čáry (sr. *hranice vojenská*). ... — **H.** přirozené, ve smyslu polit. jako je pro Francouze Rýn, pro Italy Alpy, n. vůbec čára zahrnující části země, jež poskytují obranné výhody proti útoku, bez ohledu na to, zda jde o území cizího státu, stejně jako při oblastech jazykových. — **H.** státu, myšlené čáry na povrchu země, oddělující území jednoho státu od území státu druhého, od země bez vlastníka n. od širého moře; směr těchto čar naznačuje se obyč. hraničními znameními a podle toho, jsou-li přirozená n. umělá, mluvíme o **h**-ích přirozených (voda, hory, pouště, kraj lesa ap.) n. umělých (sloupy, kameny, cesty, průplavy, bóje ve vodě, zdi — čínska ap.). ... Hraniční spory vedly často k válkám; v novější době urovnávají se však již smírnou cestou (hraniční smlouvy, arbitráž, condominium sporného pruhu země, mezinár. komise rozhraničovací). Mírové smlouvy po Svět. vál. přijaly praxi určovati **h.** slovy, pokud to bylo možno, a ponechati delimitaci rozhraničovacím komisím, jež určují hraniční čáru na místě samém, v souhlase se smlouvami ...

Masarykův slovník náučný. Lidová encyklopedie všeobecných vědomostí. Díl III, (Prague. 1927), pp. 332–33

hranice, -ce, ž., 1. = hromada: h. dříví; zapáliti, pod- hranici; Hus zemřel na –ci; 2. = podstavec: h. ve mlýně, zvonová h.; 3. = nejvyšší n. nejnižší bod, mez, ke které něco sahá: h. teploty, lomu, věková h.; 4. = konec nějakého území, konečné body, čára vyznačující konec; tu zpravidla pomn. *–nice*, -nic: okresní, zemské, státní –ce; země se od sebe dělí –cemi; celní dozor na –cích; vytknouti, vymeziti, vyměřiti –ce; jazykové h.; vše splývá, nevíš kde jsou hranice (Nezval); *H.*, -nic, pomn., ves v č., město na Mor.; zdrob. *hranička*, -ky, ž.: h. dříví v kamnech; *H-čky*, -ček, pomn., ves na M.;

Pavel Váša / František Trávníček, *Slovník jazyka Českého. A–K*, (Prague, 1937), p. 520

Czech

Expression

Nowhere did the concept of individuality in art manifest itself more strongly than in Expressionism. This movement emerged as a global phenomenon. Defined by the free expression of the artist's own experience, Expressionism became a mirror for a world that seemed to be falling apart.

Expressionist painting was characterized by an active, deeply involved style, that could be applied equally to landscape, portrait, and figurative composition. Through its constant focus on the perceived (of a natural scene, for instance), using dynamic lines or jarring contrasts of color, Expressionism was able to evoke an emotional tension that could never be achieved with the same intensity by a purely naturalistic depiction. Figurative Expressionist art likewise aimed to reproduce not only the outward appearance of the human subject, but also their emotional traits. (MH)

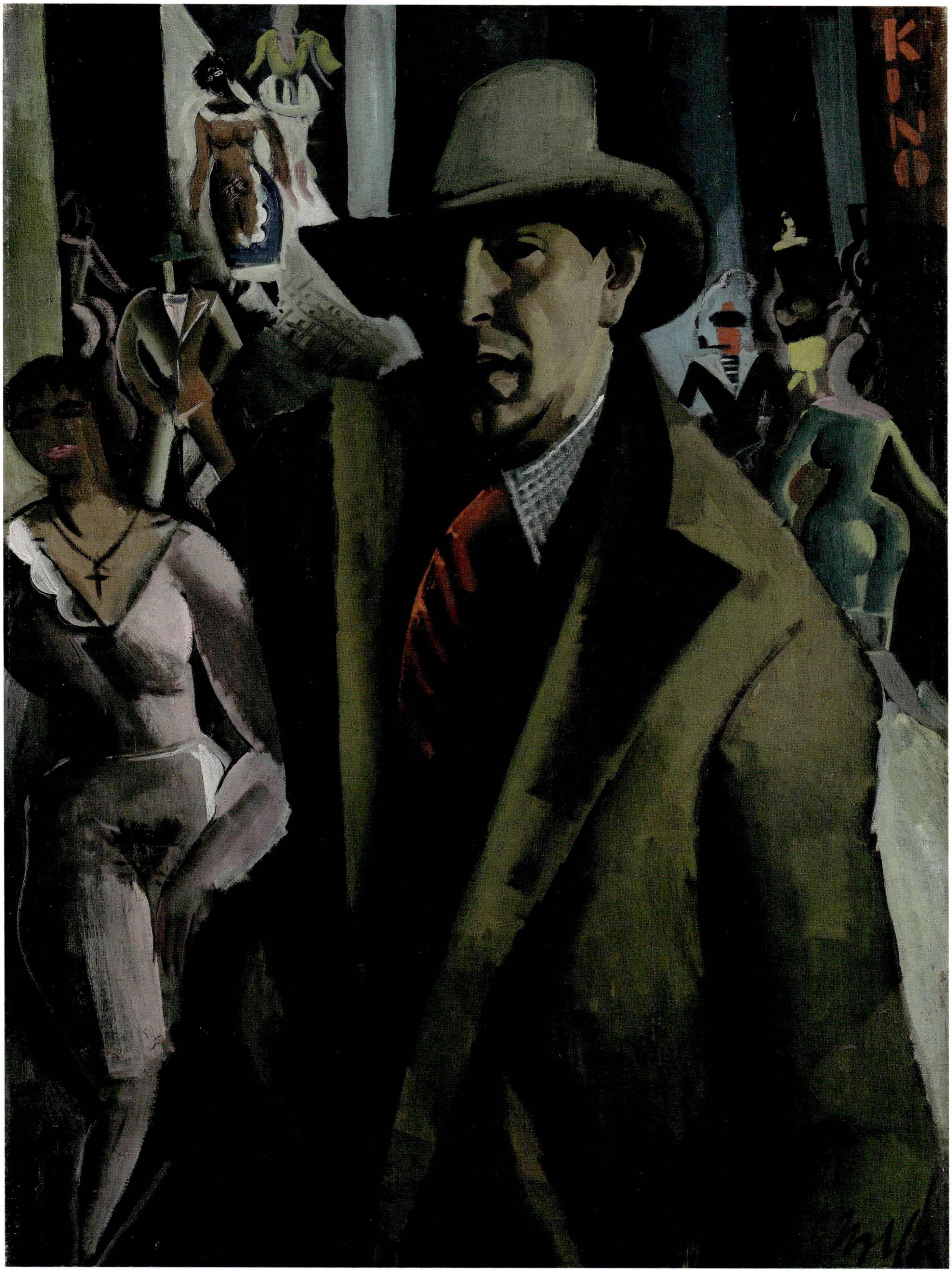

E1

Milivoj Uzelac
Self-Portrait in front of the Bar, 1923
National Museum of Modern Art, Zagreb

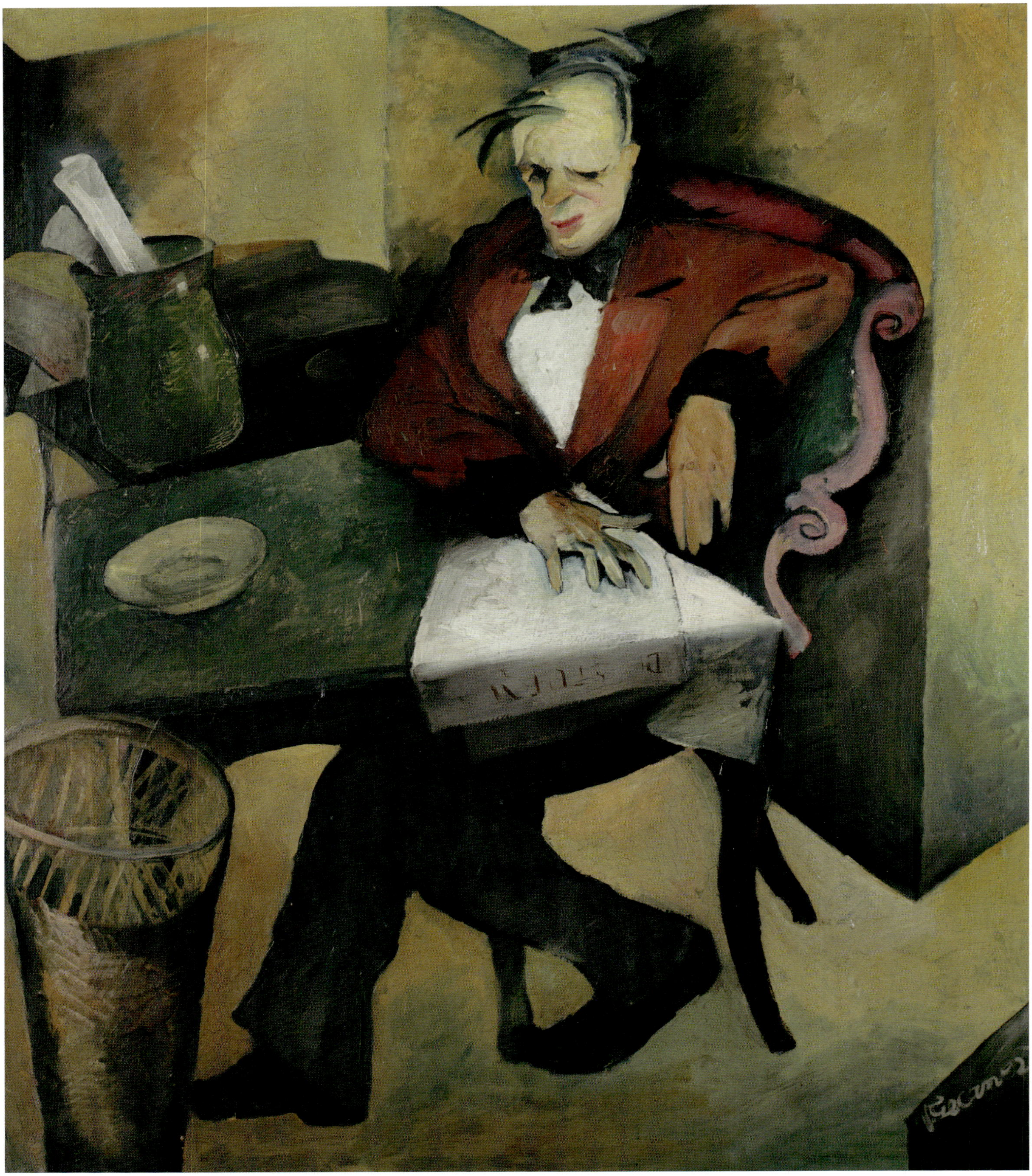

E1

Vilko Gecan
The Cynic, 1921
National Museum of Modern Art, Zagreb

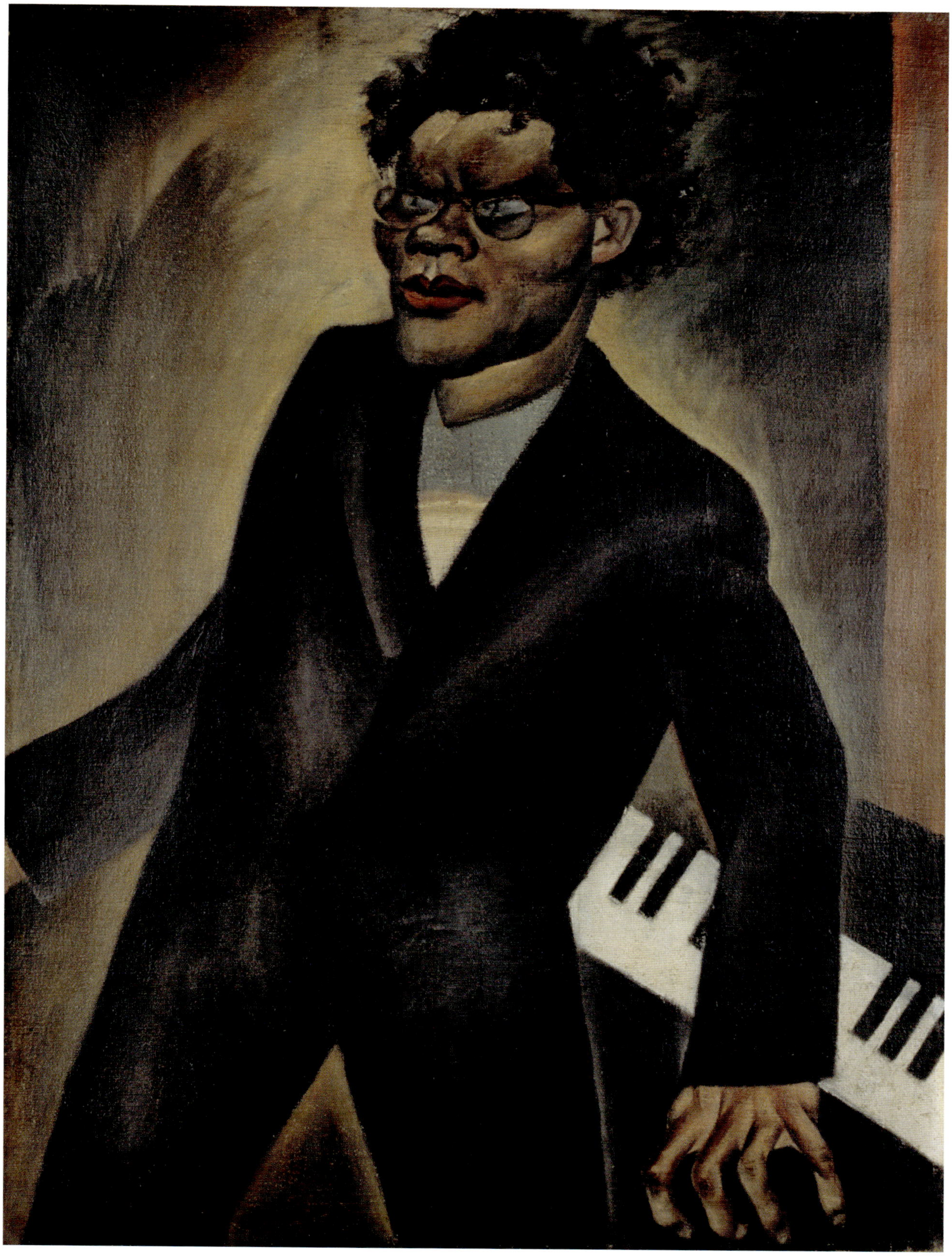

Veno Pilon
Portrait of the Composer Marij Kogoj, 1923
Moderna galerija/Museum of Modern Art, Ljubljana

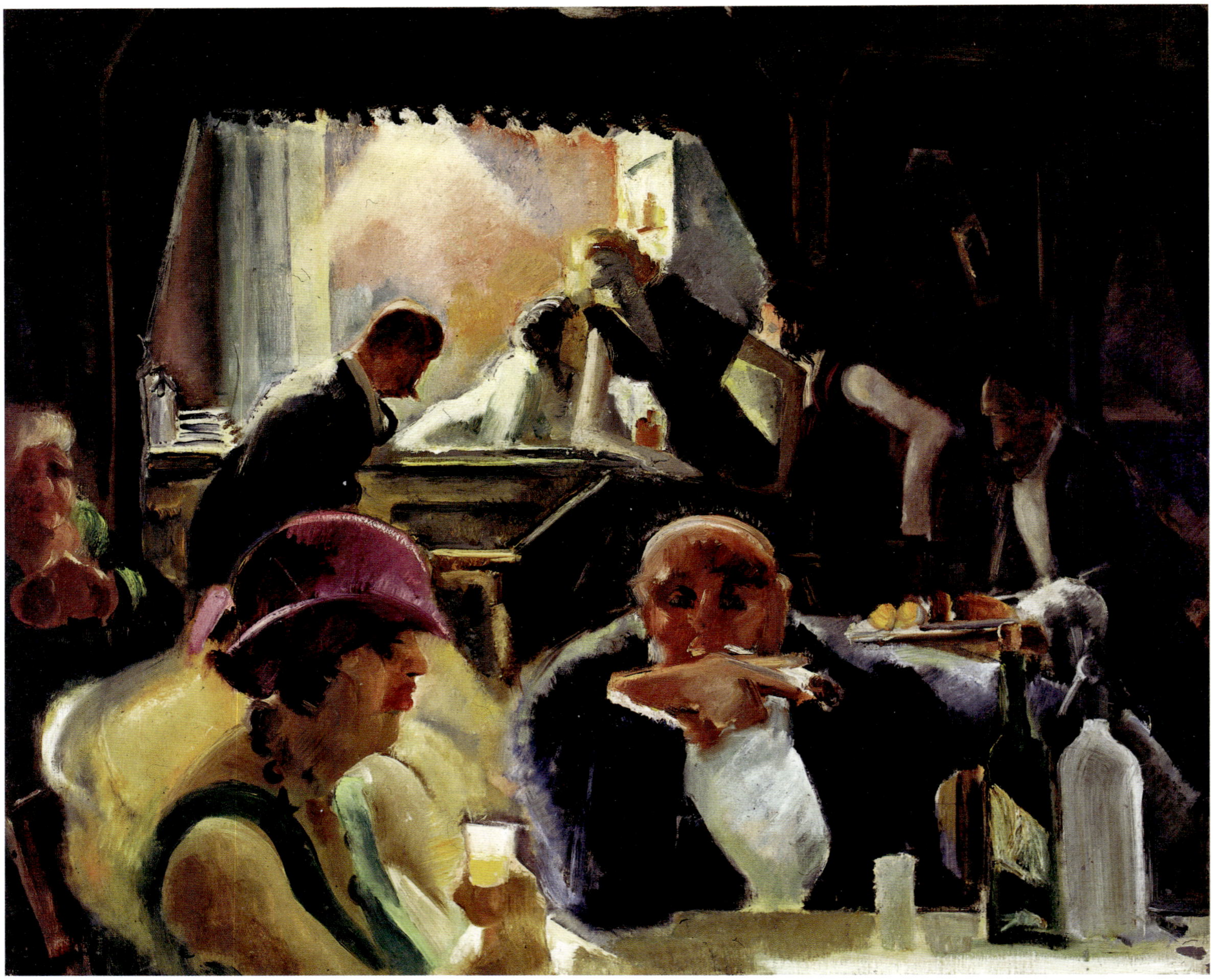

E1

István Farkas
Coffeehouse Scene, c. 1922
St. Stephen´s King Museum —
Deák Collection, Székesfehérvár

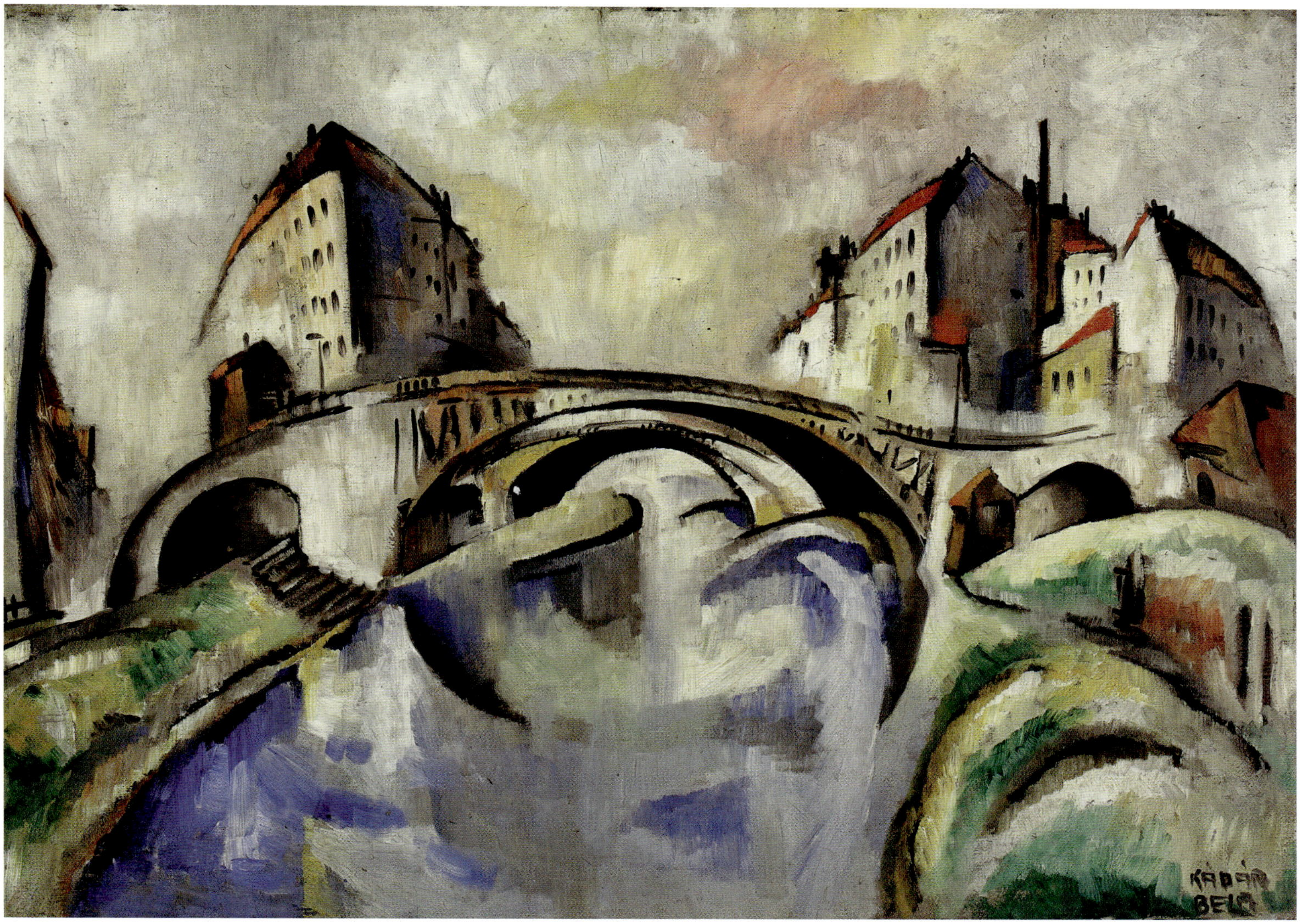

Béla Kádár
Cityscape with Bridges, c. 1921
St. Stephen´s King Museum —
Deák Collection, Székesfehérvár

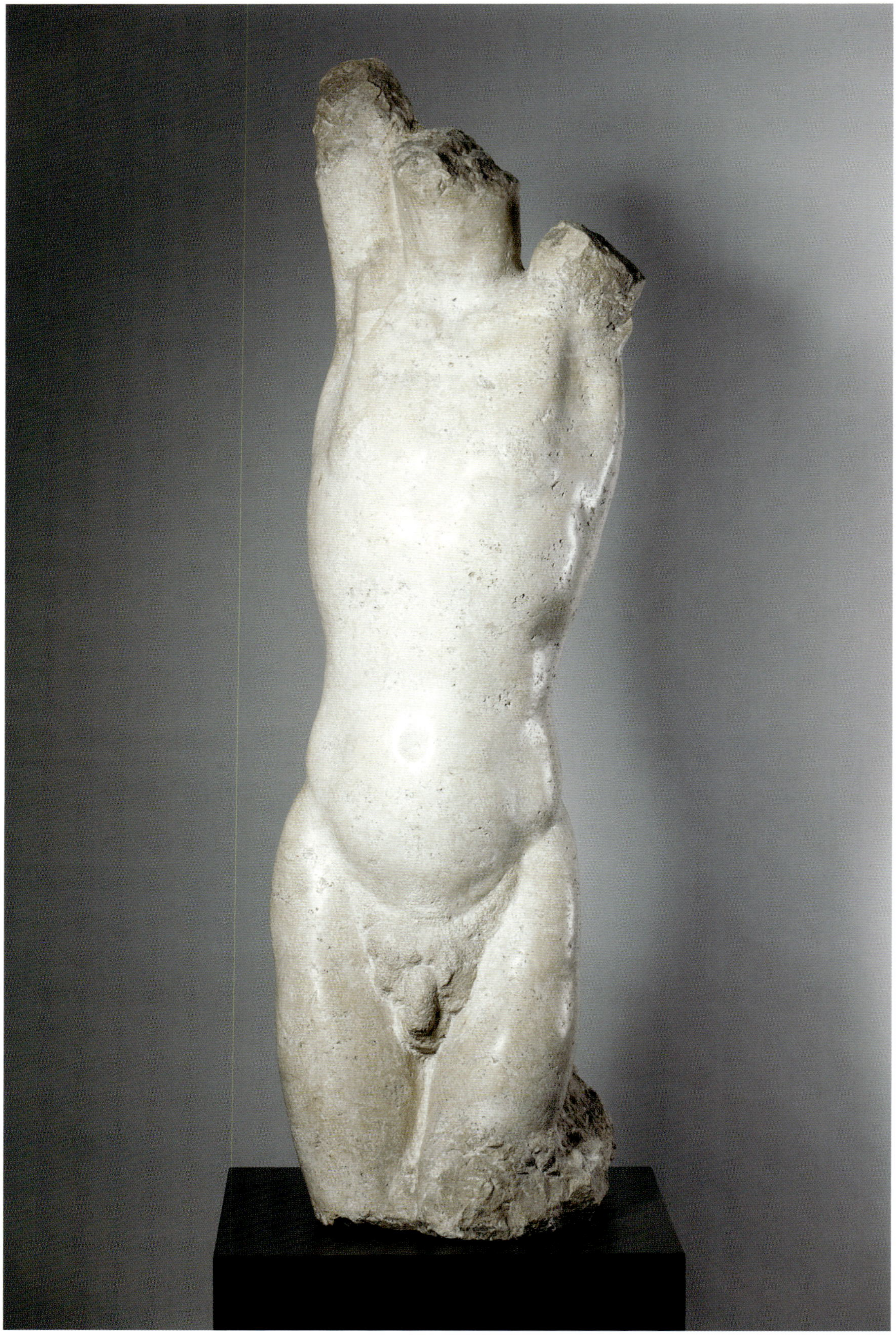

Fritz Wotruba
Torso, 1928/29
Belvedere, Vienna, on permanent loan from the Fritz Wotruba Private Foundation

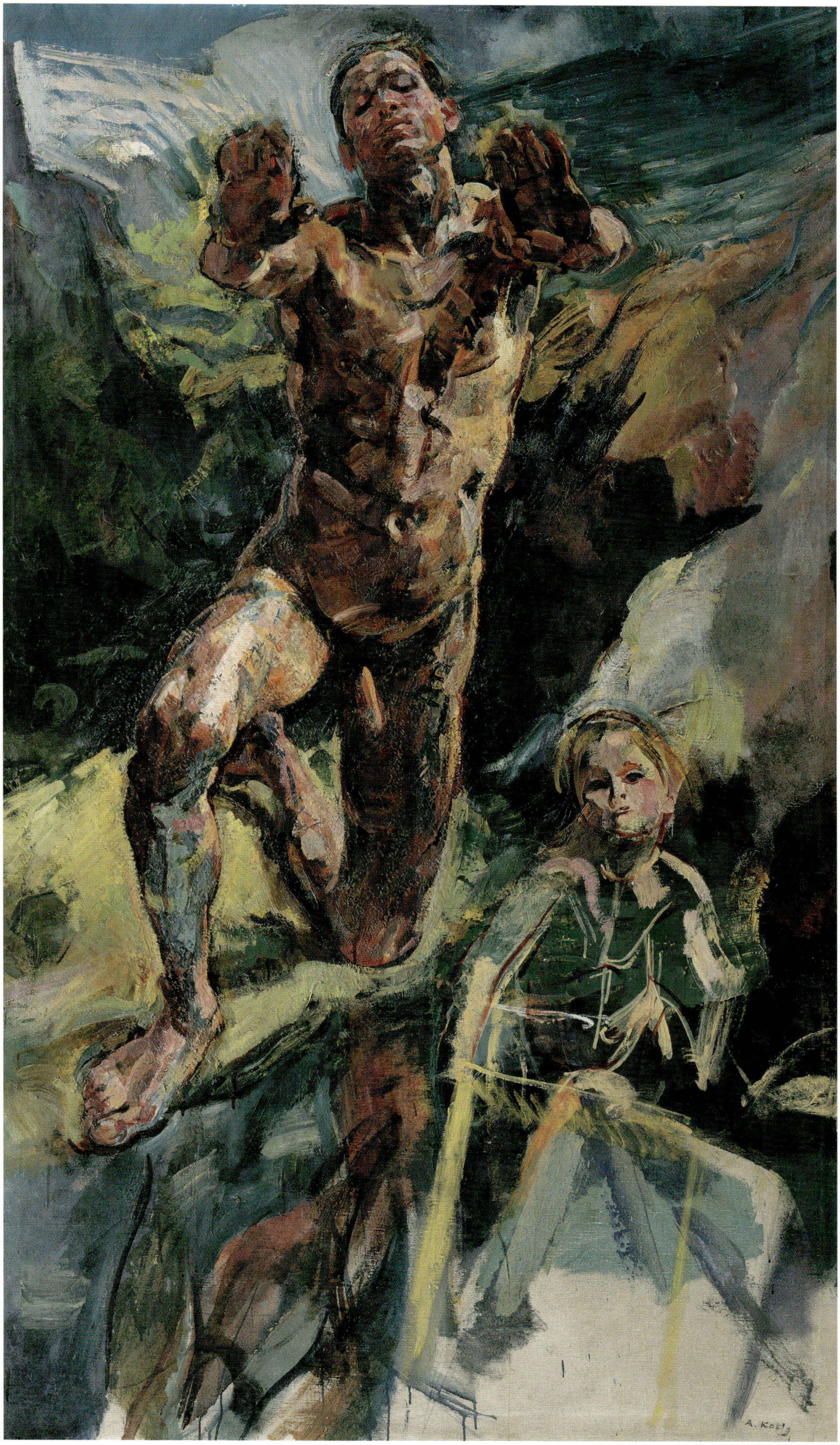

E1

Anton Kolig
Longing, 1921
Belvedere, Vienna

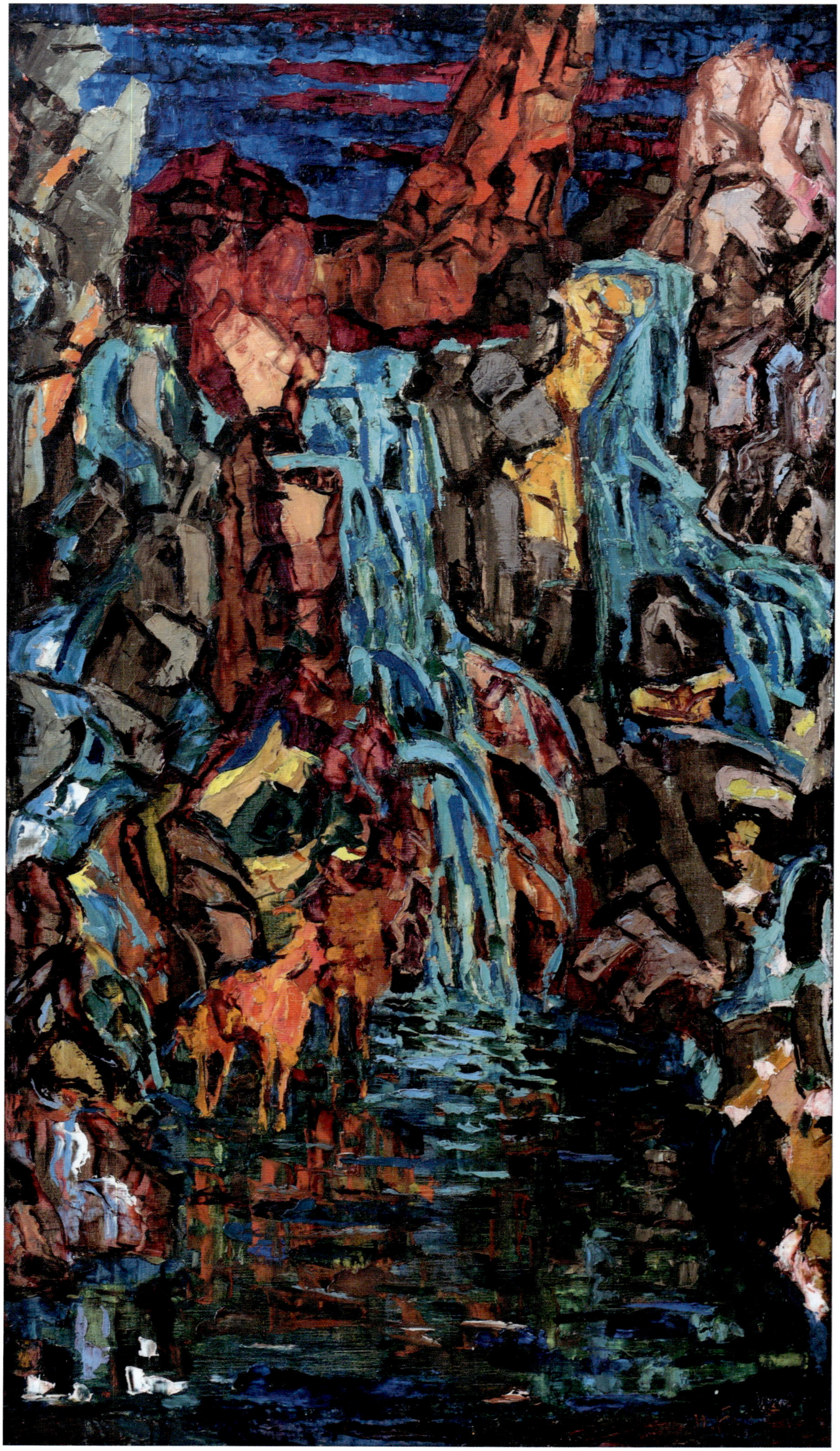

E1

Helene Funke
Waterfall, c. 1922
Courtesy of
Kunsthandel Hieke

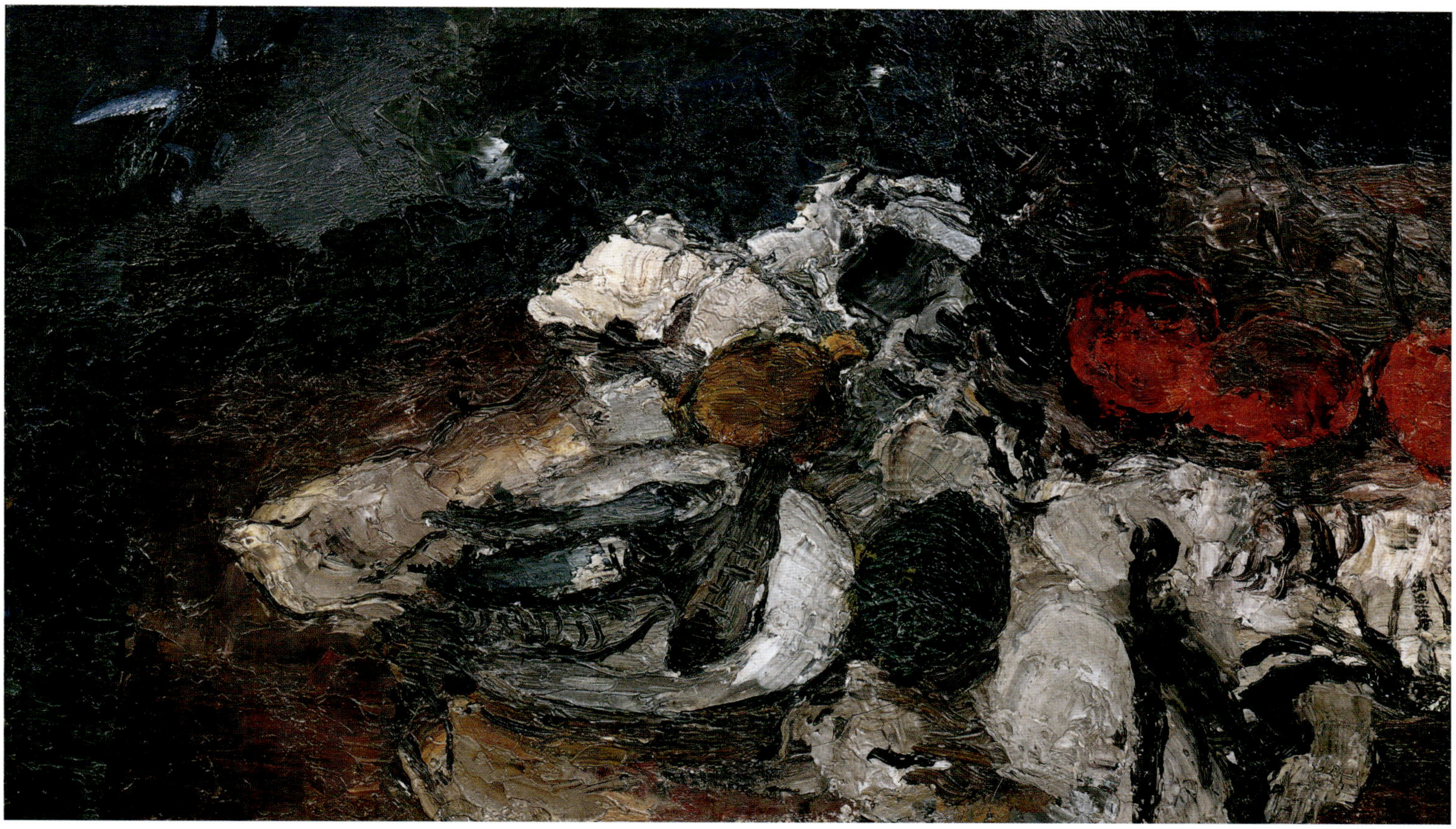

E1

Herbert Boeckl
Still Life with Fish, 1922
Belvedere, Vienna

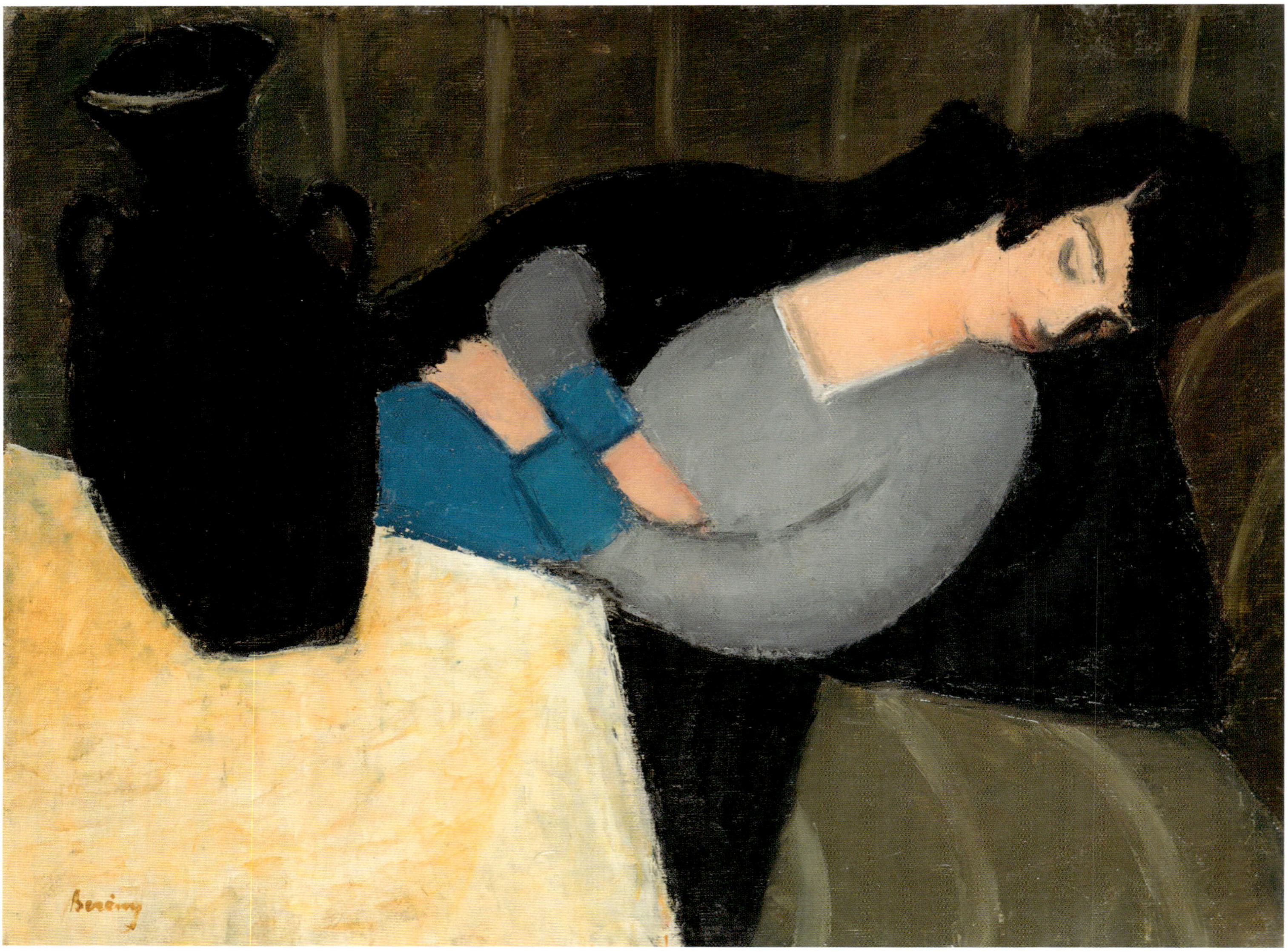

E1

Róbert Berény
Sleeping Lady with Black Vase, 1927/28
Private collection

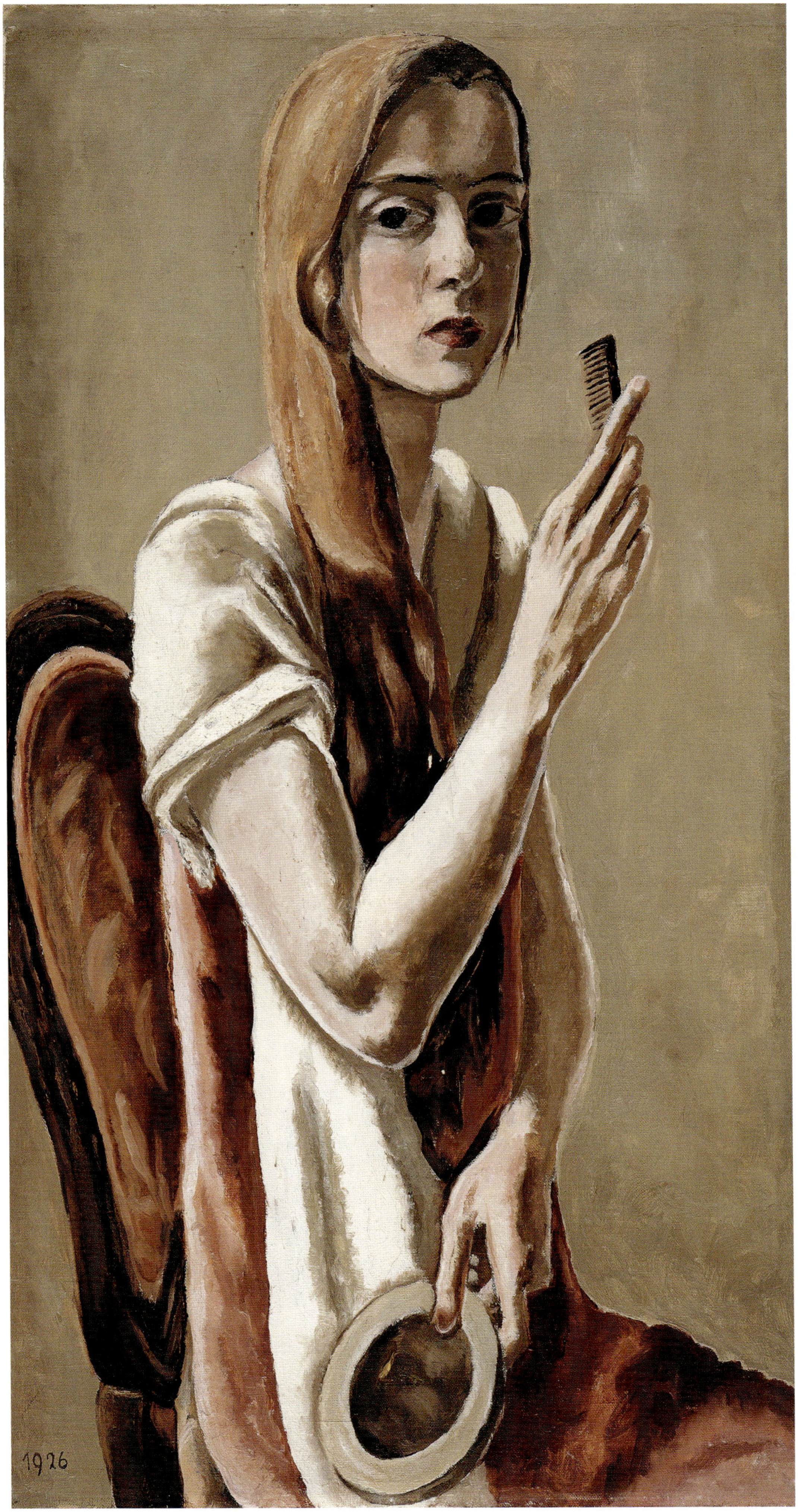

E1

Marie-Louise von Motesiczky
Self-Portrait with Comb, 1926
Belvedere, Vienna

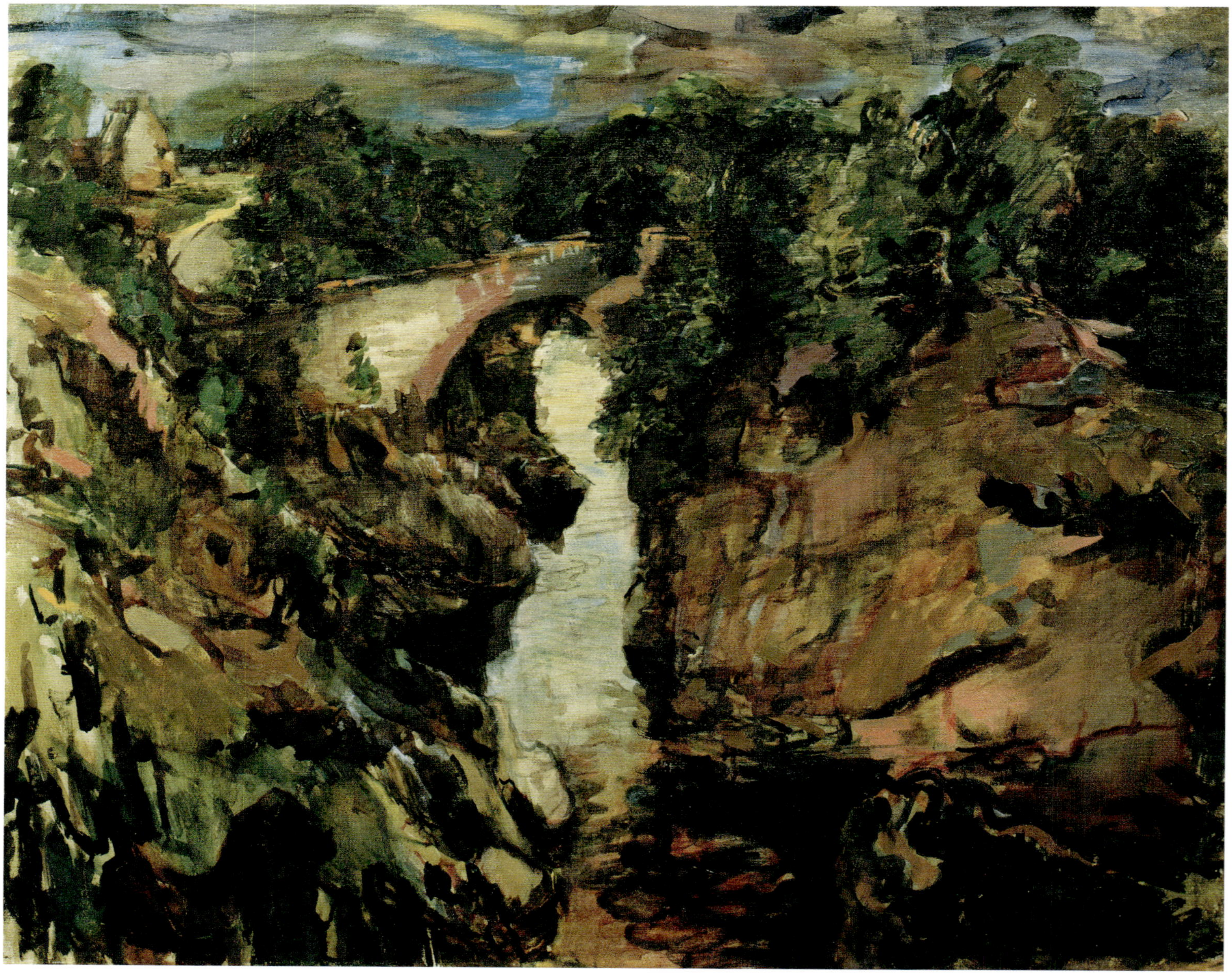

E1

Oskar Kokoschka
Dulsie Bridge, 1929
Belvedere, Vienna

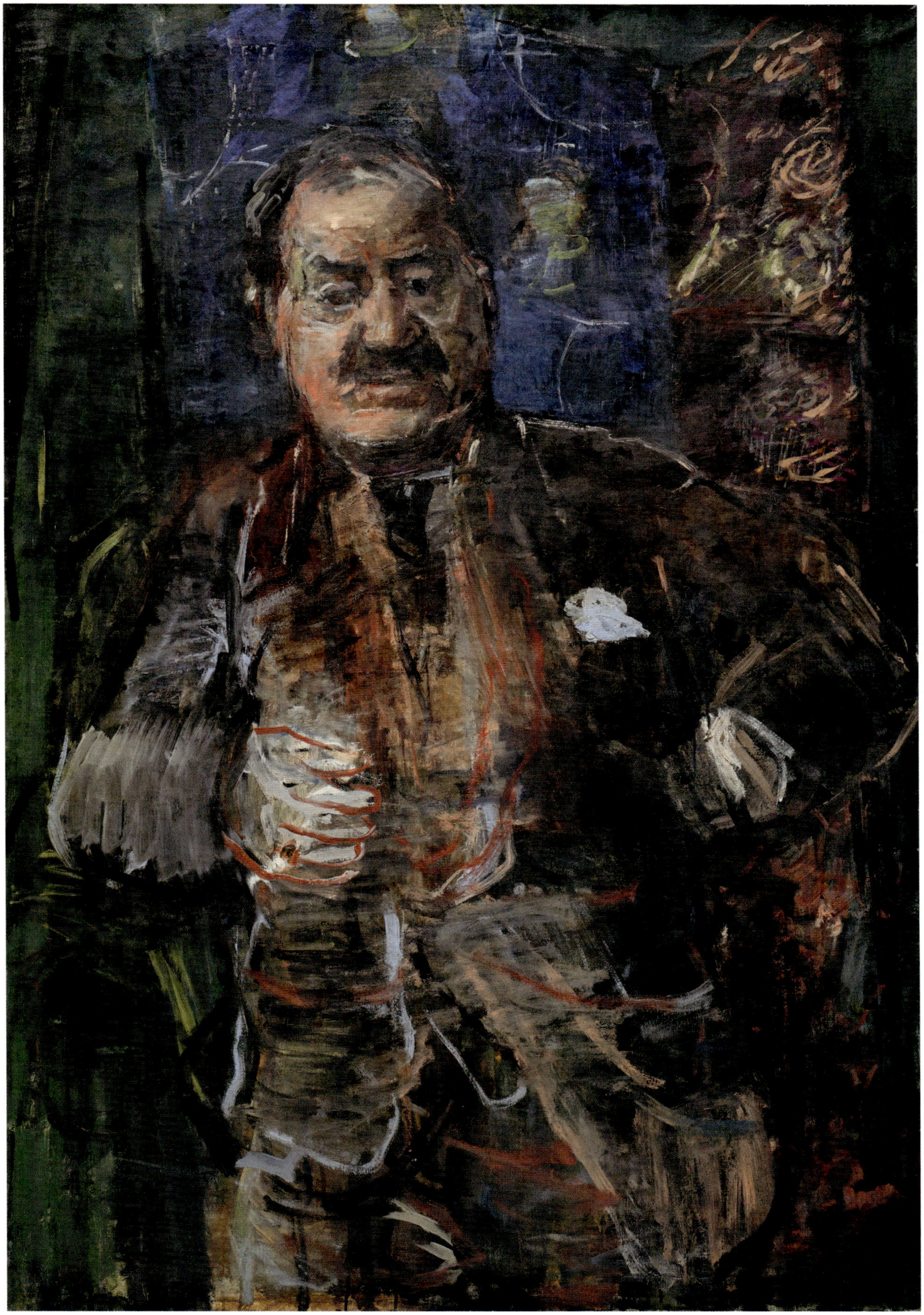

Oskar Kokoschka
Portrait of Marcel von Nemes, 1929
LENTOS Kunstmuseum Linz

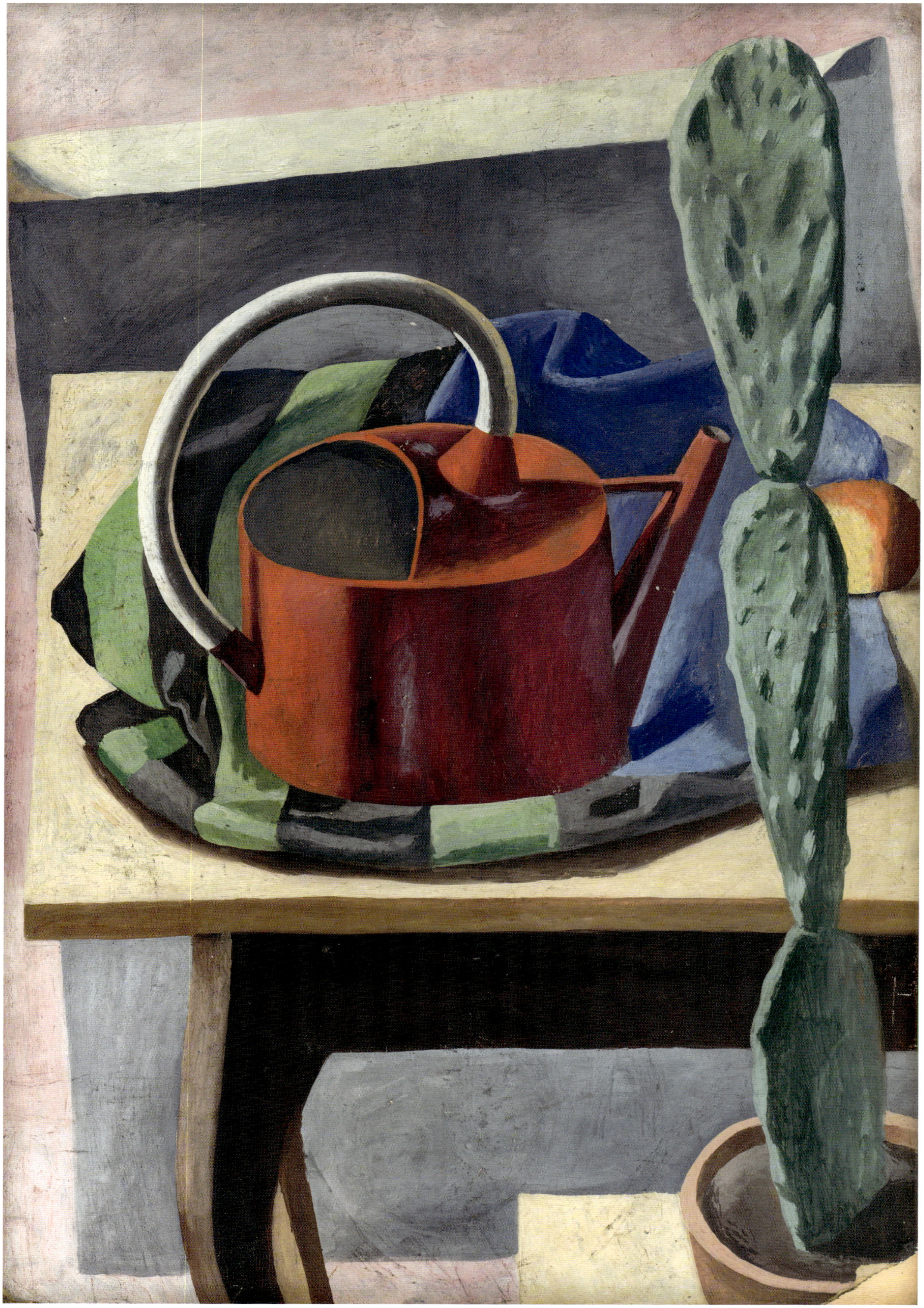

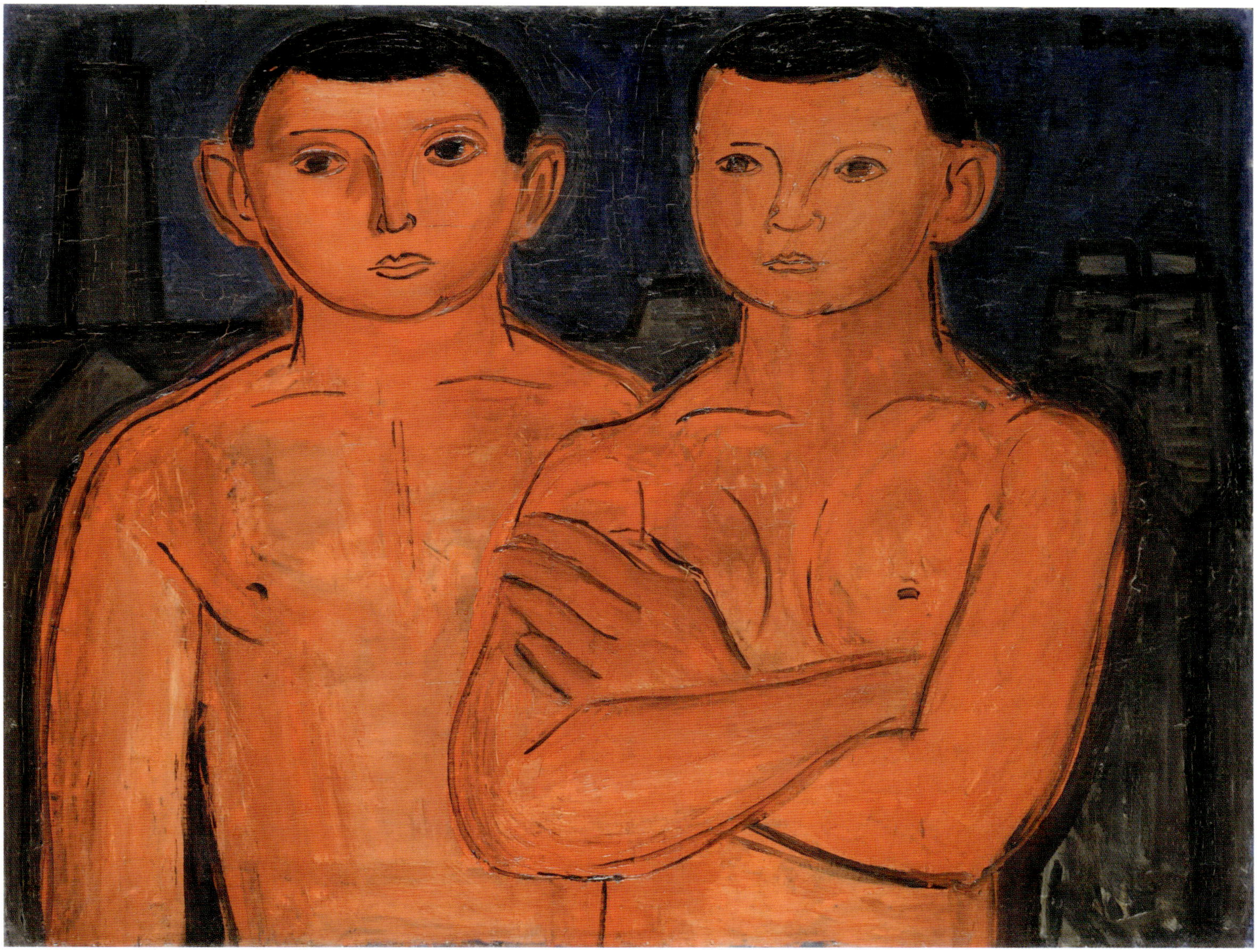

◂ Péter Pálffy
Still Life with Watering Can and Cactus, 1935
Slovak National Gallery, Bratislava

Jenő Barcsay
Red Youths (Workers), c. 1928
Museum of Fine Arts—Hungarian National Gallery, Budapest

New Realisms

The term "Expressionism" has become established, more or less worldwide, in connection to a very specific style of art. By contrast, the artistic tendencies that emerged after the end of the First World War and were grouped together under the heading "Realist art," are rather more multilayered. Sweeping these artistic movements under the umbrella term "New Objectivity" is just as broad brush and not appropriate for all forms of artistic production. The art of Europe's newly created, rapidly changing nation-states was far too complex and varied. Today, there is a tendency to view New Objectivity art as primarily a "German" phenomenon. However, a trend for perplexing depictions of reality can also be clearly identified in the art of the Austro-Hungarian successor states. Although these New Realisms arose out of different circumstances, and were accepted and propagated to different degrees, social criticism and political or objective commentary featured in art from Košice to Pilsen and from Vienna to Ljubljana, Budapest, Belgrade, and Zagreb. (MH)

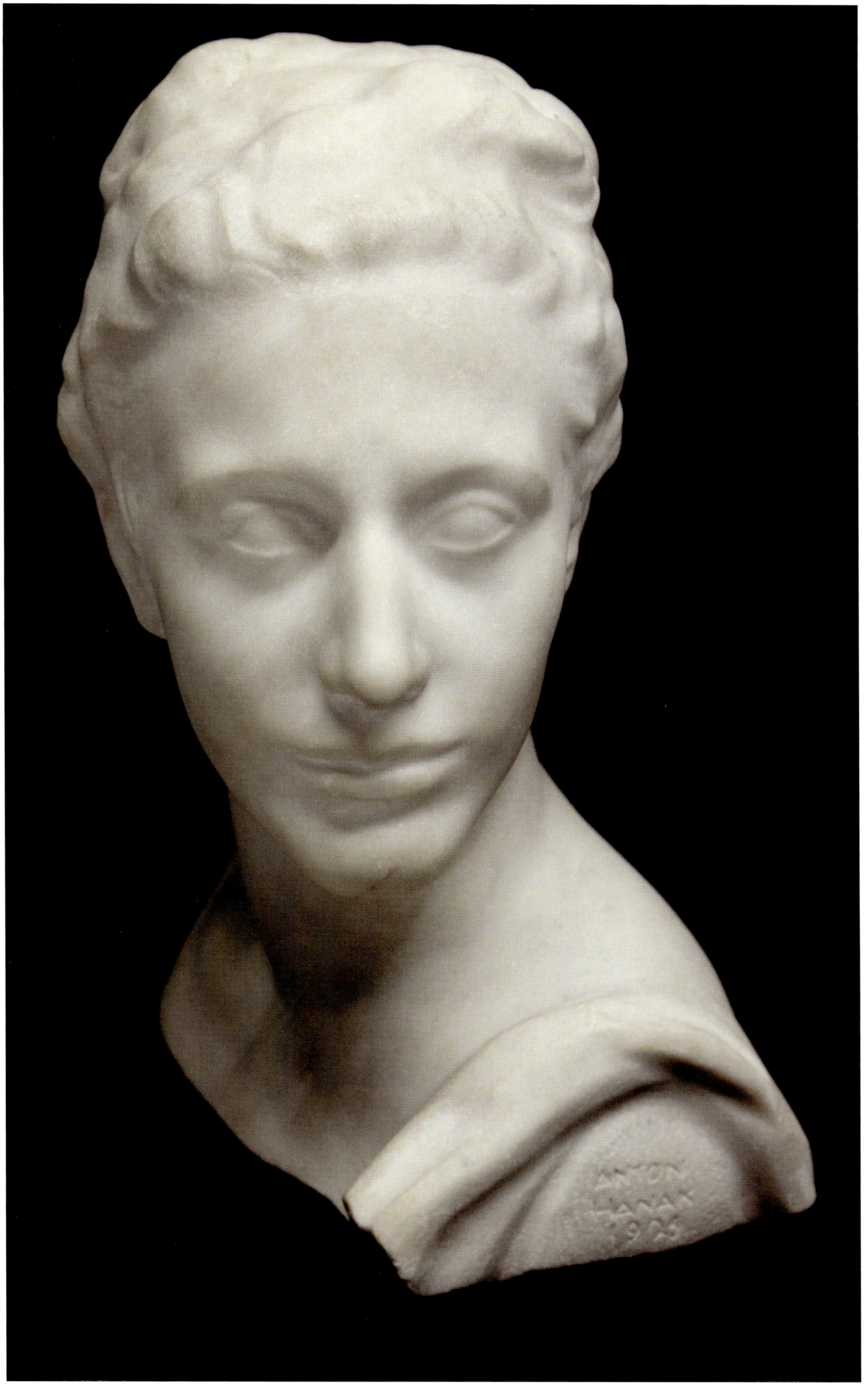

Anton Hanak
Margarete Stonborough-Wittgenstein, 1925
Belvedere, Vienna

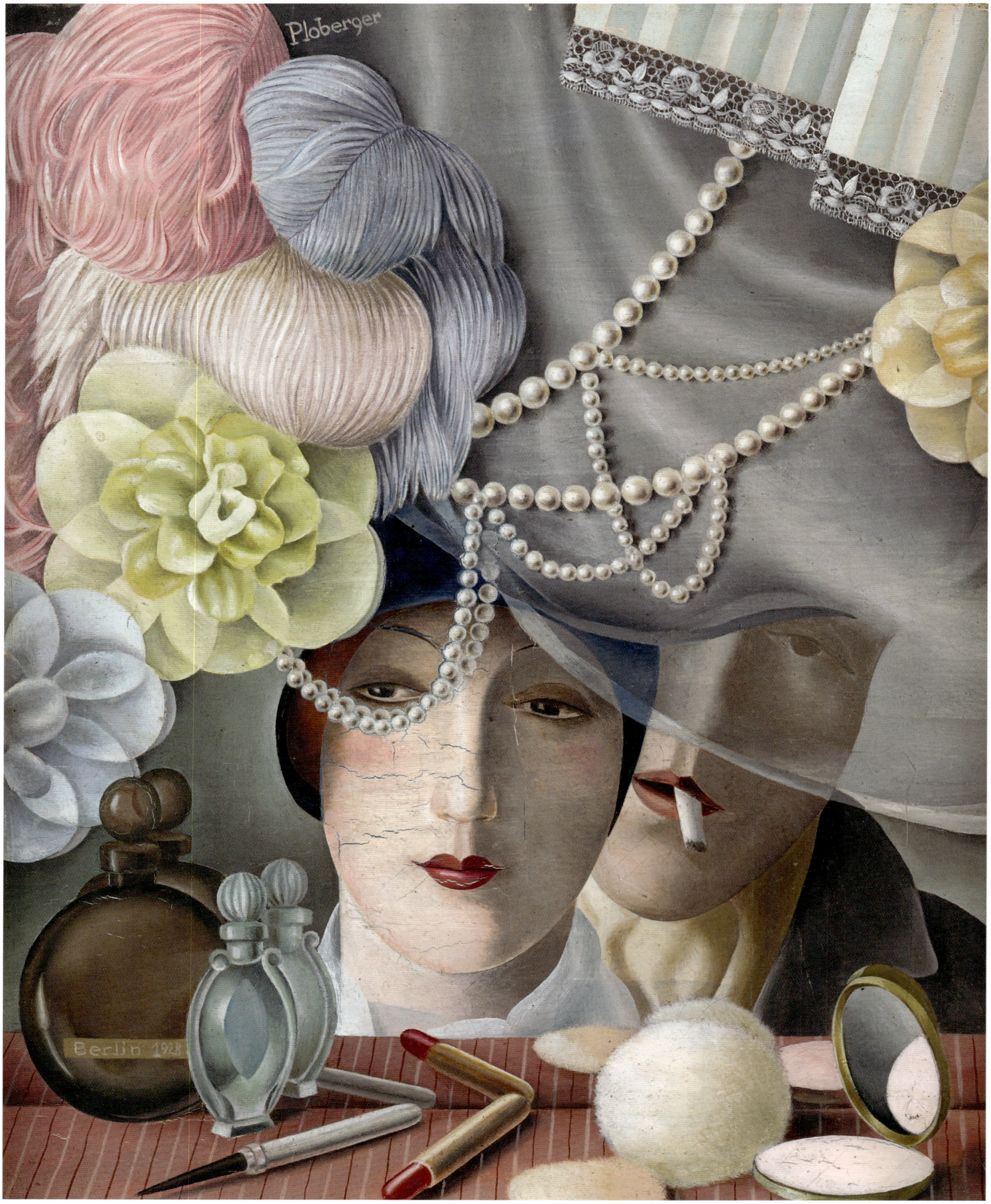

E2

Herbert Ploberger
Window Shopping, 1928
Private collection, Vienna

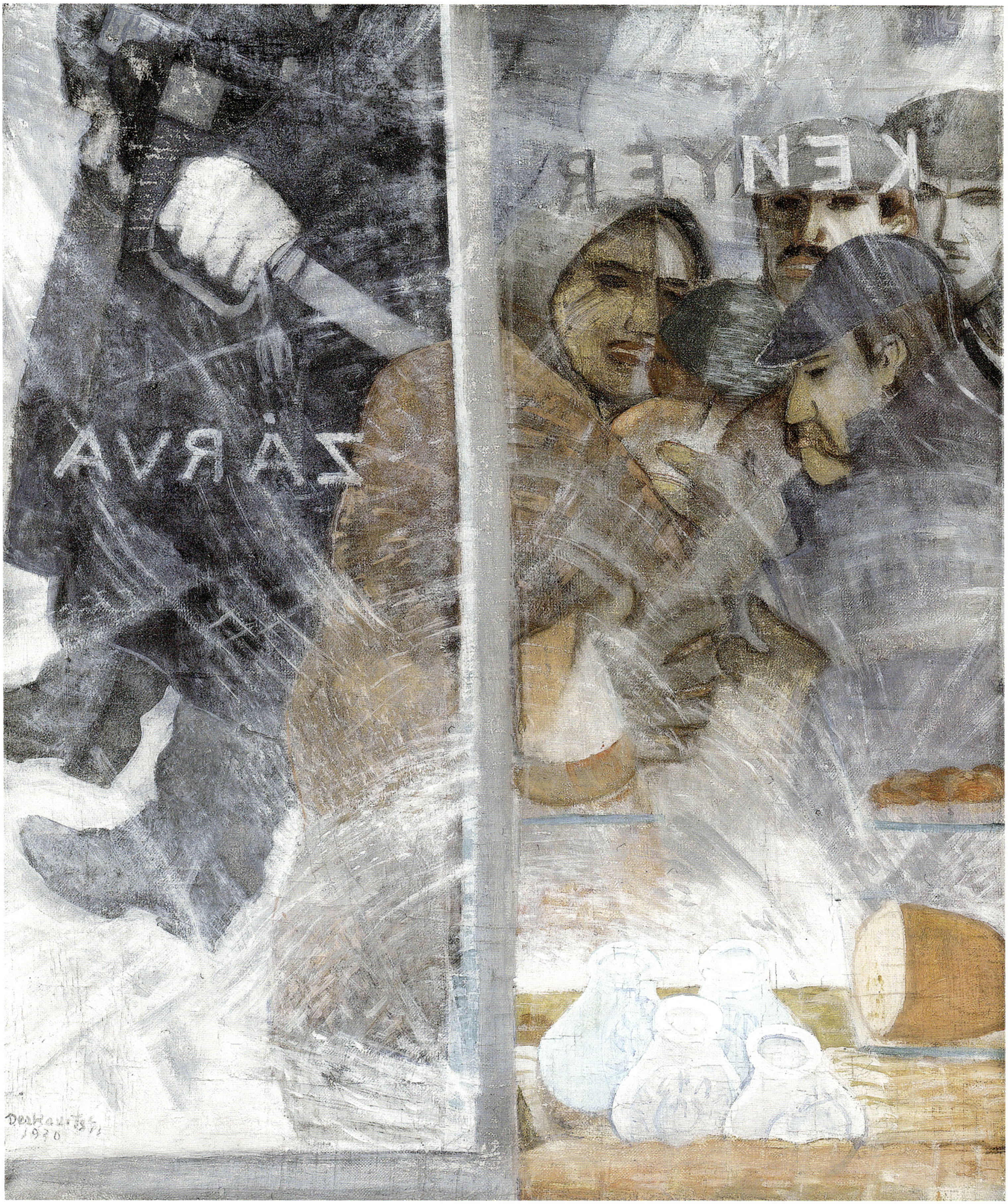

Gyula Derkovits
Starving People in Winter
(In front of the Bakery, Starving People), 1930
Szombathely Art Gallery

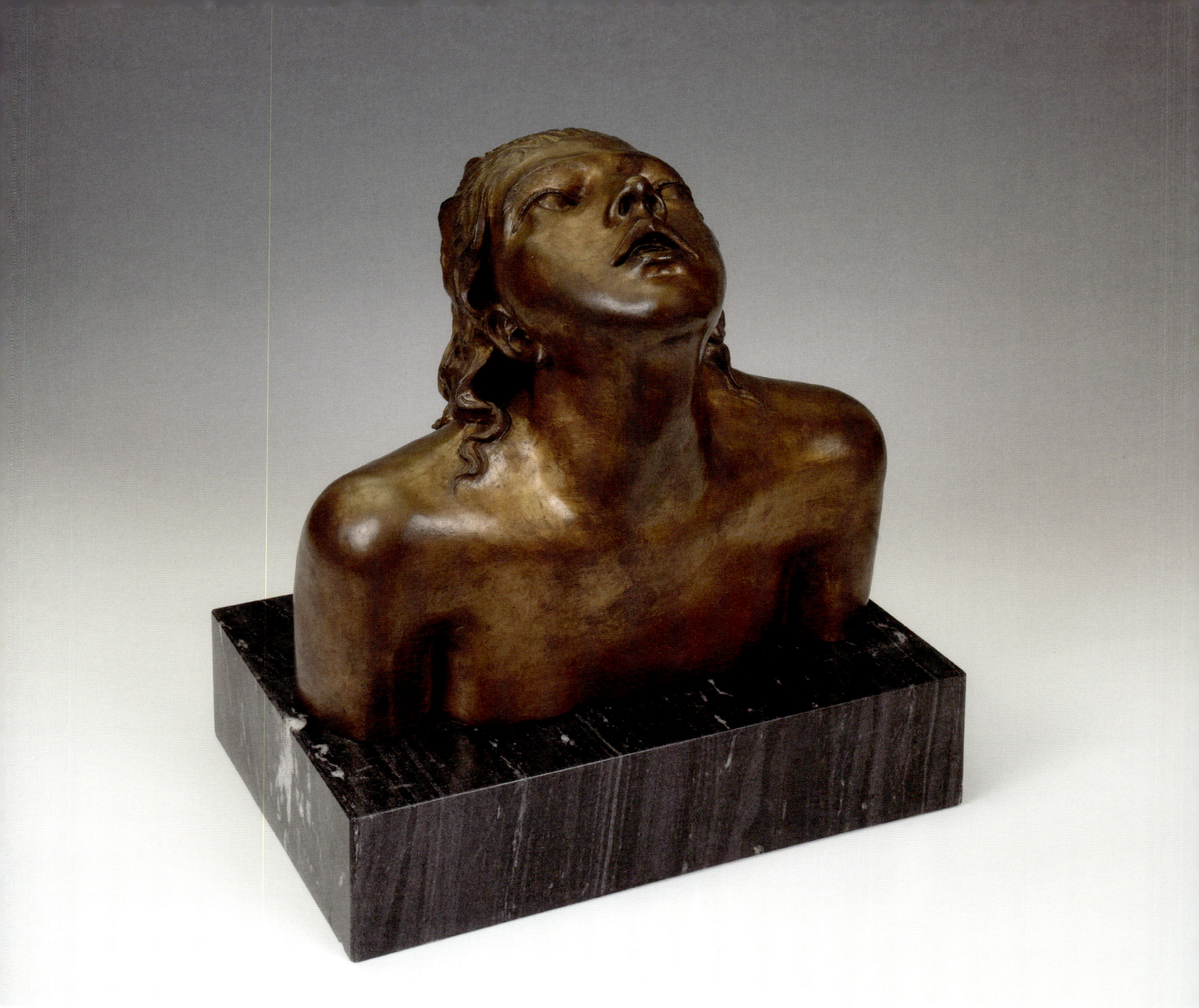

E2

Otto Gutfreund
Girl Looking Up, 1924
Moravian Gallery, Brno

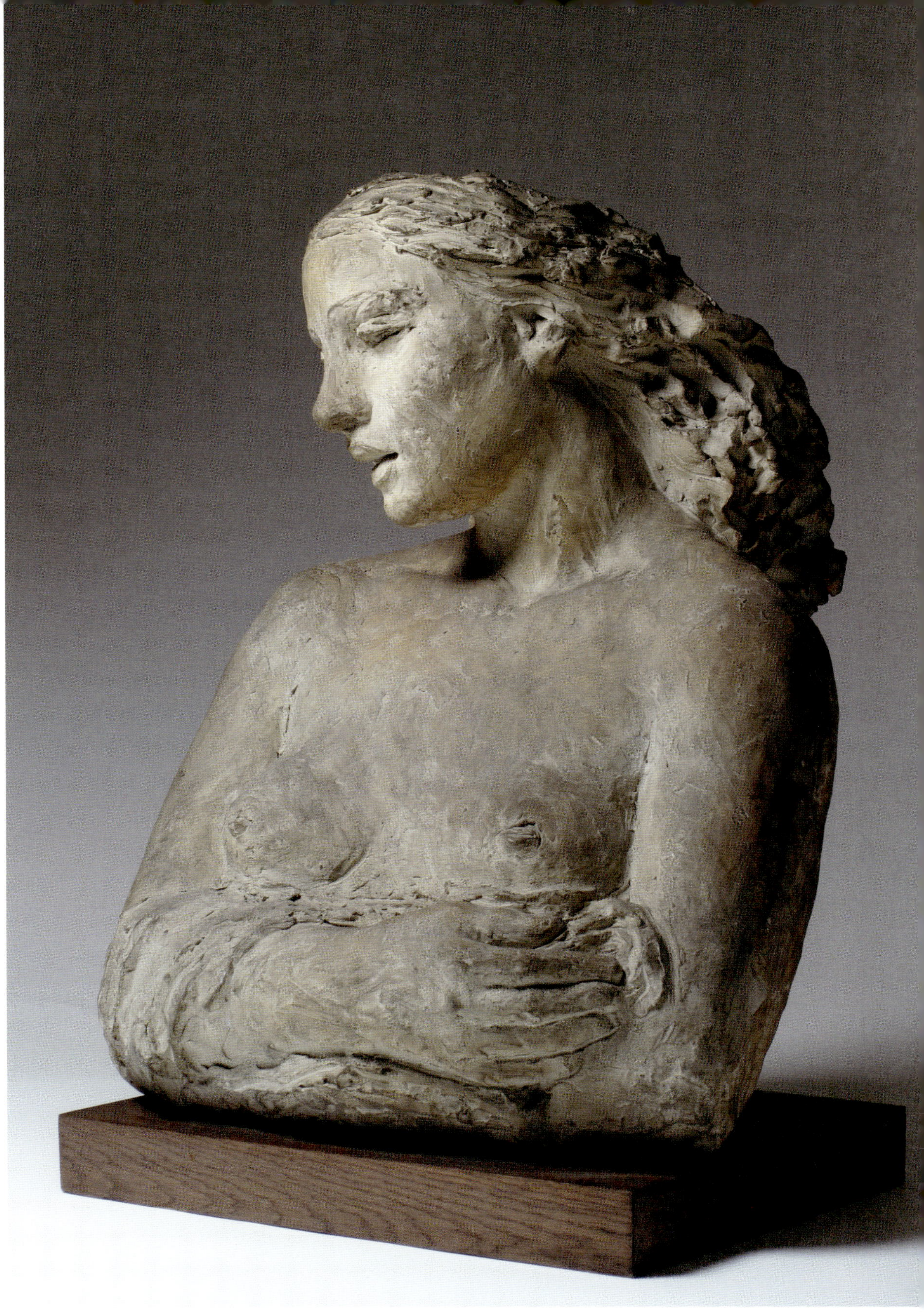

Mary Duras
Musing Woman, 1931
The Regional Art Gallery Liberec

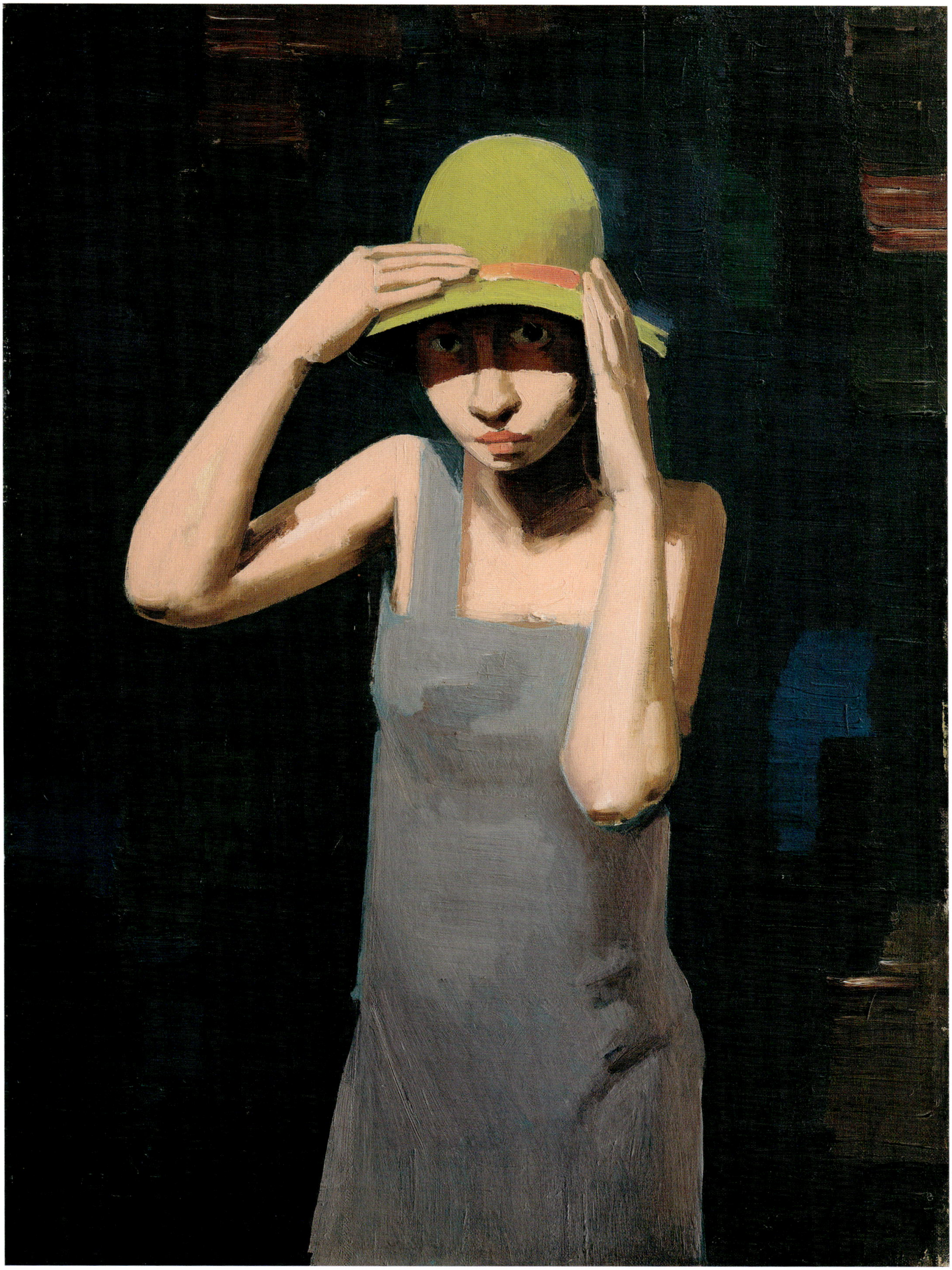

E2

Franz Lerch
Girl with Hat, 1929
Belvedere, Vienna

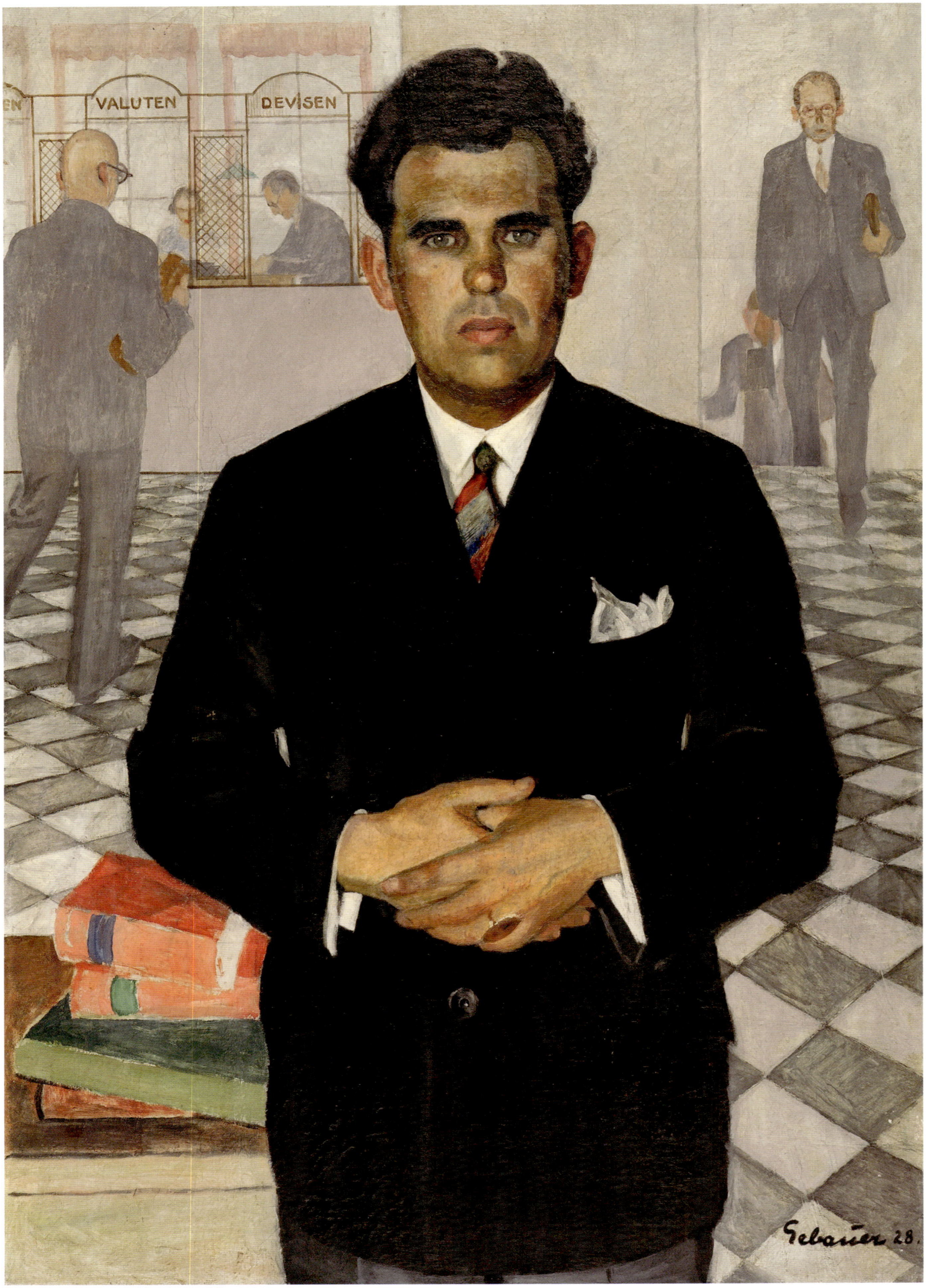
VALUTEN
DEVISEN
Gebauer 28.

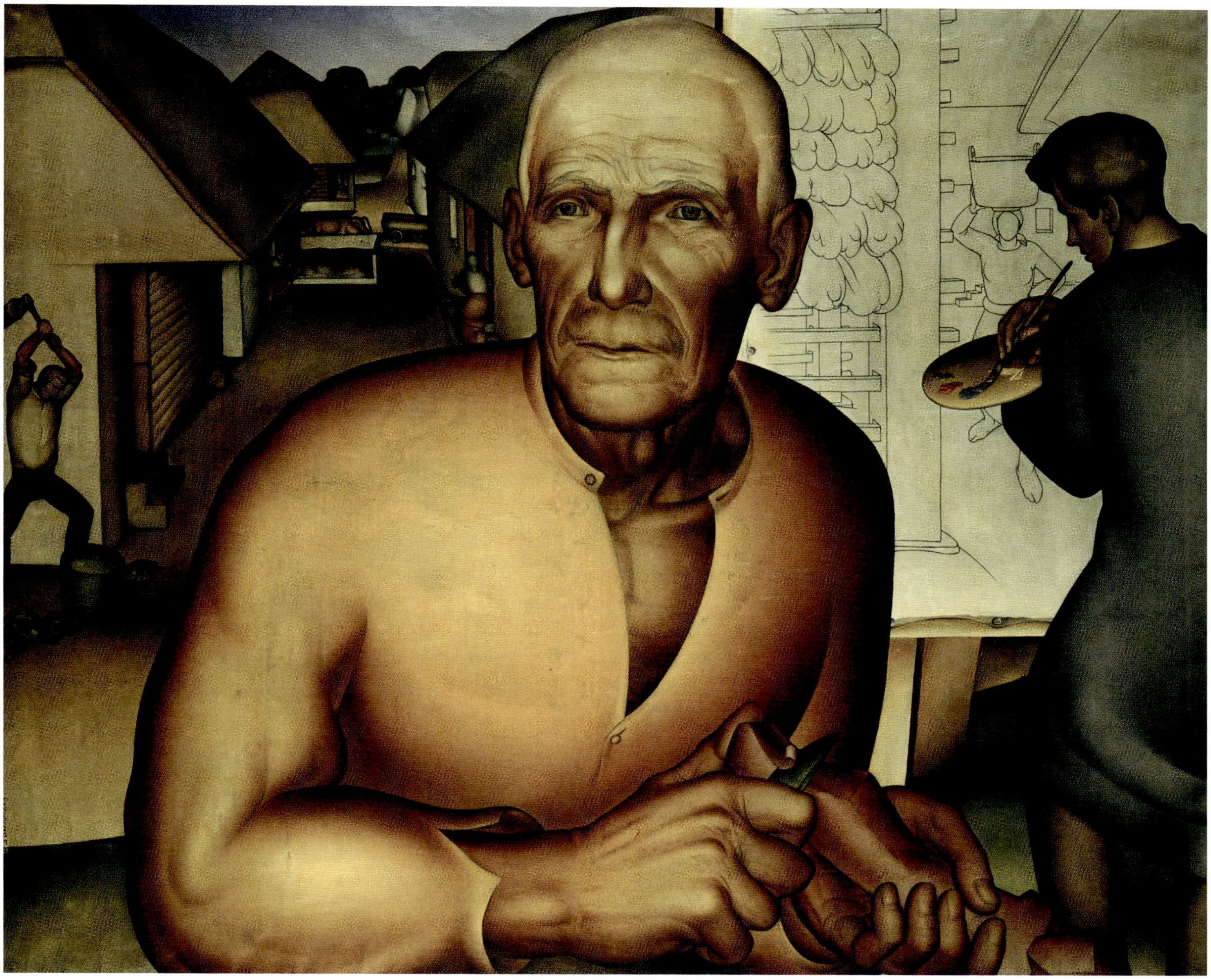

◂ Paul Gebauer
Portrait of Bank Director Koch, 1928
Collection of Slezské zemské museum / Silesian Museum, Opava

Tone Kralj
My Father, 1929
City Museum of Ljubljana (MGML)

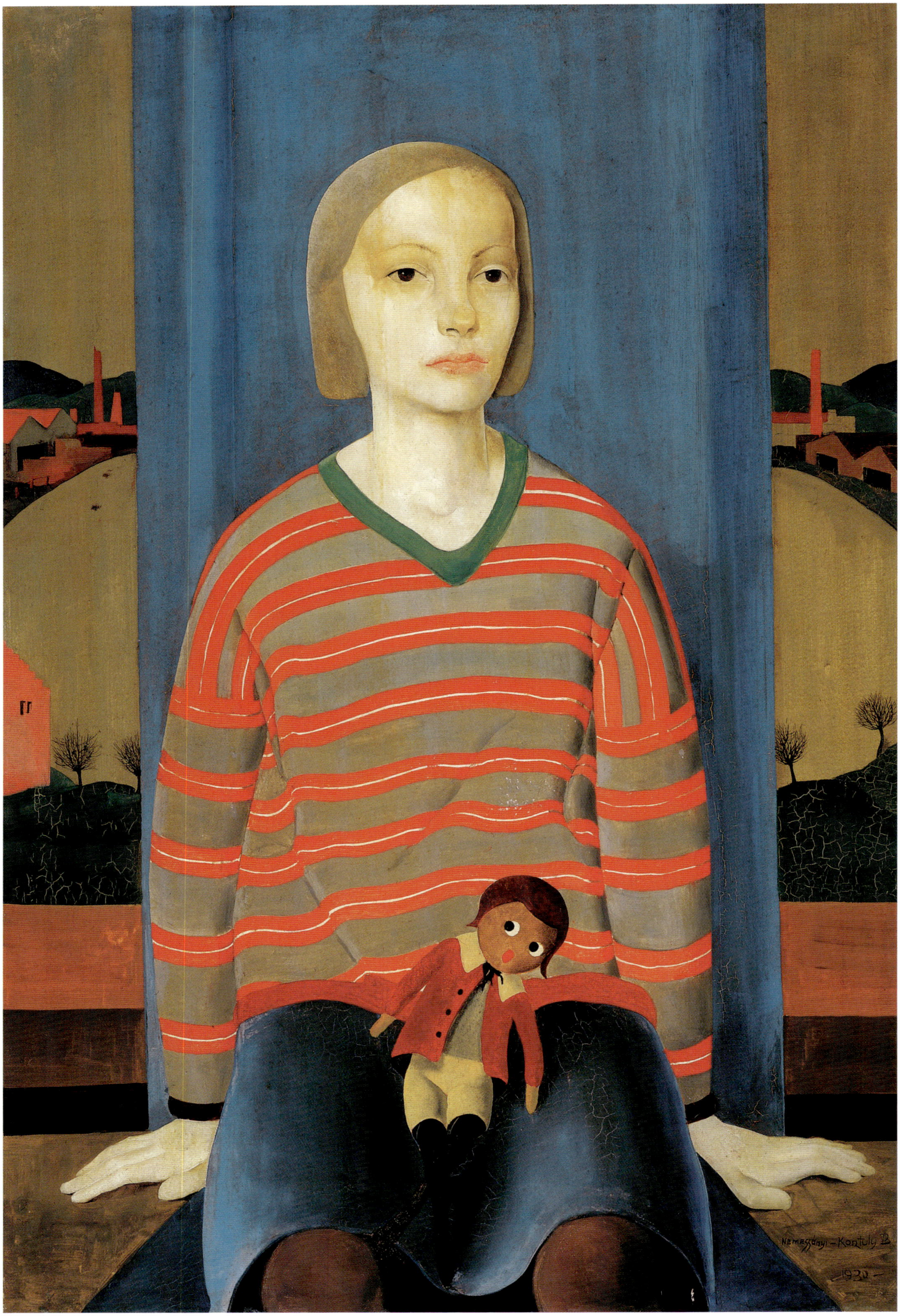
Nemesszényi - Kontuly B.
-1930-

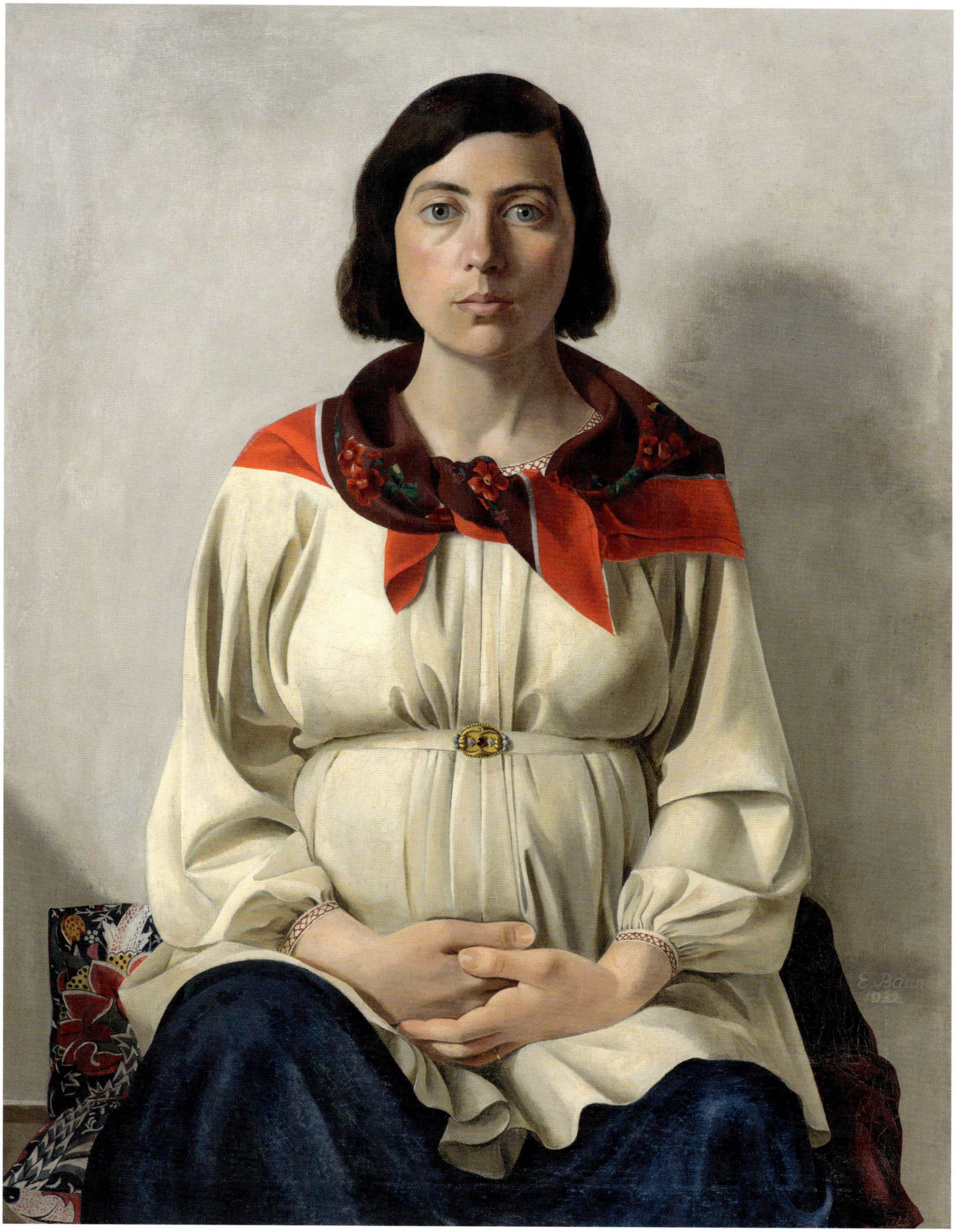

◂ Béla Kontuly
Working-Class Girl
(Girl with Striped Top), 1930
Private collection

Eduard Bäumer
Portrait of Valerie Bäumer, 1932
Private collection

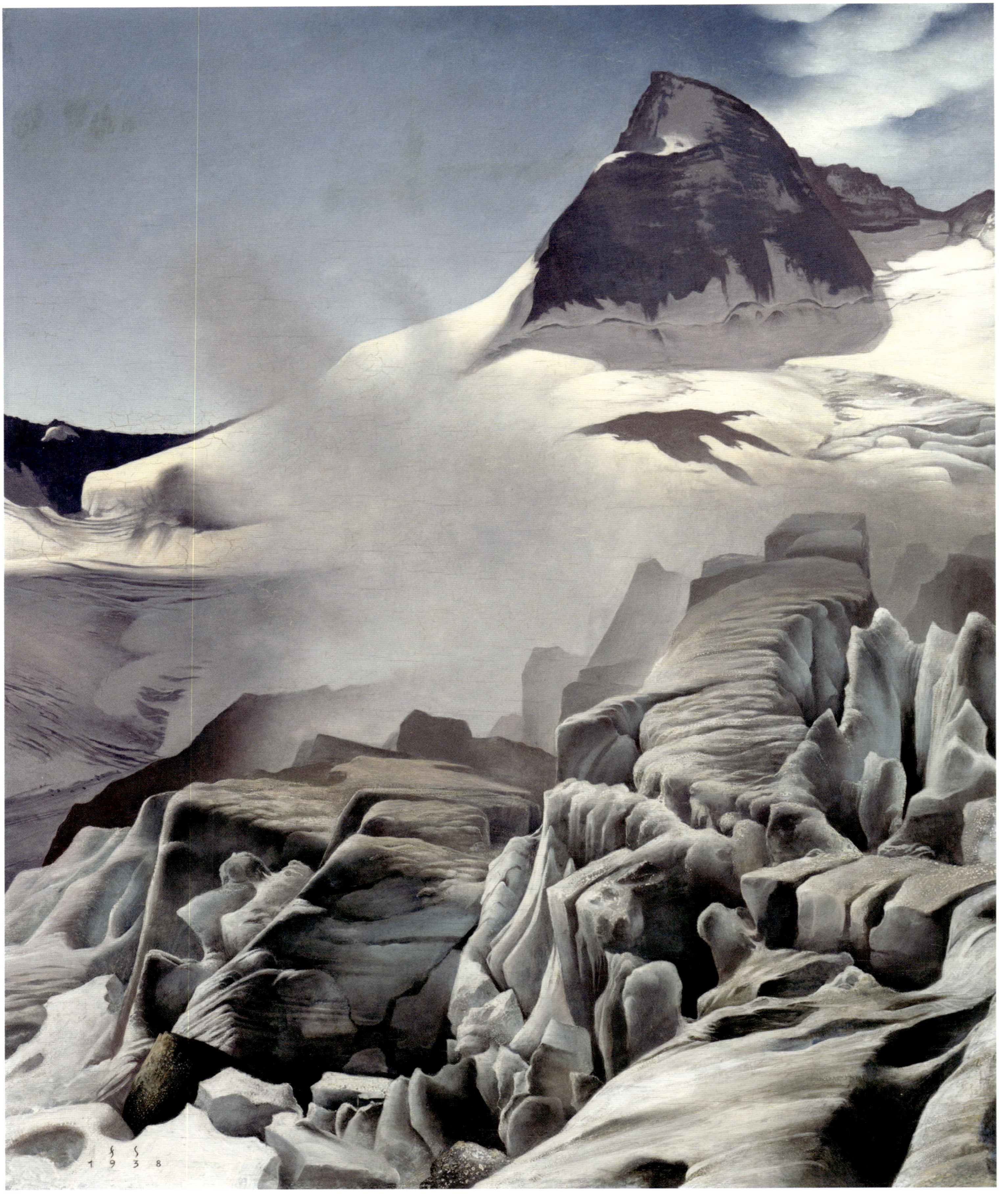

Franz Sedlacek
The Grosser Geiger (Venediger Group),
second version, 1938
Private collection

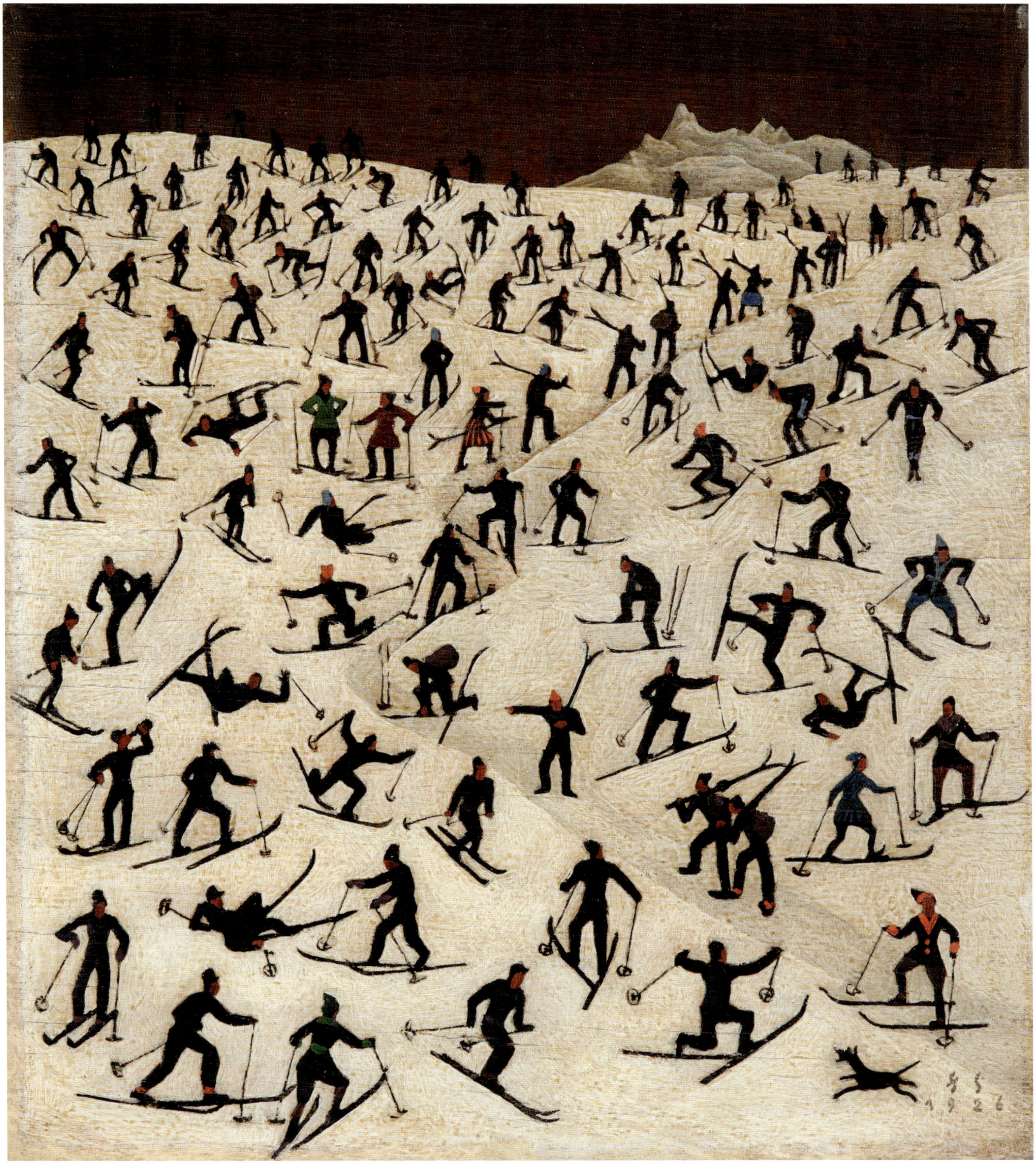

Franz Sedlacek
Practice Slope, 1926
LENTOS Kunstmuseum Linz

The Fantastic

The hopelessness and social malaise hanging over Europe in the interwar years was reflected in art in a profound, almost prophetic manner, using the means of the Fantastic. Militant politics combined with exaggerated nationalism were threatening to drag the global world order into a new, even deadlier, conflict. The nightmare of the First World War had scarcely passed before even darker clouds were gathering along the horizon of a fragile peace. Depictions of strange, unidentifiable threats, such as those by Franz Sedlacek, the disintegration of the individual or of the objective integrity of everyday life, as in the work of Rudolf Wacker, and the symbolic fragmentation of an already delicate equilibrium were unsettling omens of the totalitarian systems to come. These systems, founded on ideological, ethnic, and religious persecution, called all morality into question and led, ultimately, to the next World War. (MH)

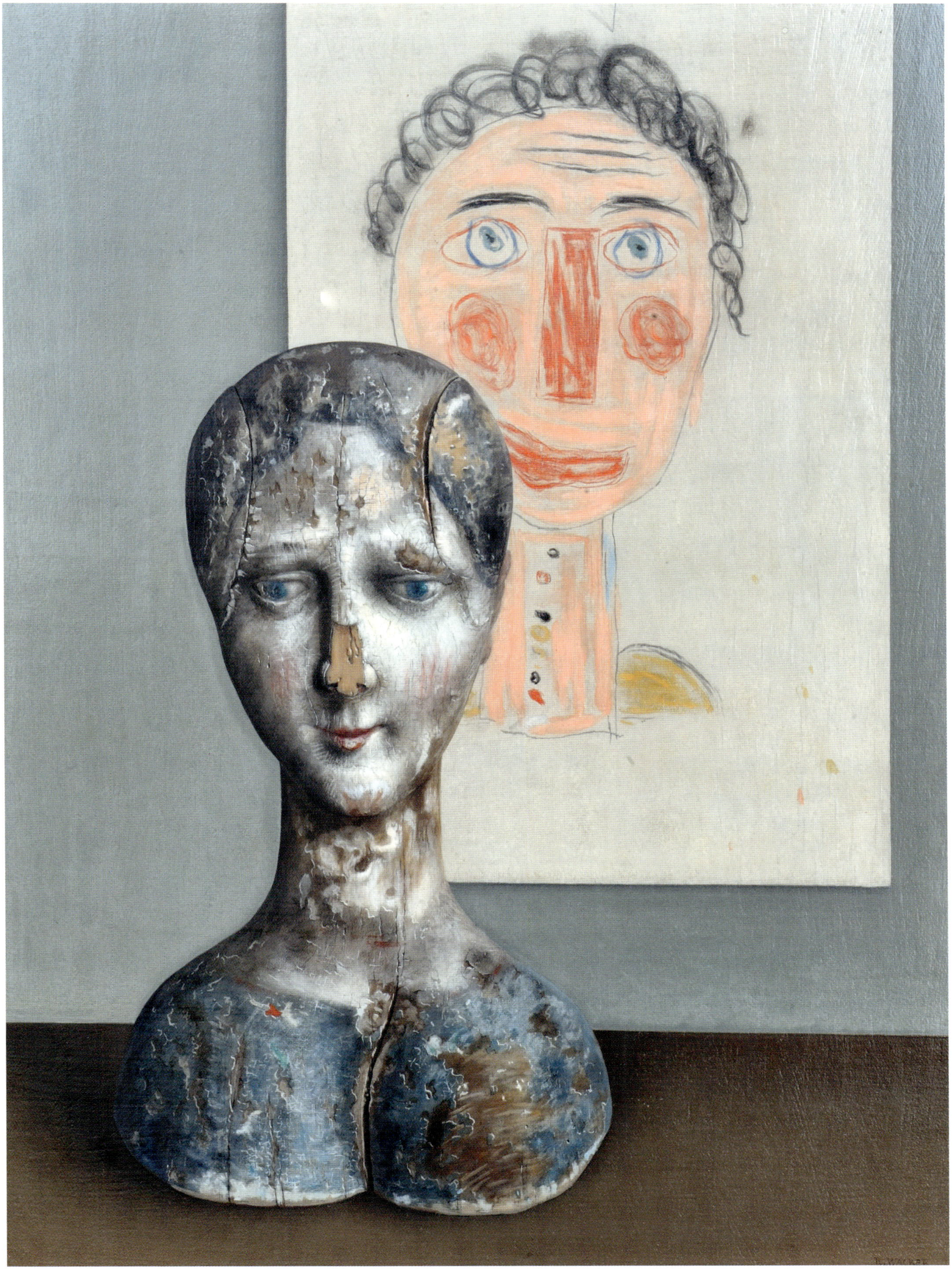

Rudolf Wacker
Two Heads (Wooden Head and Children's Drawing), 1936
Private collection

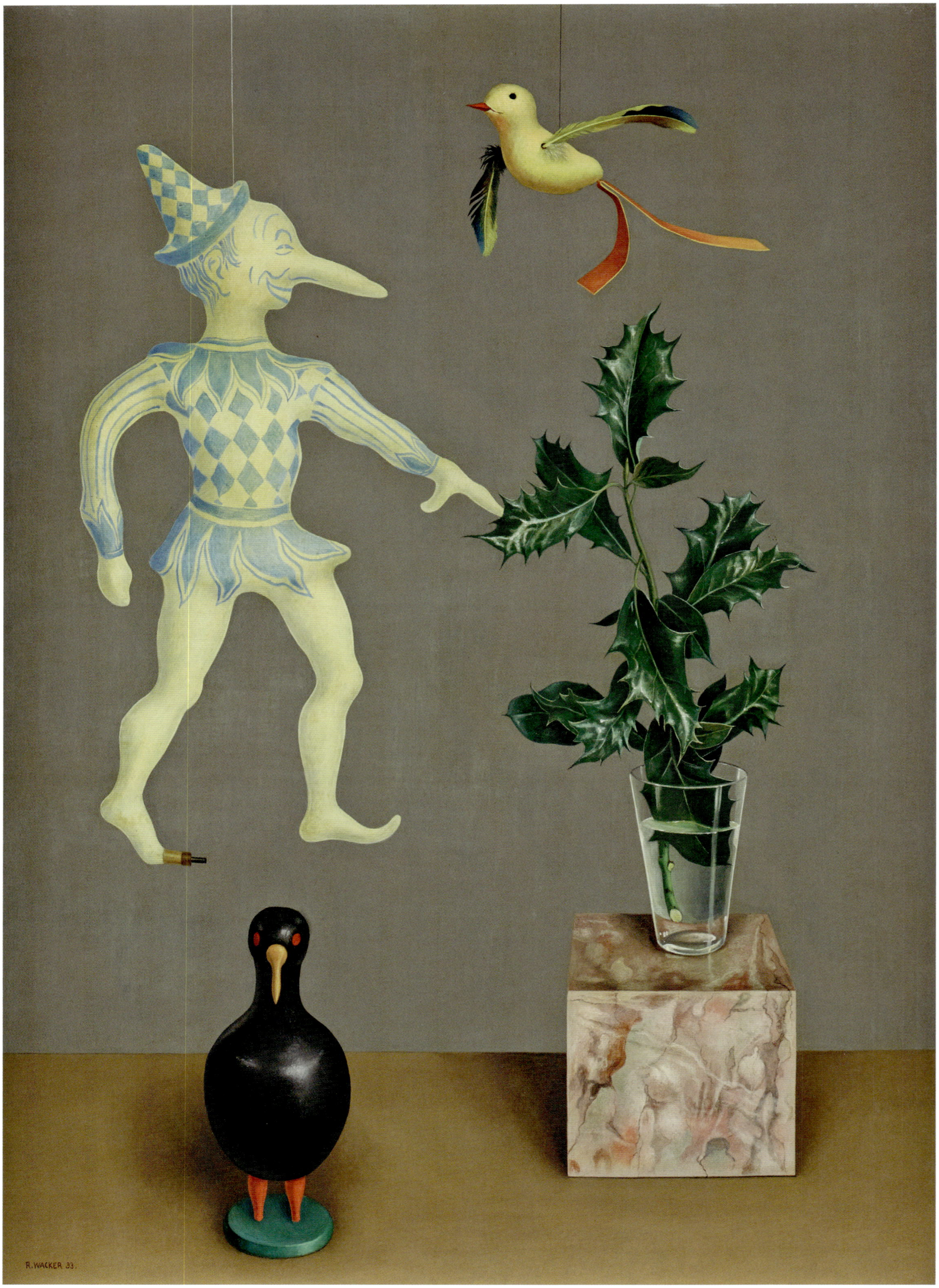
R. WACKER 33.

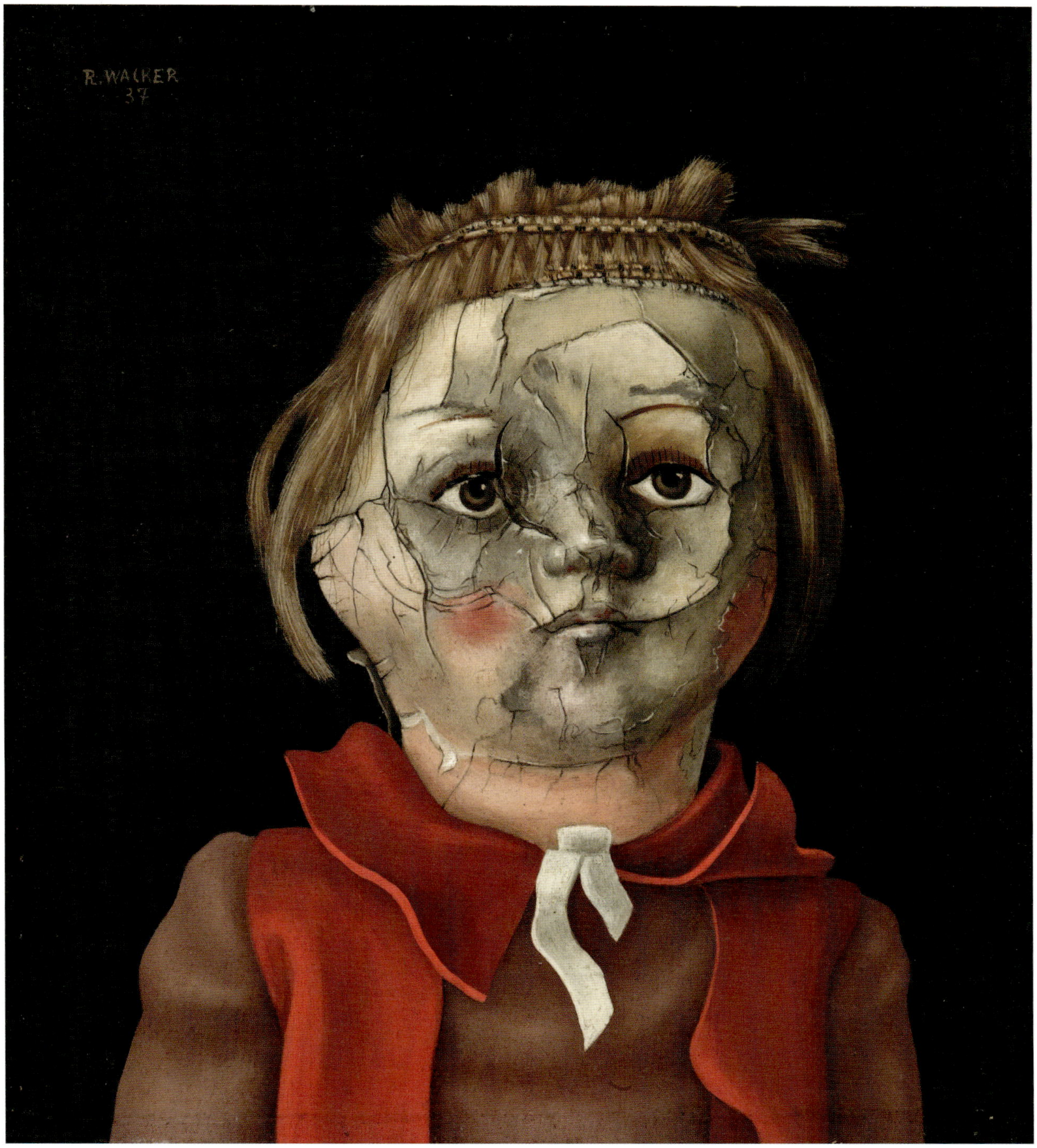

◂ Rudolf Wacker
Still Life with Holly, 1933
Private collection

Rudolf Wacker
Cracked Doll's Head, 1937
Private collection, Vienna, courtesy of
Kunsthandel Giese & Schweiger, Vienna

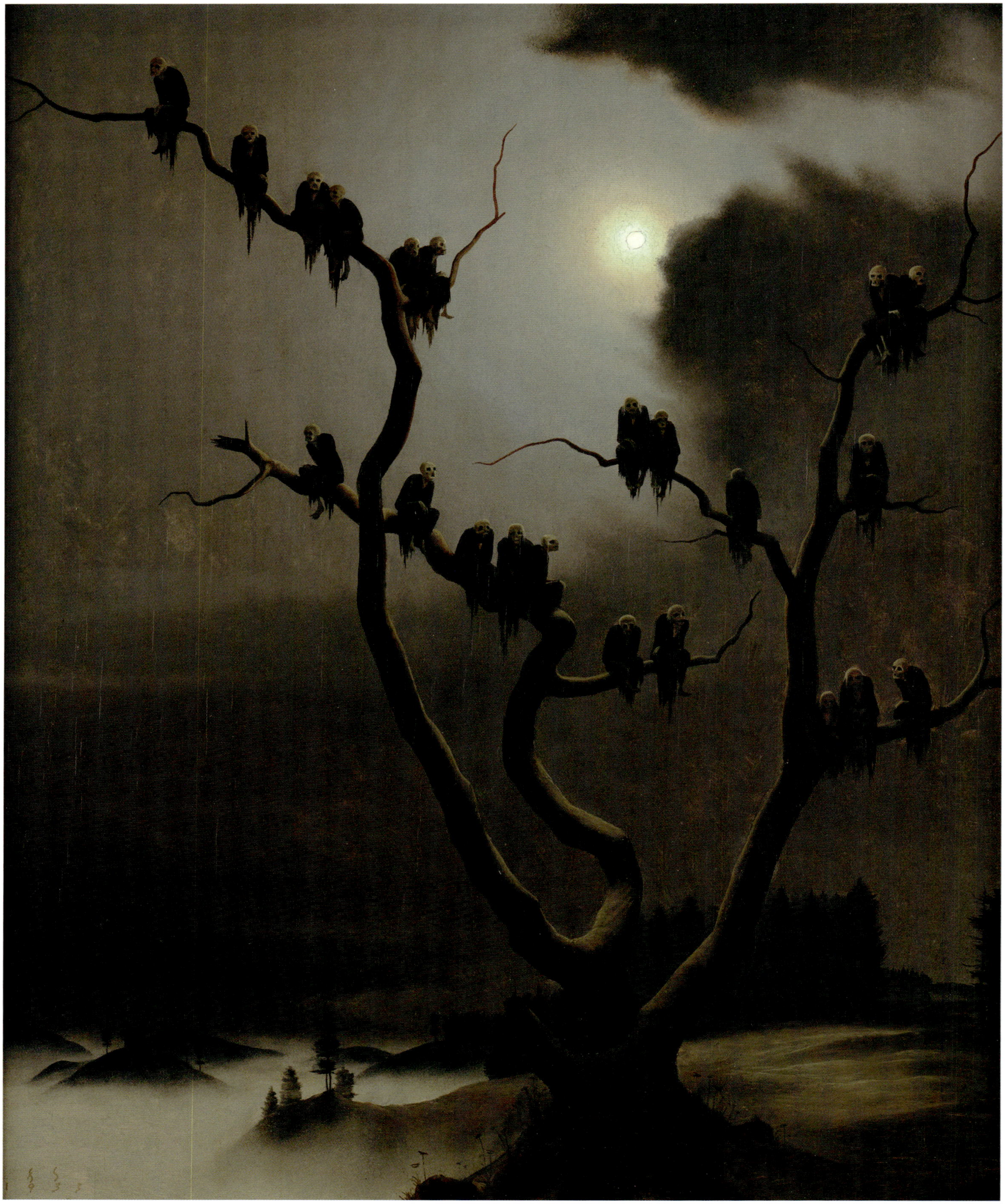

E3

Franz Sedlacek
Ghosts on the Tree, 1933
Albertina, Vienna, loan from E. Ploil

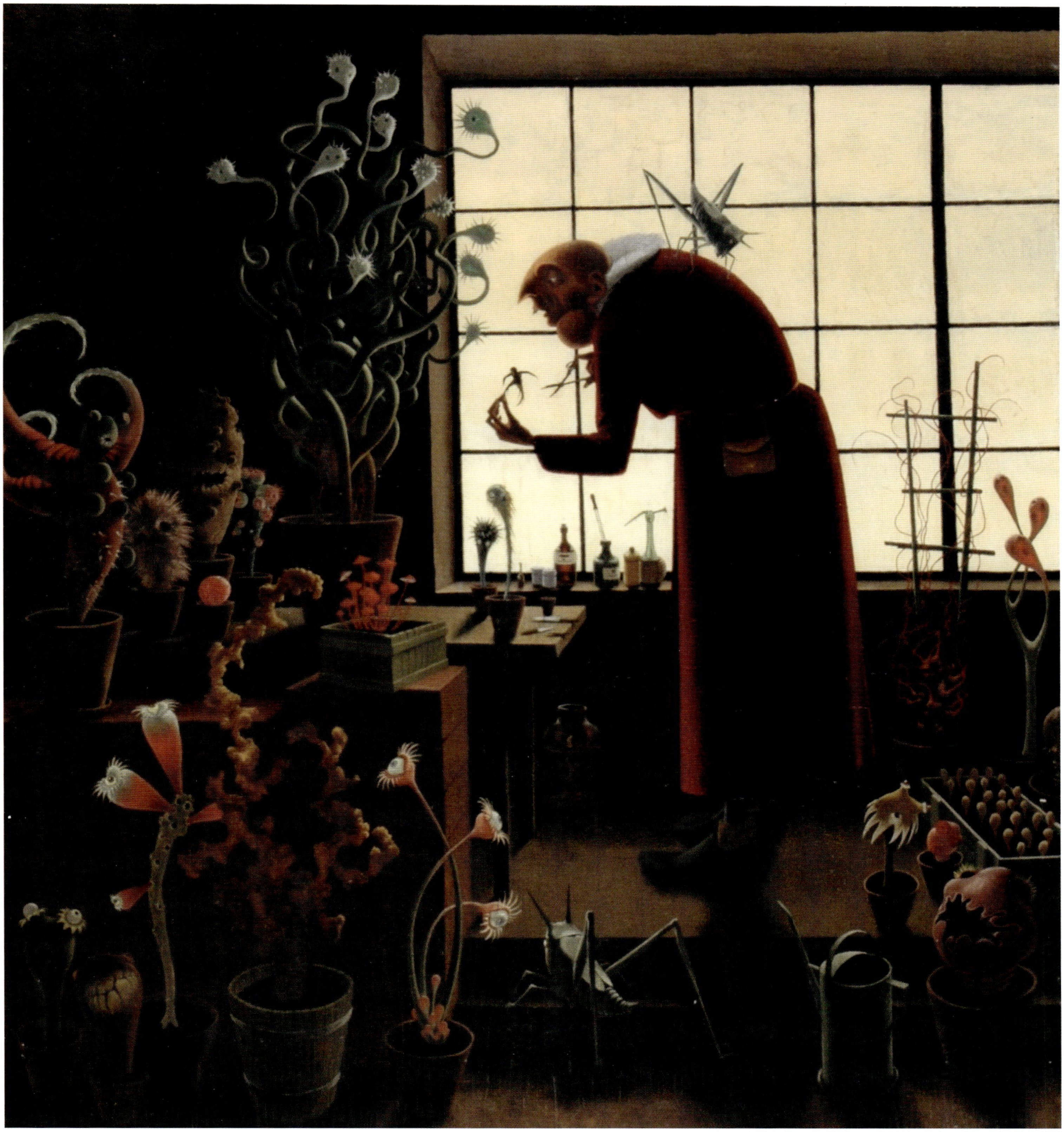

E3

Franz Sedlacek
The Gardener, 1928
Private collection, Seligenstadt

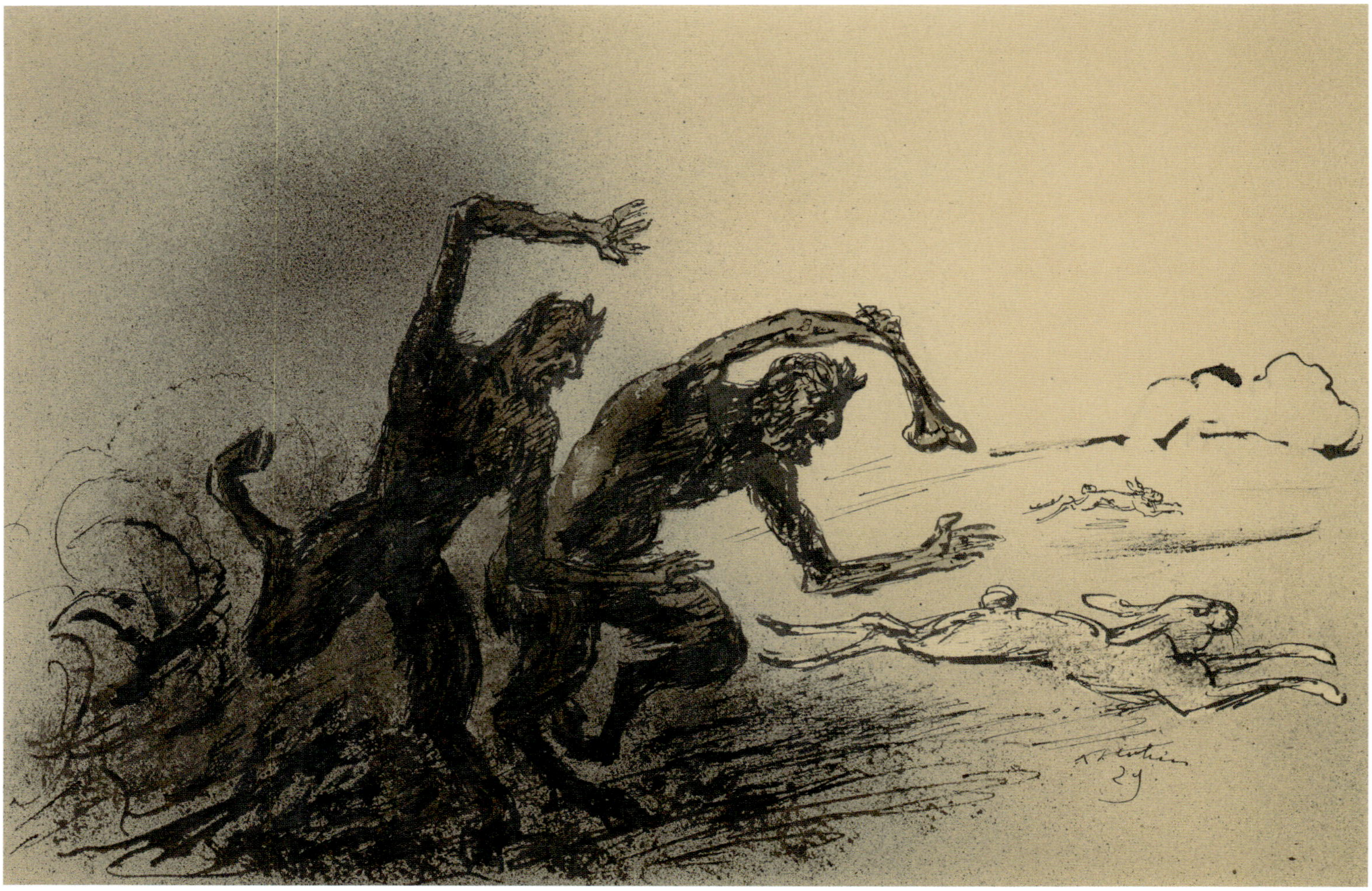

Alfred Kubin
Hare Hunting, 1929
Albertina, Vienna

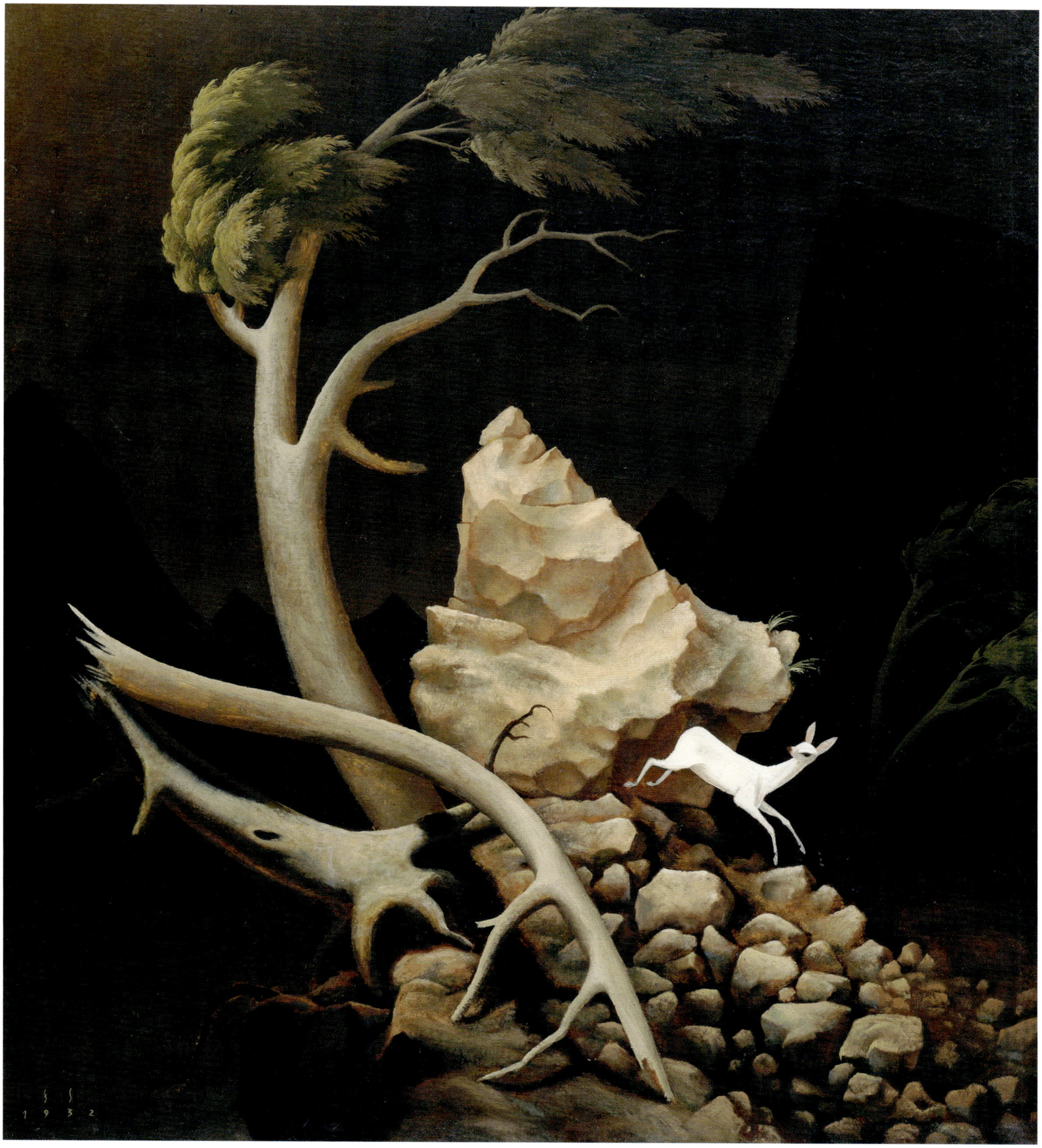

E3

Franz Sedlacek
Storm, 1932
Belvedere, Vienna

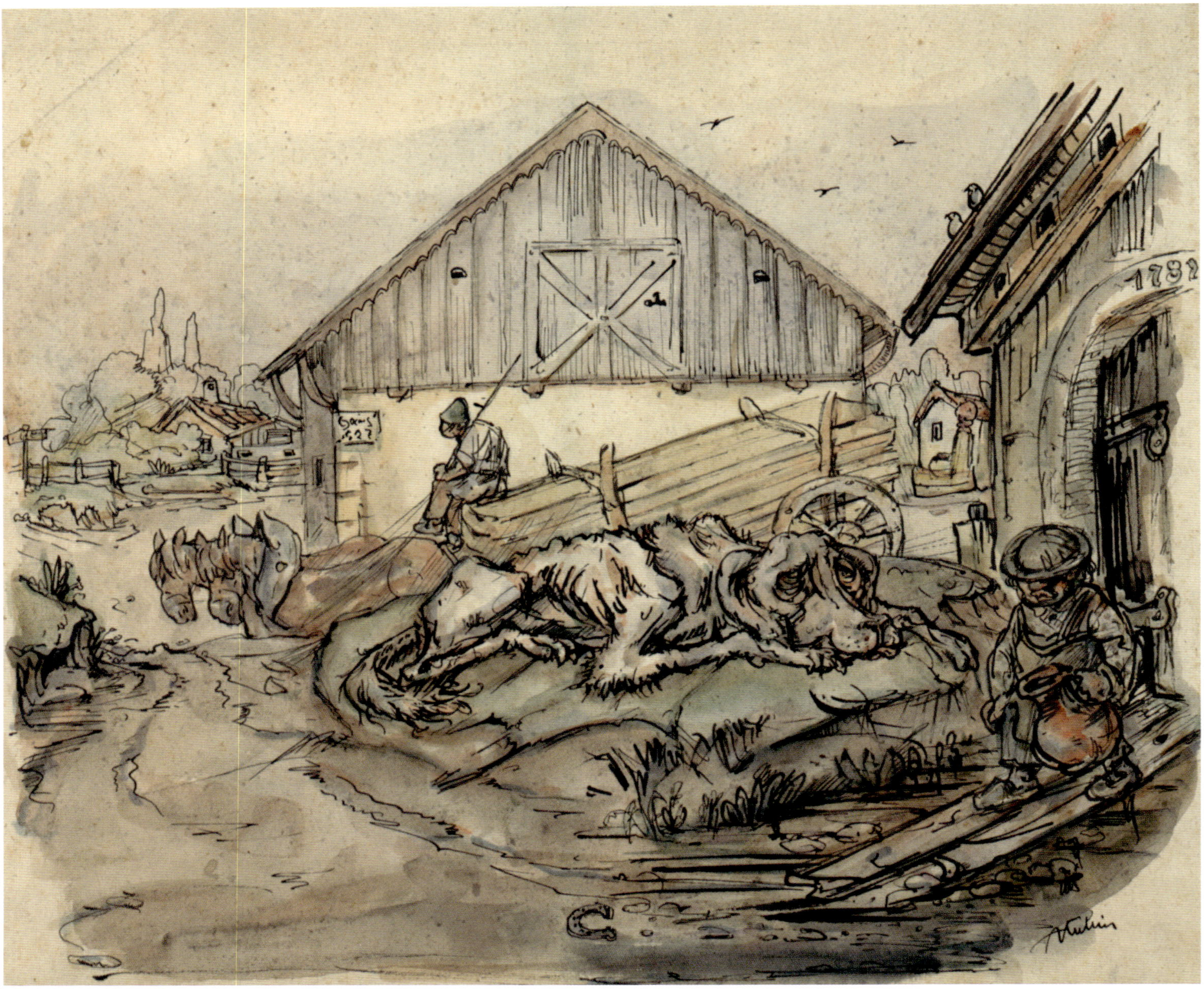

E3

Alfred Kubin
The Old Yard Dog, c. 1928
Belvedere, Vienna

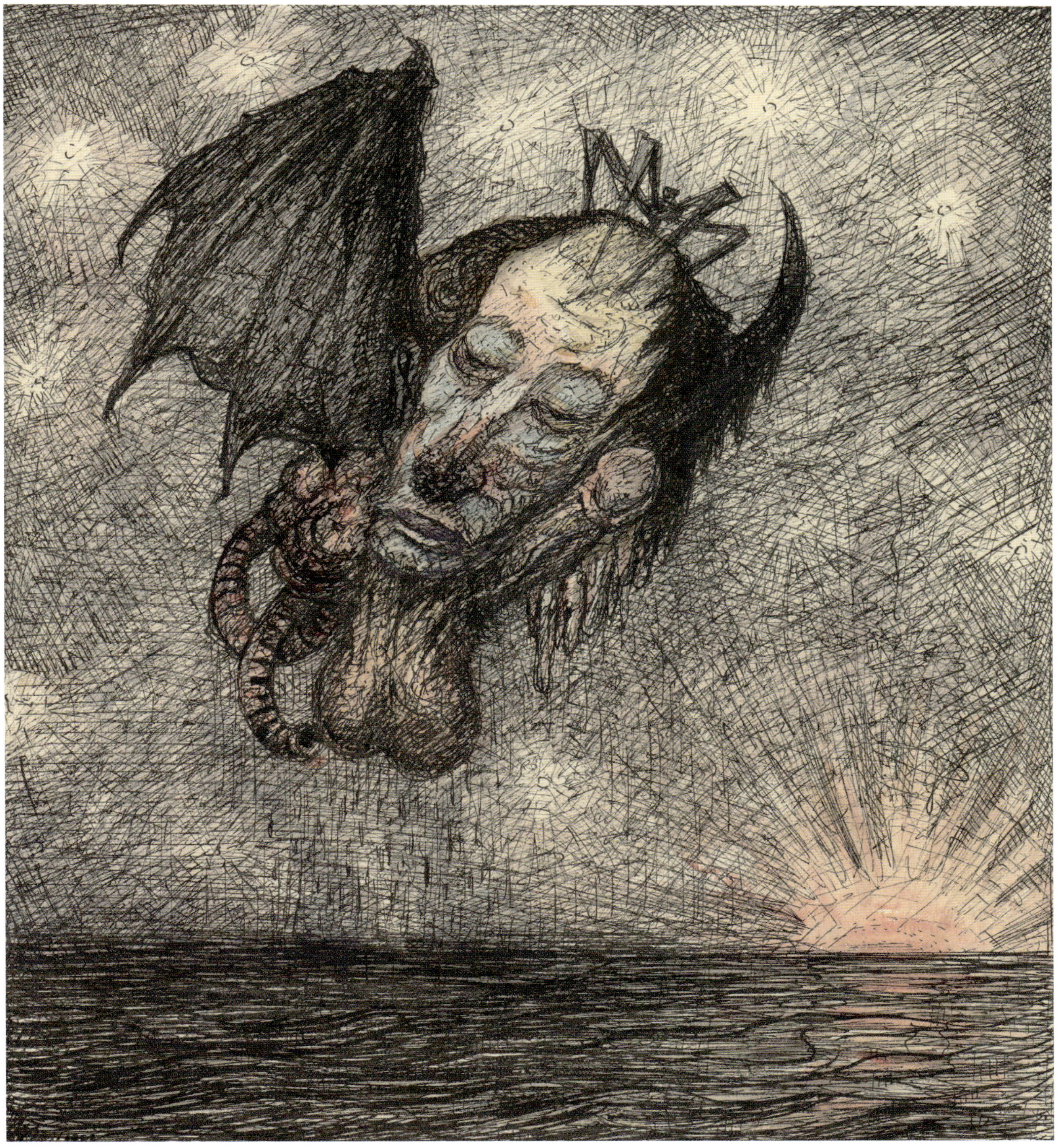

Alfred Kubin
The Fool of the World, c. 1920
Albertina, Vienna

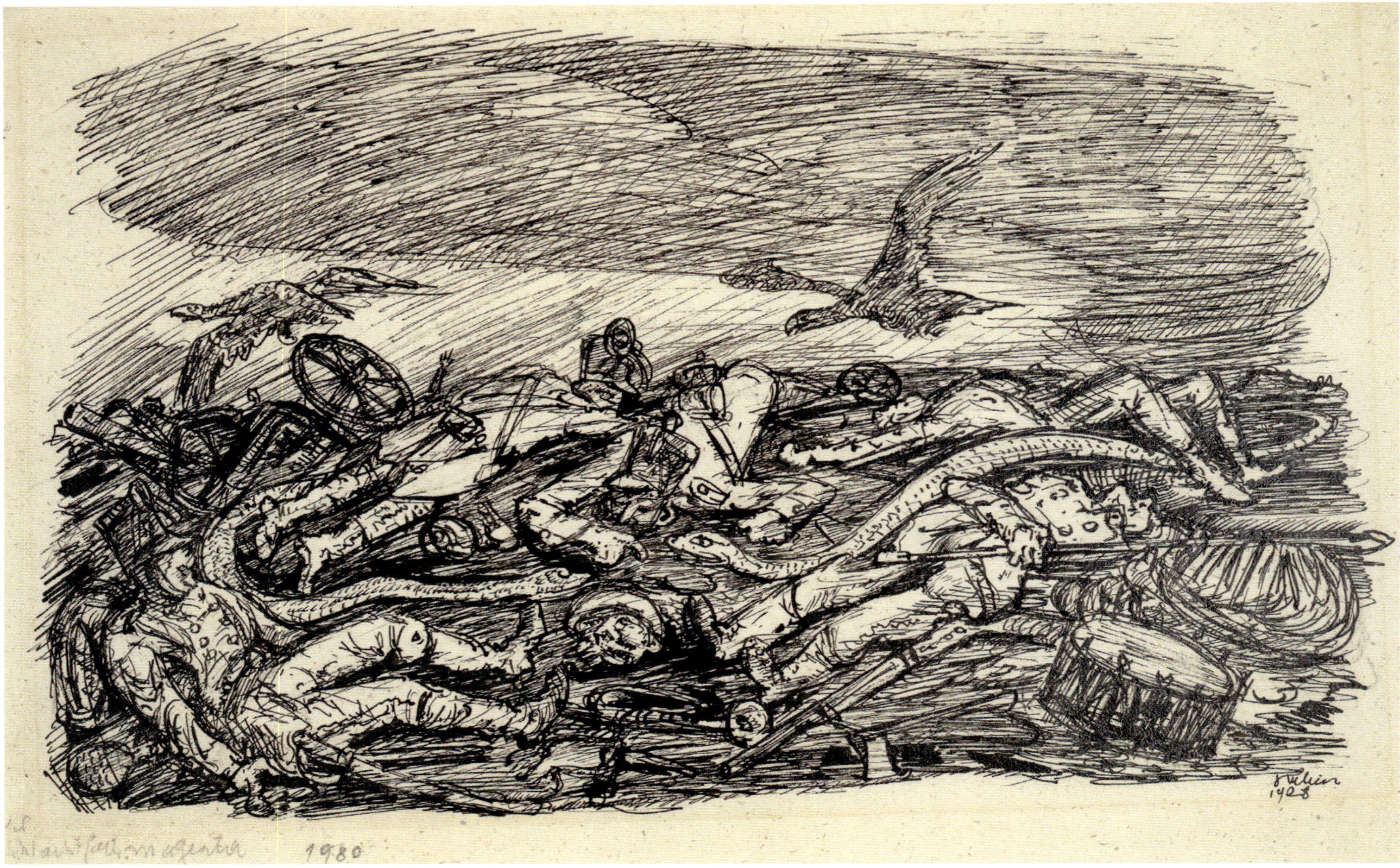

E3

Alfred Kubin
The Battlefield of Magenta, 1928
Landesgalerie Linz, Graphic Arts Collection

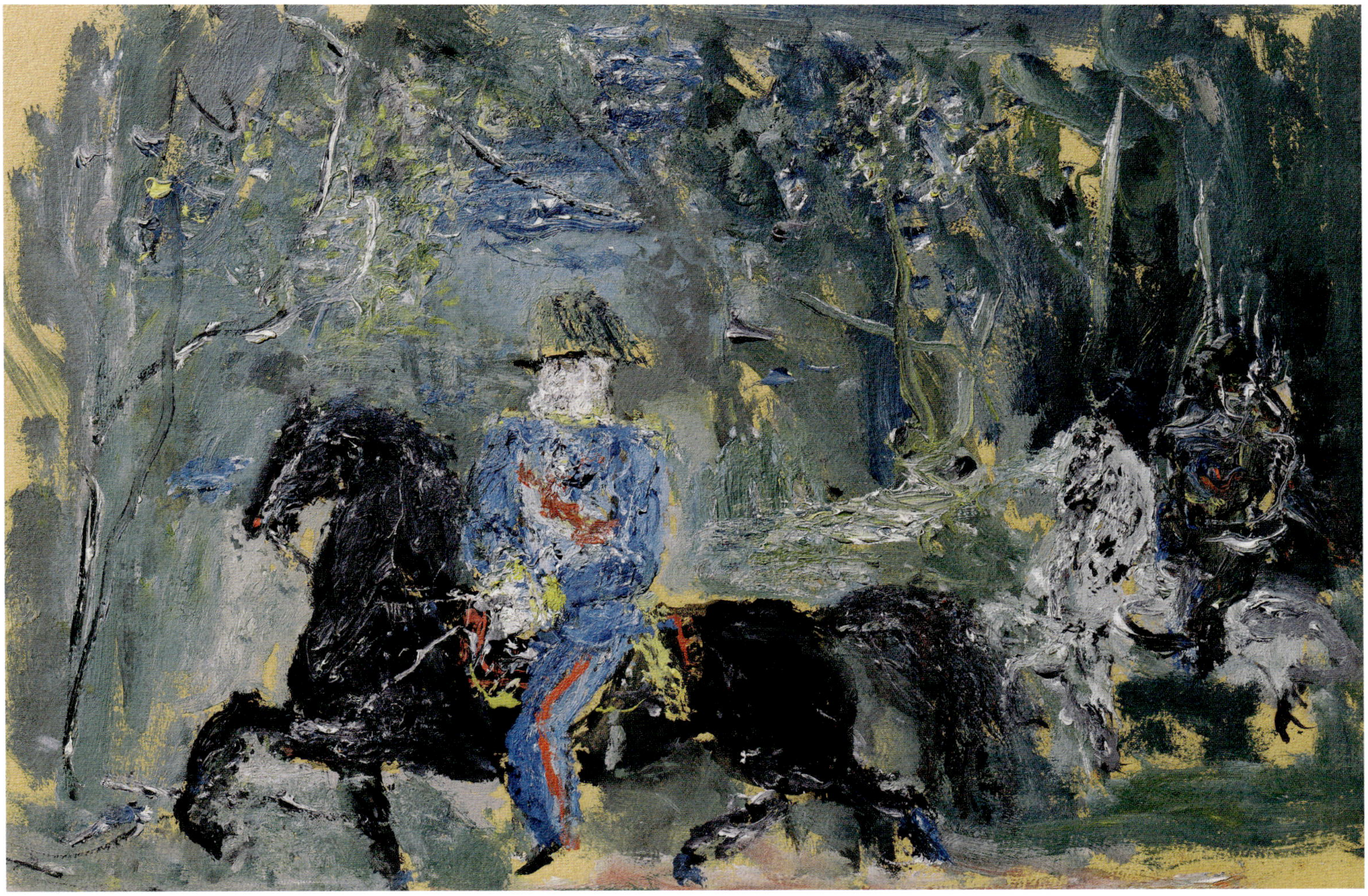

E3

Wilhelm Thöny
Emperor Franz Joseph at the Vienna Prater, 1931–33
Belvedere, Vienna

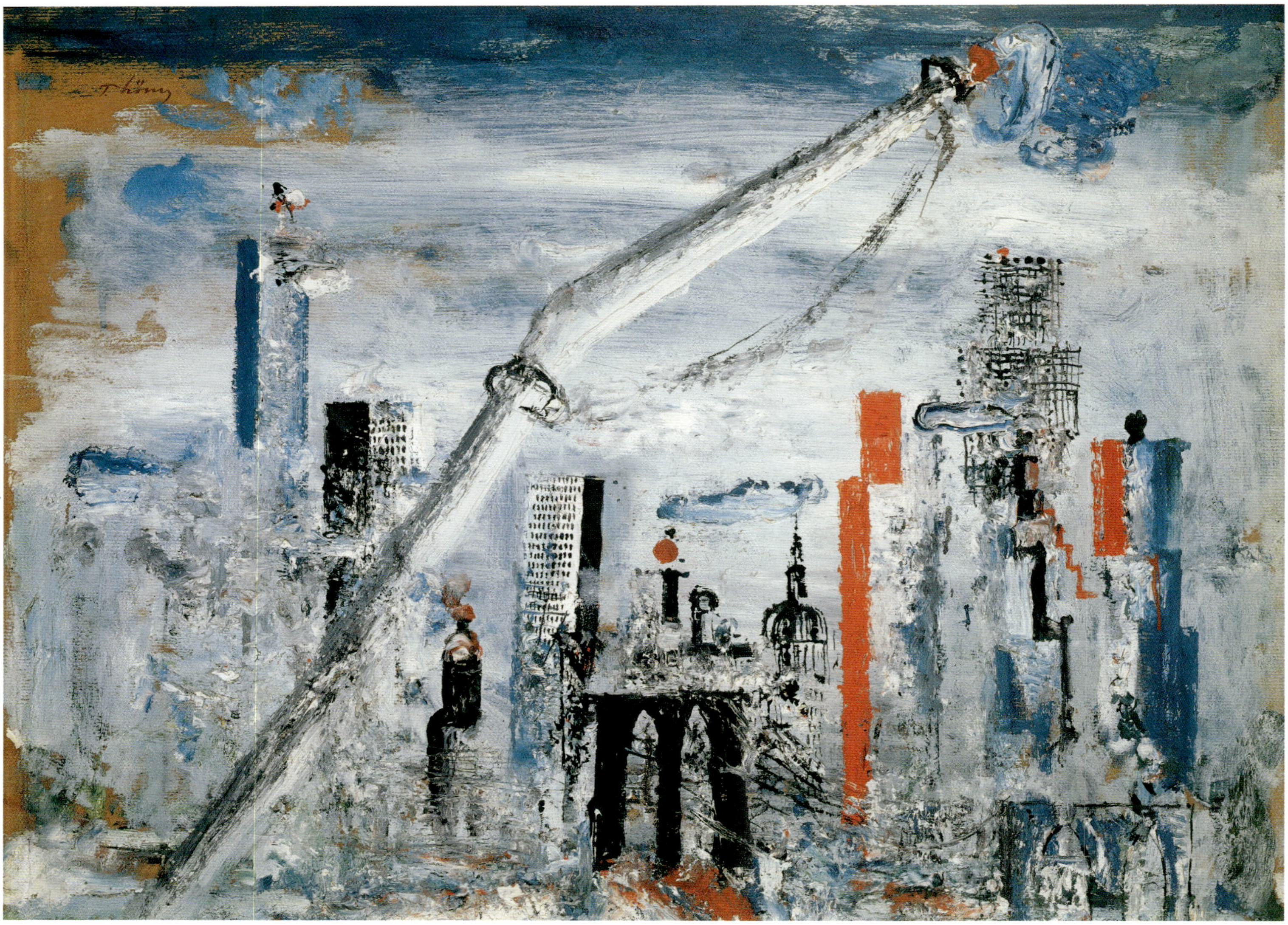

E3

Wilhelm Thöny
View of Manhattan (East River), 1935–38
Belvedere, Vienna

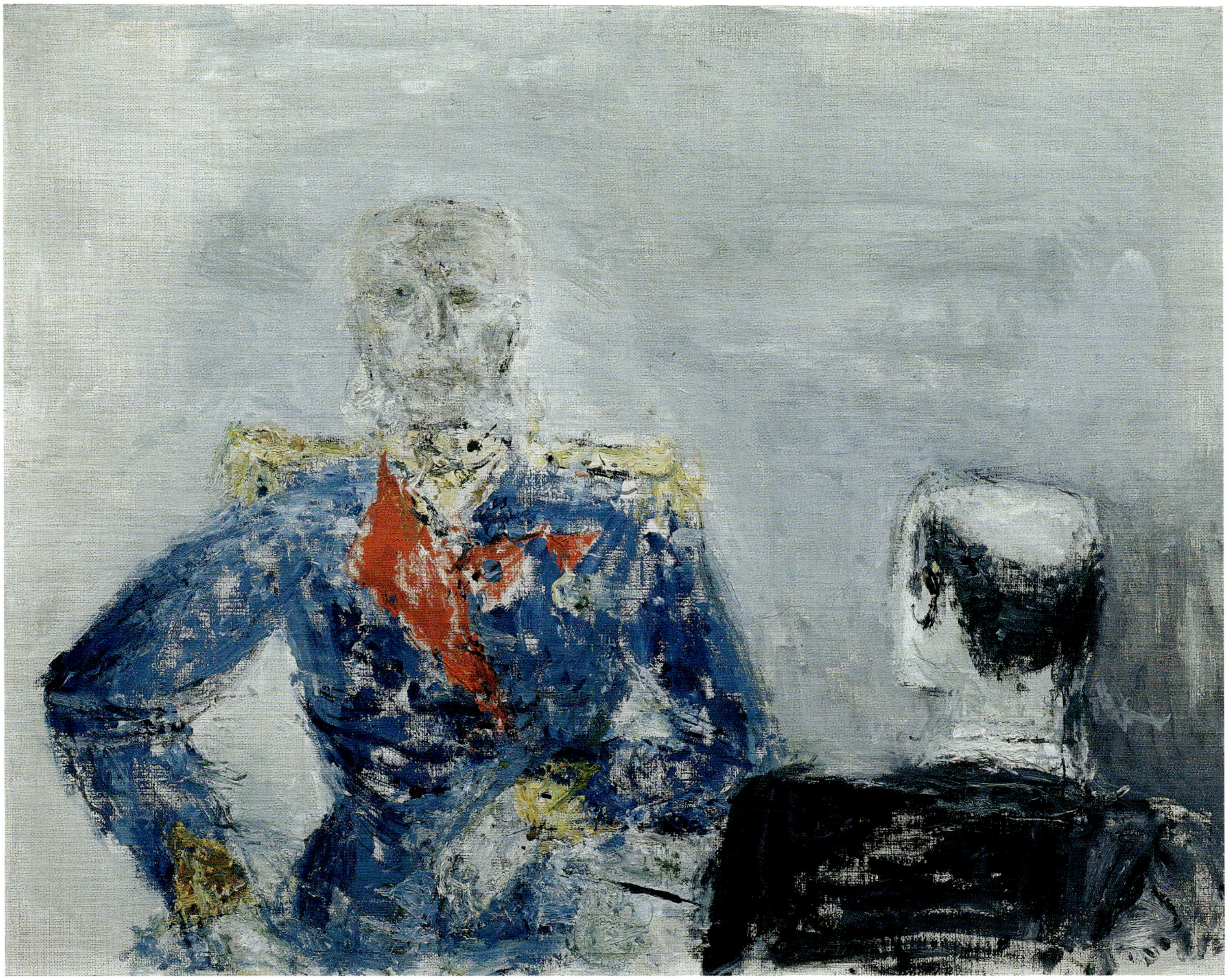

Wilhelm Thöny
General and Diplomat, c. 1930–40
Belvedere, Vienna

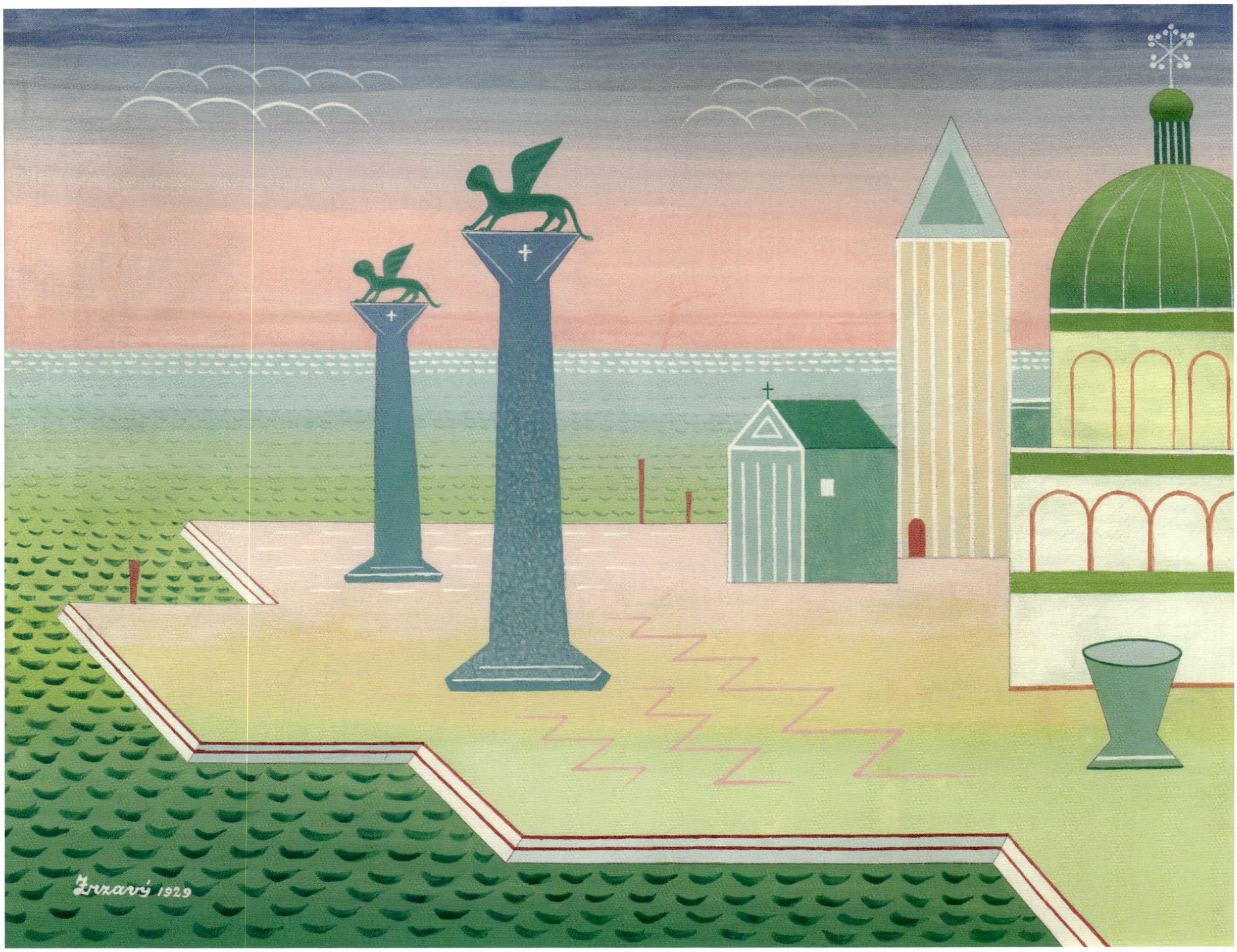

Jan Zrzavý
Piazza San Marco, Venice, 1929
Belvedere, Vienna,
on permament loan from
the Rotter Collection

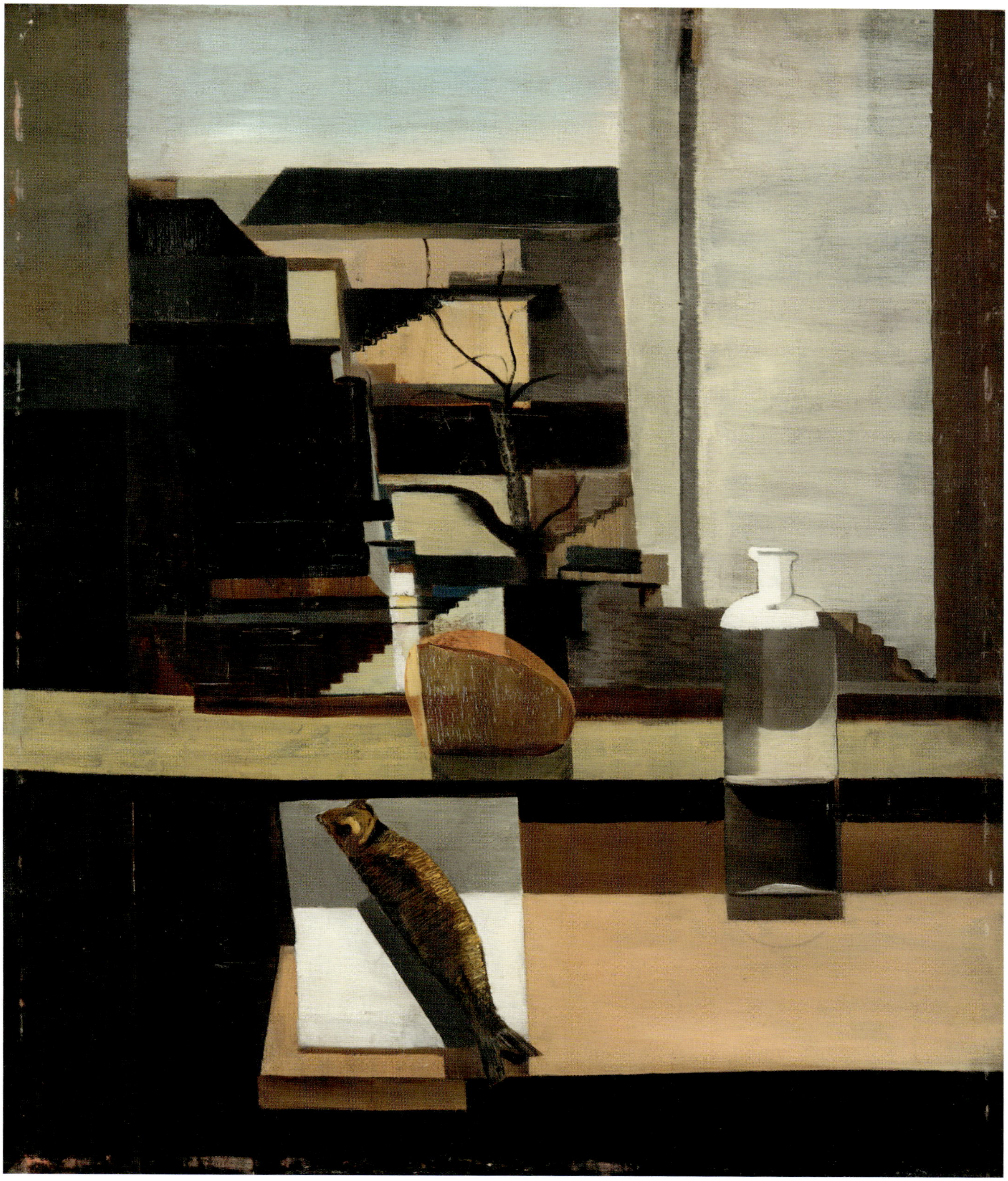

Ernő Schubert
Suburb, 1928–32
Museum of Fine Arts—Hungarian
National Gallery, Budapest

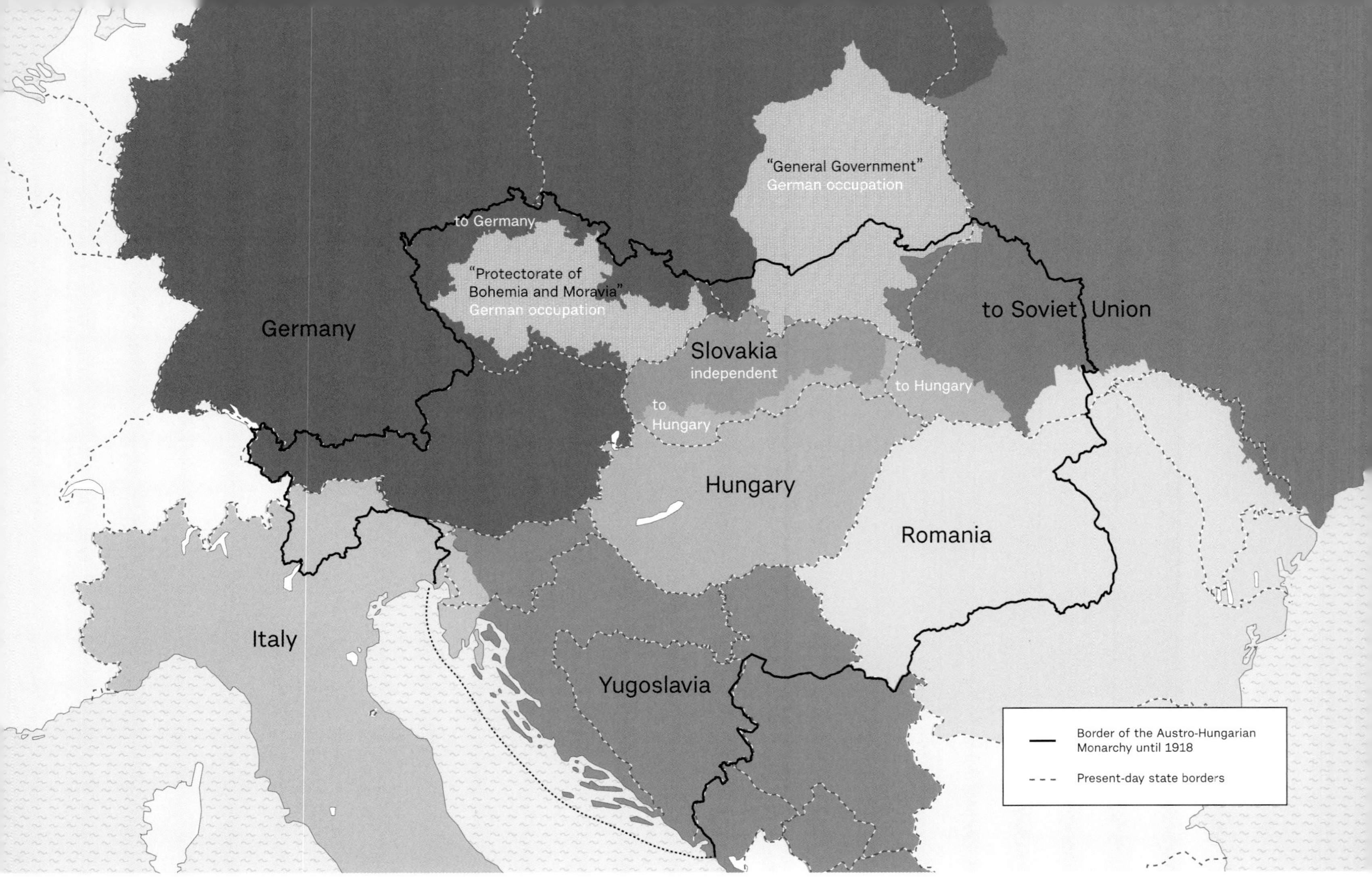
"General Government"
German occupation
to Germany
"Protectorate of
Bohemia and Moravia"
German occupation
Germany
Slovakia
independent
to Soviet Union
to Hungary
to
Hungary
Hungary
Romania
Italy
Yugoslavia
Border of the Austro-Hungarian Monarchy until 1918
Present-day state borders

nation—národ:

Národ, společenská skup., která si na zákl. urč. znaků objektivních a v duchu jisté ideologie uvědomuje, že tvoří celek, rozdílný od takových skup. jiných, a která má tendenci vytvořiti si vlastní stát. Žádný objektivní znak ani kombinace takových znaků nemohou samy o sobě vytvořiti pojem **n**-a. Znakem **n**-a není tedy: 1. řeč, ježto něk. **n**-ů mívá často řeč společnou a přesto se pokládají za **n**-y rúz. (*frc.* mluví Valoni, Frc. a část Švýc.); kdežto jiní **n**-ové mluví něk. jazyky a pokládají se za **n.** jeden (Američané, Švýc., Židé); 2. rasa, neboť každý nynější **n.** je výsledkem složitého rasového křížení; 3. kultura, ježto kult. celky často **n**-ní hranici přesahují n. se s ní kříží (ukazují to nesnáze v **n**-ních státech, sloučených po Svět. vál. z růz. kult. oblastí); 4. dějiny n. tradice, neboť části **n**-ů dnes jednotných měly často odlišný historický vývoj (Češi a Slováci, Italové); 5. stát n. náb., neboť dosud žije mn. **n**-ů n. jejich částí v státech cizích a hranice náb. se neshodují s hranicemi **n**-ními. Kromě toho se setkáváme i uvnitř **n**-ních celků se mn. odchylkami (jedn. dialekty, menší oblasti kult.), jež jednotnost objektivních znaků **n**-a vel. porušují. Znakem **n**-a jest tedy jen vědomí osobitého celku, vznikající v duchu urč. ideologie, jež si někt. z oněch objektivních znaků vybírá za svůj zákl. ...

Masarykův slovník náučný. Lidová encyklopedie všeobecných vědomostí. Díl V, (Prague, 1931), p. 46

národ, a || zastar. -u, 1. mn. (všechny) -dy || (všichni) -dové, m. = společenstvo lidí stejného jazyka, kultury, často tvořících i jeden stát; zdrob. *-růdek*, -dku, m.; *národní* [*-ně*]: n. vědomí, myšlenka, stát, majetek, svátek, škola ...; *N.* museum (v Praze), listy, rada, shromáždění (= čsl. parlament); pracovati, uvědomiti se -ně; 2 stup. *-nější*: nejnárodnější svatý (Ner.); *-dnář*, -e, m., počesť. slov. *narodniar* = národovec, člen sloven. národní politické strany; **-dník*, -a, m. = národovec (Kollár); *-dnický*: -ké umění (šal.); *-národniti*, 3. mn. -ní, slož. dokon. *od-* = zbaviti národního vědomí; od- se = ztratiti národ. vědomí; *z-* co = učiniti národním, státním, znacionalisovati; *národnost*, -i, ž., 1. = národní příslušnost: býti české, německé... -sti; 2. = národ, hlavně část národa ve státě, kde má převahu národ jiný: německá n. u nás; ...

Pavel Váša/František Trávníček, *Slovník jazyka Českého. L–Ž*, (Prague, 1937), p. 1054

Czech

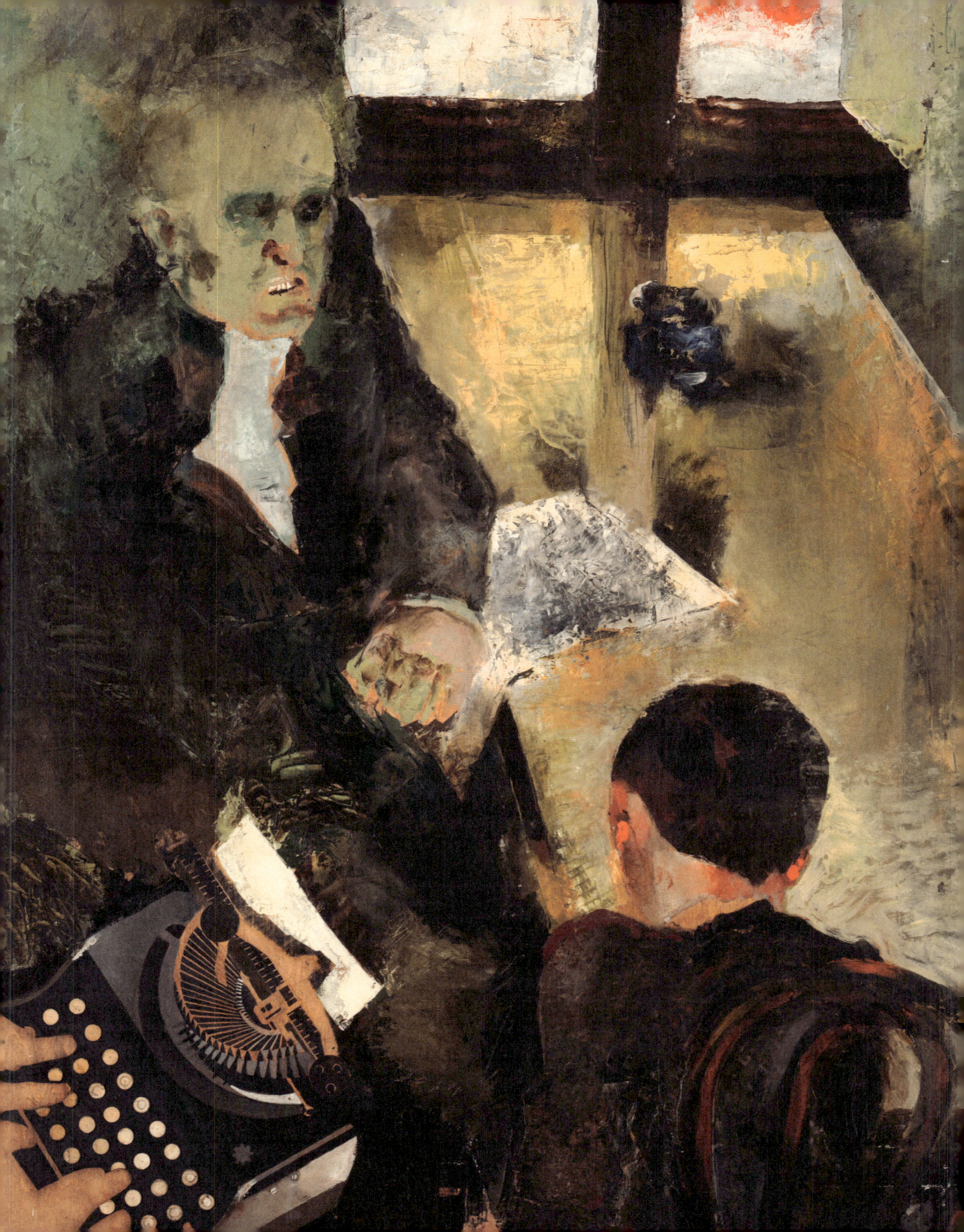

Friedl Dicker-Brandeis, *Interrogation I*, 1934 (detail), Jewish Museum in Prague

F Emigration—Persecution—Resistance

Migration: Motivation and Artists' Fates

Alexander Klee

This essay looks at the diverse and often complex circumstances leading to the emigration of artists between 1914 and 1938, particularly with reference to the Austro-Hungarian Monarchy and its successor states, such as Austria, Czechoslovakia, and Hungary. It takes no account of the internal migration within Austria-Hungary and the attraction of centers like Budapest, Prague, or Vienna.[1]

Although the reasons for migration were usually diverse, some basic patterns can be discerned in the decision to migrate and the manner of its accomplishment. A list of these patterns was compiled by Jochen Oltmer, although only a few of them apply specifically to artists. Some of these aspects merge, while additional motives can also be identified. As each case and fate was distinctive, only tendencies can be described, rather than statistically verifiable generalizations.[2] The main reasons for migration by artists during the time of the Austro-Hungarian Monarchy and in the successor states between the wars may be summed up as follows:[3]

- *Labor migration* in search of work
- *Training and education migration* in search of further qualifications and artistic development
- *Forced migration* as a result of political, ethnic, racist, or religious persecution

This categorization needs to be seen in its historical and political context, in this case the period from 1914 to around 1938. Within this period, certain phases, such as the outbreak of World War I, its end in 1918, the dwindling power of democratic forces in the early 1930s, and the increased power of populist movements leading to the rise of dictatorships, forced artists to migrate and left deep traces in their lives. The individual fate of some of the artists presented in this exhibition offers good examples of this phenomenon.

Artists left Austria-Hungary even before World War I, in many cases to further their artistic development, for example in Paris. This was the case with František Kupka, who followed László Mednyánszky, Ivan Meštrović, Alfons Mucha, and József Rippl-Rónai to the French capital. They generally passed through Vienna or Munich, which propelled them to continue to the center of the avant-garde in Paris. In line with typical migration scenarios, Kupka moved to Paris to look up Mucha, and Étienne Beothy to study under Rippl-Rónai. Networks of artists were created there, founded on unifying elements such as language or background.

Economic reasons also incited artists to emigrate. Vojtěch Preissig traveled to the USA in 1910, remaining there until 1930, and Adolf Hölzel accepted a position as professor of composition at the Royal Württemberg Academy of Fine Arts. Later on, Frederick Kiesler and Erika Giovanna Klien moved to New York, Walter Trier and Max Oppenheimer went to Berlin, and Anton Kolig obtained a position, like Hölzel, at the Academy in Stuttgart.

In many cases, migration was prompted by war. Max Oppenheimer, for example, moved to neutral Switzerland in 1915, while fellow artists Egon Schiele, Oskar Kokoschka, and Anton Kolig had to serve in the military. Emil Filla fled in 1914 from Paris via Belgium to the Netherlands. Exceptionally, František Kupka and Otto Gutfreund fought for the Entente, while most of their colleagues, such as Bohumil Kubišta or Jan Štursa, were on the side of the Central Powers.

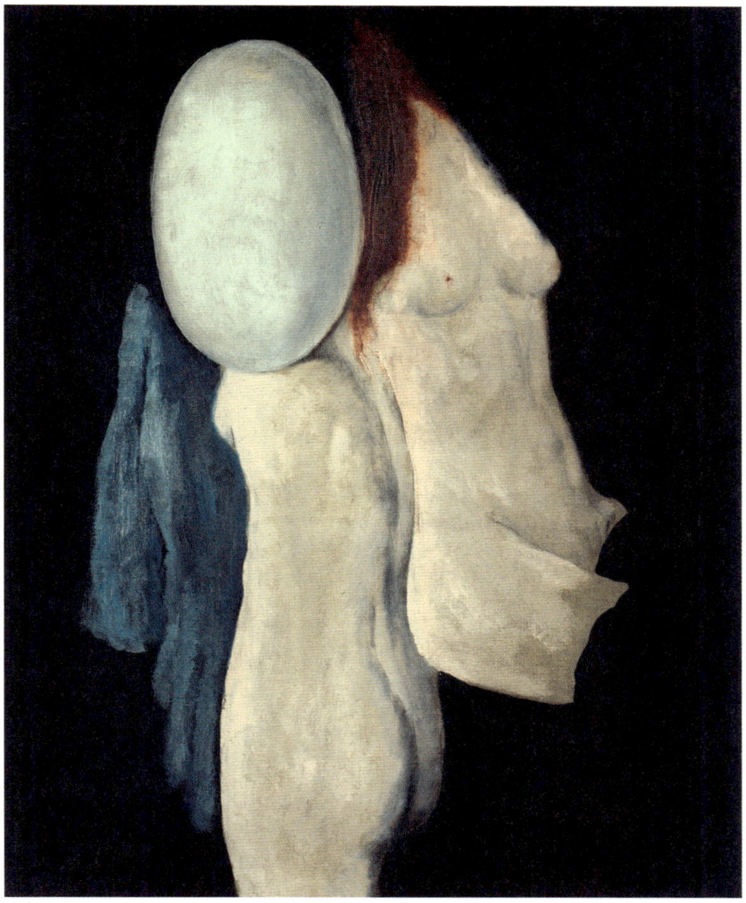

Fig. 1
Josef Šíma
Europe, 1927
Moravian Gallery
in Brno

The political collapse of the Austro-Hungarian Monarchy resulted in the formation of new nation-states, which prompted further migrations, as was the case, for example, in Hungary. Traditional focal points, of which Vienna was one, became network nodes and first ports of call. After the defeat of the Hungarian Republic of Councils in 1919 most of the members of the Hungarian avant-garde—Róbert Berény, Mihály Bíró, Sándor Bortnyik, Béla Kádár, Lajos Kassák, László Moholy-Nagy, Lajos Tihanyi, and Béla Uitz, for example—settled in Vienna.

The network spread further to Berlin. This explains the strong presence of former citizens of the Austro-Hungarian Monarchy at the Bauhaus: Herbert Bayer, Sándor Bortnyik, Marcel Breuer, Friedl Dicker-Brandeis, László Moholy-Nagy, Farkas Molnár, Franz Singer, and Andor Weininger, to mention but a few.

Although Berlin also exerted a strong attraction on artists from other countries of former Austria-Hungary, such as Herbert Boeckl, Ernst Neuschul, Fritz Schwarz-Waldegg, and Rudolf Wacker, Paris had not lost its reputation after World War I as a platform for the avant-garde. A significant number of Surrealist artists moved there,[4] including Josef Šíma

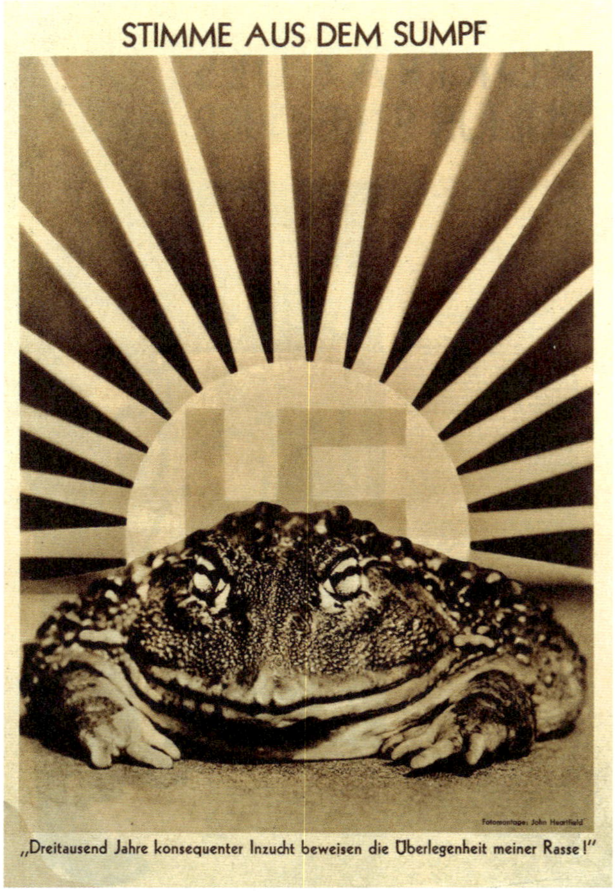

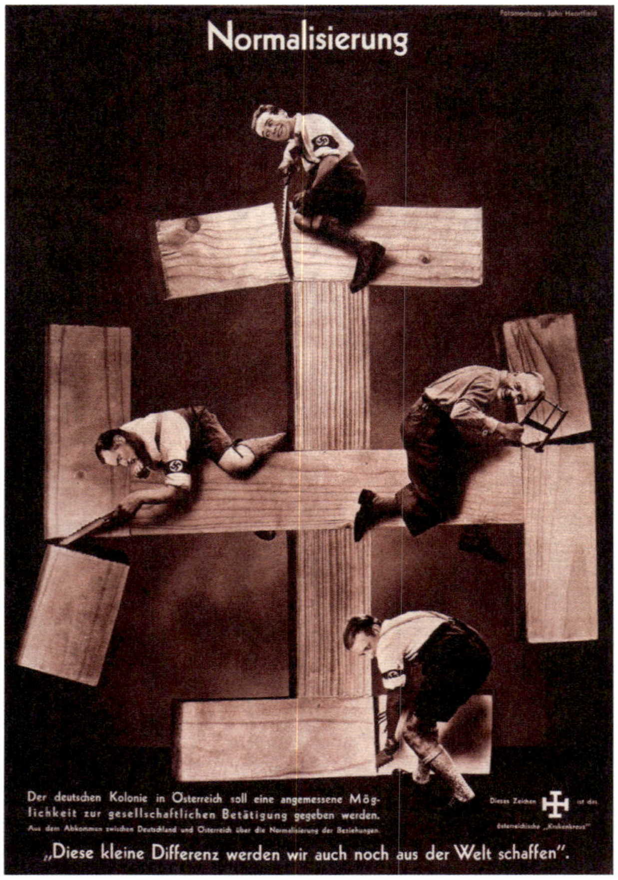

Fig. 2
John Heartfield
Voice of the Swamp
From *Arbeiter-Illustrierte-Zeitung* (AIZ), no. 12, Prague 1936

Fig. 3
John Heartfield
Normalization
From *Arbeiter-Illustrierte-Zeitung* (AIZ), no. 31, Prague 1936

(fig. 1), Jindřich Štyrský, Toyen, Wolfgang Paalen, and Frederick Kiesler.[5] They were in close contact, united by their attachment to Surrealism, and there were also crossovers with Abstraction-Création,[6] represented by Paalen, František Foltýn, Lajos Tihanyi, Étienne Beothy, and others, members of the group associated with the Paris gallery Au sacré du printemps owned by Hans Effenberger from Vienna.

Artists will have been assisted in their endeavors by the fact that contact and exchange of ideas in the centers like Paris, Prague, Budapest, Berlin, and Vienna had become much easier. Difficulties in communicating because of the new national borders after the war were compensated by the rise of art magazines and journals.[7]

Not only economic pressure, but also political and ethnic persecution increased between the wars. Eduard Bäumer emigrated with his family from Germany to Austria in 1933, and John Heartfield (figs. 2, 3) from Berlin to Prague. Otto Neurath fled from the Dollfuss regime in Austria in 1934 via the Netherlands to Britain, and Mihály Bíró and Oskar Kokoschka emigrated from Austria to Czechoslovakia. They were to be followed by many other artists (fig. 4).

In 1938, after the occupation of rump Czechoslovakia, those who could fled to Britain (Gerhart Frankl, Oskar Kokoschka; fig. 5, Franz Singer), Switzerland (Max Oppenheimer, Fritz Wotruba), or the USA (Herbert Bayer, Franz Lerch, Wilhelm Thöny, in 1939 also Wolfgang Paalen).

A few artists, including Beothy, Preissig, and Nande Vidmar, were active in the resistance. Many were murdered on account of their political persuasion, religion, or the beliefs of their ancestors, or died violent deaths (Mihály Bíró, Josef Čapek, Friedl Dicker-Brandeis, Zdeněk Dvořák, István Farkas, Alfons Mucha, Vojtěch Preissig, Fritz Schwarz-Waldegg). Only a few survived internment—Emil Filla was one—or remained hidden in Austria, as was the case with the family of Eduard Bäumer.

For many, the countries that had offered them shelter became their new homes: the USA in the case of Herbert Bayer, Marcel Breuer, and László Moholy-Nagy, and Great Britain in the case of Marie-Louise von Motesiczky, Otto Neurath, and Ernst Neuschul. Art networks also formed in the new countries: For example, Marie-Louise von Motesiczky was in contact in Britain with Elias Canetti, Mary Duras, who lived nearby, and Oskar Kokoschka.

Others were fortunate enough to be able to choose where they emigrated to, be it for personal reasons, the better living conditions or the fertile artistic environment. Some settled in the new countries: Étienne Beothy, František Kupka, Lilly Steiner, Lajos Tihanyi, Toyen, Victor Vasarely, and Milivoj Uzelac, for example, in France, and Paris in particular.

Others, by contrast, failed to find their feet: Max Oppenheimer, for example (fig. 6), Oskar Kokoschka, or Ivan Meštrović. Return was difficult or impossible for some. Gerhart Frankl

In a free and liberal environment, migration can therefore be seen as a stimulus for progress.

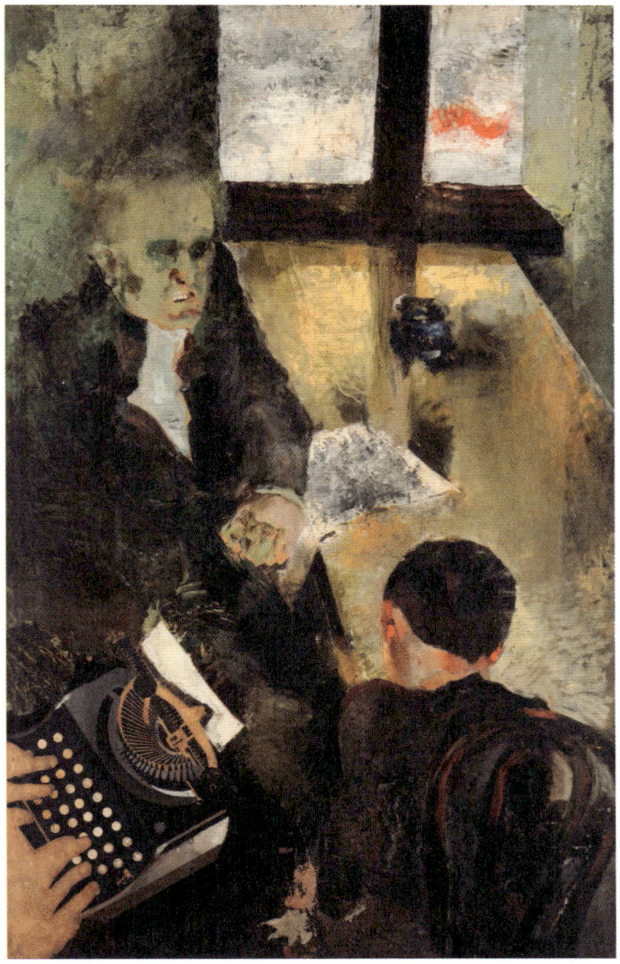

Fig. 4
Friedl Dicker-Brandeis
Interrogation I, 1934
Jewish Museum
in Prague

Fig. 5
Oskar Kokoschka
The Red Egg, 1940
National Gallery
in Prague

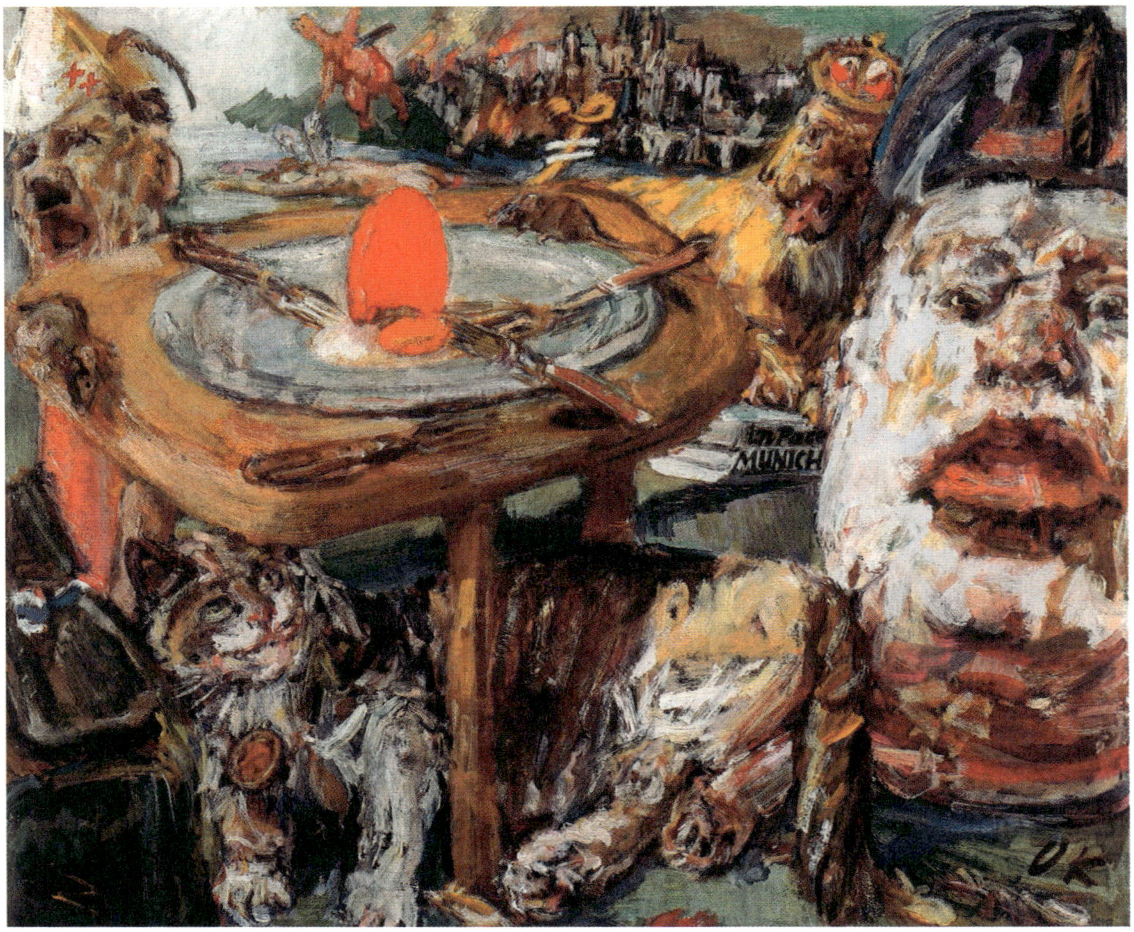

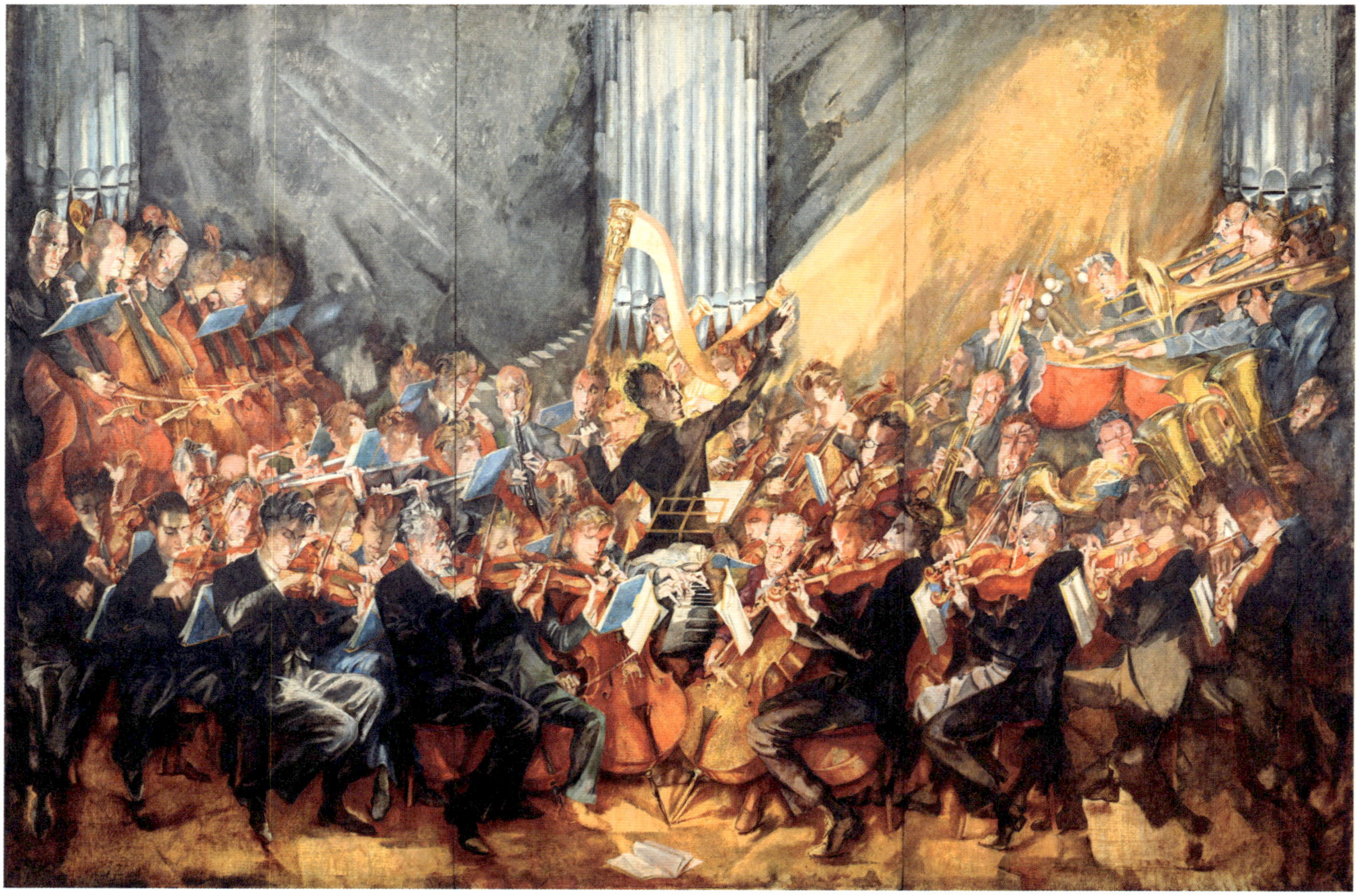

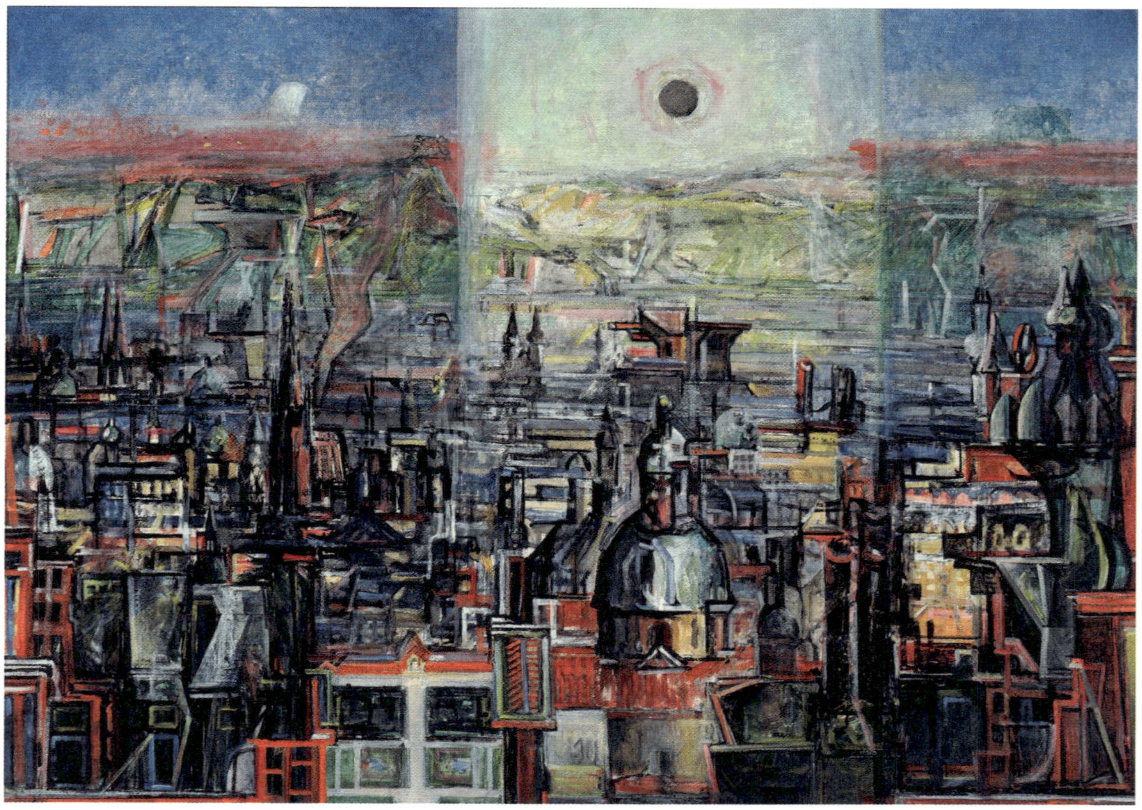

Fig. 6
Max Oppenheimer
The Philharmonic Orchestra, 1926–52
Property of the Artothek des Bundes, permanent loan to the Belvedere, Vienna

Fig. 7
Gerhart Frankl
Revisiting Vienna II, 1947/48
Belvedere, Vienna

(fig. 7) failed in his attempt to return to Vienna, and Mary Duras, who returned to Prague in 1945, emigrated again in 1963, this time to Austria. The consequences of the forced migration left their mark on those affected, leaving them permanently unsettled and restless, their careers interrupted, in many cases with lasting impact.

The forced migration as a result of dictatorship and war prevented many artists from continuing to develop, and in some cases they were not able to resume their activities until the early 1950s.

Under politically stable conditions, migration gave artists a large degree of freedom of movement and scope for development and exchange of ideas with like-minded colleagues. Until 1938, this openness led to progressive developments in art. In a free and liberal environment, migration can therefore be seen as a stimulus for progress.

1 Moritz Csaky, *Das Gedächtnis der Städte: Kulturelle Verflechtungen—Wien und die urbanen Milieus in Zentraleuropa* (Vienna/Cologne/Graz, 2010); Elisabeth Röhrlich, ed., *Migration und Innovation um 1900: Perspektiven auf das Wien der Jahrhundertwende* (Vienna/Cologne/Weimar, 2016).

2 Jochen Oltmer, "Einführung: Europäische Migrationsverhältnisse und Migrationsregime," in Jochen Oltmer and Ute Frevert, eds., *Europäische Migrationsregime: Geschichte und Gesellschaft—Zeitschrift* für *Historische Sozialwissenschaft*, 35th year, no. 1, 2009, p. 8.

3 Jochen Oltmer, *Geschichte und Zukunft der Gegenwart* (Darmstadt, 2017), pp. 30–31.

4 See essay by Judith Elisabeth Weiss in this catalogue.

5 Figurative painters, such as Jenő Barcsay, István Farkas, Marie-Louise von Motesiczky, and Lilly Steiner, were also attracted to Paris.

6 See essay by Flóra Mészáros in this catalogue.

7 See essay by Gábor Dobó and Merse Pál Szeredi in this catalogue.

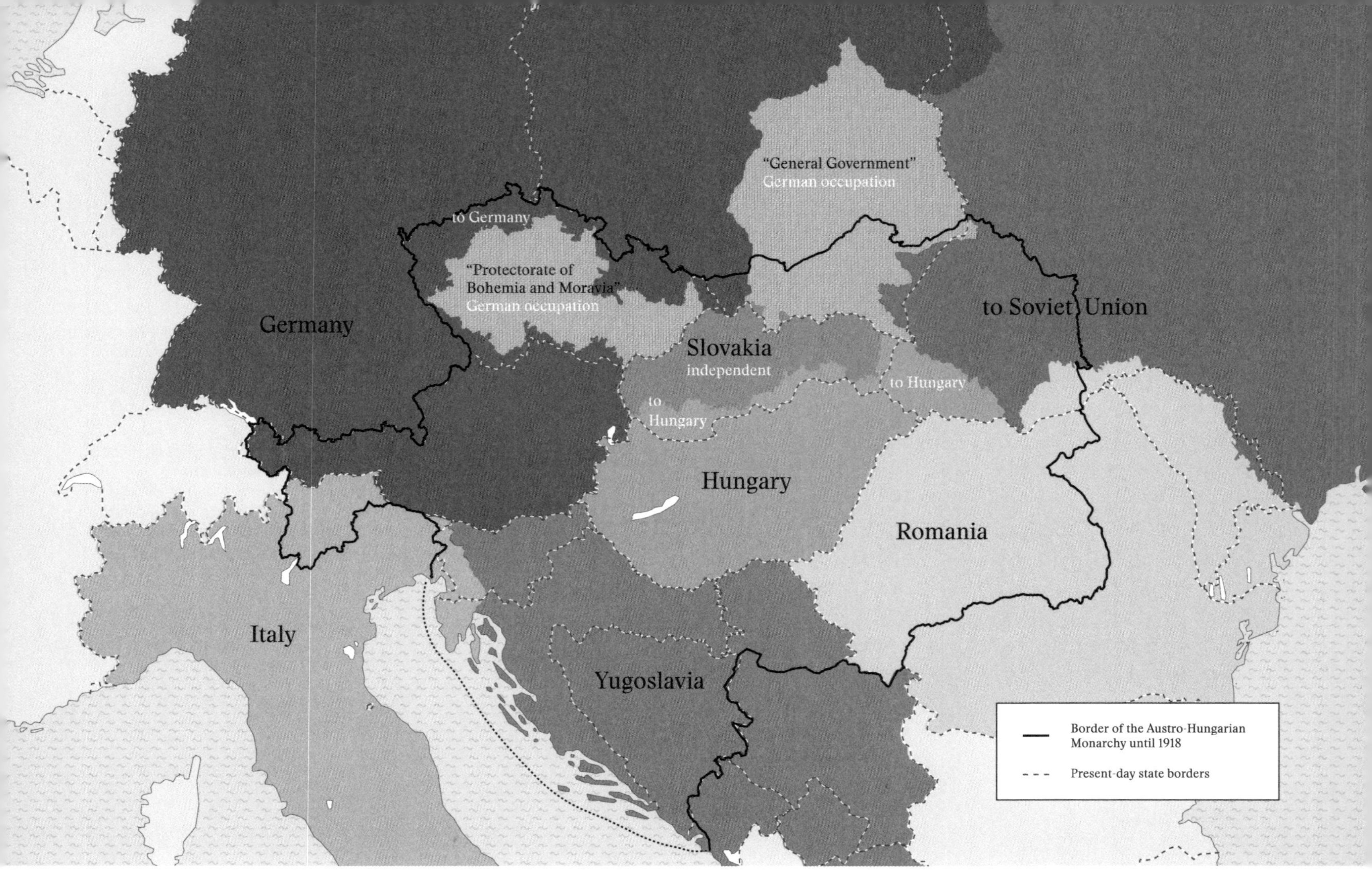

F 1938–39 From Munich Agreement
to World War II.

border—határ:

Határ, az a képzelt v. jelzett vonal, mely valamely területet körülfog, vagy az a terü-letsáv, amely két állam közigazgatási területét elválasztja egymástól. ... A H.-ok természetének nagy hatása van a népek történetére. Politikai tekintetben legked-vezőbbek a zártabb H.-ok, azaz olyanok, amelyek a területhez képest minél rövidebbek, minél inkább megközelítik a körvonalat, továbbá a hegységi és egyéb természeti H.-ok, mert a H.-ok hosszával és könnyü átlépésével egyenes arányban van a más népekkel való surlódások, összekoccanások valószinüsége. Nagy országok politikailag biztosabbak ebben a tekintetben is, mint a hasonló alakú és határú kis országok, mert nagyságukhoz képest kisebb a H.-uk. A más népekkel való érintkezés szempontjából, a művelődés, kölcsönös érintkezés, csiszolódás, kereskedelem szempontjából éppen *ellenkezőleg* a nyiltabb, hosszab H.-ok, tehát a kisebb területek kedvezőbbek. Magyarország H.-a lefolyt századokban többször ment át lényeges átalakuláson.

Révai Nagy Lexikona. Az Ismeretek Enciklopédiája. IX. Kötet. Gréc–Herold, (Budapest, 1913), p. 578

Határ, a téregységeket elválasztó vonal v. sáv megjelölése. A földrajzi tájegységek elválasztóját *természeti*, a kitűzött politikai területekét *politikai* H.-nak szokták nevezni. Utóbbi éles vonal, míg a természeti H. csak a legritkább esetben, éles sziklagerinceken vonalszerű, rendesen szélesebb sáv. Tengerek, sivatagok, mocsarak, erdőségek az alacsonyabb polgárosodás területein egész szélességükben H. szerepét játszák. Ilyen volt a középkori magy. gyepűelve, a kitűzött H.-vonal, gyepű mögötti lakatlan terület. Mesterséges H.-nak az olyanokat nevezik, melyeket az önkény a természeti tájegységek tekintetbe vétele nélkül szabott ki. Közöttük legszembetűnőbbek azok a többnyire a térképezés előtt készült mértani (fokhálózati) vonalak, melyek a tényleges birtokbavételt megelőzték (gyarmatállamok.) Prinz Gy.

László Dormándi / Vilmos Juhász, *Uj lexikon. A tudás és a gyakorlati élet egyetemes enciklopédiája 6 kötetben*, (Budapest, 1936), pp. 1677–78.

Hungarian

▸
Otto Neurath
Mächte der Erde
From *Gesellschaft und Wirtschaft. Bildstatistisches Elementarwerk*, Leipzig, 1930 (detail)

Mächte der Erde

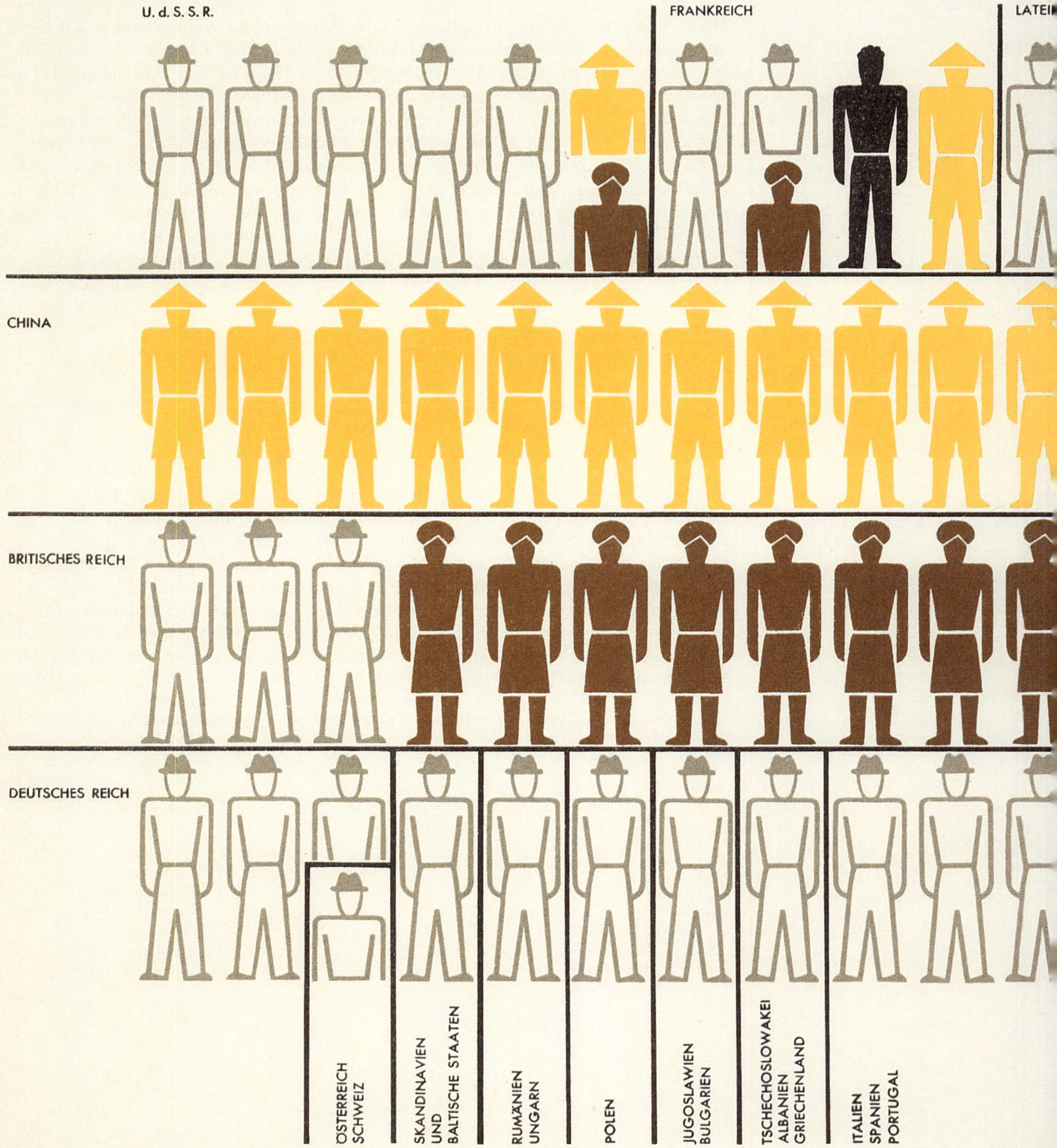

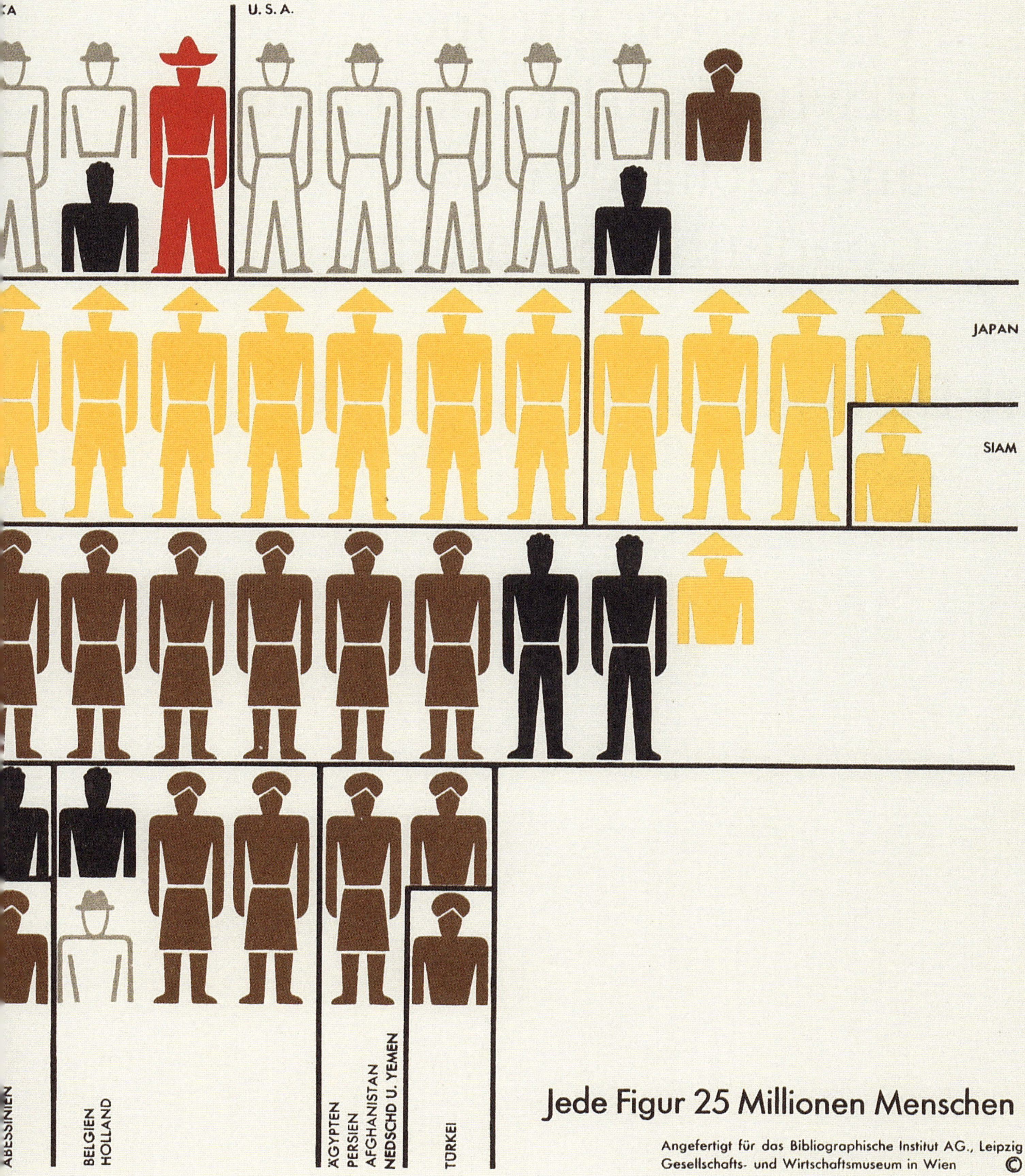

Jede Figur 25 Millionen Menschen

Angefertigt für das Bibliographische Institut AG., Leipzig
Gesellschafts- und Wirtschaftsmuseum in Wien ©

Gesellschaft or *Gemeinschaft?* Visions for Europe: Erwin Hanslik, Otto Neurath, and Richard von Coudenhove-Kalergi

Kurt De Boodt and Paul Dujardin

The First World War cut straight through the transnational networks of avant-garde artists. Although the three basic movements had a national point of departure—Cubism in France, Expressionism in Germany, Futurism in Italy—the artistic exchanges within and between cities ran across the positions adopted by these countries during the First World War: the conflict between the Central Powers and the Allies.

The avant-garde movements in smaller countries like Belgium and in the crown lands of Austria-Hungary only really broke loose after the war. Painters, who had been under the spell of Neo-Impressionism for too long, hungered for the new art. After the suspension of hostilities, they molded the pre-war art movements to their will, completed by Dada and Geometric Abstraction, which had emerged during the war (mainly) in the neutral countries. After the Armistice, the field was wide open. New avant-garde magazines, international congresses, the artistic diaspora, and humanist movements such as Clarté made the art networks even more international than before. The new world map in no way corresponded to the new artistic mapping based on kindred spirits. Take, for example, *Le monde au temps des surréalistes*, the world map published in 1929 in the Surrealism issue of Brussels' *Variétés: Revue mensuelle illustrée de l'esprit contemporain*: it literally reshapes the world through the eyes of the Surrealists.

Avant-garde, nationalism, and a hunger for a united Europe do not exclude each other. It would be hard to imagine the avant-garde explosion in Flanders after the First World War without the Flemish Movement, which the war had rekindled.[1] The demand for more Flemish autonomy was essentially European in purpose and intent: Flanders within Belgium within Europe. Not until the first state reform in 1970 did Belgium become the long-aspired federal state. And the Belgian state structure remains work in progress. Even after six state reforms, refederalization is still a regular item on the political agenda.

Belgium and the Danube Monarchy are sometimes referred to as laboratories for Europe, the economic and political "peace project" embarked upon after the Second World War, with all the internal and external tensions this entailed. After World War I, little Belgium had continued to exist as a buffer country enlarged by the East Cantons, while the defeated Austria-Hungary collapsed. The shot fired by the Bosnian-Serb nationalist Gavrilo Princip on June 28, 1914, had hit its target. Besides killing Archduke Franz Ferdinand, the bullet triggered an international chain reaction which provoked a world war and, in 1918, dealt the final blow to the Imperial and Royal Monarchy—the Dual Monarchy of Austria-Hungary—satirically transformed into Kakania in Robert Musil's *The Man Without Qualities*. The Habsburg myth was born, an idealized vision of an empire where different peoples lived together in harmony, irrespective of borders.

What was envisioned during and shortly after the First World War was a European community based on a global citizenship. Outlined below are the world views of three former Habsburgers: cultural geographer Erwin Hanslik's *Weltkulturgesellschaft* (Society of World Culture), Otto Neurath's *Gesellschafts- und Wirtschaftsmuseum* (Museum for Society and Economy) and his belief in the solidarity of urban communities, and Count Richard Coudenhove-Kalergi's *Pan-Europa*, as a forerunner of the Council of Europe and the European Union. Each in his own way pondered on society in the new, post-war Europe. How could the international spirit find acceptance again among a people torn apart by war? How could a *Gemeinschaft* (community) be created from the European *Gesellschaft* (society)?

ACT 1—ERWIN HANSLIK: *MITTELEUROPA* AND THE *WELTKULTURGESELLSCHAFT*

During the First World War, Oskar Kokoschka became artistic director of the Weltkulturakademie (Academy of World Culture) in Vienna. The academy was one chapter in a megalomaniac project: the Weltkulturgesellschaft (Society of World Culture) under the chairmanship of Erwin Hanslik. A professor of cultural geography in Vienna, Hanslik explains the ambitious plan in a typewritten document in 1918.[2] The document begins by stating that the most urgent challenge of the day is the development of an all-embracing world culture. That is the only way we can resolve the differences brought about by the world war. Nations are not in a position to create a universal culture, since they are engaged in an ongoing battle to maintain or extend their political influence: "Such a task can only be approached—and undertaken successfully—by a society liberated from the political limitations of a single state; in a sense, this kind of society fulfills the function of a world state." All ranks of civil society, but first and foremost scientists and artists, should join forces to achieve the society of world culture. In this way, according to artistic director Oskar Kokoschka, one witnesses the growing "awareness of visions."

Also, a universal culture has to start somewhere. And where better than in multicultural Vienna? "The geographic location of Vienna, as well as its old and rich culture that has grown up out of the commingling of races, make the city the ideal starting point for this purpose." Establishing a world culture during a world war is rather utopic: it requires scientific research, the exchange of knowledge and thus a suitable organization. The Institut für Kulturforschung (Institute for Cultural Research) was founded in 1915. The Forschungsinstitut für Osten und Oriënt (Oriental and Eastern Research Institute) followed a year later. There were even plans for a library, a publishing house, a film workshop, a travel agency, a world school, a biographical archive, an ethics department, and a museum of world knowledge, but most of these never progressed beyond good intentions. However, with the cooperation of leading figures from Vienna's intellectual elite, the

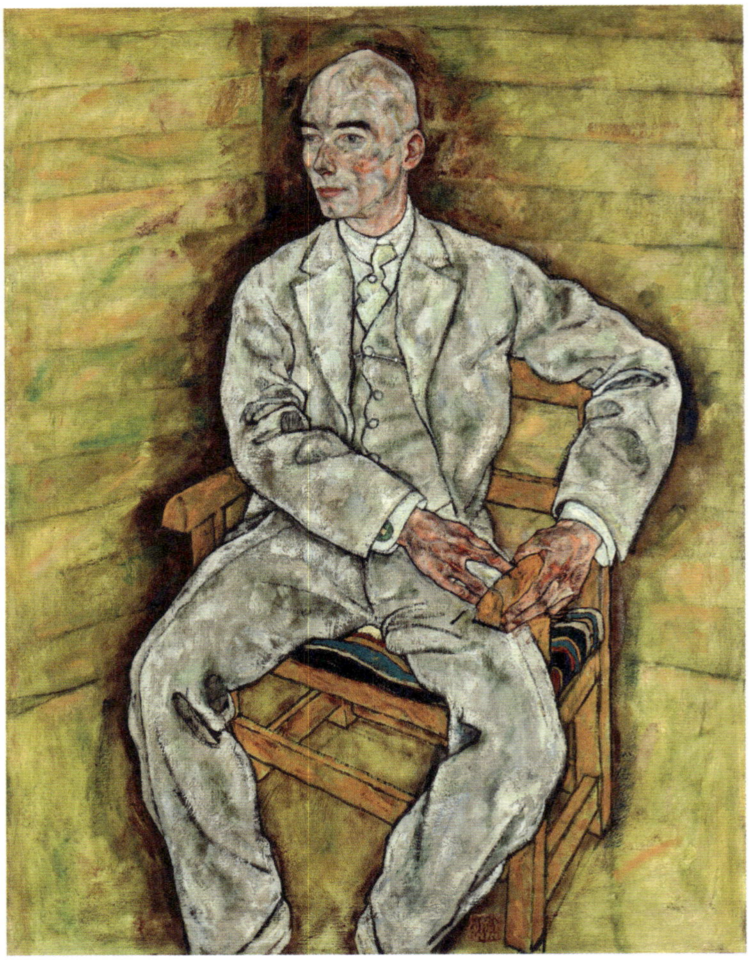

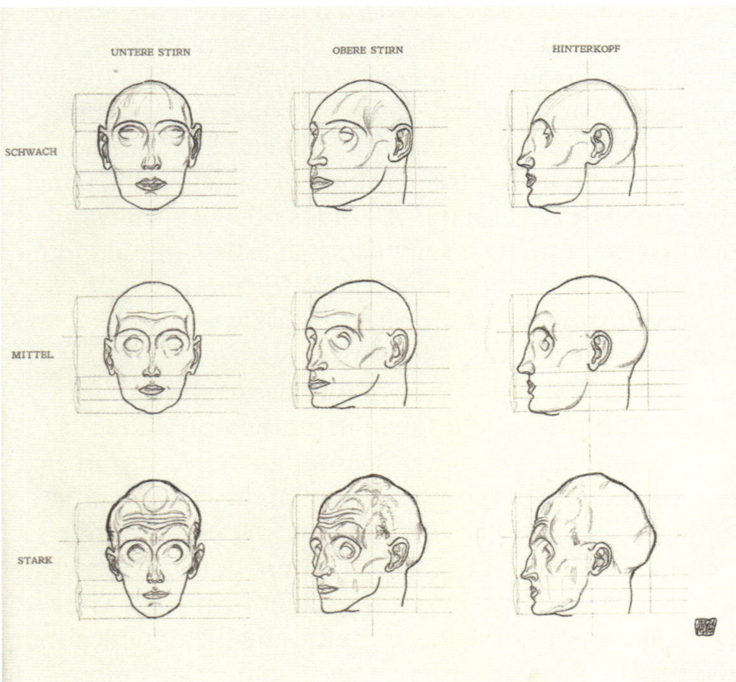

Weltkulturakademie did materialize. The driving forces behind the academy were Kokoschka, Jozef Hoffmann, and Franz Cizek. The year Hanslik was typing out his document, three founding members had just died: Otto Wagner, Egon Schiele, and Gustav Klimt. Vienna had lost three of its most famous artists. The post-war society of world culture had to be established *beyond Klimt*.

So far so good. The intentions sound highly idealistic and humanistic. The cultural model seemed to bring world peace within arm's reach. But in the background Hanslik was toying with very different, anti-modernist influences and downright racist fantasies. As professor of cultural geography, he was greatly influenced by Friedrich Ratzel, the founder of anthropogeography. Ratzel developed a social Darwinism which taught that the natural environment has a determining influence on people. So peoples—*Völker*—are not equal nor equally able to act. The world population can be divided into a hierarchy of civilizations. This pseudoscientific typology was increasingly applied politically and played out imperialistically. Just as there are strong and weak animal species, so too are there strong and weak nations. The weaker specimens will become extinct. In 1901, Ratzel coined the concept of *Lebensraum* or "space to live": the space a people needs to meet its requirements for food and raw materials. A country can also look for that space beyond its borders. The British and the French built colonial empires. There was a growing consensus among Pan-Germans à la Ernst Hasse, author of the visionary *Großdeutschland und Mitteleuropa um das Jahr 1950* (1895), that the most natural development for Germany lay not on the other side of an ocean but in Eastern Europe. According to the Pan-German discourse, there was a border colony for the taking in the East. The term *Mitteleuropa*—Central Europe—acquired an imperialistic undertone.[3] It no longer related to the region that roughly corresponded to the borders of the Danube Monarchy, but to an alliance between both "German" states.

The world war brought both states together in the same camp. This opened up post-war prospects. In the political pamphlet *Mitteleuropa* (1915), the German liberal politician Friedrich Naumann presented the confederate model as a means of restoring peace and prosperity. In this shared economic and cultural space, the large and the small nations would live side by side on an equal footing. In *Mitteleuropa*, social justice would go beyond internal military and economic gain. Neither would Germanization take the upper hand in the *vielgegliedertes Bruderland*—the brotherhood of many members. On an administrative level, decisive Germany would have to take the drowsy Double Monarchy under its wing. Naumann: "Mid-Europe will be German at the core, will voluntarily use the German language, which is known all over the world and is already the language of intercourse within Central Europe, but from the outset it must display tolerance and flexibility with regard to all the neighboring languages associated with it. For only in this way can the fundamental harmony grow

Fig. 1
Egon Schiele
Victor Ritter von Bauer, 1918
Belvedere, Vienna

Fig. 2
Egon Schiele
Kopfformen (*Head Shapes*), 1917
From Erwin Hanslik,
Wesen der Menschheit, Vienna, 1917

that is essential for a great state, pressed and threatened from all sides."[4]

The anthropogeographer Erwin Hanslik (pseudo-)scientifically underpinned Naumann's *Mitteleuropa*. In studies such as *Die Kulturpflichten Wiens und Österreich-Ungarns* and *Österreich, Erde und Geist,* Hanslik emphasized the cultural strength of the eastern areas of the Danube Monarchy. Hanslik was born in Bielitz in the crown land of Galicia, now Bielsko-Biała in Southern Poland, and was not immune to nostalgic ideas about a new Byzantine Empire. In his mind, the eastern part of Austria-Hungary would determine the Europe of the future, but this had to happen under German-speaking rule. Only then could the gap between East and West be closed.[5]

Wesen der Menschheit appeared at the end of 1917 as the first volume in a series of publications by the Institut für Kulturforschung. Erwin Hanslik took the bold but very slippery path from the macro to the micro level: from the Earth's surface through a range of environmental factors to typologies of peoples and races. He visualized all his findings in world maps. The "Talent" chapter features photographs and drawings of skulls. Egon Schiele drew the *Kopfformen*—"head shapes" (figs. 1, 2): three skulls in frontal, three-quarter, and side view, ranging from "Weak," "Middling" to "Strong." On the basis of their skull, individuals were reduced to types, along the lines of Friedrich Ratzel's nations. It is still surprising that a portraitist like Schiele, with his keen eye for striking differences in cheekbones, pelvises, chests and buttocks, espoused this dubious theory. Franz Smola speaks of a quantum leap: "Imagine: all of a sudden, the Expressionist Schiele—the master of the expressive portrait, the great analyst of humanity's most intimate psychological conditions—invests his artistic energies in producing a schema of human physiognomy for an illustration in an academic paper. Now, as an artist, he is no longer to concern himself with the human face as the communicator of subjective messages, but is to focus solely on skull shape as an object of scientific analysis. In an empirical academic illustration of this nature, the human face is reduced to a schematic physiognomy and head shape becomes an empirical category defined by measurements of forehead height, nose length, and chin position." In several symmetrically constructed double portraits produced in 1917, Schiele appears to be more interested in a type than in the subjective disposition of the model.

As a "weak" and vulnerable individual, Hanslik became the victim of the intellectual climate and racial prejudice he had helped create with his research.

We can only surmise on the direction Schiele's art might have taken after the war. We do know Hanslik's fate. He developed psychological problems and ended up in Am Steinhof, an institution for mental disorders in Vienna. In 1940, together with thousands of fellow patients, he was deported and murdered by the Nazis. Thus, as a "weak" and vulnerable individual, he became a victim of the intellectual climate and racial prejudice he had helped create with his research. Hitler sought *Lebensraum im Osten*—"living space in the East"—for his Thousand-Year Reich. There was room in it for just one race: the Aryan.

ACT 2—OTTO NEURATH: THE GLOBAL POLIS AND THE ATLAS OF WORLD CULTURE

Otto Neurath saw the ideal city as giving rise to the future world community.[6] That was new. Usually, the anonymous city was regarded as a source of social alienation and standardization. *Gemeinschaft und Gesellschaft* (Community and Society, 1887), the influential study by his sociologist friend Ferdinand Tonniës, emphasized this dichotomy. *Gesellschaft* is founded on rational calculation, self-interest, and the standardization of human interaction. *Gemeinschaft* stems from a sense of kinship, trust, and empathy. The ideal environment for this is the village. His study of the economic situation during the Balkan Wars and the First World War led Neurath to conclude that this dichotomy no longer held true in the twentieth century. Modernity and a sense of community are not necessarily mutually exclusive. Paradoxically enough, it was the wars that led Neurath to this insight. War economies are highly inefficient. In a city cut off from the rest of the world an informal economy flourishes, based on trust and informal relationships. It is these sort of grassroots initiatives which today embody the urban reality of the commons: the barter and sharing economy, the swap shops, and a whole raft of citizens' initiatives.

In 1918, Neurath headed the General War and Economics Section of the Scientific Committee for War Economy in the Austrian War Ministry. As an exhibition maker, he set to work in Serbia and Hungary to spread the knowledge about war economy. In mid-1918, the German War Ministry invited him to become director of the Deutsches Kriegswirtschaftsmuseum (German Museum of War Economy) in Leipzig. Neurath advocated an interactive presentation that made use of a variety of visual media. He wanted to help shape a modern urban population that would understand the necessity of Taylorism while at the same time getting acquainted with the informal economy of local communities. August 1918 saw the opening of the Kriegswirtschaftsmuseum's first—and last—exhibition: *Weltblockade und Kriegswirtschaft* (World Blockade and War Economy). The war was coming to an end.

Otto Neurath had seen the light: Museums and exhibitions can visually highlight social relations and interactively convey a sense of solidarity to the working classes. His images were a form of *Bildung* (self-education or cultivation of the mind): only people who fully understand human relationships and their own role in the community are able to embrace solidarity. Statistics of all kinds should thus be communicated in a simple and universally intelligible manner. At the beginning of 1925, Neurath turned the Siedlungsmuseum (Settlement Museum) into the Gesellschafts- und Wirtschaftsmuseum (Museum for Society and Economy). Its educational purpose was much broader than simply providing information about town planning in Vienna. According to Neurath, the remit of the new museum was to inform the working masses about a raft of socio-economic issues: "Modern democracy demands that broad sections of the population should be objectively instructed in production, emigration, morality, interior design, unemployment, the fight against tuberculosis and alcoholism, diet, the importance of sports, physical, and mental development, schooling ... (and) the state of industry."[7] Neurath developed a new visual language of planar figures or geometrical shapes with well-defined contours (fig. 2). His principal rule for depicting statistical proportions was: "larger quantities = more symbols." The larger the numbers, the more figures were drawn. Color and background provided additional information. This system pioneered by Neurath was known as the "Vienna Method of Society and Economy," which in 1935 became the International System of Typographic Picture Education (ISOTYPE).

> "In my opinion, there are only three countries in Europe that might be considered 'visionary': Switzerland, Austria and Belgium."
>
> (Harald Szeemann)

Initially, Neurath wanted to show Vienna to the Viennese, Austria to the Austrians. But in an age of technology and reproducibility, a museum could also be reproduced in its entirety. His kind of museum was no longer concerned with uniqueness and the exclusiveness of the authentic art object, intended for a middle-class audience, but with the dissemination of visual information among the working classes. In 1927, the Gesellschafts- und Wirtschaftsmuseum found a permanent home in the Neues Rathaus in Vienna, where it became the base for world-wide operations. The architect Joseph Frank designed a modular system of wooden panels with built-in lighting which could be transported easily. Copies of the museum appeared in Moscow, Berlin-Kreuzberg, Amsterdam, London, The Hague, and New York. Neurath's attention gradually shifted from a local and socio-educational mandate—the instruction of the working classes—to the universal expressiveness and expansion of a world community, a global polis.

The dream of a city or an exhibition that showcases the whole world was not new. It was the rationale behind the World Fairs and the Crystal Palace, built in London in 1851. In 1911, the Belgian visionary Paul Otlet set up the Palais Mondial, a repository for objects from the 1910 Brussels World Fair. Otlet was looking to concentrate global knowledge in one place, arranged according to country or region and field of research. In 1895, Otlet and Henri La Fontaine had founded the International Institute of Bibliography in a bid to compile a complete record of human knowledge. At the time, this visionary idea was implemented in a tangible way: by 1912 the cabinets contained more than nine million index cards.[8] Today, Otlet and La Fontaine are seen as the grandfathers of the World Wide Web. The next step was a Musée Mondial—the Mundaneum—to provide open access to the information. In the 1920s, Otlet campaigned for a city of world knowledge, a "Cité Mondiale," in the belief that the promotion of science, culture, and progress would make a substantial contribution to world peace. Le Corbusier and Pierre Jeanneret drew up the plans. The World City was to be built in Antwerp, Brussels, Geneva, or Paris, but it remained a pipe dream.

In 1929, Otto Neurath and Paul Otlet joined forces. The intellectual father of the Internet and the inventor of infographics were a dream team. Together they wanted to create an *Atlas of World Culture* and to that end they set up a new organization, "*Novus Orbis Pictus* N.O.P., Brussels, Geneva, Vienna Protocol." Neurath insisted on having two separate structures, which could also be promoted as such: the Orbis Institute would take on the *World Atlas of Civilization*, the Mundaneum the expansion of regional museums and exhibitions. The stock market crash in 1929 and disagreements between the founders drove a wedge between dream and deed, although, in 1931, Neurath did establish the Vienna Mundaneum. He continued to champion greater worldwide understanding by means of his pictorial language ISOTYPE. In 1939, he published his magnum opus, *Modern Man in the Making*.

N.O.P. brought together two visionary men of the sort only encountered in visionary countries. Indeed, the Protocol united the three countries which the leading Swiss curator Harald Szeemann brackets together as "visionary." In 1991, Szeemann, director of the Kunsthalle Bern and "permanent freelance curator" at the Museum for Modern Art in Zurich, made *Visionäre Schweiz*, "an exhibition that doesn't

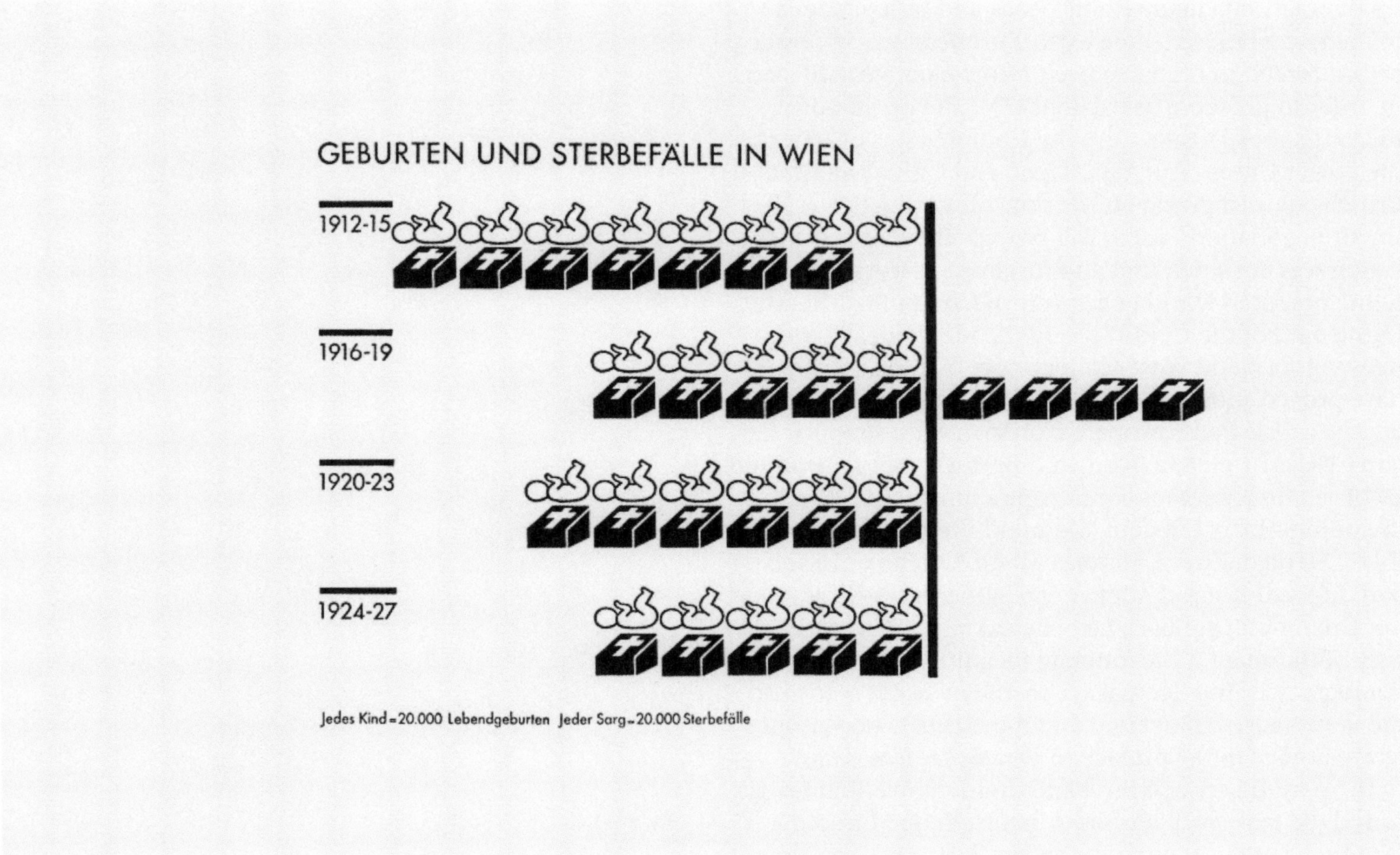

Fig. 3
Otto Neurath
Geburten und Sterbefälle in Wien
From *Bildstatistik nach Wiener Methode*, Vienna, 1931

take the more usual, purely (art-)historical approach to a country's creativity by tracing successive developments."[9] The Austrian Chancellor asked Szeemann if he could also apply this poetic concept to Austria. He could. In his preface to the catalogue, Szeemann clarifies his concept: "In my opinion, there are only three countries in Europe that might be considered 'visionary': Switzerland, Austria and Belgium. A 'visionary' Germany, Russia, France, etc. is unthinkable, and the Netherlands is more a society than a nation. I am not an expert when it comes to organizing exhibitions about countries, but in the case of Austria I simply had to say yes." Szeemann also kept his word for Belgium. In 2005, to mark 175 years of Belgium and 25 years of federalism, he put together the exhibition *La Belgique visionnaire / Visionair België: C'est arrivé pres de chez nous*. The subtitle alludes to Benoît Poelvoorde's film *C'est arrivé près de chez vous* (English title: *Man Bites Dog*). Szeemann made the *vous* (you) into *nous* (we), as if we were all accomplices. The film is a cynical and shocking portrayal of the media's increasing voyeurism: in a fictitious documentary, a film crew follows a serial killer (played by Benoît Poelvoorde) and becomes caught up in the violence. Paul Otlet's Mundaneum was given a place of honor in *La Belgique visionnaire*. While preparing the show, Szeemann was taken ill. *La Belgique visionnaire* turned out to be his last exhibition. BOZAR is still very grateful to Harald Szeemann and his son Jérôme. *La Belgique visionnaire* helped put BOZAR's European mission on the international map—for visionary artists, scientists, and countries are not deterred by borders. Artistic and scientific creativity in border nations like Belgium, Switzerland, and Austria, countries that are located at historical crossroads, provide a better understanding of twentieth-century history and the challenges facing modern-day Europe.[10]

ACT 3—RICHARD COUDENHOVE-KALERGI'S PAN-EUROPA UNION

The development of a Society of World Culture and a Cité Mondiale proved slightly too ambitious for the interwar years. The League of Nations got off to a reluctant start, and it was 1945 before the United Nations was formed. But what about the European project? These days we have this notion that the European Community only began to take shape in the minds of founding fathers such as Robert Schumann, Jean Monnet, and Konrad Adenauer after the Second World War. But this is not entirely true. It was a Count, born in Tokyo to a Japanese mother and an Austro-Hungarian father with Belgian aristocratic roots, who planted the European idea. A noble gentleman who became a citizen of Czechoslovakia in 1919 and who, after the *Anschluss* of Austria, took French nationality: Richard Nikolaus Eijiro Coudenhove-Kalergi. He set out his proposal for the first time in the article "Pan-Europa—A Proposal" (1922). The basic argumentation has a surprisingly topical ring. If the European nations want to continue to play a real role on the world stage, they must unite in a confederation, Coudenhove-Kalergi wrote a year later in his book *Pan-Europa* (1923): "Can Europe—in its political and economic fragmentation—maintain its peace and independence in the face of the growing extra-European world powers, or is it forced to organize itself into a federation of states in order to preserve its existence?"[11] The world powers in Coudenhove's time were the United States of America, the Soviet Union, Pan Asia (Japan and China), and the British colonial power (at the time of writing this essay, Brexit negotiations are in full swing). The Pan-Europa Union was designed first and foremost as a response to the potential world hegemony of Communist Russia. In the light of the Cold War and the ideological divide between East and West, Coudenhove-Kalergi's insights have proved spot on.

The Pan-Europa Union won wide support. Its congresses in Vienna (1926) and Berlin (1930) were attended by leading members of Europe's intellectual elite, including Albert Einstein, Sigmund Freud, Rainer Maria Rilke, Stephan Zweig, Thomas Mann, Ortega y Gasset, and (indeed) Konrad Adenauer. Coudenhove-Kalergi was not a democrat at heart; he believed more in the aristocracy of the spirit. "The ultimate meaning of political democracy is: intellectual aristocracy; its aim is to give the materialists enjoyment and the idealists power," he wrote in 1925 in the preface to *Praktischer Idealismus*.[12] In the period between the wars, Coudenhove-Kalergi sat round the table with authoritarian leaders: Mussolini, who in the end did not join the Pan-European movement, and the dictatorial Austrian Chancellor Engelbert Dollfuss and his successor Kurt Schuschnigg. He made the latter chairman of the Austrian department of Pan-Europa. Adolf Hitler was unimpressed by the Pan-Europa Union and Coudenhove-Kalergi, whom he referred to as "everybody's bastard." The cosmopolitan Coudenhove-Kalergi's racial view of the European of the future was at odds with the racial purity the Nazis had in mind. Coudenhove-Kalergi believed that miscegenation was more beneficial, as he wrote in *Praktischer Idealismus*: "The man of the future will be of mixed race. Today's races and classes will gradually disappear owing to the vanishing of space, time, and prejudice. The Eurasian-Negroid race of the future, similar in its appearance to the Ancient Egyptians, will replace the diversity of people with a diversity of individuals."[13] Thus Coudenhove-Kalergi turned around Erwin Hanslik's reductionist view: from race and type to a multiplicity of individuals.

The International Paneuropean Union still exists today. After Richard Coudenhove-Kalergi's death, Otto von Habsburg-Lorraine, the last Crown Prince of Austria-Hungary, became its chairman. Today, Karl von Habsburg is its vice-president; the Habsburg spirit lingers on in Europe. The twenty-eight-strong EU goes way beyond "Brussels" and the French-German axis. The European center often lies on the periphery. Or rather: in the middle, as the exhibition *Beyond Klimt: New Horizons in Central Europe* illustrates during the Austrian Presidency of the Council of the European Union in Brussels.

1 Kurt De Boodt and Paul Dujardin, "Committing Sacrilege in the 'Cubist and Flemish Nationalist Church,'" in *The Power of the Avant-Garde: Now and Then* (Tielt, 2016).
2 Estate of Franz Cizek, Wienbibliothek im Rathaus, Handschriftensammlung, ZPH 489, Archivbox 16, Materialien Weltkulturgesellschaft 4.4. My thanks to Alexander Klee for this reference.
3 See, for example, Moritz Csáky, *Das Gedächtnis der Städte: Kulturelle Verflechtungen—Wien und die urbanen Milieus in Zentraleuropa* (Vienna/Cologne/Weimar, 2010).
4 Friedrich Naumann, *Mitteleuropa* (Berlin, 1915), p. 3. Translated by Christabel Margaret (Iles) Meredith as *Central Europe: A Translation* (London, 1917).
5 Naumann 1915 (see note 4), p. 108
6 Nader Vossoughian, *Otto Neurath—The Language of the Global Polis* (Rotterdam, 2011).
7 Otto Neurath, "Aufgaben des Gesellschafts- und Wirtschaftsmuseums in Wien," in *Der Aufbau*, no. 8/9 (1926), pp. 169–170.
8 Harald Szeemann, ed. *La Belgique visionnaire / Visionair België*, exh. cat., Palais des Beaux-Arts / Paleis voor Schone Kunsten, Brussels (Brussels, 2005).
9 Harald Szeemann, *Austria im Rosennetz*, exh. cat., Palais des Beaux-Arts / Paleis voor Schone Kunsten, Brussels; Museum of Applied Arts (MAK), Vienna; Kunsthaus Zurich, Zurich (under the title *Wunderkammer* Österreich) (Vienna/New York, 1996).
10 Olivier Boehme, *Europa een geschiedenis van grensnaties* (Antwerp, 2016). Boehme defines border nations as follows: "(Those) border nations owe their past, present, and future existence and *raison d'être* to a position in the zone where cultures and peoples meet. It is no coincidence that the Netherlands, Belgium, Luxembourg, and Switzerland lie wholly or partially in the zone that once formed a middle state between two other zones which would become France on the one side and Germany on the other [...] The German and Habsburg areas formed a second European seam, a zone which held together *and* divided several parts of the continent. [...] It is interesting to note how many junctions surfaced in Europe and how various countries, large and small, used them to make claims on transnational missions."
11 R. N. Coudenhove-Kalergi, *Pan-Europa* (Vienna, 1923).
12 R. N. Coudenhove-Kalergi, *Praktischer Idealismus: Adel—Technik—Pazifismus* (Vienna/Leipzig, 1925).
13 R. N. Coudenhove-Kalergi 1925 (see note 12), pp. 22–23.

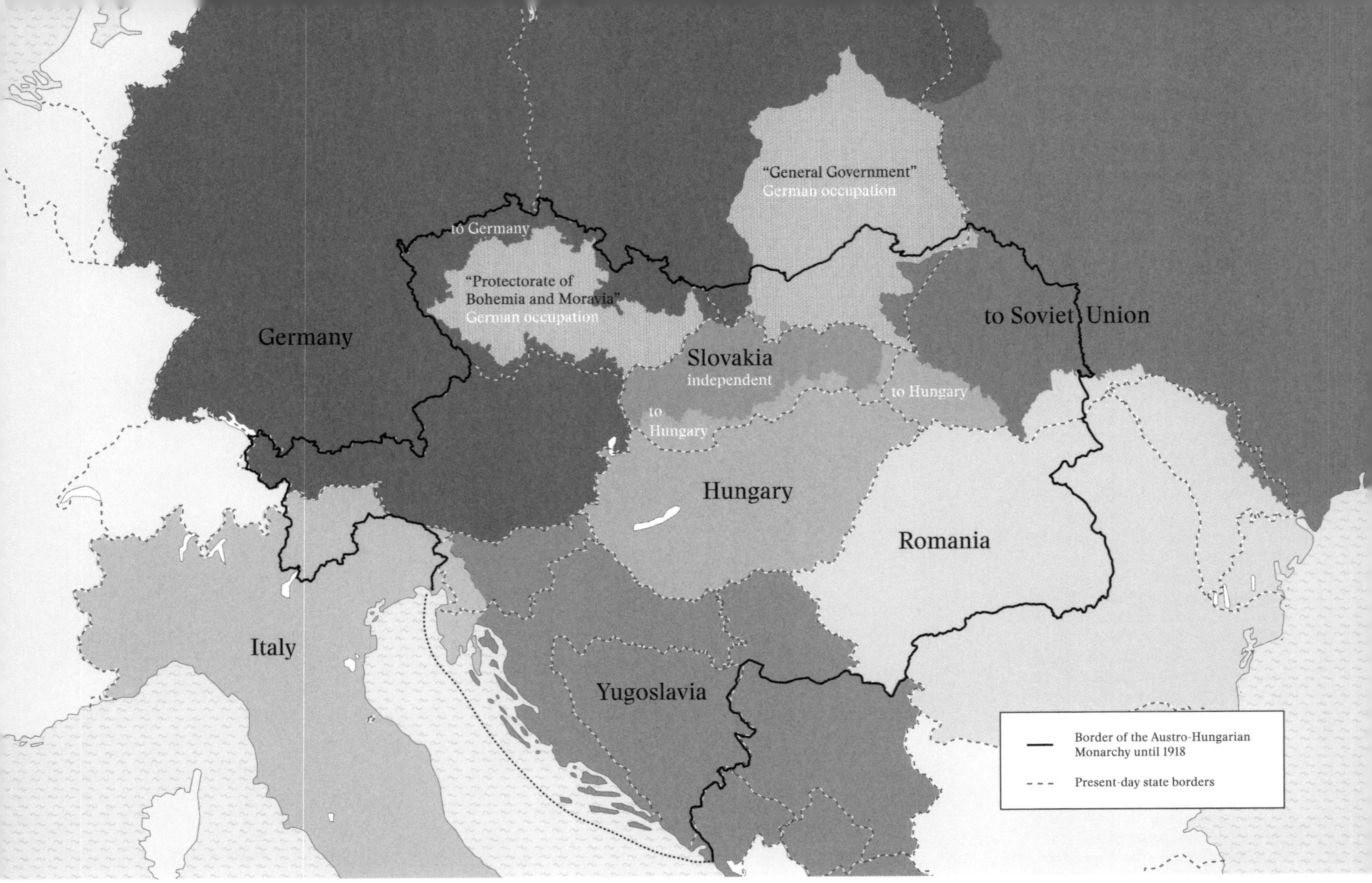

F 1938–39 From Munich Agreement
to World War II.

nation—nemzet:

Nemzet és *nemzetiség*. Nemzetiség: a nép fajbeli jelleme szerint, melynek lényeges ismérve a nyelv. Nemzet: az államotalkotó, az államnak személyi és alanyi tényezőjét, szubjektiv erejét alkotó nép. Nemzetiség a nép természetrajzi, N. a nép politikai tekintetben. A N. több nemzetiségből állhat, a N. egységének egyáltalán nem feltétele a nemzetiség egysége. Kedvezőbb azoknak az államoknak a helyzete, amelyekben a N.-et alkotó nemzetiségek egyikének fizikai v. pszichikai v. mindkét szempontból túlsúlyánál fogva sikerült a vezérszerepet magához ragadni s az államra, állami intézményeire, politikai szervezetére reá ütni kiváló, hatalmas egyéniségének bélyegét. Az ily állam N.-i állam; ellentéte a nemzetiségi állam, melyben a politikai N.-et alkotó különböző nemzetiségek az anyagi és szellemi erőegyenlőség viszonyában az anyagi és szellemi erőegyenlőseg viszonyában állanak egymáshoz. ... Erős N.-i állam: Magyarország.

Révai Nagy Lexikona. Az Ismeretek Enciklopédiája. XIV. Kötet. Mons-Ottó, (Budapest, 1916), p. 390

Nemzet, Szent István korában a nemes főtisztek, földesurak, birtokos szabadok, más birtokán jobbágyok, katonák, bérlők, vendégek és szabadosok összesége, tehát csak a rabszolgák voltak kizárva a N.-ből. A rendi alkotmány kialakulása mind szűkebbre szorította a N. fogalmát, de a Hunyadiak azonosították az országlakókkal. Csak a Hármaskönyv választja külön jogilag is a nemzetet *(natio)* a köznéptől *(plebs)*, a nép addigi fogalmát *(populus)* a nemzetre, a kiváltságolt rendekre korlátozva. A 48-as alkotmány folytán a N. fogalma újból azonosult az országlakóval, de a közben elszaporodott és önállóságra törekvő idegen anyanyelvű országlakók törekvései a nemzetiség megkülönböztető fogalmát szülték. Ma N. a közös származású, történeti múltú, gazd. és pol. érdekközösségű, azonos célközösségű polgárok összessége.

László Dormándi / Vilmos Juhász, *Uj lexikon. A tudás és a gyakorlati élet egyetemes enciklopédiája 6 kötetben*, (Budapest, 1936), pp. 2870–71.

Hungarian

In 1938, the stripping-away of democratic and humanist principles from Germany's national and international politics took its inevitable course. Following the Munich Agreement, not only entire states fell victim to the aggression of the Nazi regime, but also—most crucially—their people. After the euphoria of the "Roaring Twenties"—a time when artists traveled the world, formed free groups and associations, and cultivated a dynamic environment of intellectual exchange—the situation for free-thinking citizens and, increasingly, for Jews, Romani, and opposition forces, became increasingly perilous. Toward the end of the 1930s, artists traveled much less for studies or inspiration, but rather in response to persecution and threats to their lives. Sadly, exile was not an option open to all of them. Many artists also attempted to oppose the decay of democracy by becoming part of the Resistance movement. Political activity of any form spelled doom for those artists who refused to collaborate with the Nazi regime. The following names are given in lieu of the many more murdered by the Nazis in concentration camps: Josef Čapek (died 1945 in Bergen-Belsen), Friedl Dicker-Brandeis (died 1944 in Auschwitz), Zdeněk Dvořák (died 1943 in Auschwitz), István Farkas (died 1944 in Auschwitz), Vojtěch Preissig (died 1944 in Dachau), Fritz Schwarz-Waldegg (died 1942 in Malý Trostinec extermination camp near Minsk). (MH)

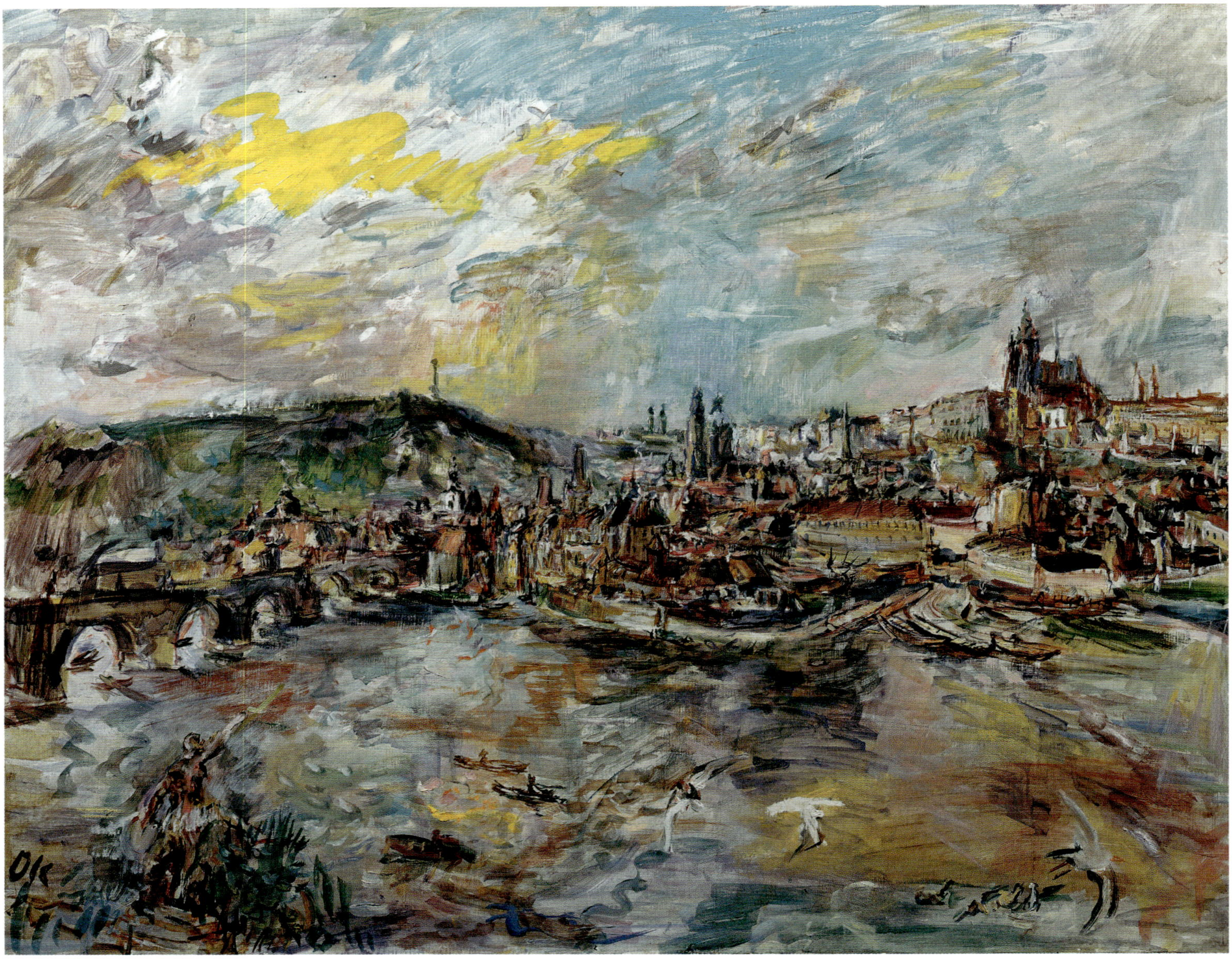

F

Oskar Kokoschka
Prague Harbor, 1936
Belvedere, Vienna

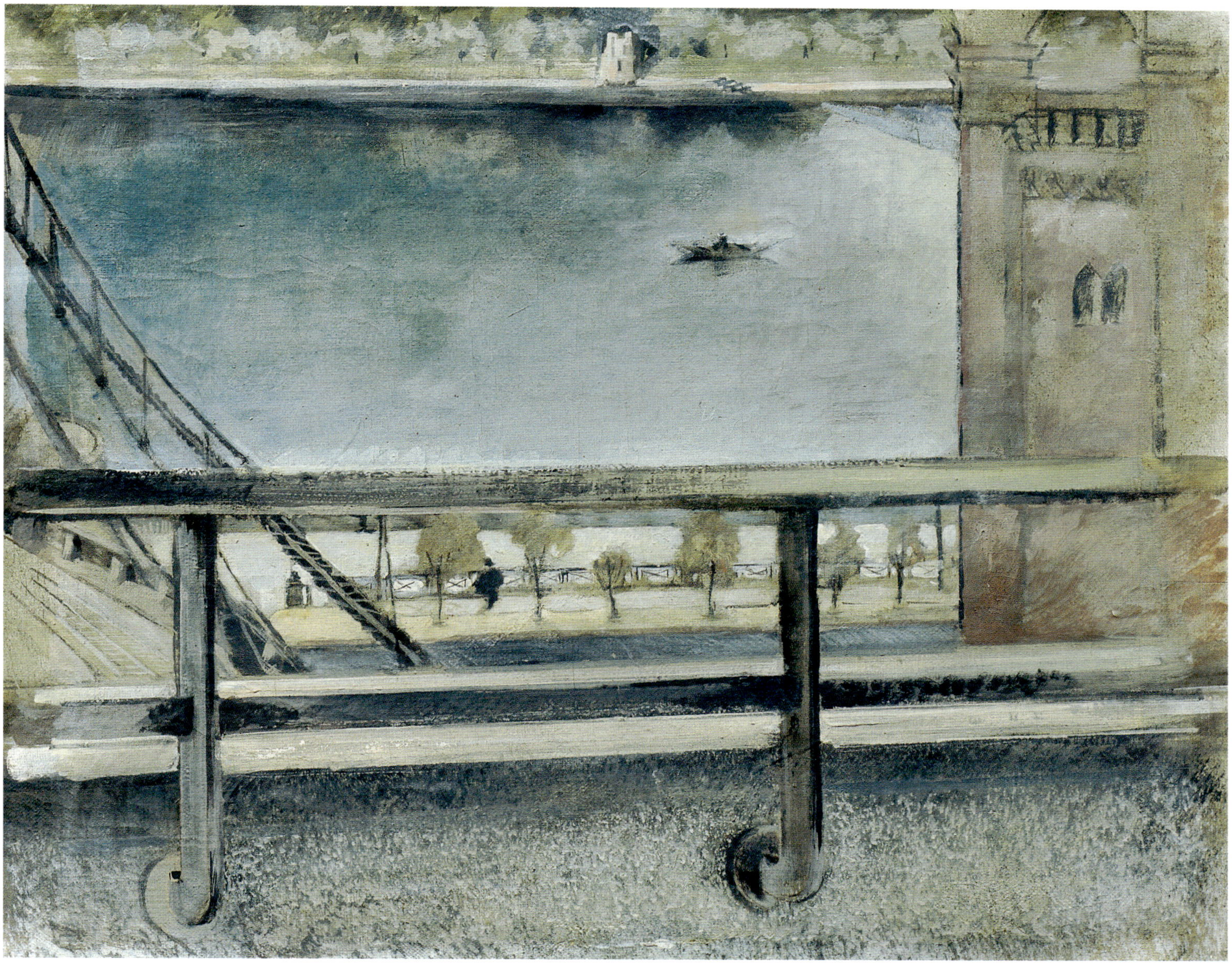

F

Friedl Dicker-Brandeis
Picture of Prague—Iron Bridge, Vltava, undated
Belvedere, Vienna, gift of Dr. Hildegard Angelini Kothny

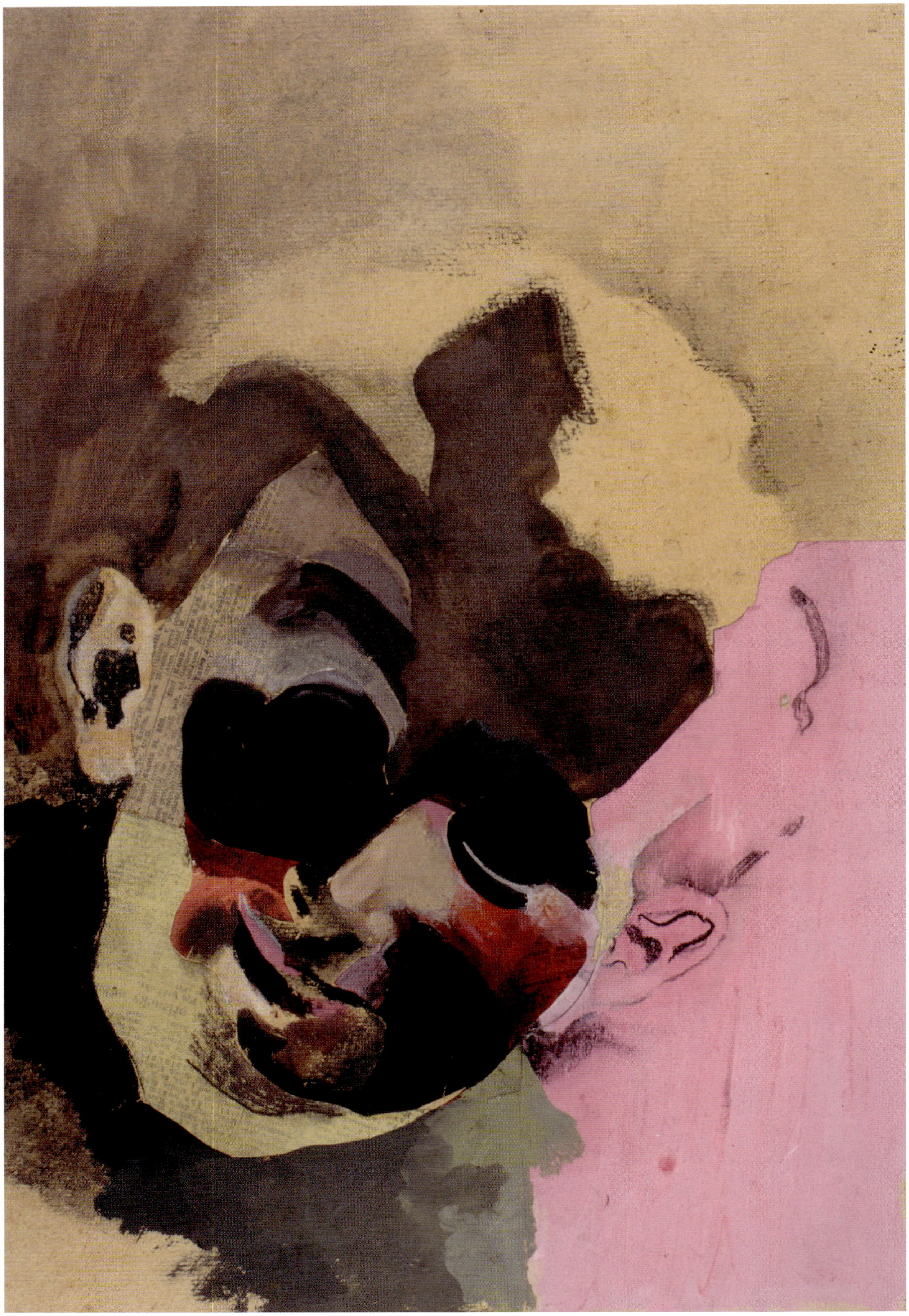

Friedl Dicker-Brandeis
Interrogation, 1934
University of Applied Arts Vienna,
Collection and Archive

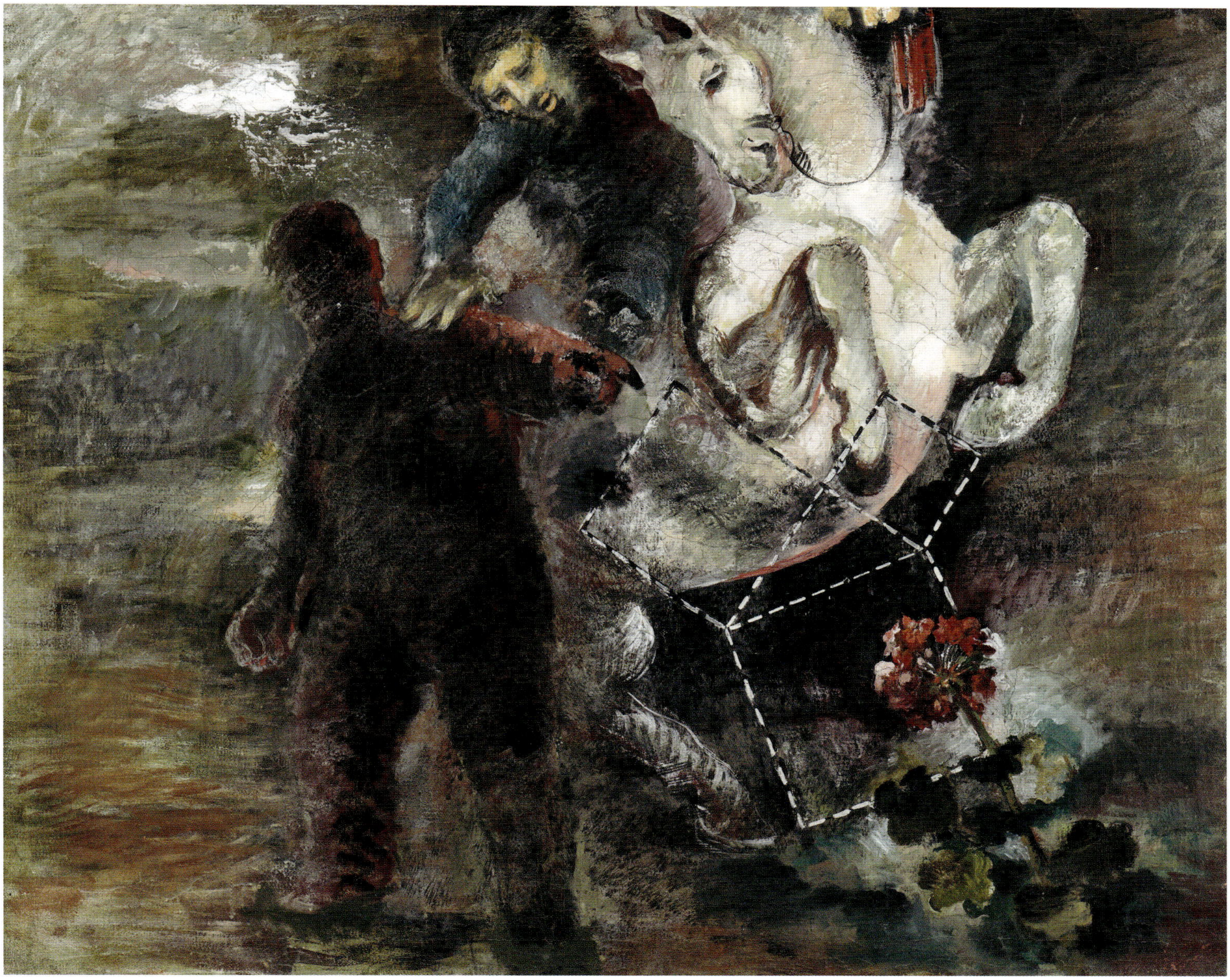

F

Friedl Dicker-Brandeis
Don Quixote and Lenin, c. 1940
Peter Lachnit, Vienna

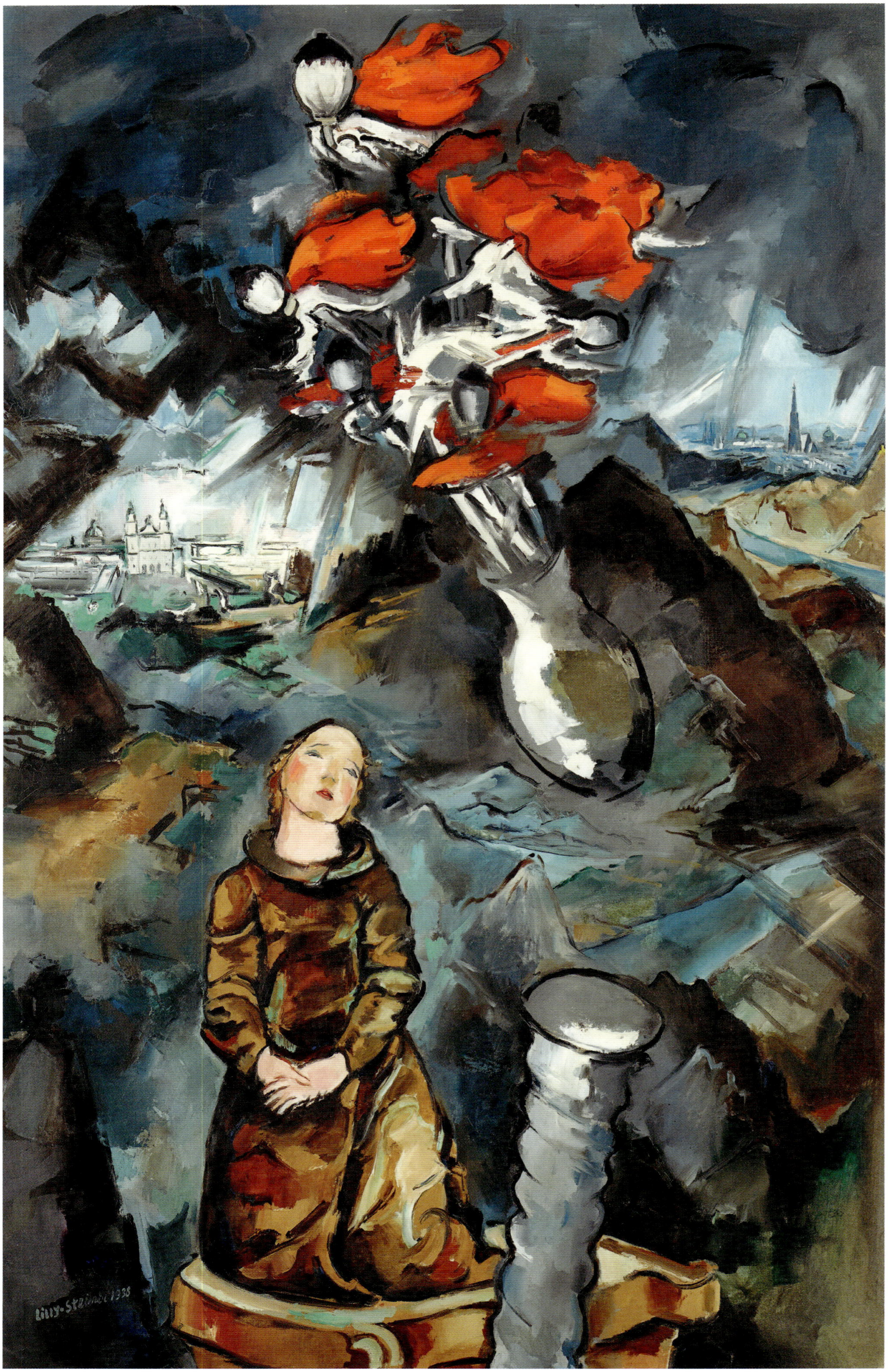

Lilly Steiner
Composition Baroque, 1938
Belvedere, Vienna

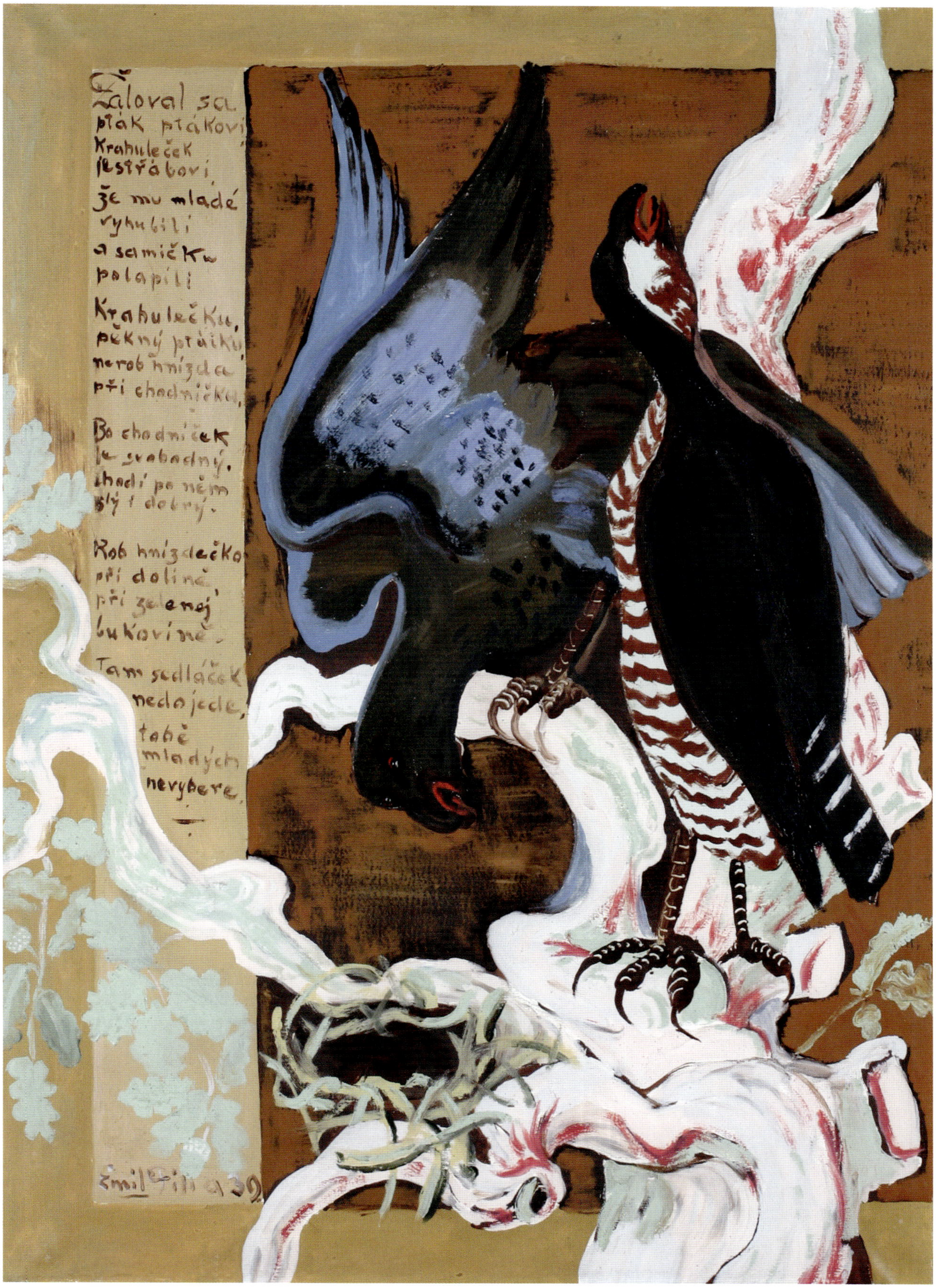

Emil Filla
Variation on a Moravian Folk Song, 1939
Regional Gallery of Fine Arts in Zlín

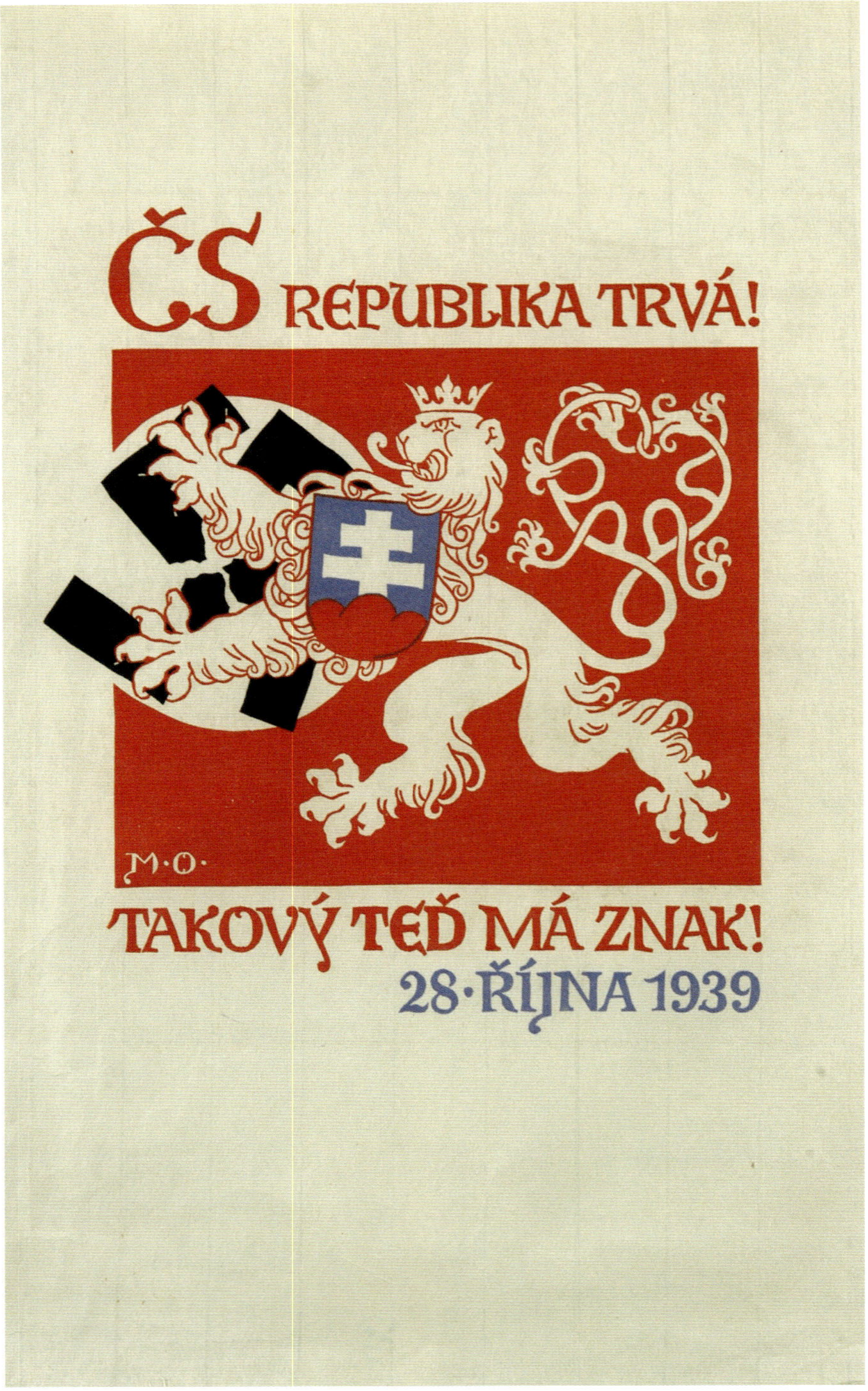

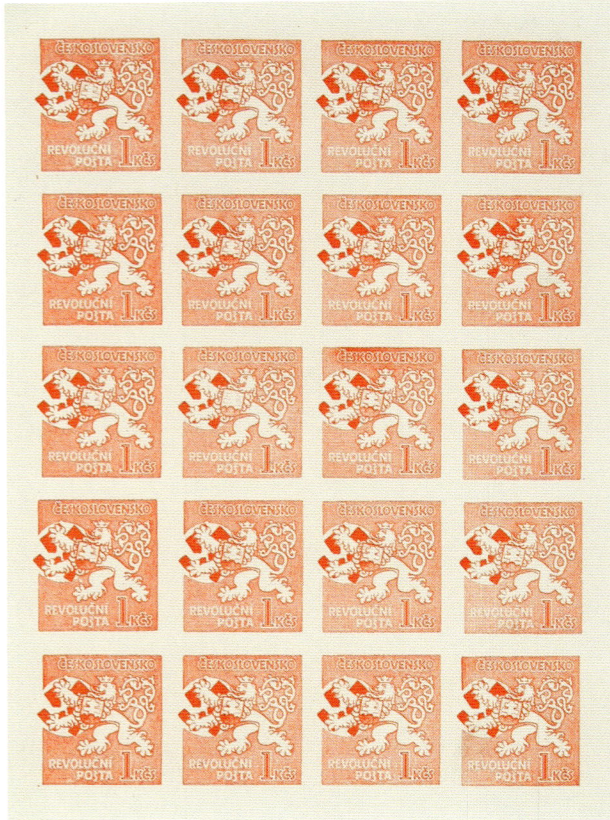

Vojtěch Preissig
The Czechslovak Republic Will Prevail! This is its New Coat of Arms, 1939
The Museum of Decorative Arts in Prague

Vojtěch Preissig
Stamps for Czechoslovakia— "resistance post," 1939
The Museum of Decorative Arts in Prague

Appendices

Artists and List of Works

B exhibited only in Brussels
V exhibited only in Vienna

ROBERT ANGERHOFER
1895 Hinterstoder — 1987 Linz
1914–18 military service; 1918 Munich; then moved to Linz.

Dead Soldier in Barbed Wire, c. 1920
Oil on canvas, 107 × 147 cm
NORDICO Stadtmuseum Linz, inv. no. G 139
‣ p. 125

GERD ARNTZ
1900 Remscheid — 1988 Den Haag
1919 relocated to Düsseldorf; 1921/22 Barmen-Elberfeld; 1924 returned to Düsseldorf; 1929 moved to Vienna; 1932 and 1933 several extended visits to Moscow (Москва); 1934 Den Haag; 1943 forcibly conscripted into the Wehrmacht; 1944–46 prisoner of war; returned to Den Haag.

JENŐ BARCSAY
1900 Cătina — 1988 Szentendre
1918 Târgu Mureș; 1920 Budapest; 1926/27 Paris; 1928–30 Paris; from 1929 Szentendre and Budapest; 1931–45 Pécs; 1945 Budapest.

Red Youths (Workers), c. 1928
Oil on canvas, 75 × 100.7 cm
Museum of Fine Arts—Hungarian National Gallery, Budapest, inv. no. 81.27T
‣ p. 305

EDUARD BÄUMER
1892 Kastellaun — 1977 Munich
1895 relocated to Frankfurt am Main; 1914–18 military service; then returned to Frankfurt; 1927/28 Berlin; 1930/31 Paris, then Frankfurt a. M. and Berlin; 1933 emigrated to Salzburg; 1943–45 military service; 1948 Vienna; 1958–75 annual visits to Tropea.

Portrait of Valerie Bäumer, 1932
Oil on canvas, 92.5 × 73.5 cm
Private collection
‣ p. 317

HERBERT BAYER
1900 Haag am Hausruck — 1985 Montecito (California)
1912 relocated to Linz; 1917/18 military service; 1919/20 Linz; 1921 Darmstadt; 1921–28 at the Bauhaus Weimar and Dessau; until 1938 Berlin; 1938 emigrated to the USA (New York); 1946–74 Aspen (Colorado); 1974 moved to Montecito.

Backdrops, 1925
Tempera on paper, 46.5 × 66 cm
LENTOS Kunstmuseum Linz, inv. no. 1638
‣ p. 247
B

Floating Architecture, 1926
Gouache on paper, 49 × 36 cm
mumok—Museum moderner Kunst Stiftung Ludwig Wien, inv. no. G 247/0
‣ p. 246
V

Blue 1926/II, 1926
Gouache, paper on cardboard, 51 × 62 cm
mumok—Museum moderner Kunst Stiftung Ludwig Wien, inv. no. G 248/0
‣ p. 248
V

Composition in Space, 1928
Pen and ink, watercolor, and opaque white on paper, 27.3 × 43.8 cm
LENTOS Kunstmuseum Linz, inv. no. 1637
‣ p. 249
B

ÉTIENNE BEOTHY
1897 Heves — 1961 Paris
1915/16 military service; 1918–24 Budapest; 1925 Paris; 1939–45 part of the French Resistance; 1945 Paris.

Danse Cosaque (Danse Russe, Paraboles, Op. 45), 1930
Bronze, H: 60.3 cm, W: 39.2 cm, D: 10.6 cm
Courtesy of Galerie Le Minotaure
‣ p. 252

RÓBERT BERÉNY
1887 Budapest — 1953 Budapest
1905 Paris; 1907 Budapest; 1914–18 military service; 1919 emigrated via Vienna to Berlin; 1926 returned to Budapest.

Sleeping Lady with Black Vase, 1927/28
Oil on canvas, 64 × 87 cm
Private collection
‣ p. 300

To Arms! To Arms!, 1919
Lithograph on paper, 124 × 184 cm
Museum of Fine Arts—Hungarian National Gallery, Budapest, inv. no. 61.01
‣ p. 168
V

MIHÁLY BÍRÓ
1886 Budapest — 1948 Budapest
1908–10 visits to Munich, Berlin, London, and Chipping Campden; 1910 returned to Hungary; 1915–17 military service; 1919 emigrated to Vienna; 1928 moved to Berlin; 1932 returned to Vienna; 1934 fled from Vienna to Czechoslovakia; from 1936 resided in Nitra; 1938 fled to Paris; 1943 interned in German-occupied France; 1944 liberated; 1947 returned to Budapest.

HERBERT BOECKL
1894 Klagenfurt — 1966 Vienna
1912 Vienna; 1915–18 military service; 1918 Klagenfurt; 1921/22 Berlin; 1923/24 Palermo; 1924 Klagenfurt; 1926 Maria Saal bei Klagenfurt; 1929 Töschling; 1930 Perchtoldsdorf; 1935 Unterkrain and Klagenfurt; 1937 Vienna.

Still Life with Fish, 1922
Oil on canvas, 40.5 × 70.5 cm
Belvedere, Vienna, inv. no. 2514
‣ p. 299

SÁNDOR BORTNYIK
1893 Târgu Mureș — 1976 Budapest
1910 Budapest; 1920 emigrated to Vienna; 1922 Weimar; 1924 Košice; 1925 returned to Budapest.

The New Adam, 1924
Oil on canvas, 48.3 × 38 cm
Museum of Fine Arts—Hungarian National Gallery, Budapest, inv. no. 64.85T
‣ p. 223
V

Green Donkey, 1924
Oil on canvas, 60 × 55 cm
Museum of Fine Arts—Hungarian National Gallery, Budapest, inv. no. 64.84T
‣ p. 221
B

The Architect Alfréd Forbát and his Wife, 1924
Oil on cardboard, 44 × 58 cm
Museum of Fine Arts—Hungarian National Gallery, Budapest, inv. no. 70.48T
‣ p. 220

MARCEL BREUER
1902 Pécs — 1981 New York
1920–28 Weimar and Dessau; 1928 Berlin; 1933 Budapest; 1934 Zurich; then Budapest; 1935–37 London; 1937 Harvard, Cambridge (Massachusetts); 1946 New York.

Marcel Breuer, Anton Lorenz
Cantilever chair, model no. 317 (B34); produced by: J. A. Talos, Vienna, 1928
Chrome-plated tubular steel; wood, blue varnish; original eisengarn covering, H: 83 cm, W: 56 cm, D: 60 cm

MAK—Austrian Museum of Applied Arts / Contemporary Art, Vienna, inv. no. H 2239-1
▸ p. 217

JOSEF ČAPEK
1887 Hronov — 1945 Bergen-Belsen concentration camp
1890 Úpice; 1901–03 Vrchlabí; 1903/04 Úpice; 1904 Prague; 1910/11 Paris; 1911 Prague; 1939 Dachau concentration camp, then Buchenwald; 1942 Sachsenhausen; 1945 Bergen-Belsen.

Portrait of a Girl (Cubist Landscape on verso*)*, 1915
Oil on canvas, 68 × 47 cm
Private collection
▸ p. 94

The Drinker, 1918/19
Oil on wood, 60.5 × 36 cm
Moravian Gallery, Brno, inv. no. A 2569
▸ p. 95

Guilty Conscience, 1926
Oil on canvas, 59.8 × 74.8 cm
Moravian Gallery, Brno, inv. no. A 978
▸ p. 203

GYULA DERKOVITS
1894 Szombathely — 1934 Budapest
1914–16 military service; 1917 Budapest; 1923–26 Vienna; 1926 returned to Budapest.

Starving People in Winter (In front of the Bakery, Starving People), 1930
Oil, tempera, silver powder paint on canvas, 76 × 64.5 cm
Szombathely Art Gallery, inv. no. K 76.57.1.
▸ p. 309

FRIEDL DICKER-BRANDEIS
1898 Vienna — 1944 Auschwitz concentration camp
1914 Vienna; 1919–23 Weimar; from 1923 Berlin; 1925 returned to Vienna; 1936 emigrated to Prague; 1938 Hronov; 1942 deported to Theresienstadt; 1944 Auschwitz concentration camp.

Virgin and Child with Saint Anne, 1915–25
Collage, gouache, pencil on paper, 149 × 34 cm (folded 61 × 34 cm)
University of Applied Arts Vienna, Collection and Archive, inv. no. 12.192
▸ p. 215

From *Utopia: Dokumente der Wirklichkeit*, 1921
Lithograph, 32.4 × 24 cm
Georg Schrom, Vienna
▸ p. 214

Friedl Dicker-Brandeis, Franz Singer
Models for Two Chairs and for Stools, c. 1932–34
Metal, paper, H: 20.5 cm, W: 8.5 cm, D: 9.5 cm
Georg Schrom, Vienna
▸ p. 216

Interrogation, 1934
Gouache, collage on brown cardboard, 46 × 33 cm
University of Applied Arts Vienna, Collection and Archive, inv. no. 8703
▸ p. 364

Don Quixote and Lenin, c. 1940
Oil on canvas, 77 × 100 cm
Peter Lachnit, Vienna
▸ p. 365

Picture of Prague—Iron Bridge, Vltava, undated
Oil on canvas, 44 × 56.5 cm
Belvedere, Vienna, gift of Dr. Hildegard Angelini Kothny, inv. no. 9656
▸ p. 363

MARY DURAS
1898 Vienna — 1982 Graz
1900 relocated to Lviv (Львів); 1904 Prague; 1908 Hradec Králové; 1911 Mostar; 1914 Prague; 1916–22 Prague; 1922 Dresden; 1923/24 New York; 1924–27 Paris; 1927 returned to Prague; 1939 fled to Britain; from 1940 Wendover Dean; 1945 returned to Prague; 1963 emigrated to Austria (Vienna); 1964 Bochum and Hamburg; 1974 Graz.

Musing Woman, 1931
Terracotta, H: 57.5 cm
The Regional Art Gallery Liberec, inv. no. P 132
▸ p. 311

ZDENĚK DVOŘÁK
1897 Hlušice — 1943 Auschwitz concentration camp
1901 Nový Bydžov; 1916–18 military service; 1919–43 Prague; 1943 deported to Auschwitz.

Plastron, c. 1935
Relief, bronze, 42 × 49 cm
National Gallery in Prague, inv. no. P 5957
▸ p. 250

ALBIN EGGER-LIENZ
1868 Stribach — 1926 St. Justina
1884–99 Munich; 1899 Vienna; 1911 Hall in Tirol; 1912/13 Weimar; 1913 St. Justina-Rentsch in Bolzano, Italy; 1915 military service; 1916/17 war painter.

Finale, 1918
Oil on canvas, 140 × 227 cm
Leopold Private Collection
▸ pp. 114 (detail), 134

Women of War, 1918–22
Oil on tempera on canvas, 124 × 247 cm
Museum der Stadt Lienz Schloss Bruck, inv. no. AEL 52
▸ p. 135

ISTVÁN FARKAS
1887 Budapest — 1944 Auschwitz concentration camp
1906 Baia Mare; 1907 Budapest; 1908 Italy; 1909/10 Budapest; 1910/11 Munich; from 1911 Paris; 1914–18 military service; 1920–25 Hungary and Bordighera; 1925–31 Paris; 1932 Budapest; 1942 Szigliget and Budapest; 1944 deported to Auschwitz.

Coffeehouse Scene, c. 1922
Oil on canvas, 98.5 × 124 cm
St. Stephen's King Museum — Deák Collection, Székesfehérvár, inv. no. 94.93.1
▸ p. 294

EMIL FILLA
1882 Chropyně — 1953 Prague
1898–1902 Brno; 1903–06 Prague; 1908 Dalmatia; 1909 Prague; 1914 Paris, fled to Belgium and the Netherlands; 1915 Amsterdam; 1918 Den Haag; 1920 Prague; 1939 deported to Dachau concentration camp, then to Buchenwald concentration camp; 1945 Prague.

Still Life Bols, 1914
Oil on canvas, 30.5 × 46 cm
The Gallery of West Bohemia in Pilsen, inv. no. O 633
▸ p. 91

Still Life with Book (Jack London, The Son of the Wolf), 1921
Oil on canvas, 63 × 62.5 cm
Belvedere, Vienna, on permanent loan from the Rotter Collection, inv. no. Lg 1401
▸ p. 204

Variation on a Moravian Folk Song, 1939
Oil on canvas, 129 × 96.5 cm
Regional Gallery of Fine Arts in Zlín, inv. no. O 23
▸ p. 367

FRANTIŠEK FOLTÝN
1891 Stachy — 1976 Brno
1905–13 Plzeň (?); 1913/14 Prague; 1914–18 military service; 1918–21 Bratislava; 1921–23 Košice, Mukachevo (Мукачево), and Uzhhorod (Ужгород); 1923 Brno; 1924–34 Paris; 1934–36 Prague, Tábor, and Brno; 1937–76 Brno.

Composition, 1928
Oil on canvas, 81.5 × 65 cm
Belvedere, Vienna, on permanent loan from the Rotter Collection, inv. no. Lg 1407
▸ p. 251

Abstract Composition, 1936/37
Oil on canvas, 114 × 87.5 cm
Belvedere, Vienna, on permanent loan from the Rotter Collection, inv. no. Lg 1408
▸ p. 253

HELENE FUNKE
1869 Chemnitz — 1957 Vienna
1899–1906 Munich; 1906–11 Paris; 1911 Vienna.

Still Life with Melon, c. 1918
Oil on wood, 67 × 80 cm
Courtesy of Kunsthandel Hieke
▸ p. 81

Waterfall, c. 1922
Oil on canvas, 108 × 63.5 cm
Courtesy of Kunsthandel Hieke
▸ p. 298

PAUL GEBAUER
1888 Sosnová/Opava — 1951 Harburg
1910/11 Dresden and Vienna; 1914–18 military service; 1919 Sosnová; 1945 Harburg.

Portrait of Bank Director Koch, 1928
Oil on canvas, 119 × 85 cm
Collection of Slezské zemské museum / Silesian Museum, Opava, inv. no. U 2433 A
▸ p. 314

VILKO GECAN
1894 Kuželj — 1973 Zagreb
1899–1902 Australia; 1902–10 Karlovac, Glogovnica, Zagreb, and Dubica (Bosnia); 1910–12 Banja Luka; 1912 Zagreb; 1913/14 Munich; 1914 Dubica; 1914–18 military service; 1918 Gomirje; 1919 Prague; 1920 Zagreb; 1922 Berlin; 1924–32 New York and Chicago; 1932 Zagreb.

The Cynic, 1921
Oil on canvas, 110.5 × 99 cm
National Museum of Modern Art, Zagreb, inv. no. MG-2668
▸ p. 292

OTTO GUTFREUND
1889 Dvůr Králové nad Labem — 1927 Prague
1903–06 Bechyně; 1906–09 Prague; 1909/10 Paris; 1910 Prague; 1912/13 Germany; 1914 Paris; 1914/15 voluntary military service for

the Entente; 1915–18 interned at Saint-Michel-de-Frigolet, France. After the end of the war, he moved between Prague and Paris.

Head II, 1919
Bronze, 37 × 16 × 26 cm
Belvedere, Vienna, on permanent loan from the Rotter Collection, inv. no. Lg 1414
▸ p. 202

Girl Looking Up, 1924
Bronze, H: 32,5 cm
Moravian Gallery, Brno, inv. no. E 811
▸ p. 310

ANTON HANAK
1875 Brno — 1934 Vienna
1878–89 Bystřice nad Pernštejnem, Pohořelice, and Mikulov; 1889–93 Vienna; 1901 Langenzersdorf bei Wien; 1904/05 Rome; 1905 returned to Langenzersdorf; 1923 moved to Hetzendorf (Vienna).

The Last Human (Ecce Homo), 1917–24
Bronze, H: 230 cm, W: 240 cm, D: 100 cm
Belvedere, Vienna, inv. no. 2495
▸ p. 161

Margarete Stonborough-Wittgenstein, 1925
Marble, H: 44.5 cm, W: 34 cm, D: 23 cm
Belvedere, Vienna, inv. no. 8374
▸ p. 307

JOHN HEARTFIELD
1891 Berlin-Schmargendorf — 1968 Berlin
1895 Weggis; 1896 Aigen; 1898 Salzburg; 1905 Wiesbaden; 1911 Munich; 1912 Mannheim; 1913 Berlin; 1914/15 military service; 1915–30 Berlin; 1931/32 visit to the Soviet Union; 1933 returned to Berlin and fled to Prague; 1935 visit to Paris; 1938 fled from Prague to London; 1940 interned for two months; 1950 returned to Germany (Leipzig).

ADOLF HÖLZEL
1853 Olomouc — 1934 Stuttgart
1868–71 Gotha; 1871–75 Vienna; 1876–82 Munich; 1887–1905 Dachau; 1905 Stuttgart.

Abstraction I, c. 1915
Oil on cardboard, 48.5 × 40 cm
Private collection
▸ p. 89

ANTON JASUSCH
1882 Košice — 1965 Košice
1898–1906 Budapest; 1906 Munich; 1907 Paris; 1908–14 Košice; 1914–16 military service; 1916–20 prisoner of war in Russia and Japan; from 1920 Košice.

The Symphony, 1922
Oil on cardboard, 61.2 × 75.5 cm
Slovak National Gallery, Bratislava, inv. no. O 2701
▸ p. 262

BÉLA KÁDÁR
1877 Budapest — 1956 Budapest
1903 Munich; 1910 Szolnok; 1912 Budapest; 1914–18 military service; 1921 Vienna and Berlin; 1921 Budapest; 1944/45 Budapest ghetto.

Cityscape with Bridges, c. 1921
Oil on canvas, 69 × 98.5 cm
St. Stephen's King Museum — Deák Collection, Székesfehérvár, inv. no. 89.82.1
▸ p. 295

LAJOS KASSÁK
1887 Nové Zámky — 1967 Budapest
1904–09 Budapest; 1909 Paris, Budapest at the end of the year; 1920 emigrated to Vienna; 1926 returned to Hungary, Budapest.

Lajos Kassák (ed.)
MA, yr. 7, no. 2, Vienna, 1922
Avant-garde journal, 30 × 23 cm
Petőfi Literary Museum— Kassák Museum, Budapest, inv. no. KM-P-2014-3-1
▸ p. 163

Fortieth Anniversary, 1927
Paper, ink, collage, 33 × 49.5 cm
Petőfi Literary Museum— Kassák Museum, Budapest, inv. no. KM-M-79.3.1.1
▸ pp. 164–165

FRIEDRICH/FREDERICK KIESLER
1890 Chernivtsi (Чернівці) — 1965 New York
1908–20 Vienna; 1914–18 military service; 1918 Vienna; 1921–23 Berlin; 1924 Vienna; 1925 Paris; 1926 New York; 1930 visit to Paris return to New York.

R.U.R. (Rossum's Universal Robots) (*W.U.R.* [*Werstands Universal Robots*] in German), 1923
Play: Karel Čapek, production: John Gottwort, set: Friedrich Kiesler, Theater am Kurfürstendamm, backdrop for the final act
Gelatin silver print on baryta paper, 20.5 × 25.4 cm
Austrian Friedrich and Lillian Kiesler Private Foundation, Vienna, inv. no. PHO 2921/12
▸ p. 235

Side view of the *Electro-Mechanical Set* for *R.U.R.* (*W.U.R.* in German), 1923
Play: Karel Čapek, production: John Gottwort, set: Friedrich Kiesler, Theater am Kurfürstendamm, backdrop for the final act
Gelatin silver print on baryta paper, 25.4 × 20.4 cm
Austrian Friedrich and Lillian Kiesler Private Foundation, Vienna, inv. no. PHO 2921/3
▸ p. 234

Sketch for a Table, 1935
Ink on paper, 14 × 21.5 cm
Austrian Friedrich and Lillian Kiesler Private Foundation, Vienna, inv. no. SFP 5251/0
▸ p. 254 (top left)

Sketch for a Table, 1935
Pencil on paper, 21.3 × 27.6 cm
Austrian Friedrich and Lillian Kiesler Private Foundation, Vienna, inv. no. SFP 5732/0
▸ p. 254 (below left)

Sketch for a Table, 1935
Pencil and color pencil on paper, 14 × 21.5 cm
Austrian Friedrich and Lillian Kiesler Private Foundation, Vienna, inv. no. SFP 5286/0
▸ p. 254 (top right)

Sketch for a Table, 1935
Pencil on paper, 14 × 21.5 cm
Austrian Friedrich and Lillian Kiesler Private Foundation, Vienna, inv. no. SFP 5249/0
▸ p. 254 (below right)

Two-Part Occasional Table, 1935–38
Table 1: H: 24.5 cm, W: 89.5 cm, D: 60 cm
Table 2: H: 24.5 cm, W: 57 cm, D: 41 cm
Part of an installation by Plamen Dejanov & Swetlana Heger
Belvedere, Vienna, inv. no. 9537
▸ p. 255

ERIKA GIOVANNA KLIEN
1900 Borgo Valsugana — 1957 New York
1912–13 Salzburg; 1918–26 Vienna; 1926–29 Klessheim; 1929 New York; 1931 Paris and Klessheim; 1932 New York.

Composition with String Instruments, 1923/24
Oil on canvas laid down on cardboard, 29.5 × 14 cm
Belvedere, Vienna, inv. no. 6088
▸ p. 210

Figurine *The Human Being, the Walker*, c. 1924
Charcoal, pencil, color pencil on paper, 32.2 × 19.5 cm
University of Applied Arts Vienna, Collection and Archive, inv. no. 2669
▸ p. 240

Kinetic Puppet Theater, 1926
Black chalk on paper, 62 × 43.5 cm
Private collection, Vienna
▸ p. 243

Kinetic Puppet Theater, 1926
Pencil, black chalk, charcoal and watercolor on paper, 49 × 65 cm
Private collection, Vienna
▸ p. 241

Kinetic Puppet Theater, 1926
Charcoal on paper, 50.3 × 20.1 cm
University of Applied Arts Vienna, Collection and Archive, inv. no. 11.620
▸ p. 242

GUSTAV KLIMT
1862 Vienna — 1918 Vienna

Adam and Eve, 1917/18
Oil on canvas (unfinished), 173 × 60 cm
Belvedere, Vienna, inv. no. 4402
▸ p. 63

Amalie Zuckerkandl, 1917/18
Oil on canvas (unfinished), 128 × 128 cm
Belvedere, Vienna, 1988 gift of Vita and Gustav Künstler, inv. no. 7700
▸ p. 64
V

Johanna Staude, 1917/18
Oil on canvas (unfinished), 70 × 50 cm
Belvedere, Vienna, inv. no. 5551
▸ p. 65

Lady in White, 1917/18
Oil on canvas (unfinished), 70 × 70 cm
Belvedere, Vienna, inv. no. 4286
no plate
B

OSKAR KOKOSCHKA
1886 Pöchlarn — 1980 Montreux
1886 Vienna; 1910 Berlin; 1911 returned to Vienna; 1914–16 military service; 1917–23 Dresden; 1933 returned to Vienna after travels abroad; 1934 Prague; 1938 fled to London; 1939 Polperro (Cornwall); 1940–45 London; 1952 Villeneuve (Switzerland).

Romana Kokoschka, the Artist's Mother, 1917
Oil on canvas, 112 × 75 cm
Belvedere, Vienna, inv. no. 5840
▸ p. 78

The Power of Music, 1918–20
Oil on canvas, 100 × 151.5 cm

Van Abbemuseum Collection, Eindhoven, inv. no. 1.0194
▸ p. 79

Dulsie Bridge, 1929
Oil on canvas, 74 × 93 cm
Belvedere, Vienna, inv. no. 5384
▸ p. 302

Portrait of Marcel von Nemes, 1929
Oil on canvas, 135 × 96 cm
LENTOS Kunstmuseum Linz, inv. no. 5
▸ p. 303

Prague Harbor, 1936
Oil on canvas, 91 × 117 cm
Belvedere, Vienna, inv. no. 3378
▸ p. 362

ANTON KOLIG
1886 Nový Jičín — 1950 Nötsch im Gailtal
1904–11 Vienna; 1912–14 Paris; 1916–18 military service; 1918–28 Nötsch im Gailtal; 1928–43 Stuttgart; 1943 returned to Nötsch.

Otto von Aichelburg-Zossenegg as First Lieutenant of the Cavalry, 1916
Oil on canvas, 144 × 91 cm
Belvedere, Vienna, inv. no. 4797
▸ p. 128

Kneeling Narcissus, 1920
Oil on canvas, 93 × 65.5 cm
Belvedere, Vienna, inv. no. 4558
▸ p. 157

Longing, 1921
Oil on canvas, 191.5 × 118 cm
Belvedere, Vienna, inv. no. 4456
▸ p. 297

BÉLA KONTULY
1904 Miskolc — 1983 Budapest
1921 studied in Prague and Budapest; 1928–30 Rome; 1941 Budapest.

Working-Class Girl (Girl with Striped Top), 1930
Oil on cardboard, 99 × 69 cm
Private collection
▸ p. 316

TONE KRALJ
1900 Zagorica — 1975 Ljubljana
1921–23 Academy of Fine Arts, Prague.

My Father, 1929
Oil on canvas, 147.5 × 181.3 cm
City Museum of Ljubljana (MGML), inv. no. 510: LIU; 0018665
▸ p. 315

ALFRED KUBIN
1877 Litoměřice — 1959 Zwickledt
1879–83 Salzburg; 1883–88 Zell am See; 1888–90 Salzburg; 1891 Zell am See, then Salzburg again; 1892–96 Klagenfurt; 1897 Zell am See; 1898–1906 Munich; 1906 Zwickledt.

Attack on the Infantry, 1914
Pen and ink and watercolor on paper, 31.3 × 39.5 cm
Albertina, Vienna, inv. no. 34309
▸ p. 107
V

Fury of War with Blazing Torch, c. 1914
Watercolor and ink on cadastre paper, 31.4 × 19.8 cm
Landesgalerie Linz, Graphic Arts Collection, inv. no. Ha II 3336
▸ p. 108
B

Entering Brussels, 1914
Color ink, watercolor, pen and black ink, 30.9 × 19.6 cm
Albertina, Vienna, inv. no. 33442
▸ p. 109
V

In the Casemates of Przemyśl, c. 1914/15
Pen and ink on cadastre paper, 19.5 × 31 cm
Landesgalerie Linz, Graphic Arts Collection, inv. no. Ha II 3344
▸ p. 111
B

Bavarian Soldiers, c. 1914/15
Ink and wash on cadastre paper, 31.4 × 19.7 cm
Landesgalerie Linz, Graphic Arts Collection, inv. no. Ha II 3328
▸ p. 112
B

Witch Transforming Herself, c. 1915
Pen and ink on paper, 26 × 36.2 cm
Albertina, Vienna, inv. no. 33246
▸ p. 106
V

Russian Advance Guard, 1915
Watercolor and ink on cadastre paper, 39.5 × 31.7 cm
Landesgalerie Linz, Graphic Arts Collection, Rombold Collection, inv. no. Ha II 13188
▸ p. 110
B

Balkan Crises, 1915–25
Color ink, watercolor, black pen and ink on paper, 36.8 × 26.5 cm
Albertina, Vienna, inv. no. 34111
no plate
V

Needle Phobia, 1915–18
Ink on paper, 36.5 × 26.4 cm
Albertina, Vienna, inv. no. 33294
no plate
V

Battle of Dwarves, 1915–20
Pen and ink and watercolor on paper, 31 × 39.2 cm
Albertina, Vienna, inv. no. 33298
no plate
V

Abyss, c. 1918–20
Watercolor and ink on cadastre paper, 19.9 × 31 cm
Landesgalerie Linz, Graphic Arts Collection, inv. no. Ha II 3320
no plate
B

The Fool of the World, c. 1920
Pen and ink and watercolor on paper, 39 × 30.8 cm
Albertina, Vienna, inv. no. 34316
▸ p. 329
V

In the Casemates, c. 1920
Color ink, wash, pen and black ink, 31.6 × 39.4 cm
Albertina, Vienna, inv. no. 34297
no plate
V

The Battlefield of Magenta, 1928
Ink on paper, 20.7 × 33.7 cm
Landesgalerie Linz, Graphic Arts Collection, inv. no. Ha 3487 II
▸ p. 330
B

The Old Yard Dog, c. 1928
Ink and watercolor, 31 × 38.3 cm
Belvedere, Vienna, inv. no. 4186
▸ p. 328

Hare Hunting, 1929
Pen and black and brown ink, wash and spray on paper, 30.3 × 40.6 cm
Albertina, Vienna, inv. no. 33713
▸ p. 326
V

Arrest, c. 1930
Pen and black and brown ink, wash and spray on paper, 37.8 × 31.3 cm
Albertina, Vienna, inv. no. 33896
no plate
V

BOHUMIL KUBIŠTA
1884 Vlčkovice — 1918 Prague
1903 Prague; 1906/07 Florence; 1913–18 military service in Pula.

Head, 1915
Patinated plaster of Paris, H: 36 cm, base: 15 cm (H: 51 cm)
The Gallery of West Bohemia in Pilsen, inv. no. P 145/b
▸ p. 93

Meditation, 1915
Oil on canvas, 50 × 30 cm
National Gallery in Prague, inv. no. O 9355
▸ p. 92

Coastal Canons Firing Against the Fleet, 1915
Oil on canvas, 37 × 49.3 cm
National Gallery in Prague, inv. no. O 3327
▸ p. 122
V

Air Raid Attack on Pula, 1915
Oil on canvas, 55.5 × 34 cm
The Gallery of West Bohemia in Pilsen, inv. no. O 832
▸ p. 123

FRANTIŠEK KUPKA
1871 Opočno — 1957 Paris-Puteaux
1884 Dobruška; 1887 Domažlice; 1888 Jaroměř; then Prague; 1893 Vienna; 1896 Paris; 1906 Puteaux; 1914/15 voluntary military service; 1940–45 Beaugency, France.

Lines, Planes, Depth, 1911/12
Oil on canvas, 82 × 69 cm
Museum Kampa—The Jan and Meda Mládek Foundation, Prague, inv. no. O 213
▸ p. 83
V

Study for *Around a Point*, 1911–30
Gouache, watercolor on paper, 30.7 × 31.2 cm
Museum Kampa—The Jan and Meda Mládek Foundation, Prague, inv. no. 354/ O 100.
▸ p. 84
V

Study for *Around a Point*, 1911–30
Gouache, watercolor on paper, 28 × 28.3 cm
Museum Kampa—The Jan and Meda Mládek Foundation, Prague, inv. no. 356/ O 102
▸ p. 85
B

Study for *Around a Point*, 1911–30
Gouache and watercolor on paper, 30.8 × 32 cm
Museum Kampa—The Jan and Meda Mládek Foundation, Prague, inv. no. 355/ O 101
no plate
V

L'Acier boit (Drinking Steel), 1927
Oil on canvas, 46.5 × 55 cm
Private collection, Prague
▸ p. 229

Study for *Circles and Straight Lines,* 1928–30
Gouache on paper, 49 × 50 cm
Museum Kampa—The Jan and Meda Mládek Foundation, Prague, inv. no. 452/ O 198
▸ p. 228 (top)
V

Study for *Circles and Straight Lines,* 1928–30
Gouache on paper, 50 × 50 cm
Museum Kampa—The Jan and Meda Mládek Foundation, Prague, inv. no. 453/ O 199
▸ p. 228 (below)
V

Abstraction, c. 1930
Gouache on paper, 28.3 × 28 cm
Museum Kampa—The Jan and Meda Mládek Foundation, Prague, inv. no. K305/ O 607
▸ p. 224 (top right)
V

Abstraction, c. 1931
Gouache on paper, 28 × 27.9 cm
Museum Kampa—The Jan and Meda Mládek Foundation, Prague, inv. no. K306/ O 608
▸ p. 224 (top left)
V

Abstraction, c. 1932
Gouache on paper, 28 × 27.9 cm
Museum Kampa—The Jan and Meda Mládek Foundation, Prague, inv. no. K307/ O 609
▸ p. 225
V

Abstraction, c. 1933
Gouache on paper, 28 × 27.9 cm
Museum Kampa—The Jan and Meda Mládek Foundation, Prague, inv. no. K308/ O 610
▸ p. 224 (below left)
V

Abstraction, c. 1934
Gouache on paper, 28 × 27.9 cm
Museum Kampa—The Jan and Meda Mládek Foundation, Prague, inv. no. K309/ O 611
▸ p. 226 (right)
B

Abstraction, c. 1935
Gouache on paper, 28 × 27.9 cm
Museum Kampa—The Jan and Meda Mládek Foundation, Prague, inv. no. K310/ O 612
▸ p. 224 (below right)
B

Abstraction, c. 1936
Gouache on paper, 28 × 27.9 cm
Museum Kampa—The Jan and Meda Mládek Foundation, Prague, inv. no. K311/ O 613
▸ p. 226 (left)
B

JOSEF LADA

1887 Hrusice — 1957 Prague
1902 Prague.

Jaroslav Hašek
Die Abenteuer des braven Soldaten Schwejk während des Weltkrieges (German translation of the Czech novel *The Good Soldier Švejk*), with illustrations by Josef Lada, vol. 3, Prague, 1926
Private collection
▸ p. 11

FRANZ LERCH

1895 Vienna — 1977 New York
1915–18 military service; 1938 emigrated to the Netherlands; then New York.

Girl with Hat, 1929
Oil on canvas, 80 × 60 cm
Belvedere, Vienna, inv. no. 6075
▸ p. 313

JÁNOS MATTIS-TEUTSCH

1884 Brașov — 1960 Brașov
1901–03 Budapest; 1903–05 Munich; 1905–08 Paris; 1908 Berlin; 1909 Brașov; 1916 Budapest and returned to Brașov; 1925 extended visit to Paris, then back in Brașov.

Landscape, c. 1917
Oil on cardboard, 50 × 50 cm
Museum of Fine Arts—Hungarian National Gallery, Budapest, inv. no. FK772
▸ p. 87
V

Landscape, c. 1917
Oil on plywood, 50 × 60 cm
Museum of Fine Arts—Hungarian National Gallery, Budapest, inv. no. 75.2 B
▸ p. 86

Solitary Tree, c. 1917
Oil on canvas, 20 × 30 cm
Flóris Rómer Museum of Art and History, Győr, inv. no. K. 85.29.1.
▸ p. 88

Symmetry, 1927
Oil on canvas, 145 × 90 cm
Rechnitzer Collection Hungary, Győr
▸ p. 209

Calling, 1928
Oil on canvas, 100 × 70 cm
Rechnitzer Collection Hungary, Győr
▸ p. 208

LÁSZLÓ MEDNYÁNSZKY

1852 Beckov — 1919 Vienna
1862 Strážky; 1872 Miskolc; 1872–74 Munich; 1874 Paris; 1875 Barbizon, then Paris; 1877 Barbizon and then returned to Hungary (Szolnok and Budapest); 1914–18 worked for the War Press Office.

In Serbia, 1914
Oil on canvas, 67.6 × 100 cm
Museum of Fine Arts—Hungarian National Gallery, Budapest, inv. no. 5245
▸ p. 132

Christmas of the Prisoners-of-War c. 1915
Oil on canvas, 80 × 100 cm
Tamás Kieselbach Collection
▸ p. 133

IVAN MEŠTROVIĆ

1883 Vrpolje — 1962 South Bend (Indiana)
1883–1900 Otavice; 1900 Split; 1900 Vienna; 1908 Paris; 1912 Rome; 1915 returned to Paris; 1919 Zagreb; 1925 visit to the USA; 1942 fled from Zagreb to Italy, where he lived in Venice, then Rome; 1943 Lausanne and Geneva; 1946 emigrated to the USA; 1947–55 New York; 1956–62 South Bend, Indiana.

Vestal Virgin, 1915
Bronze, H: 35.5 cm, W: 26.9 cm, D: 18.2 cm
The Ivan Meštrović Museums—Meštrović Atelier, Zagreb, inv. no. AMZ 185
▸ p. 103

FRANZ METZNER

1870 Všeruby — 1919 Berlin
1886 Plzeň; 1890–94 Wrocław, Zwickau, Dresden, and Leipzig; 1894 Berlin; 1903 Vienna; 1906 returned to Berlin.

Breakdown, 1919
Sandstone, H: 51.2 cm, W: 44.3 cm, D: 38.5 cm
Kunstforum Ostdeutsche Galerie Regensburg
▸ p. 159

LÁSZLÓ MOHOLY-NAGY

1895 Bácsborsód — 1946 Chicago (Illinois)
Until 1912 Mol; 1912 Budapest; 1915–17 military service; 1918 Budapest; 1919 fled to Vienna; 1920 Berlin; 1923 Bauhaus Weimar; 1925 Bauhaus Dessau; 1928 Berlin; 1933 emigrated to the Netherlands, Amsterdam; 1935 London; 1937 Chicago.

Composition A 17, 1927
Tempera on hessian, 74.5 × 93 cm
Kunstmuseum Gelsenkirchen
▸ p. 227

Kinetic Constructive System (Structure for Moving Parts for Play and Movement), 1922–28
Photomontage, ink, and watercolor on cardboard, 76 × 54.5 cm
Theater Collection, University of Cologne, inv. no. 5261 a
▸ p. 236

László Moholy-Nagy, István Sebök
Electrical Stage Lighting, 1922–30
Collage on tracing paper, 65.2 × 49.9 cm
Theater Collection, University of Cologne, inv. no. 5262 b
▸ p. 237

Electrical Stage Lighting, 1922–30
Collage, ink on tracing paper, 60.4 × 59.5 cm
Theater Collection, University of Cologne, inv. no. 5262 a
▸ p. 233

FARKAS MOLNÁR

1897 Pécs — 1945 Budapest (following an air raid)
1915–21 Budapest; 1921–25 Bauhaus Weimar.

KURI Collage with Self-Portrait, 1929
Oil and collage on paper, 33 × 50 cm
Petőfi Literary Museum—Kassák Museum, Budapest, inv. no. KM-M-83.31
▸ p. 219

KOLOMAN MOSER

1868 Vienna — 1918 Vienna
1892/93 Reichenau an der Rax; 1893 Vienna.

Self-Portrait, c. 1916
Oil on canvas, laid down on cardboard, 74 × 50 cm
Belvedere, Vienna, inv. no. 5569
▸ p. 73

MARIE-LOUISE VON MOTESICZKY

1906 Vienna — 1996 London
1925–27 extended visits to Paris; 1927/28 Frankfurt am Main; 1928 Berlin;; 1930 returned to Vienna; 1938 fled to the Netherlands; 1939 London; 1940 Amersham; 1945 London; 1958 Chesterford Gardens, Hampstead.

Self-Portrait with Comb, 1926
Oil on canvas, 83 × 45 cm
Belvedere, Vienna, inv. no. 9094
▸ p. 301

ALFONS MUCHA
1860 Ivančice — 1939 Prague
1871 Brno; 1879 Vienna;
1882 Hrušovany nad Jevišovkou;
1883 Eppan;
1885 Munich; 1887 Paris;
1900/01 Zagreb; 1904–09 moved frequently between Europe and the USA; 1910 returned to Bohemia, lived and worked in Prague and at Zbiroh Castle; 1919–21 visit to the USA; 1932–34 Nice, then Paris; 1938 returned to Prague.

Study for the Slav Epic No. 14:
The Defense of Szigetvár against the Turks by the Ban of Croatia Nikola Šubić Zrinski in 1566, c. 1913/14
Oil on canvas, 24 × 35.5 cm
Courtesy of Mucha Trust,
inv. no. O-020
▸ p. 66

The War, 1917
Pen and ink on paper, 47 × 40 cm
Courtesy of Mucha Trust,
inv. no. D-002
▸ p. 68

Study for the Slav Epic No. 8:
After the Battle of Grunwald in 1410, 1923/24
Pencil and watercolor on paper,
35 × 56 cm
Courtesy of Mucha Trust,
inv. no. W-077
▸ p. 67

JÓZSEF NEMES-LAMPÉRTH
1891 Budapest — 1924 Sátoraljaújhely
1911 Baia Mare; 1911/12 Budapest; 1913/14 Paris; 1914–17 military service; 1917 Budapest; 1919 fled to Berlin; 1920 Stockholm; 1921 Budapest; 1923 Sátoraljaújhely.

Standing Female Nude (Frontal View), 1916
Oil on canvas, 131 × 79.5 cm
Museum of Fine Arts—Hungarian National Gallery, Budapest,
inv. no. 59.147T
▸ p. 71

Landscape (with View of Horgony Street), 1917
Oil on canvas, 98.5 × 106.5 cm
Museum of Fine Arts—Hungarian National Gallery, Budapest,
inv. no. 66.26T
▸ p. 70

OTTO NEURATH
1882 Vienna — 1945 Oxford
1903–06 Berlin; 1907 Vienna; 1914 military service; 1914 professorship in Heidelberg; 1918 Leipzig; 1920 returned to Vienna; 1934 fled to the Netherlands, emigrated to Britain.

Die bunte Welt: Mengenbilder für die Jugend (Colorful World), Vienna, 1929
Dieter and Gertraud Bogner Collection at the mumok, since 2007,
inv. no. MD 124/0
no plate

MAX OPPENHEIMER
1885 Vienna — 1954 New York
1900–03 Vienna; 1903–08 Prague, then Vienna until 1911; 1912 moved to Berlin. 1915 moved to Switzerland; 1924 returned to Vienna; 1926 Berlin; 1932 returned to Vienna; 1938 fled to Switzerland; 1939 emigrated to the USA, New York.

Klingler Quartet, 1917
Oil and tempera on canvas,
70 × 80 cm (oval)
Belvedere, Vienna, inv. no. 2493
▸ p. 77

WOLFGANG PAALEN
1905 Vienna — 1959 Taxco de Alarcón (Guerrero)
1912 Berlin and Żagań; 1919 Italy, Rome; 1922 Berlin; 1926 Paris; 1927/28 Munich and Saint-Tropez; 1928 La Ciotat and Paris; 1939 emigrated to the USA, Canada, and then Mexico; 1948 San Francisco; 1951 returned to Mexico; 1951–54 Paris; 1954 returned to Mexico.

Paysage totémique, 1938
Fumage and oil on canvas,
130 × 100 cm
Private collection
▸ p. 259

PÉTER PÁLFFY
1899 Seebarn — 1987 Vienna
1921/22 Munich; 1923/24 Berlin; 1924–33 Paris; 1933 Czechoslovakia, Bratislava; 1945 fled to Austria, Kitzbühel; 1962 Vienna.

Still Life with Watering Can and Cactus, 1935
Pastel on paper, 69 × 49 cm
Slovak National Gallery, Bratislava,
inv. no. 0.3938
▸ p. 304

VENO PILON
1896 Ajdovščina — 1970 Ajdovščina
Attended school in Gorizia until 1915; 1915–18 military service; 1918 Ljubljana; 1919/20 Prague; 1920/21 Florence; 1921/22 Vienna, then Ajdovščina; 1930 lived in Paris; 1947 returned to Slovenia; 1949–67 returned to Paris; 1967 Ajdovščina.

Portrait of the Composer Marij Kogoj, 1923
Oil on canvas, 94 × 72 cm
Moderna galerija / Museum of Modern Art, Ljubljana,
inv. no. MG 546/S
▸ p. 293

HERBERT PLOBERGER
1902 Wels — 1977 Munich
1921–26 Vienna; 1925 Paris (?); 1927 Berlin; 1950 Munich.

Window Shopping, 1928
Oil on wood, 40 × 34 cm
Private collection, Vienna
▸ p. 308

JAN PREISLER
1872 Popovice / Králův Dvůr — 1918 Prague
From 1887 Prague;
1902 traveled through Italy.

The Good Samaritan, 1910–14
Oil on cardboard, 30.4 × 21 cm
The Gallery of West Bohemia in Pilsen,
inv. no. O 781
▸ p. 69

VOJTĚCH PREISSIG
1873 Světec — 1944 Dachau concentration camp
1884–97 Prague; 1897–1903 Paris; 1903–10 Prague; 1910–30 Chicago, Philadephia, and New York; 1930–40 Prague; 1940 held as a political prisoner in Goleniów, Dresden, Prague, and ultimately Dachau concentration camp.

"Who burns for the truth"— Now or never!, 1916
Color linocut, 87 × 60 cm
The Museum of Decorative Arts in Prague, inv. no. GP8970
▸ p. 136

Stamps for Czechoslovakia— "resistance post," 1939
Zincograph on paper, 26.2 × 19.1 cm
The Museum of Decorative Arts in Prague, inv. no. G2228
▸ p. 368 (below right)
V

The Czechslovak Republic Will Prevail! This is its New Coat of Arms, 1939
Color linocut, plate: 28 × 25 cm, sheet: 49.5 × 30.6 cm
The Museum of Decorative Arts in Prague, inv. no. G2227
▸ p. 368 (top left)

Stamps for Czechoslovakia— "resistance post," 1939
Linocut on paper,
8.6 × 14.7 cm, 8.8 × 15 cm,
8.7 × 14.8 cm
The Museum of Decorative Arts in Prague
B

ANTONÍN PROCHÁZKA
1882 Vážany u Vyškova — 1945 Brno
1889–1902 Kroměříž; 1902–06 Prague; 1906/07 traveled through Europe; 1907–09 Prague; 1910–21 Ostrava; 1921–24 Nové Město na Moravě; from 1924 Brno.

The Singer, 1916
Oil on canvas, 68.2 × 54.5 cm
Brno City Museum, inv. no. 50.770
▸ p. 90

The Soldier, c. 1916
Oil on cardboard, 30 × 24 cm
The Regional Art Gallery Liberec,
inv. no. O 964
▸ p. 127

Still Life with Kerosene Lamp, 1921
Oil on canvas, 63 × 49 cm
Belvedere, Vienna, on permanent loan from the Rotter Collection,
inv. no. Lg 1446
▸ p. 205

JÓZSEF RIPPL-RÓNAI
1861 Kaposvár — 1927 Kaposvár
1879–81 Budapest; 1884–87 Munich; 1887–92 Paris; 1892–1900 Neuilly; 1900–02 Budapest; from 1902 Kaposvár.

Place de l'Observatoire (Parc Monceau), 1914
Oil on paper, 75 × 105 cm
Museum of Fine Arts—Hungarian National Gallery, Budapest,
inv. no. FK8946
▸ p. 60

French Soldiers Marching, 1914
Oil on cardboard, 69 × 96.5 cm
Musée d'Orsay, Paris,
inv. no. RF MO P 2015-37
▸ p. 61
V

The Coronation of Charles IV, 1916
Oil on paper and canvas, 102 × 72 cm
BHM, Museum Kiscell, Municipal Gallery, Budapest, Hungary,
inv. no. IN: 15738
▸ p. 59

WOLFGANG SCHAUKAL
1900 Brno — 1981 Graz
1903 Vienna; 1922/23 Nötsch im Gailtal; 1928–31 Vienna and Berlin; 1934–37 Vienna, then Styria; from 1945 Graz.

Self-Portrait in a Dragoon's Uniform, 1918
Oil on canvas, softboard,
58.5 × 45.8 cm
Belvedere, Vienna, inv. no. 8686
▸ p. 129

EGON SCHIELE

1890 Tulln — 1918 Vienna
1902–06 Klosterneuburg; 1906–11 Vienna; 1911/12 Český Krumlov and Neulengbach, then Vienna; 1915 war duties.

Russian Prisoner of War, 1915
Gouache and pencil on paper, 44.5 × 31 cm
Belvedere, Vienna, inv. no. 1965c
▸ p. 126
V

Squatting Men (Double Self-Portrait), 1918 (completed by another hand)
Oil on canvas, 100 × 171 cm
Private collection, courtesy of Richard Nagy Ltd., London
▸ p. 74

The Family (Squatting Couple), 1918
Oil on canvas, 150 × 160.8 cm
Belvedere, Vienna, inv. no. 4277
▸ p. 75
V

ALOIS HANS SCHRAMM

1864 Vienna — 1919 Vienna
1889/90 Rome; 1891 Vienna.

Guard of the Carpathians, 1914/15
Oil on canvas, 105 × 75 cm
Belvedere, Vienna, inv. no. 8084
▸ p. 130

ERNŐ SCHUBERT

1903 Báč — 1960 Budapest
From 1924 Budapest.

Suburb, 1928–32
Oil on cardboard, 80 × 68 cm
Museum of Fine Arts—Hungarian National Gallery, Budapest, inv. no. 78.115 T
▸ p. 335

FRITZ SCHWARZ-WALDEGG

1889 Vienna — 1942 Malý Trostinec extermination camp
1915–18 military service; 1928–32 Berlin and Vienna; 1929 Basque Country; 1942 deported to the Malý Trostinec extermination camp near Minsk.

Confession, 1920
Oil on canvas, 117 × 88 cm
Belvedere, Vienna, inv. no. 5408
▸ p. 156

FRANZ SEDLACEK

1891 Wrocław — 1945 (?)
1894 Nuremberg; 1897 Linz; 1910 Vienna; 1914–18 military service; from 1918 Vienna; winter 1941/42 conscripted for military service; 1942–45 military service; 1945 missing in action since the battle at Toruń Fortress, Poland; 1965 pronounced dead.

Practice Slope, 1926
Oil on plywood, 26.5 × 23.3 cm
LENTOS Kunstmuseum Linz, inv. no. 462
▸ p. 319

The Gardener, 1928
Oil on plywood, 79.5 × 74 cm
Private collection, Seligenstadt
▸ p. 325

Storm, 1932
Oil on plywood, 102 × 95 cm
Belvedere, Vienna, inv. no. 4618
▸ p. 327
B

Ghosts on the Tree, 1933
Oil on plywood, 65 × 55 cm
Albertina, Vienna, loan from E. Ploil, inv. no. GE453DL
▸ p. 324
V

The Grosser Geiger (Venediger Group), second version, 1938
Oil on wood, 66.5 × 56 cm
Private collection
▸ p. 318

FRANZ SINGER

1896 Vienna — 1954 Berlin
1915–17 military service; 1919–23 Weimar; from 1923 Berlin; 1925 returned to Vienna; 1938 Britain; early 1950s Salzburg; then Berlin.

Franz Singer, Friedl Dicker-Brandeis
Models for Two Chairs and for Stools, c. 1932–34
Metal, paper, H: 20.5 cm, W: 8.5 cm, D: 9.5 cm
Georg Schrom, Vienna
▸ p. 216

LILLY STEINER

1884 Vienna — 1961 Paris
1927 Paris.

Composition Baroque, 1938
Oil on canvas, 146 × 97 cm
Belvedere, Vienna, inv. no. 4156
▸ p. 366

JAN ŠTURSA

1880 Nové Město na Moravě — 1925 Prague; 1894–98 Hořice; 1898/99 Mittelstein and Berlin; 1899–1914 Prague; 1914–16 military service; from 1916 Prague.

Wounded Man, 1916
Bronze, H: 49.5 cm
Belvedere, Vienna, inv. no. 2019
▸ p. 124

JINDŘICH ŠTYRSKÝ

1899 Dolní Čermná — 1942 Prague
1914–17 Hradec Králové; 1917/18 military service; 1918–20 Dolní Čermná; 1920–25 Prague; 1925–28 Paris; 1929–35 Prague; 1935 Paris; from 1935 Prague.

Flood, 1927
Oil on canvas, 110 × 54.8 cm
Moravian Gallery, Brno, inv. no. A 1346
▸ p. 260

Palmette, 1931
Oil on canvas, 97.8 × 74.7 cm
Moravian Gallery, Brno, inv. no. A 1347
▸ p. 261

JÁNOS TÁBOR (TAUPHERT)

1890 Budapest (?) — 1956 Budapest (?)

Red Soldiers Advance!, 1919
Lithograph on paper, 127 × 96 cm
Museum of Fine Arts—Hungarian National Gallery, Budapest, inv. no. XY.58.187
▸ p. 167
V

KÁROLY TAMKÓ SIRATÓ

1905 Novi Sad (Нови Сад) — 1980 Budapest
1922–28 Budapest; 1928 Debrecen; 1930 Paris; from 1942 (?) Budapest.

Epic about Humanity, "Planpoemes IX," 1929
Mixed media on paper, 40.6 × 52.4 cm
Private collection, Switzerland
▸ p. 218 (below)
V

Self-Portrait, 1930
Mixed media on paper, 23 × 35 cm
Private collection, Switzerland
▸ p. 218 (top)
V

RICHARD TESCHNER

1879 Karlovy Vary — 1948 Vienna
1884 Litoměřice; 1895–99 Prague; 1900 Vienna; 1901 Litoměřice; 1902 Prague; 1909 Vienna.

Nawang Wulan rod puppet from the play *Nawang Wulan*, 1912
Limewood, polychromy, fabric, H: 44 cm
Theatermuseum, Vienna, inv. no. PFS O 2880
▸ p. 101

Study for the *Nude Princess*, 1913 (?)
Pencil and watercolor on paper, laid down on cardboard, 65 × 50 cm
Theatermuseum, Vienna, inv. no. HZ HS16598
▸ p. 99
B

Study for the *Wassermann* (Water Elf), 1913 (?)
Pencil and watercolor on paper, 65 cm × 47.5 cm
Theatermuseum, Vienna, inv. no. HZ HS16593
▸ p. 100
B

Study for the figures *Princess, Sorcerer,* and *Wassermann* (Water Elf), 1913 (?)
Pencil, watercolor, and gold paint on cardboard, 66 × 50 cm
Theatermuseum, Vienna, inv. no. HZ HS16595
no plate
V

Study for the *Nude Princess*, 1913 (?)
Pencil and watercolor on paper, laid down on cardboard, 66 × 50 cm
Theatermuseum, Vienna, inv. no. HZ HS16597
no plate
V

WILHELM THÖNY

1888 Graz — 1949 New York
1908 Munich; 1915–18 military service; from 1918 Munich; 1919 Weggis (Switzerland); 1922 Munich; 1923 Graz; 1928–29 Graz and Munich; 1931 Paris; 1938 New York.

Emperor Franz Joseph at the Vienna Prater, 1931–33
Oil on cardboard laid down on hardboard, 35 × 45 cm
Belvedere, Vienna, inv. no. 5823
▸ p. 331

General and Diplomat, c. 1930–40
Oil on canvas, 36 × 45.5 cm
Belvedere, Vienna, inv. no. 5824
▸ p. 333

View of Manhattan (East River), 1935–38
Oil on cardboard, 56 × 78.2 cm
Belvedere, Vienna, inv. no. 4624
▸ p. 332

LAJOS TIHANYI

1885 Budapest — 1938 Paris
Until 1919 Budapest; 1919–24 Vienna and Berlin; from 1925 Paris.

Portrait of Magdolna Leopold, 1914
Oil on canvas, 70.5 × 59.5 cm
St. Stephen's King Museum — Deák Collection, Székesfehérvár
▸ p. 72

Composition in Blue and Yellow, 1934
Oil on plywood, 38.5 × 46 cm
Museum of Fine Arts—Hungarian National Gallery, Budapest, inv. no. 70.198T
▸ p. 213

Composition, 1937
Oil on canvas, 43.5 × 50.5 cm
Museum of Fine Arts—Hungarian National Gallery, Budapest, inv. no. 70.202T
▸ p. 212

TOYEN (MARIE ČERMÍNOVÁ)
1902 Prague — 1980 Paris
Until 1925 Prague; 1925–34 Paris; 1934–47 Prague; from 1947 Paris.

Painting, 1929
Oil on canvas, 71 × 98 cm
Belvedere, Vienna, on permanent loan from the Rotter Collection, inv. no. Lg 1461
▸ p. 258

Voice of the Forest, 1934
Oil on canvas, 92 × 72 cm
Moravian Gallery, Brno, inv. no. A 1472
▸ p. 256

Abandoned Cave, 1937
Oil on canvas, 113 × 77.5 cm
Gallery of Fine Arts in Cheb
▸ p. 257
B

WALTER TRIER
1890 Prague — 1951 Collingwood
1907 Munich, 1910 Berlin, 1936 London, 1947 Canada

Lilliput. The pocket magazine.
Stefan Lorant & Walter Trier Ed., London, Vol. 3, No. 1, 13 July 1938, Birthday Number
Private collection

Lilliput. The pocket magazine.
Stefan Lorant & Walter Trier Ed., London, Vol. 4, No. 1, 19 January 1939
Private collection

BÉLA UITZ
1887 Mehala — 1972 Budapest
1908–12 Budapest; 1914–18 (?) military service; 1918–20 Budapest; 1920 Vienna; 1921 Berlin and Moscow (Москва́); 1922/23 Vienna; 1924 Paris; 1926–36 Moscow (Москва́); 1936–38 Bishkek (Бишкек); 1938/39 imprisonment; 1970–72 Pécs and Budapest.

Icon Analysis on a Purple Background, 1922
Oil on canvas, 158 × 141 cm
Museum of Fine Arts—Hungarian National Gallery, Budapest, inv. no. 72.36T
▸ p. 206
B

Fight, 1922
Oil on canvas, 155.5 × 144.5 cm
Museum of Fine Arts—Hungarian National Gallery, Budapest, inv. no. 72.37 T
▸ p. 207
V

MARIANNE (MY) ULLMANN
1905 Vienna — 1995 Konstanz
1930 Munich; 1933–34 Berlin; 1944 Lübeck and Travemünde; until 1945 Gdańsk; 1947–50 Munich; from 1960 Münster.

Modest, 1925
Tempera on canvas, 60 × 60 cm
University of Applied Arts Vienna, Collection and Archive, inv. no. 10.008/B
▸ p. 211

MILIVOJ UZELAC
1897 Mostar — 1977 Cotignac
1903 Banja Luka; 1912–15 Zagreb; 1915–19 Prague; 1921 Paris; 1922 Zagreb; 1923 Paris; from 1935 southern France; from 1963 Cotignac.

Self-Portrait in front of the Bar, 1923
Oil on canvas, 93 × 69 cm
National Museum of Modern Art, Zagreb, inv. no. MG-1012
▸ p. 291

VICTOR VASARELY
1908 Pécs — 1997 Paris
Until 1919 Piešťany; 1920–30 Budapest; 1930–42 Paris; 1942–44 Saint-Céré; 1945–61 Arcueil; 1961 Annet-sur-Marne; from 1976 Aix-en-Provence.

Mitín, 1938
Gouache, lead white, black paint, airbrush on paper, 59.7 × 40 cm
Museum of Fine Arts—Vasarely Museum, Budapest, inv. no. VAS_V.24
▸ p. 231

JÁNOS VASZARY
1867 Kaposvár — 1939 Budapest
1885–87 Budapest; 1887/88 Munich; 1889/90 Paris; 1891 Venice, Florence, and Rome; 1891 Esztergom; 1893 Paris; 1896 Esztergom; 1898 Budapest; 1914–16 military service; 1916–25 Budapest; 1925 Paris; 1934/35 Rapallo, Venice, and Assisi; until 1939 Budapest.

Soldiers in the Snow, 1916
Oil on canvas, 101.5 × 121 cm
Museum of Fine Arts—Hungarian National Gallery, Budapest, inv. no. 59.40T
▸ p. 131

RUDOLF WACKER
1893 Bregenz — 1939 Bregenz
1910/11 Vienna; 1911–14 Weimar; 1914 military service; 1915–20 prisoner of war in Tomsk (Томск; Siberia); 1920 Nizhny Novgorod (Ни́жний Но́вгород) and Moscow (Москва́); 1920–24 Berlin; 1924 Vienna and Sibiu; from 1925 Bregenz.

Still Life with Holly, 1933
Oil on plywood, 65 × 50 cm
Private collection
▸ p. 322

Two Heads (Wooden Head and Children's Drawing), 1936
Mixed technique on wood, 65 × 50 cm
Private collection
▸ p. 321

Cracked Doll's Head, 1937
Mixed technique on wood, 24 × 26 cm
Private collection, Vienna, courtesy of Kunsthandel Giese & Schweiger, Vienna
▸ p. 323

IMRICH WEINER-KRÁĽ
1901 Považská Bystrica — 1978 Bratislava
1919–22 Prague; 1922 Düsseldorf; 1923 Berlin; 1924 Paris; 1924–29 Považská Bystrica; 1929–37 Bratislava; 1937 Berlin; 1938–50 Paris; 1951–61 Prague and Považská Bystrica; from 1961 Bratislava.

Tatra, 1933
Oil on canvas, 64.5 × 55 cm
Slovak National Gallery, Bratislava, inv. no. O 2640
▸ p. 263

ANDOR WEININGER
1899 Karanac — 1986 New York
1917–21 Pécs and Budapest; 1921–25 Weimar; 1925 Schönau, Berchtesgaden, and Pécs; 1926–28 Dessau; 1928–38 Berlin; 1938–42 Scheveningen; 1942–51 Amsterdam; 1951–58 Toronto; from 1958 New York.

De-Stijl Composition, 1922/62
Oil on cardboard, 101 × 26 cm
Museum of Fine Arts—Hungarian National Gallery, Budapest, inv. no. F83.14
▸ p. 238
B

Mechanical Stage Revue, phase I–III, n.d. (Dessau)
Pencil, gouache, watercolor, ink, and gold bronze on paper, 40.4 × 56.5 cm
Theater Collection, University of Cologne, inv. no. G 5254
▸ p. 239

ALFRED WICKENBURG
1885 Bad Gleichenberg — 1978 Graz
1891 Vienna; 1900–04 Graz; 1904 Munich; 1905 Dachau; 1905–09 Paris; 1909–14 Stuttgart; 1914–18 military service; 1919 Graz and Bad Gleichenberg; 1920–23 Rome, Florence, Milan, Naples, and Venice; from 1923 Graz.

Narcissus, 1922
Oil on canvas, 159 × 105 cm
Private collection
▸ p. 155

FRITZ WOTRUBA
1907 Vienna — 1975 Vienna
1932 Venice; 1933 Zürich and Rüschlikon; 1937 Zürich, Bern, Taubenberg, Düsseldorf, and Berlin; 1938 Essen, Düsseldorf, Berlin, and Zürich; 1939–45 Zug; 1940 Chêne-Bougeries; from 1945 Vienna.

Torso, 1928/29
Mannersdorf limestone, H: 139.5 cm, W: 40.5 cm, D: 44 cm
Belvedere, Vienna, on permanent loan from the Fritz Wotruba Private Foundation
▸ p. 296

JAN ZRZAVÝ
1890 Okrouhlice — 1977 Prague
1896–1905 attended school in Kutná Hora, Přibislav, and Havlíčkův Brod; 1905 Brno; 1906–77 Prague; 1942 repeated stays in Vodňany, 1947 in Olomouc, and 1955 in Okrouhlice.

Obsession (Lovers), 1914
Oil on canvas, 44 × 32 cm
Gallery of Fine Arts in Ostrava, inv. no. O 680
▸ p. 104

Meditation (Prayer), 1915
Oil on canvas, 50.2 × 37.5 cm
National Gallery in Prague, inv. no. O 8603
▸ p. 102

Suffering, 1916
Oil on canvas, 40 × 33 cm
National Gallery in Prague, inv. no. O 9245
▸ p. 105
V

Piazza San Marco, Venice, 1929
Oil on canvas, 48.5 × 63 cm
Belvedere, Vienna, on permanent loan from the Rotter Collection, inv. no. Lg 1472
▸ p. 334

Index of Persons

Concordance of Place Names

The following gives an overview of the places mentioned throughout this catalogue and their historical and modern names in the various different languages spoken in the lands of the former Austro-Hungarian Monarchy. The languages represented and place names researched can only give a general impression of the linguistic diversity of the multiethnic Austro-Hungarian Empire. Providing a complete record of it would be an almost impossible task.

Names of locations outside the boundaries of the Austro-Hungarian Empire are also listed in the languages spoken in the countries of the former Empire.

In a few cases, for example, if a name is ordinarily written in Cyrillic or if the English variant is widely known, a place is listed by its English name first and marked with an *.

(A) Austria
(H) Hungary
(RO) Romania
(BIH) Bosnia and Herzegovina
(CZ) Czech Republic
(HR) Croatia
(I) Italy
(PL) Poland
(SLO) Slovenia
(SRB) Serbia
(SK) Slovakia
(UA) Ukraine
(BY) Belarus
(CDN) Canada
(CH) Switzerland
(D) Germany
(F) France
(GB) United Kingdom
(KG) Kyrgyzstan
(MEX) Mexico
(NL) Netherlands
(PL) Poland
(RUS) Russia
(S) Sweden
(USA) United States of America

1 German
2 Hungarian
3 Czech
4 Croatian
5 Slovenian
6 Slovak
7 Italian
8 Polish
9 Romanian
10 Ukrainian
11 Serbian
12 Russian
13 Hebrew/Yiddish
14 Ladin

Aigen (A)
Aigen[1]

Ajdovščina (SLO)
Haidenschaft[1], Ajdovščina[5]

Auschwitz (PL)*
Auschwitz[1], Oświęcim[8], אוישוויץ[13]

Báč (SK)
Bacsfa[2], Báč[6]

Bácsborsód (H)
Bácsborsód[2], Boršot[4], Бачборшод[11]

Bad Gleichenberg (A)
Bad Gleichenberg[1]

Baia Mare (RO)
Frauenbach/Groß-Neustadt[1], Nagybánya[2], Baia Mare[9]

Banja Luka (BIH)
Weina Luka/Luka[1], Бањa Лука[11]

Bechyně (CZ)
Bechin/Beching[1], Bechyně[3]

Beckov (SK)
Beckow[1], Beckó[2], Beckov[6]

Bozen (I)*
Bozen[1], Bolzano[7], Bulsan[14]

Borgo Valsugana (I)
Burg im Suganertal[1], Al Bórgo[7]

Brașov (RO)
Kronstadt[1], Brassó[2], Brașov[9]

Bratislava (SK)
Pressburg[1], Pozsony[2], Požun[4], Bratislava[6], Братислава[11], Братисла́ва[12], בראטיסלאווא / ברטיסלאבה[13]

Braunau (A)
Braunau[1]

Brno (CZ)
Brünn[1], Brno[3], ברין / ברנו[13]

Budapest (H)
Budapest[1], Budapest[2], Budapešť[3], Budimpešta[4], Budapešť[6], Budapesta[9], Будимпешта[11], Будапе́шт[12], בודאַפּעשט / בּוּדַפֶּשְׁט[13]

Bystřice nad Pernštejnem (CZ)
Bistritz ob Pernstein/Wistritz[1], Bystřice nad Pernštejnem[3]

Cătina/Cetina (RO)
Katona[2], Cătina[9]

Česká Lípa (CZ)
Leipa[1], Česká Lípa[3]

Cieszyn (PL)
Teschen[1], Těšín[3], Cieszyn[8]

Chropyně (CZ)
Chropin/Kropin[1], Chropyně[3]

Czernowitz (UA)
Tschernowitz/Czernowitz[1], Czerniowce[8], Cernăuți[9], Чернівці[10], Черновцы[12], טשערנאָוויץ / צֶ׳רְנוֹבִיץ[13]

Debrecen (H)
Debrezin[1], Debrecen[2], Debrecín[6], Debrețin[9]

Dobruška (CZ)
Gutenfeld[1], Dobruška[3]

Dolní Čermná (CZ)
Niedertscherma/Böhmisch Rothwasser[1], Dolní Čermná[3]

Domažlice (CZ)
Taus[1], Domažlice[3]

Dubica (Kozarska Dubica) (BIH)
Bosanska Dubica[4], Козарска Дубица[11]

Dvůr Králové nad Labem (CZ)
Königinhof an der Elbe[1], Dvůr Králové nad Labem[3]

Eppan (I)
Eppan an der Weinstraße[1], Appiano sulla Strada del Vino[7]

Esztergom (H)
Gran[1], Esztergom[2], Ostrihom[4 11], Ostrihom[6], Strigonio/Strigonia[7]

Glogovnica (HR)
Donja Glogovnica / Gornja Glogovnica[4]

Gomirje (HR)
Gomirje[4], Гомирје[11]

Görz (I)
Görz[1], Gorica[5], Gorizia[7]

Graz (A)
Graz[1], Grác[2], Štýrský Hradec[3], Gradac[4], Grádec[5], Štajerský Hradec[6], Grodziec[8]

Haag am Hausruck (A)
Haag am Hausruck[1]

Hall in Tirol (A)
Hall in Tirol[1]

Havlíčkův Brod (CZ)
Deutschbrod[1], Havlíčkův Brod/Německý Brod[3]

Heves (H)
Hewesch[1], Heves[2], Heveš[6]

Hinterstoder (A)
Hinterstoder[1]

Hlušice (CZ)
Groß Hluschitz[1], Hlušice[3]

Hodonín (CZ)
Göding[1], Hodonín[3]

Hořice (CZ)
Horschitz[1], Hořice v Podkrkonoší[3]

Hradec Králové (CZ)
Königgrätz[1], Hradec Králové[3]

Hronov (CZ)
Hronow[1], Hronov nad Metují[3]

Hrusice (CZ)
Hrusice[3]

Hrušovany nad Jevišovkou (CZ)
Grusbach[1], Hrušovany nad Jevišovkou[3]

Ivančice (CZ)
Eibenschütz[1], Ivančice[3]

Jaroměř (CZ)
Jermer[1], Jaroměř[3]

Kaposvár (H)
Kopisch/Ruppertsberg / Ruppertsburg[1], Kaposvár[2], Kapošvár[6]

Karanac (HR)
Karancs[2], Karanac[4], Каранац[11]

Karlovac (HR)
Karlstadt/Carlstadt[1], Károlyváros[2], Karlovac[4], Carlostadio[7]

Karlovy Vary (CZ)
Karlsbad[1], Karlovy Vary[3]

Kitzbühel (A)
Kitzbühel[1], Kobylí[3]

Klagenfurt (A)
Klagenfurt[1], Celovac[4], Celovec ob Vrbskem jezeru[5]

Kleßheim (A)
Kleßheim[1]

Klosterneuburg (A)
Klosterneuburg[1]

Komárom (H) **/ Komárno** (SK)
Komorn[1], Komárom[2], Komárno[6]

Košice (SK)
Kaschau[1], Kassa[2], Košice[6], Koszyce[8], קאשוי / קוֹשִיצֶה[13]

Krakau (PL)*
Krakau[1], Krakkó[2], Krakov[3 4 6 11 12], Cracovia[7 9], Kraków[8], Krakiv[10], קראקע / קרקוב[13]

Králův Dvůr (CZ)
Königshof[1], Králův Dvůr[3]

Kroměříž (CZ)
Kremsier[1], Kroměříž[3]

Krumau (CZ)*
Krumau[1], Český Krumlov[3]

Kutná Hora (CZ)
Kuttenberg[1], Kutná Hora[3]

Kuželj (SLO)
Kuschel[1], Kuželj[5]

Langenzersdorf (A)
Langenzersdorf[1], Dlouhý Enčesdorf[3]

Linz (A)
Linz[1], Linec[3], Linec[6]

Litoměřice (CZ)
Leitmeritz[1], Litoměřice[3]

Ljubljana (SLO)
Laibach[1], Lublaň[3], Ljubljana[5], Ľubľana[6], Lubiana[7] Lublana[8]

Lemberg (UA)*
Lemberg[1], Ľvov[6], Ĺwow[8], Львів/Lwiw[10], לעמבערג / לְבוּב[13]

Maria Saal bei Klagenfurt (A)
Maria Saal bei Klagenfurt[1], Gospa Sveta[5]

Maribor (SLO)
Marburg an der Drau[1], Maribor[5]

Mehala (RO)
Neu-Warosch[1], Mehála[2], Mehala[9]

Mikulov (CZ)
Nikolsburg[1], Mikulov[3]

Miskolc (H)
Mischkolz[1], Miskolc[2], Miškovec[6]

Mol (SRB)
Mohol[2], Мол[11]

Mostar (BIH)
Mostar[4], Мостар[11]

Mukatschewo (UA)*
Mukatschewo/Munkatsch[1], Munkács[2], Mukačevo[3], Mukačevo[6], Muncaeg[9], Мукачево[10], [13]מוקצ׳בו / מונקאטש

Neulengbach (A)
Neulengbach[1]

Nitra (SK)
Neutra[1], Nyitra[2], Nitra[6]

Nötsch (AT)
Nötsch im Gailtal[1], Čajna[5]

Nové Město na Moravě (CZ)
Neustadtl[1], Nové Město na Moravě[3]

Nové Zámky (SK)
Neuhäusel[1], Érsekújvár[2], Uyvar[4], Nové Zámky[6]

Novi Sad (SRB)
Neusatz[1], Újvidék[2], Nový Sad[6], Нови Сад / Novi Sad[11]

Nový Bydžov (CZ)
Neubidschow/Bischowe[1], Nový Bydžov[3]

Nový Jičín (CZ)
Neu Titschein/Neutitschein[1], Nový Jičín[3]

Olomouc (CZ)
Olmütz[1], Olomouc[3], Ołomuniec[8]

Opočno (CZ)
Opotschno/Opotschen[1], Opočno[3]

Ostrava (CZ)
Ostrau/Mährisch Ostrau[1], Ostrava[3]

Otavice (HR)
Otavice[4]

Pécs (H)
Fünfkirchen[1], Pécs[2], Pečuh[4], Печуј[11]

Perchtoldsdorf (A)
Perchtoldsdorf[1]

Piešťany (SK)
Pistyan/Pistian/Püschtin[1], Pöstyény[2], Píšťany[3], Piešťany[4 6], Pieszczany[8]

Plzeň (CZ)
Pilsen[1], Plzeň[3], Pilsen[7], Pilzno[8]

Pöchlarn (A)
Pöchlarn[1]

Pohořelice (CZ)
Pohrlitz/Porlitz[1], Pohořelice[3]

Popovice
(CZ – ORTSTEIL VON KRÁLŮV DVŮR)
Popovice[3]

Považská Bystrica (SK)
Waagbistritz[1], Vágbeszterce[2], Považská Bystrica[6]

Prag (CZ)*
Prag[1], Prága[2], Praha[3], Prag[4], Praga[5], Praha[6], Praga[9], Праг[11], Πράγα[12], [13]פראג / פראג

Přibislav / Dolní Dvořiště (CZ)
Zibisschlag/Unterhaid[1], Přibislav/Dolní Dvořiště[3]

Pula (HR)
Pula[4], Pulj[5], Pola[7]

Reichenau a. d. Rax (A)
Reichenau a. d. Rax[1]

Rijeka (HR)
Fiume[2 7], Rijeka[4], Reka[5]

Salzburg (A)
Salzburg[1], Salcburk/Solnohrad[3], Solnograška[5], Soľnohrad[6], Salisburghese[7]

Sankt Justina / Zwölfmalgreien (I)
Sankt Justina/Zwölfmalgreien[1], Sankt Justina/Dodiciville[7]

Sátoraljaújhely (H)
Neustadt am Zeltberg[1], Sátoraljaújhely[2], Nové Mesto pod Šiatrom[6]

Schönau (A)
Schönau[1]

Seebarn/Harmannsdorf (A)
Seebarn/Harmannsdorf[1]

Sibiu (RO)
Hermannstadt[1], Nagyszeben[2], Sibiu[9]

Sosnová/Opava (CZ)
Zossen/Troppau[1], Sosnová / Opava[3], Sosnová/Opawa[8]

Split (HR)
Split[4], Spalato[7]

Stachy (CZ)
Stachau[1], Stachy[3]

Strážky (SK)
Nehrer[1], Nagyör[2], Strážky[6]

Stribach (A)
Stribach[1]

Světec (CZ)
Schwaz[1], Světec[3]

Szeged (H)
Szegedin/Segedin[1], Szeged[2], Segedín[3], Seghedino[7], Segedyn/Szegedyn[8], Seghedin[9], Сегедин[11]

Szentendre (H)
Sankt Andrä[1], Szentendre[2], Svätý Ondrej[6], Senandrija[9]

Szigliget (H)
Szigliget[2]

Szolnok (H)
Sollnock[1], Szolnok[2], Solnoca[9]

Szombathely (H)
Steinamanger[1], Szombathely[2], Sambotel[4], Sombotel[5], Kamenec[6]

Tábor (CZ)
Tabor/Taber[1], Tábor[3]

Târgu Mureș (RO)
Neumarkt am Mieresch[1], Marosvásárhely[2], Târgu Mureș[9]

Theresienstadt (CZ)*
Theresienstadt[1], Terezín[3]

Töschling (A)
Töschling/Techelsberg am Wörthersee[1], Došenče / Teholica ob Vrbskem jezeru[5]

Triest (I)*
Triest[1], Terst[3], Trst[4 5 11], Trieste[7]

Tulln (A)
Tulln[1]

Unterkrain (A)
Unterkrain — Gallizien[1],
Podkrinj — Galicija[5]

Úpice (CZ)
Eipel[1], Úpice[3]

Uschhorod (UA)*
Ungwar[1], Ungvár[2], Užhorod[3],
Užhorod[6], Ужгород[10], Уґґрад[12],
[13]אוז'הורוד / אונגוואַר

Vádin — Okrouhlice (CZ)
Vádin — Okrouhlice[3]

Vážany u Vyškova (CZ)
Waschan[1], Vážany u Vyškova[3]

Villach (A)
Villach[1], Bělák[3], Beljak[5], Villaco[7]

Vlčkovice (CZ)
Witschkowitz[1], Vlčkovice[3]

Vodňany (CZ)
Wodnian[1], Vodňany[3]

Vrchlabí (CZ)
Hohenelbe[1], Vrchlabí[3]

Vrpolje (HR)
Vrpolje[4]

Všeruby (CZ)
Wscherau/Scherau[1], Všeruby[3]

Wels (A)
Wels[1]

Wien (A)
Wien[1], Bécs[2], Vídeň[3], Beč[4],
Dunaj[5], Viedeň[6], Vienna[7],
Wiedeń[8], Viena[9], Відень[10], Беч[11],
Вéна[12], [13]וינה / וויען

Zagorica (SLO)
Sagoritz[1], Zagorica[5]

Zadar (HR)
Zára[2], Zadar[4], Zara[7]

Zagreb (HR)
Agram[1], Zágráb[2], Záhřeb[3],
Zagreb[4], Záhreb[6], [13]זאגרב / זאַגרעב

Zbiroh (CZ)
Zbirow[1], Zbiroh[3]

Zell am See (A)
Zell am See[1]

Zwickledt (A)
Zwickledt[1]

Places outside the Austro-Hungarian Empire

In this section, the flag denotes only the languages listed in the introduction to the previous section. Names in all other languages, including regional names, have been ignored.

Aix-en-Provence (F)

Amersham (GB)

Amsterdam (NL)
Amsterdam[1], Amszterdam[2],
Amsterodam[3],
אמסטרדם / אַמסטערדאַם[13]

Annet-sur-Marne (F)

Antwerpen (B)
Antwerpen[1], Antverpy[3 6], Anversa[7],
Antwerpia[8], Antverpen[10 11]

Arcueil (F)

Aspen (USA)

Assisi (I)
Assisi[7]

Barbizon (F)

Barmen (D)
Barmen[1]

Beaugency (F)

Belgrad (SRB)*
Belgrad[1 8 9], Belgrád[2], Bělehrad[3],
Beograd[4 5], Belehrad[6], Belgrado[7],
Bjelhrad[10], Beograd/Београд[11]

Berchtesgaden (D)
Berchtesgaden[1]

Bergen an Zee (NL)

Bergen-Belsen (D)
Bergen-Belsen[1]

Berlin (D)
Berlin[1], Berlín[3], Berlín[6], Berlino[7],
[13]בֶּרְלִין / בערלין

Bern (CH)
Bern[1], Berna[7], Berno[8], Berna[9]

Bischkek (KG)*
Bischkek/Frunse[1], Biškek[3 6],
Biszkek[8], Бишкек[12]

Bochum (D)
Bochum[1]

Bordighera (I)

Bregenz (CH)
Bregenz[1], Břežnice[3]

Brüssel (B)*
Brüssel[1], Brüsszel[2], Brusel[3 6],
Bruxelles[7 9], Bruksela[8],
Брюссель[10 12], Brisel[11]

Bukarest (RO)*
Bukarest[1 2], Bukurešť[3 6],
Bukurešt[4 11], Bucarest[7],
Bukareszt[8], Bucureşti[9],
Бухарест[12], [13]בוקרשט / בוקאַרעשט

Cambridge (USA)

Chemnitz (D)
Chemnitz[1], Saská Kamenice[3],
Kamienica Saska[8]

Chêne-Bougeries (CH)

Chicago (USA)

Chipping Campden (GB)

Cotignac (F)

Dachau (D)
Dachau[1], Dahava[4]

⚑⚑⚑⚑
Danzig (PL)*
Danzig[1], Gdańsk[3], Gdańsk[8], Danzica[7]

⚑
Darmstadt (D)
Darmstadt[1]

⚑⚑⚑⚑⚑⚑⚑⚑⚑⚑
Den Haag (NL)
Den Haag[1], Hága[2], Haag[3], Hag[4], Haag[6], L'Aia[7], Haga[8], Хаг[11], Гаáга[12], [13]דען האג / האג

⚑
Dessau (D)
Dessau[1]

⚑⚑⚑⚑⚑⚑⚑⚑
Dresden (D)
Dresden[1], Drezda[2], Drážďany[3], Draždane[4], Drážďany[6], Dresda[7], Drezno[8], Дрезден[11]

⚑
Düsseldorf (D)
Düsseldorf[1]

⚑
Essen (D)
Essen[1]

⚑⚑⚑⚑⚑⚑⚑⚑⚑⚑
Florenz (I)*
Florenz[1], Florencie[3], Firenca[4], Firence[5], Florencia[6], Firenze[7], Florencja[8], Florența[9], Фиренца[11], Флоре́нция[12]

⚑⚑⚑⚑⚑⚑⚑⚑⚑⚑
Frankfurt am Main (D)
Frankfurt am Main[1], Majna-Frankfurt[2], Frankfurt nad Mohanem[3], Frankfurt na Majni[4], Frankfurt ob Majni[5], Frankfurt nad Mohanom[6], Francoforte sul Meno[7], Frankfurt nad Menem[8], Frankfurt pe Main[9], Фра́нкфурт-на-Ма́йне[12]

⚑⚑
Gdynia (PL)
Gdingen[1], Gdynia[8]

⚑⚑⚑⚑⚑⚑⚑⚑⚑⚑
Genf (CH)
Genf[1 2], Ženeva[3 4 6], Ginevra[7], Genewa[8], Женева[10 11 12]

⚑⚑
Gollnow (PL)
Gollnow[1], Goleniów[8]

⚑
Gotha (D)
Gotha[1]

⚑
Hamburg (D)
Hamburg[1]

⚑
Harburg (D)
Harburg[1]

Harvard, Massachusetts (USA)

⚑
Heidelberg (D)
Heidelberg[1]

⚑
Kastellaun (D)
Kastellaun/Castellaun[1]

⚑⚑⚑⚑⚑⚑⚑⚑⚑
Köln/Cöln (D)
Köln[1 2 9], Kolín nad Rýnem[3], Kolín nad Rýnom[6], Colonia[7], Keln[11], Кёльн[12], Kolonia nad Renem[8]

⚑⚑⚑⚑
Konstanz (D)
Konstanz[1], Kostnice[3], Costanza[7], Konstancja[8]

⚑
KZ Buchenwald (D)
KZ Buchenwald[1]

⚑
KZ Sachsenhausen (D)
KZ Sachsenhausen[1]

La Ciotat (F)

⚑⚑⚑⚑
Lausanne (CH)
Lozana[5], Losanna[7], Lozanna[8], Лоза́нна[12]

⚑⚑⚑⚑⚑
Leipzig (D)
Leipzig[1], Lipcse[2], Lipsko[3], Lipsko[6], Lipsk[8]

⚑⚑⚑⚑⚑⚑⚑⚑⚑
London (GB)
London[1], Londýn[3], Lóndon[5], Londýn[6], Londra[7], Londyn[8], Londra[9], Ло́ндон[12], [13]לאנדאן / לונדון

⚑⚑⚑
Lübeck (D)
Lübeck[1], Lubek[3], Lubeka[8]

⚑⚑⚑⚑⚑
Mailand (I)*
Mailand[1], Milánó[2], Milán[3], Miláno[6], Milano[7]

⚑⚑⚑⚑
Malý Trostinec (BY)*
Maly Trostenez[1], Malý Trostinec[3], Maly Traszjanez[8], Малый Тростенец[12]

⚑
Mannheim (D)
Mannheim[1]

⚑⚑⚑⚑
Marseille (F)
Marsiglia[7], Marsylia[8], Marsilia[9], Marselj[11]

⚑⚑⚑⚑⚑
Minsk (BY)*
Minsk[1], Minszk[2], Mińsk[8], Минск[12], [13]מינסק / מינסק

⚑⚑
Mittelsteine (PL)*
Mittelsteine[1], Ścinawka Średnia[8]

Montecito — Santa Barbara (USA)

Montreux (CH)

⚑⚑⚑⚑⚑⚑⚑⚑⚑⚑⚑
Moskau (RUS)*
Moskau[1], Moszkva[2], Moskva[3 4 6], Moskwa[8], Moscova[9], Москва[11], Москва́[12], [13]מאסקווע / מוסקבה, Mosku[14]

⚑⚑⚑⚑⚑⚑⚑⚑
München (D)
München[1], Mnichov[3], Mníchov[6], Monaco[7], Monachium[8], Минхен[11], Мю́нхен[12], Minca[14]

⚑
Münster (D)
Münster[1]

⚑⚑⚑⚑⚑⚑⚑
Neapel (I)
Neapel[1], Nápoly[2], Neapol[3], Napulj[4], Neapelj[5], Neapol[6], Napoli[7]

Neuilly (F)

⚑
New York (USA)
[13]שטאָט נוי־יאָרק / נְוּי יוֹרְק

⚑⚑⚑⚑⚑⚑⚑⚑⚑⚑⚑
Nischni Nowgorod (RUS)*
Nischni Nowgorod[1], Nyizsnyij Novgorod[2], Nizhny Novgorod[3 5], Niżny Nowogród[4 8 9], Nižný Novgorod[6 7], Ни́жний Но́вгород[12]

⚑⚑⚑⚑⚑
Nizza (F)
Nizza[1], Nica[4], Nice[6], Nicea[8], Nisa[9]

⚑⚑⚑⚑⚑⚑
Nürnberg (D)
Nürnberg[1], Nürnberg[2], Norimberk[3], Norimberg[5], Norimberga[7], Norymberga[8]

Oxford (GB)

⚑
Palermo (I)
Palermo[7]

⚑⚑⚑⚑⚑⚑⚑⚑
Paris (F)
Párizs[2], Paříž[3], Pariz[4], Paríž[6], Parigi[7], Paryż[8], Пари́ж[12], [13]פריז / פאַריז

⚑⚑
Philadephia (USA)
Filadelfija[5], Filadelfia[7]

Polperro — Cornwall (GB)

Puteaux (F)

Rapallo (I)

Remscheid (D)
Remscheid[1]

Rom (I)
Rom[1], Róma[2], Řím[3], Rim[4], Rím[6], Roma[7], Rzym[8], Рим[12], רוים / רומא[13]

Rüschlikon (CH)
Rüschlikon[1]

Sagan (PL)*
Sagan[1], Żagań[8]

Saint-Michel de Frigolet (F)

Saint-Céré (F)

Saint-Tropez (F)

San Francisco (USA)

Sankt Petersburg (RUS)*
Sankt Petersburg[1 8 9], Leningrad[1] (Bezeichnung 1917–90), Szentpétervár[2], Sankt Petěrburk[3], Sankt-Peterburg[5], San Pietroburgo[7], Sankt-Peterburg / Санкт-Петербург[11 12]

Sarajevo (BIH)*
Sarajevo/Sarajewo[1], Szarajevó[2], Sarajevo[4], Сарајев/Sarajevo[11], Sarajewo[8]

Scheveningen (NL)

South Bend (USA)

Stockholm (S)
Stockholm[1], Štokholm[6], Stoccolma[7], Sztokholm[8], Stockholmul[9]

Stuttgart (D)
Stuttgart[1], Štíhrad[3], Stoccarda[7]

Taubenberg (D)
Taubenberg[1]

Taxco (MEX)

Tel Aviv-Jaffa / תל אביב-יפו (IL)
תל אביב / תֵּל אָבִיב-יָפוֹ[13]

Tomsk (RUS)
Tomsk[1], Tomszk[2], Tomsk[3 4 5 6 7 8 9], Томськ[10], Томск[11 12], טומסק[13]

Toronto (CDN)

Toruń (PL)
Thorn[1], Toruň[3], Torunj[5], Toruń[8]

Travemünde (D)
Travemünde[1]

Tropea (I)
Tropea[7]

Venedig (I)*
Venedig[1], Velence[2], Benátky[3], Venecija[4], Benétke[5], Benátky[6], Venezia[7], Wenecja[8], Veneția[9], Венеција[11], Венéция[12]

Villeneuve, Waadt (CH)

Warschau (PL)*
Warschau[1], Varsó[2], Varšava[3 4 6], Warszawa[8], Varșovia[9], Варшава[11], Варшáва[12], וואַרשע / ורשה[13]

Weggis (CH)
Weggis[1]

Weimar (D)
Weimar[1], Výmar/Vejmar[3]

Wendover Dean (GB)

Wiesbaden (D)
Wiesbaden[1]

Wrocław (PL)
Breslau[1], Vratislav[3], Wroclaw[5], Vratislavia/Vratislav/Vroclav[6], Wrocław[8], ברעסלוי / ורוצלב[13]

Zug (CH)
Zug[1], Zugo[7]

Zürich (CH)
Zürich[1], Curych[3], Zurigo[7], Zurych[8], Цирих[11], Цюрих[10 12], ציריך[13]

Zwickau (D)
Zwickau[1], Cvikov[3], Ćwików[8], Цвиккау[12]

Authors

STEPHANIE AUER

Stephanie Auer studied art history and Romance studies at the universities of Innsbruck and Granada. She completed her master's dissertation in 2006, spending several months in Madrid conducting research into Federico García Lorca as a visual artist. She was a project researcher at the Oskar Kokoschka Center, University of Applied Arts Vienna and curator of the exhibition *Oskar Kokoschka—Von der Moderne zu Antike* at the Kokoschka Haus Pöchlarn. Since 2007, she has been a curatorial assistant for the collections of nineteenth- and twentieth-century art at the Belvedere, contributing to numerous catalogues and helping to research and curate various exhibitions, including *Gustav Klimt–Josef Hoffmann: Pioneers of Modernism*, 2011; *Vienna–Berlin: The Art of Two Cities*, 2014; and *Klimt and Antiquity*, 2017. Her research focuses on European painting from the second half of the nineteenth and the early twentieth century.

ÉVA BAJKAY

Éva Bajkay has a degree in art history from Eötvös Loránd University in Budapest and habilitated at the Academy of Sciences in Budapest in 1983. Since graduating, she has worked at the Hungarian National Gallery, from 1980 until 1984 as Associate Director and from 1984 until 2000 as Director of the Graphic Art Collection. Until 2008, she was Senior Director, and since then has contributed to numerous academic projects. Since 2003, she has been a lecturer at the Doctoral School of the Moholy-Nagy University of Art and Design. She has curated numerous exhibitions in Hungary and abroad, for example in Innsbruck, Paris, Kassel, Vienna, Tokyo, Delaware, Cleveland, Brussels, Munich, and Berlin, and has published numerous books and articles.

GERGELY BARKI

Gergely Barki is an independent curator and curator at the Czóbel Múzeum in Szentendre. He is a Ph.D. candidate in art history at the ELTE University, Budapest. His dissertation is a monograph and catalogue raisonné on Róbert Berény, a prominent figure of Hungarian Modernism. Barki has curated exhibitions and published essays on Fauvism and Hungarian Modernism: *Magyar Vadak Párizstól Nagybányáig (Hungarian Fauves from Paris to Nagybánya) 1904–1914*, Magyar Nemzeti Galéria, Budapest, 2006. *A NYOLCAK — Cézanne és Matisse bűvöletében (THE EIGHT, In the Enchantment of Cézanne and Matisse)* Janus Pannonius Múzeum, Pécs, 2010. *A NYOLCAK (THE EIGHT)*, Szépművészeti Múzeum, Budapest, 2011. *Fauves Hongrois*, Musée d'art moderne, Céret; Musée Matisse, Le Cateau-Cambrésis; Musée des beaux-arts, Dijon, 2008–2009, *Dialogue de fauves—Fauvisme hongrois 1904–1914*, L'hôtel de ville de Bruxelles, 2010. *DIE ACHT—Ungarns 'Highway' in die Moderne*, Kunstforum, Vienna, 2012. *Béla Bartók and the Hungarian Modernism 1905–1920*, Musée d'Orsay, Paris, 2013.

KURT DE BOODT

Kurt De Boodt is a poet, art critic, and artistic advisor to the CEO of the Centre for Fine Arts in Brussels (BOZAR). Until 1999 he was chief editor of the monthly cultural magazine *Kunst & Cultuur*. As a freelance curator he has organized several exhibitions on Belgian artists, including an exhibition on young Flemish art movements as part of Expo 58 (2008), about Rik Wouters and his fellow sculptors in Mechelen (2011) and a retrospective about the Modernist painter Prosper De Troyer (2013), accompanied by the monographic study *Prosper De Troyer: Schilder in beweging* (Painter on the move). He has published six volumes of poetry, including *Waarop the klok ontwaakt!*, the epic poem *Minnezang* (2011) and *Ghostwriter* (2015). In his latest collection of poems he investigates the private, social, and avant-garde potentials of the sonnet today. De Boodt is researching the Flemish avant-garde and its complex ideological implications during and in between the two world wars.

GÁBOR DOBÓ

Gábor Dobó has studied at universities in Budapest, Florence, and Angers, and holds an MA in literary history from the University of Florence and Eötvös Loránd University. He is currently a Ph.D. candidate at Eötvös Loránd University, Budapest, and has been a researcher at the Kassák Museum since 2014. In his research, he applies the methods of periodical studies to the magazines of the Hungarian avant-garde. His doctoral research focuses on the international network of Lajos Kassák's magazine *Dokumentum* (Document), published in 1926/27. His work explores how the examination of Hungarian intellectual history contributes to an understanding of twentieth-century Hungarian art.

PAUL DUJARDIN
Paul Dujardin has been CEO and artistic director of the Centre for Fine Arts (BOZAR) in Brussels since 2002. Before that, he was CEO of the Société Philharmonique de Bruxelles and in charge of the annual Ars Musica contemporary music festival. Under his direction the BOZAR has become an internationally recognized, multidisciplinary arts center—a platform for exchange and debate between citizens, artists, political decision-makers, and personalities from other sectors. Dujardin represents the BOZAR in various forums, such as the European Concert Hall Organisation (ECHO), the International Society of Performing Arts (ISPA), the Réseau Européen de Musique Ancienne (R.E.M.A.) and ASEMUS—Asia-Europe Museum Network. Since 2013, he has been President of the International Music Council (IMC) and since February 2014 a member of the board of the European Festivals Association (EFA). A passionate advocate of the European project, Paul Dujardin has made the BOZAR into an agent for European cultural cooperation and the defense of cultural values in the European project. This is expressed by BOZAR's involvement, for example, in the European research project "The role of culture in EU external relations" and in extensive collaborations with networks and organizations such as the Goethe Institute, Culture Action Europe, EUNIC, the European Cultural Foundation, or the European Foundation Centre. Dujardin also chairs the cultural committee of the "New Narrative for Europe" project, a pilot initiative of the European Parliament implemented with the European Commission to develop a new vision for Europe through the prisms of art and science. In 2014, he received an honorary doctorate from the Université Libre de Bruxelles (ULB).

ARNIKA GROENEWALD-SCHMIDT
Arnika Groenewald-Schmidt has been assistant curator at the Belvedere since 2015. Prior to that she worked at the National Gallery in London. She studied art history in Freiburg im Breisgau and completed her Ph.D. in Dresden. Her research focuses on nineteenth- and twentieth-century art, the development of landscape painting and transnational exchange among artists and their peers.

IVO HABÁN
Ivo Habán holds an MA in art history from the Faculty of Arts at Masaryk University in Brno. From 2008 to 2013, he completed the Theory and History of Art doctorate program at the same university, having worked as an art historian at the Zezula Auction House from 2003 to 2005. Since 2005 he has worked at the National Heritage Institute's regional office in Liberec, where he is responsible for the preservation of movable cultural heritage. He specializes in visual art of the first half of the twentieth century, focusing on the work of German-speaking artists from Bohemia, Moravia, and Silesia. Together with his wife Anna Habánová he has participated as an author and curator in the project *Mladí lvi v kleci (Young Lions in a Cage)*. He is author of the monograph and curator of an exhibition on the sculptor Mary Duras (2014, 2015). Since 2011, he has been a member of the editorial board and executive editor of the peer-reviewed periodical *Fontes Nissae*. Together with Anna Habánová he has been organizing international symposiums on the visual culture of Czech-Germans since 2012.

MIROSLAV HAĽÁK
Miroslav Haľák studied art history and art theory at the University of Trnava (Slovakia) and participated in the interdisciplinary study program "AISTHESIS: Historische Kunst- und Literaturdiskurse" at the Ludwig-Maximilian University of Munich, the University of Augsburg, the University of Regensburg, the Catholic University of Eichstätt–Ingolstadt, and the Zentralinstitut für Kunstgeschichte in Munich. He gained his doctorate with a thesis about the semiotic foundations of anthropomorphism in modern landscape painting. He has been a curatorial assistant at the Belvedere since 2017. In addition to nineteenth- and twentieth-century art, his research focuses on visual semiotics and psychological aesthetics.

ALEXANDER KLEE
Alexander Klee has been the Belvedere's curator for the second half of the nineteenth century and the early twentieth century since 2010. A founding member of the Adolf Hölzel Foundation in Stuttgart, he is in the process of compiling a catalogue raisonné of Adolf Hölzel's works. He has produced numerous publications on Hölzel, Emil Jakob Schindler, Georg Karl Pfahler, and the artists of Classical Modernism. His research focuses on the nineteenth and twentieth centuries. He recently curated the exhibitions *Vienna–Berlin: The Art of Two Cities* in collaboration with the Berlinische Galerie and *Klimt, Kupka, Picasso and others—Form Art* as well as *Sin and Secession: Franz von Stuck in Vienna* (both 2016).

BARBARA LESÁK

Barbara Lesák studied theater, art history, and philosophy and wrote her doctoral thesis on the early work of the Austro-American visionary architect and theater designer Frederick Kiesler. From 1991 to 1992 she worked on an Austrian Science Fund project about the collection of Russian objects at the Österreichisches Theatermuseum. She was head of the graphic collection at the Theatermuseum until 2009. Barbara Lesák participated in the international research projects "Das deutschsprachige Musiktheater in der ersten Hälfte des 20. Jahrhunderts" (German Research Foundation DFG) and "Transdisziplinäre Konstellation in der österreichischen Literatur und Kultur der Zwischenkriegszeit," Alpen-Adria-Universität Klagenfurt (Austrian Science Fund, FWF). She has published on the subject of twentieth-century avant-garde theater and curated many exhibitions, including *Russische Theaterkunst 1910–1930*, 1993; *Von der Pose zum Ausdruck: Theaterfotografie 1900–1930*, 2004; *Kabarett Fledermaus: Gesamtkunstwerk der Wiener Werkstätte*, 2008; *Frederick Kiesler: Theatervisionär—Architekt—Künstler*, 2013.

FLÓRA MÉSZÁROS

Flóra Mészáros is an art historian, senior lecturer, and independent curator. She completed her Ph.D. on Hungarian Artists in Abstraction-Création in cotutelle at Eötvös Loránd University in Budapest and the Sorbonne in Paris. She has lectured at the Breuer Marcell Doctoral School in Pécs and became a senior lecturer at the Károli Gáspár University of the Reformed Church in Budapest in 2016. In her research and curatorial practice she focuses on Hungarian and international non-figurative art and has curated the exhibition *Ferenc Martyn and the Parisian abstraction* at the Hungarian Institute in Paris, among others. However, she also deals with contemporary art, for example, in exhibitions such as *Worldless, Talking Dead*. She has worked as an assistant curator at the Budapest Hall of Art and is the author of *Ferenc Martyn and Paris* (2014) and editor of *Modern Art and Internationalism* (2017). She also works as an art critic and essayist writing on contemporary art for art magazines.

STELLA ROLLIG

Stella Rollig has been CEO and Artistic Director of the Belvedere since January 2017. She studied German and art history at the University of Vienna and later worked as an arts journalist (for ORF, *Der Standard*, and others). From 1994 to 1996, Rollig was the Austrian Federal Curator for the Fine Arts; during this time she also founded "Depot, Kunst und Diskussion" at MuseumsQuartier Wien. From 2004 to 2016, she was Artistic Director of the LENTOS art museum in Linz and from 2011 also Director of NORDICO Stadtmuseum Linz. In addition to her curatorial roles, Rollig has taught at numerous institutions.

FRANZ SMOLA

Franz Smola studied art history and law in Vienna, Bologna, and Washington DC. He was a curator at the Österreichische Galerie Belvedere in Vienna from 2001 to 2009 and at the Leopold Museum, Vienna, from 2009 to 2017, where he was also Interim Director from 2013 to 2015. Franz Smola has been a curator at the Belvedere since 2017. His research focuses on Vienna around 1900 and Austrian and international Modern art. He has contributed to many catalogues both as publishing editor and author.

GABRIELE SPINDLER

Gabriele Spindler studied art history and Italian at the University of Salzburg. She was the public relations officer at the Österreichische Galerie Belvedere, Vienna, from 1995 to 1999. From 2000 to 2012 she was head of the collection of modern and contemporary art at the Landesgalerie Linz. In 2006, she was a visiting curator at the Künstlerhaus Bethanien, Berlin. In 2009/10, she was the curator in charge of art acquisitions for the City of Linz. Since 2012 she has been Director of the Landesgalerie Linz. Many exhibitions and publications about twentieth- and twenty-first-century art with a focus on the Austrian interwar period and contemporary art.

ARNOLD SUPPAN

Arnold Suppan, Dr. phil., Professor emeritus of East-European History, University of Vienna; visiting professor at the universities of Leiden, Freiburg, Stanford, and Budapest; President of the Austrian Institute of East- and South-East-European Studies, Vienna (1988–2002), board member at the Institute of East-European History, University of Vienna (2002–2008); corresponding (1998) and full member (2003) of the Austrian Academy of Sciences/AAS; Chairman of the Historical Commission, AAS (2003–2011), Secretary General (2009–2011) and Vice President of the AAS (2011–2013); honorary member of the Hungarian Academy of Sciences (2013). Publications include: *Die österreichischen Volksgruppen: Tendenzen ihrer gesellschaftlichen Entwicklung im 20. Jahrhundert* (Vienna, 1983); *Jugoslawien und Österreich 1918–1938: Außenpolitik im europäischen Umfeld* (Vienna–Munich, 1996); *Deutsche Geschichte im Osten Europas: Zwischen Adria und Karawanken* (Berlin, 1998, 2002); *Hitler–Beneš–Tito: Konflikt, Krieg und Völkermord in Ostmittel- und Südosteuropa*

(Vienna, 2014, 2017); *1000 Jahre Nachbarschaft. "Tschechen" und "Österreicher" in historischer Perspektive: Eine Synthese* (Vienna, 2016); numerous co-edited volumes, such as *Das Bild vom Anderen: Identitäten, Mentalitäten, Mythen und Stereotypen in multiethnischen europäischen Regionen* (Frankfurt a. M., 1999); *The Austrian State Treaty 1955: International Strategy, Legal Relevance, National Identity* (Vienna, 2005); *Osteuropäische Geschichte in Wien. 100 Jahre Forschung und Lehre an der Universität* (Innsbruck/Vienna/Bozen, 2007); *Außenpolitische Dokumente der Republik Österreich 1918–1938*, 12 vols. (Vienna, 1993–2016); *The Revolutions of 1989: A Handbook* (Vienna, 2015).

MERSE PÁL SZEREDI
Merse Pál Szeredi holds an MA in art history, is a Ph.D. candidate at Eötvös Loránd University, Budapest, and a researcher at the Kassák Museum. He has studied at universities in Budapest and Berlin, and completed internships at the Berlinische Galerie, the Hungarian National Gallery, and the Hungarian National Museum. His research focuses on the international networks of the early avant-garde, and his Ph.D. explores the history and local reception of Hungarian avant-garde artists in Viennese exile in the first half of the 1920s.

MARKÉTA THEINHARDT
Markéta Theinhardt has been a lecturer since 1995 and, since 2015, professor of museology and art history of Central Europe at the Sorbonne in Paris, having previously been custodian of the National Gallery in Prague. She has published numerous works on Czech, German, and Austrian art of the nineteenth and twentieth centuries; her monographs focus in particular on the work of František Kupka. She is co-author with Pierre Brullé and Sergiusz Michalski of a comprehensive history of Central European art entitled *L'art de l'Europe centrale* (Paris 2008).

JUDITH ELISABETH WEISS
Judith Elisabeth Weiss is a researcher at the Center for Literary and Cultural Research Berlin (ZfL), where she is in charge of the project Archetype and Transformation. Between 2000 and 2011 she was curator for modern and contemporary art at various museums, and she has published widely on these subjects. She has taught at the universities in Karlsruhe, Heidelberg, and Berlin and is also the editor and guest publishing editor of *Kunstforum International*. Her research focuses on contemporary art, the avant-garde, and Surrealism, cultures of refusal, art and nature, and the pictorial and cultural history of the face. Her most recent publications include "Figurationen der Wiederholung im Werk von Max Ernst: Analogien zur Psychoanalyse und ihre Überschreitung," in *Wiederholungstäter: Die Selbstwiederholung als künstlerische Praxis in der Moderne*, eds. Verena Krieger and Sophia Stang (Cologne, 2017); *Randgänge des Gesichts: Kritische Perspektiven auf Sichtbarkeit und Entzug* (with Mona Körte), (Paderborn, 2017).

Notes on Typography

Manuel Radde

BAUER GROTESK

Thomas Ackermann, Felix Bonge
FontShop, DE, 2014
www.fontshop.com
Introductory Section & Appendices

In 1934, the German type designers Friedrich Bauer designed *Friedrich Bauer Grotesk* for the Hamburg type foundry Trennert & Sohn. It was not as successful as comparable typefaces of the time, such as *Futura* or *Nobel,* which in Europe became synonymous with the emergence of Modernism, and after Bauer's death in 1943, Friedrich Bauer Grotesk gradually faded into obscurity. The two German type designers Thomas Ackermann and Felix Bonge rediscovered the typeface in an old type specimen book and digitized it based on the original design. This contemporary update was released by FontShop in 2014 under the name *Bauer Grotesk.*

LARISH NEUE

Radim Peško, Willi Schmid
RP Digital Type Foundry, CZ, 2007
www.radimpesko.com
Chapter A

Larish Neue **is a reinterpretation of the** ***Plinius*** **typeface, created for the Imperial-Royal Court and State Printing Office in Vienna in 1903.** ***Plinius*** **was the creation of the Austrian type designer Rudolf von Larisch, who initially worked as a civil servant at the Ministry of the Interior and taught himself type design in his free time. He later designed printed materials for institutions such as the Wiener Werkstätte, and in 1905 was appointed professor of typography and heraldry at the Vienna School of Applied Arts. Larisch had a major influence on Austrian type design. He died in 1934 in Vienna. In 2006, the Czech type designer Radim Peško and the Austrian graphic designer Willi Schmid revived the old metal type as part of their redesign of the Vienna Secession gallery's visual identity.**

PREISSIG ANTIKVA

Storm Type Foundry, CZ, 2012
František Štorm, Otakar Karlas
www.stormtype.com
Chapter B

The Czech artist Vojtěch Preissig frequently incorporated typography in his works (see pp. 136, 368). His artistic output included work as a painter, graphic artist, illustrator, and type designer. He spent over two years developing *Preissig Antikva,* which in 1925 was cast in lead by the State Printing Office in Prague. Particular attention was paid during its design to integrating the special characters of the Czech alphabet. The angular, idiosyncratic typeface is considered a milestone in Czech type design and also proved to be highly influential beyond the country's borders. In 2012, it was reworked as a digital type by Prague designers František Štorm and Otakar Karlas.

EUCLID FLEX

Swiss Typefaces, CH, 2013
www.swisstypefaces.com
Chapter C

Rather than being based on a particular historical model, the concept for this contemporary typeface takes its cues from Euclid, the "father of geometry." It comprises a choice of over five hundred alternate letterforms, which, combined with OpenType features, offers almost infinite variations. Several characters show clear references to the avant-garde typography of the 1920s. *Euclid Flex* is sold by Swiss Typefaces, a type design company founded in Lausanne in 2006 by Maxime Buechi and Ian Party. All its typefaces are designed by an in-house team.

FF BAU

Christian Schwartz, Erik Spiekermann
Fontshop, DE, 2002
www.fontshop.com
Chapter D

The visual appearance of the printed material produced by the Bauhaus was strongly influenced by ***Scheltersche Grotesk,*** **a typeface designed by the Leipzig type foundry Schelter & Giesecke. From 1925, the typeface was frequently used in Dessau. It was also popular with the famous type designer Jan Tschichold. In the late 1950s, Max Miedinger used it as his starting point when he designed the world-famous** ***Helvetica.*** **In 1999, the designer Erik Spiekermann came across an original type specimen for Scheltersche Grotesk from Leipzig, which he passed on to the German type designer Christian Schwartz. In 2002, Schwartz developed** ***FF Bau,*** **a redesign of the original that brought the lead type into the digital age for the very first time.**

URBAN GROTESK

Tomáš Brousil
Suitcase Type Foundry, CZ, 2014
www.suitcasetype.com
Chapter E

In the early twentieth century an increasing number of sans-serif typefaces were being developed, also known as "grotesque" typefaces. These broke with established typographic convention in their simpler, more reduced letterform—a formal language that remains relevant to this day. In *Urban Grotesk,* the Slovak type designer Tomáš Brousil has brought together characteristic features of key sans-serif types from the early twentieth century in a new, contemporary typeface.

STANLEY

Ludovic Balland
Optimo, CH, 2012
www.optimo.ch
Chapter F

In 1931, the British newspaper *The Times* commissioned Stanley Morison from the Monotype Corporation to develop a new typeface, after he had published an article criticizing the paper's existing design and typography as outdated. Morison modeled his design on an older Antiqua typeface, *Plantin,* which he reworked and updated. The result, *Times New Roman,* is widely known today as one of the preinstalled fonts on most desktop computers and is considered one of the twentieth century's most used serif typefaces. Eighty years later, the Swiss designer Ludovic Balland revisited *Times New Roman* and used it as a starting point for *Stanley,* his reinterpretation of the classic.

Sources:
- Paul McNeil, *The Visual History of Type,* (London, 2017)
- Websites of the various type foundries

Image Rights

PICTURE CREDITS

Albertina, Vienna: pp. 106, 107, 109, 147 (Sign. 1156195-C), 324, 326, 329 • Art Gallery Karlovy Vary: p. 35 (Bořivoj Hořínek) • Bauhaus-Archiv Berlin: p. 179 (top) (Atelier Schneider) • Belvedere, Vienna: pp. 25, 26 (top), 29 (top), 30 (top), 51 (top), 63, 64, 65, 73, 75, 77, 78, 124, 126, 128, 129, 130, 146 (below), 155, 156, 157, 161, 202, 204, 205, 210, , 243, 251, 253, 255, 258, 273, 297; 299, 301, 302, 307, 308, 313, 322, 327, 328, 331, 332, 333, 334, 344, 352 (top), 362, 363, 366 (Johannes Stoll) • BHM, Museum Kiscell, Municipal Gallery, Budapest: p. 59 • bpk/RMN — Grand Palais: p. 61 (Patrice Schmidt) • bpk/The Metropolitan Museum of Art, New York: p. 178 (top) • bpk: pp. 342 • Brno City Museum: p. 90 • Collection Museo Franz Mayer: p. 198 • Collection Van Abbemuseum, Eindhoven: p. 79 (Peter Cox) • Courtesy Kunsthandel Hieke: p. 81, 298 • Damjanich János Museum, Szolnok: p. 118 (center) (Róbert Csiszár) • Deutsches Architekturmuseum, Frankfurt/Main: p. 178 (below) (Uwe Dettmar) • Flóris Rómer Museum of Art and History, Győr: p. 88 • Fritz Wotruba Privatstiftung, Vienna: p. 296 (Harald Eisenberger) • Galerie Le Minotaure: p. 252 • Gallery of Fine Arts in Cheb: p. 257 • Gallery of Fine Arts in Ostrava: p. 104 (Archive GVUO) • Georg Schrom, Vienna: pp. 214, 216 (Johannes Stoll) • IMAGNO/Austrian Archives: p. 2 • Jewish Museum in Prague: pp. 281 (below), 338 (detail), 343 (top) • Kunstbibliothek, Staatliche Museen zu Berlin: p. 145 (top) (Dietmar Katz) • Kunstforum Ostdeutsche Galerie, Regensburg: p. 159 (Wolfram Schmidt) • Kunsthandel Giese & Schweiger, Vienna: p. 323 • Kunsthandel Widder, Vienna: p. 283 (top) • Kunstmuseum Bern, Donation ofNell Walden: p. 46 (right) • Kunstmuseum Gelsenkirchen: p. 227 • Province of Carinthia Art Collection / MMKK: p. 50 (below) • Landesgalerie Linz, Graphic Arts Collection: pp. 108, 110, 111, 112, 269, , 272, 330 • Landesgalerie Linz, Oberösterreichisches Landesmuseum: pp. 270 • Le Corbusier Foundation: p. 44 (top) • LENTOS Kunstmuseum Linz: pp. 49 (below), 247, 249, 303, 319 (Reinhard Haider) • Leopold Museum, Vienna: pp. 26 (below), 27, 31, 114 (detail), 134 • Leopold-Hoesch-Museum & Papiermuseum Düren: p. 50 (top) (Reinhard Haider) • MAK — Österreichisches Museum für angewandte Kunst / Gegenwartskunst, Vienna: pp. 28 (right), 217 (Georg Mayer) • Moravian Gallery, Brno: pp. 95, 203, 256, 260, 261, 310, 341 • Mucha Trust: pp. 66, 67, 68 • mumok — Museum moderner Kunst Stiftung Ludwig Wien: pp. 246, 248 • Municipal Museum of Ústí nad Labem: p. 281 (top) • Museum and Galleries of Ljubljana — Museum of Modern Art, Ljubljana: pp. 293, 315 • Museum der Stadt Lienz Schloss Bruck: pp. 118 (below) (Vaverka), 135 (Martin Lugger) • Museum Kampa — The Jan and Meda Mládek Foundation, Prague: pp. 83, 84, 85, 224, 225, 226, 228 • Museum of Fine Arts — Hungarian National Gallery, Budapest: pp. 45 (below), 60, 70, 71, 86, 87, 131, 132, 167, 168, 189 (below), 206, 207, 212, 213, 220, 221, 223, 238, 284 (below), 305, 335 • Museum of Fine Arts — Vasarely Museum, Budapest: p. 231 • Museum Ulm: p. 176 (below) (Armin Buhl) • National Gallery in Prague: pp. 22 (detail), 29 (below), 30 (below), 92, 102, 105, 122, 145 (below), 250, 343 (below) • National Museum of Modern Art, Zagreb: pp. 291, 292 (Goran Vranić) • Neue Galerie, New York: p. 28 (left) • NORDICO Stadtmuseum Linz: pp. 125, 271 (below) (Thomas Hackl) • Österreichische Friedrich und Lillian Kiesler-Privatstiftung, Vienna: pp. 191, 234, 235, 254, • Österreichische Nationalbibliothek, Vienna: pp. 11 (Sign. 562.890-A.Neu Mag), 45 (top) (Sign. 570.489-D), 352 (below) (Sign.521.268-B.5) • Österreichisches Gesellschafts-und Wirtschaftsmuseum, Vienna: pp. 348–349, 355 • Petőfi Literary Museum — Kassák Museum, Budapest: pp. 43, 144, 146 (top), 163, 164–165, 219 • Peter Lachnit, Vienna: p. 365 (Johannes Stoll) • Prague City Gallery: p. 36 • Private Collection, Courtesy Richard Nagy Ltd., London: p. 74 • Rechnitzer Collection Hungary, Győr: pp. 208, 209 • Regional Gallery of fine Arts in Zlín: p. 367 • Privatbesitz: Rudolf Sagmeister: p. 321 (Rudolf Sagmeister) • Silesian Museum, Opava: pp. 279, 314 • Slovak National Gallery, Bratislava: pp. 262, 263, 304 • South Bohemian Gallery: p. 38 (archive) • St. Stephen's King Museum — Deák Collection, Székesfehérvár: pp. 72, 294, 295 • Staatsbibliothek zu Berlin — Preußischer Kulturbesitz, Abteilung Historische Drucke: p. 140 (detail), 148 (4" Ad 5195®), 176 (top) (4" Ny 1236/8 ®) • Szombathely Art Gallery: p. 309 • The Gallery of West Bohemia in Pilsen: pp. 69, 91, 93, 123 • The Ivan Meštrović Museums — Meštrović Atelier, Zagreb: p. 103 (Filip Beusan) • The Museum of Decorative Arts in Prague: p. 136, 368 • The Regional Art Gallery Liberec: pp. 127, 311 (Jaroslav Trojan) • Theatermuseum, Vienna: pp. 99, 100, 101, 189 (top), 190 (below), 271 (top) • Theaterwissenschaftliche Sammlung, Universität zu Köln: pp. 192, 233, 236, 237, 239 • Tiroler Landesmuseum Ferdinandeum: pp. 117, 266 (detail), 283 (below) • ullstein bild: pp. 195, 196 • University of Applied Arts, Vienna: pp. 211, 215, 240, 364 • Východoslovenská galéria/East Slovak Gallery, Košice: p. 282 • WIENER STÄDTISCHE Versicherung AG — Vienna Insurance Group: p. 54 • Collection László & Hajni Ivan, Monaco: p. 41 • Collection Ferenc Kiss, Budapest: p. 46 (left) • Collection Emmanuelle & Jérôme de Noirmont, Paris: p. 185 • Tamás Kieselbach Collection: p. 133

LITERATURE

© Csilla Markója (Hrsg.), Mednyánszky (Ausst.-Kat. Slovenská Národná Galéria, Bratislava), Bratislava 2004, p. 413.: p. 118 (top) © Österrikiska Konstutställningen (Ausst.-Kat. Liljevalchs Konsthall, Stockholm) Stockholm 1917: p. 49 (top) © Krisztina Passuth, Etienne Beothy. Le Sculpteur de la SÉRIE D'OR, Budapest 2011, p. 101.: p. 187 © Karel Srp, Toyen. Praha 2000, p. 175.: p. 199 (top) Maps: pp. 20, 56, 96, 138, 150, 170, 264, 276, 288, 336, 346, 358

DICTIONARY DEFINITIONS

The texts about the words *border* and *nation* were taken from the dictionaries of each respective language. The aim here was to illustrate the changing use and definition of these terms. These definitions are interspersed throughout the catalogue in the following languages: German, English, Hungarian, Czech, Slovakian, Slovenian, Croatian, Romanian.

If, in spite of our thorough research, any individual illustrations have not been correctly attributed or acknowledged, we offer our apologies and would appreciate any information that will allow us to rectify the matter in future editions.

Colophon

This catalogue was published on the occasion of the exhibitions

Beyond Klimt: New Horizons in Central Europe from March 23 to August 26, 2018, at the Lower Belvedere, Vienna.

Beyond Klimt: New Horizons in Central Europe 1914–1938, from September 21, 2018, to January 20, 2019, at BOZAR, Centre for Fine Arts, Brussels.

An exhibition by the Belvedere, Vienna and the Centre for Fine Arts, Brussels (BOZAR) in cooperation with the Museum of Fine Arts, Budapest — Hungarian National Gallery

In the framework of the Austrian Presidency of the Council of the European Union

---

EXHIBITION AT THE BELVEDERE

Artistic Director, CEO: Stella Rollig
CFO: Wolfgang Bergmann
Curator: Alexander Klee
Curatorial Assistants: Stephanie Auer, Miroslav Haľák
Exhibition Management and Loans: Stephan Pumberger
Exhibition Production: Kristof Viola, Tanja Angermann-Cekinmez
Education: Susanne Wögerbauer
Marketing: Markus Wiesenhofer
Visitor Services: Margarete Stechl
Communications and Digital Belvedere: Monika Voglgruber
Research Center: Christian Huemer
Conservation Department: Stefanie Jahn

Belvedere
Prinz Eugen-Straße 27
1030 Vienna
www.belvedere.at

EXHIBITION AT BOZAR

Head of Exhibitions: Sophie Lauwers
Curator: Alexander Klee
Exhibition Coordinator: Ann Geeraerts
Head of Production: Evelyne Hinque
Technical Coordination: Nicolas Bernus
Press Officer: Leen Daems
Audience Developer: Sylvie Verbeke
Publications Coordinator: Gunther De Wit
BOZAR EXPO Team: Axelle Ancion, Nicolas Bernus, Helena Bussers, Francis Carpentier, Marie Claes, Christophe De Jaeger, Gunther De Wit, Colin Fincoeur, Ann Flas, Ann Geeraerts, Evelyne Hinque, Bart Janssen, Anne Judong, Vera Kotaji, Grégoire Legrain, Kathleen Louw, Alberta Sessa, Maïté Smeyers, Iwan Strauven, Pamela Stuyck, Christel Tsilibaris

Chief Executive Officer & Artistic Director: Paul Dujardin
Director of Operations: Albert Wastiaux
Director of Finance: Jérémie Leroy
Head of Exhibitions: Sophie Lauwers
Head of Music: Ulrich Hauschild
Head of Cinema: Juliette Duret
Head of Marketing & Communication: Johan Van Roy
Commercial Director: Luc Préaux
Director of Investments, Safety & Security: Stéphane Vanreppelen
Director Human Resources: Ignace De Breuck
Secretary General: Didier Verboomen

BOZAR, Centre for Fine Arts, Brussels
Rue Ravensteinstraat 23
1000 Brüssel
www.bozar.be

PUBLICATION

Editors: Stella Rollig, Alexander Klee
Authors: Stephanie Auer, Éva Bajkay, Gergely Barki, Kurt De Boodt, Gábor Dobó, Paul Dujardin, Arnika Groenewald-Schmidt, Ivo Habán, Alexander Klee, Barbara Lesák, Flóra Mészáros, Stella Rollig, Franz Smola, Gabriele Spindler, Arnold Suppan, Merse Pál Szeredi, Markéta Theinhardt, Judith Elisabeth Weiss
Chapter Texts: Miroslav Haľák (MH)
Graphic Design: Manuel Radde
Publication Management: Eva Lahnsteiner
Translation (German ▸ English): Rebecca Law (Auer, Barki, Smola, Spindler), Nick Somers (Dobó/Szeredi, Groenewald-Schmidt, Klee, Rollig, Weiss), Jessica West (Bajkay, Habán, Haľák, Lesák, Theinhardt)
Translation (English ▸ German): Michaela Alex (De Boodt/Dujardin, Suppan), Susanne Watzek (Mészáros)
Translation (Dutch ▸ English): Alison Mouthaan (De Boodt/Dujardin)
Translation (Czech ▸ German): Johanna Posset (Habán)
Translation (Hungarian ▸ German): György Buda (Bajkay, Barki, Dobó/Szeredi)
Copy Editing (German): Katharina Sacken
Copy Editing (English): Betti Moser
Lithography: Pixelstorm, Vienna
Printing and Binding: Printer Trento
Paper: Sappi Magno Volume 135g, Salzer Design Natural 100g

Published by Hirmer Verlag GmbH
Nymphenburgerstrasse 84
D-80636 Munich
www.hirmerverlag.de
www.hirmerpublishers.com

Bibliographic information published by the Deutsche Nationalbibliothek
The Deutsche Nationalbibliothek lists this publication in the Deutsche Nationalbibliografie; detailed bibliographic data are available online at http://dnb.de.
Printed in Italy

ISBN 978-3-7774-3058-4
(German retail edition)

ISBN 978-3-7774-3059-1
(English retail edition)

ISBN 978-3-903114-56-2
(German museum edition)

ISBN 978-3-903114-57-9
(English museum edition)

ISBN 978-3-903114-59-3
(Museum edition Bozar)

Cover (retail & museum edition): Gustav Klimt, *Johanna Staude*, 1917/18, Belvedere, Vienna & Marianne (My) Ullmann, *Modest*, 1925, University of Applied Arts Vienna, Collection and Archive

Cover (museum edition BOZAR): Gustav Klimt, *Johanna Staude*, 1917/18, Belvedere, Vienna & Gustav Klimt, *Johanna Staude* (detail), 1917/18, Belvedere, Vienna

belvedere
BOZAR CENTRE FOR FINE ARTS BRUSSELS
2018 EUROPÄISCHES KULTURERBEJAHR #EuropeForCulture
.be
KINGDOM OF BELGIUM Federal Public Service Foreign Affairs, Foreign Trade and Development Cooperation
BUNDESKANZLERAMT ÖSTERREICH
FEDERAL CHANCELLERY OF AUSTRIA